T3-BOA-062
3 0301 00029977 2

SCIENCE AND CULTURE TEXTS

JOSEPH HUSSLEIN, S.J., PH.D., GENERAL EDITOR

LITERARY READINGS IN ENGLISH PROSE

LITERARY READINGS
• IN ENGLISH PROSE •

INEZ SPECKING, M.A., Ph.D.
Professor of English, Harris Teachers College,
Lecturer in English at St. Louis University

THE BRUCE PUBLISHING COMPANY
New York Milwaukee Chicago

PRINTED IN THE UNITED STATES OF AMERICA

PREFACE BY THE GENERAL EDITOR

The first purpose in the compilation of this text has been to make available for home study and classroom use a copious selection of the various types of English prose that might serve as aids in college composition. But beyond this consideration the compiler has gathered, with fine discrimination, a rare treasure of literary prose, rich in cultural values, original, imaginative, and inspiring.

Volumes of this nature have frequently been devoted largely to specialized topics: to political problems, economic questions of the day, and scientific discussions. All these may have their proper place in such a book. But what is of foremost importance for the student in our English courses is a familiarity with the best things of the heart, the mind, and the spirit of man, expressed in a language and stylistic form which transmute them into literature.

Nor is it advisable to restrict the range of classroom study to contemporary authors only, of whom all but a few will be quickly forgotten. While obviously present-day writers are not to be neglected in the training of the student, yet only such models should be chosen as may seem best to conform to the eternal norms of truth and beauty. As for the coarse, impressionistic types of writing and the forms that blatantly discard the reticences and the hallowed sanctities of life, the less said of them the better. These works are not art but literary abnormalities. Their cult implies decadence.

Ample attention, it will be found, has been given to modern writers in the present volume, but the classics of English prose are generously represented. Their muster roll might in fact be compiled with fair completeness from its table of contents. It thus illustrates to best effect the wisdom of the tried housekeeper of the Scriptures whose example meets with the approval of the ages—"who bringeth forth out of his treasure new things and old."

In determining the proper scope of this work, inquiry was cautiously made among teachers of English to learn what development might best suit their needs. The result has been to carry out the original plan as herewith presented. It is the method most naturally called for and supplies whatever is essential for classroom use. Briefly stated, it consists in offering adequate models of practically all the various kinds of English prose composition, included here under the five main divisions: Exposition, Argument, Description, Narrative, and Letters.

Since much of the composition work undertaken by the pupils will probably be devoted to different forms of expository writing, the entire first half of this volume is given over to selections of such a nature. It is here the student learns to define his terms, to deal with a proposed subject by way of synthesis or of analysis, to group his thoughts and marshal his facts in artistic essay form, to write a readable and correct review of the book assigned to him, or even to give expression in editorial style to his calmly reasoned convictions or more impulsive thoughts, now held by him in dignified control. For all these uses the models here collected will prove an admirable preparation.

Due significance is attached, in fine, to that spiritual revival which the world is witnessing today in reaction to the stark materialism of an earlier period. Authors representative of this movement are allotted the attention they deserve. Included in this spiritual élite are: Coventry Patmore, Francis Thompson, John Henry Newman, Louise Imogen Guiney, Joyce Kilmer, Helen Parry Eden, Alice Meynell, Katherine Brégy, Gilbert Keith Chesterton, Hilaire Belloc, and a goodly company of others.

All desirable selections can naturally not be compressed between the covers of a single volume. Yet Miss Inez Specking, M.A., Ph.D., Professor of English at Harris Teachers College and for years intimately connected with the English Department of St. Louis University, offers herewith a book that will be found remarkably comprehensive and richly illustrative of the finest work that English prose literature has produced for the imitation and emulation of the new generation.

JOSEPH HUSSLEIN, S.J., PH.D.,
General Editor, Science and Culture Texts

St. Louis University
April 11, 1935

CONTENTS

I. EXPOSITION

A. Technical Exposition

B. Definition

II. ARGUMENT

PAGE

III. DESCRIPTION

A. BRIEF DESCRIPTIONS

1. BUILDINGS AND PLACES

2. PERSONS

IV. NARRATIVE

V. LETTERS

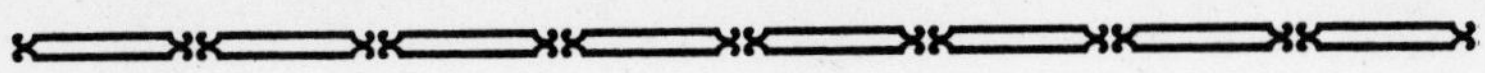

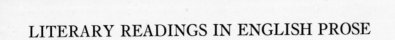

LITERARY READINGS IN ENGLISH PROSE

I. EXPOSITION
II. ARGUMENT
III. DESCRIPTION
IV. NARRATIVE
V. LETTERS

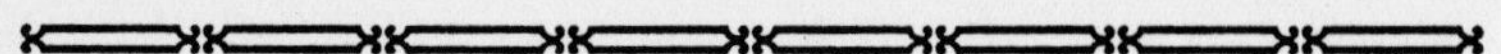

1. EXPOSITION

A. Technical Exposition

B. Definition

C. Analysis

D. The Informal Essay

E. The Formal Essay

F. The Editorial

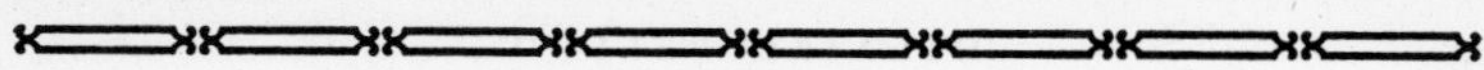

A. TECHNICAL EXPOSITION

THE MOWING OF A FIELD[1]

Hilaire Belloc

There is a valley in South England remote from ambition and from fear, where the passage of strangers is rare and unperceived, and where the scent of the grass in summer is breathed only by those who are native to that unvisited land. The roads to the Channel do not traverse it; they choose upon either side easier passes over the range. One track alone leads up through it to the hills, and this is changeable: now green where men have little occasion to go, now a good road where it nears the homesteads and barns. The woods grow steep above the slopes; they reach sometimes the very summit of the heights, or, when they cannot attain them, fill in and clothe the combes. And, in between, along the floor of the valley, deep pastures and their silence are bordered by lawns of chalky grass and the small yew trees of the Downs.

The clouds that visit its sky reveal themselves beyond the one great rise, and sail, white and enormous, to the other, and sink beyond that other. But the plains above which they have traveled and the Weald to which they go, the people of the valley cannot see and hardly recall. The wind, when it reaches such fields, is no longer a gale from the salt, but fruitful and soft, an inland breeze, and those whose blood was nourished here feel in that wind the fruitfulness of our orchards and all the life that all things draw from the air.

In this place, when I was a boy, I pushed through a fringe of beeches that made a complete screen between me and the world, and I came to a glade called No Man's Land. I climbed beyond it,

[1]Reprinted from *Hills and the Sea,* by permission of Charles Scribner's Sons.

and I was surprised and glad, because from the ridge of that glade I saw the sea. To this place very lately I returned.

The many things that I recovered as I came up the countryside were not less charming than when a distant memory had enshrined them, but much more. Whatever veil is thrown by a longing recollection had not intensified nor even made more mysterious the beauty of that happy ground; not in my very dreams of morning had I, in exile, seen it more beloved or more rare. Much also that I had forgotten now returned to me as I approached—a group of elms, a little turn of the parson's wall, a small paddock beyond the graveyard close, cherished by one man, with a low wall of very old stone guarding it all around. And all these things fulfilled and amplified my delight, till even the good vision of the place, which I had kept so many years, left me and was replaced by its better reality. "Here," I said to myself, "is a symbol of what some say is reserved for the soul: pleasure of a kind which cannot be imagined save in the moment when at last it is attained."

When I came to my own gate and my own field, and had before me the house I knew, I looked around a little (though it was already evening), and I saw that the grass was standing as it should stand when it is ready for the scythe. For in this, as in everything that a man can do—of those things at least which are very old—there is an exact moment when they are done best. And it has been remarked of whatever rules us that it works blunderingly, seeing that the good things given to man are not given at the precise moment when they would have filled him with delight. But, whether this be true or false, we can choose the just turn of the seasons in everything we do of our own will, and especially in the making of hay. Many think that hay is best made when the grass is thickest; and so they delay until it is rank and in flower, and has already heavily pulled the ground. And there is another false reason for delay, which is wet weather. For very few will understand (though it comes year after year) that we have rain always in South England between the sickle and the scythe, or say just after the weeks of east wind are over. First we have a week of sudden warmth, as though the South had come to see us all; then we have the weeks of east and southeast wind; and then we have more or less rain of which I spoke, and which always astonishes the world. Now it is just before, or during, or at the very end of that rain — but not later — that grass should be cut for hay. True, upland grass, which is always thin, should be cut earlier than the grass in the bottoms and along the water meadows; but not even the latest, even in the wettest seasons, should be left (as it is) to flower and even to seed. For what we get when we store our grass is not a harvest of something ripe, but a thing just caught in its prime before maturity: as witness that our corn and straw are best yellow, but our hay is best green. So also Death should be represented with a scythe and Time with a sickle; for Time can only take what is ripe, but Death comes always too soon. In a word, then, it is always much easier to cut grass too late than too early; and I, under that evening and come back to these pleasant fields, looked at the grass and knew that it was time. June was in full advance: it was the beginning of that season when the night has already lost her foothold of the earth and hovers over it, never quite descending, but mixing sunset with the dawn.

Next morning, before it was yet broad day, I awoke, and thought of the mowing. The birds were already chattering in the trees beside my window, all except the nightingale, which had left and flown away to the Weald, where he sings all summer by days as well as by night in the oaks and the hazel spinneys, and especially along the little river Adur, one of the rivers of the Weald. The birds and thought of the mowing had awakened me, and I went down the stairs and along the stone floors to where I could find a scythe, and when I took it from its nail, I remembered how, fourteen years ago, I had last gone out with my scythe, just so, into the fields at morning. In between that day and this were many things, cities and armies, and a confusion of books, mountains and the desert, and horrible great breadths of sea.

When I got out into the long grass the sun was not yet risen, but there were already many colors in the eastern sky, and I made haste to sharpen my scythe, so that I might get to the cutting before the dew should dry. Some say that it is best to wait till all the dew has risen, so as to get the grass quite dry from the very first. But, though it is an advantage to get the grass quite dry, yet it is not worth while to wait till the dew has risen. For, in the first place, you lose many hours of work (and those the coolest), and next — which is more important — you lose that great ease and thickness in cutting which comes of the dew. So I at once began to sharpen my scythe.

There is an art also in the sharpening of a scythe, and it is worth describing carefully. Your blade must be dry, and that is why you will see men rubbing the scythe-blade with grass before they whet it. Then also your rubber must be quite dry, and on this account it is a good thing to lay it on your coat and keep it there during all your day's mowing. The scythe you stand upright, with the blade pointing away from you, and you put your left hand firmly on the back of the blade, grasping it: then you pass the rubber first down one side of the blade-edge and then down the other, beginning near the handle and going to the point and working quickly and hard. When you first do this you will, perhaps, cut your hand; but it is only at first that such an accident will happen to you.

To tell when the scythe is sharp enough, this is the rule. First the stone clangs and grinds against the iron harshly; then it rings musically to one note; then, at last, it purrs as though the iron and stone were exactly suited. When you hear this, your scythe is sharp enough; and I, when I heard it in that June dawn, with everything quite silent except the birds, let down the scythe and bent myself to mow.

When one does anything anew, after so many years, one fears very much for one's trick or habit. But all things once learnt are easily recoverable, and I very soon recovered the swing and power of the mower. Mowing well and mowing badly—or rather not mowing at all—are separated by very little; as is also true of writing verse, of playing the fiddle, and of dozens of other things, but of nothing more than of believing. For the bad or young or untaught mower without tradition, the mower Promethean, the mower original and contemptuous of the past, does all these things: He leaves great crescents of grass uncut. He digs the point of the scythe hard into the ground with a jerk. He loosens the handles and even the fastening of the blade. He twists the blade with his blunders, he blunts the blade, he chips it, dulls it, or breaks it clean off at the tip. If anyone is standing by he cuts him in the ankle. He sweeps up into the air wildly, with nothing to resist his stroke. He drags up earth with the grass, which is like making the meadow bleed. But the good mower who does things just as they should be done and have been for a hundred thousand years, falls into none of these fooleries. He goes forward very steadily, his scythe-blade just barely missing the ground, every grass falling; the swish and rhythm of his mowing are always the same.

So great an art can only be learnt by continual practice; but this much is worth writing down, that, as in all good work, to know the thing with which you work is the core of the affair. Good verse is best written on good paper with an easy pen, not with a lump of coal on a whitewashed wall. The pen thinks for you; and so does the scythe mow for you if you treat it honorably and in a manner that makes it recognize its service. The manner is this. You must regard the scythe as a pendulum that swings, not as a knife that cuts. A good mower puts no more strength into his stroke than into his lifting. Again, stand up to your work. The bad mower, eager and full of pain, leans forward and tries to force the scythe through the grass. The good mower, serene and able, stands as nearly straight as the shape of the scythe will let him, and follows up every stroke closely, moving his left foot forward. Then also let every stroke get well away. Mowing is a thing of ample gestures, like drawing a cartoon. Then, again, get yourself into a mechanical and repetitive mood: be thinking of anything at all but your mowing, and be anxious only when there seems some interruption to the monotony of the sound. In this mowing should be like one's prayers — all of a sort and always the same, and so made that you can establish a monotony and work them, as it were, with half your mind: that happier half, the half that does not bother.

In this way, when I had recovered the art after so many years, I went forward over the field, cutting lane after lane through the grass, and bringing out its most secret essences with the sweep of scythe until the air was full of odors. At the end of every lane I sharpened my scythe and looked back at the work done, and then carried my scythe down again upon my shoulder to begin another. So, long before the bell rang in the chapel above me — that is, long before six o'clock, which is the time for the *Angelus* — I had many swathes already lying in order parallel like soldiery; and the high grass yet standing, making a great contrast with the shaven part, looked dense and high. As it says in the Ballad of Val-ès-Dunes, where —

The tall son of the Seven Winds
Came riding out of the Hither-hythe,

and his horse-hoofs (you will remember) trampled into the press and made a gap in it, and his sword (as you know)

> . . . was like a scythe
> In Arcus when the grass is high
> And all the swathes in order lie,
> And there's the bailiff standing by
> A gathering of the tithe.

So I mowed all that morning, till the houses awoke in the valley, and from some of them rose a little fragrant smoke, and men began to be seen.

I stood still and rested on my scythe to watch the awakening of the village, when I saw coming up to my field a man whom I had known in older times, before I had left the Valley.

He was of that dark silent race upon which all the learned quarrel, but which, by whatever meaningless name it may be called —Iberian, or Celtic, or what you will—is the permanent root of all England, and makes England wealthy and preserves it everywhere, except perhaps in the Fens and in a part of Yorkshire. Everywhere else you will find it active and strong. These people are intensive; their thoughts and their labors turn inward. It is on account of their presence in these islands that our gardens are the richest in the world. They also love low rooms and ample fires and great warm slopes of thatch. They have, as I believe, an older acquaintance with the English air than any other of all the strains that make up England. They hunted in the Weald with stones, and camped in the pines in the green-sand. They lurked under the oaks of the upper rivers, and saw the legionaries go up, up the straight paved road from the sea. They helped the few pirates to destroy the towns, and mixed with those pirates and shared the spoils of the Roman villas, and were glad to see the captains and the priests destroyed. They remain; and no admixture of the Frisian pirates, or the Breton, or the Angevin and Norman conquerors, has very much affected their cunning eyes.

To this race, I say, belonged the man who now approached me. And he said to me, "Mowing?" And I answered, "Ar." Then he also said "Ar," as in duty bound; for so we speak to each other in the Stenes of the Downs.

Next he told me that, as he had nothing to do, he would lend me a hand; and I thanked him warmly, or, as we say, "kindly." For it is a good custom of ours always to treat bargaining as though it were a courteous pastime; and though what he was after was money, and what I wanted was his labor at the least pay, yet we both played the comedy that we were free men, the one granting a grace and the other accepting it. For the dry bones of commerce, avarice and method and need, are odious to the Valley; and we cover them up with a pretty body of fiction and observances. Thus, when it comes to buying pigs, the buyer does not begin to decry the pig and the vendor to praise it, as is the custom with lesser men; but tradition makes them do business in this fashion:

First the buyer will go up to the seller when he sees him in his own steading, and, looking at the pig with admiration, the buyer will say that rain may or may not fall, or that we shall have snow or thunder, according to the time of year. Then the seller, looking critically at the pig, will agree that the weather is as his friend maintains. There is no haste at all; great leisure marks the dignity of their exchange. And the next step is, that the buyer says: "That's a fine pig you have there, Mr. ——" (giving the seller's name). "Ar, powerful fine pig." Then the seller, saying also "Mr." (for twin brothers rocked in one cradle give each other ceremonious observance here), the seller, I say, admits, as though with reluctance, the strength and beauty of the pig, and falls into deep thought. Then the buyer says, as though moved by a great desire, that he is ready to give so much for the pig, naming half the proper price, or a little less. Then the seller remains in silence for some moments; and at last begins to shake his head slowly, till he says: "I don't be thinking of selling the pig, anyways." He will also add that a party only Wednesday offered him so much for the pig—and he names about double the proper price. Thus all ritual is duly accomplished; and the solemn act is entered upon with reverence and in a spirit of truth. For when the buyer uses this phrase: "I'll tell you what I *will* do," and offers within half a crown of the pig's value, the seller replies that he can refuse him nothing, and names half a crown above its value; and the difference is split, the pig is sold, and in the quiet soul of each runs the peace of something accomplished.

Thus do we buy a pig or land or labor or malt or lime, always with elaboration and set forms; and many a London man has paid double and more for his violence and his greedy haste and very unchivalrous higgling. As happened with the land at Underwaltham, which the mortgagees had begged and implored the estate to take at twelve hundred, and had privately offered to all the world at a thousand, but which a sharp direct man, of the kind that makes great fortunes, a man in a motor car, a man in a fur coat, a man of few words, bought for two thousand three hundred before my very eyes, protesting that they might take his offer or leave it; and all because he did not begin by praising the land.

Well then, this man I spoke of offered to help me, and he went to get his scythe. But I went into the house and brought out a gallon jar of small ale for him and for me; for the sun was now very warm, and small ale goes well with mowing. When we had drunk some of this ale in mugs called "I see you," we took each a swathe, he a little behind me because he was the better mower; and so for many hours we swung, one before the other, mowing and mowing at the tall grass of the field. And the sun rose to noon and we were still at our mowing; and we ate food, but only for a little while, and we took again to our mowing. And at last there was nothing left but a small square of grass, standing like a square of linesmen who keep their formation, tall and unbroken, with all the dead lying around them when a battle is over and done.

Then for some time I rested after all those hours; and the man and I talked together, and a long way off we heard in another field the musical sharpening of a scythe.

The sunlight slanted powdered and mellow over the breadth of the valley; for the day was nearing its end. I went to fetch rakes from the steading; and when I had come back the last of the grass had fallen, and all the field lay flat and smooth, with the very green short grass in lanes between the dead and yellow swathes.

These swathes we raked into cocks to keep them from the dew against our return at daybreak; and we made the cocks as tall and steep as we could, for in that shape they best keep off the dew, and it is easier also to spread them after the sun has risen. Then we raked up every straggling blade, till the whole field was a clean floor for the tedding and the carrying of the hay next morning. The grass we had mown was but a little over two acres; for that is all the pasture on my little tiny farm.

When we had done all this, there fell upon us the beneficent and deliberate evening; so that as we sat a little while together near the rakes, we saw the valley more solemn and dim around us and all the trees and hedgerows quite still, and held by a complete silence. Then I paid my companion his wage, and bade him a good night, till we should meet in the same place before sunrise.

He went off with a slow and steady progress, as all our peasants do, making their walking a part of the easy but continual labor of their lives. But I sat on, watching the light creep around toward the north and change, and the waning moon coming up as though by stealth behind the woods of No Man's Land.

HOW A GONDOLA IS ROWED[1]

John Ruskin

A gondola is in general rowed only by one man, standing at the stern, those of the upper classes having two or more boatmen, for greater speed and magnificence. In order to raise the oar sufficiently, it rests, not on the side of the boat, but on a piece of crooked timber like the branch of a tree, rising about a foot from the boat's side, and called a *fórcola*. The *fórcola* is of different forms, according to the size and uses of the boat, and it is always somewhat complicated in its parts and curvature, allowing the oar various kinds of rests and catches on both its sides, but perfectly free play in all cases; as the management of the boat depends on the gondolier's being able in an instant to place his oar in any position. The *fórcola* is set on the right-hand side of the boat, some six feet from the stern: the gondolier stands on a little flat platform or deck behind it, and throws nearly the entire weight of his body upon the forward stroke. The effect of the stroke would be naturally to turn the boat's head round to the left, as well as to send it forward; but this tendency is corrected by keeping the blade of the oar under the water on the return stroke, and raising it gradually, as a full

[1]From *Stones of Venice.*

spoon is raised out of any liquid, so that the blade emerges from the water only an instant before it again plunges. A downward and lateral pressure upon the *fórcola* is thus obtained, which entirely counteracts the tendency given by the forward stroke; and the effort, after a little practice, becomes hardly conscious, though, as it adds some labor to the back stroke, rowing a gondola at speed is hard and breathless work, though it appears easy and graceful to the looker-on.

If then the gondola is to be turned to the left, the forward impulse is given without the return stroke; if it is to be turned to the right, the plunged oar is brought forcibly up to the surface, in either case a single stroke being enough to turn the light and flat-bottomed boat. But as it has no keel, when the turn is made sharply, as out of one canal into another very narrow one, the impetus of the boat in its former direction gives it an enormous leeway, and it drifts laterally up against the wall of the canal, and that so forcibly, that if it has turned at speed, no gondolier can arrest the motion merely by strength or rapidity of stroke of oar; but it is checked by a strong thrust of the foot against the wall itself, the head of the boat being of course turned for the moment almost completely round to the opposite wall, and greater exertion made to give it, as quickly as possible, impulse in the new direction.

A LETTER IN REPLY TO A YOUNG GENTLEMAN OF YALE UNIVERSITY[1]

William McFee

My Dear Sir:

I do not remember any letter among the many I have received from Americans which has given me so much pleasure as yours,

[1]From *Swallowing the Anchor*. Copyright, 1923, by William McFee, reprinted by permission of Doubleday, Doran and Company, Inc., Publishers.

or which has led me to scrutinize so narrowly the understructure of the career of authorship. I like your letter, not only because you reveal the engaging candor that seems to me to be in the New Haven air, not only because your calligraphy is so exquisitely lucid and attractive to a jaded eye, but because you are one of a numerous company of young Americans who have honored me with their letters and who have all endeared themselves to my memory by a singularly charming and slightly antique style of writing. And it is of that I would speak at first.

I am not unmindful that most of you come from New England, though several who are tinged with this eighteenth-century turn of phrase and attitude of mind hail from distant colleges. It is my desire to congratulate you upon preserving, in a syncopating era of the world, those decencies of word and thought which, in my opinion, are a not unpleasant feature of civilization.

It will be difficult, of course, for me to extract from your letter adequate examples of what I mean without quoting some of those graceful compliments that you have so ingeniously embedded in the text. But I can attempt it.

"How, my dear sir," you say, "did you begin to write? I have read a partial account in one of your books and have picked up strands here and there from time to time. Did you 'write and burn,' as Joseph Conrad advised all undergraduates here a few days ago? And again — you see I am a human question mark — do you think travel necessary to a good writer? Are newspapers advisable as a means of sharpening style? I mean, of course, writing for them — no one would read them for literary merit. You see I am seriously considering the literary life — not really considering it because I can't possibly keep out of it, i.e., when desire and not ability is the criterion — and have had considerable difficulty in matters to write about. Life, I suppose, is teeming all around me, and yet my experience is confined to a few adolescent amours. . . . Do you think it necessary to be old to write a novel?"

Here, I think, we have the mainspring and alarm of your interrogative epistle. At all events, it was this paragraph that gave me most reason for taking a retrospect of the road over which I have been traveling for twenty-five years.

It is, of course, quite unnecessary for you, as a young undergraduate, to apologize for such questions as being possibly "impertinent." That is very polite on your part, but permit me to waive it as unnecessary. Such questions are in the highest degree pertinent. Upon what rational plea can an author resent them? He is an artist, he works for the public pleasure and edification, and by these tokens the youth of the land who desire to be instructed in the art have every right to ask his counsel. And so we come to your first question —how does one begin to write?

I assume, young sir, that you have more than once turned away from those empty and windy nostrums that are at times sent floating about the literary causeways by folk who are—to put it humanely —not very scrupulous in their thinking. As, for instance, that the way to learn to write is to write. Or that writing, like everything else, is a trade. You know the sort of thing. Even the perfectly sound and valuable advice that you quote—to "write and burn"—is open to the criticism that it reverberates in young hearts like the clang of a heavy door closing, rather than the cheerful rattle of an opening casement.

I can offer you none of these formidable and epigrammatic instruments for penetrating the veils that conceal the mysteries of our art. All I can do is to light a candle and lead the way back along the corridors of memory to the magic period when, like you, I was afflicted with the passion for writing and yet had, as you phrase it so felicitously, "considerable difficulty in matters to write about."

And who has not? My first word is entirely of encouragement. I think myself it is a wise provision of nature that when we are young we lack power. Life, you suppose, is teeming all around you and yet your experience is confined to a few adolescent amours. Well, the other amours will come along in due course, and although I am not one of those who hold that art is merely a manifestation of sex, falling in love is undoubtedly a factor in the problem. But in the beginning I imagine that writing, or music, or the plastic arts, come to us unconsciously, growing out of the universal instinct for imitation.

So I recall it, rather ruefully, I may tell you. Of course, you may be informed by the modern school of psychology that I am wrong, that my memories are suspect, and that it is all a question of glands. Perhaps it is. But to me it is a picture of a small boy reading and reading and reading, much of it reading aloud to a shrewd and competent mother, and then the instinctive act of taking a pen and imitating the phrases and emotions for himself.

We can get a hint of the mechanism of literary inception, I think, from the fact that a boy—or a girl—tends to grandiose themes—the invention of improbable regions and gigantic beings, or horrors and sheeted phantoms. It is my own theory that our imaginations, like our bodies, pass rapidly through the whole gamut of evolutionary phases during adolescence. There is a period at the threshold of the introspective life when the mind is scarcely differentiated from sensation, and the things imagined are as crude as the sagas. It is these early spiritual contortions and monstrous inventions of which the fairy stories are made, which give them their power over every generation.

The next stage, however, is much more interesting to you and to me, since it takes place in the world of living men. You ask how one begins to write. Well, there are two sources of inspiration, and it is because one or other of them is forgotten in the excitement of the controversy that one derives so little profit from the precepts of eminent artists. For if dreams are the indispensable basis of the act of creation, our life in this world is the mold into which most of us must run our thoughts. I do not deny that there are masters of pure fantasy, poets of the caliber of Francis Thompson and William Butler Yeats, who move with singular ease and beauty among legends of ancient days, prose writers like De Quincey and William Blake, who float clear of our earthly levels and entrance our souls, and who, as Goethe says in *Faust,* "beckon to far-off shores with smiles from other skies."

But you and I had better keep our feet on the ground yet awhile, I think, and since the problem is the genesis of authorship, we may describe it as the imitative instinct acting upon the intimate external world of action.

And here it is proper to put in a plea for the gentlemen who are lying in wait for you, and who will demand with wistful doggedness an abundance of that same action. One of the most difficult things in the world, to my mind, is to sit down and tell a child an impromptu story. And why? Well, because the child wants us to tell it what happened. We have to invent action. The story a child makes up for itself is all action. There was once a little girl and she was crying because she had been invited to a lovely ball and her mother said she couldn't go because she was naughty. And while she was crying, suddenly a little old woman came up the garden path, a little old woman dressed in a blue cloak and with a basket on her arm full of — and so on. That is the way a child makes up a story, and with very little modification that is what you will have to do to pacify those estimable and warm-hearted editors who will insist upon something happening in your stories. The principle behind this apparently despotic demand is an eternal one. It is nothing less than the practical application of the theory that writing is an art. I am aware that modern critical jargon tends to confuse this issue and proclaims that since life is apparently formless and incomprehensible, a novel should develop along those lines. But I would here quote Goethe again, and remark in passing that the more you read that remarkable genius the better. In *Wilhelm Meister,* he observes dryly that "art is called art because it is not nature," and I suggest you never forget it.

The editor, then, who insists upon action in the story, who wants you, as a modern critic naïvely puts it, to begin at the beginning and end at the end, to have it clear in your mind before you begin to tell it, is merely requiring you to be an artist. The notion that a story leaps into existence, like Minerva springing full armed from the head of Jove, is attractive but not founded upon experience. I am inclined myself to accept the personal narratives of inspired authors with a grain of salt. You may "get an idea," as they say, and write it at white heat in a few hours. But I very much doubt whether it will be worth much after you have written it. This illusion of rapid creation is fostered by the fact that conceptions do actually come to one in a flash and at the most unexpected moments. But I would point out that the artist's mind, in these cases, is continuously preoccupied with his theme: his story, as I am fond of saying, is cooking over a slow fire, day after day, week after week, perhaps for years, before he experienced these authentic and sudden revelations of the minor syntheses. You will discover infinitely more comfort and nourishment in my own favorite theory of growth. Art is fundamentally a product of meditation. We are apt to lose sight of this point because all the machinery of modern publishing, even the vocabulary of literary processes, tends to conceal the gradual inception, the years of silent gestation, the travail of soul, that precede all genuine achievements in the imaginative sphere. It flatters our vanity to have people think we dashed it off. We are anxious to avoid any suspicion of being irresponsible loafers, and so we sit at our desks every day at certain hours, exactly as though we were engaged in merchandising. Now, industry is as important in authorship as in any other department of life, but it cannot be regulated quite so deftly as that. Nevertheless, I am not about to deliver any vaporings concerning inspiration. My idea, derived from a rather strenuous pursuit of hard manual labor and executive responsibility far removed from writing, is that success even in bench work, say, is very much a matter of inspiration. Else, how can one account for those days when a job is done by magic, when work moves forward in oiled grooves, and you reflect with amazement at the facility of your achievement? The artisan is as much the victim of temperament and inspiration as the artist, but the convention is that only the latter can claim it, and there I think the convention is wrong.

Your question, however, "did you 'write and burn,'" can be answered boldly and without any loss of honor. It is the lot of mankind to "write and burn," but I am unable to recall any formal pyre. There appears to be a ritual in these matters. The sight of the burning pages vanishing up the chimney seems to exercise a soothing and propitiatory influence upon the spirit that provides over such functions. I am unable to attribute any peculiar significance to the actual incineration of one's 'prentice work, though I confess to standing by the rail at night and dropping it overboard. The fact is, an apprentice, whether to authorship or cabinetmaking or blacksmithing, makes many "wasters" that have to be destroyed, or at least stowed away out of sight. To make it a romantic and semireligious gesture is to my mind a foolish thing to do. There need be no regret if you derived pleasure from the writing and profit from the disillusion that followed.

The next interrogation, whether travel is "necessary to a good writer," is full of danger for one who has been about the world more or less and whose work bears the mark of so many alien impressions. The cobbler believes there is nothing like leather. But candor demands that a fair judgment be delivered, and it must be confessed that while travel is desirable to afford a wide culture and a trained eye, it is by no means essential to the creation of great art. Indeed, I am able to make an excellent case for the writer who stays right in his home town. I can recall to your memory Robert Burns, for example, Mrs. Gaskell, and Thomas Hardy. Perhaps Hardy is of all modern masters of prose the best example of the artist who has achieved his greatest triumphs at his own door. But I need not labor this point. You will be able to think of many others, like Flaubert, and Maupassant in Rouen, George W. Cable in New Orleans, Arthur Machen in his garret in London, who have gone to neither China nor Peru. There is no greater fallacy than that romance lies on the other side of the world. And just as he who is a failure in business at home may imagine success beyond the ranges, so the artist who sees nothing in his native vale may dream of masterpieces conceived in the shadow of the Andes. Each is the victim of an illusion. They seek neither wealth nor fame, but the satisfaction of that strange migratory instinct —

For to admire an' for to see,
 For to be'old this world so wide —
It never done no good to me,
 But I can't drop it if I tried.

Be very sure indeed it is not that, rather than art, which propels you from port to port.

It is with the next query, as to the use of newspapers, that I must offer, in all sincerity and honest regard, an adverse criticism. Are they "advisable as a means of sharpening style," you ask, adding, rather to my annoyance, "I mean, of course, writing for them — no one would read them for literary merit." Now, I am unable to understand how writing for a newspaper can be good for a style if the newspaper has no literary merit. On the contrary, I am happy to inform you that I am a voracious reader of newspapers, of magazines, of house organs, and of advertisements. I am of the opinion that never was newspaper writing of so high a standard as at the present moment, and that your average morning or evening journal in America far transcends anything to be found elsewhere. With a few exceptions, such as, for example, an essay on the chemical nature of Water Soluble B., or a libelous attack upon an honored citizen, the metropolitan dailies will print and pay for articles upon any subject under the sun. The curiosity and enthusiasm of the editors are insatiable, and the better you write the better they will like it. So vast and so heterogeneous is the available market that no ready writer need be idle or impoverished.

For the forming of taste, however, there is something to be said for moderation in reading the papers. The reason is obvious. Children should be sparingly supplied with rich food. They should have an abundance of staples. Here we might allude to a question I have frequently seen in the correspondence columns of magazines devoted to "red-blooded stories for he-men," as they are sometimes called. These correspondents are usually the husky students of some western university and they demand ruthlessly why their courses at college contain so much dry stuff about old has-beens like Chaucer and Spenser, Shakespeare and Wordsworth. Why, they ask, can they not take a course in modern authors? And here they mention the writers who appeal to them most strongly in their favorite magazine. I suspect the professors whom you disparage so disdainfully in your letter would ignore such suggestions. I think it more to the purpose, not being a professor, to answer the question. The reason why we must acquire a knowledge of those old "has-beens" (as one indignant westerner calls them) is that nothing can be done in any profession without a standard. The whole business of education beyond the elements is designed, not to fill the brains with facts as a bin is filled with beans, but to fashion in the mind an instrument by which a work of art or literature can be gauged. Only by means of this gauging, this trained instinct for fineness, can we attain to the permanent enjoyments of life. It is, in a measure, discipline and drill. The "wild ass of the desert" doubtless enjoys life in his own way, but our civilization and culture are built up on the theory that "the acquired memories of the artist," as La Farge phrased it, are of value, and the only way to acquire memories is to read what has been done.

The practice, however, of deliberately imitating certain models, "playing the sedulous ape," as R. L. S. called it, I don't regard with any enthusiasm. I am aware Stevenson did it himself, and Walter Pater devoted long periods to translating from foreign tongues into the English of some admired master. Whether they profited by this course it is not possible to declare. In a general way the young writer imitates in spite of himself, and unconsciously. He will have his "periods." He will drink deep of Ruskin or Carlyle, Emerson or

Keats, and industriously bay the moon in these various styles, happily oblivious that the style is only the mark of the character and not to be copied. The use of these early exercises is to give suppleness of movement. It was a rule when I was taught cricket that the business of playing the ball, the stance, the swing, the muscular effort of the stroke, had to be practiced until, when at the wicket, the whole operation took place with the precision of instinct. It had to be relegated to the subconscious mind, as in operating an automobile at high speed, let us say. And one of the marks of a good writer, to my mind, is that he gets his results in this way. The phrase, the paragraph, the chapter, grow in his mind in orderly and largely unconscious sequence, not because he has had an inspiration from on high, but because he has been practicing the swing until it has become second nature.

Here I might make a brief plea for the paragraph in particular.

It fell to my lot, not long since, to read a book of considerable recent fame. The energy and personal magnetism of the author were incontestable. His life, which he elected to recount in the form of fiction, was a miracle of tempestuous and emotional uproar. One of the prevailing conceits of his character was that he was above all things an artist. And yet the book was one of the most difficult I have ever read, because the author had not the remotest conception of balance and rhythm. The book had divisions neither of chapter nor paragraph. Everything was hurled down upon the paper pell-mell and spattered with rows of the little dots which Mr. H. G. Wells used so deftly in some of his books, and which his imitators abuse so cruelly. The result was a constant strain upon the nerves. The mind was kept at full stretch so long that attention sagged and was finally severed. The material was there, piled up and chaotic, but the artist was unaware that he had not finished his job. Doubtless he would seek justification in the trend of modern literature, which seems to regard with impatience the minor but admirable task of fashioning the *mot juste,* the pregnant phrase, and welding them into the cadence of the paragraph.

"Do you think it necessary to be old to write a novel?" you ask, and I am aware of the pathos in that question. I am aware of it all the more poignantly because I see on my desk, as I write, the manuscript of a novel written by a young lady of seventeen. It is an excellent story of its kind and she is becomingly modest about her achievement. Neither she nor I would admit that any special virtue attaches to precocity. The word *novel* covers so many kinds of composition, we are entitled to persevere until extreme old age.

I would venture, with your permission, to advance a proposition which is the fruit of experience, that in the beginning equipment is of more importance than ephemeral acceptance for publication. There is nothing in life or in art that is unimportant to the novelist. All is grist that comes to his mill. His culture cannot be too wide, or his reading too various. Sooner or later the apparently sterile stuff will be of service, will fructify and grow. He must have, to quote La Farge again, an abundance of "acquired memories." He is, more than most of us care to admit, very like the fabricator of a mosaic. The fingers of his mind are forever reaching back into the heaps of colored fragments in the storerooms, trying to make them fit his design, discovering a piece of unusual shape or tint and modifying the design to bring it in. And then, when it is all in, in the rough, it must be cemented, and scoured, and smoothed, and polished.

Am I depressing? Do I present to your youthful imagination a series of perilous ascents to the hills of fair renown? That is not my design, at all events. I am not unmindful of the charming confidence you have reposed in my omniscience, and I consider it an honorable charge to give the best counsel in my power. "There is no Excellent Beauty that hath not some Strangeness in the Proportion" is an epigram I commend to your careful attention. We shall assume that you are sufficiently intelligent to understand what Lord Bacon meant when he said it. And in turning over in my mind that part of your letter in which you say you are so seriously considering the literary life that you are unable to keep out of it, it occurs to me to repeat what I have already said in some place, that the best training for literature is to take up something else. And by that I mean you will become more easily a thinker, which is indispensable to the artist, if you get your store of "acquired memories" by way of a settled and secular calling. Perhaps the further removed from literature the better, as Keats was a druggist, you will remember, and Bunyan a tinker. So you will secure for yourself a means of living and a long apprenticeship.

And now, as I look back over the pages I have written and the years I have lived, I am not sure I have given you the key, after all! I am not confident, I fear, that I know just what art is or how it can be defined. For that is your need. If we could only find a nice, concise, and noncorroding definition, how happy we should be! I am reminded by that of one I read many years ago, incongruous enough in its origin, for George Gissing could, by no stretch of word meanings, be said to have had a great deal of joy. But in that wonderful little book he wrote toward the end, *The Private Papers of Henry Ryecroft,* a book that was like the last sudden roseate glow in a somber western sky after a stormy day, he gives us his creed, that art is the expression of the joy in life.

I offer it to you with reservations. It has many votaries and will serve you for a few years. But at the back of my mind I think the truth is more subtle than Gissing suspected, fine artist that he was. For it may be doubted if a human being saturated with the joy of life, a perfectly happy person, could create anything at all. Indeed Gissing's own life affords evidence that one of the most potent incentives to the creation of works of art is grief, sorrow. I do not mean that we should be forever composing lamentations, but that grief is a lens of extraordinary power through which we can behold the workings of our own hearts.

Perhaps you now see the point toward which I have been working—that your book or your poem, if it is to have any appeal at all, must be a product of your character. All the long weary road you are about to travel, the slow accretion of "acquired memories," the perception of analogies and the comprehension of the mechanism of metaphor are but the preliminary skirmishes in the great business of becoming a writer. And when you have learned your trade as apprentice and improver, when you have grown inured to the singular fact that no measure of acceptance can ever destroy the anxiety in your heart because your work is not better, then perhaps you may begin cautiously to regard yourself as an artist. And the test is this—that in darkness and trouble, when the amenities of life are withdrawn, when love and friendship are uncertain, you can turn to your writing and find therein an indestructible consolation.

WHAT KEEPS YOU SAFE IN THE SUBWAY RUSH?[1]

Robert B. Peck

The encroachment of mechanical devices upon man power in a rapid-transit era, which sees ten-car trains operated by two men and the linked, fiery-eyed monsters of the underground taking turn-off switches apparently of their own volition, has not yet driven the towerman from his battery of switches.

He survives by reason of his brain and faithfulness, as does the lighthouse keeper in an age of automatic lighting and extinguishing devices, which may keep an untended beacon light in the hours of darkness for months on end.

No engine of human invention has been contrived which can be relied upon, month in and month out, to sort out trains at the rate of fifty-six a minute, as does the B.-M. T. towerman at the Essex Street station at the Manhattan end of the Williamsburg Bridge.

No automotion has been invented upon which the B.-M. T. will rely to play the intricate chess game, with populous trains as pieces, which three nonchalant young men play in the tower at East New York, where three rapid-transit lines converge, their tracks depressed or elevated in great arcs like the tracks of a roller coaster, so that no track crosses another at the same level.

There the trains of the Lexington Avenue, the Fulton Street, and the Broadway lines hump themselves and leap or swoop in leisurely dignity like so many inch worms playing leapfrog, as they pick their way to Jamaica, Richmond Hill, or Canarsie.

High above the tracks, where Jamaica Bay lies spread out below on one side and all of Brooklyn on the other, is the signal tower in the topmost room of which, glassed in like the light chamber of a lighthouse, is the battery of 168 signals, which controls the movement of the trains.

The handles project in a long, narrow row and are shaped much like those of a compass saw, though made of steel and far heavier.

---

[1]From The New York *Herald-Tribune.*

When one is pulled out the mechanism of a distant switch begins to move, but the movement of the handle cannot be completed nor the switch signal set to go ahead until a sharp click like a cocked pistol informs the towerman the switch is locked.

Once the train has started forward to take the switch in obedience to the signal, the switch cannot be unlocked. This guard, which is automatic, is to prevent such accidents as the one which occurred recently in the Sunnyside yards of the Long Island Railroad, where a switch was thrown while a train was passing over it.

Although the inception of every train movement is of human origin, every such movement is hedged about with automatic safety devices, designed to eliminate so far as possible the factor of human fallibility. Only human brains and faithfulness are utilized.

The entire signal system operated from the tower is interlocked so that conflicting signals cannot be shown. The signal levers must be operated in a predetermined order.

"They're on roller skates up there during the rush hour," is the way an official of the signal department described the haste which the growing burden of trains imposed upon the three men on duty at such times in the tower. But it is a haste which cannot be misdirected. Swift as are the movements of the men, they are restrained by an invisible barrier of automatic safeguards on every side which guide them in precisely the right direction at all times.

The towermen do not have to glance aside from their work to note the approach of a train. Before each of them is a map of the tracks in the section governed by the signals under his hand and a light flashes at the proper spot on it when a train is approaching.

Dusk of a fall evening is the time to see the towerman at work. Glowing trainloads of homeward-bound humanity stream smoothly below him, converging, diverging, weaving above and below each other, like the pattern in some gayly crocheted shawl. For a moment they pause and goggle at the tower with eyes of red or green or orange and then, in obedience to the slurring click of the signal lever, slide smoothly on their way.

The towerman has small time to marvel at the brilliant sequence of looping glow-worms that passes his eyrie. His eyes are upon the map before him on the wall, where bulbs suddenly burn white to show a train is waiting for the signal. With a dead cigaret pendant and forgotten on his lower lip, the towerman hastens from lever to lever, the slave of the vast mechanism, of which he also is master.

Everywhere throughout the rapid-transit system the human element operates within certain safety zones, established by mechanical devices. It is a balanced system of operation.

The subway motorman, approaching a block signal that shows red, might possibly be suddenly stricken with some mental affliction, causing him to ignore it. But his train would not pass the danger signal. Regardless of the human element in the driver's cab, the power would be shut off, the brakes applied and the train would come to a stop.

This miracle is accomplished by a tripping device similar to that in use in the Interborough subways. When the block signal, which is set automatically by the last train to pass it, shows red, a track current sets in operation a small but powerful motor buried in a steel case at the tie level.

The motor raises from the roadbed beside the rail a steel arm, tipped with a head like that of a heavy hammer. The head comes to rest in the air at exactly the level of a pipe connected with the air-brakes which protrudes from the side of the subway car. If the train starts to enter the closed block, the hammer head comes in contact with the brake pipe, setting the brakes, and at the same time shutting off the power.

Only with full knowledge of where he is going can a motorman enter a block on which the signal shows red. There is a button on the side of the signal which he can reach out and press after bringing his train to a stop. Pressure on the button releases the upthrust hammer beside the track, and his train passes into the block unhindered, the hammer rising behind it to bring the next train to a stop. Such a counter device is necessary in order to prevent tie-ups which might be caused by faulty signals.

The signal system, however, is seldom at fault. Modifications of the trip-stop motor have been made recently, and some of those of the new design have remained sealed for almost a year without being touched by a repair man. The B.-M. T. has about a thousand such motors, which cost it $500 apiece.

There is another device which is installed on stretches of track where the speed is limited, which prevents the train from exceeding that limit.

As on the Interborough lines, the B.-M. T. subway trains are protected by the "dead man's button," which will cut off the power and apply the brakes the moment the motorman relinquishes his grip upon the controller. Only the pressure of his fingers keeps the button flush with the handle of the controller. The moment it springs out from its socket the brakes are applied and the power cut off.

Even the passengers themselves come directly under the sway of the automatic rules of the subways. By means of a device in use on no other subway in the world, the force with which the brakes are applied on B.-M. T. trains is regulated by the weight of the load carried by the cars.

The heavier the load, the more pressure is exerted upon the brakes automatically. The momentum gathered by a heavily laden train is thus counterbalanced, and it may be brought to a stop with the same facility as a lighter train.

The automatically adjusted brakes are of especial value in the subway, where the steel cars are of comparatively light construction. The huge cars used by the B.-M. T. weigh 85,000 pounds apiece and have a capacity of 38,000 pounds of humanity. When crowded, therefore, they weigh about 45 per cent more than when empty.

A nice adjustment of the brake to the load is most necessary, the airbrake being the most powerful adjunct of a train. It has been figured that the airbrake on a passenger train is capable of more work in twenty seconds than the locomotive can accomplish in seven minutes.

Swift, smooth, accurate stops are necessary to the comfort of passengers in the subway and to the maintenance of the headway of trains. A constant braking power might lock the brake shoes on a light train so tight as to cause the wheels to slide, and, when the train was heavily loaded, might not be sufficient to bring it to a neat stop.

The efficacy of the combination of man and machine in the subways is testified to by the rarity of fatal accidents on the subway lines. It is far safer to ride in the subway than to cross the street. In the first six months of this year 448 persons were killed by automobiles in this city, while vehicular accidents of all other kinds, including subway accidents, resulted in only eighteen deaths.

Numerous as are the mechanisms governing the operation of the subways, there are numerous ambitious inventors with schemes to increase them. Frequent suggestions are received by officers of the B.-M. T. as to methods of operating their trains without either guards or motormen.

A typical plan was one submitted recently by a man who suggested a break in the third rail ahead of each station. As the power was thus shut off the brakes would be applied automatically with exactly the right force to bring the train to a stop at the station. The stopping of the train would bring into action another circuit which would open the doors of the cars for a certain specified time and the closing of the doors would complete another circuit which would release the brakes and gradually apply the power.

Scores of persons have written in to suggest the use of phonographs to announce the stations.

The B.-M. T., like other transit corporations, continually is experimenting along such lines. Not long ago it had the representative of the manufacturers who supply the London underground with its automatic station announcer experimenting with his device in B.-M. T. trains. It worked well in London, but conditions here were against it. The device consists of a list of stations, posted in each car, the name of the next station being illuminated as soon as the train pulls out of a station.

The London underground system consists of a central belt line from which radiate other lines to various parts of the city. Each line is operated independently as far as equipment goes. Cars used on a spoke are never transferred to the hub, or to any other spoke. Consequently, the roll of stations to be posted in each car is comparatively short, consisting only of the stations on that particular line.

Owing to the plan of the New York subway system, to the storage facilities for cars and to the demands of traffic, not only are cars transferred from one line to another with great frequency, but at certain hours, on the B.-M. T. system, trains skip certain stations at which, at other hours, they stop.

The London scheme was tried on the Bay Ridge line and, under the conditions existing here, was far from satisfactory. The list of stations was so long as to be confusing. It was impossible to adapt the illuminating device to the practice of skipping certain stations at certain hours.

The plan was abandoned, as many inventions, which seemed promising at first, have been. Nevertheless, the advances made in automatic equipment since the first subway was opened in this city twenty years ago are tremendous and rapid-transit officials are not prepared to deny that the future may see subway trains as devoid of human control as the escalator in a department store.

Even the towerman may go. Already a tower here and there at turn-off switches on the Brooklyn elevated system has been abandoned, the switches being operated automatically, in much the same way that trolley switches are.

IDEAL AND MATERIAL GREATNESS IN ARCHITECTURE[1]

Coventry Patmore

St. Thomas Aquinas writes: "Great riches are not required for the habit of magnificence; it is enough that a man should dispose of such as he possesses greatly, according to time and place." As in life, so in art, and especially in architecture, greatness of style is quite independent of wealth of material; indeed, wealth of material is constantly found by true artists to be a fatal hindrance to grandeur of effect. Hence great poets and painters are usually very shy of what commonly pass for great subjects—that is, subjects full of obvious interest and splendor; and, if they treat such subjects at all, they begin by denuding them as far as possible of all that makes them attractive to the novice in art, until they come to a simple greatness which was hitherto a secret.

Now I wish to point out what I conceive to be a principal condition of great effect with small means and in small or comparatively small buildings. It is magnificence in the expenditure of such material as the architect possesses, and especially of stone, brick, and timber. It is commonly supposed, even by architects, that a solidity of wall and roof sufficient to put far out of sight any idea of in-

[1]From *Principles in Art.*

security or decay, if properly shown forth and expressed by chamfer, molding, cornice, shafted recess, and the many other "decorations" which are principally methods of showing the thickness of wall and weight of roof, is all that noble building calls for; and that the frequent — nay, general — practice of ancient architecture in going much further than this was simply waste of material caused by want of mechanical knowledge. But those who know most of ancient architecture know best that there was no want of mechanical knowledge displayed in it, but quite the reverse. Not only is mechanical knowledge, equal to if not beyond our own, proved by such buildings as York and Salisbury Cathedrals, but the house and cottage builder of the sixteenth and seventeenth centuries seems to have known all the details of his business fully as well as the most ingenious economist of material that ever "scamped" a modern tenement of the same order. He was fully aware that the strength of a joist or rafter lay rather in its depth than in its breadth, and that, for a time at least, a few boards two inches thick and ten inches deep, set edgeways, would suffice to carry the roof, which nevertheless it pleased him better to lay upon a succession of beams ten inches square. It is the reality, and the modest ostentation of the reality, of such superfluous substantiality that constitutes the secret of effect in many an old house that strikes us as "architectural" though it may be almost wholly without architectural ornament; and, in the very few instances in which modern buildings have been raised in the same fashion, the beholder at once feels that their generous regard for the far future is of almost as poetical a character as the aged retrospect of a similar house of the time of Henry VIII or Elizabeth. A man now hires a bit of ground for eighty or ninety years; and, if he has something to spare for spending on beauty, he says to himself: "I will build me a house that will last my time, and what money I have over I will spend in decorating it. Why should I waste my means in raising wall and roof which will last five times as long as I or mine shall want them?" The answer is: Because that very "waste" is the truest and most striking ornament; and though your and your family's usufruct of a house thus magnanimously built may be but a fifth of its natural age, there lies in that very fact an "ornament" of the most noble and touching kind, which will be obvious at all seasons to yourself and every beholder, though the consciousness of its cause may be dormant; whereas the meanness of your own plan will be only the more apparent with every penny you spend in making it meretricious.

I have said that a modest ostentation of extreme substantiality is also an element of architectural effect in the kind of building contemplated. This, indeed, is the properly architectural or artistic element. A house will look respectable, and something more than respectable, which has only the reality of being built somewhat better than well. But consciousness is the life of art, and there must be a quiet rejoicing in strength, solidity, and permanence, to give these characters that power over the imagination which a work of art must have. A laborer's cottage or the smallest village church which has this character is an artistic and rightly architectural work; and the nobleman's mansion or the cathedral which wants it is not. Here comes in that true "decoration" which scarcely the humblest house of the sixteenth or early part of the seventeenth century was altogether without. In out-of-the-way villages and roadside inns of that period, you will find your attention directed to the thickness and weight of the roof timbers by a carved or molded cornice, that measures and expatiates upon the depth and substance of the rafters terminating there; or one or more of the brackets supporting the joists of the overhanging bedroom floor will have a touch of carving, to declare with what ease and pleasure the burthen is borne upon their sturdy shoulders; or the lintel of the door will show and boast of the thickness of the wall by a molded chamfer. A single touch of such decoration glorifies the whole, and puts the living spirit of art into the body of an honest building, however humble it may be.

So far is size from being needful to greatness in architecture, that one of the very grandest pieces of domestic building I ever saw is a little village inn of extremely early date in a Sussex village which scarcely anybody has ever heard of, though it stands but two miles from Berwick Station on the South Coast Railway. This village is Aldfriston. It has in its little market place an extremely ancient stone cross, far gone in decay, having never been touched by restorer. The whole village has an air of antiquity such as breathes from no other English village I have ever seen; but older than anything, except the cross, is its hostelry — no bigger than a well-to-do bailiff's cottage, showing no Elizabethan "variety" in its ground plan, and the front to the street having but three windows above and one on either side of the doorway. When I came upon it quite unprepared for seeing anything particular in the village, this house fairly took my breath away by its exemplification of the way in which ideal and material greatness differ. It was like coming, in a newspaper article, upon three or four lines, of great and unknown poetry. Yet it was nothing but a cottage built mightily, and with a mighty consciousness of being so built. It seems never to have been touched, except here and there by the house painter, since the date at which it was raised, which was probably in the fifteenth century, the carved foliage in the spandrels of the small arched doorway indicating that period. An architect learned in moldings might perhaps fix the date to within twenty-five years, from those of the cornice. The bedroom story projects considerably over the ground floor, and is borne by great oak brackets, the faces of which are adorned with painted carvings of figures in miters, one being St. Hubert, as is shown by the stag at his feet. The spaces between these brackets are ceiled with a great plaster "cavetto," which, together with the brackets, springs from a wide timber cornice above the door and windows of the ground floor. In the hollow of this cornice are four or five grotesque faces, the painting of which, though fresh, seems, like the painting of all the other decorations, to be nothing but the original coloring faithfully transmitted. The three windows of the upper floor are bays, and are carried by great spread brackets, carved and painted with most curiously quaint and simple representations of St. George and the Dragon and symbols of his tradition, the tails of two dragons in the central bracket running in their extremities into the outlines of a pointed and foliated arch. The roof is covered in with slabs of ragged stone, thick enough for a London pavement. The dimensions of the timbers of the roof are proved inferentially by the fact that the roof tree has not sagged an inch under some four hundred years of this burthen; and their mass and power are expressed artistically by their termination in a cornice of immense depth, and consisting of a greater number of molded "members" than I remember to have seen in any other feature of the kind. The walls are plastered in their plain spaces, but indicate their construction of solid oak—which, by the way, is far more durable than either brick or any ordinary stone—by the chance appearance in one place of a strange animal which runs up the face of the wall and is obviously carved out of a beam otherwise hid by the plaster.

There is nothing heavy in the total effect of this extraordinary piece of cottage architecture; for there is artistic animation everywhere, and the expression of its strength is that of living power and not mere passive sufficiency.

To build such a cottage now might cost about three times as much as it does to build a common country inn of the same dimensions. It would not, of course, suit a London citizen so well as a Chiselhurst villa of like size and cost; but it would be a fit abode for a duke in difficulties.

THE PHILOSOPHY OF COMPOSITION

Edgar Allan Poe

Charles Dickens, in a note now lying before me, alluding to an examination I once made of the mechanism of *Barnaby Rudge,* says: "By the way, are you aware that Godwin wrote his *Caleb Williams* backwards? He first involved his hero in a web of difficulties, forming the second volume, and then, for first, cast about for some mode of accounting for what had been done."

I cannot think this is the *precise* mode of procedure on the part of Godwin—and indeed what he himself acknowledges is not altogether in accordance with Mr. Dickens' idea; but the author of *Caleb Williams* was too good an artist not to perceive the advantage derivable from at least a somewhat similar process. Nothing is more clear than that every plot, worth the name, must be elaborated to its *dénouement* before anything be attempted with the pen. It is only with the *dénouement* constantly in view that we can give a plot its indispensable air of consequence, or causation, by making the incidents, and especially the tone at all points, tend to the development of the intention.

There is a radical error, I think, in the usual mode of constructing a story. Either history affords a thesis, or one is suggested by an incident of the day, or, at best, the author sets himself to work in the combination of striking events to form merely the basis of his narrative, designing, generally, to fill in with description, dialogue, or authorial comment whatever crevices of facts or action may from page to page render themselves apparent.

I prefer commencing with the consideration of an *effect*. Keeping originality *always* in view — for he is false to himself who ventures to dispense with so obvious and so easily attainable a source of interest — I say to myself, in the first place, — "Of the innumerable effects, or impressions, of which the heart, the intellect or (more generally) the soul is susceptible, what one shall I, on the present occasion, select?" Having chosen a novel, first, and secondly, a vivid effect, I consider whether it can be best wrought by incident or tone — whether by ordinary incidents and peculiar tone, or the converse, or by peculiarity both of incident and tone — afterward looking about me (or rather within) for such combination of event, or tone, as shall best aid me in the construction of the effect.

I have often thought how interesting a magazine paper might be written by any author who would — that is to say, who could — detail step by step, the processes by which any one of his compositions attained its ultimate point of completion. Why such a paper has never been given to the world, I am much at a loss to say, but, perhaps, the authorial vanity has had more to do with the omission than any one other cause. Most writers — poets in especial — prefer having it understood that they compose by a species of fine frenzy — an ecstatic intuition; and would positively shudder at letting the public take a peep behind the scenes at the elaborate and vacillating crudities of thought, at the true purposes seized only at the last moment, at the innumerable glimpses of idea that arrived not at the maturity of full view, at the fully matured fancies discarded in despair as unmanageable, at the cautious selections and rejections, at the painful erasures and interpolations — in a word, at the wheels and pinions, the tackle for scene-shifting, the step-ladders and demon-traps, the cock's feathers, the red paint and the black patches, which in ninety-nine cases out of the hundred constitute the properties of the literary *histrio*.

I am aware, on the other hand, that the case is by no means common in which an author is at all in condition to retrace the steps by which his conclusions have been attained. In general, suggestions, having arisen pell-mell, are pursued and forgotten in a similar manner.

For my own part, I have neither sympathy with the repugnance alluded to, nor at any time the least difficulty in recalling to mind the progressive steps of any of my compositions; and, since the interest of an analysis, or reconstruction, such as I have considered a *desideratum,* is quite independent of any real or fancied interest in the thing analyzed, it will not be regarded as a breach of decorum on my part to show the *modus operandi* by which some one of my own works was put together. I select *The Raven* as most generally known. It is my design to render it manifest that no one point in its composition is referable either to accident or intuition; that the work proceeded, step by step, to its completion, with the precision and rigid consequence of a mathematical problem.

Let us dismiss, as irrelevant to the poem *per se,* the circumstance — or say the necessity — which in the first place gave rise to the intention of composing *a* poem that should suit at once the popular and the critical taste.

We commence, then, with this intention.

The initial consideration was that of extent. If any literary work is too long to be read at one sitting, we must be content to dispense with the immensely important effect derivable from unity of impression; for, if two sittings be required, the affairs of the world interfere, and everything like totality is at once destroyed. But since, *ceteris paribus,* no poet can afford to dispense with *anything* that may advance his design, it but remains to be seen whether there is, in extent, any advantage to counterbalance the loss of unity which attends it. Here I say no, at once. What we term a long poem is, in fact, merely a succession of brief ones — that is to say, of brief poetical effects. It is needless to demonstrate that a poem is such, only inasmuch as it intensely excites, by elevating, the soul; and all intense excitements are, through a psychal necessity, brief. For this reason, at least one half of the *Paradise Lost* is essentially prose — a succession of poetical excitements interspersed, *inevitably,* with corresponding depressions — the whole thing deprived, through the extremeness of its length, of the vastly important artistic element, totality, or unity, of effect.

It appears evident, then, that there is a distinct limit, as regards length, to all works of literary art — the limit of a single sitting; and that, although in certain classes of prose composition, such as *Robinson Crusoe* (demanding no unity), this limit may be advantageously overpassed, it can never properly be overpassed in a poem. Within this limit, the extent of a poem may be made to bear mathematical relation to its merit — in other words, to the excitement or elevation — again, in other words, to the degree of the true poetical effect which it is capable of inducing; for it is clear that the brevity must be in direct ratio of the intensity of the intended effect: — this, without proviso — that a certain degree of duration is absolutely requisite for the production of any effect at all.

Holding in view these considerations, as well as that degree of excitement which I deemed not above the popular while not below the critical taste, I reached at once what I conceived the proper *length* for my intended poem — a length of about one hundred lines. It is, in fact, a hundred and eight.

My next thought concerned the choice of an impression, or effect, to be conveyed: and here I may as well observe that, throughout the construction, I kept steadily in view the design of rendering the work *universally* appreciable. I should be carried too far out of my immediate topic were I to demonstrate a point upon which I have repeatedly insisted, and which with the poetical stands not in the slightest need of demonstration — the point, I mean, that Beauty is the sole legitimate province of the poem. A few words, however, in elucidation of my real meaning, which some of my friends have evinced a disposition to misrepresent. That pleasure which is at once the most intense, the most elevating, and the most pure, is, I believe, found in the contemplation of the beautiful. When, indeed, men speak of Beauty, they mean, precisely, not a quality, as is supposed, but an effect; they refer, in short, just to that intense and pure elevation of *soul* — *not* of intellect, or of heart — upon which I have commented, and which is experienced in consequence of contemplating "the beautiful." Now I designate Beauty as the province of the poem, merely because it is an obvious rule of Art that effects should be made to spring from direct causes — that objects should be attained through means best adapted for their attainment — no one as yet having been weak enough to deny that the peculiar elevation alluded to is *most readily* attained in the poem. Now the object, Truth, or the satisfaction of the intellect, and the object, Passion, or the excitement of the heart, are, although attainable to a certain extent in poetry, far more readily attainable in prose. Truth, in fact, demands a precision, and Passion, a *homeliness* (the truly passionate will comprehend me), which are absolutely antagonistic to that Beauty which, I maintain, is the excitement, or pleasurable elevation, of the soul. It by no means follows from anything here said that passion, or even truth, may not be introduced, and even profitably introduced, into a poem — for they may serve in elucidation, or aid the general effect, as do discords in music, by contrast; but the true artist will always contrive, first, to tone them into proper subservience to the predominant aim, and, secondly, to enveil them, as far as possible, in that Beauty which is the atmosphere and the essence of the poem.

Regarding, then, Beauty as my province, my next question referred to the *tone* of its highest manifestation; and all experience has shown that this tone is one of *sadness*. Beauty of whatever kind, in its supreme development, invariably excites the sensitive soul to tears. Melancholy is thus the most legitimate of all the poetical tones.

The length, the province, and the tone, being thus determined, I betook myself to ordinary induction, with the view of obtaining some artistic piquancy which might serve me as a keynote in the construction of the poem — some pivot upon which the whole structure might turn. In carefully thinking over all the usual artistic effects — or more properly *points*, in the theatrical sense — I did not fail to perceive immediately that no one had been so universally employed as that of the *refrain*. The universality of its employment sufficed to assure me of its intrinsic value, and spared me the necessity of submitting it to analysis. I considered it, however, with regard to its susceptibility of improvement, and soon saw it to be in a primitive condition. As commonly used, the *refrain*, or burden, not only is limited to lyric verse, but depends for its impression upon the force of monotone — both in sound and thought. The pleasure is deduced solely from the sense of identity — of repetition. I resolved to diversify, and so heighten, the effect, by adhering, in general, to the monotone of sound, while I continually varied that of thought: that is to say, I determined to produce continuously novel effects, by the variation *of the application* of the *refrain* — the *refrain* itself remaining, for the most part, unvaried.

These points being settled, I next bethought me of the *nature* of my *refrain*. Since its application was to be repeatedly varied, it was clear that the *refrain* itself must be brief, for there would have been an insurmountable difficulty in frequent variations of application in any sentence of length. In proportion to the brevity of the sentence, would, of course, be the facility of the variation. This led me at once to a single word as the best *refrain*.

The question now arose as to the *character* of the word. Having made up my mind to a *refrain*, the division of the poem into stanzas was, of course, a corollary; the *refrain* forming the close to each stanza. That such a close, to have force, must be sonorous and susceptible of protracted emphasis, admitted no doubt; and these considerations inevitably led me to the long *o* as the most sonorous vowel in connection with *r* as the most producible consonant.

The sound of the *refrain* being thus determined, it became necessary to select a word embodying this sound and at the same time in the fullest possible keeping with that melancholy which I had predetermined as the tone of the poem. In such a search it would have been absolutely impossible to overlook the word "Nevermore." In fact, it was the very first which presented itself.

The *desideratum* was a pretext for the continuous use of the one word "Nevermore." In observing the difficulty which I at once found in inventing a sufficiently plausible reason for its continuous repetition, I did not fail to perceive that this difficulty arose solely from the pre-assumption that the word was to be so continuously or monotonously spoken by a *human* being; I did not fail to perceive, in short, that the difficulty lay in the reconciliation of this monotony with the exercise of reason on the part of the creature repeating the word. Here, then, immediately arose the idea of a *non*-reasoning creature capable of speech; and very naturally, a parrot, in the first instance, suggested itself, but was superseded forthwith by a Raven as equally capable of speech and infinitely more in keeping with the intended *tone*.

I had now gone so far as the conception of a Raven — the bird of ill omen — monotonously repeating the one word, "Nevermore," at the conclusion of each stanza, in a poem of melancholy tone, and in length about one hundred lines. Now, never losing sight of the object *supremeness*, or perfection, at all points, I asked myself: "Of all melancholy topics what, according to the universal understanding of mankind, is the *most* melancholy?" Death — was the obvious reply. "And when," I said, "is the most melancholy of topics poetical?" From what I have already explained at some length, the answer here also is obvious — "When it most closely allies itself to *Beauty;* the death, then, of a beautiful woman is, unquestionably, the most poetical topic in the world — and equally is it beyond doubt that the lips best suited for such a topic are those of a bereaved lover."

I had now to combine the two ideas, of a lover lamenting his deceased mistress and a Raven continuously repeating the word "Nevermore." I had to combine these, bearing in mind my design of varying at every turn the *application* of the word repeated; but the only intelligible mode of such combination is that of imagining the Raven employing the word in answer to the queries of the lover. And here it was that I saw at once the opportunity afforded for the effect on which I had been depending — that is to say, the effect of the *variation of application.* I saw that I could make the first query propounded by the lover — the first query to which the Raven should reply "Nevermore" — that I could make this first inquiry a commonplace one, the second less so, the third still less, and so on, until at length the lover, startled from his original nonchalance by the melancholy character of the word itself, by its frequent repetition and by a consideration of the ominous reputation of the fowl that uttered it, is at length excited to superstition, and wildly propounds queries of a far different character — queries whose solution he has passionately at heart — propounds them half in superstition and half in that species of despair which delights in self-torture — propounds them, not altogether because he believes in the prophetic or demoniac character of the bird (which, reason assures him, is merely repeating a lesson learned by rote), but because he experiences a frenzied pleasure in so modeling his questions as to receive from the *expected* "Nevermore" the most delicious, because the most intolerable, of sorrow. Perceiving the opportunity thus afforded me — or, more strictly, thus forced upon me in the progress of the construction — I first established in mind the climax, or concluding query — that query to which "Nevermore" should be in the last place an answer — that query in reply to which this word "Nevermore" should be in the last place an answer — that query in reply to which this word "Nevermore" should involve the utmost conceivable amount of sorrow and despair.

Here then the poem may be said to have its beginning—at the end, where all works of art should begin; for it was here at this point of my preconsiderations, that I first put pen to paper in the composition of the stanza:—

"Prophet," said I, "thing of evil—prophet still, if bird or devil.
By that Heaven that bends above us, by that God we both adore,
Tell this soul with sorrow laden if, within the distant Aiden,
It shall clasp a sainted maiden whom the angels name Lenore,
Clasp a rare and radiant maiden whom the angels name Lenore!"
Quoth the Raven, "Nevermore."

I composed this stanza, at this point, first, that by establishing the climax I might the better vary and graduate, as regards seriousness and importance, the preceding queries of the lover, and, secondly, that I might definitely settle the rhythm, the meter, and the length and general arrangement of the stanza, as well as graduate the stanzas which were to precede so that none of them might surpass this in rhythmical effect. Had I been able, in the subsequent composition, to construct more vigorous stanzas, I should, without scruple, have purposely enfeebled them, so as not to interfere with the climacteric effect.

And here I may as well say a few words of the versification. My first object (as usual) was originality. The extent to which this has been neglected in versification, is one of the most unaccountable things in the world. Admitting that there is little possibility of variety in mere rhythm, it is still clear that the possible varieties of meter and stanza are absolutely infinite—and yet, *for centuries, no man, in verse, has ever done, or ever seemed to think of doing, an original thing*. The fact is, that originality (unless in minds of very unusual force) is by no means a matter, as some suppose, of impulse or intuition. In general, to be found, it must be elaborately sought, and, although a positive merit of the highest class, demands in its attainment less of invention than negation.

Of course, I pretend to no originality in either the rhythm or meter of the *Raven*. The former is trochaic, the latter is octometer acatalectic, alternating with heptameter catalectic repeated in the refrain of the fifth verse, and terminating with tetrameter catalectic. Less pedantically—the feet employed throughout (trochees) consist of a long syllable followed by a short; the first line of the stanza consists of eight of these feet, the second of seven and a half (in effect two thirds), the third of eight, the fourth of seven and a half, the fifth the same, the sixth three and a half. Now, each of these lines, taken individually, has been employed before, and what originality the *Raven* has is in their *combination into stanza;* nothing even remotely approaching this combination has ever been attempted. The effect of this originality of combination is aided by other unusual and some altogether novel effects, arising from an extension of the application of the principles of rime and alliteration.

The next point to be considered was the mode of bringing together the lover and the Raven; and the first branch of this consideration was the *locale*. For this the most natural suggestion might seem to be a forest, or the fields; but it has always appeared to me that a close *circumspection of space* is absolutely necessary to the effect of insulated accident:—it has the force of a frame to a picture. It has an indisputable moral power in keeping concentrated the attention, and of course, must not be confounded with mere unity of place.

I determined, then, to place the lover in his chamber—in a chamber rendered sacred to him by memories of her who had frequented it. The room is represented as richly furnished—this is mere pursuance of the ideas I have already explained on the subject of Beauty, as the sole true poetical thesis.

The *locale* being thus determined, I had now to introduce the bird, and the thought of introducing him through the window was inevitable. The idea of making the lover suppose in the first instance that the flapping of the wings of the bird against the shutter is a "tapping" at the door, originated in a wish to increase, by prolonging, the reader's curiosity, and in a desire to admit the incidental effect arising from the lover's throwing open the door, finding all dark, and thence adopting the half-fancy that it was the spirit of his mistress that knocked.

I made the night tempestuous, first, to account for the Raven's seeking admission, and secondly, for the effect of contrast with the (physical) serenity within the chamber.

I made the bird alight on the bust of Pallas, also for the effect of contrast between the marble and the plumage—it being understood that the bust was absolutely *suggested* by the bird; the bust of *Pallas* being chosen, first, as most in keeping with the scholarship of the lover, and secondly, for the sonorousness of the word, Pallas, itself.

About the middle of the poem, also, I have availed myself of the force of contrast with a view of deepening the ultimate impression. For example, an air of the fantastic, approaching as nearly to the ludicrous as was admissible, is given to the Raven's entrance. He comes in "with many a flirt and flutter."

Not the *least obeisance made he;* not a minute stopped or stayed he;
But, with mien of lord or lady, perched above my chamber door.

In the two stanzas which follow, the design is more obviously carried out:

Then this ebony bird beguiling my sad fancy into smiling
By the *grave and stern decorum of the countenance it wore*—
"Though thy *crest be shorn and shaven,* thou," I said, "are sure no craven,
Ghastly grim and ancient Raven wandering from the nightly shore:
Tell me what thy lordly name is on the Night's Plutonian shore!"
Quoth the Raven, "Nevermore."

Much I marvelled *this ungainly fowl* to hear discourse so plainly,
Though its answer little meaning—little relevancy bore;
For we cannot help agreeing that no living human being
Ever yet was blessed with seeing bird above his chamber door,
Bird or beast upon the sculptured bust above his chamber door,
With such name as "Nevermore."

The effect of the *dénouement* being thus provided for, I immediately drop the fantastic for a tone of the most profound seriousness:—this tone commencing in the stanza directly following the one last quoted, with the line,

But the Raven, sitting lonely on the placid bust, spoke only, etc.

From this epoch the lover no longer jests—no longer sees anything even of the fantastic in the Raven's demeanor. He speaks of him as a "grim, ungainly, ghastly, gaunt, and ominous bird of yore," and feels the "fiery eyes" burning into his "bosom's core." This revolution of thought, or fancy, on the lover's part, is intended to induce a similar one on the part of the reader—to bring the mind into a proper frame for the *dénouement* which is now brought about as rapidly and as *directly* as possible.

With the *dénouement* proper—with the Raven's reply "Nevermore," to the lover's final demand if he shall meet his mistress in another world — the poem, in its obvious phase, that of a simple narrative, may be said to have its completion. So far, everything is within the limits of the accountable, of the real. A raven, having learned by rote the single word "Nevermore" and having escaped from the custody of its owner, is driven at midnight through the violence of a storm to seek admission at a window from which a light still gleams — the chamber window of a student, occupied half in poring over a volume, half in dreaming of a beloved mistress deceased. The casement being thrown open at the fluttering of the bird's wings, the bird itself perches on the most convenient seat out of the immediate reach of the student, who, amused by the incident and the oddity of the visitor's demeanor, demands of it, in jest and without looking for a reply, its name. The raven addressed, answers with its customary word, "Nevermore" — a word which finds immediate echo in the melancholy heart of the student, who, giving utterance aloud to certain thoughts suggested by the occasion, is again startled by the fowl's repetition of "Nevermore." The student now guesses the state of the case, but is impelled, as I have before explained, by the human thirst for self-torture, and in part by superstition, to propound such queries to the bird as will bring him, the lover, the most of the luxury of sorrow, through the anticipated answer "Nevermore." With the indulgence, to the extreme, of this self-torture, the narration, in what I have termed its first or obvious phrase, has a natural termination, and so far there has been no overstepping of the limits of the real.

But in subjects so handled, however skillfully, or with however vivid an array of incident, there is always a certain hardness or nakedness, which repels the artistical eye. Two things are invariably required: first, some amount of complexity, or more properly, adaptation; and secondly, some amount of suggestiveness, some undercurrent, however indefinite, of meaning. It is this latter, in especial, which imparts to a work of art so much of that *richness* (to borrow from colloquy a forcible term) which we are too fond of confounding with *the ideal*. It is the *excess* of the suggested meaning — it is the rendering this the upper instead of the under current of the theme — which turns into prose (and that of the very flattest kind), the so-called poetry of the so-called transcendentalists.

Holding these opinions, I added the two concluding stanzas of the poem — their suggestiveness being thus made to pervade all the narrative which has preceded them. The undercurrent of meaning is rendered first apparent in the lines:

"Take thy beak from out my heart, and take thy form from off my door!"
Quoth the Raven, "Nevermore!"

It will be observed that the words, "from out my heart," involve the first metaphorical expression in the poem. They, with the answer, "Nevermore," dispose the mind to seek a moral in all that has been previously narrated. The reader begins now to regard the Raven as emblematical — but it is not until the very last line of the very last stanza that the intention of making him emblematical of *Mournful and Neverending Remembrance* is permitted distinctly to be seen:

And the Raven, never flitting, still is sitting, still is sitting,
On the pallid bust of Pallas just above my chamber door;
And his eyes have all the seeming of a demon's that is dreaming,
And the lamplight o'er him streaming throws his shadow on the floor;
And my soul *from out that shadow* that lies floating on the floor
Shall be lifted — nevermore.

DOES BUSINESS WANT SCHOLARS?[1]

Walter S. Gifford

President of the American Telephone and Telegraph Company

I

The other day a gentleman said to a New York friend of his who is a lawyer, "My son is going to graduate from the law school this year and is looking around for a place. Could I send him in to see you?"

[1]From *Harper's Magazine*, May, 1928; copyright, 1928, by Harper and Brothers. Used by permission of the author and *Harper's Magazine*.

The lawyer replied, "Certainly, I'd be glad to see him," but there was no great enthusiasm in his tone.

The father continued, "He is on the *Law Review,* and several offices have spoken to him; but if you will tell me who in your office sees . . ." He got no farther. "You send him right in to see me," answered the lawyer. "I'd like to talk to him."

The change had come over the lawyer when the father said "He is on the *Law Review.*" That means he is a high-mark man.

The big law firms seek the high-mark men from the law schools. The profession believes that the man who stands well in his law studies will make a better lawyer than one who does not.

The hospitals take the same attitude toward medical students. A man with low marks in the medical school is not likely to get an appointment in the best hospitals, for it is the experience of the medical profession that those who stand well in the professional school are more likely to stand well in their profession later on.

But business, on the other hand, does not as a rule select men on the basis of their marks in college. Perhaps for this reason the undergraduate who intends to go into business does not always consider his scholastic standing in relation to his business career. He is somewhat apt to think of his college course as an era in itself, without influence on his life after graduation. If he does connect his college course with a business future at all, he is likely to think that his athletic or social activities, his work on college papers or in dramatic clubs, or similar extracurricular efforts, are better training for the future than his academic work. Some do the academic work merely in order that they may stay in college to do the other things. And in taking this attitude the boys reflect fairly accurately the opinion of many of their elders, under whom they are going to begin their working career.

I believe that this attitude of business toward the scholarship of college graduates differs from the attitude of the legal and medical professions toward scholarship in the graduate schools for one main reason: business believes that a law school teaches a boy law but that a college does not teach a boy business. Consequently, a boy who stands high in the law school will possess knowledge more immediately useful than one who doesn't, while no matter how high a boy stands in college he will not have much, if any, knowledge immediately useful in business.

This, of course, flies counter to the theory of the educators. They maintain that the courses in college are so conducted that a boy who gets high marks will have had to use his brains and that the habit and ability to use his brains will make him valuable and successful in whatever he tries to do. The legal and medical professions rather sustain this contention, for they say that it is not so much what the men of high standing know that makes them valuable when they leave the professional schools, but the fact that they have the habit of successful mental accomplishment. The academic folk believe that, while a knowledge of history or philosophy may not be immediately applicable to the shoe business, a boy who did good work in history and philosophy is more likely to do well in the shoe business than one who did poorly in those subjects.

The educators believe that the process of education is a continuous interrelated process beginning early in school and ending late in life. They have figures to prove that the boys who do well in school generally do well in college, and that those who do well in college generally rank high in the professional schools, and that those who rank high in the professional schools generally succeed in the professions—law, medicine, and teaching. In fact, a high-grade man in school has much the best chance of being a high-grade man in college, in professional school, in practice, and all through life.

A very high percentage of the membership of the Phi Beta Kappa Society are mentioned in *Who's Who.* This does not necessarily bear directly upon the relationship between scholarship and business, because *Who's Who* is not intended as a guide to business distinction, but it does indicate that the high-mark men who chose the activities favored by *Who's Who* gained more distinction in those activities than the low-mark men.

Phi Beta Kappa claims 40 per cent of the Justices of the Supreme Court between 1800 and 1922, and 40 per cent of the Secretaries of State. Considering the small numbers of the Society, that is an amazing showing.

In 1911 President A. Lawrence Lowell of Harvard published an article on "College Studies and Professional Training" which showed that men who ranked high in their college studies were apt to rank high in the law and medical schools and that, in spite of exceptions, those who ranked lower in college ranked on the average lower in the professional schools. This deduction might reasonably make business wonder whether in preparing for business it makes much difference what subjects are mainly pursued in college—if these subjects, whatever they are, are pursued with sufficient success. A study of the statistics he presented must make any business man at least wonder whether, if high-rank men are so certain to do better in the professional schools and in the professions, it might not be that they are more likely to do better than the average in business.

In 1917 Dr. William Trufant Foster, then President of Reed College, published a book under the arresting title *Should Students Study?* In the chapter "Success in Studies and in Life" he presents material concerning graduates of West Point, of the Yale School of Forestry, of an engineering school, and of several colleges. In the case of each institution the high-scholarship men were mainly those who attained later eminence. Doctor Foster concludes, "Indeed it is likely that the first quarter in scholarship of any school or college class will give to the world as many distinguished men as the other three-quarters."

Last year Professor Hugh A. Smith of the University of Wisconsin published the results of a test based on 1,800 alumni of a large university. These men had received their bachelors' degrees over a period of 45 years, and all of them were at least 15 years out of college when the study was made. As it progressed, the committee compiling the information became more and more convinced of an almost invariable consistency between scholarship and success in life. To quote Professor Smith:

> A few representative figures will show the reason for these convictions. For the first two classes of 54 graduates, a number of persons were asked opinions concerning the career and success of the members, and 8 of these alumni were quite generally agreed on, and one other was suggested by at least two correspondents, as the most worthy. The college marks showed that the 8 universally approved had the highest average in the two classes, 6 being over 91 and 2 being 89. The other one, who won partial approval had a mark of 85, which was no higher than that of 4 or 5 not suggested as eminent.
>
> From a later class of 75 members, a final list was submitted to a number of people; 11 won general approval as to their eminence in life, and 5 others received 2 or more votes. Ten of the 11 were the first 10 in the class in grades, all averaging above 90.

These data indicate that in many fields college scholarship is a significant index of later success. But even they include relatively few cases of men in business.

II

Clearly, to tell whether high scholarship has a direct relationship to success in business, more comprehensive and more rigorous evidence is needed. Business itself can most easily collect that evidence. Furthermore, it can hardly afford not to do so. Each year at least half of the 40,000 young men graduating from our colleges are entering its ranks. Their selection and training require an extremely large investment. One of the most readily available objective measures of their past achievement is their college scholastic record. It measures the results in what, after all, has been their major task for four years. Its value for indicating future achievement is surely worth determining.

With this point of view, the personnel department of the American Telephone and Telegraph Company, under the direction of Mr. E. K. Hall, for the past two years has been making such a study of the relation of college scholarship to success in the Bell System. A large part of the study, covering the record of 4,125 of the college graduates in the Bell System from 104 colleges is completed. Additional records from a number of other colleges are expected, but there is no reason to believe that these additional cases will alter materially the general results already obtained.

When this study of the relation of college scholarship to progress in the business has been completed it is proposed, if the necessary data are obtainable, to make a somewhat similar study of the relation between school record and progress in the business. A great many of the higher positions in the System are held by men who did not go to college, and the real picture of the relationship between scholarship and subsequent progress cannot be completed without some data as to the scholarship records of the men who did not have a college education. The scholastic records of the college men were studied first.

Of the 4,125 graduates, 319 were at once eliminated from the study because more than half of their business careers had been outside the Bell System. Of the 3,806 included, 1,662 were less than five years out of college, 2,144 were from five to thirty years out. In obtaining these men's records we asked the colleges to classify them in four groups:

1. Those graduating in the first tenth of their class;
2. Those graduating in the first third but not the first tenth;
3. Those graduating in the middle third of their class;
4. Those graduating in the lower third of their class.

Chart I shows the median salaries of these men grouped in accordance with their scholarship rank at college. Each group's median is

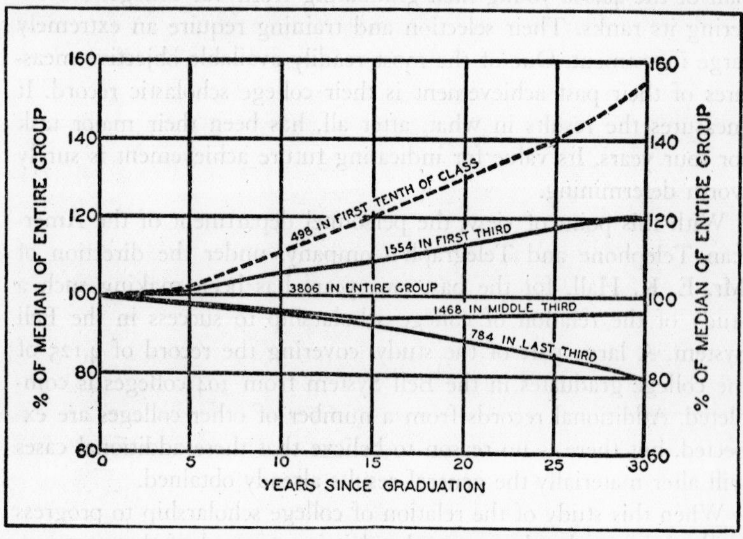

CHART I. MEDIAN SALARIES BY COLLEGE SCHOLARSHIP RANK

The median salary of the entire group studied is shown by the horizontal 100 per cent line. Thirty years after graduation, the median salary of the men in the first tenth of their college classes is 155 per cent, that of the men in the lowest third of their classes is 79 per cent of this median.

expressed as a percentage of the median of all the men included in the study. Median salaries, which show the salary of the man in the middle of his group, for example the fiftieth man in a group of ninety-nine, have been used instead of average salaries, which are sometimes greatly affected by one or two especially high salaries.

As is indicated on Chart I, of the 3,806 men studied, 498 had graduated in the first tenth of their respective classes. By about the fifth year of their employment this group began to earn more than the other college men. They continued to increase their advantage little by little until they were twenty-five years out of college. Then they began to go ahead still more rapidly. The line in the chart represents, of course, the median man in the group. Many individuals did better and many poorer than this man, but the group as a whole averaged substantially higher earnings than the rest of the 3,800.

Next to the men who graduated in the first tenth of their classes come those who were in the first third of their classes, including the first tenth, 1,554 men. Their average earnings in the Bell System are also in relation to their scholarship in college. They are lower than the earnings of the men in the first tenth of their classes, but better than any other group.

Of the 3,806 men studied, 1,468 graduated in the middle third of their classes and the median man's earnings in this group by the time they are thirty years out of college is somewhat less than two thirds that of the median man among those in the first tenth of their classes.

The 784 men who graduated in the lowest third of their classes have earned the least, and the curve of the earnings of the median man in this group has exactly the opposite trend to that of the median man in the upper tenth of their classes: the longer the best students are in business, the more rapidly their earnings rise. The longer the poorer students are in business, the slower their earnings rise.

It cannot be stated too emphatically that these lines on the charts represent the averages of the performances of the men in the different groups and that the records of individuals in each group vary very widely from the averages. It is clear, however, that in the Bell System, on the average, men who were good students have done better than those who were not. There are, of course, exceptions—men who were poor students who are succeeding well and men who were good students succeeding less well—but on the whole the evidence is very striking that there is a direct relation between high marks in college and salaries afterward in the Bell System.

In general the normal expectation is that any college graduate entering business has one chance in three of standing in salary among the highest third of all the college graduates in his company. From this study, as illustrated by the Chart II, it appears that the man in the first third in scholarship at college, five years or more after graduation, has not merely one chance in three, but about one in two of standing in the first third in salary. On the other hand, the man in the lowest third in scholarship has, instead of one chance

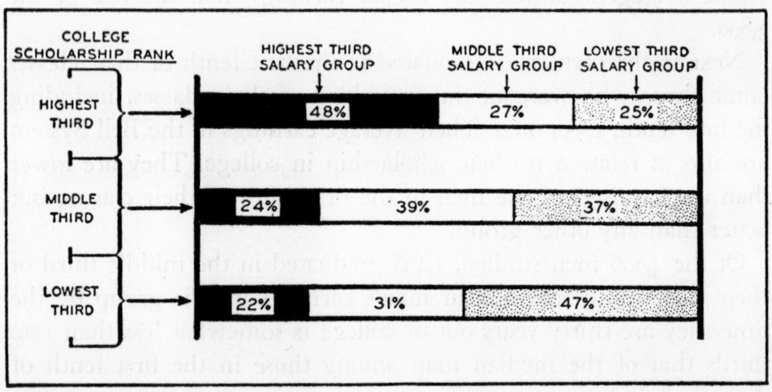

Chart II. Distribution of College Graduates into Salary Groups.

In general, men in the first third of their college classes are most likely to be found in the highest third of their group in salary, those in the middle third in scholarship to be in the middle third in salary, and those in the lowest third in scholarship to be in the lowest third in salary. The above chart is based on the record of 2,144 Bell System employees over five years out of college.

in three, only about one in five of standing in the highest third in salary. There is also nearly one chance in two that he will stand in the lowest third in salary.

In the same way, as shown by Chart III, the man in the highest tenth in scholarship at college has not one chance in ten, but nearly two chances in ten of standing in the highest tenth in salary. The man in the lowest third in salary, on the other hand, has instead of one chance in ten, only one in twenty-two of standing in the first tenth in salary.

Strikingly enough, almost exactly the same results as those just given were obtained separately for the engineering graduates and the graduates in arts and business who together make up the whole group studied.

This analysis may not answer Doctor Foster's academic question, *Should Students Study?* but it has some bearing upon whether industry should seek students who had studied. I hope it has bearing enough on the subject to lead other companies, associations, trades, and industries to make studies along similar lines. It would undoubtedly be helpful if such studies could cover men who did not go to college as well as college graduates.

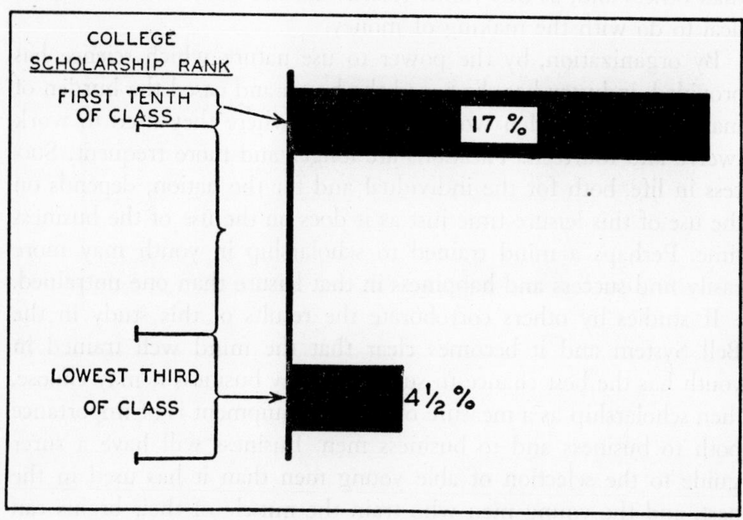

CHART III. PERCENTAGE OF SCHOLARSHIP GROUPS NOW IN HIGHEST TENTH SALARY GROUP.

Men from the first tenth of their college classes have four times the chance of those from the lowest third to stand in the highest tenth salary group.

In this particular study made by the Bell System salary has been used as a measure of success. While I do not believe that success in life can be rated by income, I do believe that as between one man and another working in the same business organization, success and salary—while not the same thing—will, generally speaking, parallel each other.

In studying the relationship between success in scholarship and in business it is necessary, therefore, to study the results of good and poor scholars in the same line of work, or perhaps even within one company; for general comparisons of men under different conditions in different business will not produce very valuable results. For instance, if scholarship were an exact measure of business ability, it would not mean that a fine scholar who had entered the cotton-mill business recently would have made as much money as if he had been in the automobile business. He might have been as great a success, however. He might achieve what he set out to do equally well. At certain times some businesses make more money than others and, as Mr. Julius Rosenwald has said, luck has a great deal to do with the making of money.

By organization, by the power to use nature which science has provided, industry has shortened the hours and eased the burden of making a living. Men work eight hours where they used to work twelve and fourteen. Vacations are longer and more frequent. Success in life, both for the individual and for the nation, depends on the use of this leisure time just as it does on the use of the business time. Perhaps a mind trained to scholarship in youth may more easily find success and happiness in that leisure than one untrained.

If studies by others corroborate the results of this study in the Bell System and it becomes clear that the mind well trained in youth has the best chance to succeed in any business it may choose, then scholarship as a measure of mental equipment is of importance both to business and to business men. Business will have a surer guide to the selection of able young men than it has used in the past, and the young men who train the muscle of their brains can feel reasonably certain that such training will add to their success in business and, in all probability, to the fruitful and happy use of the leisure which success in business will give them.

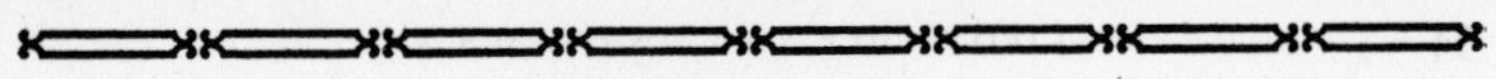

B. DEFINITION

A UNIVERSITY[1]

John Henry Newman

A university is a place of concourse, whither students come from every quarter for every kind of knowledge. You cannot have the best of every kind everywhere; you must go to some great city or emporium for it. There you have all the choicest productions of nature and art all together, which you find each in its own separate place elsewhere. All the riches of the land, and of the earth, are carried up thither; there are the best markets, and there the best workmen. It is the center of trade, the supreme court of fashion, the umpire of rival talents, and the standard of things rare and precious. It is the place for seeing galleries of first-rate pictures, and for hearing wonderful voices and performers of transcendent skill. It is the place for great preachers, great orators, great nobles, great statesmen. In the nature of things, greatness and unity go together; excellence implies a center. And such, for the third or fourth time, is a university; I hope I do not weary out the reader by repeating it. It is the place to which a thousand schools make contributions; in which the intellect may safely range and speculate, sure to find its equal in some antagonist activity, and its judge in the tribunal of truth. It is a place where inquiry is pushed forward, and discoveries verified and perfected, and rashness rendered innocuous, and error exposed, by the collision of mind with mind, and knowledge with knowledge. It is the place where the professor becomes eloquent, and is a missionary and a preacher, displaying his science in its most complete and most winning form, pouring it forth with the zeal of enthusiasm, and lighting up his own love of it in the

[1]From *The Idea of a University.*

breasts of his hearers. It is the place where the catechist makes good his ground as he goes, treading in the truth day by day into the ready memory, and wedging and tightening it into the expanding reason. It is a place which wins the admiration of the young by its celebrity, kindles the affections of the middle-aged by its beauty, and rivets the fidelity of the old by its associations. It is a seat of wisdom, a light of the world, a minister of the faith, an Alma Mater of the rising generation. . . .

A GENTLEMAN[1]

John Henry Newman

Hence it is that it is almost a definition of a gentleman to say that he is one who never inflicts pain. This description is both refined and, as far as it goes, accurate. He is mainly occupied in merely removing the obstacles which hinder the free and unembarrassed action of those about him; and he concurs with their movements rather than takes the initiative himself. His benefits may be considered as parallel to what are called comforts or conveniences in arrangements of a personal nature: like an easy-chair or a good fire, which do their part in dispelling cold and fatigue, though nature provides both means of rest and animal heat without them. The true gentleman in like manner carefully avoids whatever may cause a jar or a jolt in the minds of those with whom he is cast; all clashing of opinion, or collision of feeling, all restraint, or suspicion, or gloom, or resentment; his great concern being to make everyone at his ease and at home. He has his eyes on all his company; he is tender towards the bashful, gentle towards the distant, and merciful towards the absurd; he can recollect to whom he is speaking; he guards against unreasonable allusions, or topics which may irritate; he is seldom prominent in conversation, and never wearisome. He

[1]From *Scope and Nature of University Education.*

makes light of favors while he does them, and seems to be receiving when he is conferring. He never speaks of himself by a mere retort, he has no ears for slander or gossip, is scrupulous in imputing motives to those who interfere with him, and interprets everything for the best. He is never mean or little in his disputes, never takes unfair advantage, never mistakes personalities or sharp sayings for arguments, or insinuates evil which he dare not say out. From a long-sighted prudence, he observes the maxim of the ancient sage, that we should ever conduct ourselves towards our enemy as if he were one day to be our friend. He has too much good sense to be affronted at insults, he is too well employed to remember injuries, and too indolent to bear malice. He is patient, forbearing, and resigned, on philosophical principles; he submits to pain, because it is irreparable, and to death, because it is his destiny. If he engages in controversy of any kind, his disciplined intellect preserves him from the blundering discourtesy of better, perhaps, but less educated minds; who, like blunt weapons, tear and hack instead of cutting clean, who mistake the point in argument, waste their strength on trifles, misconceive their adversary, and leave the question more involved than they find it. He may be right or wrong in his opinion, but he is too clear-headed to be unjust; he is as simple as he is forcible, and as brief as he is decisive. Nowhere shall we find greater candor, consideration, indulgence: he throws himself into the minds of his opponents, he accounts for their mistakes. He knows the weakness of human reason as well as its strength, its province and its limits. If he be an unbeliever, he will be too profound and large-minded to ridicule religion or to act against it; he is too wise to be a dogmatist or fanatic in his infidelity. He respects piety and devotion; he even supports institutions as venerable, beautiful, or useful, to which he does not assent; he honors the ministers of religion, and it contents him to decline its mysteries without assailing or denouncing them. He is a friend of religious toleration, and that, not only because his philosophy has taught him to look on all forms of faith with an impartial eye, but also from the gentleness and effeminacy of feeling, which is the attendant on civilization.

TACT

New York Times[1]

There are always two ways of saying a thing. The existing tension between Signor Cippico and Professor East of Harvard at the Williamstown Conference would not have arisen if the latter had chosen to make his approach somewhat indirect. Instead of saying that Italy has been sending us the dregs of her population, Professor East should have said what a pity it is that the superb qualities of the Italian people which have manifested themselves so strikingly and beneficently throughout her history should be only imperfectly represented in the emigrants whom she has sent to this country. And Signor Cippico, instead of declaring that Professor East's remarks were beneath contempt, should have suggested that a broader acquaintance with the character of the Italian immigrant than can be secured in the secluded shades of Cambridge would be bound to modify the opinion of an eminent scholar whose familiarity with the high realms of thought is probably superior to his knowledge of the facts of the real world.

ON FAMILIAR STYLE[1]

William Hazlitt

It is not easy to write a familiar style. Many people mistake a familiar style for a vulgar style, and suppose that to write without affectation is to write at random. On the contrary, there is nothing that requires more precision, and, if I may so say, purity of expression, than the style I am speaking of. It utterly rejects not only the

[1]August 9, 1929.
[1]From *Essays.*

unmeaning pomp, but all low, cant phrases, and loose, unconnected, *slipshod* allusions. It is not to take the first word that offers, but the best word in common use; it is not to throw words together in any combinations we please, but to follow and avail ourselves of the true idiom of the language. To write a genuine familiar or truly English style is to write as anyone would speak in common conversation who had a thorough command and choice of words, or who could discourse with ease, force, and perspicuity, setting aside all pedantic and oratorical flourishes. Or to give another illustration, to write naturally is the same thing in regard to common conversation as to read naturally is in regard to common speech. It does not follow that it is an easy thing to give the true accent and inflection to the words you utter, because you do not attempt to rise above the level of ordinary life and colloquial speaking. You do not assume, indeed, the solemnity of the pulpit, or the tone of stage declamation; neither are you at liberty to gabble on at a venture, without emphasis or discretion, or to resort to vulgar dialect or clownish pronunciation. You must steer a middle course. You are tied down to a given and appropriate articulation, which is determined by the habitual associations between sense and sound, and which you can only hit by entering into the author's meaning, as you must find the proper words and style to express yourself by fixing your thoughts on the subject you have to write about. Anyone may mouth out a passage with a theatrical cadence, or get upon stilts to tell his thoughts; but to write or speak with propriety and simplicity is a more difficult task. Thus it is easy to affect a pompous style, to use a word twice as big as the thing you want to express: it is not so easy to pick upon the very word that exactly fits it. Out of eight or ten words equally common, equally intelligible, with nearly equal pretensions, it is a matter of some nicety and discrimination to pick out the very one, the preferableness of which is scarcely perceptible, but decisive. The reason why I object to Dr. Johnson's style is that there is no discrimination, no selection, no variety in it. He uses none but "tall, opaque words," taken from the "first row of the rubric"—words with the greatest number of syllables, or Latin phrases with merely English terminations. If a fine style depended on this sort of arbitrary pretension, it would be fair to judge of an author's elegance by measurement of his words and the substitutions of foreign circumlocutions (with no precise associations) for the mother-tongue. How simple it is to be dignified without ease, to be pompous with meaning! Surely it is but a mechanical rule for avoiding what is low, to be always pedantic and affected. It is clear you cannot use a vulgar English word, if you never use a common English word at all. A fine tact is shown in adhering to those which are perfectly common, and yet never falling into any expressions which are debased by disgusting circumstances, or which owe their signification and point to technical or professional allusions. A truly natural or familiar style can never be quaint or vulgar, for this reason, that it is of universal force and applicability, and that quaintness and vulgarity arise out of the immediate connection of certain words with coarse and disagreeable or with confined ideas. The last form what we understand by *cant* or *slang* phrases. To give an example of what is not very clear in the general statement, I should say that the phrase "To cut with a knife" or "To cut a piece of wood" is perfectly free from vulgarity, because it is perfectly common; but to "cut an acquaintance" is not quite unexceptionable, because it is not perfectly common or intelligible, and has hardly yet escaped out of the limits of slang phraseology. I should hardly there use the word in this sense without putting it in italics as a license of expression, to be received *cum grano salis*. All provincial or by-phrases come under the same mark of reprobation — all such as the writer transfers to the page from his fireside or a particular *coterie,* or that he invents for his sole use and convenience. I conceive that words are like money, not the worse for being common, but that it is the stamp of custom alone that gives them circulation or value. I am fastidious in this respect, and would almost as soon coin the currency of the realm as counterfeit the King's English.

. . . .

The proper force of words lies not in the words themselves, but in their application. A word may be a fine-sounding word, of an unusual length, and very imposing from its learning and novelty, and yet in the connection in which it is introduced may be quite pointless and irrelevant. It is not pomp or pretension, but the adaptation of the expression to the idea, that clinches a writer's meaning — as it is not the size or glossiness of the materials, but their being fitted each to its place, that gives strength to the arch; or as the pegs and nails are as necessary to the support of the building as the larger timbers, and more so than the showy, unsubstantial ornaments. I hate anything that occupies more space than it is worth. I hate to see a load of bandboxes go along the street, and I hate to see a parcel of big words without anything in them.

. . . .

It is as easy to write a gaudy style without ideas as it is to spread a palette of showy colors, or to smear in a flaunting transparency. "What do you read?" "Words, words, words." "What is the matter?"—"Nothing," it might be answered. The florid style is the reverse of the familiar. The last is employed as an unvarnished medium to convey ideas; the first is resorted to as a spangled veil to conceal the want of them. When there is nothing to be set down but words, it costs little to have them fine. *Rouge* high enough, and never mind the natural complexion. The vulgar, who are not in the secret, will admire the look of preternatural health and vigor; and the fashionable, who regard only appearances, will be delighted with the imposition. Keep to your sounding generalities, your tinkling phrases, and all will be well. Swell out an unmeaning truism to a perfect tympany of style. A thought, a distinction is the rock on which all the brittle cargo of verbiage splits at once. Such writers have merely *verbal* imaginations, that retain nothing but words.

ON JARGON[1]

Sir Arthur Quiller-Couch

I remember to have heard somewhere of a religious body in the United States of America which had reason to suspect one of its churches of accepting spiritual consolation from a colored preacher—an offense against the laws of the Synod—and dispatched a Disciplinary Committee with power to act; and of the Committee's

[1]From *On the Art of Writing,* G. P. Putnam's Sons, 1916. Reprinted by permission.

returning to report itself unable to take any action under its terms of reference, for that while a person undoubtedly colored had undoubtedly occupied the pulpit and had audibly spoken from it in the Committee's presence, the performance could be brought within no definition of preaching known or discoverable. So it is with that infirmity of speech — that flux, that determination of words to the mouth, or to the pen — which, though it be familiar to you in parliamentary debates, in newspapers, and as the staple language of Blue Books, Committees, Official Reports, I take leave to introduce to you as prose which is not prose and under its real name of Jargon.

You must not confuse this Jargon with what is called Journalese. The two overlap, indeed, and have a knack of assimilating each other's vices. But Jargon finds, maybe, the most of its votaries among good douce people who have never written to or for a newspaper in their life, who would never talk of "adverse climatic conditions" when they mean "bad weather"; who have never trifled with verbs such as "obsess," "recrudesce," "envisage," "adumbrate," or with phrases such as "the psychological moment," "the true inwardness," "it gives furiously to think." It dallies with Latinity — *"sub silentio," "de die in diem," "cui bono?"* (always in the sense, unsuspected by Cicero, of "What is the profit?") — but not for the sake of style. Your journalist at the worst is an artist in his way; he daubs paint of this kind upon the lily with a professional zeal; the more flagrant (or, to use his own word, arresting) the pigment, the happier is his soul. Like the Babu he is trying all the while to embellish our poor language, to make it more floriferous, more poetical — like the Babu, for example, who, reporting his mother's death, wrote, "Regret to inform you, the hand that rocked the cradle has kicked the bucket."

There is metaphor; *there* is ornament; *there* is a sense of poetry, though as yet groping in a world unrealized. No such gusto marks — no such zeal, artistic or professional, animates — the practitioners of Jargon, who are, most of them (I repeat), douce, respectable persons. Caution is its father, the instinct to save everything and especially trouble, its mother, Indolence. It looks precise, but is not. It is, in these times, *safe:* a thousand men have said it before and not one of your knowledge has been prosecuted for it. And so, like respectability in Chicago, Jargon stalks unchecked in our midst. It is becoming the language of Parliament; it has become the medium through which Boards of Government, County Councils, Syndicates, Committees, Commercial Firms, express the processes as well as the conclusions of their thought and so voice the reason of their being.

Has a Minister to say "No" in the House of Commons? Some men are constitutionally incapable of saying no; but the Minister conveys it thus: "The answer to the question is in the negative." That means "no." Can you discover it to mean anything less, or anything more except that the speaker is a pompous person?—which was no part of the information demanded.

That is Jargon, and it happens to be accurate. But, as a rule, Jargon is by no means accurate, its method being to walk circumspectly around its target; and its faith, that having done so it has either hit the bull's-eye or at least achieved something equivalent, and safer.

Thus the clerk of a Board of Guardians will minute that—

In the case of John Jenkins deceased the coffin provided was of the usual character.

Now, this is not accurate. "In the case of John Jenkins deceased," for whom a coffin was supplied, it is wholly superfluous to tell us that he is deceased. But actually John Jenkins never had more than one case, and that was the coffin. The clerk says he had two—a coffin in a case; but I suspect the clerk to be mistaken, and I am sure he errs in telling us that the coffin was of the usual character; for coffins have no character, usual or unusual.

Have you begun to detect the two main vices of Jargon? The first is that it uses circumlocution rather than short, straight speech. It says: "In the case of John Jenkins deceased, the coffin" when it means "John Jenkins's coffin"; and its yea is not yea, neither is its nay nay; but its answer is in the affirmative or in the negative, as the foolish superfluous "case" may be. The second vice is that it habitually chooses vague, woolly, abstract nouns rather than concrete ones. I shall have something to say by-and-by about the concrete noun, and how you should ever be struggling for it whether in prose or in verse. For the moment I content myself with advising you, if you would write masculine English, never to forget the old tag of your Latin Grammar—

Masculine will only be
Things that you can touch and see.

But since these lectures are meant to be a course in First Aid to writing, I will content myself with one or two extremely rough rules; yet I shall be disappointed if you do not find them serviceable.

The first is: Whenever in your reading you come across one of these words, *case, instance, character, nature, condition, persuasion, degree*—whenever in writing your pen betrays you to one or another of them—pull yourself up and take thought. If it be "case" (I choose it as Jargon's dearest child—"in Heaven yclept Metonymy") turn to the dictionary, if you will, and seek out what meaning can be derived from *casus,* its Latin ancestor; then try how, with a little trouble, you can extricate yourself from that case. The odds are, you will feel like a butterfly who has discarded his chrysalis.

Here are some specimens to try your hand on:

(1) All those tears which inundated Lord Hugh Cecil's head were dry in the case of Mr. Harold Cox.

Poor Mr. Cox! left gasping in his aquarium!

(2) [From a cigar-merchant.] In any case, let us send you a case on approval.

(3) It is contended that Consols have fallen in consequence: but such is by no means the case.

"Such," by the way, is another spoilt child of Jargon, especially in Committee's Rules—"Coopted members may be eligible as such; such members to continue to serve for such time as"—and so on.

(4) Even in the purely Celtic areas only in two or three cases do the Bishops bear Celtic names.

For "cases" read "dioceses."

Instance. In most instances the players were below their form.

But what were they playing at? Instances?

Character—Nature. There can be no doubt that the accident was caused through the dangerous nature of the spot, the hidden character of the by-road, and the utter absence of any warning or danger signal.

Mark the foggy wording of it all! And yet the man hit something and broke his neck! Contrast that explanation with the verdict of a coroner's jury in the west of England on a drowned postman:

"We find that deceased met his death by an act of God, caused by sudden overflowing of the river Walkham and helped out by the scandalous neglect of the way-wardens."

The Aintree course is notoriously of a trying nature.

On account of its light character, purity, and age, Usher's whisky is a whisky that will agree with you.

Order. The mésalliance was of a pronounced order.

Condition. He was conveyed to his place of residence in an intoxicated condition.

"He was carried home drunk."

Quality and *Section.* Mr. —, exhibiting no less than five works, all of a superior quality, figures prominently in the oil section.

—This was written of an exhibition of pictures.

Degree. A singular degree of rarity prevails in the earlier editions of this romance.

That is Jargon. In prose it runs simply "The earlier editions of this romance are rare"—or "are very rare"—or even (if you believe what I take leave to doubt), "are singularly rare"; which should mean that they are rarer than the editions of any other work in the world.

Now, what I ask you to consider about these quotations is that in each the writer was using Jargon to shirk prose, palming off periphrases upon us when with a little trouble he could have gone straight to the point. "A singular degree of rarity prevails," "the accident was caused through the dangerous nature of the spot," "but such is by no means the case." We may not be capable of much; but we can all write better than that, if we take a little trouble. In place of, "the Aintree course is of a trying nature" we can surely say "Aintree is a trying course" or "the Aintree course is a trying one"—just that and nothing more.

Next, having trained yourself to keep a lookout for these worst offenders (and you will be surprised to find how quickly you get into the way of it), proceed to push your suspicions out among the whole cloudy host of abstract terms. "How excellent a thing is sleep," sighed Sancho Panza; "it wraps a man round like a cloak"—an excellent example, by the way, of how to say a thing concretely; a Jargoneer would have said that "among the beneficent qualities of sleep its capacity for withdrawing the human consciousness from the contemplation of immediate circumstances may perhaps be accounted not the least remarkable." How vile a thing—shall we say?—is the abstract noun! It wraps a man's thoughts round like cotton wool.

Here is a pretty little nest of specimens, found in *The Times* newspaper by Messrs. H. W. and F. G. Fowler, authors of that capital little book *The King's English:*

One of the most important reforms mentioned in the rescript is the unification of the organization of judicial institutions and the guarantee for all the tribunals of the independence necessary for securing to all classes of the community equality before the law.

I do not dwell on the cacophony; but, to convey a straightforward piece of news, might not the editor of *The Times* as well employ a man to write:

One of the most important reforms is that of the Courts, which need a uniform system and to be made independent. In this way only can men be assured that all are equal before the law.

I think he might.

A day or two ago the musical critic of the *Standard* wrote this:

MR. LAMOND IN BEETHOVEN

Mr. Frederick Lamond, the Scottish pianist, as an interpreter of Beethoven has few rivals. At this second recital of the composer's works at Bechstein Hall on Saturday afternoon he again displayed a complete sympathy and understanding of his material that extracted the very essence of esthetic and musical value from each selection he undertook. The delightful intimacy of his playing and his unusual force of individual expression are invaluable assets, which, applied to his technical brilliancy, enable him to achieve an artistic triumph. The two lengthy Variations in E flat major (Op. 35) and in D major, the latter on the Turkish March from *The Ruins of Athens,* when included in the same program, require a master hand to provide continuity of interest. *To say that Mr. Lamond successfully avoided moments that might at times, in these works, have inclined to comparative disinterestedness, would be but a moderate way of expressing the remarkable fascination with which his versatile playing endowed them,* but *at the same time* two of the sonatas given included a singular form of composition, and no matter how intellectually brilliant may be the interpretation, the extravagant use of a certain mode is bound in time to become somewhat ineffective. In the Three Sonatas, the E major (Op. 109), the A major (Op. 2), No. 2, and C minor (Op. 111), Mr. Lamond signalized his perfect insight into the composer's varying moods.

Will you not agree with me that here is no writing, here is no prose, here is not even English, but merely a flux of words to the pen?

Here again is a string, a concatenation — say, rather, a tiara of gems of purest ray serene from the dark unfathomed caves of a Scottish newspaper:

The Chinese viewpoint, as indicated in this letter, may not be without interest to your readers, because it evidently is suggestive of more than an academic attempt to explain an unpleasant aspect of things which, if allowed to materialize, might suddenly culminate in disaster resembling the Chang-Sha riots. It also ventures to illustrate incidents having their inception in recent premature endeavors to accelerate the development of Protestant missions in China; but we would hope for the sake of the interests involved that what my correspondent describes as "the irresponsible ruffian element" may be known by their various religious designations only within very restricted areas.

Well, the Chinese have given it up, poor fellows! and are asking the Christians — as today's newspapers inform us — to pray for them. Do you wonder? But that is, or was, the Chinese "viewpoint" — and what a willow-pattern viewpoint! Observe its delicacy. It does not venture to interest or be interesting; merely "to be not without interest." But it does "venture to illustrate incidents" — which, for a viewpoint, is brave enough; and this illustration "is suggestive of something more than an academic attempt to explain an unpleasant aspect of things which, if allowed to materialize, might suddenly culminate." *What* materializes? The unpleasant aspect? or the things? Grammar says the "things," "things which if allowed to materialize." But things are materialized already, and as a condition of their being things. It must be the aspect, then, that materializes. But, if so, it is also the aspect that culminates, and an aspect, however unpleasant, can hardly do that, or at worst cannot culminate in anything resembling the Chang-Sha riots. . . . I give it up.

Let us turn to another trick of Jargon; the trick of Elegant Variation, so rampant in the sporting press that there, without needing to attend these lectures, the undergraduate detects it for laughter: —

Hayward and C. B. Fry now faced the bowling, which apparently had no terrors for the Surrey crack. The old Oxonian, however, took some time in settling to work. . . .

Yes, you all recognize it and laugh at it. But why do you practice it in your essays? An undergraduate brings me an essay on Byron. In an essay on Byron, Byron is (or ought to be) mentioned many times. I expect, nay exact, that Byron shall be mentioned again and again. But my undergraduate has a blushing sense that to call Byron Byron twice on one page is indelicate. So Byron, after starting bravely as Byron, in the second sentence turns into "that great but unequal poet" and thenceforward I have as much trouble with Byron as ever Telemachus with Proteus to hold and pin him back to his proper self. Half-way down the page he becomes "the gloomy master of Newstead"; overleaf he is reincarnated into "the meteoric darling of society"; and so proceeds through successive avatars—"this arch-rebel," "the author of *Childe Harold,*" "the apostle of scorn," "the ex-Harrovian, proud, but abnormally sensitive in his clubfoot," "the martyr of Missolonghi," "the pageant-monger of a bleeding heart." Now this again is Jargon. It does not, as most Jargon does, come of laziness; but it comes of timidity, which is worse. In literature as in life he makes himself felt who not only calls a spade a spade but has the pluck to double spades and redouble.

For another rule—just as rough and ready, but just as useful: Train your suspicions to bristle up whenever you come upon "as regards," "with regard to," "in respect of," "in connection with," "according as to whether," and the like. They are all dodges of Jargon, circumlocutions for evading this or that simple statement; and I say that it is not enough to avoid them nine times out of ten, or nine-and-ninety times out of a hundred. You should never use them. That is positive enough, I hope? Though I cannot admire his style, I admire the man who wrote to me, "Re Tennyson—your remarks anent his *In Memoriam* make me sick"; for though *re* is not a preposition of the first water, and *anent* has enjoyed its day, the finish crowned the work. But here are a few specimens far, very far, worse:

> The special difficulty in Professor Minocelsi's case [our old friend "case" again] arose *in connection with* the view he holds *relative to* the historical value of the opening pages of Genesis.

That is Jargon. In prose, even taking the miserable sentence as it stands constructed, we should write "the difficulty arose over the views he holds about the historical value," etc.

From a popular novelist:

> I was entirely indifferent *as to* the results of the game, caring nothing at all *as to* whether *I had losses or gains*—

Cut out the first "as" in "as to," and the second "as to" altogether, and the sentence begins to be prose—"I was indifferent to the results of the game, caring nothing whether I had losses or gains."

But why, like Dogberry, have "had losses"? Why not simply "lose." Let us try again. "I was entirely indifferent to the results of the game, caring nothing at all whether I won or lost."

Still the sentence remains absurd; for the second clause but repeats the first without adding one jot. For if you care not at all whether you win or lose, you must be entirely indifferent to the results of the game. So why not say, "I was careless if I won or lost," and have done with it?

> A man of simple and charming character, he was fitly *associated with* the distinction of the Order of Merit.

I take this gem with some others from a collection made three years ago, by the *Oxford Magazine;* and I hope you admire it as one beyond price. "He was associated with the distinction of the Order of Merit" means "he was given the Order of Merit." If the members of that Order make a society then he was associated with them; but you cannot associate a man with a distinction. The inventor of such fine writing would doubtless have answered Canning's Needy Knife-grinder with:—

> I associate thee with sixpence! I will see thee in another association first!

But let us close our *florilegium* and attempt to illustrate Jargon by the converse method of taking a famous piece of English (say, Hamlet's soliloquy) and remolding a few lines of it in this fashion:

> To be, or the contrary? Whether the former or the latter be preferable would seem to admit of some difference of opinion; the answer in the present case being of an affirmative or of a negative character according as to whether one elects on the one hand to mentally suffer the disfavor of fortune, albeit in an extreme degree, or on the other to boldly envisage adverse conditions in the prospect of eventually bringing them to a conclusion. The condition of sleep is similar to, if not indistinguish-

able from that of death; and with the addition of finality the former might be considered identical with the latter: so that in this connection it might be argued with regard to sleep that, could the addition be effected, a termination would be put to the endurance of a multiplicity of inconveniences, not to mention a number of downright evils incidental to our fallen humanity, and thus a consummation achieved of a most gratifying nature.

That is Jargon: and to write Jargon is to be perpetually shuffling around in the fog and cotton-wool of abstract terms; to be forever hearkening, like Ibsen's Peer Gynt, to the voice of the Boyg exhorting you to circumvent the difficulty, to beat the air because it is easier than to flesh your sword in the thing. The first virtue, the touchstone of masculine style, is its use of the active verb and the concrete noun. When you write in the active voice, "They gave him a silver teapot," you write as a man. When you write "He was made the recipient of a silver teapot," you write Jargon. But at the beginning set even higher store on the concrete noun. Somebody — I think it was Fitz-Gerald — once posited the question, "What would have become of Christianity if Jeremy Bentham had had the writing of the Parables?" Without pursuing that dreadful inquiry I ask you to note how carefully the Parables — those exquisite short stories — speak only of "things which you can touch and see" — "A sower went forth to sow," "The Kingdom of Heaven is like unto leaven, which a woman took" — and not the Parables only, but the Sermon on the Mount and almost every verse of the Gospel. The Gospel does not, like my young essayist, fear to repeat a word, if the word be good. The Gospel says "Render unto Cæsar the things that are Cæsar's" — not "Render unto Cæsar the things that appertain to that potentate." The Gospel does not say "Consider the growth of the lilies," or even "Consider how the lilies grow." It says "Consider the lilies, how they grow."

Or take Shakespeare. I wager you that no writer of English so constantly chooses the concrete word, in phrase after phrase forcing you to touch and see. No writer so insistently teaches the general through the particular. He does it even in *Venus and Adonis* (as Professor Wendell, of Harvard, pointed out in a brilliant little monograph on Shakespeare, published some ten years ago). Read any page of *Venus and Adonis* side by side with any page of Marlowe's *Hero and Leander* and you cannot but mark the contrast: in Shakespeare the definite, particular, visualized image, in Marlowe the beautiful generalization, the abstract term, the thing seen at a literary remove. Take the two openings, both of which start out with the sunrise. Marlowe begins:

> Now had the Morn espied her lover's steeds:
> Whereat she starts, put on her purple weeds,
> And, red for anger that he stay'd so long,
> All headlong throws herself the clouds among.

Shakespeare wastes no words on Aurora and her feelings, but gets to his hero and to business without ado.

> Even as the sun with purple-color'd face—

(You have the sun visualized at once),

> Even as the sun with purple-color'd face
> Had ta'en his last leave of the weeping morn,
> Rose-cheek'd Adonis hied him to the chase;
> Hunting he loved, but love he laugh'd to scorn.

When Shakespeare has to describe a horse, mark how definite he is:

> Round-hoof'd, short-jointed, fetlocks shag and long,
> Broad breast, full eye, small head and nostrils wide,
> High crest, short ears, straight legs and passing strong;
> Thin mane, thick tail, broad buttock, tender hide.

Or again, in a casual simile, how definite:

> Upon this promise did he raise his chin,
> Like a dive-dipper peering through a wave,
> Which, being look'd on, ducks as quickly in.

Or take, if you will, Marlowe's description of Hero's first meeting Leander:

> It lies not in our power to love or hate,
> For will in us is over-ruled by fate . . . ,

and set against it Shakespeare's description of Venus's last meeting with Adonis, as she came on him lying in his blood:

> Or as a snail whose tender horns being hit
> Shrinks backward in his shelly cave with pain,
> And there, all smother'd up, in shade doth sit,

Long after fearing to creep forth again;
So, at his bloody view—

I do not deny Marlowe's lines (if you will study the whole passage) to be lovely. You may even judge Shakespeare's to be crude by comparison. But you cannot help noting that whereas Marlowe steadily deals in abstract, nebulous terms, Shakespeare constantly uses concrete ones, which later on he learned to pack into verse, such as:

Sleep that knits up the ravell'd sleeve of care.

Is it unfair to instance Marlowe, who died young? Then let us take Webster for the comparison; Webster, a man of genius or of something very like it, and commonly praised by the critics for his mastery over definite, detailed, and what I may call *solidified sensation*. Let us take this admired passage from his *Duchess of Malfy:*

Ferdinand. How doth our sister Duchess bear herself
In her imprisonment?
Basola. Nobly: I'll describe her.
She's sad as one long wed to 't, and she seems
Rather to welcome the end of misery.
Than shun it: a behavior so noble
As gives a majesty to adversity.[2]
You may discern the shape of loveliness
More perfect in her tears than in her smiles;
She will muse for hours together;[3] and her silence
Methinks expresseth more than if she spake.

Now set against this the well-known passage from *Twelfth Night* where the Duke asks and Viola answers a question about someone unknown to him and invented by her—a mere phantasm, in short: yet note how much more definite is the language:

Viola. My father had a daughter lov'd a man;
As it might be, perhaps, were I a woman,
I should your lordship.
Duke. And what's her history?
Viola. A blank, my lord. She never told her love,
But let concealment, like a worm i' the bud,

[2]Note the abstract terms.

[3]Here we first come on the concrete: and beautiful it is.

Feed on her damask cheek; she pined in thought,
And with a green and yellow melancholy
She sat like Patience on a monument
Smiling at grief. Was not this love indeed?

Observe (apart from the dramatic skill of it) how, when Shakespeare *has* to use the abstract noun "concealment," on an instant it turns into a visible worm "feeding" on the visible rose; how, having to use a second abstract word "patience," at once he solidifies it in tangible stone.

Turning to prose, you may easily assure yourselves that men who have written learnedly on the art agree in treating our maxim — to prefer the concrete term to the abstract, the particular to the general, the definite to the vague — as a canon of rhetoric. Whately has much to say on it. The late Mr. E. J. Payne, in one of his admirable prefaces to Burke (prefaces too little known and valued, as too often happens to scholarship hidden away in a schoolbook), illustrated the maxim by setting a passage from Burke's speech *On Conciliation with America* alongside a passage of like purport from Lord Brougham's *Inquiry into the Policy of the European Powers.* Here is the deadly parallel: —

BURKE

In large bodies the circulation of power must be less vigorous at the extremities. Nature has said it. The Turk cannot govern Ægypt and Arabia and Curdistan as he governs Thrace; nor has he the same dominion in Crimea and Algiers which he has in Brusa and Smyrna. Despotism itself is obliged to truck and huckster. The Sultan gets such obedience as he can. He governs with a loose rein, that he may govern at all; and the whole of the force and vigour of his authority in his centre is derived from a prudent relaxation in all his borders.

BROUGHAM

In all the despotisms of the East, it has been observed that the further any part of the empire is removed from the capital, the more do its inhabitants enjoy some sort of rights and privileges; the more inefficacious is the power of the monarch; and the more feeble and easily decayed is the organization of the government.

You perceive that Brougham has transferred Burke's thought to his own page; but will you not also perceive how pitiably, by dissolving Burke's vivid particulars into smooth generalities, he has enervated its hold on the mind?

"This particularizing style," comments Mr. Payne, "is the essence of poetry; and in prose it is impossible not to be struck with the energy it produces. Brougham's passage is excellent in its way: but it pales before the flashing lights of Burke's sentences." The best instances of this energy of style, he adds, are to be found in the classical writers of the seventeenth century. "When South says, 'An Aristotle was but the rubbish of an Adam, and Athens but the rudiments of Paradise,' he communicates more effectually the notion of the difference between the intellect of fallen and of unfallen humanity than in all the philosophy of his sermons put together."

You may agree with me, or you may not, that South in this passage is expounding trash; but you will agree with Mr. Payne and me that he uttered it vividly.

Let me quote to you, as a final example of this vivid style of writing, a passage from Dr. John Donne far beyond and above anything that ever lay within South's compass:—

> The ashes of an Oak in the Chimney are no epitaph of that Oak, to tell me how high or how large that was; it tells me not what flocks it sheltered while it stood, nor what men it hurt when it fell. The dust of great persons' graves is speechless, too; it says nothing, it distinguishes nothing. As soon the dust of a wretch whom thou wouldest not, as of a prince whom thou couldest not look upon will trouble thine eyes if the wind blow it thither; and when a whirlewind hath blown the dust of the Churchyard into the Church, and the man sweep out the dust of the Church into the Churchyard, who will undertake to sift those dusts again and to pronounce, This is the Patrician, this is the noble flowre [flour], this the yeomanly, this the Plebeian bran? So is the death of *Iesabel* (*Iesabel* was a Queen) expressed. They shall not say *This is Iesabel:* not only not wonder that it is, nor pity that it should be; but they shall not say, they shall not know, *This is Iesabel.*

Carlyle noted of Goethe, "his emblematic intellect, his never-failing tendency to transform into *shape,* into *life,* the feeling that may dwell in him. Everything has form, has visual excellence: the poet's imagination bodies forth the forms of things unseen, and his pen turns them into shape."

Perpend this, Gentlemen, and maybe you will not hereafter set it down to my reproach that I wasted an hour of a May morning in a denunciation of Jargon, and in exhorting you upon a technical matter at first sight so trivial as the choice between abstract and definite words.

A lesson about writing your language may go deeper than language; for language (as in a former lecture I tried to preach to you) is your reason, your λόγος. So long as you prefer abstract words, which express other men's summarized concepts of things, to concrete ones which lie as near as can be reached to things themselves and are the first-hand material for your thoughts, you will remain, at the best, writers at second-hand. If your language be Jargon, your intellect, if not your whole character, will almost certainly correspond. Where your mind should go straight, it will dodge: the difficulties it should approach with a fair front and grip with a firm hand it will be seeking to evade or circumvent. For the style is the man, and where a man's treasure is there his heart, and his brain, and his writing, will be also.

THE TRUE EDUCATION[1]

A. Lawrence Lowell

I was asked to say something about the relation of colleges to business, but if I may be permitted I should rather talk about business — my business — for I am a manufacturer, as my forbears were before me, and I want to advertise — no, that is not the proper word — I want to let people know the quality of the goods that we produce.

My forbears made cotton goods. The concern that I belong to has a different kind of product, but it is an old and well established concern; it is the oldest corporation now existing in the United

[1]An address delivered before the Chamber of Commerce of the State of New York. Reprinted by permission.

States. In eight years the business will be 300 years old, which is more, I think, than any other here represented.

What we produce is men. I am speaking not of the professional schools, but simply of the college. We make men. It is a curious product. It is one that you cannot standardize, because it is a biological product and, therefore it cannot be wholly standardized. Nevertheless, there are different grades in the goods we produce, and one of the difficulties we find in marketing our product is that business men are very apt to prefer our second-class goods and then complain that they are not first rate.

I remember some years ago a business man said to me, "You are not teaching your students as you ought to. A good many of them go into brokers' offices, and they sell stocks and bonds to their fathers' friends, but they do not progress much." I began to think that over and said: "If you let us do what all other manufacturers do, recommend our own goods, you will find a very different result."

Mr. Walter Gifford has made some very interesting statistics, which he published in *Harper's Magazine,* and which, perhaps, some of you have seen. He employs some thousands of college graduates, and it occurred to him that, being an honor graduate from college himself, he might see how other men did in relation to their rank in college. He graded these men for the periods they had been in his employ and compared that with the rank that they had obtained while in college. He found that for the five first years, while men were learning their business, there was little difference, but from that time on the better students in college got larger salaries. By the way, the comparison was wholly made not by estimates but by salaries actually paid. He found that from that time on they departed more and more; that the men who had been in the first third of their class in college were earning larger salaries than those in the second third, and those in the second third more than those in the third third; and that this divergence continued until they had been out about twenty years, when it accentuated itself very much, the better scholars rising and the lower scholars falling off relatively more.

The goods we produce are of a peculiar character. The machine, if you choose to call it so, that we place upon the market does not run very smoothly for the first hundred miles or so, by which I mean that it will not run as well as an inferior machine which has already been running for some time, but try it and let it run a while and then see how it compares. I think you will see that the difference is very considerable by that time.

Now, what is our process of manufacture? How do we try to make these queer and uncertain goods? We pursue a policy which is not wholly understood by those who do not know the constitution of the human mind. I was very much struck, in reading Trevelyan's *History of England,* at a remark he made about the medieval universities, and if I may I will simply read it because I do not want to massacre the words of a man like George Macaulay Trevelyan. He says:

> The chief study of the medieval universities was a peculiar school of logic. . . .
>
> The great work of medieval logic and scholasticism was to train and subtilize the crude intellect of Europe. The intellectual progress by the Middle Ages is to be measured not by results in original thought, which was under an interdict, or at least in strict confinement, but by the skill with which men learned to handle their philosophic material. Though much of the subject matter of their disputes seems to us as vain and nugatory as the much debated problem "how many angels can stand on the point of a needle," the debt we owe to these ancient choppers of logic is nŏne the less great for being strictly inestimable.

There is a theory, at one time called "The Recapitulation Theory," which was that all people growing up recapitulated the history of the human race, that the child starts as a savage, then becomes a barbarian, then semicivilized, and so on. That theory has been naturally discarded because we know that infants are not savages. Nevertheless, there is something true about it in that the evolution of the individual mind is not very unlike the evolution of the mind of the race, just as the medieval universities trained men to think abstractly and to handle and deal with their material, to entertain abstract ideas, to think clearly and to develop a power of dealing with things which could not be perceived by the material senses, which was later of value when applied to useful results; so it is true that the cultivation of the mind by the colleges is an attempt to make men think accurately, to discern between the essential and accidental in phenomena, and to train the imagination to grasp things that cannot be felt or perceived by the material senses. That is the great object of college education. It is not merely to give knowledge. Knowledge vanishes away, but wisdom remains, and that, I take it, is, after all, a perception of the relative value of things. I know that some of you are saying to yourselves: "This is very well, but why not teach a man to think on subjects that he can apply? Why will not things that are useful train the mind as well as things that are useless?" The answer is simply that dealing with the concrete does not lead to the knowledge of the abstract. The study of that which is directly applicable does not tend to give a grasp of things which are not perceived by the senses. The mind that is directed toward the practical does not indulge itself in flights of imagination and thereby enlarge its scope.

I remember well when I was in college studying comparative anatomy and physiology with William James. He told me that he could pick out of the class the men who intended to be doctors because they spent their time in studying human bones, and thereby failed to grasp, as the rest of us did, the physiology, that is, the functions of animal life, which were, after all, the essential and valuable things in the course.

Let me put it in a different way. The real thing we want is not knowledge but resourcefulness. What I mean by that is that the art of life, the art which creates things both great and small, is not the capacity for solving problems. That may seem a curious statement, but the real art of life consists in finding out what is the question to be solved, and the person who can find out what the problem to be solved is, is the man who can make the real contributions to life. It is comparatively easy to train people to solve problems when they are stated, but the man who can see a new problem and state it is the man who makes the real advance. And that is true in everything. You all know perfectly well that the young man you want in your business is the man who will perceive something that needs to be done and has not been done. Finding out how to do it is comparatively simple.

It happened to be my good fortune to meet some time ago two men who have made great contributions to medicine. One of them was Banting. I took the privilege of an older man and said: "Tell me how you found it," and he told me how he made the discovery of insulin. It was a marvelous story. Shortly after that I happened to ask our Dr. Minot how he happened to get hold of the use of the liver treatment for pernicious anemia, which has practically abolished the disease, always fatal before, but now banished. He told me how he did it, and in each case the great thing was finding out what the problem to be solved was. The solving it afterward took more time, but the really great thing was finding out what the problems were to be solved. That, we say is resourcefulness, and that is what we really are attempting to impart.

How can resourcefulness be acquired? Is it by pumping into a man information? Not at all. There is only one thing which will really train the human mind, and that is the voluntary use of the mind by the man himself. You may aid him, you may guide him, you may suggest to him, and, above all, you may inspire him; but the only thing that is worth having is that which he gets by his own exertions, and what he gets is proportionate to the effort he puts into it. It is the voluntary exercise of his own mind, and I care very little about what he exercises it upon.

In his study I noticed that Mr. Gifford paid no attention whatever to what subjects his men had studied, and I fancy the reason was he did not consider that important. I myself made some studies twenty-five years ago about the relation between rank in college and rank in our law and medical schools, where I could easily get the figures, and I found just the same thing he found, that the men who had ranked high in college — of course, with many exceptions — were on the average the men who ranked high in the law and medical schools. I took also in that case the subjects they had studied, and I found that it made no difference. There was no perceptible difference between the men who had studied one subject or another, but there was a great superiority on the part of the men who really had done well in college, who had sharpened their minds by hard thought.

Given a certain voltage of intellectual power and, save in men who are unusually constituted, you can turn it into almost any channel and make it effective. The important thing is the degree of voltage, and that must come by making the men desire to educate themselves.

At one time there was a theory that the way to make men educate themselves was to let them select the subject in which they were interested and study that. The trouble is that nine boys out of ten at that age have no real interest, and if you ask them what their interest is they will select the thing which offers the least obstacle. In other words, their object, instead of being to cultivate their minds by effort, is to attempt to cultivate their minds with the least expenditure of energy. Now, that is the wrong way. Anyone who deals with young men who have an occupation realizes that almost anyone will become interested in that which he really does earnestly. In other words, doing comes not from interest, but interest comes from doing. That is, all of you are interested in the things you are doing. It is not because you were born with a natural interest for that particular kind of business. You know perfectly well you could have slid into something else; but as soon as you do a thing and try to do it well, you become interested in doing it. You feel that it is worth while.

Such is the way we are trying to educate in our factory, and when I say "our" I mean the colleges of the United States. We are today aware of the fact that there has been a great deal too little energy put by students voluntarily into their work. We think that our product has improved, and to revert to what I said in the beginning, if it costs more, try it and see whether it is worth the cost.

And, above all, let us ask you one thing: Help us to make a good product. When your son goes to college do not be satisfied that he gets by, creeps through and obtains those other very substantial advantages which come from college; but feel that he goes there to get an education, and let him understand that it is the education you expect him to get.

The great trouble that we have is with parents who do not desire that their son shall get an education. Why, then, do they send him to college? I will not attempt to answer that question. You can answer it better than I can. But the fact is that many parents do not seriously care whether their boy obtains the best education of which he is capable. In other words, they do not seriously care that he should leave college with a well-trained and a self-trained brain which can be turned into fields of great utility for this country.

Now, I think — any man is entitled to think — that the particular thing in which he is engaged is the most important for the country, and, therefore, you will pardon me if I believe our product of men is the most important for the future, and I bespeak your assistance in helping to hold up our hands in making good that product which will determine the fate of America in the next century.

THE NATURE OF POETIC DICTION[1]

Samuel Taylor Coleridge

Little of what I have here written concerns myself personally; the narrative is designed chiefly to introduce my principles of politics, religion, and poetry. But my special purpose is to decide what is the true nature of poetic diction, and to define the real poetic character of the works of Mr. Wordsworth, whose writings have been the subject of so much controversy.

At school I had the advantage of a very sensible though severe master. I learned from him that poetry, even that of the loftiest odes, had a logic of its own as severe as that of science, and more difficult, because more subtle. In the truly great poets, he would say, there is a reason assignable, not only for every word, but for the position of every word. In our English compositions he showed no mercy to phrase, metaphor, or image, where the same sense might have been conveyed with equal force and dignity in plainer words. In fancy, I can almost hear him now exclaiming: "Harp? Lyre? Pen and ink, boy, you mean!" Nay, certain introductions, similes, and examples were placed by name on a list of interdiction.

I had just entered my seventeenth year when the sonnets of Mr. Bowles were made known to me, and the genial influence of his poetry, so tender, yet so manly, so natural and real, yet so dignified and harmonious, recalled me from a premature bewilderment in metaphysics and theology. Well were it for me, perhaps, if I had never relapsed into the same mental disease.

The poetry of Pope and his followers, a school of French poetry invigorated by English understanding, which had predominated from the last century, consisted of prose thoughts translated into poetic language. I was led to the conjecture that this style had been kept up by, if it did not wholly arise from, the custom of writing Latin verses. I began to defend the use of natural language, such as "I will remember thee," instead of "Thy image on her wing, Before my fancy's eye shall memory bring"; and adduced, as exam-

[1]From *Biographia Literaria.*

ples of simplicity, the diction of Greek poets, and of our elder English poets, from Chaucer to Milton. I arrived at two critical aphorisms, as the criteria of poetic style: first, that not the poem which we have read with the greatest pleasure but that to which we return with the greatest pleasure possesses the genuine power; and, second, that whatever lines can be translated into other words of the same language, without diminution of their significance, are so far vicious in their diction.

One great distinction between even the characteristic faults of our elder poets and the false beauties of the moderns is this. In the former, from Donne to Cowley, we find the most fantastic out-of-the-way thoughts, but the most pure and genuine mother English; in the latter, the most obvious thoughts, in language the most fantastic and arbitrary. Our faulty elder poets sacrificed the passion, and passionate flow of poetry, to the subtleties of intellect and to the starts of wit; the moderns to the glare and glitter of a perpetual yet broken and heterogeneous imagery. The one sacrificed the heart to the head, the other both heart and head to drapery.

THE HIGHEST OF THE ARTS[1]

Francis Clement Kelley

What is the highest of the arts? Each art will answer the question by a claim to the superiority for itself. I shall answer it by saying that the art which does most to develop all the arts is the highest. Architecture is that art. Architecture is the Pantheon of all the arts. Under the roof of its own masterpieces that lift its message above the earth, it shelters the works it inspires. Sculpture carves its arches and fills its niches, fashions its solid adornment within and without. Painting beautifies its altars and brightens its shrines. Ceramics calls the glory of the sun through the painted glass to fill

[1]From *The Forgotten God,* the Religion and Culture Series. the Bruce Publishing Co., Milwaukee.

its dim spaces with magic colors. Music rolls melody through its pillared cloisters. No art that appeals to the soul is a stranger in the palace of architecture, from the tapestry that hangs over a balcony to the chased chalice upon the altar. Architecture alone can make such a sweeping claim to leadership. The ten centuries recognized this and gave us the glory of architecture, not in the heavy but beautiful horizontal and vertical lines of the worldly Greek, but in the curves of the Roman and Gothic that suggest the rainbow starting its brilliant upward climb from two points on earth and meeting in a blaze of beauty high in the heavens. Christian architecture is Christian thought. It animates the dumb stone, bids it preach and teach, organizes and spiritualizes matter to give it a soul of its own, and joins all the arts and all the inert materials with which they work in a psalm without words which God hears as another *Benedictus.* It is only the world of Christ that could produce such a triumph.

ASTHORE[1]

Leonard Feeney, S.J.

I am, if I may be allowed to stress one of my qualities, a good companion for an old person. My early life, up to my eleventh year, was spent in constant association with an aged grandfather. In those years of our childhood (his second and my first), my grandfather and I took a sympathetic interest in each other's joys and miseries. He preferred me to any of his old cronies and I him to any of my playmates. We were kindred spirits and loved each other dearly.

It was my business when his memory became unreliable to solve my grandfather's bewilderments concerning the time of day, the hour of dinner, and the whereabouts of his spectacles. I had not

[1]From *America,* Dec. 10, 1932, reprinted in *Fish on Friday,* by permission of Sheed and Ward Publishers, New York.

only exclusive access to his thoughts but also extraordinary privileges about his person. I was allowed to tie his boot laces, dust his hat, wind his watch, and light his pipe. And my youthful ear had a monopoly on his stories.

His stories were invariably about Ireland, and rigidly Irish in flavor; but there was universal stuff in them: ghosts, fairies, christenings, wakes, weddings, famines, battles. The battles were my favorites, fought, it seems, from the beginning of the world, against an army of ruffians called "low Briddish." The "low Briddish" kept coming across the sea in order to persecute our people, the "high Bernians." We were a peaceful and gentle race. They were unkind and cruel. They killed our orators. They poisoned our potatoes. Many a summer's afternoon my grandfather and I sat on the front doorstep, with our chins in our hands, shaking our heads and hating the "low Briddish," wishing them bad luck, and calling them the names they deserved.

From my grandfather I acquired many of my personal characteristics: the habit, for instance, of licking back my hair with my hand when I am annoyed, or of putting my thumbs behind my suspenders when I am amused. From him, too, I derived my sole musical talent, the art of humming Irish tunes. My grandfather took pains to teach me these ancestral arias with great thoroughness; and though I never tried to put words to them (nor did he), I learned to manage them in melody behind a closed mouth with unmistakable authenticity and sweetness. Even to this day native-born Irishmen will testify that I am a splendid Celtic hummer, with an extraordinary nasal range, and a most interesting repertory of hums.

Every child in the course of his development makes at least one precocious remark. Some children, provided they be unusually bright or abnormally stupid, make many. But no child fails to make at least one. I made one, I am quite sure *only* one, but I think it was a very good one.

My grandfather and I were sitting — need I say? — on the front doorstep one drowsy afternoon in July. It was getting late. The sun was ready to go down. Our voices were weary and our emotions tired. Finn McCool, a large-jowled Irish chieftain, had just executed some fine stunts for us in the movies of our imaginations. At intervals we had cleared our soft palates and strummed a little music, keeping it in time with a metronome accompaniment of heel and toe. My grandfather had made a few meditative remarks on his favorite holy topic, the Blessed Mother of God, at the mention of whose name he invariably raised his hat, even though it occurred twice in a sentence. I, being hatless, was in the habit of paying my devoir to any spoken syllables indicating Our Lady's reality by making her a reverential flick of my hair. But, as I said, at last we grew tired, tired of talk and romantics. And we lapsed into one of those long silences we often had together when the conversation lagged.

My grandfather sighed. It was a long, deep sigh, indicating not the fatigue of a day but the fatigue of a whole life. He was growing very feeble at the time, only six months before his death. He sighed again, and looked at me for ten intense minutes that were full of flashes issuing from the core of his soul to the kernel of mine. "I am all through!" he said without speaking, "you must carry on. You must keep alive the thoughts, the dreams, the stories we once shared together."

I sighed back at my grandfather to show him that I understood his message, and was assuming my burden with pride and regret. And in some dim way I promised him with my eyes that if ever I had a grandson I would see to it that our stories were kept alive and that our tradition did not die. I did not know at that time that it was God's holy design to make me the last of my line.

When this sacred trust had been executed and I had in silence received it, my grandfather shriveled, and for some moments after seemed to lose his individuality. His hands grew cold, his face expressionless, and his head dropped dismally on his breast. For a little while he stopped being anybody's grandfather, even mine, and became just an old hulk of a body with a spirit floating somewhere inside it, a soul unrelated to material dimensions and movements, without a function on any human purpose. I pulled his head down, and putting my mouth close to his ear, whispered, "Is it lonely in there, grandfather?" . . . I hope I am allowed to consider this a remarkable question, very precocious, and, indeed, deeply mystical.

My grandfather saw to a nicety the point of my strange query. He wiped his bad eye with the back of his hand — he had one bad eye which for the last ten years of his life was constantly inflamed, and which my mother had to bathe three times a day with boric acid and warm water — and answered, "It is, *asthore!*"

There is, in Irish, no expression of endearment so delicate in its nuance or so extravagant in its meaning as the term *asthore*. It is very probably the loveliest word in that language. It is elusive in its emotional significance and impossible to translate straightforwardly into English, much like the word *doux* in French. I once heard Hilaire Belloc struggling to render in good Anglo-Saxon the expression *le doux air d'Anjou*. "The *sweet* air of Anjou," he said, would never do. Nor would "the *gentle* air of Anjou." But possibly "the *quiet kindness* of the Angevin air" would, in roundabout fashion, indicate the spirit of the word. "Asthore" is even more difficult.

The best way to convey the meaning of "asthore" is to state the relationship which must exist in persons between whom its employment is warranted. "Asthore" supposes in general what I may call "an affectionate, protective superiority" on the part of the one using it toward the one to whom it is used. A young person never calls another young person "asthore"; nor would a child use it to an elder, nor elder people among themselves. There are three situations in which the word achieves its power and its point, which usages I may designate as (1) The Lover-Beloved; (2) The Parent-Child; and (3) The Grandparent-Grandchild.

(1) The L-B use of "asthore" is always dead serious. It is, in this case, never a mere pet word, nor one to be employed in any light flirtation. For instance, an Irish lad would never think of saying to a pretty girl at a cross-roads dance, "You have nice eyes, asthore," or "What are you doing next Tuesday evening, asthore?" This would be an utter profanation of the word. It would be in impossible bad taste, much as though a young American "fresh guy" should say to an indefinite blonde waitress in a cafe, "Hello, bright eyes! I can see right on the spot that God meant you from all eternity to be my comfort, my joy, and my delight. Would you mind telling me your name and letting me take you to the movies?"

No. When a young man calls his sweetheart "asthore" it is required (*a*) that she be not merely his sweetheart, but his "sweet soul"; and (*b*) that they be realizing for the moment some phase of the spiritual quality of love, its sacrificial character, its burden, its rapture, and its mystery. "And will you love me when I am a weeshy, scrawny, wither-may-jingle old woman?" says she. If she has asked it smilingly, he will answer: "Yes, acushla (or mavourneen or machree)" meaning "Yes, my darling, or my honey, or my sweet one." But if she asked this question *with tears in her eyes,* his answer is "I will, asthore!" That's the way the word goes among lovers.

(2) The Parent-Child use of "asthore" is playful. It is the term of affection by which fathers and mothers (or their equivalents: aunts or uncles, or very close neighbors) indicate to youngsters what adorable annoyances they are, what agreeable nuisances. When a father calls his little son "asthore" he means: "I love you because you are my little son. I love you because you are at once such a joy to me, and such a bother. I wouldn't swap you for ten million pounds. And I wouldn't give tuppence for ten more like you!" This is the second meaning of "asthore."

(3) The Grandparent-Grandchild use of "asthore" is the most sacred of all. It is a word of ritual, the love cry of a tribe, the call of the blood overleaping a generation. It is the means by which an aged human heart asks its own posterity, not for affection but for existence, not for companionship but for continuation. It makes vocable an act, not of love alone, but of love and faith fused into one virtue, which we call "hope," and which we rightly set highest of all the operations of the human spirit in its present condition of probation and exile. If King David had written his psalms in Irish he would have called his Royal Grandchild "asthore."

The night my grandfather died, just before the death rattle began in his throat, he raised a blessed candle and waved good-by to all his neighbors and kindred, to the whole world and all its countries and peoples. And then with the last bit of strength left in him he whispered "Good-by, asthore" to me. Shortly afterward the undertaker arrived to dress his lifeless body in its coffin clothes, surround it with candles, and give it a parlor respectability. I have never had a grandfather since that time. . . .

Freudians, psychoanalysts, and chemical philosophers who are anxious to dissect and desecrate all forms of honorable human affection will be interested in this personal confession. It may give rise to a whole new department in the field of behavioristic studies hitherto left untouched: "The little-boy-old-man neurosis"; or maybe "the atavistic perversion"; or more likely "the Abraham complex." And if their textbooks can prove that the implications of any psychic irregularity are sufficiently degenerate and gloomy to arouse popular interest, science will hand over a fresh inspiration to literature. A new form of melancholy will develop among our novelists. America's leading dramatist will put me in a play.

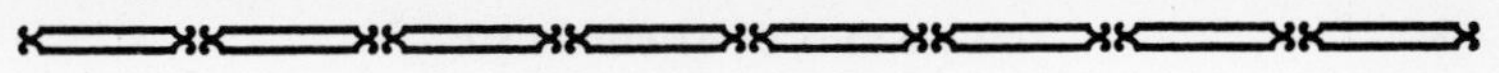

C. ANALYSIS

GOSSIP

Cardinal Manning

"Noblest things find vilest using." And certainly it is a rigorous destiny that *Gossipred* should have come to signify the worst of social vices. There is something venerable in the pious confabulation of godfathers and godmothers over caudle cups and postle spoons: but there is something murderous in the conspiracy of gossips. It may be that the christening of an infant may have usually let loose a flood of small talk, and volumes of charitable hopes that the son may be better than his father, and the daughter less intolerable than her mother. This mixture of detraction and prophecy is the original sin of gossiping: and it has descended with rapid propagation to all races and languages among Christian men.

There are many varieties in the Gossip kingdom. First, there is the Harmless Gossip, who, being good-hearted but empty-headed, talks incessantly in a kindly, bird-witted, scatter-brained way of all sorts and conditions of men. Such a one cannot talk of subjects scientific, literary, or historical, for he knows nothing about them; nor of things generally, for he is habitually unobservant; but his whole talk is of persons. What such a one has done, is doing, is about to do, would do, or will do: and what such another has said, or is saying, and so on, through all the moods and tenses: how Mr. Gladstone entered Parliament as a supralapsarian, but has gone over to the social democracy: and how no Duchess of Sutherland would ever have in her wardrobe less than one hundred and forty-four pocket handkerchiefs, every one of which cost twenty-five guineas: how Sir Wilfred Lawson in early life tried to be a Dominican, but was sent away because of his hard drinking and contagious melancholy. Such gossips are, however, as free from guile or malice as they are from common sense or discernment of what in men or things is credible, probable, or possible. Nothing comes amiss to them. Gossip they must, by a second nature. If they have anything to say, they will say it: if nothing, it is all one: they buzz on amiably, *sicut chimaera bombitanes in vacuo;* amiable buzzing creatures, the bluebottles of social life.

There is next the Unconscious Gossip, who repeats all he hears to all he meets, with no greater perception of the fitness of time, place, or person, than he has of colors in the dark. What somebody told him he tells to everybody; mostly to the person who ought last to hear it, and whom it most concerns. The unconscious gossip is an adult *enfant terrible* — a sort of *petroleur* or *petroleuse* on a large scale, sprinkling society with petroleum, believing it to be as harmless as salad oils. Such innocents have not even the vice of curiosity. They have not sufficient perception of either the eternal or the transient relations of things to excite curiosity, or to make them conscious of the social explosions, earthquakes, conflagrations they are daily causing. The law against arson ought to be extended to such unconscious incendiaries. Their only plea at bar is: "Who could have ever thought that the man I met in the train was accused of the crime or afflicted with the unhappiness of which I told him? I did not even know who he was."

To these must be added the Professional Gossip. This is the kind known to the Clubs. He knows everybody; is particularly intimate with the people you are talking of; he saw them yesterday; or is going to dine with them, to meet the Russian Ambassador, tomorrow. He puts no handle to any man's name: they are his familiars and clients, patients and penitents, Lords, Commons, and Lions. They all consult him; tell him everything, do nothing without him. He was called last night after twelve o'clock by telegram to Hawarden Castle or to Alnwick, but was not able to go, being sent for from Buckingham Palace. He knows the outline of the Bill of the Session; and how many Peers will be made to carry it; and who are to be made Peers. Such gossips have one fatality. Their prophecies never come to pass; and of their secrets, what is true is not new, and what is new is not true. Each day wipes them out; but they are like tales of fiction, a pleasant excitement for the moment. Such gossips are not malicious. They are too well pleased with themselves to bear ill will. A quarrel, or even a duel now and then, they may create without meaning it; but they make it up by sacrificing themselves, which costs them nothing, and they begin again the old trade with new capital.

But Gossipdom has inner *bolge* or circles less innocuous. As we enter further, we encounter next the Malignant Gossip. Of this kind there are two sorts — men who murder the reputations of others, and women who throw vitriol over it. They have an ear always wide open to catch all evil that is said, truly or falsely in the world. Their ears are spread in the dark, like the nets of bat-folders; nothing escapes them. It is enough to be ten minutes in a room with them, to see the rent in every man's coat, or the wrinkle in every woman's temper. As a sponge sucks in water, so these malignant gossips draw in, by affinity, all malignant histories. They have, too, a laboratory in the brain, and a chemical acid by which all that is malignant is at once detected, and drawn out for use in a concentrated form. Such men are man-slayers: for to a good man and an honorable man a fair name is dearer than life. And such women are domestic *vitrioleuses,* more guilty than the male malignities, as the nature and dignity of woman is mercy, tenderness, and compassion. The distortion of their nature is there more intense.

There remains one more kind — the Mendacious Gossip. We put him last, not because he is necessarily worse, but because he makes more havoc, and provides, both willingly and unwillingly, weapons and vitriol for the use of the malignants. For such gossips by no means are always conscious or intentional liars. They have gaping ears, and itching tongues, and wandering wits. They are never sure of what they hear, and never accurate in what they repeat. They magnify, and multiply, and put carts before horses, and all things upside down, first in their own minds, and next in their histories. They would not misrepresent if they knew it, nor do mischief if they were aware of it; but all their life long they do mischiefs of lesser or greater magnitudes. They are not false, for they have no intention to be untruthful; but they are not true, for a great part of what they say is false. With all their good intentions they are dangerous as companions, and still more dangerous as friends. But there is another kind of mendacious gossip, who knows that he is inventing, inverting, exaggerating, supplementing with theories and explanations of his own, the words and actions of other men. The Italians call such a man *uomo finto.* He is a living fiction; and all he touches turns to fiction, as all that Midas touched turned to gold. He is reckless of the name, and fame, and feelings, and dignity of other men, having none of his own: and he is hardly conscious of the pain he inflicts, though he would still inflict it even if he could feel it himself: for in him the malignant and mendacious gossip meet in one brain—and a miserable brain it is. *Quisque suos patimur manes.* Self is our worst scourge.

WHY A CLASSIC IS A CLASSIC[1]

Arnold Bennett

The large majority of our fellow citizens care as much about literature as they care about airplanes or the program of the Legislature. They do not ignore it; they are not quite indifferent to it. But their interest in it is faint and perfunctory; or, if their interest happens to be violent, it is spasmodic. Ask the two hundred thousand persons whose enthusiasm made the vogue of a popular novel ten years ago what they think of that novel now, and you will gather that they have utterly forgotten it, and that they would no more dream of reading it again than of reading Bishop Stubbs's *Select Charters*. Probably if they did read it again they would not enjoy it—not because the said novel is a whit worse now than it was ten years ago; not because their taste has improved—but because they have not had sufficient practice to be able to rely on their taste as a means of permanent pleasure. They simply don't know from one day to the next what will please them.

In the face of this one may ask: Why does the great and universal fame of classical authors continue? The answer is that the fame of classical authors is entirely independent of the majority. Do you suppose that if the fame of Shakespeare depended on the man in the street it would survive a fortnight? The fame of classical au-

[1]From *Literary Taste and How to Form It*, by Arnold Bennett, reprinted by permission of Doubleday, Doran and Company, Inc.

thors is originally made, and it is maintained, by a passionate few. Even when a first-class author has enjoyed immense success during his lifetime, the majority have never appreciated him so sincerely as they have appreciated second-rate men. He has always been reënforced by the ardor of the passionate few. And in the case of an author who has emerged into glory after his death, the happy sequel has been due solely to the obstinate perseverance of the few. They could not leave him alone; they would not. They kept on savoring him, and talking about him, and buying him, and they generally behaved with such eager zeal, and they were so authoritative and sure of themselves, that at last the majority grew accustomed to the sound of his name and placidly agreed to the proposition that he was a genius; the majority really did not care very much either way.

And it is by the passionate few that the renown of genius is kept alive from one generation to another. These few are always at work. They are always rediscovering genius. Their curiosity and enthusiasm are exhaustless, so that there is little chance of genius being ignored. And, moreover, they are always working either for or against the verdicts of the majority. The majority can make a reputation, but it is too careless to maintain it. If, by accident, the passionate few agree with the majority in a particular instance, they will frequently remind the majority that such and such a reputation has been made, and the majority will idly concur: "Ah, yes. By the way, we must not forget that such and such a reputation exists." Without that persistent memory-jogging the reputation would quickly fall into the oblivion which is death. The passionate few only have their way by reason of the fact that they are genuinely interested in literature, that literature matters to them. They conquer by their obstinacy alone, by their eternal repetition of the same statements. Do you suppose they could prove to the man in the street that Shakespeare was a great artist? The said man would not even understand the terms they employed. But when he is told ten thousand times, and generation after generation, that Shakespeare was a great artist, the said man believes — not by reason, but by faith. And he, too, repeats that Shakespeare was a great artist, and he buys the complete works of Shakespeare and puts them on his shelves, and he goes to see the marvelous stage effects which accompany *King Lear* or *Hamlet,* and comes back religiously convinced that Shakespeare was a great artist. All because the passionate few could not keep their admiration of Shakespeare to themselves. This is not cynicism; but truth. And it is important that those who wish to form their literary taste should grasp it.

What causes the passionate few to make such a fuss about literature? There can be only one reply. They find a keen and lasting pleasure in literature. They enjoy literature as some men enjoy beer. The recurrence of this pleasure naturally keeps their interest in literature very much alive. They are forever making new researches, forever practicing on themselves. They learn to understand themselves. They learn to know what they want. Their taste becomes surer and surer as their experience lengthens. They do not enjoy today what will seem tedious to them tomorrow. When they find a book tedious, no amount of popular clatter will persuade them that it is pleasurable; and when they find it pleasurable no chill silence of the street-crowds will affect their conviction that the book is good and permanent. They have faith in themselves. What are the qualities in a book which give keen and lasting pleasure to the passionate few? This is a question so difficult that it has never yet been completely answered. You may talk lightly about truth, insight, knowledge, wisdom, humor, and beauty. But these comfortable words do not really carry you very far, for each of them has to be defined, especially the first and last. It is all very well for Keats in his airy manner to assert that beauty is truth, truth beauty, and that that is all he knows or needs to know. I, for one, need to know a lot more. And I never shall know. Nobody, not even Hazlitt or Sainte-Beuve, has ever finally explained why he thought a book beautiful. I take the first fine lines that come to hand—

> The woods of Arcady are dead,
> And over is their antique joy—

and I say that those lines are beautiful because they give me pleasure. But why? No answer! I only know that the passionate few will broadly agree with me in deriving this mysterious pleasure from these lines. I am only convinced that the liveliness of our pleasure in those and many other lines by the same author will ultimately cause the majority to believe, by faith, that W. B. Yeats is a genius. The one reassuring aspect of the literary affair is that the passionate few are passionate about the same things. A continuance of interest does, in actual practice, lead ultimately to the same judgments. There is only the difference in width of interest. Some of the passionate few lack catholicity, or, rather, the whole of their interest is confined to one narrow channel; they have none left over. These men help specially to vitalize the reputations of the narrower geniuses such as Crashaw. But their active predilections never contradict the general verdict of the passionate few; rather they reënforce it.

A classic is a work which gives pleasure to the minority which is intensely and permanently interested in literature. It lives on because the minority, eager to renew the sensation of pleasure, is eternally curious and is therefore engaged in an eternal process of rediscovery. A classic does not survive for any ethical reason. It does not survive because it conforms to certain canons, or because neglect would not kill it. It survives because it is a source of pleasure, and because the passionate few can no more neglect it than a bee can neglect a flower. The passionate few do not read "the right things" because they are right. That is to put the cart before the horse. "The right things" are the right things solely because the passionate few *like* reading them. Hence—and I now arrive at my point—the one primary essential to literary taste is a hot interest in literature. If you have that, all the rest will come. It matters nothing that at present you fail to find pleasure in certain classics. The driving impulse of your interest will force you to acquire experience, and experience will teach you the use of the means of pleasure. You do not know the secret ways of yourself; that is all. A continuance of interest must inevitably bring you to the keenest joys. But, of course, experience may be acquired judiciously or injudiciously, just as Putney may be reached *via* Walham Green or *via* St. Petersburg.

LITERATURE OF KNOWLEDGE AND LITERATURE OF POWER[1]

Thomas De Quincey

What is it that we mean by *literature?* Popularly, and among the thoughtless, it is held to include everything that is printed in a book. Little logic is required to disturb *that* definition. The most thoughtless person is easily made aware that in the idea of *literature* one essential element is some relation to a general and common interest of man — so that what applies only to a local, or professional, or merely personal interest, even though presenting itself in the shape of a book, will not belong to literature. So far the definition is easily narrowed; and it is as easily expanded. For not only is much that takes a station in books not literature, but inversely, much that really *is* literature never reaches a station in books. The weekly sermons of Christendom, that vast pulpit literature which acts so extensively upon the popular mind — to warn, to uphold, to renew, to comfort, to alarm — does not attain the sanctuary of libraries in the ten-thousandth part of its extent. The drama again — as, for instance, the finest part of Shakespeare's plays in England, and all leading Athenian plays in the noontide of the Attic stage — operated as literature on the public mind, and were (according to the strictest letter of that term) *published* through the audiences that witnessed their representation some time before they were published as things to be read; and they were published in this scenical mode of publication with much more effect than they could have had as books during ages of costly copying or of costly printing.

Books, therefore, do not suggest an idea coextensive and interchangeable with the idea of literature; since much literature, scenic, forensic, or didactic (as from lecturers and public orators), may never come into books, and much that does come into books may connect itself with no literary interest. But a far more important correction, applicable to the common vague idea of literature, is to be sought not so much in a better definition of literature as in a

[1]From *Essays.*

sharper distinction of the two functions which it fulfills. In that great social organ which, collectively, we call literature, there may be distinguished two separate offices, that may blend and often do so, but capable, severally, of a severe insulation, and naturally fitted for reciprocal repulsion. There is, first, the literature of *knowledge,* and secondly, the literature of *power.* The function of the first is to *teach;* the function of the second is to *move;* the first is a rudder, the second an oar or a sail. The first speaks to the *mere* discursive understanding; the second speaks ultimately, it may happen, to the higher understanding or reason, but always through affections of pleasure and sympathy. Remotely, it may travel toward an object seated in what Lord Bacon calls "dry light"; but proximately it does and must operate—else it ceases to be a literature of *power*—on and through that *humid* light which clothes itself in the mists and glittering *iris* of human passions, desires, and genial emotions. Men have so little reflected on the higher functions of literature as to find it a paradox if one should describe it as a mean or subordinate purpose of books to give information. But this is a paradox only in the sense which makes it honorable to be paradoxical. Whenever we talk in ordinary language of seeking information or gaining knowledge, we understand the words as connected with something of absolute novelty. But it is the grandeur of all truth which *can* occupy a very high place in human interests that it is never absolutely novel to the meanest of minds; it exists eternally by way of germ or latent principle in the lowest as in the highest, needing to be developed, but never to be planted. To be capable of transplantation is the immediate criterion of a truth that ranges on a lower scale.

Besides which, there is a rarer thing than truth—namely *power,* or deep sympathy with truth. What is the effect, for instance, upon society, of children? By the pity, by the tenderness, and by the peculiar modes of admiration which connect themselves with the helplessness, with the innocence, and with the simplicity of children, not only are the primal affections strengthened and continually renewed, but the qualities which are dearest in the sight of heaven—the frailty, for instance, which appeals to forbearance, the innocence which symbolizes the heavenly, and the simplicity which is most alien from the worldly—are kept up in perpetual remembrance, and their ideals are continually refreshed. A purpose of the same nature is answered by the higher literature, viz., the literature of power. What do you learn from *Paradise Lost?* Nothing at all. What do you learn from a cookery book? Something new, something that you did not know before, in every paragraph. But would you therefore put the wretched cookery book on a higher level of estimation than the divine poem? What you owe to Milton is not any knowledge, of which a million separate items are still but a million of advancing steps on the same earthly level; what you owe is *power* — that is, exercise and expansion to your own latent capacity of sympathy with the infinite, where every pulse and each separate influx is a step upward, a step ascending as upon a Jacob's ladder from earth to mysterious altitudes above the earth. All the steps of knowledge from first to last, carry you further on the same plane, but could never raise your one foot above your ancient level of earth; whereas the very *first* step in power is a flight — is an ascending movement into another element where earth is forgotten.

Were it not that human sensibilities are ventilated and continually called out into exercise by the great phenomena of infancy, or of real life as it moves through chance and change, or of literature as it recombines these elements in the mimicries of poetry, romance, etc., it is certain that, like any animal power or muscular energy falling into disuse, all such sensibilities would gradually droop and dwindle. It is in relation to these great *moral* capacities of man that the literature of power, as contradistinguished from that of knowledge, lives and has its field of action. It is concerned with what is highest in man; for the Scriptures themselves never condescended to deal by suggestion or coöperation with the mere discursive understanding. When speaking of man in his intellectual capacity, the Scriptures speak not of the understanding, but of "the understanding heart" — making the heart, i.e., the great *intuitive* (or non-discursive) organ, to be the interchangeable formula for man in his highest state of capacity for the infinite. Tragedy, romance, fairy tale, or epopee, all alike restore to man's mind the ideals of justice, of hope, of truth, of mercy, of retribution, which else (left to the support of daily life in its realities) would languish for want of sufficient illustration.

What is meant, for instance, by *poetic justice?* It does not mean a justice that differs by its object from the ordinary justice of human jurisprudence, for then it must be confessedly a very bad kind of justice; but it means a justice that differs from common forensic justice by the degree in which it attains its object — a justice that is more omnipotent over its own ends, as dealing, not with the refractory elements of earthly life, but with the elements of its own creation, and with materials flexible to its own purest preconceptions. It is certain that, were it not for the literature of power, these ideals would often remain among us as mere arid notional forms; whereas, by the creative forces of man put forth in the literature, they gain a vernal life of restoration, and germinate into vital activities. The commonest novel, by moving in alliance with human fears and hopes, with human instincts of wrong and right, sustains and quickens those affections. Calling them into action, it rescues them from torpor. And hence the preëminency over all authors that merely *teach,* of the meanest that *moves,* or that teaches, if at all, indirectly by moving. The very highest work that has ever existed in the literature of knowledge is but a provisional work — a book upon trial and sufferance, and *quamdiu bene se gesserit.*[2] Let its teaching be even partially revised, let it be but expanded — nay, even let its teaching be but placed in a better order — and instantly it is superseded. Whereas the feeblest works in the literature of power, surviving at all, survive as finished and unalterable among men. For instance, the *Principia* of Sir Isaac Newton was a book *militant* on earth from the first. In all stages of its progress it would have to fight for its existence: first, as regards absolute truth; secondly, when that combat was over, as regards its form or mode of presenting the truth. And as soon as a Laplace, or anybody else, builds higher upon the foundations laid by this book, effectually he throws it out of the sunshine into decay and darkness, by weapons won from this book he superannuates and destroys this book, so that soon the name of Newton remains as a mere *nominis umbra,*[3] but his book, as a living power, has transmigrated into other forms. Now, on the contrary, the *Iliad,* the *Prometheus* of Æschylus, the *Othello* or *King Lear,* the *Hamlet* or *Macbeth,* and the *Paradise Lost,* are not militant, but triumphant forever, as long as the languages exist in which they speak or can be taught to speak. They never *can* transmigrate into new incarnations. To reproduce *these* in new forms, or variations, even if in some things they should be im-

---

[2]"During good behavior."

[3]"The shadow of a name."

proved, would be to plagiarize. A good steam engine is properly superseded by a better. But one lovely pastoral valley is not superseded by another, nor a statue of Praxiteles by a statue of Michelangelo. These things are separated not by imparity, but by disparity. They are not thought of as unequal under the same standard, but as different in *kind,* and, if otherwise equal, as equal under a different standard. Human works of immortal beauty and works of nature in one respect stand on the same footing: they never absolutely repeat each other, never approach so near as not to differ, and they differ not as better and worse, or simply by more and less—they differ by undecipherable and incommunicable differences, that cannot be caught by mimicries, that cannot be reflected in the mirror of copies, that cannot become ponderable in the scales of vulgar comparison.... At this hour, five hundred years since their creation, the tales of Chaucer, never equaled on this earth for their tenderness and for life of picturesqueness, are read familiarly by many in the charming language of their natal day, and by others in the modernizations of Dryden, of Pope, and Wordsworth. At this hour, one thousand eight hundred years since their creation, the pagan tales of Ovid, never equaled on this earth for the gayety of their movement and the capricious grace of their narrative, are read by all Christendom. This man's people and their monuments are dust, but *he* is alive; he has survived them, as he told us that he had it in his commission to do, by a thousand years, "and shall a thousand more."

All the literature of knowledge builds only ground nests, that are swept away by floods, or confounded by the plow; but the literature of power builds nests in aërial altitudes of temples sacred from violation, or of forests inaccessible to fraud. This is a great prerogative of the *power* literature, and it is a greater which lies in the mode of its influence. The *knowledge* literature, like the fashion of this world, passeth away. An encyclopedia is its abstract; and, in this respect, it may be taken for its speaking symbol—that before one generation has passed, an encyclopedia is superannuated; for it speaks through the dead memory and unimpassioned understanding, which have not the repose of higher faculties, but are continually enlarging and varying their phylacteries. But all literature properly so called—literature *κατ' ἐξοχήν*[4]—for the very reason that

[4]*Par excellence,* "preëminently."

it is so much more durable than the literature of knowledge, is (and by the very same proportion it is) more intense and electrically searching in its impressions. The directions in which the tragedy of this planet has trained our human feelings to play, and the combinations into which the poetry of this planet has thrown our human passions of love and hatred, of admiration and contempt, exercise a power for bad or good over human life that cannot be contemplated, when stretching through many generations, without a sentiment allied to awe. And of this let everyone be assured—that he owes to the impassioned books which he has read many a thousand more of emotions than he can consciously trace back to them. Dim by their origination, these emotions yet arise in him, and mold him through life, like forgotten incidents of his childhood.

THE RABID VERSUS THE HARMLESS SCHOLAR[1]

Louise Imogen Guiney

A philosopher now living, and too deserving for any fate but choice private oblivion, was in Paris, for the first time, a dozen years ago; and having seen and heard there, in the shops, parks, and omnibus stations, much more baby than he found pleasing, he remarked, upon his return, that it was a great pity the French, who are so in love with system, had never seen their way to shutting up everything under ten years of age! Now, that was the remark of an artist in human affairs, and may provoke a number of analogies. What is in the making is not a public spectacle. It ought to be considered criminal, on the death of a painter or a poet, to exhibit those rough first drafts, which he, living, had the acumen to conceal. And if, to an impartial eye, in a foreign city, native innocents seem too aggressively to the fore, why should not the seclu-

[1]From *Patrins*. Reprinted by permission of Miss Grace Guiney.

sion desired for them be visited a thousandfold upon the heads, let us say, of students, who are also in a crude transitional state, and undergoing a growth much more distressing to a sensitive observer than the physical? Youth is the most inspiring thing on earth, but not the best to let loose, especially while it carries swaggeringly that most dangerous of all blunderbusses, knowledge at half-cock. There is, indeed, no more melancholy condition than that of healthy boys scowling over books, in an eternal protest against their father Adam's fall from a state of relative omniscience. Sir Philip Sidney thought it was "a piece of the Tower of Babylon's curse that a man should be put to school to learn his mother-tongue." The throes of education are as degrading and demoralizing as a hanging, and when the millennium sets in, will be as carefully screened from the laity. Around the master and the pupil will be reared a portly and decorous Chinese wall, which shall pen within their proper precincts the din of *hic, haec, hoc,* and the steam of suppers sacrificed to Pallas.

The more noxious variety of student, however, is not young. He is "in the midway of this our mortal life"; he is fearfully foraging, with intent to found and govern an academy; he runs in squads after Anglo-Saxon or Comparative Mythology; he stops you on 'change to ask if one has not good grounds for believing that there was such a person as Pope Joan? He can never let well enough alone. Heine must be translated and Junius must be identified. The abodes of hereditary scholars are depopulated by the red flag of the *nouveau instruit*. He infests every civilized country: the army worm is nothing to him. He has either lacked early discipline altogether, or gets tainted, late in life, with the notion that he has never shown sufficiently how intellectual he really is. In every contemplative-looking person he sees a worthy victim, and his kindling eye, as he bears down upon you, precludes escape: he can achieve no peace unless he is driving you mad with all which you fondly dreamed you had left behind in old S.'s accursed lecture room. You may commend to him, in vain, the reminder which Erasmus left for the big-wigs, that it is the quality of what you know which tells, and never its quantity. It is inconceivable to him that you should shut your impious teeth against First Principles, and fear greatly to displace in yourself the illiteracies you have painfully acquired.

Judge, then, if the learner of this type (and in a bitterer degree, the learneress) could but be safely cloistered, how much simpler would become the whole problem of living! How profoundly would it benefit both society and himself could the formationary mind, destined, as like as not, to no ultimate development, be sequestered by legal statute in one imperative limbo, along with babes, lovers, and training athletes! *Quicquid ostendis mihi sic, incredulus odi.*

For the true scholar's sign-manual is not the midnight lamp on a folio. He knows; he is baked through; all superfluous effort and energy are over for him. To converse consumedly upon the weather, and compare notes as to "whether it is likely to hold up for tomorrow" — this, says Hazlitt, "is the end and privilege of a life of study." Secretly, decently, pleasantly, has he acquired his mental stock; insensibly he diffuses, not always knowledge, but sometimes the more needful scorn of knowledge. Among folk who break their worthy heads indoors over Mr. Browning and Madame Blavatsky, he moves cheerful, incurious, and free, on glorious good terms with arts and crafts for which he has no use, with extraneous languages which he will never pursue, with vague Muses impossible to invite to dinner. He is strictly non-educational.

> Thou wast not born for death, immortal bird!
> No hungry generations tread thee down.

He loathes information, and the givers and takers thereof. Like Mr. Lang, he laments bitterly that Oxford is now a place where many things are "being taught and learned with very great vigor." The main business, to him, is to live gracefully, without mental passion, and to get off alone into a corner for an affectionate view of creation. A mystery serves his turn better than a history. It is to be remembered that had the Reverend Laurence Sterne gone to gaze upon the spandrils of Rouen, we should have lost the *fille de chambre,* the dead ass, and Maria by the brookside. Any one of these is worth more than hieroglyphics; but who is to attain that insight that these are so, except the man of culture, who has the courage to forget at times even his sole science, and fall back with delight upon a choice assortment of ignorances?

The scholar's own research, from his cradle, clothes him in privacy; nor will he ever invade the privacy of others. It is not with a light heart that he contemplates the kindergarten system. He himself, holding his tongue, and fleeing from Junius and Pope Joan, from cubic roots and the boundaries of Hindostan, must be an evil sight to Chautauquans, albeit approved of the angels. He has little to utter which will sound wise, the full-grown, finished soul! If he had, he would of his own volition seek a cell in that asylum for protoplasms, which we have made bold to recommend.

The truth is, very few can be trusted with an education. In the old days, while this was a faith, boredom and nervous prostration were not common, and social conditions were undeniably dramatic. Then, as now, quiet was the zenith of power: the mellow mind was unexcursive and shy. Then, as now, though young clerical masters of arts went staggering abroad with heads lolling like Sisyphus' stone, the ideal worth and weight grew "lightly as a flower." Sweetly wrote the good Sprat of his famous friend Cowley: "His learning sat exceedingly close and handsomely upon him: It was not embossed on his mind, but enamelled." The best to be said of any knowing one among us, is that he does not readily show what deeps are in him; that he is unformidable, and reminds those whom he meets of a distant or deceased uncle. Initiation into noble facts has not ruined him for this world nor the other. It is a beautiful brag which James Howell, on his first going beyond sea, March the first, in the year sixteen hundred and eighteen, makes to his father. He gives thanks for "that most indulgent and costly Care you have been pleased, in so extraordinary a manner, to have had of my Breeding, (tho' but one child of Fifteen) by placing me in a choice Methodical Schoole so far distant from your dwelling, under a Learned (tho' Lashing) Master; and by transplanting me thence to Oxford to be graduated; and soe holding me still up by the chin, until I could swim without Bladders. This patrimony of liberall Education you have been pleased to endow me withal, I now carry along with me abroad as a sure inseparable Treasure; nor do I feele it any burden or incumbrance unto me at all!"

There, in the closing phrase, spoke the post-Elizabethan pluck. Any man does well since, who can describe the aggregated agonies of his brain as *no incumbrance,* as less, indeed, than a wife and posterity! To have come to this is to earn the freedom of cities, and to sink the schoolmaster as if he had never been.

THE MIND OF THE UNDERGRADUATE[1]

George Pierce Baker

I wish to state certain conditions which I find in the minds of Harvard undergraduates as some one hundred and fifty of them come before me, year after year, in the various courses on argumentation and public address which it is my fortune to have in charge. Whenever I consider the states of mind which confront me in these courses, certain queries and problems instantly arise. Understand, please, that what I am saying this morning I am not saying about the brilliant undergraduate, nor about the dull undergraduate. I am talking about the rank and file of the undergraduate body as it comes before me. I am talking, too, about youths who are not sophomores, but juniors and seniors, and sometimes even graduate students; that is, the maturer of our college men. It is becoming clear to our undergraduate that he had better keep out of the debating, certainly out of the higher forms of debating work, until he, or somebody else, recognizes that he is somewhat matured.

As I work, year by year, with these youths, there is a sentence which keeps recurring to me with renewed significance. It is: "Now and then be idle; sit and think." Unless you have recently been reading in the eighteenth-century literature, I doubt if you will associate that with the right person. It doesn't sound like the meteoric career and the varied activities of Richard Brinsley Sheridan; but he is the man who wrote it. I should like to see that verse written large somewhere upon the walls of Harvard College, because as I work with these undergraduates I am more and more surprised to find, not that they do not know how to think accurately, cogently (I suppose they would not be in classes in argumentation if they knew how to think well), but that many of them have no real interest in knowing how to think well. Many of them mean to enter the law school and therefore wish training in debate. Many suspect that some day they will have to speak often in public and wish the requisite training. Far too many of both groups desire the end but care nothing

[1]Reprinted from *The Educational Review,* Vol. 30, p. 189 (September, 1905), by permission of the author and of the publishers.

for means, the process by which it may best be attained. It is only by forcing, coaxing, that one can develop in these youths any interest in thinking for thinking's own sake, can make them appreciate the fact that there is a delicate pleasure in the process of thinking. I meet often the type — which you must all know perfectly well, only he is a little more mature with me and therefore, I suppose, a little less pliable — who sits in front of you with an amiably receptive expression, who smiles gently at all your neat terms of praise, who gives you a feeling that, on the whole, your lecture is really well fitted to the needs of the class, and then comes to the desk to ask you just one question which shows his mind has not taken in one important idea from the entire hour. Not only that; sometimes, and here is where his real genius comes in, he shows you that (despite his receptive appearance throughout your lectures) he has not taken in anything new for two or three weeks. It sometimes seems to me that the undergraduate of this type approaches more nearly to the delicious state of Nirvana than anybody outside of the East, perhaps than anybody in the East: his mind is not somewhere else, but simply nowhere; it is taking an absolute rest. What makes this Buddhist of the West especially difficult to deal with is that he is not boorish or inconsiderate toward the instructor, but usually quite the opposite. Clad in intellectual oilskins, he is almost blithesome in his absolute imperviousness to the ideas for which he is supposed to be taking the course.

There is another closely related group, those who, when choosing a question for a forensic or debate, instantly balk when I say: "I think we have had enough of the Panama Canal, the control of Manchuria, and the Merger Case; let us try something now that will really test you, let us try a question of college life." They don't want it at all, and they don't take it unless I insist. I have been asked just once in three years to approve a question on a college matter. When asked, I was quite overwhelmed and immensely encouraged. That is to say, then, if I suggest to the undergraduate that he take this question, which is of vital moment to us at Harvard at the present day: Is the new plan for assigning rooms in the Yard likely to draw the representative men to the Yard? that is, Are we likely to succeed in endeavoring to get back in the Yard the representative men and the larger body of students? he does not take it unless I force him. In that case, he works over it for a while and finally comes to tell me that he is very sorry but he must change the question: there is no evidence at all to be found on it, he says. When I suggest that I have supposed his mind is his own kingdom, and that he, surely, can discuss the question inasmuch as he applied for a room under this plan and is by choice, supposedly, living inside rather than outside the Yard, he says: "Well, you know there is nothing written upon this subject at all; I've got to spin it all out of my own head! I can't do that." That happens over and over again. A year or two ago we were discussing the question: Shall we enforce training in the gymnasium for the freshmen? When I talked with juniors and seniors who certainly had all been freshmen, some of the freshmen who had carefully and conscientiously done work in the gymnasium, urging them to take that question, they at first said they knew absolutely nothing about it. They could tell me how they had exercised when they had exercised, but as for getting their experience into any relationship with undergraduate life in general, or looking at the question from the point of view of another undergraduate, that seemed to them quite impossible. This means that among undergraduates there is a curious lack of correct information about current topics in college life, and particularly about the relation of undergraduate life to the larger interests of the university. Often a student comes to me in an intense state of enthusiasm over some scheme regarding a college organization: after listening to it, I point out that it seems admirable, but that four years before we tried identically that scheme—which failed dismally, for reasons which still hold good. He had never heard of all this, though any investigation of the history of his organization would have given him the information. He has simply developed his own scheme for the immediate moment, with no look backward and no thought forward.

Recently I asked some of my students to note simply in three hundred words, exactly why the writer was rooming inside or outside the Yard, that I might see whether the class could put the matter clearly in that compass. The exercise was very well done indeed. Then I said: "Now suppose you are writing to a friend whom you wish to induce to room with you either inside or outside the Yard. Take some real person whose peculiarities and habits you know well. So present your reasons that they shall have persuasive value for the individual just because he is himself and not another person." Result: a dire failure. Most of those exercises were simply repetitions of letter number one. A few were very gentle attempts at the art of persuasion. The majority gave a reader no suggestion of the personality addressed. These illustrations show, it seems to me, not only no pleasure at all in thinking as thinking, but almost an unwillingness to think. When I point out to such students that some clear statement of their ideas is all very well, but that I don't see why I should accept their views since other unanswered ideas occur to me, they too often seem to regard me as a little contrary, a little misinformed, uninformed perhaps — very rarely with a suspicion that I may be a little more informed. After all, the state of mind of the undergraduate beginning this matter of argumentation always reminds me of those lines on old Daniel Hanks down on Cape Cod.

> Some fellows reckon, more or less,
> Before they speak their mind,
> And sometimes calculate or guess,
> But they ain't Daniel's kind.
> Says I: "How do you know you're right?"
> "How do I know?" says he;
> "Well now, I vum, I know by gum
> I'm right, because I be."

When I ask these students to look at the ideas, if possible, from the other person's side, not that they must necessarily go over to the other man's position, but just to see if they can imagine what the other man might think on the subject, they can't do it. Only after long training can they see the idea in more than one way. Yet in the whole field of persuasion certainly one of the great demands upon public speakers is so to present an idea that it shall seem true to the other person, not simply because of the truth of the idea, but because of the method of presentation. How can they do that, if they can't begin to imagine what the other man is likely to think about any particular subject?

This lack of coöperation between the imagination and thought is illustrated over and over again in our undergraduate life. At the preliminary Boylston Prize speaking, which we have in Cambridge every spring, it has often been difficult to distinguish between selections from George William Curtis, Demosthenes, and Mr. Bryan.

One listens for hours to thirty or forty young men doing admirably just this: reading, rather than speaking, their selections so that the meaning is perfectly clear, but so that neither the special qualities of the style nor the special conditions for which the speech was prepared are equally clear. The result is that these men's speeches are almost exactly alike. When perhaps you suggest to one of the young men the desirability of recalling that when George William Curtis delivered his address in New York on "The Puritant Principle: Liberty Under the Law," excitement over the Hayes-Tilden controversy was at fever heat and that Mr. Curtis, fitting his speech to the needs of the occasion, poured oil on the troubled waters, the student looks at you puzzled. He has learned his lines. He delivers them in his own way. What more can you ask? The few to whom this criticism does not apply so stand out from their competitors that they are sure to appear in the list of those chosen for the final contest.

These conditions have some interesting results in undergraduate life. I do not know how much you may have read the undergraduate editorial. It is not to be recommended unless you have plenty of time. I have read a great many and they almost all fall into one of two classes. They are either wonderfully noncommittal, balanced so delicately that the editor can fall either way with rapidity as college sentiment moves one way or the other; or else are a skillful clouding of a very slight idea in a mist of words. Once in a while a man comes forward who has the editorial instinct. Giving himself some trouble, he writes editorials that say something, either summarizing existing conditions so that you are thoroughly informed, or summarizing and commenting at the same time. Very rarely, some of these men write an editorial which states an opinion, and maintains it clearly, perhaps leading off in a movement. Is it too much to ask sometimes for the last kind of editorial? It might be if I did not know most of these editors to be personally intelligent, alert and responsive, assiduous in gathering news, alive to the changes of undergraduate life. Yet when it comes to a significant editorial statement from them you look almost in vain. These men seem to have no interest in relating the particular phenomena of the movement to what has gone before or to the conditions that are likely to come. So, too, it is with the undergraduate applying, under the new plan, for a room in the Yard. He has a paper to sign which states the new plan. He reads, signs, and that is the end of the work for him. Consideration of the new policy as likely to lead to different conditions in undergraduate life, as likely to make the undergraduate life of his successor somewhat different from his own, any consideration perhaps whether his own college life has been pleasanter because he has roomed where he has — there is little of that kind of thinking in the college papers. It is done, if at all, by a few thoughtful men — who are not always, in their college days, the most prominent men.

There is another curious manifestation of this neglect of thinking. One great difficulty which I find in my teaching is the restless activity of the undergraduate. Some of the best men, who really might do admirable work in their courses and win distinction in their undergraduate career, don't get these results simply because they are like a student of mine in recent years, always so busy with the other thing that the immediate piece of work never was done properly. That is the most common difficulty in undergraduate work; of course we know the excuse for it. It is, that these are young people. They are; but they are getting older, and I take it that, in so far as age means judgment, discretion, we are here in these colleges largely to assist in making these youths somewhat older. I see no reason why they should not begin this training early in their college career. Instead they plunge into every kind of activity. When I meet an undergraduate who is able to say: "These things I will do, and these things I will put aside," I know that man is going to rise. I have seen him rise, year after year, and college generation after college generation. The past students whom I take most pride in are those who are beginning to be able to make this thoughtful choice even in their college days. The majority of undergraduates cannot do it at all. They think themselves vitally interested in a special subject they are studying, and get small results in it. Certainly some of them say often enough there is no subject in which they are so much interested as debating and the practice of public address, and that they mean to do the very best possible work, yet they prove ineffective in the courses. One student, for instance, says: "I am taking the history of economics in order that my work may be better in this debating." I put him on an early debate and his contribution is the thinnest imaginable. Nor has he in the least meant to deceive me. Not at all. Investigating, I find he is president of one club, secretary of another; belongs to ten different organizations, and has accepted an office in every one. He has so many things to do that he cannot possibly do any of them well. Even while he is taking a course in debating he belongs to his own class debating club, which debates weekly and depends for its interest upon the activity of four or five men. He is one of the officers of the Debating Union which embraces all the undergraduate debating clubs. He is full of schemes for the improvement of Harvard debating. Here, then, is a man of A capacity, who is able to obtain a grade of B, if he simply does nothing but follow his own natural bent, who barely gets his B, because he comes to me with poorly prepared debates, over which he grieves greatly two hours after the fiasco is passed. Has not lack of thought something to do with that? How can the undergraduate who thinks about the possibilities of his undergraduate career, realizing what his chances are, fail to see that to behave in this way is to lose just the special chances for which he would once have told you he was coming to college? I don't care, in the least, whether he settles down upon his philosophical club, his musical organization, debating or something else, if he will only settle down, concentrating upon something; then we shall be able to get results from him. This mental dissipation, this American hustle, which keeps interested in everything with small, because scattered, results, is a very unsatisfactory feature of the undergraduate world of today.

I do not contend for a moment that some of the undergraduates in the colleges I know do not understand thoroughly how to fulfill the first half of Richard Brinsley Sheridan's sentence: "Now and then be idle." But to sit apart and think is the troublesome operation. Watch them in their reading; watch them attending the theaters; you will find them reading mainly the books of ephemeral popularity, books they can skim, and attending musical burlesque, melodrama, vaudeville. Negation of thought is a science with this group. You face an interesting social question. We are developing curious citizens, unless we can, in some way, arouse these men to more responsibility. Now, it is quite fair to say, of course, that the awakening comes in many cases as graduate students and in the graduate school of life. I think it is perhaps a question with all of us teachers whether that is not a slightly late awakening. I never can fully share in the joy of the friends of a young man who has wasted most of his college time, when they say: "He is working hard, I assure you, in the Law School," as if somehow that were a satisfactory solution for everything. Does that recovery fully offset all the wasted opportunities of his college life?

There is another way in which this unwillingness to think works out. The growth of the tutorial system in this country is both interesting and a little alarming. A father said to me, recently: "How is it that when I went to —— school (a preparatory school), it was not at all necessary that I should have a tutor every summer in order to get into Harvard College, nor necessary for my friends either? But my boy has to have a tutor. He is as bright as I was, and the others boys are bright — yet they all have tutors. What is the matter?" Of course we know what the fathers want to do — they want to hold you and me responsible. But first of all the boy is responsible; he wants to get his results as far as possible without thinking; at least he wishes somebody else to stand over him to see that he does. As a result we have this curious development at our colleges — the tutor who drags his young men along until he drags them through. The ethics of this custom need not be discussed here, but surely it is self-evident that such tutelage cannot be desirable.

Nor do I believe that this general attitude of mind among undergraduates is temporary. When I have sometimes spoken about these matters to graduates, of course they have said: "You must not take the situation too seriously. Boys will be boys. We have had numerous curious phases of undergraduate life. You must remember, when you were in college, what was known as 'Harvard indifference.' It was a peculiar kind of pose that held the stage for a time." That is true; it was temporary. It was a pose, something superimposed. We did it; we knew all the time we were doing it, and we had a good deal of fun out of it. But, watching this lack of pleasure in thinking, I don't think it is superimposed but exceedingly basal. No choice whatever is involved in it. It is the state of mind in which these youths come to college. Often a student says: "That was an interesting principle you explained at the last lecture and I should like to carry it out in my work." "Why don't you? If it is good for anything, it is applicable for you." He answers: "I tried to carry it out the other day, but somehow I couldn't see how it fits into my work." Surely if he can't learn in his college days to make the application of general principles to his own needs, if you must stand over him, explaining, coaxing, aiding, he will have an odd time with the outside world where taskmasters are more plentiful than teachers — or tutors. If this were the state of one, two, or ten undergraduates, it would not be important; but when there is a large group, and I believe an increasing group, of this sort, it is time to ask the source of this weakness. I am clear in my own mind that back of the responsibility of the boy lies the responsibility of the college, school, and home.

It is rather hard on a boy to plunge him into such a maze of possibilities as the Harvard elective pamphlet. I have sometimes wondered that the freshman bears everything as bravely as he does. Of course he wants to take everything, all the higher mathematics courses before he has completed the initial courses, the most advanced Latin courses before he has finished Cæsar, all the courses in Anglo-Saxon before he has even a rudimentary knowledge of English Literature. Although he is not permitted to do this, it is one of the weaknesses of the Elective System — everything that is wrong has its weaknesses — that it seems to suggest variety and not solidity as of first importance in education, so that youth deduces as a corollary that variety is not only the spice of college life but the great essential. That may in part lead to the dissipation of energies of which I have spoken — wasteful, dangerous. The big lecture courses are enervating for the student. They are, for the teachers, the toughest problem he has to face. Given three or four hundred young men so crowded into a room where the temperature is so high that the air grows close before the hour is half over; given a subject necessarily a little hard to grasp; given an instructor who speaks in a voice not audible for all, or with a dry, uninteresting manner, and such conditions are a forcing house for that look of apparent attention which really marks vacuity of mind.

But would so many develop so rapidly this indifference to thinking if other causes had not prepared the way, before college days? I sometimes wonder, and that is one reason I am here this morning, whether it is possible that the colleges have set such rigid standards for the various entrance examinations that the schools must give all their time to cramming the boys for them, and cannot teach them to see the relation or bearing of one subject upon another. If, instead, the boy came up to college with fewer facts, but an interest in thinking for its own sake, respect for learning and literature, and some responsibility in citizenship, would not the gain be great? The schools now send him up with his mind like a desk with pigeonholes, some of them perhaps a trifle dusty, but undoubtedly with contents, yet not as a human being who has a relation to learning, literature, and the facts of existence, and who is able and eager to make for himself applications of the ideas he has learned. Whatever may be the cause, I believe that our secondary education at present spends too much time on facts as facts, far too little on creating an attitude of mind toward life and learning. Surely when one sees large numbers of our boys and girls alike rushing nervously from activity to activity; unable or unwilling to think quietly about the ideas taught them, or what they see about them, avid of ephemeral but strong sensation and superficial information, all is not well. One may spoil a child's mind even as one may spoil a child's digestion. The appetite for food and the appetite for information are much alike in the normal child. Each is insistent, will be fed, and takes what is given as it is given. The normal child has its keen interests and will absorb anything which bears on them. If he is interested in birds, you will find him in his enthusiasm reading the Latin names or scientific descriptions of them long before he can properly pronounce the Latin or understand the long technical terms. But in other subjects his interest may be only languid. It is dangerously easy to let this languor, which means ultimate superficiality, pass over even into what was once a subject so absorbing that it, at least, meant thoroughness. Some of our present-day so-called aids to study — certain conditions permitted, or at least not counteracted, in secondary schools, such as the rapid increase in tutoring to piece out the schoolwork — are insidious.

Of course one must admit that in any case the secondary school is between the upper millstone of the rigid and severe college requirements and the nether millstone of the irresponsible home. It is amusing to hear occasional lamentation that today we Americans do not read with enjoyment the contemplative poetry of the eighteenth century — "The Pleasure of Hope," "The Pleasures of Memory," etc. What has the American, who cannot utter the word *hustle* without affectionate stress upon its syllables as a word created by his people to describe a quality which they assume to be an American monopoly, to do with such poetry? Much today in American business life and, consequently, in its social life is but superficiality and sham concealed in a dust storm of innumerable activities. Business and social responsibilities make it impossible for many parents, we are told, to train their children, and they are left to the schools, tutors, and themselves. Moreover, all this *hustle* is self-conscious, childlike. It thrives on living in the eye of the public, it is satisfied only with constant, evident results of its activity which the public will surely acclaim. Consequently we are only beginning to value properly the life of the scholar. Not long ago an American, after some years of study abroad, returned with his family to one of our cities most priding itself on its "culture." He tried to devote himself to historical research preparatory to a book, and yet to see something of society. After a winter he told me he was going abroad again. He and his family were tired of the insistent: "What are you doing? Oh, writing! A history? Really! When will it be out?" The combination of restrained incredulity that a man financially able to do what he pleased with his life should devote it to scholarship, and of demand for the instant results from his work, was too much for him.

I believe, then, that the causes for this heedlessness in undergraduates lie back of college and school, in the home, in the very nature of maturer American life of today. Whether we can get at the conditions in the home, or not, we certainly can in the school and college. But first we must recognize the condition and our present failure to grapple with it. Grant all the force exerted by the upper and nether millstones, is the secondary school resisting as stoutly as it might? That is worthy of serious consideration. Is there not danger that, in much of the higher education, we teachers are like the builders fitting marble plates to stucco walls or him who makes bricks without straw?

ON THE WRITING OF ESSAYS[1]

Alexander Smith

I have already described my environments and my mode of life, and out of both I contrive to extract a very tolerable amount of satisfaction. Love in a cottage, with a broken window to let in the rain, is not my idea of comfort; no more is Dignity, walking forth richly clad, to whom every head uncovers, every knee grows supple. Bruin in winter time fondly sucking his own paws, loses flesh; and love, feeding upon itself, dies of inanition. Take the candle of death in your hand, and walk through the stately galleries of the world, and their splendid furniture and array are as the tinsel armor and pasteboard goblets of a penny theater; fame is but an inscription on a grave, and glory the melancholy blazon on a coffin lid. We argue fiercely about happiness. One insists that she is found in the cottage which the hawthorn shades. Another that she is a lady of fashion, and treads on cloth of gold. Wisdom, listening to both, shakes a white head, and considers that "a good deal may be said on both sides."

There is a wise saying to the effect that "a man can eat no more than he can hold." Every man gets about the same satisfaction out of life. Mr. Suddlechops, the barber of Seven Dials, is as happy as Alexander at the head of his legions. The business of the one is to depopulate kingdoms, the business of the other to reap beards seven days old; but their relative positions do not affect the question. The one works with razors and soap lather, the other with battle cries and well-greaved Greeks. The one of a Saturday night counts up his shabby gains and grumbles; the other on *his* Saturday night sits down and weeps for other worlds to conquer. The pence to Mr. Suddlechops are as important as are the worlds to Alexander. Every condition of life has its peculiar advantages and wisdom points these out and is contented with them. The varlet who sang—

A king cannot swagger
Or get drunk like a beggar,
Nor be half so happy as I—

---

[1]From *Dreamthorp.*

had the soul of a philosopher in him. The harshness of the parlor is revenged at night in the servants' hall. The coarse rich man rates his domestic, but there is a thought in the domestic's brain, docile and respectful as he looks, which makes the matter equal, which would madden the rich man if he knew it — make him wince as with a shrewdest twinge of hereditary gout. For insult and degradation are not without their peculiar solaces. You may spit upon Shylock's gaberdine, but the day comes when he demands his pound of flesh; every blow, every insult, not without a certain satisfaction, he adds to the account running up against you in the daybook and ledger of his hate — which at the proper time he will ask you to discharge. Every way we look we see evenhanded nature administering her laws of compensation. Grandeur has a heavy tax to pay. The usurper rolls along like a god, surrounded by his guards. He dazzles the crowd — all very fine but look beneath his splendid trappings and you see a shirt of mail, and beneath *that* a heart cowering in terror of an air-drawn dagger. Whom did the memory of Austerlitz most keenly sting? The beaten emperor? or the mighty Napoleon, dying like an untended watch-fire on St. Helena?

Giddy people may think the life I lead here staid and humdrum, but they are mistaken. It is true, I hear no concerts, save those in which the thrushes are performers in the spring mornings. I see no pictures, save those painted on the wide sky-canvas with the colors of sunrise and sunset. I attend neither rout nor ball; I have no deeper dissipation than the tea table; I hear no more exciting scandal than quiet village gossip. Yet I enjoy my concerts more than I would the great London ones. I like the pictures I see, and think them better painted, too, than those which adorn the walls of the Royal Academy; and the village gossip is more after my turn of mind than the scandals that convulse the clubs. It is wonderful how the whole world reflects itself in the simple village life. The people around me are full of their own affairs and interests; were they of imperial magnitude, they could not be excited more strongly. Farmer Worthy is anxious about the next market; the likelihood of a fall in the price of butter and eggs hardly allows him to sleep o' nights. The village doctor — happily we have only one — skirrs hither and thither in his gig, as if man could neither die nor be born without his assistance. He is continually standing on the confines of existence, welcoming the newcomer, bidding farewell to the goer-away. And the robustious fellow who sits at the head of the table when the Jolly Swillers meet at the Blue Lion on Wednesday evenings is a great politician, sound of lung metal, and wields the village in the tap room, as my Lord Palmerston wields the nation in the House. His listeners think him a wiser personage than the Premier, and he is inclined to lean to that opinion himself. I find everything here that other men find in the big world. London is but a magnified Dreamthorp.

And just as the Rev. Mr. White took note of the ongoings of the seasons in and around Hampshire Selborne, watched the colonies of the rooks in the tall elms, looked after the swallows in the cottage and rectory eaves, played the affectionate spy on the private lives of chaffinch and hedge-sparrow, was eavesdropper to the solitary cuckoo; so here I keep eye and ear open; take note of man, woman, and child; find many a pregnant text imbedded in the commonplace of village life; and, out of what I see and hear, weave in my own room my essays as solitarily as the spider weaves his web in the darkened corner. The essay, as a literary form, resembles the lyric, insofar as it is molded by some central mood—whimsical, serious, or satirical. Give the mood, and the essay, from the first sentence to the last, grows around it as the cocoon grows around the silkworm. The essay writer is a chartered libertine, and a law unto himself. A quick ear and eye, an ability to discern the infinite suggestiveness of common things, a brooding meditative spirit, are all that the essayist requires to start business with. Jacques, in "As You Like it," had the makings of a charming essayist. It is not the essayist's duty to inform, to build pathways through metaphysical morasses, to cancel abuses, any more than it is the duty of the poet to do these things. Incidentally he may do something in that way, just as the poet may, but it is not his duty and should not be expected of him. Skylarks are primarily created to sing, although a whole choir of them may be baked in pies and brought to table; they were born to make music, although they may incidentally stay the pangs of vulgar hunger. The essayist is a kind of poet in prose, and if questioned harshly as to his uses, he might be unable to render a better apology for his existence than a flower might. The essay should be pure literature as the poem is pure literature. The essayist wears a lance, but he cares more for the sharpness of its point than for the pennon that flutters on it, than for the banner of the captain under whom he serves. He plays with death as Hamlet plays with Yorick's skull, and he reads the morals — strangely stern, often, for such fragrant lodging — which are folded up in the bosoms of roses. He has no pride, and is deficient in a sense of the congruity and fitness of things. He lifts a pebble from the ground, and puts it aside more carefully than any gem; and on a nail in a cottage door he will hang the mantle of his thought, heavily brocaded with the gold of rhetoric. He finds his way into the Elysian fields through portals the most shabby and commonplace.

The essayist plays with his subject, now in whimsical, now in grave, now in melancholy mood. He lies upon the idle grassy bank, like Jacques, letting the world flow past him, and from this thing and the other he extracts his mirth and his moralities. His main gift is an eye to discover the suggestiveness of common things; to find a sermon in the most unpromising texts. Beyond the vital hint, the first step, his discourses are not beholden to their titles. Let him take up the most trivial subject, and it will lead him away to the great questions over which the serious imagination loves to brood — fortune, mutability, death — just as inevitably as the runnel, trickling among the summer hills, on which sheep are bleating, leads you to the sea; or as, turning down the first street you come to in the city, you are led finally, albeit by many an intricacy, out into the open country, with its waste places and its woods, where you are lost in a sense of strangeness and solitariness. The world is to the meditative man what the mulberry plant is to the silkworm. The essay writer has no lack of subject matter. He has the day that is passing over his head; and, if unsatisfied with that, he has the world's six thousand years to depasture his gay or serious humor upon. I idle away my time here, and I am finding new subjects every hour. Everything I see or hear is an essay in bud. The world is everywhere whispering essays, and one need only be the world's amanuensis. The proverbial expression which last evening the clown dropped as he trudged homeward to supper, the light of the setting sun on his face, expands before me to a dozen pages. The coffin of the pauper, which today I saw carried carelessly along, is as good a subject as the funeral procession of an emperor. Craped drum and banner add nothing to death; penury and disrespect take nothing away. Incontinently my thought moves like a slow-paced hearse with sable nodding plumes. Two rustic lovers, whispering between the darkening hedges, is as potent to project my mind into the tender passion as if I had seen Romeo touch the cheek of Juliet in the moonlight garden. Seeing a curlyheaded child asleep in the sunshine before a cottage door is sufficient excuse for a discourse on childhood; quite as good as if I had seen infant Cain asleep in the lap of Eve with Adam looking on. A lark cannot rise to heaven without raising as many thoughts as there are notes in its song. Dawn cannot pour its white light on my village without starting from their dim lair a hundred reminiscences; nor can sunset burn above yonder trees in the west without attracting to itself the melancholy of a lifetime. When spring unfolds her green leaves I would be provoked to indite an essay on hope and youth, were it not that it is already writ in the carols of the birds; and I might be tempted in autumn to improve the occasion, were it not for the rustle of the withered leaves as I walk through the woods. Compared with that simple music, the saddest-cadenced words have but a shallow meaning.

The essayist who feeds his thoughts upon the segment of the world which surrounds him cannot avoid being an egoist; but then his egotism is not unpleasing. If he be without taint of boastfulness, of self-sufficiency, of hungry vanity, the world will not press the charge home. If a man discourses continually of his wines, his plate, his titled acquaintances, the number and quality of his horses, his menservants and maidservants, he must discourse very skillfully indeed if he escapes being called a coxcomb. If a man speaks of death — tells you that the idea of it continually haunts him, that he has the most insatiable curiosity as to death and dying, that his thought mines in churchyards like a "demon mole" — no one is specially offended, and that this is a dull fellow is the hardest thing likely to be said of him. Only the egotism that overcrows you is offensive, that exalts trifles and takes pleasure in them, that suggests superiority in matters of equipage and furniture; and the egotism is offensive, because it runs counter to and jostles your self-complacency. The egotism which rises no higher than the grave is of a solitary and a hermit kind — it crosses no man's path, it disturbs no man's *amour propre*. You may offend a man if you say you are as rich as he, as wise as he, as handsome as he. You offend no man if you tell him that, like him, you have to die. The king, in his crown and coronation robes, will allow the beggar to claim that relationship with him. To have to die is a distinction of which no man is proud. The speaking about oneself is not necessarily offensive. A modest, truthful man speaks better about himself than about anything else, and on that subject his speech is likely to be most profitable to his hearers. Certainly, there is no subject with which he is better acquainted, and on which he has a better title to be heard. And it is this egotism, this perpetual reference to self, in which the charm of the essayist resides. If a man is worth knowing at all, he is worth knowing well. The essayist gives you his thoughts, and lets you know, in addition, how he came by them. He has nothing to conceal; he throws open his doors and windows, and lets him enter who will. You like to walk round peculiar or important men as you like to walk round a building, to view it from different points, and in different lights. Of the essayist, when his mood is communicative, you obtain a full picture. You are made his contemporary and familiar friend. You enter into his humors and his seriousness. You are made heir of his whims, prejudices, and playfulness. You walk through the whole nature of him, as you walk through the streets of Pompeii, looking into the interior of stately mansions, reading the satirical scribblings on the walls. And the essayist's habit of not only giving you his thoughts, but telling you how he came by them, is interesting, because it shows you by what alchemy the ruder world becomes transmuted into the finer. We like to know the lineage of ideas, just as we like to know the lineage of great earls and swift race horses. We like to know that the discovery of the law of gravitation was born of the fall of an apple in an English garden on a summer afternoon. Essays written after this fashion are racy of the soil in which they grow, as you taste the lava in the vines grown on the slopes of Etna, they say. There is a healthy Gascon flavor in Montaigne's Essays; and Charles Lamb's are scented with the primroses of Covent Garden. . . .

OF STUDIES[1]

Francis Bacon

Studies serve for delight, for ornament, and for ability. Their chief use for delight is in privateness and retiring; for ornament, is in discourse; and for ability, is in the judgment and disposition of business; for expert men can execute, and perhaps judge of particulars, one by one; but the general counsels, and the plots and marshaling of affairs come best from those that are learned. To spend too much time in studies is sloth; to use them too much for ornament is affectation; to make judgment wholly by their rules is the humor of a scholar. They perfect nature, and are perfected by experience; for natural abilities are like natural plants, that need pruning by study; and studies themselves do give forth directions too much at large, except they be bounded in by experience. Crafty men contemn studies, simple men admire them, and wise men use them; for they teach not their own use; but that is a wisdom without them and above them, won by observation. Read not to contradict and confute, nor to believe and take for granted, nor to find talk and discourse, but to weigh and consider. Some books are to be tasted, others to be swallowed, and some few to be chewed and digested; that is, some books are to be read only in parts; others to be read but not curiously, and some few to be read wholly, and with diligence and attention. Some books also may be read by deputy, and extracts made of them by others; but that would be only in the less important arguments and the meaner sort of books; else distilled books are, like common distilled waters, flashy things. Reading maketh a full man; conference a ready man; and writing an exact man. And, therefore, if a man write little, he had need have a great memory; if he confer little, he had need have a present wit; and if he read little, he had need have much cunning, to seem to know that he doth not. Histories make men wise; poets, witty; the mathematics, subtle; natural philosophy, deep; moral, grave; logic and rhetoric, able to contend: *Abeunt studia in mores!*[2] Nay, there is no

[1]From Bacon's *Essays.*
[2]"Studies develop into habits."

stand or impediment in the wit but may be wrought out by fit studies; like as diseases of the body may have appropriate exercises. Bowling is good for the stone and reins, shooting for the lungs and breast, gentle walking for the stomach, riding for the head and the like. So if a man's wit be wandering, let him study the mathematics; for in demonstrations, if his wit be called away never so little, he must begin again. If his wit be not apt to distinguish or find differences, let him study the schoolmen; for they are *cymini sectores!*[3] If he be not apt to beat over matters, and to call up one thing to prove and illustrate another, let him study the lawyers' cases; so every defect of the mind may have a special receipt.

BEDE: THE SCHOLAR[1]

John Richard Green

Under the peaceful reigns of Ecgfrith's successors, Aldfrith and Ceolwulf, their kingdom became the literary center of western Europe. No schools were more famous than those of Jarrow and York. The whole learning of the age seemed to be summed up in a Northumbrian scholar. Baeda — the Venerable Bede, as later times styled him — was born about ten years after the Synod of Whitby, beneath the shade of a great abbey which Benedict Biscop was rearing by the mouth of the Wear. His youth was trained, and his long tranquil life was wholly spent in an offshoot of Benedict's house which was founded by his scholar Ceolfrid. Baeda never stirred from Jarrow. "I spent my whole life in the same monastery," he says, "and while attentive to the rule of my order and the service of the Church, my constant pleasure lay in learning, or teaching, or writing." The words sketch for us a scholar's life, the more touching in its simplicity that it is the life of the first great English scholar. The quiet grandeur of a life consecrated to knowledge, the tranquil

[3]"Splitters of cummin seed" — hair splitters.
[1]From *History of the English People.*

pleasure that lies in learning and teaching and writing, dawned for Englishmen in the story of Baeda. While still young he became a teacher, and six hundred monks, besides strangers that flocked thither for instruction, formed his school of Jarrow. It is hard to imagine how among the toils of the schoolmaster and the duties of the monk Baeda could have found time for the composition of the numerous works that made his name famous in the West. But materials for study had accumulated in Northumbria through the journeys of Wilfred and Benedict Biscop and the libraries which were forming at Wearmouth and York. The tradition of the older Irish teachers still lingered to direct the young scholar into that path of Scriptural interpretation to which he chiefly owed his fame. Greek, a rare accomplishment in the West, came to him from the school which the Greek Archbishop Theodore founded beneath the walls of Canterbury. His skill in the ecclesiastical chant was derived from a Roman cantor whom Pope Vitalian sent in the train of Benedict Biscop. Little by little the young scholar thus made himself master of the whole range of the science of his time; he became, as Burke rightly styled him, "the father of English learning." The tradition of the older classic culture was first revived for England in his quotations of Plato and Aristotle, of Seneca and Cicero, of Lucretius and Ovid. Virgil cast over him the same spell that he cast over Dante; verses from the Æneid break his narratives of martyrdoms, and the disciple ventures on the track of the great master in a little eclogue descriptive of the approach of spring. His work was done with small aid from others. "I am my own secretary," he writes; "I make my own notes. I am my own librarian." But forty-five works remained after his death to attest his prodigious industry. In his own eyes and those of his contemporaries the most important among these were the commentaries and homilies upon various books of the Bible which he had drawn from the writings of the Fathers. But he was far from confining himself to theology. In treatises compiled as textbooks for his scholars Baeda threw together all that the world had accumulated in astronomy and meteorology, in physics and music, in philosophy, grammar, rhetoric, arithmetic, medicine. But the encyclopedic character of his researches left him in heart a simple Englishman. He loved his own English tongue, he was skilled in English song, his last work was a translation into English of the Gospel of St. John, and almost the last words that broke from his lips were some English rhymes upon death.

But the noblest proof of his love of England lies in the work which immortalizes his name. In his *Ecclesiastical History of the English Nation,* Baeda was at once the founder of medieval history and the first English historian. All that we really know of the century and a half that follows the landing of Augustine we know from him. Wherever his own personal observation extended, the story is told with admirable detail and force. He is hardly less full or accurate in the portions which he owed to his Kentish friends, Alcwine and Nothelm. What he owed to no informant was his exquisite faculty of story-telling, and yet no story of his own telling is so touching as the story of his death. Two weeks before the Easter of 735 the old man was seized with an extreme weakness and loss of breath. He still preserved, however, his usual pleasantness and gay good-humor, and in spite of prolonged speechlessness continued his lectures to the pupils about him. Verses of his own English tongue broke from time to time from the master's lips — rude rhymes that told how before the "need-fare," Death's stern "must go," none can enough bethink him what is to be his doom for good or ill. The tears of Baeda's scholars mingled with his song. "We never read without weeping," writes one of them. So the days rolled on to Ascension-tide, and still master and pupils toiled at their work, for Baeda longed to bring to an end his version of St. John's Gospel into the English tongue and his extracts from Bishop Isidore. "I don't want my boys to read a lie," he answered those who would have had him rest, "or to work to no purpose after I am gone." A few days before Ascension-tide his sickness grew upon him, but he spent the whole day in teaching, only saying cheerfully to his scholars, "Learn with what speed you may; I know not how long I may last." The dawn broke on another sleepless night, and again the old man called his scholars round him and bade them write. "There is still a chapter wanting," said the scribe, as the morning drew on, "and it is hard for thee to question thyself any longer." "It is easily done," said Baeda; "take thy pen and write quickly." Amid tears and farewells the day wore on to eventide. "There is yet one sentence unwritten, dear master," said the boy. "Write it quickly," bade the dying man. "It is finished now," said the little scribe at last. "You speak truth," said the master; "all is finished now." Placed upon the pavement, his head supported in his scholar's arms, his face turned to the post where he was wont to pray, Baeda chanted the solemn "Glory to God." As his voice reached the close of his song he passed quietly away.

First among English scholars, first among English theologians, first among English historians, it is in the monk of Jarrow that English literature strikes its roots. In the six hundred scholars who gathered round him for instruction he is the father of our national education. In his physical treatises he is the first figure to which our science looks back.

GEORGE MEREDITH[1]

Brother Leo

Henley himself, no unworthy commentator of the cryptic sage of Box Hill, has written that an epigram is at best a half truth that looks like a whole one. Of course, that is an epigram, too; so that it needs a mathematician or an economist or a psychic analyst or some other utterly superior and unhuman person to discover just what proportion of truth inheres in the Henleyan formula. As for those of us who are human and who know the English novelists of the last century, the only practical solution, however logical, is to paraphrase Henley thus: An epigram may contain less than half the truth, but it contains nearly all the truth concerning George Meredith, when it has been written by him or written about him.

Even the most casual reader of Meredith—and he is one of those non-Dickensian writers who can survive even the onslaughts of the casual reader—knows that the man who wrote *The Ordeal of Richard Feverel* culled many a truth-crammed nut from the garden of his fancy, knows that many a page in that novel alone makes slow reading because it demands fast thinking, knows that a generous proportion of Meredith's epigrams, though precious hard to

[1]Reprinted by kind permission of the author.

crack, are precious worth the cracking. And the casual reader may even know likewise that their excessively epigrammatic envisaging of truth is one of the things which keep Meredith's poems from being poetry.

But the epigrams achieved by Meredith are less startlingly true than the epigrams achieved about him. Indeed, Meredith criticism has so generally, almost inevitably, assumed the epigrammatic form that to lecture on him or to write on him or to converse on him is one of the easiest things in the world. All one need to do is to quote judiciously. And even should one quote injudiciously, one could not well go seriously astray.

Let the critics rave and the reviewers devise vain things concerning such topics as the Baconian theory of Shakespeare, the literary significance of Whitman or the permanence of the "Main Street" school in American letters, and there will doubtless be epigrams; but they will be epigrams diverse and contradictory. But with Meredith as the topic, the lion and the lamb will lie down together and all the epigrams, however clever or however otiose, will say substantially the same thing. This is so, not because the critics seek to agree, but because in this instance they cannot help agreeing. To know George Meredith at all is to know that here was a marvelously mellow violin that by some freak of fortune never managed to have its full complement of strings.

Henley himself said as much in his *Academy* review of *The Egotist* in 1879. And long before Henley, as J. A. Hammerton has shown in his *George Meredith in Anecdote and Criticism,* other reviewers had promulgated the same obvious truth. It remained for Oscar Wilde to point the moral and adorn the tale: "Meredith! Who can define him? His style is chaos illumined by flashes of lightning. As a writer he has mastered everything except language: as a novelist he can do everything, except tell a story: as an artist he is everything, except articulate." And in the same vein — for Meredith criticism the absolutely inevitable and consistent vein — Mr. Arthur Symons must say: "He thinks in flashes and writes in shorthand. He has an intellectual passion for words, but he has never been able to accustom his mind to the slowness of their service; he tosses them about the page in his anger, tearing them open and gutting them with a savage pleasure."

Such is the truth; the truth concerning the keen-eyed, retiring man who could, Cassius-like, look quite through the deeds of men, who could prick unerringly the bubble of pretension, who could expose to scathing ridicule the worship of formalism in education and social life, who was an astonishingly accurate and sagely competent critic of ever so many things except his own books and their incredible artistic deficiencies. As we say nowadays, Meredith had a message; but he lacked power to preach the gospel. He had ever so much to say; but, for the very life of him, he could not say it.

To explain that irritating phenomenon, to show just why it was that Meredith resembled a bottle of precious fluid with an abnormally small neck, is a task impressive but never satisfactorily essayed. It was easy for Andrew Lang to remark that "the fairies of literature gave him all good gifts, but added a Celtic wilfulness"; but the difficulty cannot be rationalized thus. Lang was an authority on fairies; but the "Celtic wilfulness" is another story. It is pretty generally recognized that both at his best and his worst, the Celt is pronouncedly articulate. Rather it is more salutary to believe that but for the Celtic strain in his blood Meredith would have been able to say absolutely nothing whatever — another reason, possibly, why God loves the Irish!

No, the why of Meredith's lack of expression is quite beyond the mere bookman. Some day, perchance, a bespectacled young candidate for the doctorate at a German university may undertake to solve the Meredithian complex by the aid of futuristic psychoanalysis, and then the world may wonder and understand. Meanwhile it must suffice to recognize that Meredith's style, both in prose and verse, is a style that reveals by concealments, that illuminates by obscurities, that seduces by exasperations. To know that is to be truly wise.

From the novels of Meredith we get no unity of impression, no sense of totality or finality as generally we get from the novels of Flaubert and Thackeray and Jane Austen, from the novels of Mr. Wells and Mr. Maxwell and young Mr. Walpole. Wilde was right; we get simply "chaos illumined by flashes of lightning." Our impressions are lightninglike in their suddenness, in their blinding brilliancy, in their enduring enthronement in the halls of memory. To give an ordered account of the progress of a Meredith story is impossible two weeks after reading the book; but it is even more impossible ever to forget the first meeting of Richard Feverel and

Lucy by the river, the peregrinations of the dyspeptic uncle with the wedding cake, the newspaper episode in *Diana of the Crossways,* the preposterous symbolism of Sir Willoughby's leg. (It is morally impossible to discuss Meredith without a flourish of Sir Willoughby's leg.) We forget plots, or rather we never get them; but scenes and characters remain forever.

Perhaps, after all, this is as it should be. Perhaps the Meredithian manner is a closer approximation to life than we are prone to believe. Perhaps the man who looks back toward childhood through the dust of the mounded years, across the valley of humiliation and the hill of the triumph and the meadow of the harvest moon, sees also a thing of chronological chaos, a thing of untented shadows, a thing that is a nameless thing save only where the piercing lightning falls. Perhaps it is the way of life; it were ungracious, almost irrelevant, to urge that it is not the way of art.

The epigrammatic critics have stressed Meredith's perversity of manner, his ardent admirers, quantitatively small but qualitatively important, have dilated on his rarity of matter; but the secret of his power and of his impotence, of his greatness and his littleness, really lies in the inconsistency of his mood. Theoretically, Meredith had a clear-cut conception of the rôle of novelist he essayed; he worked out to a nicety the office of the impartial satirist who was to find in every manifestation of the comic spirit his inspiration and his lure. He had the tremendous advantage of knowing what he wanted to do; and what he wanted to do was in every sense worthy.

But in the doing of it his mood too often radically changed. His Olympian impartiality of attitude could not be maintained — a fact which may reflect credit on the man in him however much it militates against his supremacy as a writer. He waxed indignant, as the true satirist can never afford to do, as the principles of the comic-spirit philosophy will not permit the satirist to do, against the malice of social gossip, against the subjugation of woman, against the cruelty and self-sufficiency of egoism, against blindly complacent parents who put their trust in meticulously devised systems of child training. And so, as an artist, he lost his poise. And of that loss the famous Meredith style — the style wherein the human heart is an "inward flutterer" and de-feminization is characterized as "the flowering up of that hard rough jaw from the tender blooming promise of a petticoat" — is an effect and not a cause. 'Tis the gods of our making who bless or ban. Meredith's literary deity was the god of aloofness and scrutiny and imperturbable show; and Meredith failed to placate that difficult divinity with appropriate gifts. Had he been a little less sure of the functions of the comic spirit, had he endowed his titular dæmon with a frankly human heart, had he, even at a distance, offered his libations to the idol of Dean Swift and suffered that great Irishman's *sæva indignatio* to suffuse with its righteous glow the pale, cold marble of his Victorian shrine—then!

Well, then the epigrams coined by George Meredith would have been less hard and brilliant and the epigrams coined about Meredith would be less of the nature of half truths than even Henley would concede. Then, both in his prose and his verse, there would be genius and felicity. Then in his portraits of human life there would be less flash and more glow. Then we ordinary mortals, whose philosophy of life is rather more pragmatic than formally consonant and complete, might be able to read him otherwise than in homeopathic doses. Then we should feel surer of his vogue and his power a hundred years from now.

D. THE INFORMAL ESSAY

OLD CHINA[1]

Charles Lamb

I have an almost feminine partiality for old china. When I go to see any great house, I enquire for the china closet, and next for the picture gallery. I cannot defend the order of preference, but by saying, that we have all some taste or other, of too ancient a date to admit of our remembering distinctly that it was an acquired one. I can call to mind the first play, and the first exhibition, that I was taken to; but I am not conscious of a time when china jars and saucers were introduced into my imagination.

I had no repugnance then — why should I now have? — to those little, lawless, azure-tinctured grotesques, that under the notion of men and women, float about, uncircumscribed by any element, in that world before perspective — a china teacup.

I like to see my old friends — whom distance cannot diminish — figuring up in the air (so they appear to our optics), yet on *terra firma* still — for so we must in courtesy interpret that speck of deeper blue — which the decorous artist, to prevent absurdity, had made to spring up beneath their sandals.

I love the men with women's faces, and the women, if possible, with still more womanish expressions.

Here is a young and courtly Mandarin, handing tea to a lady from a salver — two miles off. See how distance seems to set off respect! And here the same lady, or another — for likeness is identity on teacups — is stepping into a little fairy boat, moored on the hither side of this calm garden river, with a dainty mincing foot, which in a right angle of incidence (as angles go in our world) must in-

[1]From *The Essays of Elia.*

fallibly land her in the midst of a flowery mead—a furlong off on the other side of the same strange stream!

Farther on—if far or near can be predicated of their world—see horses, trees, pagodas, dancing the hays.

Here—a cow and rabbit couchant, and coextensive—so objects show, seen through the lucid atmosphere of fine Cathay.

I was pointing out to my cousin last evening, over our Hyson (which we are old-fashioned enough to drink unmixed still of an afternoon), some of these *speciosa miracula*[2] upon a set of extraordinary old blue china (a recent purchase) which we were now for the first time using; and could not help remarking, how favorable circumstances had been to us of late years, that we could afford to please the eye sometimes with trifles of this sort—when a passing sentiment seemed to overshade the brows of my companion. I am quick at detecting these summer clouds in Bridget.

"I wish the good old times would come again," she said, "when we were not quite so rich. I do not mean, that I want to be poor; but there was a middle state"—so she was pleased to ramble on—"in which I am sure we were a great deal happier. A purchase is but a purchase, now that you have money enough and to spare. Formerly it used to be a triumph. When we coveted a cheap luxury (and, oh! how much ado I had to get you to consent in those times!)—we were used to have a debate two or three days before, and to weigh the *for* and *against,* and think what we might spare it out of, and what saving we could hit upon, that should be an equivalent. A thing was worth buying then, when we felt the money that we paid for it.

"Do you remember the brown suit, which you made to hang upon you, till all your friends cried shame upon you, it grew so threadbare—and all because of that folio Beaumont and Fletcher, which you dragged home late at night from Barker's in Covent Garden? Do you remember how we eyed it for weeks before we could make up our minds to the purchase, and had not come to a determination till it was near ten o'clock of the Saturday night, when you set off from Islington, fearing you should be too late—and when the old bookseller with some grumbling opened his shop, and by the twinkling taper (for he was setting bedwards) lighted out the relic from

[2] "Pretty marvels."

his dusty treasures — and when you lugged it home, wishing it were twice as cumbersome — and when you presented it to me — and when we were exploring the perfectness of it (*collating* you called it) — and while I was repairing some of the loose leaves with paste, which your impatience would not suffer to be left till daybreak — was there no pleasure in being a poor man? or can those neat black clothes which you wear now, and are so careful to keep brushed, since we have become rich and finical, give you half the honest vanity, with which you flaunted it about in that overworn suit — your old corbeau — for four or five weeks longer than you should have done, to pacify your conscience for the mighty sum of fifteen — or sixteen shillings was it? — a great affair we thought it then — which you had lavished on the old folio. Now you can afford to buy any book that pleases you, but I do not see that you ever bring me home any nice old purchases now.

"When you came home with twenty apologies for laying out a less number of shillings upon that print after Lionardo, which we christened the 'Lady Blanch'; when you looked at the purchase, and thought of the money — and thought of the money, and looked again at the picture — was there no pleasure in being a poor man? Now, you have nothing to do but to walk into Colnaghi's, and buy a wilderness of Lionardos. Yet do you?

"Then, do you remember our pleasant walks to Enfield, and Potter's Bar, and Waltham, when we had a holyday — holydays, and all other fun, are gone, now we are rich — and the little hand-basket in which I used to deposit our day's fare of savory cold lamb and salad — and how you would pry about at noontide for some decent house, where we might go in, and produce our store — only paying for the ale that you must call for — and speculate upon the looks of the landlady, and whether she was likely to allow us a tablecloth — and wish for such another honest hostess, as Izaak Walton has described many a one on the pleasant banks of the Lea, when he went a fishing — and sometimes they would prove obliging enough, and sometimes they would look grudgingly upon us — but we had cheerful looks still for one another, and would eat our plain food savorily, scarcely grudging Piscator his Trout Hall? Now, — when we go out a day's pleasuring, which is seldom moreover, we *ride* part of the way — and go into a fine inn, and order the best of dinners, never debating the expense — which, after all, never has half the relish of those chance country snaps, when we were at the mercy of uncertain usage, and a precarious welcome.

"You are too proud to see a play anywhere now but in the pit. Do you remember where it was we used to sit, when we saw the Battle of Hexham, and the Surrender of Calais, and Bannister and Mrs. Bland in the Children in the Wood — when we squeezed out our shillings apiece to sit three or four times in a season in the one-shilling gallery — where you felt all the time that you ought not to have brought me — and more strongly I felt obligation to you for having brought me — and the pleasure was the better for a little shame — and when the curtain drew up, what cared we for our place in the house, or what mattered it where we were sitting, when our thoughts were with Rosalind in Arden, or with Viola at the Court of Illyria? You used to say, that the gallery was the best place of all for enjoying a play socially — that the relish of such exhibitions must be in proportion to the infrequency of going — that the company we met there, not being in general readers of plays, were obliged to attend the more, and did attend, to what was going on, on the stage — because a word lost would have been a chasm, which it was impossible for them to fill up. With such reflections we consoled our pride then — and I appeal to you, whether, as a woman, I met generally with less attention and accommodation, than I have done since in more expensive situations in the house? The getting in indeed, and the crowding up those inconvenient staircases, was bad enough — but there was still a law of civility to woman recognised to quite as great an extent as we ever found in the other passages — and how a little difficulty overcome heightened the snug seat, and the play, afterwards! Now we can only pay our money and walk in. You cannot see, you say, in the galleries now. I am sure we saw, and heard too, well enough then — but sight, and all, I think, is gone with our poverty.

"There was pleasure in eating strawberries, before they became quite common — in the first dish of peas, while they were yet dear — to have them for a nice supper, a treat. What treat can we have now? If we were to treat ourselves now — that is, to have dainties a little above our means, it would be selfish and wicked. It is very little more that we allow ourselves beyond what the actual poor can get at, that makes what I call a treat — when two people living together, as we have done, now and then indulge themselves in a cheap luxury, which both like; while each apologises, and is willing to take both halves of the blame to his single share. I see no harm in people making much of themselves in that sense of the word. It may give them a hint how to make much of others. But now — what I mean by the word — we never do make much of ourselves. None but the poor can do it. I do not mean the veriest poor of all, but persons as we were, just above poverty.

"I know what you were going to say, that it is mighty pleasant at the end of the year to make all meet — and much ado we used to have every thirty-first night of December to account for our exceedings — many a long face did you make over your puzzled accounts, and in contriving to make it out how we had spent so much — or that we had not spent so much — or that it was impossible we should spend so much next year — and still we found our slender capital decreasing — but then, betwixt ways, and projects, and compromises of one sort or another, and talk of curtailing this charge, and doing without that for the future — and the hope that youth brings, and laughing spirits (in which you were never poor till now) we pocketed up our loss, and in conclusion, with 'lusty brimmers' (as you used to quote it out of *hearty cheerful Mr. Cotton,* as you called him), we used to welcome in the 'coming guest.' Now we have no reckoning at all at the end of the old year — no flattering promises about the new year doing better for us."

Bridget is so sparing of her speech on most occasions, that when she gets into a rhetorical vein, I am careful how I interrupt it. I could not help, however, smiling at the phantom of wealth which her dear imagination had conjured up out of a clear income of a poor hundred pounds a year. "It is true we were happier when we were poorer, but we were also younger, my cousin. I am afraid we must put up with the excess, for if we were to shake the superflux into the sea, we should not much mend ourselves. That we had much to struggle with, as we grew up together, we have reason to be most thankful. It strengthened, and knit our compact closer. We could never have been what we have been to each other, if we had always had the sufficiency which you now complain of. The resisting power — those natural dilations of the youthful spirit, which circumstances cannot straiten — with us are long since passed away. Competence to age is supplementary youth, a sorry supplement indeed, but I fear the best that is to be had. We must ride, where we formerly walked: live better, and lie softer—and shall be wise to do so—than we had means to do in those good old days you speak of. Yet could those days return—could you and I once more walk our thirty miles a day—could Bannister and Mrs. Bland again be young, and you and I be young to see them—could the good old one-shilling gallery days return—they are dreams, my cousin, now—but could you and I at this moment, instead of this quiet argument, by our well-carpeted fireside, sitting on this luxurious sofa—be once more struggling up those inconvenient staircases, pushed about, and squeezed, and elbowed by the poorest rabble of poor gallery scramblers—could I once more hear those anxious shrieks of yours—and the delicious *Thank God, we are safe,* which always followed when the topmost stair, conquered, let in the first light of the whole cheerful theater down beneath us—I know not the fathom line that ever touched a descent so deep as I would be willing to bury more wealth in than Crœsus had, or the great Jew R—— is supposed to have, to purchase it. And now do just look at that merry little Chinese waiter holding an umbrella, big enough for a bed-tester, over the head of that pretty insipid half-Madonna-ish chit of a lady in that very blue summer house."

DREAM CHILDREN: A REVERIE

Charles Lamb

Children love to listen to stories about their elders, when *they* were children; to stretch their imagination to the conception of a traditionary great-uncle, or grandame whom they never saw. It was in this spirit that my littles ones crept about me the other evening to hear about their great-grandmother Field, who lived in a great house in Norfolk (a hundred times bigger than that in which they and papa lived) which had been the scene—so at least it was generally believed in that part of the country—of the tragic incidents which they had lately become familiar with from the ballad of the

Children in the Wood. Certain it is that the whole story of the children and their cruel uncle was to be seen fairly carved out in wood upon the chimney-piece of the great hall, the whole story down to the Robin Redbreasts, till a foolish rich person pulled it down to set up a marble one of modern invention in its stead, with no story upon it. Here Alice put out one of her dear mother's looks, too tender to be called upbraiding. Then I went on to say, how religious and how good their great-grandmother Field was, how beloved and respected by everybody, though she was not indeed the mistress of this great house, but had only the charge of it (and yet in some respects she might be said to be the mistress of it too), committed to her by the owner, who preferred living in a newer and more fashionable mansion which he had purchased somewhere in the adjoining county; but still she lived in it in a manner as if it had been her own, and kept up the dignity of the great house in a sort while she lived, which afterwards came to decay, and was nearly pulled down, and all its old ornaments stripped and carried away to the owner's other house, where they were set up, and looked as awkward as if someone were to carry away the old tombs they had seen lately at the Abbey, and stick them up in Lady C.'s tawdry gilt drawing-room. Here John smiled, as much as to say, "that would be foolish indeed." And then I told how, when she came to die, her funeral was attended by a concourse of all the poor, and some of the gentry too, of the neighborhood for many miles round, to show their respect for her memory, because she had been such a good and religious woman; so good indeed that she knew all the Psaltery by heart, ay, and a great part of the Testament besides. Here little Alice spread her hands. Then I told what a tall, upright, graceful person their great-grandmother Field once was; and how in her youth she was esteemed the best dancer — here Alice's little right foot played an involuntary movement, till, upon my looking grave, it desisted — the best dancer, I was saying, in the county, till a cruel disease, called a cancer, came, and bowed her down with pain; but it could never bend her good spirits, or make them stoop, but they were still upright, because she was so good and religious. Then I told how she was used to sleep by herself in a lone chamber of the great lone house; and how she believed that an apparition of two infants was to be seen at midnight gliding up and down the great staircase near where she slept, but she said, "Those innocents would do her no harm," and how frightened I used to be, though in those days I had my maid to sleep with me, because I was never half so good or religious as she—and yet I never saw the infants. Here John expanded all his eyebrows and tried to look courageous. Then I told how good she was to all her grandchildren, having us to the great house in the holydays, where I in particular used to spend many hours by myself, in gazing upon the old busts of the Twelve Cæsars, that had been Emperors of Rome, till the old marble heads would seem to live again, or I to be turned into marble with them; how I never could be tired with roaming about that huge mansion, with its vast empty rooms, with their worn-out hangings, fluttering tapestry, and carved oaken panels, with the gilding almost rubbed out—sometimes in the spacious old-fashioned gardens, which I had almost to myself, unless when now and then a solitary gardening man would cross me—and how the nectarines and peaches hung upon the walls, without my ever offering to pluck them, because they were forbidden fruit, unless now and then—and because I had more pleasure in strolling about among the old melancholy-looking yew trees, or the firs, and picking up the red berries, and the fir apples, which were good for nothing but to look at—or in lying about upon the fresh grass, with all the fine garden smells around me—or basking in the orangery, till I could almost fancy myself ripening too along with the oranges and the limes in that grateful warmth—or in watching the dace that darted to and fro in the fishpond, at the bottom of the garden, with here and there a great sulky pike hanging midway down the water in silent state, as if it mocked at their impertinent friskings—I had more pleasure in these busy-idle diversions than in all the sweet flavors of peaches, nectarines, oranges, and suchlike common baits of children. Here John slyly deposited back upon the plate a bunch of grapes, which, not unobserved by Alice, he had meditated dividing with her, and both seemed willing to relinquish them for the present as irrelevant. Then in somewhat a more heightened tone, I told how, though their great-grandmother Field loved all her grandchildren, yet in an especial manner she might be said to love their uncle, John L——, because he was so handsome and spirited a youth, and a king to the rest of us; and, instead of moping about in solitary corners, like some of us, he would mount the most mettlesome horse he could get, when but an imp no bigger than themselves, and make it carry him half over the county in a morning, and join the hunters when there were any out — and yet he loved the old great house and gardens too, but had too much spirit to be always pent up within their boundaries — and how their uncle grew up to man's estate as brave as he was handsome, to the admiration of everybody, but of their great-grandmother Field most especially; and how he used to carry me upon his back when I was a lame-footed boy — for he was a good bit older than me — many a mile when I could not walk for pain; and how in after-life he became lame-footed too, and I did not always (I fear) make allowances enough for him when he was impatient, and in pain, nor remember sufficiently how considerate he had been to me when I was lame-footed; and how when he died, though he had not been dead an hour, it seemed as if he had died a great while ago, such a distance there is betwixt life and death; and how I bore his death as I thought pretty well at first, but afterwards it haunted and haunted me; and though I did not cry or take it to heart as some do, and as I think he would have done if I had died, yet I missed him all day long, and knew not till then how much I had loved him. I missed his kindness, and I missed his crossness, and wished him to be alive again, to be quarreling with him (for we quarreled sometimes) rather than not have him again, and was as uneasy without him, as he their poor uncle must have been when the doctor took off his limb. Here the children fell a crying, and asked if their little mourning which they had on was not for uncle John, and they looked up, and prayed me not to go on about their uncle, but to tell them some stories about their pretty dead mother. Then I told how for seven long years, in hope sometimes, sometimes in despair, yet persisting ever, I courted the fair Alice W——n; and, as much as children could understand, I explained to them what coyness, and difficulty, and denial meant in maidens — when suddenly, turning to Alice, the soul of the first Alice looked out at her eyes with such a reality of representment, that I became in doubt which of them stood there before me, or whose that bright hair was; and while I stood gazing, both the children gradually grew fainter to my view, receding, and still receding till nothing at last but two mournful features were seen in the uttermost distance, which, without speech, strangely impressed upon me the effects of speech: "We are not of Alice, nor of thee, nor are we children at all. The children of Alice call Bartrum father. We are nothing; less than nothing, and dreams. We are only what might have been, and must wait upon the tedious shores of Lethe millions of ages before we have existence, and a name"—and immediately awaking, I found myself quietly seated in my bachelor armchair, where I had fallen asleep, with the faithful Bridget unchanged by my side—but John L. (or James Elia) was gone forever.

ON UNANSWERING LETTERS[1]

Christopher Morley

There are a great many people who really believe in answering letters the day they are received, just as there are people who go to the movies at nine o'clock in the morning; but these people are stunted and queer.

It is a great mistake. Such crass and breathless promptness takes away a great deal of the pleasure of correspondence.

The psychological didoes involved in receiving letters and making up one's mind to answer them are very complex. If the tangled process could be clearly analyzed and its component involutions isolated for inspection, we might reach a clearer comprehension of that curious bag of tricks, the efficient masculine mind.

Take Bill F., for instance, a man so delightful that even to contemplate his existence puts us in good humor and makes us think well of a world that can exhibit an individual equally comely in mind, body, and estate. Every now and then we get a letter from Bill, and immediately we pass into a kind of trance, in which our mind rapidly enunciates the ideas, thoughts, surmises, and contradictions that we would like to write to him in reply. We think what fun it would be to sit right down and churn the inkwell, spreading speculation and cynicism over a number of sheets of foolscap to be wafted Billward.

[1]From *Mince Pie,* pp. 35–40. Copyright, 1919, by permission of Doubleday, Doran and Company, Inc.

Sternly we repress the impulse for we know that the shock to Bill of getting so immediate a retort would surely unhinge the well-fitted panels of his intellect.

We add his letter to the delta of unanswered mail on our desk, taking occasion to turn the mass over once or twice and run through it in a brisk, smiling mood, thinking of all the jolly letters we shall write some day.

After Bill's letter has lain on the pile for a fortnight or so it has been gently silted over by about twenty other pleasantly postponed manuscripts. Coming upon it by chance, we reflect that any specific problems raised by Bill in that manifesto will by this time have settled themselves. And his random speculations upon household management and human destiny will probably have taken a new slant by now, so that to answer his letter in its own tune will not be congruent with his present fevers. We had better bide a wee until we really have something of circumstance to impart.

We wait a week.

By this time a certain sense of shame has begun to invade the privacy of our brain. We feel that to answer that letter now would be an indelicacy. Better that we never got it. By-and-by Bill will write again and then we will answer promptly. We put the letter back in the middle of the heap and think what a fine chap Bill is. But he knows we love him, so it doesn't really matter whether we write or not.

Another week passes by, and no further communication from Bill. We wonder whether he does love us as much as we thought. Still — we are too proud to write and ask.

A few days later a new thought strikes us. Perhaps Bill thinks we have died and he is annoyed because he wasn't invited to the funeral. Ought we to wire him? No, because after all we are not dead, and even if he thinks we are, his subsequent relief at hearing the good news of our survival will outweigh his bitterness during the interval. One of these days we will write him a letter that will really express our heart, filled with all the grindings and gear-work of our mind, rich in affection and fallacy. But we had better let it ripen and mellow for a while. Letters, like wines, accumulate bright fumes and bubblings if kept under cork.

Presently we turn over that pile of letters again. We find in the lees of the heap two or three that have gone for six months and can safely be destroyed. Bill is still on our mind, but in a pleasant, dreamy kind of way. He does not ache or twinge us as he did a month ago. It is fine to have old friends like that and keep in touch with them. We wonder how he is and whether he has two children or three. Splendid old Bill!

By this time we have written Bill several letters in imagination and enjoyed doing so, but the matter of sending him an actual letter has begun to pall. The thought no longer has the savor and vivid sparkle it had once. When one feels like that it is unwise to write. Letters should be spontaneous outpourings: they should never be undertaken merely from a sense of duty. We know that Bill wouldn't want to get a letter that was dictated by a feeling of obligation.

Another fortnight or so elapsing, it occurs to us that we have entirely forgotten what Bill said to us in that letter. We take it out and con it over. Delightful fellow! It is full of his own felicitous kinks of whim, though some of it sounds a little oldfashioned by now. It seems a bit stale, has lost some of its freshness and surprise. Better not answer it just yet, for Christmas will soon be here and we shall have to write then anyway. We wonder, can Bill hold out until Christmas without a letter?

We have been rereading some of those imaginary letters to Bill that have been dancing in our head. They are full of all sorts of fine stuff. If Bill ever gets them he will know how we love him. To use O. Henry's immortal joke, we have days of Damon and Knights of Pythias writing those uninked letters to Bill. A curious thought has come to us. Perhaps it would be better if we never saw Bill again. It is very difficult to talk to a man when you like him so much. It is much easier to write in the sweet fantastic strain. We are so inarticulate when face to face. If Bill comes to town we will leave word that we have gone away. Good old Bill! He will always be a precious memory.

A few days later a sudden frenzy sweeps over us, and though we have many pressing matters on hand, we mobilize pen and paper and literary shock troops and prepare to hurl several battalions at Bill. But, strangely enough, our utterance seems stilted and stiff. We have nothing to say. *My dear Bill,* we begin, *it seems a long time since we heard from you. Why don't you write? We still love you, in spite of all your shortcomings.*

That doesn't seem very cordial. We muse over the pen and nothing comes. Bursting with affection, we are unable to say a word. Just then the phone rings. "Hello?" we say.

"It is Bill, come to town unexpectedly."

"Good old fish!" we cry, ecstatic. "Meet you at the corner of Tenth and Chestnut in five minutes."

We tear up the unfinished letter. Bill will never know how much we love him. Perhaps it is just as well. It is very embarrassing to have your friends know how you feel about them. When we meet him we will be a little bit on our guard. It would not be well to be betrayed into any extravagance of cordiality.

And perhaps a not altogether false little story could be written about a man who never visited those most dear to him, because it panged him so to say good-by when he had to leave.

ENGLISH IN 850 WORDS[1]

Richardson Wood

Basic English is the English language in 850 words, not taking into account special names (such as those of persons and places), words used in special fields, and words which are used internationally such as "hotel" and "telephone." The English language, as it is given in the New Oxford Dictionary, has over 400,000 words; and the normal man makes use of between 7,000 and 20,000 of these. As great a number as 50,000 may be necessary for reading a newspaper.

Basic English is *not* Pidgin English. It is good, straightforward English from which everything unnecessary has been cut out. A number of Shakespeare's lines are in Basic or near-Basic. You may go through page after page of Basic English without being conscious of anything strange. In English we may say: "He descended the gang plank." In Basic one says: "He got off the boat." Basic

[1]Basic English is an International Language now in use. The article is taken from *Review of Reviews* and *World's Work*, April, 1933.

English is the work of C. K. Ogden, of Magdalene College, Cambridge, in England.

For those of us whose natural language is English, Basic English would probably be a good training in the art of making thought clear to ourselves and to others. But we are able to get on without it, and probably will. We have knowledge of it now for reading purposes, and when it is used by others we will be able to get the sense of what is said. But we will only go to the trouble of talking and writing it if we have some special need to do so. There is a need, however, for an international language and for a fixed international form in science, engineering, trade, and all branches of business.

For trade and political purposes an international language is clearly necessary. Things could be done more quickly and with less trouble. Short-wave radio is about to put all countries in touch with one another. Today a workingman in Stuttgart, by touching a button on his radio apparatus, may get voices from Oslo, Warsaw, Paris, Rome, or Madrid. Tomorrow we may be doing the same. In what language would a truly international talk be given? If it is made in an international language of the schoolroom, such as Esperanto, only a very small number will get the sense or even make an attempt to do so. If it is made in normal English, almost 500,000,000 will get some idea of what has been said — but the rest will be quite out of the picture. If it is made in Basic English, the same 500,000,000 will still get the sense, while the rest will be in a position to get an idea of what it is all about.

What is true of radio, is true in a lesser degree of the talking pictures. It is quite possible that radio, by the use of Basic English, might be a help to the talking pictures in their attempt to get back something of the position which was taken from them when sound-recording apparatus took its place by the side of the camera. The hard-working actors will have to go to school again. They may take comfort from the thought that of the 1,800,000,000 persons on earth, one third have a knowledge of English, while another third are attempting to get that knowledge.

The need of the sciences and the trades for an international language, which is fixed for all, is more readily seen. The signs used in mathematics and engineering designs will be equally clear to experts in Berlin, Bagdad, or Boston. But there is no agreement about the notes and words which go with them. For this reason it is frequently hard for a man to be certain about what another worker in his field, even if he is of the same country and language, is attempting to get across.

The uses of Basic English, and a complete teaching system, are being worked out under Mr. Ogden's direction by the Orthological Institute, of Cambridge, England. A great interest has been taken in Basic English by persons who are politically important, and by the heads of education and science organizations in a number of different countries. The Japanese, frequently quicker to take up a good thing produced by us than we are ourselves, have now got out a paper in Basic English.

For those who are good at learning by ear, the complete Basic system has been put on six folding gramophone records. With the help of a simple apparatus which may be fixed on to any gramophone, any part of a record may be played again and again till the learner has got it into his head.

The Basic English library is chiefly in the form of small books which will go in the pocket. These books are put out under Mr. Ogden's direction by the Orthological Institute. "Basic English" is an account of the language. "Debabelization" puts forward the arguments for such a language. "Brighter Basic" gives examples for the Basic talker, and gives an idea of the elastic quality of the language. In "International Talks" the material which was put into Basic is printed opposite the Basic form of it. There is a small "Basic Dictionary" in which the Basic way round common English words not in Basic is given. Inside the cover of every one of these books there is a small piece of paper on one side of which are clearly printed all the words in Basic English, with an outline of the rules.

Mr. Ogden is in a position to give the undertaking the best possible start. He has the direction of *Psyche,* an international paper of psychology, and of two important groups of books: *The History of Civilization* and *The International Library of Psychology, Philosophy and Scientific Method,* and this work puts him in touch with men of learning in all parts of the earth.

Basic English is so simple, and so much needed, that it is only a question of time before it comes into general use as a second language. This page you have been reading is, by the way, in Basic English.

SOME NONSENSE ABOUT A DOG[1]

Harry Esty Dounce

"My hand will miss the insinuated nose."
—*Sir William Watson.*

But the dog that was written of must have been a big dog. Nibbie was just a comfortable lapful, once he had duly turned around and curled up with his nose in his tail.

This is for people who know about dogs, in particular little mongrels without pedigree or market value. Other people, no doubt, will find it disgustingly maudlin. I would have found it so before Nibbie came.

The day he came was a beautiful, bright, cool one in an August. A touring car brought him. They put him down on our corner, meaning to lose him, but he crawled under the car, and they had to prod him out and throw stones before they could drive on. So that when I came home I found, with his mistress-elect, a sort of pot-bellied bundle of tarry oakum, caked with mud, panting convulsively still from fright, and showing the whites of uncommonly liquid brown eyes and a pink tongue. There was tennis that evening and he went along—I carried him over the railroad tracks; he gave us no trouble about the balls, but lay huddled under the bench where she sat, and shivered if a man came near him.

That night he got chop bones and she got a sensible homily on the unwisdom of feeding strays, and he was left outdoors. He slept on the mat. The second morning we thought he had gone. The third, he was back, wagging approval of us and intent to stay, which

[1]By permission of the author and the *New York Evening Post.*

seemed to leave no choice but to take him in. We had fun over names. "Jellywaggles," suggested from next door, was undeniably descriptive. "Rags" fitted, or "Toby" or "Nig"—but they had a colored maid next door; finally we called him "Nibs," and soon his tail would answer to it.

Cleaned up—scrubbed, the insoluble matted locks clipped from his coat, his trampish collar replaced with a new one bearing a license tag—he was far from being unpresentable. A vet. once opined that for a mongrel he was a good dog, that a black cocker mother had thrown her cap over Scottish mills, so to speak. This analysis accounted for him perfectly. Always, depending on the moment's mood, he was either terrier or spaniel, the snap and scrap and perk of the one alternating with the gentle snuggling indolence of the other.

As terrier he would dig furiously by the hour after a field mouse; as spaniel he would "read" the breeze with the best nose among the dog folk of our neighborhood, or follow a trail quite well. I know there was retrieving blood. A year ago May he caught and brought me, not doing the least injury, an oriole that probably had flown against a wire and was struggling disabled in the grass.

Nibbie was shabby-genteel black, sunburnt as to the mustache, grizzled as to the raggy fringe on his haunches. He had a white stock and shirt-frill and a white fore paw. The brown eyes full of heart were the best point. His body coat was rough Scottish worsted, the little black pate was cotton-soft like shoddy, and the big black ears were genuine spaniel silk. As a terrier he held them up smartly and carried a plumy fishhook of a tail; as a spaniel the ears drooped and the tail swung meekly as if in apology for never having been clipped. The other day when we had to say good-by to him each of us cut one silky tuft from an ear, very much as we had so often when he'd been among the burdocks in the field where the garden is.

Burrs were by no means Nibbie's only failing. In flea time it seemed hardly possible that a dog of his size could sustain his population. We finally found a true flea bane, but, deserted one day, he was populous again the next. They don't relish every human; me they did; I used to storm at him for it, and he used, between spasms of scratching, to listen admiringly and wag. We think he supposed his tormentors were winged insects, for he sought refuge in dark clothes-closets where a flying imp wouldn't logically come.

He was willful, insisted on landing in laps when their makers wanted to read. He *would* make advances to visitors who were polite about him. He *would* get up on the living-room table, why and how, heaven knows, finding his opportunity when we were out of the house, and taking care to be upstairs on a bed—white, grimeable coverlets preferred—by the time we had the front door open; I used to slip up to the porch and catch through a window the diving flourish of his sinful tail.

One of his faults must have been a neurosis, really. He led a hard life before we took him in, as witnessed the game hind leg that made him sit up side-saddle fashion, and two such scars on his back as boiling hot grease might have made. And something especially cruel had been done to him when asleep, for if you bent over him napping or in his bed he would half rouse and growl, and sometimes snap blindly. (We dreaded exuberant visiting children.) Two or three experiments I hate to remember now convinced me that it couldn't be whipped out of him, and once wide awake he was sure to be perplexedly apologetic.

He was spoiled. That was our doing. We babied him abominably—he was, for two years, the only subject we had for such malpractice. He had more foolish names than Wogg, that dog of Mrs. Stevenson's, and heard more Little Language than Stella ever did, reciprocating by kissing proffered ears in his doggy way. Once he had brightened up after his arrival, he showed himself ready to take an ell whenever we gave an inch, and he was always taking them, and never paying penalties. He had conscience enough to be sly. I remember the summer evening we stepped outside for just an instant, and came back to find a curious groove across the butter, on the dining table, and an ever-so-innocent Nibbie in a chair in the next room.

While we were at the table he was generally around it, bulldozing for tid-bits—I fear he had reason to know that this would work. One fortnight when his Missie was away he slept on his Old Man's bed (we had dropped titles of dignity with him by then) and he rang the welkin hourly, answering far-away dog friends, and occasionally came north to lollop my face with tender solicitude, just like the fool nurse in the story, waking the patient up to ask if he was sleeping well.

More recently, when a beruffled basket was waiting, he developed an alarming trick of stealing in there to try it, so I fitted that door with a hook, insuring a crack impervious to dogs. And the other night I had to take the hook, now useless, off; we couldn't stand hearing it jingle. He adopted the junior member on first sight and sniff of him, by the way; would look on beaming as proudly as if he'd hatched him.

The last of his iniquities arose from a valor that lacked its better part, an absurd mixture of Falstaff and bantam rooster. At the critical point he'd back out of a fuss with a dog of his own size. But let a police dog, an Airedale, a St. Bernard, or a big ugly cur appear and Nibbie was all around him, black-guarding him unendurably. It was lucky that the big dogs in our neighborhood were patient. And he never would learn about automobiles. Usually tried to tackle them head on; often stopped cars with merciful drivers. When the car wouldn't stop, luck would save him by a fraction of an inch. I couldn't spank that out of him either. We had really been expecting what finally happened for two years.

That's about all. Too much, I am afraid. A decent fate made it quick the other night, and clean and close at hand, in fact, on the same street corner where once a car had left the small scapegrace for us. We tell ourselves how glad we are it happened as it did, instead of an agonal ending such as many of his people come to. We tell ourselves we couldn't have had him forever in any event; that some day, for the junior member's sake, we shall get another dog. We keep telling ourselves these things, and talking with animation on other topics. The muzzle, the leash, the drinking dish are hidden, the last muddy paw track swept up, the nose smudges washed off the favorite front windowpane.

But the house is full of a little snoofing, wagging, loving ghost. I know how the boy Thoreau felt about a hereafter with dogs barred. I want to think that somewhere, sometime, I will be coming home again, and that when the door opens Nibbie will be on hand to caper welcome.

BREAKFASTS[1]

Mary Eneth

"Breakfast was always my best meal"

I, like William Dean Howells, have always been fond of breakfasts. I can remember far-off winter mornings on the farm, when, one of a family of twelve, I sat down in a vast and chilly log room to a table that groaned, under its red-and-white-checked table cloth, with the weight of many rings of country sausage, great mounds of golden-brown cornbread, and heaped-up bowls of fried apples. I can remember the empty platters and bowls that were refilled almost as magically as the pitcher of Baucis and Philemon. Here indeed was the plenty of the gods. And here were appetites, quite prosaic but by no means lacking the poetic touch, for out of doors the zero wind whirled the snow about the windows and indoors the great fire on the hearth leaped and danced the while my father murmured over bowed heads—bowed that we might not yield to the distraction of sausages and apples—"Bless us, O Lord."

Here were no finicky appetites. Everybody came to breakfast on time and everybody ate heartily. Mother did not need to coax Jane into swallowing a glass of milk or of orange juice before she went to school, and no one had any occasion to discover that Baby Peggy would be willing to eat her Cream of Wheat if she knew that she would find the three bears or the Dutch twins at the bottom of the bowl.

And as for Roger, was there ever a time when he refused pancakes and maple syrup? How often in the dark days of Roger's exile from all proper breakfasts, did Mother say wistfully "They *don't* have sausages and pancakes in France do they?" Whimsically I hope that God has been good to Roger in the way of breakfasts. Whimsically, too, my mind plays round Roger's first morning in heaven. I know that there are no breakfasts in heaven and yet in spite of myself, I see a tall lady angel offering Roger honey and manna, and I see him waiving them aside with his good-natured grin and demanding "potato and ham and eggs," with "stacks of

[1]By permission of the author.

hot, buttered toast and real coffee, and, if you have some handy, a dozen pancakes with lots of choke-cherry jelly." Ah, that lady angel! She must have been surprised as much as old Doctor Butler was the morning he came to see a Roger covered with measles.

"Breakfast? Well, an egg, soft-boiled, perhaps, if you feel like it. What! Buckwheat cakes and maple syrup, fried ham and eggs? You'd die."

"Die nothing," Roger grinned. And he had his breakfast.

Yes, though I smile at myself and even grow a bit scrupulous over my worldly thoughts of heaven, I know that in my inmost heart there is always the hope that God and the lady angels will care for Roger who has gone, God's knight, before the great white throne to cry, "A boon, great King, a boon!"

Yes, we loved our breakfasts, all of us. I mean it. We loved them, though you, like my Aunt Sarah, may insist that we merely liked them. . . . It was Peggy who discovered California breakfasts under acacias and pepper trees, the odor of eucalyptus mingling with the fragrance of coffee and the taste of the clear blue air hovering delicately about the taste of the chilled apricots, the great blue prunes and Lee Ching's perfect Sally Lunn. It was Peggy too who discovered our pine and spruce breakfasts, that will always be connected in my mind with six o'clock beefsteak at the half-way shelf on Flagstaff, or at the bend of the road below the Arapahoes. It is true that breakfast is connected with other memories, quite impossible memories of morning hospital trays and the odor of ether, breakfasts quite different from those under the open sky at Estes, at Flagstaff, at Arapahoe glacier.

But there was that perfect breakfast, years ago, the morning when Peggy and I left the old church of Ste. Germaine de Pres and turned into the boulevard where, of a sudden, Peggy's dancing feet were still, and we stood outside a café and looked curiously within. We saw a bar with a number of men and girls standing about and drinking a dark liquid that might have been coffee but actually was chicory. We stood still for a few minutes — merely looking while people came in and went out. All within stood, gulped coffee or wine, and came out.

"Don't they ever eat?" Peggy asked at last in a startled little whisper. "I seem to remember that they eat a little later — *dejeuner* they call it."

Shall I ever forget Peggy's dismay? "But I'm hungry. They must have something. Look, there's a basket of rolls and there's a man eating one. Shall I steal that basket? At least we won't need to starve. Weren't we taught that there is no sin in taking enough to keep from the throes of death by hunger?"

And then, hopefully, "There must be something else, bacon and eggs, at least."

"I'm afraid not. You're in the Frenchiest of French Paris—just a few steps from the Seine."

"Well, faint heart ne'er won fair breakfast," she lilted; "so let's use our hearts and our French if we can find it."

It was a long time before Peggy's French made the waiter hurry out to rob a near-by *patisserie* and rush to the equivalent of our corner grocery for delicate snail-shell rolls of butter and a little pot of strawberry jam. And then, in the shadow of old Ste. Germaine, we sat while a waiter, made up largely of mustaches and gestures, poured hot chocolate from one pitcher and hot milk from another.

Fascinated, I watched the two streams mingle in my cup with the lure of Paris and of California, of Colorado and of the old farm home, and I saw again Father bending over the red-checked table—the table loaded with sausages and cornbread and apples—Father who said, "Bless us, O Lord." And bowing my head I joined in too and said "Bless us, O Lord, and these Thy gifts which we are to receive from Thy bounty, through Jesus Christ, Our Lord."

EVENING PRAYERS[1]

Mary Eneth

Evening prayers were in our home an established custom. My father had a special "Key of Heaven" prayer book, which lay on the library mantel and was brought to him each evening by Boy or Sis. I was never allowed to touch it. Even in dishwashing and table-setting I touched nothing but the knives and forks. They were unbreakable. The "Key of Heaven" was unbreakable too but, alas, not untearable. Thus it was that even on dusting days, Sis mounted the

[1]By permission of the author.

footstool and carefully dusted the mantel and the "Key of Heaven," while I wiped chair rungs and the endless spindles of the stairway.

"Key of Heaven!" Who named it? Could he have known that for one small, pig-tailed girl, at least, it actually opened heaven?

"Oh, my dear Mother, Mary, take me under thy mantle and let me rest and sleep there." Each evening the words whispered to me softly a new magic, a new comfort, and my eyes strayed from Boy sitting on his heels, one hand outstretched to keep Spot quiet, to the lovely oil painting of the Madonna over the old horsehair sofa. Each night the whispered petition brought me from far and silent travels to her, my rest. I had need of her, for I had never known a mother's care. *She* had to take me into her arms, fold her mantle around me, hold me close and warm as she held her Divine Son. As I went up the dark stairway, she was with me — a flood of light, a great silence, a mystery of love and sweetness. I lit a candle — it was only a Christmas-tree candle and not blessed — before the little plaster statue my father had given me, knelt and dreamed a long time of her and of her love. The long years fall away, and I see again quite clearly the small girl, the quaint little shrine, the little statue, veiled with mosquito-netting and crowned with braided white clovers, the buttercups and pink phlox in the jelly glasses that served as vases. I see all these things and something tugs at my heart. Oh bright, other world, that opened to me in those far days, where are you? "Oh, my dear, Mother Mary, take me under thy mantle and let me rest and sleep there."

A LADY'S HEADDRESS[1]

Joseph Addison

Tanta est quærendi cura decoris.[2] — Juv. Sat. vi. 500.

There is not so variable a thing in nature as a lady's headdress. Within my own memory I have known it rise and fall above thirty

[1]No. 98 of *The Spectator,* June 22, 1711.
[2]"So studiously their persons they adorn."

degrees. About ten years ago it shot up to a very great height, insomuch that the female part of our species were much taller than the men. The women were of such an enormous stature, that "we appeared as grasshoppers before them"; at present the whole sex is in a manner dwarfed, and shrunk into a race of beauties that seems almost another species. I remember several ladies, who were once very near seven foot high, that at present want some inches of five. How they came to be thus curtailed I cannot learn. Whether the whole sex be at present under any penance which we know nothing of; or whether they have cast their headdresses in order to surprise us with something in that kind which shall be entirely new; or whether some of the tallest of the sex, being too cunning for the rest, have contrived this method to make themselves appear sizeable, is still a secret; though I find most are of opinion, they are at present like trees new lopped and pruned, that will certainly sprout up and flourish with greater heads than before. For my own part, as I do not love to be insulted by women who are taller than myself, I admire the sex much more in their present humiliation, which has reduced them to their natural dimensions, than when they had extended their persons and lengthened themselves out into formidable and gigantic figures. I am not for adding to the beautiful edifices of nature, nor for raising any whimsical superstructure upon her plans: I must therefore repeat it, that I am highly pleased with the coiffure now in fashion, and think it shows the good sense which at present very much reigns among the valuable part of the sex. One may observe that women in all ages have taken more pains than men to adorn the outside of their heads; and indeed I very much admire, that those female architects who raise such wonderful structures out of ribands, lace, and wire, have not been recorded for their respective inventions. It is certain there have been as many orders in these kinds of building, as in those which have been made of marble. Sometimes they rise in the shape of a pyramid, sometimes like a tower, and sometimes like a steeple. In Juvenal's time the building grew by several orders and stories, as he has very humorously described it:

> Tot premit ordinibus, tot adhuc compagibus altum
> Ædificat caput: Andromachen a fronte videbis;
> Post minor est: aliam credas.
>
> —Juv. Sat. vi. 501.

With curls on curls they build her head before
And mount it with a formidable tow'r:
A giantess she seems; but look behind,
And then she dwindles to the pigmy kind.

But I do not remember in any part of my reading, that the headdress aspired to so great an extravagance as in the fourteenth century; when it was built up in a couple of cones or spires, which stood so excessively high on each side of the head, that a woman, who was but a pigmy without her headdress, appeared like a Colossus upon putting it on. Monsieur Paradin[3] says, "That these old-fashioned fontanges rose an ell above the head; that they were pointed like steeples; and had long loose pieces of crêpe fastened to the tops of them, which were curiously fringed, and hung down their backs like streamers."

The women might possibly have carried this Gothic building much higher, had not a famous monk, Thomas Conecte by name, attacked it with great zeal and resolution. This holy man traveled from place to place to preach down this monstrous commode; and succeeded so well in it, that, as the magicians sacrificed their books to the flames upon the preaching of an apostle, many of the women threw down their headdresses in the middle of his sermon, and made a bonfire of them within sight of the pulpit. He was so renowned, as well for the sanctity of his life as his manner of preaching, that he had often a congregation of twenty thousand people; the men placing themselves on the one side of his pulpit, and the women on the other, that appeared (to use the similitude of an ingenious writer) like a forest of cedars with their heads reaching to the clouds. He so warmed and animated the people against this monstrous ornament, that it lay under a kind of persecution; and, whenever it appeared in public, was pelted down by the rabble, who flung stones at the persons that wore it. But notwithstanding this prodigy vanished while the preacher was among them, it began to appear again some months after his departure, or, to tell it in Monsieur Paradin's own words, "the women, that like snails in a fright had drawn in their horns, shot them out again as soon as the

[3]Guillaume Paradin was a French writer of the sixteenth century, author of several voluminous histories. It is from his *Annales de Bourgoigne*, published in 1566, that the following passages are quoted.

danger was over." This extravagance of the women's headdresses in that age is taken notice of by Monsieur d'Argentre in his *History of Bretagne*,[4] and by other historians, as well as the person I have here quoted.

It is usually observed, that a good reign is the only proper time for the making of laws against the exorbitance of power; in the same manner an excessive headdress may be attacked the most effectually when the fashion is against it. I do therefore recommend this paper to my female readers by way of prevention.

I would desire the fair sex to consider how impossible it is for them to add anything that can be ornamental to what is already the masterpiece of nature. The head has the most beautiful appearance, as well as the highest station, in a human figure. Nature has laid out all her art in beautifying the face; she has touched it with vermillion, planted in it a double row of ivory, made it the seat of smiles and blushes, lighted it up and enlivened it with the brightness of the eyes, hung it on each side with the curious organs of sense, giving it airs and graces that cannot be described, and surrounded it with such a flowing shade of hair as sets all its beauties in the most agreeable light. In short, she seems to have designed the head as the cupola to the most glorious of her works; and when we load it with such a pile of supernumerary ornaments, we destroy the symmetry of the human figure, and foolishly contrive to call off the eye from great and real beauties, to childish gewgaws, ribands, and bonelace.

ARE THINGS AS GOOD AS THEY USED TO BE?[1]

Crag Dale

How often have you heard the remark, "They don't make 'em like they did in the good old days" and how much truth is there in it?

---

[4]Bertrand d'Argentre was an eminent French lawyer of the sixteenth century.

[1]Reprinted from *Popular Mechanics Magazine*, August, 1930, with permission.

To answer these questions, to speed up the wear and tear of time so that a few hours will reveal faults it ordinarily would take a lifetime to discover, is the job of Dr. Ellery H. Harvey, head of the "proving plant" of one of the greatest merchandising houses in the world.

There are some queer jobs in this plant. One man smashes dishes and glassware, and is paid to do it. Trunks are thrown from a roof to the ground, nine stories down, to see whether they will break. Then there is the mattress tester! Sleeping like a log is no idle phrase here, for they toss a real log upon a mattress to test its resiliency.

Doctor Harvey himself has devised many of the surprising ways of finding out just how well some 35,000 products "stand the gaff." He is a sort of commercial detective who is engaged in throwing light on any possible flaws in the cases of goods that are sent to him to be investigated. One of his most interesting tests recently was conducted to determine how long the platinum tip on fountain-pen points would last. He constructed a motor-driven hand that traveled in a changing circle over an ordinary sheet of writing paper, and which held the pen at a constant angle. Force feeding of ink kept the flow constant. One pen traveled 156 miles before it stopped writing. That, he declared, is equivalent to 123 years of average use.

The wearing qualities of silk dress goods began to give Doctor Harvey much trouble when women began to insist on bright colors. Rayon stepped in and added to the trouble because manufacturers of real silk goods, in some instances, attempted to lessen the cost of silk by using a tin "filler." This filler was the woof thread in the fabric and is made of tin chloride. Tin chloride oxidizes under sunshine, and perspiration breaks it down rapidly. Laws of trade permit the use of as much as 25 per cent of tin chloride in making silk goods, but some manufacturers, spurred by hot competition, used as high as 55 per cent of the tin. In those cases the fabric breakdown was rapid.

Chemical analysis, of course, would disclose the quantity of tin in the goods, but not the length of wear under average conditions. The public wanted silk, or something that looked mighty like it, and the merchants had to provide it — even if it were half tin. So Doctor Harvey devised another machine; one that would do in a few minutes what weeks or months of wearing would do to a silk dress. Operating at normal room heat under ultra-violet rays and in reasonable humidity, Doctor Harvey's abrasive machine would deliver 72 rubs a minute on the cloth at the friction of the material rubbing against itself. Three minutes of rubbing was enough for heavily filled silk, while that containing no more than 25 per cent tin stood from three to four times as many rubs before breaking down.

By using the same machine, without the addition of ultra-violet rays or humidity, a piece of medium-weight wool suiting for men is found to stand 50,000 rubs at the rate of 72 a minute. That gives an idea, though indefinite, since conditions must vary with individual instances, of how many times one might expect to sit down on a chair covered with like material before wearing out his trousers.

One of the most difficult methods of speeding up time has been successfully solved by Doctor Harvey in finding out the lasting qualities of paints, varnishes, lacquers, and asphalt roofing.

"The flair for bright colors on linoleums, on weatherboards, and throughout the house, gave us a lot of trouble at first," he said. "We just didn't know what we could guarantee. But now we have a machine which can tell us quickly about it. A piece of linoleum, for instance, is no better than the paint that is on it. When the paint breaks down, the whole fabric begins to go.

"In our 'weatherometer' we have effects that make one hour equivalent to one day of actual weather conditions. The painted metal panel is placed in the machine, and for three hours out of twenty-four is given a drenching downpour of rain and one hour of refrigeration at nineteen degrees, and then seventeen hours of blistering sunlight produced by ultra-violet lamps. The remainder of the time it is in the dark."

At what is considered proper intervals, the metal is taken from the machine, dry, and the unpainted side is placed on a bed of steel wool which is connected with an electric battery. Another contact is made to the metal and then fifty drops of salt or soap solution are placed at regular intervals over the area of the piece of metal. The operator then applies a platinum needle, attached to a set of radio-receiving earphones through which he listens. If there has been any breakdown or cracking of the paint, the operator hears a loud click as the electric contact is made on the wet spot by the needle.

The longest that the best grades of paint yet tested will stand under such a test is seventeen years, according to Doctor Harvey, and it took about three quarters of a year to establish that fact. Painted wall paper — or more accurately, tinted wall paper — has given much trouble, too. The few bright shades, with their many variations and mixtures, have been difficult to obtain so that they will last against the brilliance of sunshine. So far, three years has been established as the longest time such paper can be warranted not to fade.

Another apparatus of more than passing interest in this laboratory of unusual things is the machine for determining the resistance of china against breakage. For this test a four-ounce steel weight is swung against the plate in ever-increasing arcs to measure the foot-pounds of resistance. The trick is to obtain a really thin dish which will stand some bumping around — one which the hurried housewife can drop occasionally without hearing the heartbreaking clatter of crashing china. Two and a half foot-pounds is established by Doctor Harvey as the smash that a plate or cup must stand before he can accept it.

And mattresses — what they go through before Doctor Harvey will give them his official approval is enough to discourage the best of them. A log is hooked up to machinery so that it pounds the mattress from almost every conceivable angle. If a mattress stands up under that for a week, it is good for a lifetime.

"Taken as a whole, a comparison of quality between an article that is made today and the same thing of 25 years ago will show many things are not so good today," declared Doctor Harvey. "On the other hand, the public is not so much interested now in how long a thing will last as how it will look. I'm speaking of clothing now; women's clothing in particular. But bear this in mind: If the quality of silk goods has deteriorated, that very deterioration has placed silk goods in the reach of many who could not afford it years ago.

"But it is difficult to discuss the question of relative goodness of things without advancing the thought that today we have so many more things than we had 25 years ago. Every year sees additions to the list of things the public desires. What they are enabled to save by buying silk with tin in it, or a suit with shoddy and cotton, they spend for some of the other items which, after all, make life more interesting, and which put within the reach of everyone those things which once were considered available only to the very rich.

"Yes, sir, the day of the spinning wheel definitely is gone, and while the socks and fascinators that grandma used to make might have lasted longer, the things of today serve their purpose just as well, if not better. Things may not be so good, in a technical sense, as they were in times gone by, but I believe that that very truth is partly responsible for the undeniable fact that living itself is better."

OUR FRIENDS, THE BOOKS[1]

Agnes Repplier

There is a short paragraph in Hazlitt's *Conduct of Life* that I read very often, and always with fresh delight. He is offering much good counsel to a little lad at school, and when he comes to a matter upon which most counselors are wont to be exceedingly didactic and diffuse — the choice of books — he condenses all he has to say into a few wise and gentle words that are well worth taking to heart:

"As to the works you will have to read by choice or for amusement, the best are the commonest. The names of many of them are already familiar to you. Read them as you grow up with all the satisfaction in your power, and make much of them. It is perhaps the greatest pleasure you will have in life, the one you will think of longest, and repent of least. If my life had been more full of calamity than it has been (much more than yours, I hope, will be), I would live it over again, my poor little boy, to have read the books I did in my youth."

In all literature there is nothing truer or better than this, and its sad sincerity contrasts strangely with the general tone of the essay, which is somewhat in the manner of Lord Chesterfield. But here, at least, Hazlitt speaks with the authority of one whose books had

[1]Reprinted from *Essays in Miniature,* by permission of Houghton Mifflin Co.

ever been his friends; who had sat up all night as a child over *Paul and Virginia,* and to whom the mere sight of an odd volume of some good old English author, on a street stall, brought back with keen and sudden rapture the flavor of those early joys which he remembered longest, and repented least. His words ring consolingly in these different days, when we have not only ceased reading what is old, but when — a far greater misfortune — we have forgotten how to read "with all the satisfaction in our power," and with a simple surrendering of ourselves to the pleasure which has no peer. There are so many things to be considered now besides pleasure, that we have well-nigh abandoned the effort to be pleased. In the first place, it is necessary to "keep up" with a decent proportion of current literature, and this means perpetual labor and speed, whereas idleness and leisure are requisite for the true enjoyment of books. In the second place, few of us are brave enough to withstand the pressure which friends, mentors, and critics bring to bear upon us, and which effectually crushes anything like the weak indulgence of our own tastes. The reading they recommend being generally in the nature of a corrective, it is urged upon us with little regard to personal inclination; in fact, the less we like it, the greater our apparent need. There are people in this world who always insist upon others remodeling their diet on a purely hygienic basis; who entreat us to avoid sweets or acids, or tea or coffee, or whatever we chance to particularly like; who tell us persuasively that cress and dandelions will purify our blood; that celery is an excellent febrifuge; that shaddocks should be eaten for the sake of their quinine, and fish for its phosphorus; that stewed fruit is more wholesome than raw; that rice is more nutritious than potatoes; — who deprive us, in a word, of that hearty human happiness which should be ours when dining. Like Mr. Woodhouse, they are capable of having the sweetbreads and asparagus carried off before our longing eyes, and baked apples provided as a substitute.

It is in the same benevolent spirit that kind-hearted critics are good enough to warn us against the books we love, and to prescribe for us the books we ought to read. With robust assurance they offer to give our tutelage their own personal supervision, and their disinterested zeal carries them occasionally beyond the limits of discretion. I have been both amazed and gratified by the lack of reserve with which these unknown friends have volunteered to guide my own footsteps through the perilous paths of literature. They are so urgent, too, not to say severe, in their manner of proffering assistance: "To Miss Repplier we would particularly recommend"—and then follows a list of books of which I dare say I stand in open need; but which I am naturally indisposed to consider with much kindness, thrust upon me, as they are, like paregoric or a porous plaster. If there be people who can take their pleasures medicinally, let them read by prescription and grow fat! But let me rather keep for my friends those dear and familiar volumes which have given me a large share of my life's happiness. If they are somewhat antiquated and out of date, I have no wish to flout their vigorous age. A book, Hazlitt reminds us, is not, like a woman, the worse for being old. If they are new, I do not scorn them for a fault which is common to all their kind. *Paradise Lost* was once new, and was regarded as a somewhat questionable novelty. If they come from afar, or are compatriots of my own, they are equally well-beloved. There can be no aliens in the ranks of literature, no national prejudice in an honest enjoyment of art. The book, after all, and not the date or birthplace of its author, is of material importance. "It seems ungracious to refuse to be a *terræ filius,*" says Mr. Arnold; "but England is not all the world." Neither, for that matter, is America, nor even Russia. The universe is a little wider and a little older than we are pleased to think, and to have lived long and traveled far does not necessarily imply inferiority. The volume that has crossed the seas, the volume that has survived its generation, stand side by side with their newborn American brother, and there is no lack of harmony in such close companionship. Books of every age and of every nation show a charming adaptability in their daily intercourse; and, if left to themselves, will set off each other's merits in the most amiable and disinterested manner, each one growing better by contact with its excellent neighbor. It is only when the patriotic critic comes along, and stirs up dissensions in their midst, that this peaceful atmosphere is rent with sudden discord; that the English book grows disdainful and supercilious; the American, aggressive and sarcastic; the French, malicious and unkind. It is only when we apply to them a test which is neither wise nor worthy that they show all their bad qualities, and afford a wrangling ground for the ill-natured reviewers of two continents.

There is a story told of the Russian poet, Pushkin, which I like to think true, because it is so pretty. When he was carried home fatally wounded from the duel which cost him his life, his young wife, who had been the innocent cause of the tragedy, asked him whether there were no relatives or friends whom he wished to see summoned to his bedside. The dying man lifted his heavy eyes to the shelf where stood his favorite books, and murmured faintly in reply, "Farewell, my friends." When we remember that Pushkin lived before Russian literature had become a great and dispiriting power, when we realize that he had never been ordered by critics to read Turguéneff, never commanded severely to worship Tolstoï or be an outcast in the land, never even reveled in the dreadful gloom of Dostoïevsky, it seems incredible to the well-instructed that he should have loved his books so much. It is absolutely afflicting to think that many of these same volumes were foreign, were romantic, perhaps even cheerful in their character; that they were not his mentors, his disciplinarians, his guides to a higher and sadder life, but only his "friends." Why, Hazlitt himself could have used no simpler term of endearment. Charles Lamb might have uttered the very words when he closed his patient eyes in the dull little cottage at Edmonton. Sir Walter Scott might have murmured them on that still September morn when the clear rippling of the Tweed hushed his tired heart to rest. I think that Shelley bade some swift, unconscious farewell to all the dear delights of reading, when he thrust into his pocket the little volume of Keats, with its cover bent hastily backward, and rose, still dreamy with fairy land, to face a sudden death. I think that Montaigne bade farewell to the fourscore "everyday books" that were his chosen companions, before turning serenely away from the temperate pleasures of life.

For all these men loved literature, not contentiously, nor austerely, but simply as their friend. All read with that devout sincerity which precludes petulance, or display, or lettered asceticism, the most dismal self-torment in the world. In that delicious dialogue of Landor's between Montaigne and Scaliger, the scholar intimates to the philosopher that his library is somewhat scantily furnished, and that he and his father between them have written nearly as many volumes as Montaigne possesses on his shelves. "Ah!" responds the sage with gentle malice, "to write them is quite another thing; but one reads books without a spur, or even a pat from our Lady Vanity."

Could anything be more charming, or more untrue than this?

Montaigne, perched tranquilly on his Guyenne hill-slope, may have escaped the goad; but we, the victims of our swifter day, know too well how remorselessly Lady Vanity pricks us round the course. Are we not perpetually showing our paces at her command, and under the sharp incentive of her heel? Yet Charles Lamb, in the heart of London, preserved by some fine instinct the same intellectual freedom that Montaigne cherished in sleepy Gascony. He too was fain to read for pleasure, and his unswerving sincerity is no less enviable than the clearness of his literary insight. Indeed, while many of his favorite authors may have no message for our ears, yet every line in which he writes his love is pregnant with enjoyment; every word expresses subtly a delicious sense of satisfaction. The soiled and torn copies of *Tom Jones* and *The Vicar of Wakefield* from the circulating library, which speak eloquently to him of the thousand thumbs that have turned over each well-worn page; the "kind-hearted play-book" which he reaches down from some easy shelf; the old *Town and Country Magazine* which he finds in the window seat of an inn; the "garrulous, pleasant history" of Burnet; the "beautiful, bare narrative" of *Robinson Crusoe;* the antiquated, time-stained edition of "that fantastic old great man," Robert Burton; the Folio Beaumont and Fletcher — all these and many more are Lamb's tried friends, and he writes of them with lingering affection. He is even able, through some fine choice of words, to convey to us the precise degree and quality of pleasure which they yield him, and which he wins us to share, not by exhortations or reproaches, but gently, with alluring smiles, and hinted promises of reward. How craftily he holds each treasured volume before our eyes! How apt the brief, caressing sentence in which he sings its praises! — "The sweetest names, and which carry a perfume in the mention, are Kit Marlowe, Drayton, Drummond of Hawthornden, and Cowley." "Milton almost requires a solemn service of music to be played before you enter upon him. Who listens, had need bring docile thoughts, and purged ears." "Winter evenings — the world shut out — with less of ceremony the gentle Shakespeare enters. At such a season, the *Tempest,* or his own *Winter's Tale.*"

In fact, the knowledge of when to read a book is almost as valuable as the knowledge of what book to read, and Lamb, as became a true lover of literature, realized instinctively that certain hours and certain places seem created expressly for the supreme enjoyment of an author, who yields to these harmonious surroundings his best and rarest gifts. To pick up *The Faerie Queene* as a stop-gap in the five or six impatient minutes before dinner, to carry *Candide* into the "serious avenues" of a cathedral, to try and skim over Richardson when in the society of a lively girl—Lamb knew too well that these unholy feats are the accomplishments of an intellectual acrobat, not of a modest and simple-hearted reader. Hazlitt also was keenly alive to the influences of time and place. His greatest delight in poring over the books of his youth lay in the many recollections they aroused of scenes and moments rich in vanished joys. He opened a faded, dusty volume, and behold! the spot where first he read it, the day it was received, the feeling of the air, the fields, the sky, all returned to him with charming distinctness, and with them returned his first rapturous impression of that long-closed, long-neglected romance: "Twenty years are struck off the list, and I am a child again." Mr. Pater lays especial emphasis on the circumstances under which our favorite authors are read. "A book," he says, "like a person, has its fortunes with one; is lucky or unlucky in the precise moment of its falling in our way; and often, by some happy accident, ranks with us for something more than its independent value." Thus it is that Marius and Fabian, nestled in the ripened corn amid the cool brown shadows, receive from the *Golden Ass* of Apuleius a strange keen pleasure; each lad taking from the story that which he is best fitted to absorb; each lad as unmindful of the other's feelings as of the grosser elements in the tale. For without doubt a book has a separate message for every reader, and tells him, of good or evil, that which he is able to hear. Plato, indeed, complains of all books that they lack reticence or propriety toward different classes of persons, and his protest embodies the aversion of the flexible Greek mind for the precision of written literature. A poem or an oration which, crystallized into characters, speaks to all alike, and reveals itself indiscriminately to everybody, is of less value to the ancient scholar than the poem or oration which lingers in the master's mind, and maintains a delicate reserve toward the inferior portion of the community. Plato is so far removed from the modern spirit which seeks to persuade the multitude to read Shakespeare and Milton, that he practically resents their peering with rude, but pardonable curiosity, into the stately domains of genius. We have now grown so insistently generous in these matters that our unhappy brothers, harassed beyond endurance, may well envy the plebeian Greeks their merciful limitations; or wish, with the little girl in *Punch,* that they had lived in the time of Charles II, "for then education was very much neglected." But strive as we may, we cannot coerce great authors into universal complaisance. Plato himself, were he so unfortunate as to be living now, would recognize and applaud their manifest reserves. Even to the elect they speak with varying voices, and it is sometimes difficult to believe that all have read alike. When *Guy Mannering* was first given to the public, who awaited it with frantic eagerness, Wordsworth thoughtfully observed that it was a novel in the style of Mrs. Radcliffe. Murray, from whom one expects more discernment, wrote to Hogg that *Meg Merrilies* was worthy of Shakespeare; "but all the rest of the novel might have been written by Scott's brother, or any other body." Blackwood, about the same time, wrote to Murray: "If Walter Scott be the author of *Guy Mannering,* he stands far higher in this line than in his former walk." One of these verdicts has been ratified by time, but who could suppose that Julia Mannering and honest Dandy Dinmont would ever have whispered such different messages into listening ears!

And it is precisely because of the independence assumed by books, that we have need to cherish our own independence in return. They will not all be our friends, and not one of them will give itself freely to us at the dictation of a peremptory critic. Hazlitt says nobly of a few great writers, notably Milton and Burke, that "to have lived in the cultivation of an intimacy with such works, and to have familiarly relished such names, is not to have lived in vain." This is true, yet if we must seek for companionship in less august circles, there are many milder lights who shine with a steady radiance. It is not the privilege of everyone to love so great a prose writer as Burke, so great a poet as Milton. "An appreciation of *Paradise Lost,*" says Mr. Mark Pattison, "is the reward of exquisite scholarship"; and the number of exquisite scholars is never very large. To march up to an author as to the cannon's mouth is at best but unprofitable heroism. To take our pleasures dutifully is the least likely way to enjoy them. The laws of Crete, it is said, were set to music, and sung as alluringly as possible after dinner; but I doubt if they afforded a really popular pastime. The well-fed guests who listened to such decorous chants applauded them probably from the standpoint of citizenship, rather than from any undisguised sentiment of enjoyment, and a few degenerate souls must have sighed occasionally over the joys of a rousing and unseemly chorus. We of today are so rich in laws, so amply disciplined at every turn, that we have no need to be reminded at dinner of our obligations. A kind-hearted English critic once said that reading was not a duty, and had therefore no business to be made disagreeable; and that no man was under any obligation to read what another man wrote. This is an old-fashioned point of view, which has lost favor of late years, but which is not without compensations of its own. If the office of literature be to make glad our lives, how shall we seek the joy in store for us save by following Hazlitt's simple suggestion, and reading "with all the satisfaction in our power"? And how shall we insure this satisfaction, save by ignoring the restrictions imposed upon us, and cultivating, as far as we can, a sincere and pleasurable intercourse with our friends, the books?

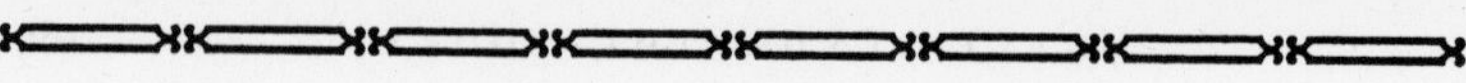

E. THE FORMAL ESSAY

SIR THOMAS MORE: SAINT AND HUMORIST[1]

James J. Daly, S.J.

"The great," says Emerson in his pontifical way, "will not condescend to take anything seriously: all must be gay as the song of a canary though it were the building of cities or the eradication of old and foolish churches and nations which have cumbered the earth long thousands of years." Still, when he wishes to illustrate this doctrine by example, the only one in all Christendom to occur to him is Thomas More, who literally laid down his life to prevent an old Church from being eradicated and supplanted by a new one. Which of those two Churches is foolish, the old one or the new, is a question which, if it has not already been settled, may be confidently left for sure solution to the processes of time. The entire paragraph, the brightest in the essay on "Heroism," leaves a strong impression of having been written with Sir Thomas More in mind. "That which takes my fancy most in the heroic class is the good humor and hilarity they exhibit. It is a height to which the common duty can very well attain, to suffer and to dare with solemnity. But these rare souls set opinion, success, and life at so cheap a rate that they will not soothe their enemies by petitions, or the show of sorrow, but wear their habitual greatness." His intuition, so often more reliable than his erratic play of intellect, brings the "sage of Concord" very close to a great spiritual truth when he goes on to say that, if we could see the whole race assembled together, the true heroes would appear "like little children frolicking together, though

[1]From *The Catholic World,* reprinted in *A Cheerful Ascetic and Other Essays,* the Science and Culture Series, published by The Bruce Publishing Co., Milwaukee.

to the eyes of mankind at large they wore a stately and solemn garb of works and influence."

The only portion of mankind which, as a class, answers to this description are the saints. It was from the saints accordingly that Emerson, with some reluctance we may suppose, selected his type of debonair and smiling hero. Blessed Thomas More was a leading statesman and politician; the first great writer of English prose; a classicist of European reputation, a philosopher, a theologian, an original thinker, a man of affairs, an eloquent pleader, a skillful parliamentarian, an honest and learned judge, a smooth and astute ambassador, and the principal adviser of a powerful monarch. It sounds preposterously fortunate. But there it stands in history with more than the usual explicitness and corroboration.

Indeed, on the evidence this is, if anything, an incomplete catalogue of the greatness of the immediate successor to that Wolsey, "who once trod the ways of glory." Nevertheless, we should look for Sir Thomas More in the "nurseries of heaven." His judicial ermine and gold chains and seals of office, the royal patronage and the homage of the Commons, the respectful and almost affectionate deference of scholars and nobles, could not induce him to take the world seriously. He proceeded on his shining way with the quizzical and detached and amused air of a curious stranger on Broadway or in the Strand, or rather like a sprightly child sent out into the country for a maying, with a keen relish for the beautiful things of life, conditioned, of course, in the expectation of a lasting City at nightfall. He glances athwart his generation like a happy and exotic being from some superior planet. His shy and subtle aloofness from the world, whose history he was making, marked him out for official beatification more surely than his martyrdom. His mask of gentle laughter still baffles the curious scrutiny of eyes that are worldly.

It is fascinating to observe how his jests multiplied with his misfortunes, as if these were your true material for comedy. When his greatness fell about him he sat among the ruins, shaking with a quiet merriment, as if the greatest joke in life had at last been perpetrated. The clouds gathering so darkly over him served no other purpose than to display the sheet-lightning of his humor. Wolsey in a similar, though less serious, situation became for all time a tragic figure. Neither history nor legend has been able to employ the properties of tragedy in the last act of Sir Thomas More's life. He whistled tragedy down all the winds with a fine and genuine unconcern. He refused to live up to the traditions of prosperity in swift collapse, of virtue in bondage and misery, of merit trampled under foot. The spectacle which he exhibits excites no pity nor terror. In Aristotle's phrase, it purifies the heart, indeed: but with feelings of serenest joy.

Only once do tears leap to your eyes: it is when his beloved daughter, Meg, meets him on the Thames landing at the tower, just after sentence of death has been passed upon him, and breaks her way through the spectators and the soldiers to fling herself upon him with passionate tears, and, after pitiful hands have loosed her grasp of him, tears herself away from those who would hold her and rushes back to embrace him again and again for the last time. The night before his execution her father wrote Meg a letter. They had, long months before, deprived him of writing material, and he had been using coal for pen and ink, finding his paper where he might. He had assured Meg that pecks of coal could not suffice to express his love for her, and now in this last letter he tells her that he never loved her so much as on that day, a week ago, when she clung to him and kissed him on the Tower-wharf.

This lovely human touch was necessary to complete the true impression of his humor and to save it from the suspicion of a proud disdain, thoughtless, as well as heartless, of the claims of life. For, it must be admitted, his high spirits which seemed to rise with the increasing imminence of death, almost disconcert a strict sense of the proprieties. A woman in the crowd that surged about him on his progress to the place of execution, cried to him about some papers she had intrusted to his keeping when he was Lord High Chancellor. "My good woman, allow me half an hour and his gracious majesty, our good King, will relieve me of all responsibility for your papers." He bade the friendly lieutenant of the Tower to be of good cheer, for they would all "be merry" together in heaven. When the scaffold was reached he showed droll alarm at its poor construction and tested the insecure steps leading up to it. He begged the lieutenant very gravely to help him up those crazy stairs. "As for my coming down," he said, "let me shift for myself." How could the woebegone lieutenant remain serious? The apparatus and customary trappings of the tragedy were made ridiculous.

On mounting the scaffold Sir Thomas asked the assembled people to pray for him, and told them simply and briefly that he died in and for the holy Catholic Church. He then called the attention of the axman to the shortness of his neck, urging him to be careful of his professional credit. After he had laid his head upon the block he stopped proceedings for a moment or two that he might dispose his beard safely from the ax, since, he said, it was not accused of treason.

The Protestant bishop, Burnet, a historian of the Reformation, was shocked at what he was pleased to consider the levity of Sir Thomas on this momentous occasion. It is true, most of us do well "to suffer and to dare with solemnity." When death confronts us we cannot hope, and perhaps ought not to desire, to be in a mood for jesting, unless we have a record like Sir Thomas's behind us. Compunction and fear are the proper and familiar sentiments of a Christian living and dying; and the most jaundiced critic of Sir Thomas More dare not hint that he ever yielded to the easy refreshment of pagan anodynes such as shallow levity, smug self-complacence, arbitrary optimism, or the illusions of a presumptuous hope. The hero and the ascetic are not always the gentle practitioners of a playful and charming humor. Human nature has to be nagged into decency: it has to be whipped with scorpions into the front line of saints and heroes; and it sometimes becomes grim under the discipline. The bright and warm comforts are so much the ordinary conditions of genial humor that when a saint smiles without self-consciousness, the remarkable phenomenon seems to demand some sort of explanation.

Has anyone noted that Coleridge's theory of humor appears to promise some light which will help us to understand how seriousness and merriment, if carried to their logical limits, meet at a common point? "There is always," he says, "in a genuine humor an acknowledgment of the hollowness and farce of the world, and its disproportion to the godlike within us." And he proceeds to make the essence of humor to consist "in a certain reference to the general and the universal, by which the finite great is brought into identity with the little, or the little with the finite great, so as to make both nothing in comparison with the infinite. The little is made great, and the great little, in order to destroy both; because all is equal in contrast with the infinite." Precisely: to Sir Thomas his beard was of as much importance as his head, or, if you wish to put it differently, his head was of as small importance as his beard, because he was thinking of the Infinite.

If Coleridge's analysis of humor has anything in it, one can perhaps see how it may be possible to be a humorist without being a saint; but it is not easy to see how anyone can be a saint without being a humorist. It would seem that solid and sober persons who are dismayed at the quips and quirks of the saints, are not what you might call good psychologists of either sanctity or humor.

It comes to this: if serious people are tempted to fling up their hands at the casual air with which saints trifle with misfortune, it is only because serious people are not serious enough. Take, for instance, Bishop Burnet. It is very probable that he did not wear a hair-shirt most of his life, nor get up every morning at two o'clock to spend most of his time in prayer and the rest in study till seven o'clock Mass. Thomas More did these things and many other hard things like them, which it is scarcely an injustice to the bishop to surmise that he never dreamed of doing. It is not, therefore, idle or paradoxical to conclude that Sir Thomas was the more serious man. If anyone is frivolous, it must be the worthy bishop who shakes his head sadly over Sir Thomas's willful sport with the mournful properties of a melancholy occasion. It has to be admitted in the bishop's favor that nearly all of Sir Thomas's world shook their sadly puzzled heads over him. You could never tell, say contemporaries, whether he was fooling or in earnest. Imagine their bewilderment when they beheld him cracking jokes in an imprisonment which he need not endure and on a scaffold which he need not have mounted, if he would only take a trifle of an oath which practically all England had swallowed without winking. Outward appearances proclaim him a *farceur* to most of the practical and sensible people of the day.

Even his wife, the estimable Alice Middleton, was on Bishop Burnet's side in her opinion of her husband's want of seriousness. Watch her in a famous passage from William Roper's delightful life of his father-in-law: "When Sir Thomas More had continued a good while in the Tower, my lady, his wife, obtained license to see him, who at her first coming, like a simple woman and somewhat worldly, too, with this manner of salutations, bluntly saluted him, 'What the good year, Mr. More,' quoth she, 'I marvel that you, that have been always hitherto taken for so wise a man, will now play the fool to lie here in a filthy prison and be content to be shut up among mice and rats when you might be abroad at your liberty, and with the favor and good will of the King and his Council, if you would do as all the bishops and best learned of his Realm have done. And seeing you have at Chelsea a right fair house, your library, your books, your gallery, your garden, your orchards, and all other necessaries so handsomely about you, where you might, in the company of me, your wife, your children, and household be merry, I muse what in God's name, you mean here still thus fondly to tarry.' After he had a while quietly heard her, with a cheerful countenance he said unto her, 'I pray thee, good Mrs. Alice, tell me one thing.' 'What is that?' quoth she. 'Is not this house as nigh heaven as mine own?' To whom she, after her accustomed fashion, not liking such talk, answered, 'Tilly vally, tilly vally.' 'How say you, Mrs. Alice, is it not so?' quoth he. 'Bone Deus, bone Deus, man, will this gear never be left?' quoth she."

Poor lady! As Francis Thompson observes, it is a grievous trial to be the near relation of a saint. To Alice, who thought of the Infinite only when she said her prayers, the too obvious difference between the pleasant park in Chelsea and the moldy cell in the Tower was not a proper subject for curious and patient speculation. I dare say Sir Thomas could not help being amused at her stout opposition, but I am sure also that her distress stretched him on a rack crueler than any in the Tower. It was not in the nature of his humor to inflict pain or draw satisfaction from any exhibition of it. When the lieutenant of the Tower announced with much confusion and embarrassment that sorely against his will he was obliged, by the King's strict command, to cut down the comforts and small liberties of his illustrious prisoner, Sir Thomas put him in countenance with a laugh and a jest: "Assure yourself, Mr. Lieutenant, I do not mislike my cheer; but whenever I do so, then thrust me out of your doors."

The Commissioners, his former friends and associates, who thought it best for worldly considerations to bend before the royal will and condemn him to death, were not elated over the performance of their task. Their pusillanimity might have stirred the scorn and contempt of a less sweet-tempered man than the doomed prisoner. The concluding portion of his speech to them shows us which of them, in Sir Thomas's mind, he or his judges, was in need of consoling words. "More have I not to say, my Lords, but like as the Blessed Apostle, St. Paul, as we read in the Acts of the Apostles, was present and consented to the death of St. Stephen, and kept their clothes that stoned him to death, and yet be they now both twain holy saints in heaven, and shall continue there friends forever, so I verily trust and shall right heartily pray that though your Lordships have now on earth been judges to my condemnation, we may yet hereafter in heaven merrily all meet together to our everlasting salvation."

The thought of the Infinite, it will be noticed, was always with him, not only conferring the gift of humor but also preserving it from the common form of degeneration into cynicism and sardonic irony. While the sun was shining on his side of the globe, he took no credit for seeing the way while antipodeans walked in darkness. He thanked the God of light and was humbled by the privilege.

Nor did he feel tempted to flaunt his privilege as a challenge. The consciences of others were not in his keeping and the issue for which he was laying down his life was, at that time, somewhat subtle for the common mind. He needed all his energy and attention for the struggle going on in his own soul that truth and justice might triumph over selfish casuistry and the fear of consequence. He sought to win no followers, even in his own family. He uttered no defiance, but walked warily, as might be expected of the shrewdest lawyer of that time, among the cunning snares of an angry King and a scorned Queen. Perjury had at last to be suborned to undo him.

Sir Thomas was of a gentle and sensitive cast of character, with a scholar's and a cultivated man's extreme dislike of violence. He shrank in all his instincts from this rough contest with the Royal Supremacy, and was troubled by the doubt whether he would be granted the grace and the strength to stand by his conscience to the end. When the end actually arrived he was surprised at the absence of all fear. The relief and exhilaration of that surprise made him more than usually mirthful, and accordingly enigmatic to people who hold that martyrs must be fanatics. Bishop Burnet called him a buffoon, since he could not call him a fanatic. The Blessed Thomas must enjoy this.

After all, where is the conundrum? As he had lived, so Sir

Thomas died — a common fate enough — measuring the finite with the Infinite. Contrary to his humble expectations, he brought to the experience of dying the same buoyant spirit which he had brought to the business of living, with some extra zest thrown in because he was so near Home after a delightful day.

ON SANDALS AND SIMPLICITY[1]

Gilbert K. Chesterton

The great misfortune of the modern English is not at all that they are more boastful than other people (they are not); it is that they are boastful about those particular things which nobody can boast of without losing them. A Frenchman can be proud of being bold and logical, and still remain bold and logical. A German can be proud of being reflective and orderly, and still remain reflective and orderly. But an Englishman cannot be proud of being simple and direct and still remain simple and direct. In the matter of these strange virtues, to know them is to kill them. A man may be conscious of being heroic or conscious of being divine, but he cannot (in spite of all the Anglo-Saxon poets) be conscious of being unconscious.

Now, I do not think that it can be honestly denied that some portion of this impossibility attaches to a class very different in their own opinion, at least, to the school of Anglo-Saxonism. I mean that school of the simple life, commonly associated with Tolstoy. If a perpetual talk about one's own robustness leads to being less robust, it is even more true that a perpetual talking about one's own simplicity leads to being less simple. One great complaint, I think, must stand against the modern upholders of the simple life — the simple life in all its varied forms, from vegetarianism to the honorable consistency of the Dukhobors. This complaint against them stands,

---

[1]From *Heretics*, by Gilbert K. Chesterton. Published by Dodd, Mead and Company, Inc. Reprinted by permission.

that they would make us simple in the unimportant things, but complex in the important things. They would make us simple in the things that do not matter — that is, in diet, in costume, in etiquette, in economic system. But they would make us complex in the things that do matter — in philosophy, in loyalty, in spiritual acceptance, and spiritual rejection. It does not so very much matter whether a man eats a grilled tomato or a plain tomato; it does very much matter whether he eats a plain tomato with a grilled mind. The only kind of simplicity worth preserving is the simplicity of the heart, the simplicity which accepts and enjoys. There may be a reasonable doubt as to what system preserves this; there can surely be no doubt that a system of simplicity destroys it. There is more simplicity in the man who eats caviar on impulse than in the man who eats Grape Nuts on principle.

The chief error of these people is to be found in the very phrase to which they are most attached — "plain living and high thinking." These people do not stand in need of, will not be improved by, plain living and high thinking. They stand in need of the contrary. They would be improved by high living and plain thinking. A little high living (I say, having a full sense of responsibility, a little high living) would teach them the force and meaning of the human festivities, of the banquet that has gone on from the beginning of the world. It would teach them the historic fact that the artificial is, if anything, older than the natural. It would teach them that the loving-cup is as old as any hunger. It would teach them that ritualism is older than any religion. And a little plain thinking would teach them how harsh and fanciful are the mass of their own ethics, how very civilized and very complicated must be the brain of the Tolstoyan who really believes it to be evil to love one's country and wicked to strike a blow.

A man approaches, wearing sandals and simple raiment, a raw tomato held firmly in his right hand, and says, "The affections of family and country alike are hindrances to the fuller development of human love"; but the plain thinker will only answer him, with a wonder not untinged with admiration, "What a great deal of trouble you must have taken in order to feel like that." High living will reject the tomato. Plain thinking will equally decisively reject the idea of the invariable sinfulness of war. High living will convince us that nothing is more materialistic than to despise a pleasure as purely material. And plain thinking will convince us that nothing is more materialistic than to reserve our horror chiefly for material wounds.

The only simplicity that matters is the simplicity of the heart. If that be gone, it can be brought back by no turnips or cellular clothing; but only by tears and terror and the fires that are not quenched. If that remain, it matters very little if a few Early Victorian armchairs remain along with it. Let us put a complex *entrée* into a simple old gentleman; let us not put a simple *entrée* into a complex old gentleman. So long as human society will leave my spiritual inside alone, I will allow it, with a comparative submission, to work its wild will with my physical interior. I will submit to cigars. I will meekly embrace a bottle of Burgundy. I will humble myself to a hansom cab. If only by this means I may preserve to myself the virginity of the spirit, which enjoys with astonishment and fear. I do not say that these are the only methods of preserving it. I incline to the belief that there are others. But I will have nothing to do with simplicity which lacks the fear, the astonishment, and the joy alike. I will have nothing to do with the devilish vision of a child who is too simple to like toys.

The child is, indeed, in these, and many other matters, the best guide. And in nothing is the child so righteously childlike, in nothing does he exhibit more accurately the sounder order of simplicity, than in the fact that he sees everything with a simple pleasure, even the complex things. The false type of naturalness harps always on the distinction between the natural and the artificial. The higher kind of naturalness ignores that distinction. To the child the tree and the lamppost are as natural and as artificial as each other; or rather, neither of them are natural but both supernatural. For both are splendid and unexplained. The flower with which God crowns the one, and the flame with which Sam the lamp-lighter crowns the other, are equally of the gold of fairy tales. In the middle of the wildest fields the most rustic child is, ten to one, playing at steam engines. And the only spiritual or philosophical objection to steam engines is not that men pay for them or work at them, or make them very ugly, or even that men are killed by them; but merely that men do not play at them. The evil is that the childish poetry of clockwork does not remain. The wrong is not that engines are too much admired, but that they are not admired enough. The sin is not that engines are mechanical, but that men are mechanical.

In this matter, then, as in all the other matters treated in this book, our main conclusion is that it is a fundamental point of view, a philosophy or religion which is needed, and not any change in habit or social routine. The things we need most for immediate practical purposes are all abstractions. We need a right view of the human lot, a right view of the human society, and if we were living eagerly and angrily in the enthusiasm of those things, we should, *ipso facto,* be living simply in the genuine and spiritual sense. Desire and danger make everyone simple. And to those who talk to us with interfering eloquence about Jaeger and the pores of the skin, and about Plasmon and the coats of the stomach, at them shall only be hurled the words that are hurled at fops and gluttons, "Take no thought what ye shall eat or what ye shall drink, or wherewithal ye shall be clothed. For after all these things do the Gentiles seek. But seek first the kingdom of God and His righteousness, and all these things shall be added unto you." Those amazing words are not only extraordinarily good, practical politics; they are also superlatively good hygiene. The one supreme way of making all those processes go right, the processes of health, and strength, and grace, and beauty, the one and only way of making certain of their accuracy, is to think about something else. If a man is bent on climbing into the seventh heaven, he may be quite easy about the pores of his skin. If he harnesses his wagon to a star, the process will have a most satisfactory effect upon the coats of his stomach. For the thing called "taking thought," the thing for which the best modern world is "rationalizing," is in its nature, inapplicable to all plain and urgent things. Men take thought and ponder rationalistically, touching remote things — things that only theoretically matter, such as the transit of Venus. But only at their peril can men rationalize about so practical a matter as health.

STORY OF A SOUL[1]

(*A Review*)

Frederic Taber Cooper

In this era prolific of biographies of all sorts and conditions, here is a volume that shines forth with the serene and steadfast radiance of a star of the first magnitude. Neither in outward structure, technique or deeper inner purpose has it any of the hall-marks of modernity, the approved twists and methods of the moment. In style and effect it is timeless and undated, a present-day little classic destined to live on through the momentum of its own sterling worth.

Edith O'Shaughnessy is always achieving the unexpected. Her results never bear quite the awaited ratio to her announced theme. In *Viennese Medley* she took the whole brutal aftermath of the Great War and reduced it by sheer magic to the dimensions of a single week out of eternity, a single family astray in a wrecked world. Here in *Marie Adelaide* she takes an adolescent girl seated on the throne of a toy kingdom and weaves an epic drama which in spirit if not in magnitude verges upon the Dantesque — the drama of a soul on its arduous pilgrimage toward saintliness.

Any portrait painter can limn in the material contours of face and figure, the fabric of a garment, the color of eyes and hair. It is the inner spirit, the hidden thought, the ruling passion that prove elusive. The salient, priceless quality of this portrait of Marie Adelaide lies in its luminous aliveness, its self-revelation. The artist has caught not merely the physical charm and beauty of youth, but the far rarer and deeper loveliness of the soul. And she has achieved this by dipping her brushes in the rich colors of love and sympathy and subtle understanding. Hence her canvas glows softly with a spiritual iridescence, an almost tangible halo.

The historic facts of Marie Adelaide's brief reign would hardly run to the dimensions of a thumb-nail sketch. Her span of life was not quite thirty years. She came to the throne in all the immaturity

[1]From *The Commonweal*, August 10, 1932.

and unpreparedness of eighteen. Endowed by heredity with a high sense of duty and the urge to rule, she had hardly grasped the reins of power when her duchy was overflowed by the mounting tides of the World War; and whichever way she moved, she was predestined to be found blameworthy. So at least the Peace Conference found her, and her abdication was demanded. Having lost her temporal kingdom, she turned for refuge to the inner kingdom of the spirit and sought peace in a Carmelite convent. But here again she was rejected; and after a few scant years of exiled wanderings, she welcomed the release of an early death.

Even in these few facts there is much that seems paradoxical in Marie Adelaide's brief career. Possessed of beauty, rank, and power, she none the less refused earthly love and marriage; despite the inborn instinct for ruling, she almost gladly surrendered her scepter to her sister; and while the "quality of sanctity" was admittedly an outstanding attribute, she was found wanting by one religious order after another. Mrs. O'Shaughnessy herself continues: "There is no key to Marie Adelaide's life. Its strange imperfections are only surpassed by its stranger imperfections." And elsewhere she admits still more definitely her sense of bafflement: "She belongs to the little company of chosen souls who take form and place in the world according to what some call the natural working of temperament on environment, others fate, others Divine decree. But from whatever vantage ground she is regarded she is one of those shrouded figures of history, and with the exception of the recorded acts of her accession, reign, and abdication, she remains mysterious to the end, passing swiftly, veiled as the nun she was not to be."

"Shrouded figure of history" is a picturesque phrase. Yet as applied to Marie Adelaide it seems somewhat exaggerated. In the light shed by this biography the enigmas of her life tend to solve themselves. She was obviously the product of a mixed heredity: "in her veins ran warmly the beautifying blood of the Braganzas . . . creating strange cross-currents and eddies with that ponderable Nassau strain." And this inner conflict between these same two opposing strains, fiery Braganza and cool, calculating Nassau, crops up repeatedly, from page to page, through the extent of this chronicle. Herein doubtless lies the key to such riddles as those mutinous silences, those gusty fits of temper which characterized the approach of adolescence—perhaps also to that momentous and unheralded decision that she reached when attending the nuptials of Charles, future heir to the Hapsburg throne, and Zita of Bourbon-Parma.

In recording the events of that brilliant function, Mrs. O'Shaughnessy writes, "The path of Marie Adelaide's destiny is revealed only occasionally in lightning flashes, in sinister reverberations." What happened then to this fifteen-year-old girl, what sudden revolt or inhibition, what mystical awakening, can never be known. But that something significant, something that changed her destiny, must have taken place is evidenced by the startling announcement she made to her mother that same night: "There is something I must tell you before I can sleep. I shall never marry. Never ask it of me. And I do not wish to reign." Mrs. O'Shaughnessy, in recording this episode, adds poignantly: "It has been remembered by many who saw her at Schwarzau that she was of such a virginal loveliness that few dared to approach her, to tread upon that dew of innocence that so visibly lay about her feet. . . . She seemed designed for early human love. How could one know that in that hour she had espoused, unwitnessed, chastity?"

There is another crucial hour over which a curtain hangs, never to be drawn aside. It was when Prince Xavier of Bourbon-Parma, who had long loved Marie Adelaide, came almost on the eve of her abdication, having been assured that marriage with him would preserve for her the throne of her fathers. Of her interview with him nothing is known save the bare fact that she refused. But adds her biographer, "There was always to be the shyest expression in her eyes at any mention of the Prince's name."

Regarding the tragedy of Marie Adelaide's novitiate in the "fiery furnace of Carmel," her inability to attain a nervous and physical adjustment and her ultimate rejection, Mrs. O'Shaughnessy says in part: "The conventual unfitness of Marie Adelaide has never been explained. . . . But broken health, disarray of nerves, nostalgia, are not sufficient explanation. . . . The reason lies deeper, hidden in the most secret workings of temperament and destiny. Frustration was signed on Marie Adelaide's forehead, stamped on her heart. Neither crown nor cloister. 'Handful of dust' indeed."

Perhaps it is true that there is no explanation, and that countless other women as frail or frailer have adjusted themselves. Yet elsewhere in this same volume the author has recorded that Marie Adelaide "clearly felt, in some peculiar nervous sense the limitations of the convent walls, something claustrophobic." And if you get from this searching and sympathetic study any one impression more persistent and enduring than any other, it is that of a spirit of freedom, a creature attuned to the sunshine, the blue sky, the breath of heaven. Even the city pavements were in a sense stifling. Always, even in girlhood, she throve upon nature, the open fields, the birds and flowers and grasses. All her life she loved the minute life all about her, studying and collecting beetles and butterflies, shells and edible fungi. And even in the Roman days of her exile, one of the few stray glimpses we have of her is of a "tall, star-eyed young woman, who always had a few grasses in her hand or was bending to watch an insect cross a sunny path." One cannot read, in the brief annals of her stay at Carmel, without a sudden painful constriction of the throat, the passage describing her love of the spreading branches of a single stone pine just outside the garden confines, and again her discovery one morning of a little green-gold lizard darting through the pink, sun-baked walls. However steadfast her soul, physically at least she was like a skylark, shut from its azure vault.

There is more than one heartbreak in this volume. The most poignant is very near the end, when, voicing her increasing desire to be under obedience, she said to the Countess Anna: "Mother, give me now thy permission to die."

It is hard to pass on to others any adequate impression of the delicate and sustained beauty, the contagious charm of this volume, done with such deep understanding and loving service. Mrs. O'Shaughnessy brings to her task a rich storehouse of culture and of research and, what is a rarer and more priceless possession, a delicately wrought and enviable style. She has the magic of the *mot juste,* the impeccable phrase, the cadenced rhythm. These pages are a colorful and jeweled casket in which she has piously enshrined the fragrance and the loveliness of "the brightest jewel in the crown of Luxemburg."

DEATH COMES FOR THE ARCHBISHOP[1]

(*A Review*)

Dorothy Foster Gilman

In the first place, this is not a novel. In the second place, it is one of the most superb pieces of literary endeavor this reviewer has ever read, regardless of language or nation. Third and finally, it is a piece of work that everyone may read with reverence and respect. Miss Cather gives us history. Yet she distills the fine essence of it so miraculously that we feel that the recorded events shaped themselves only a day or two before, that the saintly and clerical pioneers she describes might walk in our midst today were we willing to go forth into the wilderness and await them.

Nor are these words of ours the result of any previous admiration for Miss Cather's writings. We have never particularly appreciated the significance of her work until today. The art of the historian is something of which many historians know little. When Carlyle wrote his *French Revolution* the familiar and commonplace criticism by spiteful reviewers was unvarying. "Very little accurate information about the Revolution," they all declared bitterly, "but altogether too much about Carlyle." When Mr. Strachey wrote of Queen Victoria there was not a great deal of the author's personality in the biographical survey, but historical facts were selected for the express purpose of rendering ponderous, complaisant feminine royalty a little ignoble. A fashion was thereby created. Men and women have risen who fancy themselves wrapped in the mantle of the historian when they are in actual fact merely wearing the drab blue smock of the professional literary scavenger.

* * * * * * *

We assert firmly that this is not a novel. It is technically a historical biography dealing imaginatively, though accurately, with the life of a Catholic missionary in New Mexico during the years fol-

[1]From the Boston *Evening Transcript*, September 10, 1927. Reprinted by permission of the author and of the Boston *Transcript*.

lowing 1848, when the United States acquired considerable foreign territory. The Roman Catholic Church at this time looked upon this new land with some misgivings. For those blessed with missionary zeal the Vicarate of New Mexico meant a glorious opportunity. For minds more episcopal and less enthusiastic it appeared a desolate and unrewarding area where converts were few and money was constantly needed. Miss Cather begins this biography with a chapter she reasonably calls a prologue. The scene is in Rome, in the garden of a Spanish prelate high in political authority. At his dinner table sit two other cardinals, one an Italian, one a Frenchman, and also a missionary bishop whose North American diocese embraces all lands on the borders of the Great Lakes. Father Ferrand has come to suggest the appointment of a young priest from one of his own parishes as Vicar Apostolic in the new territory which the three cardinals regard as soil continuously unfruitful for the purposes of their church. Miss Cather from beginning to end writes in a poetic and simple style suitable to the theme she has selected. When she employs a simile, it is never forced. If she says, for example, in speaking of the young priest whose fate is now in the hands of these four men, that the country of New Mexico "will drink up his youth and strength as it does the rain," she tells everything in a few words.

The prologue is soon finished, and with that dramatic sense which only an artist dares to use for literary ends the author begins at once to describe the missionary labors of Father Jean Latour. First, he is seen alone on horseback riding over the dry desolation of the New Mexican desert where only little juniper trees dare to infringe upon the arid solitudes. And we are attuned to the significance of the high theme Miss Cather has chosen by our response to Father Latour's own reverence when he kneels at the foot of the cruciform tree. Shall we give you a description of the new bishop in the words chosen by Miss Cather? "Under his buckskin riding coat he wore a black vest and the cravat and collar of a churchman. A young priest, at his devotions; and a priest in a thousand one knew at a glance. His bowed head was not that of an ordinary man; it was built for the seat of a fine intelligence. His brow was open, generous, reflective, his features handsome and somewhat severe. There was a singular elegance about the hands below the fringed cuffs of the buckskin jacket. Everything showed him to be a man of gentle birth—brave, sensitive, courteous. His manners, even when he was alone in the desert, were distinguished. He had a kind of courtesy toward himself, toward his beasts, toward the juniper tree before which he knelt, and the God whom he was addressing."

We find the key to Miss Cather's mood in such a paragraph as this. Those who read must journey with her, sympathetically comprehending the consecrated ardor and the hallowed selflessness which Father Latour brought to an almost impossible task. The "Splendid Idle Forties" of California were unknown to him and his friend, Father Joseph, whose own temperament was governed by more worldly considerations, though his zeal for increasing the power of his church was no less efficient than that of the missionary bishop. Together these two men visit the different parishes under their control. They travel under the hot sun, with little food, casual shelters, and constant fatigue as their daily portion. They carry not only the spiritual benefits of the church, but also a small altar, the sacred vestments and the sacraments. In the small adobe villages they perform the ceremonies of marriage and baptism. They visit the dying. They pass judgment upon the work of local priests who occasionally fail to maintain the integrity of their calling. Other scenes described by Miss Cather are domestic moments when we return from these parochial expeditions and seat ourselves beside the bishop as he waits for his devoted assistant to prepare the evening meal. Companionship, that nectar of the soul, and courage, that ambrosia of the spirit, unite these two men in their devotion to the religious life they have chosen. Piety never flaunts itself in these pages. No hint is there of any spiritual concessions, although both he and Father Joseph are made aware only too often of those incalculable concessions which the human soul in its weakness makes to the human body.

* * * * * * *

With beautiful and delicate weaving of words the author enriches her biography with legends of the period. She gives us a portrait of the famous Kit Carson. She tells of the good priest Father Junipero Serra who was given shelter for a night by the Holy Family. We learn of the Bishop of Leavenworth, who begged for Father

Joseph's aid in bringing peace and decency to Colorado during the gold rush under the shadow of Pike's Peak. The story of all these things is narrated with restraint and simplicity, with an entire absence of religious posturing or trite phraseology. History, being a record of events, must at all times be more impressive than fiction. We find no footnotes here, no assertions on the part of the author that she is giving us facts, no elaborate references to classic authorities. In their place we recognize that amazing power of the imagination which enables Miss Cather to invest the subject of her biography with everlasting life. No unlettered critic will ever know, nor care to know, whether Father Latour, Archbishop, and his vicar, Father Joseph, in the flesh, lived and talked together in the fashion Miss Cather has portrayed or not.

We concern ourselves little with daguerreotypes, historical or fanciful. We behold the supreme expression of Miss Cather's art. She has always reverenced the days of America's pioneers. Perhaps, with her feeling for beauty, she has idealized their moods and their intentions. She has set herself the task of describing with a directness only possible for a mind perpetually conscious of the nobility of life, the accomplishments of a man who was continually and positively certain that he must spread the gospel of his church. Like all human beings who have renounced the pleasures of sense, the archbishop seems to us a little cold, perhaps a trifle detached as the years pass from the strivings and weaknesses of ordinary men and women. He is negatively good, being a man to whom temptations have appeared in their lightest guise. He feels a little closer to God because he has lost those quick fervent sympathies of youth which brought him once in more intimate touch with Man.

* * * * * * *

As the limitations of age approach, the archbishop's emotions center more on his cathedral than on the human beings in the many parishes about him. In his daily life we see a constant awareness of the demands of his faith. Yet he can always be aroused to the needs of the oppressed and he manifests again and again an Emersonian responsiveness to their supplications. Few writers in any language have selected this period in American history, and have revealed such a capacity for making that history live. Miss Cather pays thus a tribute to all those unknown soldiers of the Catholic Faith who, migrating from France or Italy, gave their lives eagerly for the glory of their church. Their form of warfare was more terrible in many instances than that carried on in Europe ten years ago. For these men entered the battle weaponless. Spiritual armor they may have had, but it is not always the protection tradition would make us believe. This story of Jean Marie Latour comes in the nature of a revelation to historians, to those who fancy they can write fiction, and to that multitude of readers who know little or nothing of that ardent fire kindled by Jesus Christ in the hearts of His apostles. "When the cathedral bell tolled just after dark, the Mexican population of Santa Fé fell upon their knees, and all American Catholics as well. Many others who did not kneel prayed in their hearts. Eusabio and the Tesuque boys went quietly away to tell their people; and next morning the old archbishop lay before the high altar in the church he had built."

THE FALLACY OF FREE VERSE[1]

Theodore Maynard

In view of the fact that Miss Harriet Monroe (who seems to be not only editor of *Poetry* but of poetry) has announced that the discussion of free verse is now closed, I feel a little diffident about forcibly reopening it. My apology is that most attacks upon free verse, like most defenses, have been unintelligent; and that mine, I venture with all due modesty to believe, will be intelligent.

The whole controversy, intelligent or not, has become so confused in its issues, so much entangled with personal ambitions and prejudices, that it is difficult as well as dangerous to make any attempt

[1]From *The Yale Review*. Reprinted, after slight revision by Professor Maynard, with permission.

to reduce the matter to orderly arrangement. It can only be done by painfully clearing, at each step, the ground of its cumbering misconceptions.

To be fair to the *vers librists* we should not take the wild eccentricities of the notoriety seekers among them as typical of the movement. It would, I think, be just to draw unfavorable conclusions from the prevalence of eccentricity among even the staider innovators who, like Miss Amy Lowell, have protested against the "nefarious persons who endeavor to keep themselves before the public by means of a more or less clever charlatanism." But it would not be just to hold Miss Lowell and her coworkers guilty of crimes that, in intention at least, they do not commit. This is an easy, often-used, and discreditable method for bringing free verse into contempt. I disdain to employ it.

Moreover, there is much to be said for the widely diffused notion that free verse is a better mode for expressing the emotions of our age than traditional metrical forms. I think it quite probable myself: so much the worse for the age!

A paradoxical circumstance about modernism, however, is that it is never modernism: it is invariably futurism. And the central doctrine of futurism is that we are all poor fools — which also is a highly tenable proposition. For the modernist is continually making violent efforts to be revolutionary, although he carries in his breast the exasperating knowledge that he must in due course appear a reactionary to his children. He is obliged, in short, to begin as a young freak merely to end up as an old fogy.

Any philosophy behind futurism is a philosophy of negation which doubts, without daring to deny, the validity of reason and the existence of all absolutes. Truth has fallen into the hands of the pragmatists; goodness into the hands of the psychoanalysts; and beauty — well, the natural result of the age's deliquescence is free verse. The one thing certain is that nothing is certain. We have fallen into the abyss of hopeless skepticism. The very title of the most characteristic of Miss Lowell's books, *Pictures of the Floating World,* is significant and appropriate.

Mr. Santayana's genius for profound criticism has noted this state of affairs and has drawn from it the correct conclusions. "The interest abroad," he says, to summarize him, "in the condition of flux, in the process of becoming rather than in what has or will result, is the unmistakeable mark of the barbarian." In saying so he touches the root of modern esthetic experimentalism.

The artist is no longer concerned with the impossible but happy task of capturing absolute beauty: he does not believe in an absolute beauty. Consequently, he is thrown back upon himself, and must use as the material of his art not reality but his personal reactions to the unsubstantial phenomena of appearances. He gives up in despair the ancient ambitions of his craft and confines himself to the narrowing circle of his own ego. It is a terrible fate; but one that has, at present, the delusive attraction of novelty. The poet is spurred on by the craving to be "original"; and as he has nothing to reflect in the distorted mirrors of his fantastic art but his reactions, he is compelled to be as idiosyncratic as possible in order to justify himself.

It is frequently asserted that free verse is lacking in form. That is an ignorant contention and one easily demolished by the exponents of modernism. The point at issue is not whether free verse has form but whether it has poetic form; whether it is a satisfactory medium for poetry. Its advocates maintain that they are able to get out of it effects of which other literary modes are incapable. They say, with a great show of reasonableness:

Stick to your traditional forms, if they are adapted to what you are trying to do. Free verse is adapted to what *we* are trying to do. We have not only the right to use it, but — since an artist must work in his medium — no right to use anything else.

It may be so. It would be partially proved to be so if the *vers librists* were able to produce any example of pure poetry that could not have been written in any other way. But one does not feel the inevitability in even "Out of the Cradle Endlessly Rocking" as one feels in it the case of the "Ode to a Nightingale." For free verse is always more or less of a *tour de force*. It has form, but unnatural form.

The mere technic of free verse is a feat. "H. D." achieves it within a small compass; few others do. Most of the so-called free verse poets write either dithyrambic prose, whose cadences they emphasize by a typographical device, or else meters mingled and broken in such a way as to be unrecognized as meters.

Far from traditional poetry concentrating on form, it is free verse that does so. The one mode accepts a convention (not perhaps, as a rule, realizing that it is more than a convention) and is in consequence at liberty to forget form. But not for an instant is free verse able to possess the carelessness of freedom. Its refusal of limitation binds it, of necessity, in the strictest of limits.

Indeed, in the latest developments of technic we have what is equivalent to an abandonment of the earlier free verse position. Imagism removes the discussion outside of the question of form to that of method; and "polyphonic prose" is nothing more than a synthesis of every conceivable method, ranging from bald statement to frank doggerel — a haggis pie into which innumerable ingredients are thrown at hazard.

Imagism brings together, with an indulgent catholicism, those who use meter with a brilliant exactness, those who use only cadence, and those who use both. But they are to a man sticklers for form. And in the tenets agreed upon among them and published in their first anthology, free verse is fought for merely as a principle of liberty. The sole rule that distinguishes them from other schools is that of the presentation of images. As Miss Lowell, their spokesman, puts it, throwing Aristotle overboard, "Imagism is presentation not representation."

No other of their six rules can be caviled at by the most conservative. Poets have never abandoned the principle of using always the exact and not the nearly exact word, though they have not always been successful in finding it. (Neither are the Imagists.) Poetic diction has practically disappeared as good usage. Every poet of consequence has invented some new rhythms. Most poets have felt free in the choice of subject. Concentration is no new poetic ambition. And poetry that is "clear and hard, never blurred nor indefinite," existed before the Imagist manifesto appeared.

Nevertheless, a restatement of these hoary precepts is to be welcomed. Like all precepts they are frequently forgotten in practice; and to do the Imagists justice they have made an attempt to carry out their rules with meticulous conscientiousness.

Moreover, their central idea — that of rendering particulars exactly without vague generalities — is valuable when not pushed too far. But the Imagists *have* pushed their doctrine too far. They are like the group of painters whose fad it was to paint sand with real sand; hair with real hair. Like them this group of poets is out for "presentation not representation." They will describe sand with words that are as sandy as possible; hair with words that are as hairy as possible. It is onomatopœia ceasing to be a casual trick and stiffening into a habit with the likelihood of freezing into a ritual.

One must, nevertheless, recognize that at the bottom of Imagism lies a hunger for actuality, for close contact. This, like the other fine elements in the movement, is not novel. "It is an odd jealousy," said Emerson, "but the poet finds himself not near enough to his object. The pine tree, the river, the bank of flowers before him, does not seem to be nature. Nature is still elsewhere." The Imagists would accept the first but not the second part of the dictum. Their hands must touch the wood of chairs, the skin of flowers—and reproduce in words the sensations of their curious fingers. So far so good. But their eyes must be pressed against the object of their love —and they will be too close to it to see it. They forget that "Nature is still elsewhere," that beyond the material substance is a mysterious essence—the beauty which should be the object of their search —and the closest scrutiny fails to yield the results that they had expected.

Along with this, as a corollary, goes a desire to strip life to the bare bones, which now and then achieves an austere economy of speech that is, in itself, wholly admirable. But while the Imagists are refining down their material from all alloy, making it ready for use, they generally do not remember that they have to go on and use it. The process is doubtless one that is necessary to poetry. But it is a preliminary process. And the Imagists usually stop there. As Miss Lowell herself states—

We will scatter little words
Upon the paper,
Like seeds about to be planted.

Unfortunately the Imagists omit to plant them.

Wakefulness, for example, is full of the material of poetry carefully prepared for use. The preliminary process is complete. (As a matter of fact all the process should be put into operation simultaneously, and the poet refine, design, and build with the same hand at the same moment. Still, one may be glad of an embryo for purposes of biological data.) A poem and a good poem is ready to be made—but where is the poem?

Jolt of market carts;
Steady drip of horses' hoofs on hard pavement;
A black sky lacquered over with blueness

And the lights of Battersea Bridge
Pricking pale in the dawn.
The beautiful hours are passing
And still you sleep!
Tired heart of my joy,
Incurved upon your dreams,
Will the day come before you have opened to me?

If anyone doubts my assertion that this is not a poem, let him read another suggested by it, Wordsworth's sonnet on Westminster Bridge. I am sure that my point will then be clear, and will be accepted by the reader.

The majority of free verse poets, however, do not follow the Imagist example in this matter. I wish they did. Much more common faults are vast prolixity and an utterly unselective dealing with life in raw slabs.

We could not take three more representative examples of the various brands of free verse than that written by Edgar Lee Masters, Carl Sandburg, and Amy Lowell, who among them cover nearly the whole field and will provide more than enough illustrations for our purpose. Their methods differ widely, as do the subject matter and the temperament of each. To classify them roughly, let us say that Masters is a free verse poet by accident; Sandburg by fate; Amy Lowell by choice; Sandburg by natural bent; Amy Lowell by cleverness; Masters by shrewdness helped out by luck.

Edgar Lee Masters, who, oddly, is one of the most famous free verse poets, once told me that he did not call himself a free verse poet at all. It is quite true that the larger part of his work is composed in formal meters. He has an ambition to be known as a poet pure and simple; and he plods along writing bad blank verse and feeble lyrics which would never attract attention were it not for the *éclat* of the *Spoon River Anthology*. Apart from the fine "Silence" (in free verse as it happens) included in *Song and Satires,* none of the other poems in this volume is worth a straw.

The *Domesday Book,* despite its glaring faults, has power. It is in many ways a remarkable performance. But out of its twelve thousand lines hardly twelve possess any distinction.

> An inquisition taken for the people
> Of the State of Illinois here in Le Roy,
> County aforesaid, on the 7th of August,
> Anno Domini, nineteen hundred nineteen,
> Before me, William Merival, coroner.

That passage has no more and no less reason for being written in blank verse than the rest of a volume which may be magnificent but which is not poetry.

Even the *Spoon River Anthology* has no technical subtlety. Mr. Masters, with rare candor, has explained that he picked up his hint from the Greek Anthology. He does not hesitate to go to the length of turning one of Meleager's epigrams into verse before our eyes as an object lesson to explain his own literary method. This is certainly a striking illustration of what typographical arrangement will do:

The holy night and thou, O Lamp, we took as witness of our vows; and before thee we swore, he that he would love me always and I that I would never leave him. We swore, and thou wert witness of our double promise. But now he says that our vows were written on the running waters. And thou, O Lamp, thou seest him in the arms of another.

This becomes:

> The holy night and thou,
> O Lamp,
> We took as witness of our vows;
> And before thee we swore,
> He that he would love me always
> And I that I would never leave him.
> We swore,
> And thou wert witness of our double promise.
> But now he says that our vows were written on the running waters.
> And thou, O Lamp,
> Thou seest him in the arms of another.

Reading this, Miss Harriet Monroe declares, with a toss of her head, that Mr. Masters has more of the authentic classic note than Tennyson, Browning, and Arnold combined! But the indication of where we are to breathe cannot make anything except prose out of a prose passage. This is still truer of the *Spoon River Anthology,* for which it served as a model but to which it did not impart its beauty. We may grant, however, that, though Mr. Masters defaced his book with a morbid preoccupation with satyriasis and nymphomania, he produced a highly interesting collection of thumbnail sketches and deserved his triumph.

To an English reader, and I suppose to many American readers as well, Mr. Carl Sandburg's three volumes, on first acquaintance, must appear to be a chaos of cacophony. The poet is at no trouble to placate his audience. He throws words as he might throw bricks at your head.

And yet, amid all this welter of verbiage, a beauty is to be discerned — a beauty often smothered by ugly jargon, but still beauty. To cite Whitman's superb phrase, one hears "a horn sounding through the tangle of the forest and the dying echoes."

A great deal of Sandburg's success is, I suspect, due to the fact that he is supposed to write "American." He does, but not nearly so often as is generally supposed. He does get, however, a considerable amount of publicity because of a tendency current in some quarters to connect free verse with "hundred-per-cent Americanism" — a tendency that can do no good either to free verse or Americanism. For metrical experiments are by no means peculiar to America. And Robert Frost and Edwin Arlington Robinson are, to say the least, as rooted in the national soil and as informed with the national spirit as Carl Sandburg. Chicago is not the world. It is not even the whole of the United States. And when Mr. Sandburg defends Chicago by bellowing "Come and show me another city with head lifted singing so proud to be alive and coarse and strong and cunning!" I feel like saying, with cold contempt, that if Chicago is what he says it is — which I have reason to doubt — then he ought not to be proud of Chicago. He speaks with the brutal violence of the barbarian.

Now, the barbarian, I hasten to add, may possess many splendid qualities which civilized men are inclined, during periods of decay, to neglect. But to exalt the barbarian at the expense of the civilized man is cosmic treason. And Mr. Sandburg, I regret to say, is guilty of that crime. He has many finer elements in him — tenderness, humor, gayety; but to me he is the barbarian.

There are signs, nevertheless, that Mr. Sandburg is mellowing. The crudity of his adolescence is gradually wearing off; and as a consequence his verse is growing more delicate and nearer to the Imagist ideal. In *Smoke and Steel* he is under the disadvantage of being less sure of himself than he was in *Chicago Poems;* but, on the other hand, he was a little too sure of himself in the earlier book. He will acquire poise in time.

Probably the best way of illustrating Carl Sandburg is to set out his poem "Good Night," and let it make its own vivid contrast with a poem bearing a similar title by Walter de la Mare, recently published in the anthology *The Enchanted Years:*

Many ways to spell good night.
Fireworks at a pier on the Fourth of July spell it with red wheels and yellow spokes.
They fizz in the air, touch the water and quit.
Rockets make a trajectory of gold and blue and then go out.
Railroad trains at night spell with a smokestack mushrooming a white pillar.
Steamboats turn a curve in the Mississippi crying in a baritone that crosses lowland cottonfields to a razorback hill.
It is easy to spell good night.
Many ways to spell good night.

Now for Mr. de la Mare's poem, "Goodbye":

The last of last words spoken is, Goodbye —
The last dismantled flower in the weed-grown hedge,
The last thin rumor of a feeble bell far ringing,
The last blind rat to spurn the mildewed rye;

A hardening darkness glasses the haunted eye,
Shines into nothing the Watchman's burnt-out candle,
Wreathes into scentless nothing the wasting incense,
The last of last words spoken is, Goodbye.

Love of its muted music breathes no sign,
Thought in her ivory tower gropes in her spinning,
Toss on in vain the whispering trees of Eden,
Last, of all last words spoken, is, Goodbye.

This is one of those few cases in which two poems can be fairly compared. They are equal in theme, in length, and in mood — but how unlike each other they are! Mr. Sandburg has all the originality of detail and of manner; Mr. de la Mare has all the originality of effect.

"Good Night," though characteristic, is not the best of Sandburg's poems. There are other pieces which would supply more vivid examples of single points, and one poem (which, though I cannot quote it here, I must in justice mention), "Flash Crimson" from *Smoke and Steel,* where all of Carl Sandburg's admirable qualities are gathered together, and the ultimate word he has to say—courage.

Miss Amy Lowell is much the most completely equipped and, therefore, the most satisfactory example of a *vers librist* to be found. For Masters writes free verse without finesse, and Sandburg without any clear understanding of his own purpose. Amy Lowell possesses both: she is dexterous and doctrinaire. Moreover, though "H. D." excels all the members of her group in exquisite restraint, Amy Lowell excels "H. D." in power and the width of her sweep. And though no one could accuse of mystical humility the author of a book on American poetry written in order to justify her private poetics, Miss Lowell is at least free of the fantastic egotism of Ezra Pond and the callow pedantry of John Gould Fletcher. In addition there is no "hundred-per-cent Americanism" nonsense about her — a Lowell does not need it. She is cosmopolitan, complicated, clever, and self-conscious. All her books have prefatory explanations; and all the poems in them are obviously written to sustain a thesis.

If Miss Lowell were unable to indicate successful instances of regular verse in her later volumes, the early work of *A Dome of Many-Colored Glass* would incline the critic to conclude that she went in for revolution because she was a failure as a conservative.

When, however, *Men, Women and Ghosts* appeared, it became demonstrated beyond question that Miss Lowell is not merely an important free verse poet, but an important poet. Indeed, the finest things in the second book are cast in a strict mold — "Patterns and Pickthorne Manor" being written in odic form, the latter actually in elaborately constructed stanzas; and "The Cremona Violin" in the Chaucerian style affected by Mr. Masefield.

"The Cremona Violin" becomes a literary curiosity by being

broken by brief interludes of *vers libre*. They are intended to represent — perhaps I should say "present" — the notes of a violin. If they are read critically they will look more like the notes the poet put down, meaning but omitting to polish in stanzas. This is a thing we come upon frequently, not only in Miss Lowell but in the other poets of her school: the jottings for incomplete poetry or the jottings for incomplete prose allowed to appear before the public as finished articles. How admirably this might have been worked into a descriptive essay:

Leaves fall,
Brown leaves,
Yellow leaves streaked with brown.
They fall,
Flutter,
Fall again.
The brown leaves,
And the streaked yellow leaves,
Loosen on their branches
And drift slowly downwards.
One,
One, two, three,
One, two, five.
All Venice is a falling of Autumn leaves —
Brown,
And yellow streaked with brown.

Almost invariably the free verse poem that is successful in making its desired effect is very short and suggestive of a translation. Miss Lowell, for her part, has studied to acquire the tang of *hokku*. She will be as delicate, as deliberate, and as limited as the art of Japan — but it is an art remote from us, one alien to the texture of our souls. Whether the *vers librist* translates from the Japanese, like Miss Lowell; or from the Chinese, like Mr. Pound; or from the Greek, like Mr. Aldington, he betrays a natural bent toward translation. And this, I think, is because his original work suggests a flower plucked from the grave of a dead language.

This tendency has made Miss Lowell grow more and more metallic. Whole pages in *Legends* are covered with plates of foil. All her prints might be called, as she calls some of them, *Lacquer*

Prints. Her handling of lifeless substances is significant. Where Shakespeare heard the lark singing at heaven's gate, she sees that

> A golden weather-cock flashes smartly,
> His open beak "Cock-a-doodle-dooing"
> Straight at the ear of Heaven.

In the final analysis it will be discovered that what is wrong with the *vers librists* is not so much their technic as their conception of poetry. It would not matter even that they rebelled against one kind of vicious virtuosity to bring in another kind equally vicious, if their fundamental understanding of art were sound.

The Imagist itch to "present" instead of represent, and the "advanced" attitude toward the limitations of meter reveal a false view of the nature of poetry. I have already tried to show that meter is much more than a convention; that though it is not the soul of verse there can be no verse without it—for it is the body which contains the soul. And hence to speak of bad poetry (as I, in this essay, for convenience have done) is a contradiction in terms. Bad poetry is an impossibility: it is either poetry, and therefore good, or nonexistent. Poetry is nothing less than perfect speech—and how rare that is! It is unique among the arts in that it cannot be tolerated unless it attains excellence.

The poet accordingly lays upon himself the most heartbreaking of labors—and the happiest. He is on fire with desire. He is tormented with frustration. Beauty is a constant lure—and forever eludes him. Thrice blest is he who once in a lifetime is able to consummate in himself the marriage of the genius of mortal language with the divine Logos!

The *vers librists,* so far from being daring innovators, are really shirkers of the vocation. They take the safe middle course, in which they will neither fail so badly as those who aspire to the highest nor succeed so well as those who attain the highest. They renounce the hope of perfection.

And yet they have performed an exceedingly useful service to literature—one for which we should be grateful: they have carried out the dead. The vogue of the loose and the sentimental and the decorative is over. The world may learn from the *vers librists'* fantasticality, sometimes, and from their frigidity, always, salutary lessons in technic. They are the schoolmasters—should I not add "and schoolmarms"?—to bring us back to poetry.

HAMLET[1]

Samuel Taylor Coleridge

The seeming inconsistencies in the conduct and character of Hamlet have long exercised the conjectural ingenuity of critics; and, as we are always loth to suppose that the cause of defective apprehension is in ourselves, the mystery has been too commonly explained by the very easy process of setting it down as in fact inexplicable, and by resolving the phenomenon into a misgrowth or *lusus* of the capricious and irregular genius of Shakespeare. The shallow and stupid arrogance of these vulgar and indolent decisions I would fain do my best to expose. I believe the character of Hamlet may be traced to Shakespeare's deep and accurate science in mental philosophy. Indeed, that this character must have some connection with the common fundamental laws of our nature may be assumed from the fact that Hamlet has been the darling of every country in which the literature of England has been fostered. In order to understand him, it is essential that we should reflect on the constitution of our own minds. Man is distinguished from the brute animals in proportion as thought prevails over sense: but in the healthy processes of the mind, a balance is constantly maintained between the impressions from outward objects and the inward operations of the intellect—for if there be an overbalance in the contemplative faculty, man thereby becomes a creature of mere meditation, and loses his natural power of action. Now one of Shakespeare's modes of creating characters is, to conceive any one intellectual or moral faculty in morbid excess, and then to place himself, Shakespeare,

[1]From *Notes and Lectures on Shakespeare and Other Old Poets and Dramatists.*

thus mutilated or diseased, under given circumstances. In *Hamlet* he seems to have wished to exemplify the moral necessity of a due balance between our attention to the objects of our senses, and our meditation on the workings of our minds — an *equilibrium* between the real and the imaginary worlds. In Hamlet this balance is disturbed: his thoughts, and the images of his fancy, are far more vivid than his actual perceptions, and his very perceptions, instantly passing through the *medium* of his contemplations, acquire, as they pass, a form and a color not naturally their own. Hence we see a great, an almost enormous, intellectual activity, and a proportionate aversion to real action, consequent upon it, with all its symptoms and accompanying qualities. This character Shakespeare places in circumstances, under which it is obliged to act on the spur of the moment — Hamlet is brave and careless of death; but he vacillates from sensibility, and procrastinates from thought, and loses the power of action in the energy of resolve. Thus it is that this tragedy presents a direct contrast to that of Macbeth; the one proceeds with the utmost slowness, the other with a crowded and breathless rapidity.

The effect of this overbalance of the imaginative power is beautifully illustrated in the everlasting brooding and superfluous activities of Hamlet's mind, which, unseated from its healthy relation, is constantly occupied with the world within, and abstracted from the world without, giving substance to shadows, and throwing a mist over all commonplace actualities. It is the nature of thought to be indefinite — definiteness belongs to external imagery alone. Hence it is that the sense of sublimity arises, not from the sight of an outward object, but from the beholder's reflection upon it — not from the sensuous impression, but from the imaginative reflex. Few have seen a celebrated waterfall without feeling something akin to disappointment: it is only subsequently that the image comes back full into the mind, and brings with it a train of grand or beautiful associations. Hamlet feels this; his senses are in a state of trance, and he looks upon external things as hieroglyphics. His soliloquy —

> O! that this too too solid flesh would melt, etc.

springs from that craving after the indefinite — for that which is not — which most easily besets men of genius; and the self-delusion common to this temper of mind is finely exemplified in the character which Hamlet gives of himself:

> It cannot be
> But I am pigeon-livered, and lack gall
> To make oppression bitter.

He mistakes the seeing his chains for the breaking them, delays action till action is of no use, and dies the victim of mere circumstance and accident. . . .

In all the best attested stories of ghosts and visions, as in that of Brutus, of Archbishop Cranmer, that of Benvenuto Cellini recorded by himself, and the vision of Galileo communicated by him to his favorite pupil Torricelli, the ghost-seers were in a state of cold or chilling damp from without, and of anxiety inwardly. It has been with all of them as with Francisco on his guard — alone, in the depth and silence of the night — " 'twas bitter cold, and they were sick at heart, and *not a mouse stirring*." The attention to minute sounds — naturally associated with the recollection of minute objects, and the more familiar and trifling, the more impressive from the unusualness of their producing any impression at all — gives a philosophic pertinency to this last image; but it has likewise its dramatic use and purpose. For its commonness in ordinary conversation tends to produce the sense of reality, and at once hides the poet, and yet approximates the reader or spectator to that state in which the highest poetry will appear, and in its component parts, though not in the whole composition, really is the language of nature. If I should not speak it, I feel that I should be thinking it; the voice is the poet's, the words are my own. That Shakespeare meant to put an effect in the actor's power in the very first words — "Who's there?" — is evident from the impatience expressed by the startled Francisco in the words that follow — "Nay, answer me: stand and unfold yourself." A brave man is never so peremptory, as when he fears that he is afraid. Observe the gradual transition from the silence and the still recent habit of listening in Francisco's — "I think I hear them" — to the more cheerful call out, which a good actor would observe, in the — "Stand ho! Who is there?" Bernardo's inquiry after Horatio, and the repetition of his name and in his own presence indicate a respect or an eagerness that implies him as one of the persons who are in the foreground; and the skepticism attributed to him—

> Horatio says, 'tis but our fantasy;
> And will not let belief take hold of him—

prepares us for Hamlet's after eulogy on him as one whose blood and judgment were happily commingled. The actor should also be careful to distinguish the expectation and gladness of Bernardo's "Welcome, Horatio!" from the mere courtesy of his "Welcome, good Marcellus!"

Now observe the admirable indefiniteness of the first opening out of the occasion of all this anxiety. The preparation informative of the audience is just as much as was precisely necessary, and no more; it begins with the uncertainty appertaining to a question:

> *Mar.* What, has *this thing* appear'd again to-night?—

Even the word *again* has its *credibilizing* effect. Then Horatio, the representative of the ignorance of the audience, not himself, but by Marcellus to Bernardo, anticipates the common solution—" 'tis but our fantasy!" upon which Marcellus rises into

> This dreaded sight, twice seen of us—

which immediately afterwards becomes "this apparition," and that, too, an intelligent spirit, that is to be spoken to! Then comes the confirmation of Horatio's disbelief—

> Tush! tush! 'twill not appear!—

and the silence, with which the scene opened, is again restored in the shivering feeling of Horatio sitting down, at such a time, and with the two eyewitnesses, to hear a story of a ghost, and that, too, of a ghost which had appeared twice before at the very same hour. In the deep feeling which Bernardo has of the solemn nature of what he is about to relate, he makes an effort to master his own imaginative terrors by an elevation of style—itself a continuation of the effort—and by turning off from the apparition, as from something which would force him too deeply into himself, to the outward objects, the realities of nature, which had accompanied it—

> *Ber.* Last night of all,
> When yon same star, that's westward from the pole
> Had made his course to illume that part of heaven
> Where now it burns, Marcellus and myself,
> The bell then beating one—

This passage seems to contradict the critical law that what is told, makes a faint impression compared with what is beholden; for it does indeed convey to the mind more than the eye can see; while the interruption of the narrative at the very moment when we are most intensely listening for the sequel, and have our thoughts diverted from the dreaded sight in expectation of the desired, yet almost dreaded tale—this gives all the suddenness and surprise of the original appearance—

> *Mar.* Peace, break thee off; look, where it comes again!—

Note the judgment displayed in having the two persons present, who, as having seen the Ghost before, are naturally eager in confirming their former opinions—while the skeptic is silent, and after having been twice addressed by his friends, answers with two hasty syllables—"Most like"—and a confession of horror:

> —It harrows me with fear and wonder.

O heaven! words are wasted on those who feel, and to those who do not feel the exquisite judgment of Shakespeare in this scene, what can be said?—Hume himself could not but have had faith in this Ghost dramatically, let his anti-ghostism have been as strong as Sampson against other ghosts less powerfully raised.

> Act i, sc. 1.
> *Mar.* Good now, sit down, and tell me, he that knows
> Why this same strict and most observant watch, etc.

How delightfully natural is the transition to the retrospective narrative! And observe, upon the Ghost's reappearance, how much Horatio's courage is increased by having translated the late individual spectator into general thought and past experience — and the sympathy of Marcellus and Bernardo with his patriotic surmises in daring to strike at the Ghost; while in a moment, upon its vanishing the former solemn awe-stricken feeling returns upon them:

> We do it wrong, being so majestical,
> To offer it the show of violence.

Ib. Horatio's speech:

> I have heard,
> The cock, that is the trumpet to the morn,
> Doth with his lofty and shrill-sounding throat
> Awake the god of day, etc.

No Addison could be more careful to be poetical in diction than Shakespeare in providing the grounds and sources of its propriety. But how to elevate a thing almost mean by its familiarity, young poets may learn in this treatment of the cock-crow.

Ib. Horatio's speech:

> And, by my advice,
> Let us impart what we have seen to-night
> Unto young Hamlet; for, upon my life,
> This spirit, dumb to us, will speak to him.

Note the inobtrusive and yet fully adequate mode of introducing the main character, "young Hamlet," upon whom is transferred all the interests excited for the acts and concerns of the king, his father.

Ib. sc. 2. The audience is now relieved by a change of scene to the royal court, in order that Hamlet may not have to take up the leavings of exhaustion. In the king's speech, observe the set and pedantically antithetic form of the sentences when touching that which galled the heels of conscience — the strain of undignified rhetoric — and yet in what follows concerning the public weal, a certain appropriate majesty. Indeed was he not a royal brother? —

Ib. King's speech:

And now, Laertes, what's the news with you? etc.

Thus with great art Shakespeare introduces a most important, but still subordinate character first, Laertes, who is yet thus graciously treated in consequence of the assistance given to the election of the late king's brother instead of his son by Polonius.

Ib.

Ham. A little more than kin, and less than kind.
King. How is it that the clouds still hang on you?
Ham. Not so, my lord, I am too much i' the sun.

Hamlet opens his mouth with a playing on words, the complete absence of which throughout characterizes Macbeth. This playing on words may be attributed to many causes or motives, as either to an exuberant activity of mind, as in the higher comedy of Shakespeare generally; or to an imitation of it as a mere fashion, as if it were said—"Is not this better than groaning?"; or to a contemptuous exultation in minds vulgarized and overset by their success, as in the poetic instance of Milton's Devils in the battle; or it is the language of resentment, as is familiar to every one who has witnessed the quarrels of the lower orders, where there is invariably a profusion of punning invective, whence, perhaps, nicknames have in a considerable degree sprung up; or it is the language of suppressed passion, and especially of a hardly smothered personal dislike. The first and last of these combine in Hamlet's case; and I have little doubt that Farmer is right in supposing the equivocation carried on in the expression "too much i' the sun," or son.

Ib.

Ham. Ay, madam, it is common.

Here observe Hamlet's delicacy to his mother, and how the suppression prepares him for the overflow in the next speech, in which his character is more developed by bringing forward his aversion to externals, and which betrays his habit of brooding over the world within him, coupled with a prodigality of beautiful words, which are the half embodyings of thought, and are more than thought, and have an outness, a reality *sui generis,* and yet retain their correspondence and shadowy affinity to the images and movements within. Note also Hamlet's silence to the long speech of the king which follows, and his respectful, but general, answer to his mother.

Ib. Hamlet's first soliloquy:

> O, that this too too solid flesh would melt,
> Thaw, and resolve itself into a dew! etc.

This *tædium vitæ* is a common oppression on minds cast in the Hamlet mold, and is caused by disproportionate mental exertion, which necessitates exhaustion of bodily feeling. Where there is a just coincidence of external and internal action, pleasure is always the result; but where the former is deficient, and the mind's appetency of the ideal is unchecked, realities will seem cold and unmoving. In such cases, passion combines itself with the indefinite alone. In this mood of his mind the relation of the appearance of his father's spirit in arms is made all at once to Hamlet: it is—Horatio's speech, in particular—a perfect model of the true style of dramatic narrative; the purest poetry, and yet in the most natural language, equally remote from the inkhorn and the plough.

Ib. sc. 3. This scene must be regarded as one of Shakespeare's lyric movements in the play, and the skill with which it is interwoven with the dramatic parts is peculiarly an excellence of our poet. You experience the sensation of a pause without the sense of a stop. You will observe in Ophelia's short and general answer to the long speech of Laertes the natural carelessness of innocence, which cannot think such a code of cautions and prudences necessary to its own preservation. . . .

Ib. Speech of Polonius:

> How prodigal the soul
> Lends the tongue vows: these blazes, daughter, etc.

A spondee has, I doubt not, dropped out of the text. Either insert "Go to" after "vows":

> Lends the tongue vows: Go to, these blazes, daughter—

or read

> Lends the tongue vows: These blazes, daughter, mark you—

Shakespeare never introduces a catalectic line without intending an equivalent to the foot omitted in the pauses, or the dwelling emphasis, or the diffused retardation. I do not, however, deny that a good actor might by employing the last-mentioned means, namely, the retardation, or solemn knowing drawl supply the missing spondee with good effect. But I do not believe that this or any other of the foregoing speeches of Polonius, Shakespeare meant to bring out the senility or weakness of that personage's mind. In the great ever-recurring dangers and duties of life, where to distinguish the fit objects for the application of the maxims collected by the experience of a long life, requires no fineness of tact, as in the admonitions to his son and daughter, Polonius is uniformly made respectable. But if an actor were even capable of catching these shades in the character, the pit and the gallery would be malcontent at their exhibition. It is to Hamlet that Polonius is, and is meant to be, contemptible, because in inwardness and uncontrollable activity of movement, Hamlet's mind is the logical contrary to that of Polonius, and besides, as I have observed before, Hamlet dislikes the man as false to his true allegiance in the matter of the succession to the crown.

Ib. sc. 4. The unimportant conversation with which this scene opens is a proof of Shakespeare's minute knowledge of human nature. It is a well-established fact, that on the brink of any serious enterprise, or event of moment, men almost invariably endeavor to elude the pressure of their own thoughts by turning aside to trivial objects and familiar circumstances: thus this dialogue on the platform begins with remarks on the coldness of the air, and inquiries, obliquely connected, indeed, with the expected hour of the visitation, but thrown out in a seeming vacuity of topics, as to the striking of the clock, and so forth. The same desire to escape from the impending thought is carried on in Hamlet's account of, and moralizing on, the Danish custom of wassailing: he runs off from the particular to the universal, and, in his repugnance to personal and individual concerns, escapes, as it were, from himself in generalizations, and smothers the impatience and uneasy feelings of the moment in abstract reasoning. Besides this, another purpose is answered; for by thus entangling the attention of the audience in the nice distinctions and parenthetical sentences of this speech of Hamlet's, Shakespeare takes them completely by surprise on the appearance of the Ghost, which comes upon them in all the suddenness of its visionary character. Indeed, no modern writer would have dared, like Shakespeare, to have preceded this last visitation by two distinct appearances, or could have contrived that the third should rise upon the former two in impressiveness and solemnity of interest.

But in addition to all the other excellences of Hamlet's speech concerning the wassel-music — so finely revealing the predominant idealism, the ratiocinative meditativeness, of his character — it has the advantage of giving nature and probability to the impassioned continuity of the speech instantly directed to the Ghost. The *momentum* had been given to his mental activity; the full current of the thoughts and words had set in, and the very forgetfulness, in the fervor of his argumentation, of the purpose for which he was there, aided in preventing the appearance from benumbing the mind. Consequently, it acted as a new impulse — a sudden stroke which increased the velocity of the body already in motion, while it altered the direction. The co-presence of Horatio, Marcellus, and Bernardo is most judiciously contrived; for it renders the courage of Hamlet and his impetuous eloquence perfectly intelligible. The knowledge, the unthought-of consciousness, the sensation — of human auditors, of flesh-and-blood sympathists — acts as a support and a stimulation *a tergo,* while the front of the mind, the whole consciousness of the speaker, is filled, yea, absorbed, by the apparition. Add too, that the apparition itself has by its previous appearances been brought nearer to a thing of this world. This accrescence of objectivity in a Ghost that yet retains all its ghostly attributes and fearful subjectivity, is truly wonderful.

Ib. sc. 5. Hamlet's speech:

> O all you host of heaven! O earth! What else?
> And shall I couple hell?

I remember nothing equal to this burst unless it be the first speech of Prometheus in the Greek drama, after the exit of Vulcan and the two Afrites. But Shakespeare alone could have produced the vow of Hamlet to make his memory a blank of all maxims and generalized truths, that "observation had copied there," followed immediately by the speaker noting down the generalized fact,

> That one may smile, and smile, and be a villain!

Ib.

> *Mar.* Hillo, ho, ho, my lord!
> *Ham.* Hillo, ho, ho, boy! come bird, come, etc.

This part of the scene after Hamlet's interview with the Ghost has been charged with an improbable eccentricity. But the truth is, that after the mind has been stretched beyond its usual pitch and tone, it must either sink into exhaustion and inanity, or seek relief by change. It is thus well known, that persons conversant in deeds of cruelty contrive to escape from conscience by connecting something of the ludicrous with them, and by inventing grotesque terms and a certain technical phraseology to disguise the horror of their practices. Indeed, paradoxical as it may appear, the terrible by a law of the human mind always touches on the verge of the ludicrous. Both arise from the perception of something out of the common order of things — something, in fact, out of its place; and if from this we can abstract danger, the uncommonness will alone remain, and the sense of the ridiculous be excited. The close alliance of these opposites — they are not contraries — appears from the circumstance, that laughter is equally the expression of extreme anguish and horror as of joy: as there are tears of sorrow and tears of joy, so is there a laugh of terror and a laugh of merriment. These complex causes will naturally have produced in Hamlet the disposition to escape from his own feeling of the overwhelming and supernatural by a wild transition to the ludicrous — a sort of cunning bravado, bordering on the flights of delirium. For you may, perhaps, observe that Hamlet's wildness is but half false; he plays that subtle trick of pretending to act only when he is very near really being what he acts.

The subterraneous speeches of the Ghost are hardly defensible: but I would call your attention to the characteristic difference between this Ghost, as a superstition connected with the most mysterious truths of revealed religion — and Shakespeare's consequent reverence in his treatment of it — and the foul earthly witcheries and wild language in *Macbeth*.

Ib. Gentleman's speech:

> And as the world were now but to begin,
> Antiquity forgot, custom not known,
> The ratifiers and props of every word —
> They cry, etc.

Fearful and self-suspicious as I always feel, when I seem to see an error of judgment in Shakespeare, yet I cannot reconcile the cool, and, as Warburton calls it, "rational and consequential," reflection in these lines with the anonymousness, or the alarm, of this Gentleman or Messenger, as he is called in other editions.

Ib. King's speech:

> There's such divinity doth hedge a king,
> That treason can but peep to what it would,
> Acts little of his will.

Proof, as indeed all else is, that Shakespeare never intended us to see the King with Hamlet's eyes; though, I suspect, the managers have long done so.

Act v. sc. 1: O, the rich contrast between the Clowns and Hamlet, as two extremes! You see in the former the mockery of logic, and a traditional wit valued, like truth, for its antiquity, and treasured up, like a tune, for use.

Ib. sc. 1 and 2. Shakespeare seems to mean all Hamlet's character to be brought together before his final disappearance from the scene—his meditative excess in the grave-digging, his yielding to passion with Laertes, his love for Ophelia blazing out, his tendency to generalize on all occasions in the dialogue with Horatio, his fine gentlemanly manners with Osrick, and his and Shakespeare's own fondness for presentiment:

> But thou would'st not think, how ill all's here about my heart: but it is no matter.

THE LAST QUESTION OF ALL[1]

C. E. Montague

All lines of thought about literature lead to one ultimate question.

---

[1]From *The Saturday Review of Literature,* October 13, 1928. Reprinted by permission of and arrangement with Doubleday, Doran & Co., Inc., and with the Estate of C. E. Montague.

It lies at the end of more roads than Rome ever did. Why are we moved so strongly and so strangely as we are by certain simple groupings of a few ordinary words?

Bacon says that the nature of things is best seen in the smallest possible quantities of them. Take, then, some unit or atom of beautiful writing — a line of verse or a sentence of prose that has stirred you uncommonly. It may be Falsta's "we have heard the chimes at midnight." Or

> The tide of pomp
> That beats upon the high shore of this world.

Or "visited all night by troops of stars," in Wordsworth's poem on Mont Blanck. How comes it that these special sequences of quite common words can take hold of you with a high hand, filling your mind and thrilling it with a poignant ecstasy, a delicious disquiet, akin to the restlessness and the raptures of lovers? When I was an idle boy going to school and discovered the lines, out of Scott,

> But the lark's shrill fife may come
> At the daybreak from the fallow
> And the bittern sound his drum
> Booming from the sedgy shallow,

they made me so drunk with delight that I had to walk up and down empty compartments of trains, saying them over and over again, as incapable as a blue-bottle either of sitting quiet or of ceasing to hum. The adult Stevenson would seem to have been bitten by much the same gadfly when first he read certain verses of Meredith's "Love in the Valley":

> Lovely are the curves of the white owl sweeping
> Wavy through the dusk lit by one large star.

He told Mr. Yeats how he went about whooping the heavenly stuff to the Dryads of the Riviera, "waking with it all the echoes of the hills about Hyères." Everybody must know the sensation. But how to account for it?

. . .

Of course you can easily go a small part of the way toward a full explanation. In the Meredith lines, for example, certain contributory lures and graces are obvious — the engaging "Sing a song o' sixpence," melody, the play that is made with a few picked consonants, winged and liquidly gliding, and the winning way the second line is retarded at its close by the three stressed monosyllables, like a well-mannered horse pulled up by a well-mannered rider. The Scott passage, too, has its taking devices of craftsmanship. There is the deftly managed consonantal chord of *bdf* pervading it, to its advantage. There is the drumlike beat of its main vowels, and the reedy hiss of the successive sibilants to help evoke the picture in the two last lines.

Such devices are not to be sniffed at. They help. They are like jewels and lace skillfully worn by a beautiful woman. But these are not the intrinsic and ultimate beauty of their wearer. The Venus of Melos had none; and some of the most lovely sentences ever written are almost as bare of any applied ornament, anything we can detach and define. The critical analyst has to throw up his hands, almost at once, when he tries to precipitate with his acids the charm of

Beauty falls from the air;
Queens have died young and fair;
Dust hath dimmed Helen's eyes

or of

She walks in beauty like the night
Of cloudless climes and starry skies.

The context, of course, counts for something: every gem is the better for a fine setting. But no gem of the first water is made by its setting. These small splinters of perfection in the art of letters would still bewitch us if they had no context at all. As if to prove as much, Shakespeare struck off one of them —

Child Rowland to the dark tower came —

and left it contextless, to haunt the minds of poets like one of the isolated granules of beauty surviving from the Greek Anthology. For it, too, has the essential gemlike quality — a kind of dazzling unreason, as it may seem at first sight — a power of taking you captive without giving you any materials for a presentable explanation of your surrender.

• • •

If we cannot say why we capitulate thus, we may at least try to fix and describe the sensations that visit us while the charm is at work.

For one thing, we are deeply excited. We are shaken or lifted out of our ordinary state of consciousness. Many of our faculties are, for the moment, enhanced. We feel keener perceptions coming into action within us. We are given the use of more than our normal stock of penetrative sympathy: we feel that we can enter into people's feelings, and understand the quality of their lives better than ever before.

Another effect of the drug is that, while it is acting strongly, the whole adventure of mankind upon the earth gains, in our sight, a new momentousness, precariousness, and beauty. The new and higher scale of power in ourselves seems to be challenged by an equal increase in the size of the objects on which it is exercised. Living becomes a grander affair than we had ever thought.

A third effect on the mind is a powerful sense—authentic or illusory—of being in the presence of extraordinary possibilities. You feel as if new doors of understanding and delight were beginning to open around you. Some sort of mysterious liberation or empowerment seems to be approaching. You are assured, in an unaccountable way, that wonderful enlightenments, still unreceived, are on their way to you, like new stars that are nearing the point in space at which they will come within the range of our sight.

These sensations may not be defined or measured as closely as doctors measure a patient's temperature, his pulse, and his blood pressure. And yet they are worth describing, if only because you will find that you are also describing something else by the way. The nearer you get to saying just what you feel, when under the spell of great writing, the nearer are you, too, to defining the state of mind and heart in which great things are written.

• • •

That state is not normal. It is not the state of each particular writer "at par." To do great things he has to be far above himself, however high his normal level of thought and feeling may be. Not of Oliver Goldsmith alone among writers might it be said that he "wrote like an angel and talked like poor Poll." Nor need we suppose that Goldsmith himself did any injustice to the normal level of his mind when he failed to shine at the club in conversation with Reynolds and Burke. More probably the angelic music and wit of his best prose came to the birth when he was worked up to an extraordinary state of mental fertility and felicity. More often than not the great writer, or other great artist, when seen and heard in the flesh, is a disappointing figure to innocent persons who seek his acquaintance under the old illusion that the living, breathing man must be greater than his work. Seek not to "see Shelly plain." He may be plain indeed. Tennyson could be a boor, and the inexpressive grunts of Turner are notorious.

And yet this state of pregnant excitement is not a mystery wholly concealed from ordinary people or absolutely excluded from their experience. Almost everyone must at some time or other have found how it feels to be utterly absorbed in the writing of a private letter —how you lose count of time and have no sense of disagreeable effort; how words of a strange rightness come easily into your head and apt quotations drift into your reach; how some scene that you describe becomes more and more amusing to yourself, in recollection, while you describe it; and how at the end you are rather tired and rather happy, and read the thing through and say to yourself that you would never have thought you could do it so well.

That common experience is not different in kind, but only in the degree of its intensity, from an onset of creative passion in a great imaginative artist. Where such an artist differs most widely from the common run of men and women is in his power of inducing that exceptional condition in himself and of working it up to a pitch that for the rest of us is quite unattainable. For most of his time he may seem, and indeed he may be, quite a dull man, a humorless egoist, or a trumpeting bore. He may cut no figure at all among the wits and sages of a country house or a bar parlor. But, with a pen in his hand, he can "have a devil" at will, or at least some of the many times he wills it. In a way he is like a car with a quite commonplace basic speed but a remarkable power of acceleration. And in a way he is like those gifted fighting men in whom the manual exercise of combat means to light a wonderful fire in the blood. To them, battle brings ecstasy. They are ravished above pain and fear; and in that temporary trance of exemption from common checks upon fury, and of immunity from common maladies of the will, they can delightedly do and endure things preposterous or impossible in the eyes of cool common sense.

. . .

It is seldom that a great artist has anything new to say about life. The things that touch or amuse him are usually those by which the greatest number of ordinary people were touched and amused before him. The minds of Virgil and Sophocles, Shakespeare and Dante and Goethe seem in the main to have brooded over just those stable themes which elicit less memorable expressions of melancholy from Smith, Brown, and Jones — lost youth and severed friends and disappointed love and the consignment of beauty to dust and the frustration of hopes that once seemed too powerful ever to fail. If a great tragic writer were to arise in England today, it is likely that his musings on the perishable splendor of man's fate and the irreparableness of action would take the form most widely prevalent among the more sensitive portion of his countrymen — perhaps an afternoon sense of sad sunshine and overblown flowers, the outlived expectations of a melting empire on an earth that is rubbing its own features down and that moves always more and more slowly round a sun that is losing its heat. The theme would be commonplace. But when the great tragic writer had brooded upon it, then it would have gained the charm of a new and extraordinary intensity.

A great and available reserve of sheer intensity — intensity of perception and of emotion — it is in his possession of this that a great artist differs most deeply from his fellows. In no vague or rhetorical sense of the words, he sees and hears more intensely. Science tells us that what we call a sight or a sound is a product of two distinct forces. As waves break upon a seacoast, certain undulatory movements, that throb through the air break upon delicate shores in a man's eyes or ears. From the beach, so to speak, word is sent thereupon by a nerve to a special bureau of the brain; and, with this material in hand, the brain builds up for itself the song of a lark or the color and form of a rose in a world that, apart from this act of the brain, is utterly silent and dark. So there is no one rose or lark, perceived identically by us all. There are as many different roses or larks as there are different brains to make them. The flower or bird of the great artist's make, when his brain is working at its best, is made with an extraordinary concentration of care and delight. It is like a lover's handiwork, done for the beloved, not a journeyman's.

This intense constructiveness of vision goes beyond objects of physical sight. From the construction of single physical things, at the instance of the eye or on the prompting of the ear, it can pass easily on to the vivid framing of their implications: in Blake's much-quoted words it can see the world in a grain of sand, and heaven in a wild flower. It can go further and build up, always with a passionate relish for what it is producing, a kind of semi-sensuous image of something abstract and vague — the *lacrimæ rerum* of Virgil, life's falling tears, or the Wordsworthian sense of the world's loss of transfiguration as we grow up. But, however somber the theme, it brings to the artist no grief in the usual sense of the word. For grief disables, and this kind of vision empowers. It has been said that God is a person who feels all the pain there is in the world without being disabled by it at all. And that much of divineness there is in a great artist. When the excitement of writing Macbeth had worked Shakespeare up to the full height and heat of his powers, he saw the frustratory aspect of most people's lives with such intensity of clearness that, if he had not been an artist at work, he might well have thrown everything up and sat down to despair. But the heat of artistic emotion is always convertible into force of the constructive order. So the climax of intensity in this tragic vision brought no incoherent cry of pity or prostration, but the extreme opposite, the passionately perfect design of one of the most famous of the writer's "purple patches":

> To-morrow, and to-morrow, and to-morrow,
> Creeps in this petty pace from day to day
> To the last syllable of recorded time,
> And all our yesterdays have lighted fools
> The way to dusty death. Out, out, brief candle!

Life's but a walking shadow, a poor player
That struts and frets his hour upon the stage
And then is heard no more: it is a tale
Told by an idiot, full of sound and fury,
Signifying nothing.

. . .

To this supernormal level of impassioned constructiveness a writer, or any other artist, mounts by an ascending scale of interaction between the technical exercise of his craft — the act of word assorting and writing, of laying on paint, or of modeling clay, and the imaginative effort of penetrating to the essence, the inmost and uttermost significance, of the "subject" before him. You may see a painter start a portrait almost apathetically. He will handle his paint in a commonplace way. He will seem to see no more than you or I can see at a glance in the personality of his sitter. But soon the feel of the paint on the canvas begins to enliven his mind; and the mind thus quickened conceives a livelier curiosity about the creature before him. And then the mind that is piqued with this curiosity transmits in turn a share of its new animation to the working hand, firing it to do feats of swift sureness, summary selection, and eloquent brilliancy beyond its ordinary powers. And so this process of mutual stimulation continues till both the faculties engaged in it are forced up far above their natural human commonness. They rise to a point at which the artist is sometimes said, in the old phrase, to be "inspired."

The phrase may be uncritical. And yet it has been a measure of aptness. It does at least convey that a painter or a writer has attained a kind of self-attesting note of authority for which we cannot easily account. His lips may not be touched, but he speaks as if they were. And we listen as if they were, too. Out of some experience not given to ourselves, and not to be easily explained to us, he has emerged with an utterance which we cannot prove to be authentic, but which still imposes itself irresistibly upon our belief and our admiration. Somehow it carries about it an indefinable certificate that it is no skimble-skamble stuff, with nothing behind its façade. There shines through it still the intensity of vision and the immense sincerity of the emotion in which it had its origin.

Think how often you have seen some slippery politician put his hand upon his heart and vow that it is only "for the cause" that he has executed this little maneuver or that. Nobody minds him. And yet when Othello says, "It is the cause, my soul, it is the cause," you do not merely believe it. You probably feel that never till now have you fully known how appallingly sincere a man may be in trying to remain judicial under a tempest of pain. It is no rare experience again, to hear someone say that he is dying, and to know that it is true. In such a case you are probably touched by the words, but unless the dying man be a dear friend you will scarcely feel any such surging of emotion as shakes you when Antony says, "I am dying, Egypt, dying." For here you have not merely truth, but truth raised to higher powers of itself; not the simple overshadowing of life by death, but the immensity of tragic import that this obscuration may have for a mind enormously more susceptible to tragic impressions than our own.

There still remains that ultimate question. In virtue of what do these intrinsically plain arrangements of quite common words carry the germs of a rare and noble fever of the soul from a person long dead to persons living in another age and perhaps at the other end of the world? Is it that, even when masked in print, the written word retains the power of the spoken voice to give a subtle guarantee of its own authenticity, if authentic it be? So that in print, as well as in speech, the same words may stir us deeply in one case, and leave us quite cold in another? Does some intimation reach us that one man has written them with authority, and another only as the Scribes? If so, is the intimation "internal," as we say of literary evidence? Can it be traced in some more elusive quality in the actual words than any that literary criticism has yet marked down? In that passage quoted already,

> Beauty falls from the air:
> Queens have died young and fair;
> Dust hath dimmed Helen's eyes,

is there some delicately expressive quality of rhythm which carries with it the same overpowering effect of momentousness that a spoken assurance sometimes derives, in part, from the modulation of the living voice? Or can criticism only say that by some means which are out of its ken these heavenly lines do somehow convey a state of passionately poignant exaltation from the writer's mind to the fit reader's — and leave us to wonder whether the apparently countless sets of possibly communicative "waves," suspected, but not yet listed, that are said to ripple endlessly about the world, may include a set that enables the passionate stir of one mind to impinge directly on some specially sensitized tissue in other brains, with the aid of no more apparatus than certain verbal memoranda playing a quite subsidiary part in the business?

"What know I?" From this cascade of tough questions I take refuge, for my own part, in the safe old question of Montaigne.

JEANNE D'ARC[1]

Katherine Brégy

On Twelfth Night, the Feast of the Magi, in the year 1412, Jeanne d'Arc was born in the little Lorraine village of Domrémy. All the world knows, or misknows, her story; for while she and the Poverello of Assisi stand at opposite poles of sainthood, they have at least this in common, that they continue down the centuries to attract every possible variety of biographer. The just and the unjust have fought over Jeanne's faithful ashes — the German poet, the American humorist, the agnostic French philosopher, the paradoxical Irish dramatist have, each in his own way, contributed to her compelling immortality. And our own century has seen the final reparation for one of the greatest crimes in history: Jeanne looks down today not only from the walls of the Pantheon but from the altars of the Catholic Church.

There was never a cult more salutary than this cult of *La Pucelle* — never a canonization more timely in our professedly feminist and profoundly hazardous age. The curious fact is that Jeanne d'Arc should not be more confidently claimed, more universally exploited

[1]From *From Dante to Jeanne D'Arc,* Science and Culture Series, The Bruce Publishing Co., Milwaukee.

by women themselves, both within and without the Church; since there is scarcely in all history a figure who embodies in so quintessential a degree the ideals toward which modern womanhood is striving. We all remember the Westminster epitaph of Margaret, Duchess of Newcastle, for whose family it was proudly claimed that "all the brothers were valiant and all the sisters virtuous." But the goal of the modern woman, at its soundest and sanest and sweetest, is both higher and more inclusive — it would have the sisters valiant as well as virtuous, the brothers virtuous as well as valiant.

This is precisely the ideal which Jeanne d'Arc so simply and whole-heartedly fulfilled. Obviously she was a *specialist* in all her public career. The work which, for particular national reasons, she was called to do lay distinctly outside the normal province of womanhood — the way she did it, as distinctly within. Indeed, it is rather important to remember that there is nothing in life or art, nothing great or humble, nothing from darning socks to writing sonnets, which would not become more beautiful, more effectual, if done in that spirit of largeness and singleness and consecration which she embodied! Through the records of her Trial and Rehabilitation a thousand intimate personal characteristics flame out like golden banners. Concerning the childhood and girlhood when she was growing up in war-torn Domrémy — used to the more or less hopeless tales of English victory and French defeat, used also to the necessity of occasional flight with her family from predatory bands of soldiers, yet learning to sew and spin and watch the flocks, as became the daughter of a prosperous peasant farmer — we have a few charming but perfectly normal anecdotes. There is, for instance, the story of the neighboring verger whom Jeanne bribed by little presents of wool to work more diligently in his belfry: he had known all her brief life in the village, and testified to her grave and gentle modesty, her devotion to the offices of the Church, her helpfulness to the poor, and her industry, whether at the loom, the plow, or the pasture. Then come the artless depositions of the women of Domrémy, who used to walk to and from Mass with "Jeannette": who remembered her kneeling in the fields when the Church bells rang, or dancing with the other village maidens, or bringing nuts and provisions for the annual picnic at the Ladies' Tree on Laetare Sunday. "I did not know of Jeanne's departure," cried one of these women tristfully after the lapse of quarter of a century: "I wept much — I loved her dearly for her goodness and because she was my friend."

From quite another angle comes the testimony of those who knew the Maid during her fifteen months of militant service. The Sieur de Metz saw Jeanne first when she traveled up to Vaucouleurs in her shabby frock of red serge, pleading with Robert de Baudricourt for the third time for soldiers to lead her to the young dauphin at Chinon. She had been twice refused, and she never argued the subject; she simply returned to the attack. But the fire of unquenchable purpose was burning beneath this maidenly calm, and it blazed up when the knight inquired with mild curiosity when she wished to start. "Better at once than tomorrow," came the characteristic retort, "and better tomorrow than later!" That was at the very beginning of her public career — she scarcely knew as yet how to balance a lance on horseback. But when her poor, dazed sovereign was celebrating the mighty victory she had won for him at Orléans, and making the peasant-maid *grande chère,* the identical spirit answered him: "Noble Dauphin, hold not such long and so many councils, but start at once for Rheims and there receive your crown."

Jeanne's swiftness of thought and directness of action were a constant marvel to the men about her — men who too well remembered Agincourt, and had ceased even to hope aggressively. Probably they were also very much confused about the real rights of the French succession. There is a sense in which Bernard Shaw was correct enough in his contention that Jeanne d'Arc was the *first nationalist;* for almost alone of her century she seems to have perceived that the old feudal order was definitely passed, that the nations of Europe had become separate entities, and that each country belonged to the people living in it and to their own legitimate rulers. How she attained this sweeping vision is one of the amazing questions of her amazing life, for an unlettered girl can scarcely have worked out the matter philosophically. But either by the intuition of genius or the direct revelation of sainthood, she knew when a page of history had been turned. "Get back to *your own country,* God with you," she dictated in the first of those astounding letters addressed to the English regent, Bedford; "and if this is not done expect news of the Maid, who will shortly go to see you to your very great damage." Her going was to besiege Orléans in that May of 1430, where after two days of fighting she and her troops were completely victorious. It was the "sign" or seal of her divine mission which she had promised the doubting dauphin. . . . And being, during her trial two years later, hypocritically questioned about inciting her king to "shed human blood," she cited her efforts to negotiate peace with the neighboring duke of Burgundy, but insisted: "As for the English, the only peace with them is by their return to their own country, *to England*."

One little incident before the attack upon Jargeau reveals the winsomeness as well as the force of the mighty Maid. "Forward, gentle duke, to the assault!" she cried, bursting in upon his grace of Alençon about nine o'clock one morning. He protested that the assault was premature, and pleaded for delay; whereupon Jeanne, with that high queenliness of hers, gave the superb answer: "It is the right time when it pleases God, we must work when it is His will. *Travaillez, et Dieu travaillera!*" Yet never a prophet was gentler to the weakness of the flesh. "Ah, gentle duke," she said, turning back when she saw that her point was gained, "dost thou not know that I promised thy wife to bring thee back whole and sound?"

No one seems to have studied Jeanne more intelligently or more sympathetically during all this time than her *"beau duc,"* as she used to call him. D'Alençon was a prince of the blood royal, commander-in-chief, until her own coming, of the French armies, and his testimony is full of significance. He was hunting quails at St. Florent — having recently been ransomed at enormous price from a three-year imprisonment by the English — when news was brought of the young peasant girl who had come to Charles VII with the dizzying message that God had sent her to raise the siege of Orléans and drive the English out of France. Not unnaturally, the duke made his own way right speedily to the impoverished little court at Chinon — and his capitulation was immediate. Seeing, he believed; or it may be that believing, he saw. . . . Side by side they followed the weary marches, the daring, glorious engagements of her campaign of the Loire. It is not certain where d'Alençon was when the Maid was captured by the Burgundians at Compiègne and later sold to the English, or while the grim tragedy of her trial was being played to its end. But some twenty-five years later, when by order of Pope Calixtus III the doctors assembled in Notre Dame to inquire into the validity of the Rouen sentence, the duke came up to Paris to give his testimony. The picture of Jeanne's white fire of purity, her hatred of blasphemy and of the evil women who followed the camp, her tact in dealing with the various generals, her reverent piety, came upon him then in a wave of impassioned memory. "I think truly, it was God who led us," he declared of her brief generalship; and the sum of his deposition fell into these momentous words:

"I always held her for an excellent Catholic and modest woman; she communicated often, and at sight of the Body of Christ, shed many tears. In all she did, except in affairs of war, she was a very simple young girl; but in warlike things — bearing the lance, assembling an army, ordering military operations . . . she was most skillful. Everyone wondered that she should act with as much wisdom and foresight as a captain who had fought for twenty or thirty years. It was above all in making use of artillery that she was so wonderful."

Of course, d'Alençon erred in this last sentence. The wonder of Jeanne d'Arc was never more preëminent than when she faced her court of accusers (it cannot be said that the tribunal boasted any judges!) in the English citadel at Rouen. To martyrdom she marched valiantly enough in all truth, but each step of the way was fought soldier-wise. Every power on earth was marshaled against the girl: learning and treachery and might and brutality and — hardest of all to bear — the *appearance* of righteous authority. For these men, whom Jeanne knew to be fighting God, fought ostensibly in God's name! That was the consummate irony of it all. Bedford, the capable English regent, and his colleague of Winchester, were not content merely to imprison or to kill the Maid: they determined to impugn her entire work. They wished to place the ban of sacrilege and illegitimacy upon her king's coronation at Rheims. Hence it was decreed to try Jeanne for heresy and witchcraft — a wave of this latter phobia having, according to Pierre Champion, reached its sinister high-water mark in fifteenth-century Europe — before a tribunal of English sympathizers carefully suborned for the end in view. She seems to have taken no great trouble to conceal her scorn of them, and answered with so high a spirit that one of Henry's own soldiers was heard to exclaim: "This is a brave woman. Would she were English!" Without legal counsel, day after day and week after week, she faced her inquisitors with the same patient fire. . . .

The matter of these Voices cannot any longer be begged, since upon their authenticity the Maid of France quite literally staked her life. She left her home to lead the French armies to victory and the French King to his crown — and in the end went to the stake rather than abjure her mission — for the single reason that she believed herself a sword chosen and wielded by the hand of God. And she believed this because, as she herself declared, she had been told, so commanded, by "her brothers in Paradise." There is small strangeness, of course, to the Catholic mind, in this more personal and intimate manifestation of the mysterious Communion of Saints. The vessel of election in every age has been wrought for service — or it may be, merely guided toward the way of service — by hands other than material. And although Jeanne was rather a silent woman, always given to deeds rather than words, her testimony about the Voices, first during the dauphin's inquiry at Chinon, and later during the endless, hostile interrogations of the Rouen trial, was full enough to be quite intelligible. The first Voice spoke to her at Domrémy one summer afternoon when she was but thirteen — suitably enough, it was the heavenly warrior, Michael — saying simply: "Be good — go often to church." With the words came a light, and the young girl, standing alone in her father's homely garden, feared at first; but it was not Jeanne's way to fear anything very long, least of all an angel. . . . A little later on came the apparitions of St. Catherine and St. Margaret, while the messages became at once more definite and more incredible: she — Jeanne — must go over from Lorraine into France — she must relieve the siege of Orléans — she must lead her dauphin to the anointing and coronation of his Kingship! For five years she kept these persistent words in her heart, telling the visions neither to her family nor even to her confessor. Then she simply but deliberately set about accomplishing the impossible.

During the first year of her military leadership, Jeanne seems to have been confirmed almost constantly by her saints. "You have been to your counsel," she said to the dissenting generals when they were trying — as usual — to hold her back from action, "and I have been to *mine,* and the counsel of God shall be accomplished." After the coronation at Rheims she acted more or less on her own authority: her divine commission was fulfilled. And it was then that she met, together with splendid victories, her first real defeats. But she was able to prophesy within some three weeks the date of her capture at Compiègne, and in prison she was not abandoned. On one occasion the Voice woke her as she "slept for sorrow" in the Rouen cell.

"Was it by touching you on the arm?" inquired her inquisitors somewhat fatuously.

"It woke me without touching," Jeanne answered: and then, with heart-shaking simplicity, she rehearsed the exquisite little drama of consolation. No, she did not fall upon her knees, but she thanked the visitant for coming. "I was sitting on the cot; I joined my hands; I implored its help. The Voice said to me: 'Answer them boldly. God will help thee!' "

So now we come close to the most fundamental point of all — the *source* of Jeanne's visions. The Rouen judges declared that these apparitions proceeded from the devil, and they dealt with her accordingly. Mr. Anatole France and his school declared they came from her own noble but unsound imagination, and *they* dealt with her accordingly. But the Maid herself said they came from God: and after one momentary weakness of denial, she sealed her faith with blood and with fire. So the mind of the Church, believing Jeanne and judging her inspiration by its fruits, has after five hundred years so dealt as to place the crown of sainthood upon her head. . . . Now it does not seem that Jeanne was particularly introspective or at all analytical. She did not question, as our modern ages question, the *how* and the *why* of Almighty God. But she listened, as few have listened in this garrulous world — then with an *Ecce ancilla Domini,* she threw herself unreservedly into the work of His will. And just this "one rapture of an inspiration" was the basic need of her disheartened people. Only a miracle could have raised fifteenth-century France to any belief in its own desperate cause, and the miracle was — "Jeannette!" By the dynamic force of her own divine and vivid certainty she lifted up the hearts of men. It was not simply her genius which ended the Hundred Years' War and saved the nationhood of France. It was not even her sanctity.

It was the supreme, God-given belief in her own mission. And modern psychology has made it at least a little easier to understand that this belief is the one universal secret of hero and of saint.

But Jeanne's methods were all rational enough. Her angelic accolade brought no immunity from the daily lot of toil and pain. Like many another mystic, she was enormously efficient — and she knew only too well that she fought with armies of men, not of angels. She was the *practical idealist:* and that is why she was, at the beginning of this paper, suggested as so intimately significant to the woman of today, rather than because she raised the siege of Orléans or baffled the University of Paris. Almost unique in history was this peasant girl's *balance* of action and vision, of pride and humility, of strength and tenderness. She loved, indeed, to help bridge a moat or build a rampart; but she loved better still to kneel beside some dying French — or English — soldier. She used to say that she loved her banner forty times better than her sword! And best of all she loved to receive Holy Communion on the days when little children were allowed to bear her company to the church. For Jeanne walked not only by faith, but by what Coventry Patmore has pregnantly named the *corollaries* of faith. She believed largely — she gave all. And oftener than not, these corollaries are very human in expression. Love, as we know upon the highest authority, is translated by deed and by truth into obedience; and the whole counsels of perfection may underlie so simple a matter as walking up instead of down the street. It is all a matter of motive, of intention. The hero does great things: he may apparently do more than the saint. The difference is that the saint does great things for God! And then, fortunately for us, it is never possible, even in the highest and most potent life, to separate the universal from the personal. One of the personal characteristics of Jeanne d'Arc was her immense capacity for good work. She left much to God, but nothing to chance. Above this, she possessed three of the noblest virtues known to manhood or to womanhood: courage, simplicity, and the love of truth. They are none too common — in fact, they are rarer than most of us care to admit — but in them lies the hope of the race. And without them heroic sanctity, at least, is inconceivable. For courage is the belief in God and in self, a free and large virtue, the daughter of hope and the mother of action. And simplicity is the grace of shooting straight, without détour or distraction or self-consciousness; in one sense it may be called divine concentration. While to love truth, and to serve truth, with a passion absorbing life and death alike, is not far from the Kingdom of Heaven.

No virtue, and no vice, is confined to any single century. But in a sense almost symbolic, Jeanne summed up the particular virtues of medievalism—its absolute and beautiful faith, its quixotically self-sacrificing devotion to a cause, its enormous, youthful energy and vitality in action: just as her persecutors summed up the medieval vices of cruelty, superstition, oversubtlety, and rapacity. In more ways than one, her passing marked the sunset of the Middle Ages—the dawn of Modernity. A little boy of Rouen, standing in the crowd before that awesome conflagration, would have witnessed in his manhood the final expulsion of the English from his country—*and* the invention of printing! He might easily have lived on to see the birth of those two typical Renaissance gentlemen, absolute egoists and absolute monarchs, Francis I of France and Henry VIII of England. Before he died, Martin Luther—champion of the religious revolt which had so long been rumbling throughout Europe—would have been born in Germany; while Spain would be rejoicing in the fall of the Moorish empire and the discovery of the New World.

SATAN AMONG THE BIOGRAPHERS[1]

Samuel McChord Crothers

By Satan I do not mean the evil spirit who goes about like a roaring lion. I have in mind the Satan who appears in the prologue to the Book of Job. He is the adversary, the one who presents the other side. When the sons of God came together, then came the adversary among them. He belonged to the assembly, but he sat on the opposition bench. He introduced questions which had occurred to him as he walked up and down the earth. His function was to challenge

[1]By permission of Houghton Mifflin Co.

generally received opinions. There was Job. Everyone looked upon him as a man who was as righteous as he was prosperous. But was he? Satan suggested that his character should be analyzed. Take away Job's prosperity and let us see what becomes of his righteousness.

Now that critical spirit has entered into the biographers and influenced their attitude toward what they used to call the subject of their sketch. It used to be taken for granted that the tone of biography should be eulogistic. "Let us praise famous men and the fathers who begat us." This indicates how closely biography is related to genealogy. The text is often transformed into, "Let us praise the fathers who begat us, and if we have sufficient literary skill we may make them famous."

The lives of the saints have a great sameness, for it is necessary that they should be saintly. Even when their adventures are of the most astonishing character, the chronicler must throw in a word now and then to show that they are not acting out of character. Thus that wild Irish saint, St. Brandan, who went careering over the Western Sea like another Sindbad the Sailor, must have a religious motive for his voyage. The chronicler declares, "seven years on the back of a whale he rode, which was a difficult mode of piety." Had Brandan been a layman, we might have admired him for his acrobatic gifts. Being a saint, we must see him balancing himself on the back of a whale as a pious exercise.

Biographers on the whole have been a rather modest folk and have had scant recognition in academic circles. Thus there are numberless professors of history — ancient and modern — but when recently a Minnesota college established a professorship of biography, the title seemed a strange one. The educational world has followed the example of Nature — so careful of the type, so careless of the single life.

But a new school of biography has arisen, and it is of interest to compare it with the old. The great difference is in the attitude of the biographer toward his subject. The attitude of the old biographer was that of a painter who was commissioned to paint the portrait of a great man. He wished to make a likeness and to make it as lifelike as possible; but he had to recognize the proprieties. The painter is frankly on the outside, and can give only so much of character as is revealed in the countenance. So the biographer was dealing frankly with externals. What the great man did or said could be recorded, but what he meant could only be guessed. Every man's mind was his castle, and there were private rooms into which the public had no right to intrude. If a person were very inquisitive, he might, if he got the chance, peep in through the windows of the soul; but that was as far as he could go. He was necessarily an outsider.

But of late the biographer has become bolder and instead of peeping in, has taken to breaking and entering. His method is described as "penetrating." We see him not only prowling in the consciousness, but penetrating into the most remote portions of the subconsciousness. We see him throwing his flashlight upon motives concealed from nearest friends. It is the era of the X-ray, and human character cannot escape the methods of research. The biographer attempts to show us a man's mind as viewed from the inside. How he gets inside is his business—not ours.

Let us compare John Morley's *Gladstone* with Mr. Strachey's *Queen Victoria.* Morley takes his subject very seriously. Gladstone was a great man, and knew it, and so did everyone else. He lived in a great period and was an important part of it. Morley was a friend who followed his career with respectful but discriminating interest. He was in a position to know a great many facts. But he did not intrude. A vast number of details are given, but the result of it all is that we feel that we are looking *at* Gladstone and not through him. We know what he did and what he said, and we know what interpretations his friend Morley put upon his words and actions; but we can only guess at his ulterior motives. We see the conclusions to which he came but not all the mental processes by which they were reached. Mr. Gladstone always appears to us clothed and in his right mind. If he had any unlucid intervals, they are not a part of the record. As for exploring Gladstone's subconscious mind, his friend would as soon have thought of poking about in his host's pantry without asking leave. What did Gladstone think when he wasn't addressing the public or preparing to address it? The biographer would say, "That is none of your business, nor is it mine."

The same impression is made by Trevelyan's *John Bright.* We feel that we know John Bright as well as his constituents knew him. It never occurs to us that we know him better.

Turn to Mr. Strachey's delightful biography of Queen Victoria. We have a surprise. We are conscious of a new sensation. To say that the book is stimulating is faint praise. It is intoxicating. Here is biography with its crudeness and irrelevancies distilled away. We get the essential spirit.

It is not that we are behind the scenes as an ordinary playgoer who is allowed this novel experience, that he may see how things look on that side of the curtain. We are behind the scenes as a playwright, who is also his own stage manager, may be behind the scenes. We feel that somehow we have an intimate knowledge of how the lights should be arranged to produce the best effect. We have no illusions ourselves, but this allows us to watch the production of the play with keener intellectual interest.

We see Queen Victoria, not as her admiring subjects, with superstitious ideas about royalty, saw her, but as she would have seen herself, had she been as clever as we are. The revelation has all the charm that an autobiography would have if a person could speak about himself without vanity and without self-consciousness.

In reading the *Confessions* of St. Augustine or Rousseau, we feel that they are trying to tell the whole truth about themselves, but we are not convinced that they have succeeded. They confess certain sins that attract their attention; but what of those failings which St. Paul describes as "the sins that so easily beset us"? Some of these beset a person so closely that he doesn't know that they are there. There are certain commonplace faults which are seldom confessed by the most conscientious. I have never come across an autobiography in which the writer drew attention to the fact that his friends often found him a little wearing.

Mr. Strachey gives us Victoria's autobiography written by somebody else who saw through her. There is an awareness of all her limitations and a cool appreciation of her middle-class virtues. We sympathize with her efforts to live up to her station in life. We see her successes and admire her pluck. When she makes mistakes we recognize that she is thoroughly conscientious. Her judgments are often shrewd. She is rather muddle-headed in regard to the new problems of the day, but not more so than her constitutional advisers. She is a real character, and we know her in the same way that we know Becky Sharp and Mrs. Proudie. We feel that we not only know what she did, but we know the moving why she did it.

We know also why she did not do more. It was because it wasn't in her to do more. And her environment was exactly fitted to her personality. We feel that it was no mere coincidence that she lived in the Victorian Age.

In *Eminent Victorians* Mr. Strachey reversed the methods practiced by writers like Walter Scott. They took some well-known historical character and allowed their imagination to play about it. The result was Historical Romance, or Romance founded on fact.

Mr. Strachey takes well-known historical characters of the last generation, like Arnold of Rugby, Cardinal Manning, Chinese Gordon, and Florence Nightingale, and shows us that they have become in a short time little better than noted names of fiction. Every man is his own myth-maker and his friends and enemies collaborate in producing something quite different from the reality. The ordinary biography is, therefore, little more than a collection of facts founded on a fiction. The problem, then, is not simply to reëxamine the facts, but to rearrange them so that they will tell a true story and not a false. The biographer is like a typesetter. He must first distribute the type and then set it up again to form new words and sentences.

No saint in the calendar had a legend more firmly fixed and authenticated than Florence Nightingale. The public not only knew what she did, but was convinced that it knew what kind of a person she was. She was the lady with the lamp, the gentle ministering angel who went about through the hospitals in the Crimea. She was the one who brought the feminine touch to war.

Mr. Strachey does not change the outlines of her story. That is a matter of historic record. She did all and more than we have been taught to believe. But he shows Florence Nightingale as an altogether different kind of person.

The feminine gives way to a masterful personality. Florence Nightingale was the stuff that successful politicians and captains of industry are made of. She appears as a formidable person, abrupt in manner, often bitter in speech, the terror of evil-doers, and still more the terror of incompetent well-doers. She was strong-minded, neurasthenic, intense in her antipathies, and not pleasant to live with; but she got things done.

She was born in a wealthy family. She wanted to have her own way, but was never quite sure what it was to be. This was an endless trouble to her family, who never knew what to do with Florence, or rather what Florence would let them do for her.

When marriage was suggested, she writes, "The thoughts and feelings I have now I can remember since I was six years old. A profession, a trade, a necessary occupation, something to fill and employ all my faculties I have always felt essential to me. Everything has been tried — foreign travel, kind friends, everything. My God, what is to become of me?"

Then came the Crimean War with the breakdown of the hospital service. At last she had her own way and it proved a gloriously right way. She won immortal fame.

The war ended, and Florence Nightingale had fifty years of invalidism. But she was the same energetic, pugnacious personality. Almost to the end she refused to wear the halo prepared for her by the public which she continued to serve faithfully and acrimoniously. We are made to feel that Florence Nightingale loved her fellowmen, but not as an amiable person loves those friends whom he finds congenial. She loved mankind as a thoroughly conscientious person might love his enemies. "Sometimes," says Mr. Strachey, "her rages were terrible. The intolerable futility of mankind obsessed her, and she gnashed her teeth at it."

This is a triumph of biographical reconstruction. We see Florence Nightingale as great and good, though with very different virtues.

When I turn to Arnold of Rugby and Chinese Gordon, I begin to have misgivings. Mr. Strachey's portraits are marvelously clear, but there is something lacking. Looking through the eyes of Thomas Hughes and Dean Stanley, we see Dr. Arnold as a great man. We cannot expect Mr. Strachey to share their awe, for Dr. Arnold was not his schoolmaster. But we do not feel that he accounts for the impression the Doctor made on those who knew him.

As for General Gordon, we see him not through the eyes of a hero worshiper, but as he appeared to one who had no sympathy with his enthusiasms. That irony which is delightful when playing around the figure of Queen Victoria seems out of place when directed toward the hero of Khartum. There was a touch of fanaticism about Gordon, just as there was about Cromwell. But Carlyle's Cromwell stands out against the background of eternity, and is justified. Strachey's Gordon stands condemned against a bleak background of common sense. Even the final tragedy is told without any relenting admiration. The whole thing was so unnecessary. When all was over, we are told of the group of Arabs whom Slatin Pasha saw, one of whom was carrying something wrapped in a cloth. "Then the cloth was lifted and he saw before him Gordon's head. The trophy was taken to the Mahdi; at last the two fanatics met face to face."

Thirteen years after, Kitchener fearfully avenged his death at Omdurman, "after which it was thought proper that a religious ceremony in honor of Gordon should be held at the Palace in Khartum. The service was conducted by four chaplains and concluded with a performance of 'Abide with Me,' General Gordon's favorite hymn. General Gordon, fluttering in some remote Nirvana the pages of a phantasmal Bible, might have ventured a satirical remark. But General Gordon had always been a contradictious person, even a little off his head perhaps—though a hero; and besides he was no longer there to contradict. But any rate, all ended happily in a glorious slaughter of twenty thousand Arabs, a vast addition to the British Empire, and a step in the peerage for Sir Evelyn Baring."

What is it that offends in this? It is the unfairness not to Gordon but to his contemporaries. Gordon represented an ideal that belonged to his generation. It was British imperialism touched with a sense of responsibility for the government of the world. We have broken with imperialism, but we ought to be touched by the heroism. In brushing aside the judgment of his contemporaries with a touch of scorn, we feel the kind of unfairness of which Cato complained when, after he had passed his eightieth year, he was compelled to defend himself in the Senate. "It is hard," he said, "to have lived with one generation, and to be tried by another."

Each generation takes itself seriously. It has its own ideals and its own standards of judgment. One who has made a great place for himself in the hearts of his contemporaries cannot be dismissed lightly because he does not conform to the standards of another period. The visitor to Colorado is taken by his friends for a drive over the high plains in sight of the mountains. Pointing to a slight rise of ground that is little more than a hillock, the Coloradian remarks: "That we call Mount Washington, as it happens to be the exact height of your New Hampshire hill."

The New Englander recalls, with shame at his provincialism, the time when he thought Mount Washington sublime. When he recovers his self-respect, he remembers that a mountain is as high as it looks. It should be measured not from the level of the sea but from the level of its surrounding country. Mount Washington seen from the Glen looks higher than Pike's Peak seen from the window of a Pullman car.

In like manner a great man is one who towers above the level of his own times. He dominates the human situation as the great mountain dominates the landscape of which it is a part.

II

A very alluring opportunity is offered for the scientific study of personages who have made a great place for themselves in history. They have all of them been more or less ailing, and have had "symptoms" of one kind and another. An American medical man has given us a number of volumes entitled *Biographic Clinics.*

Mr. Frederick Chamberlain has given us a large volume on *The Private Character of Queen Elizabeth.* Elizabeth is defended against the charges made by her enemies, but the defense is damaging to the romance which has gathered around her name. She is treated as if she were an out-patient in the General Hospital. The first thing, of course, is to take her family history. Then we have sixty pages of the medical history of Elizabeth Tudor.

The writer is most conscientious, and says, "Items are numbered consecutively, accompanied by Elizabeth's age and the date of each. It is attempted to confine each disease or illness to one group." In her long life she had a number of ailments. We are spared not one detail. Following the itemized health record, there are twenty-five pages of "The Opinions of Medical Experts." Mr. Chamberlain, who is not by profession a medical man, presented the data he had collected to the leading consultants, to get their opinion as to what was the matter with Queen Elizabeth.

Sir William Osler was rather brief in his answers to the questions. While agreeing that, judging from the records, the patient could hardly be said to be in good health, he says, "Apart from the dropsy, which may have been nephritis, and the smallpox, the descriptions are too indefinite to bear any opinion of much value." To

Question IV — What was her probable health during the years for which there are no data supplied? — Dr. Osler answers, "Impossible to say."

Sir Clifford Allbutt is equally unsatisfactory. "Would it be too much to say that after her fifteenth year she was practically an invalid with the possible exception of the years for which no data are supplied, directly or indirectly?" He answers, "It would be too much."

But Dr. Keith of the Royal College of Surgeons gives an opinion at great length, accompanied by a clinical chart. We learn that she had anemia, stomach and liver derangements, septic conditions of the teeth, and the pain in her left arm may have been from rheumatism.

The reader's apprehensions, however, are somewhat relieved by the consideration that all these ailments did not come at once but were scattered over a period of sixty-nine years. Dr. Keith adds very justly that the diagnosis would be more complete had the physician had an opportunity to personally examine the patient. "In the case of Queen Elizabeth, the modern physician is separated from his patient by more than three hundred years; he has to attempt a diagnosis on historical data."

By the way, it is interesting to see how the course of history modifies scientific opinion. When she was about eighteen, Elizabeth had an illness which Dr. Howard at first diagnosed as the most extreme form of kidney disease. "But," he adds, "it seems hardly possible that the subject of nephritis of so severe a type would live to be nearly seventy." He therefore inclines to the theory that the trouble was "acute endocarditis and mitral regurgitation"; and then he adds, with the fairness characteristic of a scientific man, "The same objection to longevity might be raised to this diagnosis also."

Modern pathology may throw light on some historical characters, but one feels that it has its limitations. Not only do the modern physicians find it difficult to make a complete diagnosis when the patient has been dead for three hundred years, but they find it difficult to keep to the highest standard of professional ethics when speaking of the practitioners of a former day.

Thus Sir Clifford, speaking of the doctors who treated Queen Elizabeth, says: "My impression is that in the sixteenth century medicine was below contempt. In Queen Elizabeth's time Clowes did somewhat, and possibly, Lowe; but really all the medicine of value was in Italy; and only by studying in Italy could our doctors then have known anything. Some few did, of course. The rest were hard-shell Galenish and quacks."

This is rather hard, coming from a consultant of the twentieth century who was called into a case that belonged to medical men of the sixteenth century. The fact that these medical men had kept the patient alive for almost seventy years, while the modern diagnosticians would have given her up at twenty, ought to count for something.

I am willing to admit that pathological inquiries may have their uses for the biographer, but there are limits. In this sphere pathology may be a good servant, but it is a bad master. The same may be said of psychology. The psychologist in his own sphere is a modest and hard-working person. The advancement of any science within its own territory is always slow work. If one is to get results he must work for them and share them with others.

III

But there is a border line between the sciences which is a fair field for adventure. The bold borderer, with a few merry men, may make a foray and return with booty. The psychiatrists and psychoanalysts have invaded the field of biography in force and are now engaged in consolidating their conquests. Biography is a particularly inviting field. To psychoanalyze a living person takes a great deal of time and patience. But to psychoanalyze historical personages and to point out their various complexes and repressions and conflicts is an inviting pastime. There is no one to contradict.

The old-time theologians in discussing predestination ventured into the recesses of the Divine Mind. Assuming that God both foreknew and foreordained man's fall, they asked which had the priority, foreknowledge or foreordination. Did God foreknow that man would fall and therefore foreordain that he should be punished everlastingly? So said the sub-lapsarians! With more rigid logic the supra-lapsarians contended that foreordination is absolute and independent of all contingencies. God foreordained man's creation, his fall, and his punishment in one decree, and of course he foreknew that the decree would be fulfilled.

Theologians today are more modest and are inclined to admit that there are some things which they do not know. But there are biographers whose minds seem to be built on the high supra-lapsarian plan. When we open the book we feel that everything is foreordained. There are no contingencies. The man's character being determined, the biographer presents us with the incidents which illustrate it. We know the kind of person he is, and his deeds are predetermined.

The clear-cut character sketches in which a man represents a single trait are interesting, but they are most sharply defined when we know only one incident. Some of the most familiar characters of the Bible are known only from a chance word or mere gesture. "Gallio cared for none of these things." Generations of preachers have held up Gallio as an example of the sin of indifference. He was the kind of man who, if he lived now, would neglect his religious privileges and forget to register at the primaries. But was Gallio that kind of man? All we know about this Roman magistrate is that he dismissed a case over which he had no jurisdiction, and in regard to which he had little interest. Had we a glimpse of him on another day, we might revise our opinion.

The name of Ananias has been used as a synonym for habitual liar. But in the Book of the Acts it is not said that Ananias *told* a lie; all that is said is that he sold his possessions and laid part of the price at the Apostle's feet. In other words, Ananias did not, on this occasion, make a complete return of his personal property.

When this method is applied to persons whose lives are well known, there will always be a great deal of skepticism. How can we be sure that the clever writer has happened on the right clue to the character he undertakes to reveal to us?

In the *Mirrors of Downing Street,* and *Painted Windows,* and *Uncensored Celebrities,* we have interesting studies of character. We have snapshots of distinguished statesmen and churchmen. But do we really get inside the minds of these persons; and, if we did, should we be as wise as we think we should be?

Take this question in regard to Mr. Lloyd George. The writer, speaking of that statesman's sudden change of front, asks, "How came it that the most pronounced pacifist of a pacifist liberal cabinet, who had, six weeks before, begun a passionate crusade against armaments, on the fateful August 4, 1914, gave his voice for war?"

Now I venture to say that no biographer, furnished with the latest instruments of psychological precision, exploring the recesses of Mr. Lloyd George's mind but ignoring the tremendous events of crowded days, could give the right answer to that question.

Why does it happen that a quiet householder in Kansas, who is shingling his kitchen roof, is seen the next moment frantically digging himself out of a mass of débris? You cannot understand the sudden change of occupation by an intensive study of the Kansas mind—you have to take into account the nature of a cyclone.

The student of Mr. Lloyd George's mind says: "He is always readier to experience than to think. To him the present tick of the clock has all the dignity of the Eternal. If thought is a malady, he is of all men most healthy. The more he advocates a policy, the less he can be trusted to carry it through."

This is clever analysis, but the question intrudes—How does the writer know so much about what goes on inside of Mr. Lloyd George's mind? Why may he not be doing a good deal of rapid thinking while he is experiencing so vividly? And why may not this thought directed to the question of the moment be fairly accurate? Granted that he changed his mind rapidly, did he change it any more rapidly than the circumstances with which he had to deal changed? Granted that he didn't bring anything to its logical conclusion. Amid the tremendous forces that were struggling in the world, could anything be brought to its logical conclusion? There is room here for honest doubt.

The biographer may well sharpen his wits by means of psychology, but he must not allow a formula to stand in the way of an individual. From the rigid supra-lapsarians we are always happy to escape to the biographers, ancient or modern, who are of the humanistic school. In their pages we see characters developing unevenly under the stress of circumstances. We cannot tell what a person is capable of doing till he does it; and even then we are not always sure that we have all his reasons. There is no program that is followed. Unexpected things are all the time turning up and bringing into play powers which we had not looked for. We are compelled to revise our first impressions both of the man and his times. The more the individual is observed, the more individualistic he appears to be. He becomes less significant as a symbol and more interesting as a personality.

There, for example, is Plutarch's Cato. No attempt is made to analyze his character or to account for his idiosyncrasies. We see him just as he happened to be. He doesn't correspond to any formula. He is just Cato.

Cato was gray-eyed and red-headed. He was a self-made man. He worked hard and liked to wear old clothes when he was in the country. He was fond of turnips and of cabbage. He was very thrifty, and when his slaves began to grow old he sold them to save the depreciation in his property. He disliked flatterers, but was not averse to praising himself. He loved sharp jests. He was a popular orator and a good soldier. When he was elected to office, he put a super-tax on articles of luxury; he cut the pipes by which wealthy householders had surreptitiously drawn water from the public fountains; he reduced the rates of interest on loans, and conducted himself with such outrageous rectitude that all the best people turned against him.

All these incidents have to do with the outward life of Cato. Plutarch is content to set them down with the remark,"Whether such things are proof of greatness or of littleness of mind, let each reader judge for himself." Yet somehow they make the red-headed Roman seem very real to us. We know him in the same way that we know a contemporary. If we were to drop into Rome on election day and be told that the paramount issue was "Anything to beat old Cato," we should feel at home. We should probably vote for Cato, and regret it after the election.

We have this sense of complete reality in the characters of statesmen and soldiers which we come upon in the crowded pages of Clarendon. Here is Clarendon's Hampden. It is the portrait of a gentleman drawn by another gentleman who was his enemy. But one would prefer to have Clarendon as an enemy rather than another man as a friend.

John Hampden "was a gentleman of good family in Buckinghamshire, and born to a fair fortune, and of a most civil and affable deportment. In his entrance into the world he indulged to himself all the license in sports, and exercises, and company, which was used by men of the most jolly conversation. Afterwards he retired to a more reserved and melancholy society, yet preserving his own natural cheerfulness and vivacity, and above all a flowing courtesy to all men. . . . He was of that rare affability and temper in debate, and of that seeming humility and submission of judgment, as if he brought no opinion with him but a desire of information and instruction; but he had so subtle a way of interrogating, and, under the notion of doubts, insinuating his objections, that he left his opinions with those from whom he pretended to learn and receive them. . . . He was indeed a very wise man and of great parts and possessed with the most absolute spirit of popularity, that is, the most absolute faculties to govern the people, of any man I ever knew."

In Clarendon's eyes John Hampden was a very dangerous man. "He begat many opinions and motions, the education of which he committed to other men." Of one thing we are not left in doubt. He was a very great man, though he fought on the wrong side.

"He was very temperate in diet, and a supreme governor over all his passions and affections, and had thereby a great power over other men. He was of an industry and vigilance not to be tired out or wearied by the most laborious; and of parts not to be imposed upon by the most subtle or sharp, and of a personal courage equal to his best parts; so that he was an enemy not to be wished wherever he might have been made a friend." It is after all these qualities have been acknowledged that Clarendon adds: *"His death therefore seemed a great deliverance to the nation."*

No psychologist by the most painstaking analysis could produce the effect that these words make upon us. We are conscious of John Hampden's personality as a force against which strong men are contending. We not only see the man himself, but we see why some men loved him and others resisted him. He was part of a mighty movement, which he largely directed.

Biography cannot be reduced to a science, but it may rise into the finest of the arts. It is the art of reproducing not merely the incidents of a great man's life, but the impression he made on those who knew him best.

SHAKESPEARE'S PROSE

Francis Thompson

It might almost be erected into a rule that a great poet is, if he please, also a master of prose. Tennyson in modern times is the great example of a poet who never spoke without his singing-robes. But we feel an instinctive conviction that Tennyson's prose would have been worth having; that it would have been terse, strong, and picturesque — in another fashion from the pictorial English of the Anglo-Saxon revivalists. Indeed, there is manifest reason why a poet should have commanded over "that other harmony of prose," as a great master of both has called it. The higher includes the lower, the more the less. He who has subdued to his hand all the resources of language under the exaltedly difficult and specialized conditions of meter should be easy lord of them in the unhindered forms of prose. Perhaps it is lack of inclination rather than of ability which indisposes a poet for the effort. Perhaps, also, the metrical restraints are to him veritable aids and pinions, the lack of which is severely felt in prose. Perhaps he suffers, like Claudio, "from too much liberty."

Though Shakespeare bequeathed us neither letters nor essays, nor so much as a pamphlet, he has not left us without means of estimating what his touch would have been in prose. The evidences of it are scattered through his plays. There is, of course, the plentiful prose-dialogue. But this can only indirectly give us any notion of what might have been his power as a prose writer. Dramatic and impersonal, it is directed to reproducing the conversational style of his period, as developed among the picturesque and varying classes of Elizabethan men and women. It is one thing with Rosalind, another with Orlando, another with Beatrice, another with Mistress Ford or Master Page, and yet another with his fools or clowns. Thersites differs from Apemantus, plain-spoken old Lafeu from plain-spoken Kent. At the most we might conjecture hence how Shakespeare talked. And if there be anywhere a suggestion of Shakespeare's talk, we would look for it not so much in the overpowering richness of Falstaff, as in the light, urbane, good-humored pleasantry of Prince Hal. Prince Hal is evidently a model of the cultivated, quick-witted, intelligent gentleman unbending himself in boon society. In his light dexterity, his high-spirited facility, one seems to discern a reminder of the nimble-witted Shakespeare, as Fuller portrays him in the encounters at the "Mermaid." No less do the vein of intermittent seriousness running through his talk, the touches of slightly scornful melancholy, conform to one's idea of what Shakespeare may have been in society. One can imagine him, in some fit of disgust with his companions such as prompted the sonnets complaining of his trade, uttering the contemptuous retort of Prince Hal to Poins: "It would be every man's thought, and thou art a blessed fellow to think as every man thinks; never a man's thought in the world keeps the roadway better than thine."

The noble speech of Brutus to the Romans would alone prove that Shakespeare had a master's touch in prose. The balance, the antithesis, the terseness, the grave simplicity of diction make it a model in its kind. Yet one can hardly say that this is the fashion in which Shakespeare would have written prose, had he used that vehicle apart from the drama. It was written in this manner for a special purpose—to intimate the laconic style which Plutarch records that Brutus affected. Its laconisms, therefore, exhibit no tendency of the poet's own. To find a passage which we do believe to show his native style we must again go to Prince Hal, in his after-character of Henry V. The whole of the King's encounter with the soldiers, who lay on his shoulders the private consequences of war, affords admirable specimens of prose. But in particular we quote his chief defensive utterance:

There is no king, be his cause never so spotless, if it come to the arbitrament of swords, can try it out with all unspotted soldiers. Some, peradventure, have on them the guilt of premeditated and contrived murder; some, of beguiling virgins with the broken seals of perjury; some, making the wars their bulwark, that have before gored the gentle bosom of peace with pillage and robbery. Now, if these men have defeated the law, and outrun native punishment, though they can outstrip men, they have no wings to fly from God: war is His beadle, war is His vengeance; so that here men are punished, for before-breach of the King's laws, in now the King's quarrel: where they feared the death, they have borne life away; and where they would be safe, they perish. Then if they die unprovided, no more is the King guilty of their damnation, than he was before guilty of those impieties for the which they are now visited. Every subject's duty is the King's, but every subject's soul is his own. Therefore should every soldier in the wars do as every sick man in his bed, wash every mote out of his conscience; and dying so, death is to him advantage: or not dying, the time was blessedly lost, wherein such preparation was gained: and in him that escapes, it were not sin to think that, making God so free an offer, He let him outlive that day to see His greatness, and to teach others how they should prepare.

The whole is on a like level, and it is obvious that Shakespeare's interest in his theme has caused him for the moment to forsake dramatic propriety by adopting a structure much more complete and formal than a man would use in unpremeditated talk. It is Shakespeare defending a thesis with the pen, rather than Henry with the tongue. And you have, in consequence, a fine passage of prose, quite original in movement and style, unlike other prose of the period, and characteristic (we venture to think) of Shakespeare himself. You would know that style again. Close-knit, pregnant, with a dexterous use of balance and antithesis, it is yet excellently direct, fluent, and various, the rhetorical arts carefully restrained, and all insistence on them avoided. Despite its closeness, it is not too close; there is space for free motion: and it has a masculine ring, a cut-and-thrust fashion, which removes it far alike from pedantry on the one hand and poetized prose on the other. Such, or something after this manner, would (we think) have been Shakespeare's native style in prose: not the ultraformal style he put (for a reason) into the mouth of Brutus.

With the Baconian dispute revived, it is interesting to ask how such passages compare with the known prose of Bacon. The speech of Brutus might possibly be Bacon's, who loved the sententious. But surely not a typical passage such as we have quoted. Take an average extract from Bacon's *Essays:*

It is worth observing that there is no passion in the mind of man so weak, but it mates and masters the fear of death; and, therefore, death is no such terrible enemy when a man hath so many attendants about him that can win the combat of him. Revenge triumphs over death; Love delights in it; Honour aspireth to it; Grief flieth to it; nay, we read, after Otho, the Emperor, had slain himself, Pity (which is the tenderest of affections) provoked many to die, out of mere compassion to their Sovereign, and as the truest sort of followers.

Grave, cold, slow, affecting an aphoristic brevity, and erring (when it does err) on the side of pedantry, could this style take on the virile energy and freedom of movement, the equipoise of concision and fluency, which we discern in Henry's speech, as in all Shakespeare's characteristic passages? We cannot think it. And that other style of Bacon's exemplified in the *Reign of Henry VII,* expanded, formal, in the slow-moving and rather cumbersome periods which he deems appropriate to historic dignity, is yet more distant from Shakespeare. The more one studies Shakespeare, the more clearly one perceives in him a latent but quite individual prose-style, which, had he worked it out, would have been a treasurable addition to the great lineage of English prose.

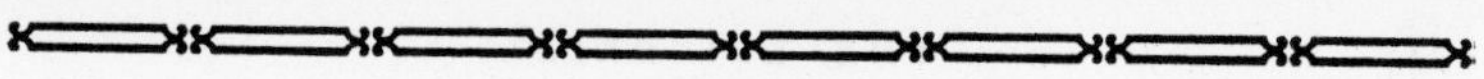

F. THE EDITORIAL

FEBRUARY 12, 1809[1]

America

One hundred years ago, Abraham Lincoln, postmaster at New Salem in the State of Illinois, was down at the heel, and at his wits' end. He had just made a few dollars on a job of surveying for John Calhoun, but work of that kind promised few fees, and those far between. There was always a welcome for him at Aunt Hannah Armstrong's, where he could play with the children, or read, as he rocked the cradle of the youngest with his big foot, and then share the family's meal of cornbread, mush, and milk. But he was now twenty-five years old, and prospects were dark.

The grocery store which he had bought in partnership with the bibulous Berry had "just winked out," leaving him with nothing but a reputation for honesty, and a crushing debt. In desperation he had turned his hand to anything that offered. He had split rails, helped in a smithy, and hired himself out as a farm hand. As postmaster of New Salem, he could easily carry all the letters delivered to the office in his hat, and he did. His emoluments for the year, even if they came to him in silver coin, he could have held in one big clenched fist. He might yet be obliged, he reflected, to make his living as a blacksmith, although that distasteful occupation would leave him little time for reading. Then there was Anne Rutledge. Did the girl really mean to marry John McNeill? The smooth-spoken, prosperous McNeill made him conscious that he was big, awkward, ill-clad, and shy, and put him at a disadvantage, he thought, with this blue-eyed, auburn-haired girl from Kentucky.

Born in a log cabin in Kentucky, Lincoln at twenty-five was inured to hardship and disappointment. As his mother held him

[1]Birthday of Abraham Lincoln. The editorial was published February 10, 1934.

in her arms, crooning to him the old songs that her people had carried with them across the seas from England, she may have dreamed, as mothers will, that this child at her breast would one day equal in renown the heroes of whom she sang to him. But it was the lot of Nancy Hanks to give us Lincoln "and never know." She did not know that he was to enkindle in the world a flame which, please God, can never be extinguished so long as men love liberty and seek after justice. She did not know that he was to live for fewer years than three score, and ending a pilgrimage over hard and lonely roads, leave a name that the world can never forget or fail to honor.

She did not know these things. Nor, looking at Lincoln in New Salem, "getting an education," as he said, "by littles," did anyone know them.

Add twenty-five to the sum of his years. On his fiftieth birthday, Lincoln was a moderately successful country lawyer. He had served four terms in the State legislature, and at the age of forty had finished his only term in Congress. Then he went back to his law office in Springfield, and kept aloof from politics until the Autumn of 1854. In the following year, he appeared before the legislature as a candidate for the Senate of the United States. He was beaten by Lyman Trumbull. Three years later, he was a candidate against Douglas, and was beaten again. At the end of that campaign he wrote a friend, "I am absolutely without money now, even for household expenses." Once more he went back to the practice of law to get his bread, "disappointed but not discouraged." At fifty years of age, Lincoln was giving a lecture now and then, usually on "Discoveries and Inventions," in some little Illinois town, but without much success. The dreams his mother dreamed seemed farther than ever from fulfillment.

But the man had long been trained to face defeat. It did not discourage, however much it disappointed him. He was growing in power of thought and in sure insight. His lawyer companions on the Illinois circuit, rising in the morning, would find him huddled over the gray embers of the open fireplace of the inn, silent and abstracted. In the turn of the night, and as the cold dawn crept over the prairies, he envisioned the glory to which he gave undying expression in the "Gettysburg Address." What he said at Gettysburg did not spring on the moment from the tired brain of a sorely tried man, nor did the occasion inspire them. Those thoughts had lived in his mind for more than forty years. They were born of the years of his childhood in Kentucky, when his mother read to him from the Bible; of the years in the clearings in Indiana, where, so soon, his mother died, bidding him with her last breath to love God, obey his father, and be good to his little sister; of the long years in Illinois, first of striving and of obscurity, then of a widening fame and greater conflict on a national field. All the years of his life, from Kentucky to Washington, with their wisdom and experience, won through hardship, disappointment, and failure, merged at last to make him

> The kindly-earnest, brave, foreseeing man,
> Sagacious, patient, dreading praise, not blame,
> New birth of our new soil, the first American.

So runs our thought, yet who can say what it was that made Lincoln Lincoln? In him was malice toward none, but charity for all, a keen intelligence, ambition without guile, a conciliating spirit that fitly tempered his unbreakable tenacity of purpose. But what made Dante a poet, Beethoven a musician? To each God gave rare opportunities for sacrifice, and after that He gave to Dante, to Beethoven, and to Lincoln, "genius." There is no other answer.

WORDS THAT LAUGH AND CRY

New York Sun

Did it ever strike you that there was anything queer about the capacity of written words to absorb and convey feeling! Taken separately they are mere symbols with no more feeling to them than so many bricks, but string them along in a row under certain mysterious conditions and you find yourself laughing or crying as your eye runs over them. That words should convey mere ideas is not so remarkable. "The boy is fat," "The cat has nine tails" are statements that seem obviously enough within the power of written language. But it is different with feelings. They are no more visible in the symbols that hold them than electricity is visible on the wire; and yet there they are, always ready to respond when the right test is applied by the right person. That spoken words, charged with human tones and lighted by human eyes, should carry feelings, is not so astonishing. The magnetic sympathy of the orator one understands; he might affect his audience, possibly, if he spoke in a language they did not know. But written words—how can they do it! Suppose, for example, that you possess remarkable facility in grouping language and that you have strong feelings upon some subject, which finally you determine to commit to paper. Your pen runs along, the words present themselves, or are dragged out, and fall into their places. You are a good deal moved; here you chuckle to yourself, and a half a dozen of lines further down a lump comes into your throat, and perhaps you have to wipe your eyes. You finish, and the copy goes to the printer. When it gets into print a reader sees it. His eye runs along the lines and down the page until it comes to the place where you chuckled as you wrote; then he smiles, and six lines below he has to swallow several times and snuffle and wink to restrain an exhibition of weakness. And then someone else comes along who is not so good a word juggler as you are, or who has no feelings, and swaps the words about a little and twists the sentences, and behold the spell is gone, and you have left a parcel of written language duly charged with facts, but without a single feeling.

No one can juggle with words with any degree of success without getting a vast respect for their independent ability. They will catch the best idea a man ever had as it flashes through his brain and hold on to it to surprise him with it long after, and make him wonder that he was ever man enough to have such an idea. And often they will catch an idea on its way from the brain to the pen point, turn, twist, and improve on it as the eye winks, and in an instant there they are, strung hand in hand across the page and grinning back at the writer: "This is our idea, old man; not yours!"

As for poetry, every word that expects to earn its salt in poetry should have a head and a pair of legs of its own, to go and find its place, carrying another word, if necessary, on its back. The most that should be expected of any competent poet in regular practice is to serve a general summons and notice of action on the language. If the words won't do the rest for him it indicates that he is out of sympathy with his tools.

But you don't find feelings in written words unless there were feelings in the man who used them. With all their apparent independence, they seem to be little vessels that hold in some puzzling fashion exactly what is put into them. You can put tears into them, as though they were so many little buckets; and you can hang smiles along them, like Monday's clothes on the line; or you can starch them with facts and stand them up like a picket fence; but you won't get the tears out unless you first put them in. Art won't put them there. It is like the faculty of getting the quality of interest into pictures. If the quality exists in the artist's mind he is likely to find means to get it into his pictures, but if the feelings are in the writer and he knows his business, they will get into the words; but they must be in him first. It isn't the way the words are strung together that makes Lincoln's Gettysburg speech immortal, but the feelings that were in the man. But how do such little, plain words manage to keep their grip on such feelings? That is the miracle.

THE HOUSE OF A HUNDRED SORROWS[1]

New York Times

The walls are grimy and discolored. The uneven floors creak and yield underfoot. Staircases and landings are rickety and black. The door of every room is open. Walk along these corridors. Walk into this room. Here is a sickly boy of five, deserted by his mother, underfed, solitary in the awful solitude of starved, neglected childhood. "Seldom talks." Strange, isn't it? Some, many children, never "prattle," like your darlings. They are already old. They are full, perhaps of long, hopeless thoughts. There are plenty of other "kids"

[1]Edward M. Kingsbury.

in this tenement. Here is one, only three. Never saw his father. His mother spurned and abused him. He is weak and "backward." How wicked of him when he has been so encouraged and coddled! Doesn't know any games. How should he? Do children play? Not this kind. They live to suffer.

In Room 24 is Rose, a housemother of ten. Father is in the hospital. Mother is crippled with rheumatism. Rose does all the work. You would love Rose if she came out of Dickens. Well, there she is, mothering her mother in Room 24. In Room 20 age has been toiling for youth. Grandmother has been taking care of three daughters who lost their mother. A brave old woman, but what with rheumatism and heart weakness, three-score-and-ten can't go out to work any more. What's going to happen to her and her charges? Thinking of that, she is ill on top of her physical illness. A very interesting house, isn't it, Sir? Decidedly "a rum sort of place," Madam? Come into Room 23. Simon, the dollmaker — but handmade dolls are "out" — lives, if you call it living, there. Eighty years old, his wife of about the same age. Their eyesight is mostly gone. Otherwise they would still be sewing on buttons and earning a scanty livelihood for themselves and two little girls, their grandchildren. The girls object to going to an orphans' home. Some children are like that.

You must see those twin sisters of sixty-five in Room 47. True, they are doing better than usual on account of the coming holidays; making as much as $10 a month, whereas their average is but $6. Still, rents are a bit high; and the twins have been so long together that they would like to stay so. In Room —, but you need no guide. Once in The House of a Hundred Sorrows you will visit every sad chamber in it.

If your heart be made of penetrable stuff, you will do the most you can to bring hope and comfort to its inmates, to bring them Christmas and the Christ.

"For I was hungry, and you gave Me to eat; I was thirsty, and you gave Me to drink; I was a stranger, and you took Me in; naked, and you covered Me; sick, and you visited Me; I was in prison, and you came to Me" (Matt. xxv. 35, 36).

THE UNKNOWN SOLDIER[1]

New York Herald

That which takes place today at the National Cemetery in Arlington is a symbol, a mystery, and a tribute. It is an entombment only in the physical sense. It is rather the enthronement of Duty and Honor. This man who died for his country is the symbol of these qualities; a far more perfect symbol than any man could be whose name and deeds we knew. He represents more, really, than the unidentified dead, for we cannot separate them spiritually from the war heroes whose names are written on their gravestones. He — this spirit whom we honor — stands for the unselfishness of all.

This, of all monuments to the dead, is lasting and immutable. So long as men revere the finer things of life the tomb of the nameless hero will remain a shrine. Nor, with the shifts of time and mind, can there be a changing of values. No historian shall rise to modify the virtues or the faults of the Soldier. He has an immunity for which kings might pray. The years may bring erosion to the granite but not to the memory of the Unknown.

It is a common weakness of humanity to ask the questions that can never be answered in this life. Probably none to whom the drama of the Unknown Soldier has appealed has not wondered who, in the sunshine of earth, was the protagonist of today's ceremony. A logger from the Penobscot? An orchardist from the Pacific coast? A well driller from Texas? A machinist from Connecticut? A lad who left his hoe to rust among the Missouri corn? A longshoreman from Hell's Kitchen? Perhaps some youth from the tobacco fields, resting again in his own Virginia. All that the army tells us of him is that he died in battle. All that the heart tells is that some woman loved him. More than that no man shall learn. In this mystery, as in the riddle of the universe, the wise wonder; but they would not know.

What were his dreams, his ambitions? Likely he shared those common to the millions: a life of peace and honest struggle, with

[1]Frank M. O'Brien.

such small success as comes to most who try; and at the end the place on the hillside among his fathers. Today to do honor at his last resting place come the greatest soldiers of the age, famous statesmen from other continents, the President, the high judges, and the legislators of his own country, and many men who, like himself, fought for the flag. At his bier will gather the most remarkable group that America has seen. And the tomb which Fate reserved for him is, instead of the narrow cell on the village hillside, one as lasting as that of Rameses and as inspiring as Napoleon's.

It is a great religious ceremony, this burial today. The exaltation of the nameless bones would not be possible except for Belief. Where were Duty and Honor, the wellsprings of Victory, if mankind feared that death drew a black curtain behind which lay nothing but the dark? So all in whom the spark of hope has not died can well believe that we, to whom the Soldier is a mystery, are not a mystery to him. They can believe that the watchers at Arlington today are not merely a few thousands of the living but the countless battalions of the departed. "Though he were dead, yet shall he live" —there is the promise to which men hold when everything of this earth has slipped away.

All the impressive ritual of today would be a mockery if we did not believe that, out in an infinity which astronomers cannot chart or mathematicians bound, the Unknown Soldier and all the glorious dead whom we honor in his dust are looking down upon this little spinning ball, conscious of our reverence. And when noon strikes, signal for the moment of silent prayer, few of those who stand with bared head will lack conviction that the rites at Arlington are viewed by other than mortal eyes. Only in that spirit may we honor the Unknown Soldier and those who, like him, died for this Republic.

Unknown, but not unknowing!

TYPES OF THE TIME

The Commonweal

If the temper of human society is really changing, we ought to see a definitely new type of representative citizen emerge. But do we? It is possible to declare that certain familiar samples are disappearing — that the supply of dapper, oily, amiable Kreugers and Insulls is dwindling rapidly, that a specific kind of business man has now virtually exhausted himself by suicide, and that the well-dressed politician, Jimmie Walker model, may henceforth make his home on the Riviera. Yes, some even hold that the spectacular desperado of the Al Capone ilk is beginning to look a bit like last year's silk shirt.

Yet this appraisal is merely tentative. Many another well-nigh institutionalized citizen is bearing up rather well. The Columnist is as chic as ever; and when, like Will Rogers in the *Times,* he grows worse and worse, people seem to laugh harder and harder. Hunk Anderson is doing nicely as Knute the Second. Bill McGeehan is making the same old funny remarks. The incoming Congress promises to be even more orthodox than usual. Campaigners for Barbasol, Listerine, and other precious additions to the American standard of living manifest no change of tactics since 1928. And, last but not least, the President-elect declares firmly that he will not endeavor to be a "new" species of chief executive but that he swears by Woodrow Wilson, model 1916.

Perhaps as much could be alleged concerning the great electorate. The jobless who knock at the back door in quest of a quarter, a meal, or an old pair of pants are just as deferential, equally as good-natured about it all, as they were in those halcyon days when everybody imagined that the "slump" was a mere hangover from a financial gin party. Collectors for community-chest drives and such worthy enterprises will tell you that the same givers are giving, and that the same pikers are piking. Nearly everybody has, to be sure, lost a little of that good old breeziness which the boys at the periscope told us was normal to the seas of American life. It used to be that if a bond salesman made forty a week he tried to have his name put on the waiting list at the Bankers Club. At present not even the lifelong members of the Club will admit that they are earning as much as that. But why put too much emphasis upon a mere loss of élan? In the secret recesses of his heart, the American citizen is waiting for the day—in German it used to be called *Der Tag* and sounded sinister—when United States Steel will climb back to 100 and a Duesenberg will no longer seem the symbol of a lost golden age.

We hate to generalize, but the conclusion to which one arrives after making the survey indicated above is that business is still the center of our intellectual and social existence. Such changes as are manifest are taking place in this center. A different variety of executive is emerging here and there—a man considerably more troubled than he has ever previously been, dubious about the vitamin value of favorite slogans, and ready to welcome the point of view of once despised "experts." It is true that he still potters around in generalities, vigorously debating questions that are a bit beside the point. But he has girded his loins with seriousness and remains determined to fight a hard battle with destiny in spite of technocracy and kindred terrors.

Europe seems to have produced one distinctively new citizen, and to have surrounded him with some other human novelties more or less interesting. The political dictator, real or would be, originally grew out of a Socialist movement tried by the war and its aftermath. There is no longer any use dwelling upon the peculiar virtues of Lenin and Mussolini, both of whom have been fathers of revolution. More recent, however, is the type of overlord, real or imaginary, which a harassed democracy seems to desire. First Poland, then Hungary, and then Germany have virtually entrusted government to a real soldier, lest one only partly real gain control of the situation. In all these cases, the underlying force has been nationalism, concentrating the more or less chaotic yearnings of a people in a single personage. And by way of compensation there have appeared a number of interesting revolutionists, most of them little known but some famous enough to get their pictures taken by American press photographers.

Of new religions the most impressive is Communism, for that is a religion. If the pseudo-deity it has enthroned happens to be nothing more concrete than a sound and deeply human ethical impulse — the demand of justice which lives on in man's heart — there is, nevertheless, every reason to believe that the creed has vitality and steadfastness. It may well be that between this vociferously godless faith and Christianity there is more common ground than lay between the doctrine of the Saviour and such philosophical cults as New Thought and Unitarianism. At all events, it is sufficiently obvious that henceforth the struggle for human souls will be fought out between this new and rebellious heresy and the Christian faith. And so it is not wholly accidental that during recent years the Church herself has witnessed a great flowering of heroic virtue among the poor and the untutored — Therese Neumann, Matt Talbot, Margaret Sinclair.

Just as the literature of the gilded decade made capital of the vices, pleasures, and quandaries of the prosperous, young and old, so is a steadily growing body of writing filled with those wide reaches of social emotion generated by the unrest of the time. In America we have, as yet, seen comparatively little of it. Some few revolutionary novels have been written in the United States, but (like the *American Spectator*) they belong to the age of the I. W. W. and the suffragettes rather than to the years in which we now live. Mr. Dreiser is not quite as out-of-date as Mr. Winston Churchill, author of *Richard Carvel;* but in a few years more, the first will be unreadable while the second may, to some extent, be reread. But if we take some such representative instance as the German Georg Rendl's *Vor den Fenstern,* it is possible to catch a glimpse of the human earth upon which millions are at this moment walking. There is something very new in this book — something at once terrible and yet sweet, echoing the going of man to his doom in the company of hope. In this book it is possible to see first the weight that lies upon the world, but second also the strength of the bearer. Christianity will not fail. It will be tried, its human exponents will sometimes be found wanting. But it will revive and remain.

Wherefore we shall not permit ourselves to be as pessimistic as appears to be the fashion. After all, there are good reasons for rewriting, in terms of our country and of the world, these lines from Mr. Chesterton's hard-fighting and still rather jovial weekly: "Despite the squalor and misery that is rampant in England, despite the danger of anarchy from men who are being driven into the ranks of Communism, despite the desperate case we are in with such 'leaders' as we have in this plight, we believe that England is still the best place to live in, for a thousand and one reasons which do not need to be told here. . . . Having observed with horror the attempts of politicians to make England a land fit for heroes to live in, we are less ambitious. We will rest content if we can make England a land fit for humans to live in. And in the words of the old song, 'We've got a long way to go!' " That is a brave note, but it is possibly the truly right one.

Fit for humans to live in! Well, it has at least become a world of men and women, mere men and women, once again. Gone are the strutters who were made up like supermen. Gone are the tricks by which wealth could be dressed into the semblance of a king. There is just one disturbing noise on earth just now—the rumble of the millions. They may do a great deal of damage. They will probably be badly mistaken, if they do not run amuck. They will say things in which there is not a grain of sense. But no one can deny to them the pleasure of speedy liberation from some recent false gods.

"HUMANITIES" IN THE TECHNICAL SCHOOLS

America

Last month, a report was published by James D. Cunningham, chairman of the trustees of Armour Institute, a Chicago school, purporting to answer the question "What is wrong with the training in our technical schools?" The report was written after the directors of sixty of the most extensive industries in the country, requiring large numbers of trained men, had been consulted. Some of our more advanced educators may be surprised to learn that what these directors found most fault with was the exclusion from the technical schools of that group of studies which our fathers called "the humanities."

The modern graduate, wrote the directors, is so narrowly trained that often he does not understand the practical application of the theories he has learned. He lacks "directness and energy" and appears to be guilty of negligence or indifference, simply because he has never learned to express himself in word or in work. At school, his range of interests has been exceedingly narrow, and he learns with difficulty after his graduation that even a technician must be a man if he hopes to succeed in his profession. Other faults pointed out by the directors are inadequate powers of observation, inability to appreciate the value of work that is not engineering work, immature judgment, and inaccuracy. "We have a mandate from those who employ our graduates," writes Mr. Cunningham. "They tell technical educators they must diversify, and pay greater attention to the human elements."

It is interesting to note the reforms suggested by the report. Since employers report that technical graduates "won't think, if they can possibly avoid it, and even then not logically," the technical school should offer compulsory courses in philosophy. Since most of them are inclined to believe that good English is not necessary in their professional work, courses in English composition and literature should be instituted. History, economics, sociology, and elementary law will be useful in broadening the interests of the student and in teaching him the meaning of human relations. The student must learn that the world is a larger place than a shop or a laboratory, and that, in fact, the real world is not made up of material things, but of men and women. In brief, the technical school must endeavor to humanize the student, to make him a man as well as a technician; and it is believed that the old-fashioned humanities are about the best means the school has of achieving these desirable ends.

Now that our professional schools are recognizing the value of the humane studies, one may hope that the colleges will soon reach the same stage of enlightenment. By reason of the elective system, bulwarked by the "credit" system, it is quite possible for a youngster to spend four years at college, and emerge from the experience untouched by culture, and with views on life which would hardly reflect credit on an unwashed pagan. The technical schools fell into the error of confounding wisdom with knowledge, but they are recognizing their error, and promise reform. When our colleges and high schools are ready to repent and confess, the reform will be complete.

AN UNSPEAKABLE ACT OF SAVAGERY[1]

Virginian Pilot

As the Democratic hosts prepare to rededicate themselves anew to fairness and justice, the bustling Southern city in which they are to meet is disgraced by an unspeakable act of savagery. There is no other way to describe the performance of the eight armed white men who yanked Robert Powell, 24-year-old Negro, from a hospital cot on which he lay with a bullet in his stomach, and hanged him from a bridge just outside the city. Powell was under the charge of killing a detective in a shooting match from which he himself emerged with an apparently mortal wound. In the event of his recovery, he was headed for the courts. But to this Texas mob neither Death nor Justice was an acceptable arbiter. Nothing would satisfy them but a loathsome act of murder carried out against a human being while he lay in agony with a bullet in his entrails.

Houston, which is said not to have had a lynching in fifty years, is understandably stirred by this foul thing laid on its doorsteps just when it was anxious to show itself to the world at its cleanest. The City Council made an immediate appropriation of $10,000 for an investigation to be carried out by a committee representative of both races. A grand jury has been ordered to drop all other business to conduct an immediate inquiry. The Governor has offered a reward for the capture of each participant in the lynching and sent a special detail of Texas Rangers to assist the Houston police in the hunt. Apparently, the spotlight that beats on Houston at this particular time has had something to do with the energy with which the authorities have acted. Ordinarily, Texas Justice proceeds in

[1]Louis I. Jaffe.

these matters with considerably less dispatch and excitement. But this is no time to inquire too closely into motives. One of the proudest cities of Texas has been polluted by one of the foulest forms of mob murder, and it is a matter for general satisfaction that the authorities are moving so energetically to repair the damage to Texas' good name. If the perseverance of the authorities is in keeping with their initial burst of energy, one or more of the group that bravely did to death a crippled man lying on a hospital cot may see the inside of the Texas penitentiary.

The year that saw four months pass without a single lynching has now accumulated five of them. Five lynchings in six months represent a proportional reduction in savagery from last year's record of sixteen lynchings in twelve months, but the year is only half gone and no one may be too confident. We have come a long way from the dark days of 1892 when America celebrated the 400th anniversary of its discovery with two hundred and fifty-five lynchings, but we have not yet arrived at that social abhorrence of this crime that must precede its practical extinction. When eight presumably decent and rational beings can gain the consent of their conscience to rob a hospital bed for the purpose of executing summary vengeance, and when, as was the case a few days ago in Louisiana, two Negroes are torn from their guards and lynched because they were brothers of another Negro who was accused of murder, it must be recognized that the rise and fall of the lynching curve is governed by racial passions that remain still to be brought under civilized control.

ADVANCING BACKWARD[1]

The Nation

It is said that toward the close of the Civil War a patriotic Southern newspaper, anxious to maintain the morale of its readers, pub-

[1]From *The Nation* (New York), December 31, 1924. Reprinted by the kind permission of the editor.

lished the following dispatch: "Our glorious army is rapidly advancing backward and the enemy is retreating after it." For the truth of this story we do not vouch, but we do give solemn assurance that a metropolitan daily recently headed an article "Rush of Progress Menace to the World, says Rockefeller."

Progress a menace? What, then, does "progress" mean? It sounds like a meaningless paradox. One would not say that a man was dying from excess of health, but one can, it appears, speak in all seriousness of a civilization which is going backward because it is "progressing" too fast. If there is any word of which the modern world has made a shibboleth, "progress" is the word, and in the language of popular thought it has no definite meaning.

Asked to define it the average man would doubtless give some fairly satisfactory reply; unconsciously he uses it to mean no more than any increase in size, in power, or in speed. Words are but counters, and sometimes it makes little difference what they are taken to mean; but it makes a great deal of difference when an important word happens to mean one thing in theory and another in practice. When progress became the religion of the modern world and came to be identified with things which are not necessarily in themselves good, the present age of confusion began. Gradually men forgot that speed might be uncomfortably hurrying them nowhere and that power might destroy civilization itself. Ceasing to criticize their definition they ceased to criticize their aims, and the result is knowledge and speed and power which are constantly increasing without any proportionate gain in happiness or virtue. There is wealth enough to make every man comfortable and power enough to relieve him of all except a comfortable minimum of work, but there is no immediate prospect that poverty will disappear or that the majority of men will be released from the necessity of deadly toil; yet the average man never doubts that the world is progressing at an ever-increasing rate. His eyes glitter with enthusiasm when he speaks of the size of his city, which is stifling him with its congestion, he points with pride to accumulated wealth, which is crushing him; he will even regard with complacency the prospect of being blown sky-high with the rest of his family by an aerial bomb because he can rejoice in the "progress" which makes such an event possible.

The present age has little use for logical subtleties; "facts, not theories" is its motto. Yet a little dialectic might save civilization. No frequenter of the Platonic Academy would ever have made a word the corner stone of his faith without first defining it. Plato did not know countless things which we know, but had he known them he would have seen to it that something better came of them than the mad world in which we live. He would have laughed at progress which goes backward and he would have called a halt in the perfection of the machine until he had learned to use it for instead of against himself. We, having already so much power that we are in danger of destroying ourselves, think of nothing except how to make it greater. We can go anywhere we like and faster than we need to go; few realize that it is time to ask where it is most worth while to go.

THE MANIA FOR CLASSIFICATION

Catholic World

It is a common practice, especially among those who have a penchant for cataloging things and persons, to divide all human beings into two groups, Good and Bad, Rich and Poor, Learned and Unlearned, Washed and Unwashed, White and Colored, Optimists and Pessimists, Conservatives and Liberals, Aristotelians and Platonists, Up-to-Daters and Old Fogies, and so on. The cataloging need cease only when one can no longer think of a brace of epithets. Of course, such classification is clumsy and scientifically inaccurate. The joke of the matter is that most of us don't fit exactly into any one of the groups. We are neither rich nor poor, not altogether good or bad; we are only semi-learned, we are not perfectly white (this paper is white but a live man is pinkish or brownish. Once I saw a white woman. She was what I think they call a platinum blonde, but the platinum was over her face as well as in her hair, and though she had beautiful features she had made herself quite ghastly). Take again the division into conservatives and radicals.

Aren't we all both? Sometimes radical, sometimes conservative, or radical and conservative at the same time.

Obviously the divisions are imaginary and arbitrary. Nevertheless they are convenient. So here goes for one more that happens to serve my purpose. All mankind is divided into realists and idealists. The realists — roughly speaking — are the business men, especially "hard-headed" business men; industrial magnates; bankers, domestic and international; soldiers, not volunteer but professional; statesmen and their little brothers the politicians; legal advisers to all the above; heads and members of governmental bureaus and departments; "steering" committees; lobbyists; bosses, district leaders and their henchmen, who are not in politics for their health; and in general all who love to call themselves "men of affairs." One and all they hold that industry, finance, government and all matters of importance are forever beyond the ken of the common people and must be left to experts — the experts being themselves. They are the knowers and the doers. There is no nonsense about them, no foolish sentiment; they are just realists.

On the other side of the invisible line of demarcation are the rest of us, poets, artists, students, dramatists (those of them who take their profession seriously), religious people (especially those who carry religion to extremes such as saints and mystics), prophets, preachers, moralists, philosophers, metaphysicians (if any remain). The realists lump them together and label them all dreamers, visionaries, unpractical people who stand idly by while the realists are running things. And it wouldn't be so bad — say the doers — if the visionaries would *only* stand by. But they interfere, they get in the way, they do fool things and mess up matters. They are all of the breed of Don Quixote — not that the realists have read the chronicle of the doings of the poor pseudo-knight of La Mancha, but they have heard that his chief exploit was tilting at windmills. Precisely! that's the sport of these crack-brained idealists. We that do things in the world ought to be thankful to — let's see what was the author's name? Cervantes? Yes, we owe Cervantes a debt of gratitude for giving us a symbol for dreamers, reformers, moralists and all other meddlers while we are trying to make things go smoothly for them.

Obviously the world today, if not always, is in the grip of the realists. They look upon idealists with the same mingling of pity and scorn that Mr. Jiggs looks upon his wife's singing teacher, or as our friend the "hard-headed business man" looks upon a matinée idol or a long-haired violinist who goes about playing his fiddle to hysterical women. Your man of affairs says with a gesture of resignation that he supposes such cracked-pots must exist — the world is full of petty nuisances — but of one thing he is sure, they must not be permitted to have anything to do with business or government. No Sir! keep them out. So the realists have held control, and the idealists have been side-tracked.

The result is what we see and what we know. Business and government and politics are in a chaotic condition, and the pompous fellows who said "Leave it to us" are now confessing one after another, "We don't know what did it, and we don't know what to do about it." But the idealists know. It is "Realism" that has wrought the devastation, shaken the financial and industrial and political world to its foundations, and it will be no credit to the realists if the whole structure doesn't come crashing down.

THE COFFIN OF THE KING

The London Times Weekly

The lid of the sarcophagus of King Tutankhamen has been raised; and Mr. Howard Carter, Mr. Mace, Mr. Burton, and the others assembled in the tomb have looked upon that which no eye had seen for thirty-two centuries — the coffin and the carved face of a monarch who was buried five hundred years before Homer sang. Beneath the shrouds lay the gigantic gilded coffin, in the form of the King's body; his face of gold, with crystal eyes, a lifelike portrait; the signs of kingship on his brow; the flail and the scepter of kingship in his crossed hands. At the moment it seems but a small matter that the coffin of King Tutankhamen is the most magnificent ever discovered. The capital fact, that which makes every reader of the news glow with something like personal pride, is that the coffin was there. For once success has been dramatic and complete. A splendid service has been done to art and history. A great undertaking has been faithfully and wisely carried out with consummate skill. The story is rich in the mysteries of the fitness of exquisite design and marvelously adjusted coincidence. For thirty-two centuries the body of the King lay undisturbed in the darkness, the dryness, the stillness, the sameness, which were the only conditions in which it could be preserved, with all those accessories whose value to knowledge is as great as their beauty, whose beauty is enhanced by their personal appeal. The sun of Egypt blazed down upon the sands, and the heavens wheeled in their course for thousands upon thousands of nights and days. The King and his treasures, "rolled round in earth's diurnal course with rocks and stones and trees," were no more known to the living men about them than their fleeting hours and ephemeral hopes and fears were known to his still, deserted frame. Other tombs were rifled; other bodies were discovered, to become material for science and gazing stocks to far peoples. King Tutankhamen's time was not yet. It was ordained that he should wait for an age that could value and use the discovery better than its forerunners, because it had sufficient knowledge, not only to gauge the importance of its treasure-trove, but to preserve the least fragment that could enrich the learning and the senses of present and future times. With a fitness very rare in mortal concerns, the time, the task, and the men came together; and after nearly sixteen years of labor, of adventure, of towering hopes and sickening disappointments, of luck both magically good and maddeningly bad, of exasperating difficulties and intoxicating successes, the work is done. The King's tomb has yielded up its secret.

Other tombs have been opened, other mummies have been found. But never before have modern eyes looked upon a Royal sarcophagus, a Royal coffin of Egypt, intact since its funeral rites. And that is not all. The body of King Tutankhamen is not, doubtless, the last kingly body of ancient Egypt that research will light upon. Yet two qualities, besides its priority in time, mark off this discovery from others that are possible. We are all by this time so well acquainted with a monarch whose very name was unknown to us less than two years ago that he appeals to us almost as closely as our own King Henry V or King Charles.

We have seen photographs of his very wine-strainers and his walking-sticks; we may see them for ourselves in Cairo, if art and science can preserve them from falling to pieces in our garish light and air after their long seclusion. We have learned of the love that lived between him and his Queen. We have realized this mighty King, who died and was buried 3,000 years and more ago, as a human being like ourselves; and it is improbable that any other Egyptian monarch will touch us with so intimate a personal appeal. Moreover, it is admitted that history and archeology are great gainers by the accident that the tomb, so nearly missed, so hazardously discovered, was the tomb of Tutankhamen and not of another. His reign fell, as we have read, at an abnormal period of marked transition in the history of his strange and world-old kingdom. He it was who turned from the new ways of an idealistic monotheism back to the old ways of the concrete and dogmatic religion of his country. Other tombs may throw equal light on the still mysterious history of the art that seems to have spread from ancient Egypt to the Mediterranean and thus has poured an influence even into our own civilization. When all the records have been examined, it will be strange if history, and especially the history of religion, which is the history of the human mind, does not learn from the tomb of Tutankhamen something which no other tomb could have revealed.

Be that as it may, the value of the discovery to art and learning may be trusted to grow only the clearer as time strips it of the excitement that naturally gathered about an event so thrilling. For the moment the excitement must hold the field. For once a human effort has made a story which might have been built up by a fine craftsman in story-telling. From the first published groping to the final triumph the tale has kept men, women, and children in many lands agog with interest; and not a man of us but has envied Mr. Howard Carter. To plan a great adventure, to set about it, to rejoice and to suffer in its course, to achieve it definitely, completely, victoriously, before the eyes of the world — that falls to the lot of few. Mr. Howard Carter is not only fortunate. He has suffered in his toil, in difficulties acknowledged and concealed, and in the loss of his friend and patron, who made the adventure possible. And besides his daring and his pertinacity, he exercised two unspectacular qualities, the lack of which might have spoiled his enterprise. The one is reverence: the other is patience. He has entered the resting-place of a King in order that human knowledge may be the richer and the human spirit the more clearly known. And, for his patience, none but they can tell how hard he and his invaluable fellow-workers must have found it again and again to be patient, when the final achievement came within reach, only to float away.

RARITY

The New Yorker

Whenever life begins to pall on Dr. Anderson and his assistants at the Public Library, some wag mentions the Ulster County *Gazette* of January 4, 1800, and everyone feels more cheerful. The *Gazette* is a standard joke at the Library. Every week from one to four people bring in copies of the January 4 issue, which announces the death of Washington, and offer to sell it for a thousand dollars or so. The joke is that, as far as is known, no original copy of that issue is in existence. (If it were, it wouldn't be worth more than fifty or a hundred dollars.) There are, however, a million bogus copies—literally. Sixty different reproductions are known. The Library has specimens of thirty of these. No two are alike. No real facsimile of the original exists because when the earliest copy was made, in July, 1825, there were no mechanical means for making facsimiles, and the original has since been lost. The counterfeit Ulster County *Gazettes* have appeared in large numbers on various festive occasions. Copies were sold at the Philadelphia Centennial Exposition in 1876 for a nickel apiece. One reason for there being so many is that apprentice printers used to set up the *Gazette* as a test of their ability as compositors. Another is that an old gentleman who hailed from Frederick, Maryland, made his living by selling copies of the *Gazette* at fairs, carnivals, pageants, and other public events all over the country. He had the copies printed and then soaked them in tan vats to make them look old.

The counterfeit *Gazette's* greatest triumph came right in New York. Two years ago it popped up in a window display of rarities in the Wurlitzer Building, alongside a Stradivarius worth thirty thousand dollars.

THE EDITORIAL WE[1]

Woman's Home Companion

The editor is used to being asked, "How do you get to be an editor?" Yet she never seems to have a satisfactory answer. Secretly I suspect she shares the opinion that editors are neither born nor made — they just happen.

It's a little difficult to say just what an editor is, for her position is largely defined by what she edits. Newspapers, trade papers, weekly or monthly magazines have different policies, schedules and methods. An editor's job on *Harper's* for example is as different from an editor's job on *Women's Wear* as the format of the publications might indicate.

Big magazines like the *Woman's Home Companion* are big business, with highly specialized departments edited by experts under the supervision of an editor-in-chief. This editor-in-chief must know something about cuts, printing, and layout. She must and does shape policy, plan editorials, edit all the material that goes into the magazine, and give to the finished product the stamp of approval. Much of the actual work of putting the book together, however, must necessarily be done by subeditors.

On a small magazine where the staff is limited this is rarely the case. The editor, with possibly one or two assistants, gets out the book. She works with the artists, the engravers, and printers. She lays out the material, manipulates the budget, writes the leads and editorials, edits the copy, reads and cuts the proof, struggles with

[1] Hazel Rawson Cades. This was not written as an editorial but as a vocational article, October, 1929.

the advertising schedule, placates subscribers and difficult directors, and literally brings up by hand this child of her editorial pencil.

It has been said that an editor must know about a lot of things. Miss Camille Davied, whom many of you probably knew as an editor of *American Girl* and who is now managing editor of *Vogue,* says, however, that the best piece of advice ever given to her was to know one thing well. This something may not necessarily be knowledge of subject matter. It may be a flair for suiting the public in the selection of material. It may be a knack for layout, or choice of illustration or type which makes her especially successful in presenting her material.

Certain qualities are pretty generally useful to an editor. Good health is essential, particularly if a girl takes her apprenticeship on a newspaper or small magazine. She must be able to work long stretches, to stand irregular hours, and not to mind work in bunches. Marguerite Moores Marshall tells of a characteristic interview with Miss Helen Taft, then dean of Bryn Mawr. Miss Taft was leaving for a western trip and time pressed. Miss Marshall went to Bryn Mawr. They talked from eight to ten in the evening. She wrote all night, got Miss Taft's O.K. at eight in the morning, caught a train for New York and delivered the article before one o'clock. Stories like this are common in newspaper legend but to the uninitiated, magazine life sounds more leisurely. It may be sometimes, on some magazines; but closing date often means a near-panic on even a well-ordered publication.

Another desirable quality of the would-be editor is willingness to work a lot and to work at anything. The editor of an important woman's magazine, who asks me not to mention her name, began by offering her services to an editor of a small publication for the privilege of learning the trade. Her offer was accepted with surprised gratitude. She worked evenings, all the time keeping at her regular daytime job. But she hurdled that objection that the young have to meet. She had experience to offer when she applied for a paying job.

There are very few editorial positions open to the inexperienced. If you want to be an editor you can try to get a job on a newspaper, preferably a small one at first. You can take a stenographic position with some publication and hope to make your editorial abilities obvious. Or you can go round and go round, besieging the editors in the hope that you will some day fall heir to one of those rare editorial apprenticeships.

Another way to begin, which perhaps I should mention, is in a printing or engraving establishment. Less is known about type, cuts, and the various processes which go into the physical making of a magazine than of most any other part of editorial work, and such knowledge is valuable. It is also fairly obvious that any experience one can get on a school or college paper is just so much free training.

Classes in various aspects of editing are given in several of the universities but so far as I know there is no one course in editing which covers the necessary training. Mrs. Mary Fanton Roberts of *Arts and Decoration* urges such a unified course which would prepare a girl in the literary aspects of the editor's job and also give her training in selection of type, cuts and papers, preparation of copy and layouts, proofreading, and all the other mechanical processes of the work. The magazines which now have to train their own people would probably welcome such a course, but the small number of available jobs is a drawback to the marketing of too many editors.

The more an editor knows, usually, the better editor she is. Education, travel, a lively interest in everything that goes on in the world, and a wide acquaintance with ideas and people are all invaluable. An editor should respect the opinions of others without being dominated. She should have a good eye and a trained pencil, a sensitiveness to the public pulse, a feeling for news and the ability to appraise it judicially, and to select it cannily. A good editor is a good executive. She is not necessarily a poet, novelist, art critic, or even a brilliant writer of editorials, but she knows who are and where to get them. Mrs. Irita Van Doren, editor of the book section of the *Herald Tribune,* expresses this in terms of her job when she says, "The book critic thinks what she can say about a book, the book editor thinks who is the best person to say it."

Having secured a working editorial foundation — anywhere — study the field and decide where you fit in. (This includes studying the publications. Don't go in to apply for a job and tell the editor you've never read her magazine. Girls do it and it doesn't make a hit.)

You may decide that a newspaper suits you. There aren't many women newspaper editors. Once in a while you hear of a woman managing editor, a city editor, or Sunday magazine editor. Woman's page editors are not so rare. The columnist, who deals in fashions, foods, babies or advice to the lovelorn does somewhat the same sort of work that the department editor does on a big magazine.

Trade papers and magazines specializing in art, fashion, architecture, gardens, or interior decoration are at the opposite poles in respect to price and form, but have one thing in common — absorption in a single idea. They are the logical goal of the editor who knows a great deal about a subject or who has a specializing mind. The cultural background demanded by the magazines devoted to many of the arts puts them out of question for the novice but the fashion publications are often looking for untrained girls with social background and clothes sense. For the girl with literary tastes and aspirations there are the small group of intellectual publications such as *Atlantic Monthly,* the larger group of fiction magazines, where the manuscript reader is especially in demand, the general weekly or monthly, such as *Collier's,* and the group which is primarily interested in economic and civic aspects such as the *New Republic*.

The big women's magazines find places for authorities on many subjects such as architecture, cooking, civic problems and politics, interior decoration, clothes, health, and care of children. They also need literary editors, managing editors, art editors, proofreaders, and a good number of editorial assistants, whose work smacks of the reporter, the copy writer, and general handy-girl.

House organs of big businesses and magazines devoted to the interests of trades, clubs, or other organizations often appeal to a girl whose interests or background happen to fit her for the work. Miss Helen Havener, for example, was publicity chairman of the Federation of Business and Professional Women before she became editor of their magazine, *Independent Woman*.

Though apprentice wages are about the same (twenty dollars is a fair average) and associate editor salaries are not usually high (seventy-five dollars is normal) there is more chance of salary advancement on the big magazines which carry a lot of advertising and earn a lot of money than on the smaller publications which sometimes find it difficult to make ends meet.

The women's magazines, appealing to women and dealing with

many subjects in which they excel, naturally find more use for women editors than do more general publications. If locality means anything to a girl, newspapers or small publications situated throughout the country may be more attractive than the big magazines which have their chief locale in New York, Philadelphia, Boston, and Chicago.

I doubt if the ordinary editorial job is much help to creative writing. Girls who see in it a chance to get next to the literary life or a blissful opportunity to write clever captions or read all the newest fiction first should be warned of the probable existence of endless word-counting and proof-cutting.

The real editor takes the drudgery as a matter of course or as spiritual meat and drink. She loves the look of a pasted-up layout. Every page that's marked up for the printer is a new achievement. Every proof that comes back is a thrill and a potential surprise. Every completed issue that's laid on her desk is her child to praise or to censure. But she, as I've said, is a real editor. If this sounds good to you, go ahead and maybe you'll be one too.

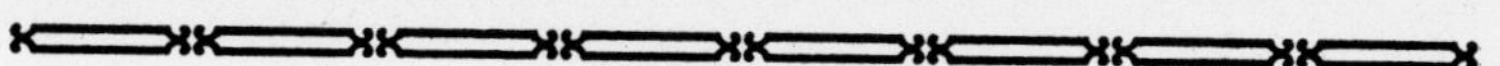

II. ARGUMENT

II. ARGUMENT

THE RICH MAN AND THE NEEDLE'S EYE[1]

Henry Somerville, M.A.

When slump comes after boom in the course of the trade cycles, nothing experiences deeper depression than the reputations of captains of industry and wizards of Finance. Kreuger, internationally idolized as the greatest of all financial geniuses, commits suicide and is discovered to be a gross swindler. The head of the "Insull Utilities Empire" in the United States, the controller of a capital of 1,500 million dollars, is a fugitive from the police. Clarence Hatry, England's post-war pioneer of "rationalization," is a convict; and Lord Kylsant, who from one only of his chairmanships drew remuneration as high as £48,000 in a year, has passed through prison. The statement occasionally appears in the press that Henry Ford is the only multimillionaire in the United States who is credited by public opinion with having obtained his fortune without recourse to antisocial means. But is the Ford fortune not really open to some criticism?

Admittedly it is not easy for an outsider to judge Henry Ford and his works, especially the largest of them in Detroit. The published evidence is hopelessly conflicting; there is the most widespread story which describes him as the model employer, and there is another which represents his workers as slaves of the conveyer belt driven at an inhuman pace, with foremen to "fire" those who slow up, and with secret service agents to "fire" any whose walk or talk or look is thought suggestive of subversive opinions. There is a certain amount of public knowledge of Ford Policies of which there can be no doubt. He pays exceedingly high wages, which is good; but

[1]From *Studies,* March, 1933.

he throws men on to the streets ruthlessly when they cannot earn him profits, which is bad. Those firms that pay moderate wages but endeavor to keep their men in employment during slack times are more socially minded than Ford, even though they do not have publicity departments to broadcast their theories of efficiency and welfare. Detroit has had the reputation of being the most distressed of American cities during the depression, not because of the greatness of the unemployment there, but because of the meagerness of the relief. Hans Wantoch, in a very able and, I believe, perfectly sincere book not emanating from a publicity department, says of Ford: "He has proved that work will keep the working classes contented; he has succeeded in producing an era of peace and in abolishing class warfare; he has founded a real community of workers and has shown up as absolute nonsense the theory that capital and labor must regard each other as enemies. There has never been a strike in the Ford factories."[2] Herr Wantoch wrote before March, 1932, when thousands of disgruntled workers, calling themselves hunger marchers, paraded against the Ford works in Detroit. Ford, like other great American capitalists, has his own armed private police. These were insufficient, though they used tear-gas bombs, to keep back the marchers. State police came as reinforcements, and the marchers were fired upon, four being killed and between fifty and a hundred wounded.

The fortune of £200,000,000 attributed to Ford is stupendous. Divide it by 20 or even 200 and it remains a debatable question whether such a fortune can ever be amassed by any man who observes the laws of justice and charity. "The ways to enrich are many, and most of them are foul," remarked Lord Bacon, who brought about his own downfall by corruptly receiving money when he held the highest judicial office in England. Ford is quite exceptional in having made his money by manufacture. The very big fortunes are nearly always made by Stock Exchange operations and company promotions, especially merger promotions. The lucky finding of rich gold mines, oil fields, and other natural sources of wealth, the prospecting for which is much like a lottery, is rarely enough to bring a seven-figure fortune. Cecil Rhodes, at the age of eighteen, realized that there was more profit in buying and selling digging rights in the diamond region than in taking a pick

[2]Wantoch: *Magnificent Money-Makers,* p. 241 (Desmond Harmsworth, 1932, 21s.).

and spade and digging himself. At the age of twenty-one he had begun his successful effort to form a combine of all the diamond producers. Without the combine the value of diamonds would have fallen very low indeed. Similarly with inventions: when they yield great wealth it is through their shrewd exploitation, which usually means cleverness in securing a position of monopoly. Inheritances apart, vast fortunes do not fall into men's laps; they are acquired by deliberate acts. We come back to the question whether they can be made justly?

Herr Wantoch's book contains a score of studies of a wide range of characters, beginning with the banking house of the Medici and ending with Ivar Kreuger. It is a well-written book, and the judgments are intelligent though they do not always command agreement. The most uncritical reader, who may not feel qualified to check the author's assertions about the Fuggers, for instance, will be put on his guard against the rest of the book by the unlucky last chapter on Kreuger. Here Kreuger is idealized, for it was written before the criminality of the Swedish financier had been revealed. The publishers of the English edition of *Magnificent Money-Makers* have shown courage in letting it appear unexpurgated. On our question of the justice of the methods by which great fortunes are made the book throws very little light. The author's ethical standpoint is not that of the Gospels. He has none of the Christian distrust of wealth; he goes curiously out of his way to glorify the Renaissance, which he surprisingly identifies with a Puritan devotion to work. Without the author intending it in the least, *Magnificent Money-Makers* is a demonstration of the deceitfulness of riches. With few exceptions, the magnificent money-makers lived mournful lives. I may take the last seven chapters in the book as a sample of the whole. One of the seven subjects, Henry Ford, may have a reasonably happy life for all we know to the contrary. We know that Kreuger's life ended in tragedy, and the other five are shown by Herr Wantoch to have had grisly skeletons in their golden cupboards. Siemens, the German telegraph king, wrote at the age of fifty: "I seem to be lacking in energy. Wealth and honor have lost their old attraction for me, and science appears to be my only interest. Even for that the old incentive has gone." Alfred Nobel, the explosives magnate, "did not live his life, he suffered it." Cecil Rhodes was tolerably happy, perhaps because money was always desired by him only as a means, not an end; but the chapter devoted to him mentions the multimillionaire Barney Barnato going mad and committing suicide. Rathenau did not like business life, and moreover he was not outstanding as a money-maker. August Thyssen, German ironmaster, "gave himself up wholly to his work; for it he sacrificed marriage, domestic peace, and the happiness of his family."

Herr Wantoch's subjects are men who count as more than money-makers. He has made his selections because of the parts they have played in the economic history of the world. Wallenstein, Richard Arkwright, and Cobden are in his gallery, but not a single American except Henry Ford: not John Jacob Astor, Cornelius Vanderbilt, Jay Gould, or J. Pierpont Morgan. Yet the fortunes made in America dwarf those made in Europe, not because Americans are abler than Europeans, or less scrupulous, or more intent on chasing the almighty dollar, but because the rapid development of new centers of industry and population in the nineteenth century gave the Americans opportunities not presented in Europe. In the twentieth century the largest fortunes have been made out of the war and new industries. The film business gives examples not only of fabulous fortunes derived from investments, but of the earning of enormous salaries. Some film directors are said to have been paid £50,000 a year at Hollywood, and the "star" performers have done even better, if newspaper statements are to be believed. No one supposes that the earning powers of Greta Garbo and Charlie Chaplin are a measure of their artistic merit. They simply happen to have the gifts that best please the hundreds of millions of people throughout the world who frequent the cinemas. A million pounds may easily be paid to see a single film that retains great popularity for a period of time, and therefore the most popular artists can name almost their own terms as remuneration for their services.

It is not drastically different with extraordinary earning powers in other spheres. Not to mention best-sellers among novelists, let us take the incomes of leaders of the Bar. There is one lawyer in England, still in public life though not practising, who was credited with earnings of from £50,000 to £100,000 a year. He is undoubtedly a man of supreme intellectual and forensic ability, but probably only a shade superior to men who had not a tenth of his earning power. The superiority, such as it was, might only be a more ingratiating manner with juries, but it would be sufficient to make all the difference. Solicitors would always try to brief him in preference to the next best man, and they would offer him larger and larger fees. In these days the amounts of money that are concerned in the issue of litigation so frequently run into tens and hundreds of thousands that the difference between paying a leading counsel £500 and £5,000 is almost immaterial.

What we have said suggests that extraordinary fortunes are due more to favorable external circumstances than to extraordinary personal abilities. The same reasoning goes far to relieve the possessors of great fortunes from the presumption of extraordinary wickedness. The evidence may point to wickedness being the rule among money-makers, but it is ordinary wickedness. Thyssen, who "gave himself up wholly to his work — for it he sacrificed marriage, domestic peace, and the happiness of his family" — only did what the multitude of small money-makers must do. The rewards of Mammon are not paid without hard service of Mammon. Even the film stars do not get their money solely for their charm and beauty and humor; they must pander to tastes that are often vicious. "Give the public what they want" is the rule of all who are out for the public's money. This is quite ordinary wickedness. Grinding avarice and the sacrifice of moral scruple can be found among those making small and moderate incomes as well as among the millionaires. This may be said without any extenuation of wickedness in high places, and without minimizing the social desirability of cutting the claws of the bigger vultures when cutting is possible.

On whom do the vultures prey? One well-known episode in financial history may be recalled to illustrate the complexity of the question. Andrew Carnegie had built up a steel business which was already gigantic by the standards of the time. It produced steel ingots and left to others the more advanced stages of manufacture. Overproduction and cut-throat competition were features of the American steel situation at the end of the nineteenth century. Carnegie was aggrieved by an invasion of what he considered his territory, the ingot field, by other steel firms. He threatened to retaliate by building plants for finished steel products. It was known he was able to make good his word, and his competitors were thrown into alarm. It was then that the idea of trustifying the American steel industry was launched, and Pierpont Morgan undertook the formation of the United States Steel Corporation, consolidating hundreds of different enterprises, the Carnegie concern among them. Morgan represented financial interests that shuddered at the prospective effects of a steel war on the general security market, and he was ready to buy peace at almost any price. Carnegie and his associates were thus able to sell their property for 303½ million dollars in bonds of the U.S. Steel Corporation *plus* stock of a par value of 200 million dollars. Carnegie personally received 218 million dollars.

Morgan paid extorted money to avoid a steel war; but it can be said for Carnegie that, if he had declared war, he would not have been the aggressor; competitors had invaded his territory first. Did Carnegie act unjustly in squeezing the last million out of Morgan or the United States Steel Corporation? Of course the money really came from all who held stock in the corporation which was floated in 1901 with a capital of over 1,000 million dollars in shares and 300 million dollars in bonds. It had to carry loads of water because of the huge price exacted by Carnegie. By good management and good luck the water was pumped out, and the corporation became able to pay reasonable dividends.

Another question that an economist may refer to the moralist is what should be a fair remuneration to the Morgan firm for putting through a deal of such magnitude. "The promoting syndicate made a profit of 62½ million dollars; the firm of Morgan, which played the leading part, received a fixed sum of 12½ million dollars and also a percentage of the remainder. Some 150 million dollars worth of stock of the Trust went to promoters and underwriters."[3] The methods employed in such a flotation presents problems in casuistry. There was manipulation of the Stock Exchange not only by getting brokers to recommend the stock to their clients, but by rigging the market. The aims of the riggers were to lift prices and to make the stock "active," that is, one in which dealings were frequent so as to make a free market. Investors are naturally attracted to a stock which can be bought and sold with the uttermost readiness. The manipulators for Morgan therefore arranged buying and selling themselves. The buyers and sellers were the same people, the transactions were faked and the prices artificial, though they were

[3]Liefmann: *Cartels, Concerns and Trusts*, p. 309.

actually available to any person who wanted to deal. In the event the stock proved good, and those who bought had no reason to repent their bargains; but if the water-logged craft had sunk, would our moral judgment of the Morgan tactics be different?

The administrators of Kreuger's bankrupt estate declared him to be not a great man of business, but only a criminal. He died with liabilities of £58½ millions against assets less than £5 millions. A man who fails to the extent of eleven pence in the shilling is a failure pretty complete. Yet even after he had become a suicide, the financial authorities of the world were still regarding Kreuger as the greatest constructive genius of the age. He moved hundreds of millions of pounds across the world from countries that had capital to spare to those where it was in urgent demand. He was doing by himself what the League of Nations sighed over its inability to do. He was hailed by the idealists and intellectuals as the great constructive exponent of international economic co-operation. The money he lent to governments he raised from the investing public on the credit of his companies. It can no longer be said in his excuse that he was a victim of the "economic blizzard"; for as early as 1926 his balance sheets were forged. One lesson of his career is that the financial world, including the great banks, are easily fooled.

No purpose would be served by denouncing here admitted criminalities which nobody defends. The useful thing would be to suggest ways of preventing them. What made Kreuger's swindles possible was the present-day system of holding and subsidiary companies. The system not only involves highly centralized control of immense enterprises, but it facilitates secrecy of accounts and allows infinite scope for financial juggling. Indeed it is for these reasons that the system is adopted on all hands today. It is judged to be conducive to commercial success. There is no reason for thinking that the system is generally abused if we judge by current business standards. Questions of the reform of company law are among the most complicated of legal and economic problems. The trouble which legislators experience is in making safeguards against abuses which will not hinder legitimate enterprise at the same time.

A Catholic student would not judge business practices only by what happen to be current business standards. We may well ask whether many of the legalities as well as illegalities of such men as Kreuger should not be prevented in the interests of justice and social welfare. Hans Wantoch tells us that when Kreuger formed his original American company: "Ostensibly its main object was to speculate in land and house property, and it proposed to use American money for purchasing real estate in the inflationist countries, particularly France and Germany. In actual fact, it wormed its way into the American match business, buying now here, now there, under all sorts of aliases for the parent concern, the Swedish Match Company." To disguise operations in business is often legitimate; to aim at a monopoly may be legitimate, but I think that a private monopoly obtained by such means will rarely be in the public interest. If there are to be monopolies, their formation, as well as their operation, should, I think, be under public scrutiny and regulation to prevent such evils as overcapitalization.

The banking practice of making loans for Stock Exchange speculations has even more responsibility than the modern system of company finance for facilitating the plunder of investors. The great financial swindlers are always speculators; they begin as speculators, and it is when their gambles go wrong that they resort to fraud. Their speculations would be very limited if they were not able to utilize the ordinary credit system. This applies to the small as well as to the large speculators. The great boom in Wall Street of 1928 and thereabouts could never have reached such dizzy heights, if it had not been for buying "on margin"; that is, buying with borrowed money. It is true that the Federal Reserve banking authorities did their best to restrict lending to Wall Street, but their efforts were stultified by other greedy lenders supplying the market.

A curious fact of some significance is that there is a tendency among business men to judge leniently the swindles that land a big financier into prison. There are people who knew Hatry who will speak as if he did nothing worse than "make a mistake" when driven into a corner through stress of circumstances. Now, Hatry's crime was the forging of share certificates and other scrip which were sold on the market or pledged with lenders as collateral. The money he raised by such means he wanted for the purpose of "supporting the market" in his various securities. He and his associates raised as much as £2½ millions by documents of title which were impugned at the trial, and it was shown that some of the biggest banks had advanced money to Hatry on the strength of this dishonest paper. The lenient judgment of such malpractices is due to a feeling that as Hatry was accustomed to manufacture scrip which had a value only because it was believed to have a value, that is to say, its value was speculative, he was only crossing a very thin line when he duplicated certificates for shares issued —he was, in fact, only adding another drop of water to the stock of his companies, and he was doing it to keep up the market value of the stock. Similarly, when he borrowed from a bank, depositing a forged bond as collateral, his intention would be to redeem the bogus document when he had got over temporary difficulties. Probably he was not taking any fresh money from the bank, but only renewing a loan for which he had to put up increased collateral, which he did by means of forged scrip. The bank was not making any present sacrifice, even if it did lend new money, for a bank is supposed, with a certain degree of accuracy, to create money by the mere act of lending.

This leniency toward criminality such as Hatry's is not logically inconsistent for the minds that accept as legitimate and right the ordinary business of such as Hatry—the manufacture of speculative securities for sale to the public at a profit to himself, and the artificial manipulation of the prices of such securities by Stock Exchange rigging. There is a difference between the manufacture of speculative securities for Stock Exchange operations, which was Hatry's business, and the issue of securities for the purpose of financing a useful industrial enterprise. An example, familiar to investors, of the difference between the two is afforded by those mining companies which are formed, in market parlance, "to mine the public" rather than the earth. The company does indeed make the show of digging a hole in the ground, though the insiders have little hope of raising valuable minerals. They get their profit not from the minerals they produce, but from the shares they sell to investors. "Mining the public" is also practised in connection with really productive mines because the prices of the shares are moved up and down by market manipulation, so that outsiders are lured into buying "high" or selling "low." In a legitimate flotation of public securities the primary object is the provision of necessary capital, and the speculativeness of the securities is only incidental and is kept to the minimum. In the Hatry type of operation the creation of securities to serve as speculative counters is itself a primary object, or the speculativeness is maximized by the terms of issue or by subsequent market "management."

The *Quadragesimo Anno* quotes St. Thomas in praise of industrial enterprises for "results which are really useful." The test of social utility, and not merely of private profit, should be applied in our judgment of economic acts. On this ground we must seriously question the ordinary practice of the banks in giving credit for Stock Exchange speculation. A bank credit creates a claim on the labor and other economic resources of the community, not simply a claim on the resources of the bank. It is an economic principle that a bank loan tends to raise the prices of goods and services generally by increasing the demands upon them. Hence in a very special way the administration of bank credit is a social function, and a bank has no right to make profits in ways detrimental to society as a whole. There are certain times when banks think it necessary to adopt a policy of deflation, and they then refuse to lend for the purchase of speculative securities. It would, therefore, be perfectly practicable for them to observe this self-denying ordinance at all times; and if they did so, they would do much toward avoiding the inflation which necessitates subsequent deflation. The buyers of securities, even when they are small investors, are not to be regarded entirely as innocent victims. More than a few of those who dabble in the wrong sort of securities are greedy or foolish speculators themselves. All of us who apply labor or capital should be directed by the consideration not only of pecuniary return but of "results which are really useful." Only when there is right motive may the miracle be possible of passing through the needle's eye.

PSYCHIATRY AND THE CONFESSIONAL[1]

John Rathbone Oliver

My maternal grandfather was a man of very deep religious convictions; a man who cultivated a constant sense of God's presence and who lived a godly, righteous, and sober life. He was a devout

[1]Copyright by Charles Scribner's Sons, 1930. Reprinted from *Scribner's*, July, 1930, with permission.

Baptist. And while I was still an undergraduate at Harvard, some thirty-odd years ago, he became greatly disturbed about what he called my "Romish practices." One night, in his dim old library, he had been holding forth to me on the evil of "auricular confession."

"I don't see why your dear mother lets you do such things," he said; for he thought of me still as a wayward boy. "And I never realized what it might lead to when she insisted on being baptized in the Episcopal Church. I can't imagine what your church is coming to anyhow. Confession! — Nonsense! Poppy-cock! — But I'll tell you one thing, my boy — No mortal man shall ever come between my soul and my God."

Thirty years ago this was the general attitude of the average devout Protestant toward what Catholics call the Sacrament of Penance. My dear old grandfather could not see that "A man" — "The Man" — God in Man incarnate — had not only come between him and his God, but had made Himself the Way by which the world had been brought back to God, had become the main channel of Man's approach to the Everlasting Father. My grandfather, like all really conscientious Protestants of his day, believed implicitly in the Divinity of Christ. But he could not draw the logical conclusions that flow from the fundamental fact of the Incarnation. He could not see that God had taken human nature unto Himself, in the Person of God the Son; that matter had become interpenetrated by the divine; that God now made use of material things, water, bread, and wine, as channels of forgiveness and of spiritual power, and that the man, the priest, who said in Christ's name *Absolvo te* was a material agent, divinely instituted, just as water had become a material agent to the mystical washing away of sin. You could reason with him about such things all night long. He would go just so far; but at the thought of "telling your sins to a priest instead of to God," he balked and would not move an inch. Not that he did not willingly and contritely confess himself a very imperfect Christian and in need of divine forgiveness. He would stand up at a prayer meeting, and say as much. But only in a general way. The details of his failings and doubts and difficulties were "nobody's business" except his own — and God's.

The trouble was that he never thought of his pastor as a trained physician of the soul. He was ready enough to go to him during some period of bereavement or discouragement, and get down on his stiff, blessed, old knees in the pastor's study, and "have a few moments of prayer." But he would never have gone to his minister with the harassing details of his daily mistakes and anxieties, as he might have gone to our family physician when his digestion was out of order and he needed "something to shake up his liver."

The Protestant attitude to this entire question has shifted mightily since I was a boy. Not long ago, at a meeting of a group of psychiatrists, I listened to an address by a distinguished Protestant "divine," who openly proclaimed his belief that the Protestant sects had lost a tremendous source of help and of spiritual growth when they had "outlawed the confessional." Thirty years ago no Protestant minister would have dared to make such a statement.

And therefore, today, one hears a great deal, among my many Protestant friends, about the necessity of providing for their people some means of allaying mental stress, of rooting out phobias and obsessions, of using "modern psychology" in the service of the soul. The need is evident enough. But I think that people are mistaken in comparing with the Catholic Sacrament of Penance the ideals of mental healing and guidance, which so many Protestant churches are endeavoring to turn into some reliable, useful institution or service.

In one of the larger Congregational churches in Washington, the pastor, who is a man of unusual power and experience, has organized what he calls "A Life Adjustment Center." It is like a mental clinic or dispensary; and yet it is something more valuable still. This Center has a large volunteer staff that consists not only of physicians for the body and psychiatrists for the mind but also of a lawyer or two, a specialist in domestic science, another specialist in child training, and so on. There is no domain of modern life which is not more or less adequately covered by some person trained to give help and advice on its distinct problems. This Center is open several times a week in the evenings. One member of it is on hand all day long in order to see anyone who drops in during the day and to make for him or her the necessary appointments with that special member of the staff whose knowledge and training can be of the greatest help to that particular patient. Hundreds of people come to this Center. It is doing a remarkably successful work. But to compare it with what people call "The Confessional" is beside the mark.

In old Trinity Church in New York, that stands like a tiny island of peace amidst the swirling tides of physical and mental hurry, noise, and tension, you will see, as you enter, a notice or announcement set in a prominent place on the wall. It reads something like this: "From ten o'clock until noon, every day, a priest will be found sitting in such and such a part of this church. He is not there to hear confessions. He is there for the convenience of anyone who wants to talk with him or who seeks advice or help of any kind." Twenty years ago, such a priest would have sat alone, unused, unnoticed. Today, as I am told, there are so many people who slip in from the hurrying stream of humanity outside—so many people who seek out the quiet figure in its black cassock—that the hours of the priest's service have been doubled, and that more than one priest will soon be necessary. Unhappy, anxious, fearful people come into Trinity Church to talk with this priest—people who would not for worlds go to their own ministers. And why? Principally, I think, because here they feel protected. They do not know the priest to whom they talk. He does not ask their names. Perhaps he cannot even see their faces clearly. In order to reach their own pastor they must make an appointment, they must come to his study, they must give their names. The pastor's wife will probably notice them, and tell the other women of the parish that "Poor Mrs. X came to see my husband today and I heard her crying in his study. I do wonder what the matter is." Or, that same afternoon, after having poured out their troubles to their minister, they may have to meet him at a Guild Tea—or at a Rummage Sale, and try to make conversation with him over the teacups in some crowded corner. All that is too much to ask. It makes the way to help too difficult. But to slip into a quiet church—to sit down in the shadows beside a man you do not know and who does not know you—a man who has been trained to understand people's difficulties, who will not pat you on the back and tell you "not to worry," but who will listen—and listen—and go on listening, until you have brought out the very last shred of your troubles and apprehensions—ah, that is easy—that is protected—and so quieting and so helpful, that you kneel to say a prayer before you leave the church, and find that at last you really can pray again.

All these things are signs of the times; signs of an awakened need in the hearts of many people who know nothing about the Catholic

Faith and who want to hear even less — but who *do* know that they need help and who are gradually learning where to look for it.

I often wonder whether many psychiatrists have so many mysterious telephone calls as I. Five or six times a week the same conversation takes place. — Yes, this is Doctor Oliver. — Doctor, I want to see you. — Very well. If you will come to my office at—. — No, I do not want to come to your office. My name? It is not necessary for me to give my name, is it? — But, if I don't know who you are, how can I make any appointment? — If I can't see you without giving my name and without sitting in a waiting-room full of patients, I can't see you at all. And I want to see you. I *want* to."

To the half-suppressed cry for help in that one word "want" it is hard indeed to be entirely deaf. As a result, I have a group of patients whose names I do not know, and whose faces I have, oftentimes, never clearly seen. They drop in at the Clergy House where I stay on Saturday nights; they slip into the darkened church itself, knowing that they will find me sitting in a dim corner — at the end of a side aisle. At the back of the church, there are groups of people around the confessional boxes, so that a stranger does not feel absolutely alone. He or she tiptoes up the aisle, slides into the pew in which I am sitting. There is enough light to show up my white hair. They know that it is I. And then, the story begins.

They take a long time, those stories, as a general rule. And one must have limitless supplies of patience. Some of these nameless patients of mine are practising Catholics, and go regularly to their confessions. But in the box, there is not time to talk at length; other penitents are waiting. But, sitting by my side, in an empty pew, they are at their ease and they can talk as long as they like. Others do not practise their religion — or have no religion to practise. If they need the grace and strength of sacramental confession and absolution, I direct their minds toward it. Still others are devout Protestants. I do not try to estrange them from their familiar ways. I only, occasionally, point out the greater happiness that is waiting for them in the fullness of the Catholic religion. More often than is perhaps right, I make no effort to change whatever type of faith they may profess; I hear — no matter how long it takes — what they have to say. I give what advice I can — and then send them to say a prayer before the high altar, where the tiny red light floats amidst the shadows. And I leave them there in the hands of Him who is the only perfect physician of body and soul, leave them kneeling there before His presence — a presence that they may neither understand nor accept nor believe — but that will bless them, just the same.

It is a curious psychological fact that it is far easier for an anxious man or woman, bothered by some inner conflict, to tell his or her story to a practically unknown or neutral person than to those who are nearest and dearest to them, and who may be reasonably expected to have their best interests at heart. This is especially true during the introverted period of adolescence. In most boys' lives, for instance, there comes a time when the free, easy intercourse of childhood with father or mother becomes clouded with a sense of restraint. A wall grows up between father and son. The son has found in sex questions a new matter of absorbing interest. But usually he has learned of these new matters in secret, shoddy ways. From whispered talks with other boys, behind the barn; from chauffeurs in his father's garage; from purloined medical books — even from the Bible itself. And because his new knowledge is tainted by smutty secretiveness, he cannot — he dares not — talk of these things to his father — much less to his mother. But even in those happy families in which the father has trained himself and his adolescent son to talk as easily and as directly about sex matters as they talk about the weather or the last baseball game — even there, the adolescent boy usually has a whole field of new interests and ambitions — daydreams and castles in Spain — which are so peculiarly his own that he cannot share the knowledge of them with his father. The older man might laugh at them, make light of things that to the boy seem more important than life itself. And even if he does not laugh the boy feels that he could never "understand." The same wall of reticence grows up between mother and daughter. And it is during this difficult period that the seeds of so many antagonisms are sown between parent and child. Oftentimes, the father is too busy to take the trouble even to try to understand his son. For it requires patience and many failures before the wall that is rising between them can be broken down, even for a time. I have known young men, tormented by some persistent source of unhappiness, who have wanted to get help from their father — who have longed for an older man's advice and sympathy — and yet who have been absolutely incapable of putting their troubles into words. Father and son, mother and daughter are too close together to make confidences easy. If the boy pours out his troubles to his father, he feels that he may read the memory of them in his father's eyes every time the family sits down to dinner. Or that he will find his mother looking at him with a new glance of poorly hidden distress, and will know that his father has not respected his confidences but has discussed him with his mother.

And so it is infinitely easier — and more natural perhaps, for the perplexed boy or girl — to tell his or her troubles to someone who does not even know his or her name; or who at least will not become a constant, ever-present reminder of the failings and mistakes that are tormenting them. It is here that the confessional has its great value. The priest behind the grating is an unseen presence; but a kindly, an understanding one. If the penitent feels afraid to go to his or her own parish priest — well, there are hundreds of other churches and thousands of other priests in other confessionals, to whom the penitent is merely the voice of a soul in distress. Among Protestants, where there is no dim confessional, no sense of absolute secrecy and protection — the troubled adolescent is likely to be as much afraid of his minister, of his study, of his wife and children, as he is of his own home and of his own parents. And often enough, unfortunately, the minister has had no training in dealing with mental difficulties. If the burden of the young man's difficulties be purely sexual the pastor will talk about sin, and saving grace, and the necessity of faith. And then he will ask the young man to get down on his knees beside the littered, disorderly desk and "have a word or two of prayer."

Far be it from me to cast the slightest aspersion or to make the lightest criticism of those devoted Protestant ministers who are aflame with a real love of souls and who have a deep desire to help "sinners." If they fail to help, it is not because of any lack of interest or of desire to do their best. The trouble is that they do not realize that one cannot become an able physician of souls simply by wishing to be one, any more than a man can perform the simplest surgical operation without a long preparatory training in anatomy and surgical technic. In the Roman Communion, not every priest is licensed to hear confessions simply because he has been ordained. The cure of souls, in the confessional, is a jealously guarded privilege. And no priest may, except of necessity, hear the confessions of religious communities — of monks and nuns — without special license from the ecclesiastical authorities. Moreover, most people do not realize that in Catholic seminaries, the young candidates for holy orders are trained for years in Moral Theology. And Moral Theology is to the physician of souls what the dissecting room and the surgical dispensary are to the medical student. Look through any good treatise on Moral Theology (Noldin, Lehmkuhl, or Tanqueray), and you will find not only the principles of mental surgery, but also imaginary case histories, in which the principles are applied to definite cases of conscience.

If our Protestant brethren are seeking to regain some of the valuable things that they lost when they "outlawed the confessional" they must realize that they must begin to train their "mental physicians" in their divinity schools. If they do not, then they will be trying to operate without definite preparation—and although they may not kill the patient's body, they may gravely injure his soul, his happiness, and his mental health.

But even Catholics are beginning to realize that the mere book-training in Moral Theology is often inadequate. Fifty years ago, in many unadvanced, unscientific, medical schools, the student spent two or three years learning Materia Medica and Therapeutics out of a book, and then, after graduation, he was supposed to get his practical knowledge by "practice." Rather hard on the patients. For such men often learned most by their mistakes. Of course, the mistakes were usually buried; and next time, the doctor, we hope, did better. Nowadays, in many of our seminaries, the theological student is being taught Moral Theology in new ways. Or at least, he is given some opportunity for coming into personal contact with definite mental cases. Not from the standpoint of sin or of morality. But from the standpoint of mental medicine. Courses are being given to theologians by psychiatrists. Given in the mental dispensaries of large hospitals where the seminarian can observe the manner in which psychiatrists examine, classify, diagnose, and treat mental illness and mental difficulties of all kinds. The theologian is learning to recognize the outstanding symptoms of serious mental disease, and how to differentiate it from mental maladjustments, phobias, and obsessions. He is also brought into contact with social service centers where he learns how experts deal with problems of domestic difficulty, with unemployment and with a hundred other matters of which he was formerly ignorant. And so, among Catholics, at least, an effort is being made to develop physicians of the mind and of the soul adequately equipped to meet and to deal with the complex problems of modern life.

Our Protestant brothers are doing something of the same kind. But it is an utter misunderstanding of the situation to imagine that the Protestant can ever undo the damage of the "outlawing of the confessional." It is possible that a Presbyterian or a Methodist pastor might set up in his church a so-called "confessional box"; he might sit on one side of it behind the grating, and might listen to the outpourings of the sins and troubles of some members of his congregation. No doubt the person who there poured out his soul, might be benefited by the procedure; might get helpful advice and go away feeling happier. But all the confessional boxes in the world could not bring back to the Protestant bodies the one thing that really matters — the one thing that is more important than confession — than all the confessional boxes in the world — the thing that we Catholics call "absolution."

It is the "absolution" that gives to the confessional its great power to help and to heal. It is the Sacrament of Penance, in which by the "power that our Lord Jesus Christ has left upon earth to absolve all sinners who truly repent and believe in Him," the priest, acting in Christ's name and by His authority, "absolves from sin" — in which he, as it were, pours upon the head of the penitent the precious blood that was shed upon the cross, in the one perfect sacrifice, oblation and satisfaction for the sins of the whole world. And where there is no priesthood, there is no absolving priest; where there is no absolving priest there is no absolute blotting out of all past sin, no complete restoration to God's grace and to complete forgiveness. To the Catholic, every confession and absolution is a fresh start. He begins his Christian life all over again. All past guilt is wiped out. And fresh grace is given him to start on the road of life once more.

It is all this that makes it so impossible to conceive of a Protestant confessional, in the true sense of the word. And yet one would not, for anything in the world, discourage those devout Protestant ministers who are trying to give their people a deeper, more scientific Cure of Souls — to meet their difficulties by training themselves in psychology and psychiatry. But the one Thing, that the Catholic prizes so highly and which is to him a constant source of divinely instituted grace — Christ's absolution and covenanted forgiveness — this the Protestant ministers can never give — not because he may not be an infinitely better, holier man than the least intelligent Catholic priest, but simply because he does not have it to give, since the power to give it has never been bestowed upon him.

Many modern people — who have no use at all for the Sacrament of Penance — are kind enough to "think highly" of the confessional. I had a medical colleague once, who consulted me about a school for his two children. "I want," he said, "to send them to one of your Anglican schools, a place where they will have to go to confession. I can't go quite as far as to send them to a Roman Catholic institution. But I won't have them trained in any Protestant atmosphere, such as I was brought up in, and in which there is no means of mental outlet, no chance for mental direction and training."

That father, acting, perhaps, from no real religious motive, gave to his children a greater gift than he realized. How great that gift is, only one can understand who has sat some Saturday afternoon or evening in a quiet church, while confessions are being heard. Watch the people when they come in; and then look at them again when they leave the church.

A few weeks ago, I was kneeling at the back of such a church. In front of me there knelt a girl of, perhaps, sixteen or less. She was tense — tormented, apparently. She twisted about; she could not keep still. The glimpse that I caught of her showed me the face of a person in great mental distress. I could not take my eyes from her. She seemed anxiety personified. A few moments later, she got up, and went into the confessional. I also got up from my knees, and walked up to the high altar to kneel before the Blessed Sacrament. Time passed quickly there. Then someone pushed by me, and knelt down on the altar steps, just a few feet away. It was the same girl. But I have never seen such a change in any human being. All her tenseness was gone; the lines of worry had been soothed from her face. No signs of mental torment now; no anxiety — only perfect relaxation, peace, and, apparently, a great happiness, for her lips were parted in a smile. If I, as a psychiatrist, could have done for that girl in three hours what had been accomplished in fifteen minutes, I should have thought myself a clever physician, indeed.

I watched her make the sign of the cross, from forehead to breast, from shoulder to shoulder, with a hand that was steady, co-ordinated, efficient, exact. Then she folded her arms on her breast, and lifted her face to the Tabernacle. That face still bore traces of dried tears; but the eyes were bright, unclouded. I left her there, with a prayer of thanksgiving; left her there at peace with man, and, if I may say so without irreverence, at home with her God.

"All magic, all superstition, all emotional self-hypnosis," my materialistic friend may say. Well, let them say so as often as they please. I shall begin to listen to them when their own particular type of magic and hypnosis gets the same results.

TIPS FOR PULLMAN PORTERS

Traffic World[1]

There is, of course, a certain justice in the plea of the Pullman porters that their salaries be such that they need not depend on tips for a living. Perhaps there is enough in it, in a legal sense, to compel the payment of reasonable salaries by the Pullman Company and the abolition of the recognized fee system as a method of compensation. That is for the lawyers to fight about. But we are wondering if the humiliation suffered by the colored gentlemen who wait on us when we travel in Pullmans, because they must accept their living from a grateful and well-fed and cared-for public, generous while traveling, is so real that, when their salaries are placed on a just basis, they will refuse to accept these tips. If so, shall we find our shoes polished when we arise in the morning? Shall we be able to get an extra blanket when our toes are frozen? May we have the window in our berth open just a little? Shall we be permitted to have the dust of travel brushed from our trousers without "digging" into these same trousers? We doubt it. That is, we are in doubt both as to whether porters would refuse the tips,

[1]September 24, 1927.

if offered, and as to whether we would get the same hospitable service if the tips were withheld. Also we doubt that the tips would be withheld. Certainly the laborer is worthy of his hire, and it would seem that the Pullman Company ought to pay anybody who works for it what his work is worth. But there is something about the nature of the work of the Pullman porter that calls for tips, whether he gets a salary or not. Probably the tips would not be as large or as frequent if the passengers knew the porter was getting a decent salary, but it would be a long time before tipping ceased. . . . What the porters will get, then, if their petition is granted, will be proper compensation in salary and tips besides — a sort of salary and fee system such as was once popular in public office. We confess that, adequate salary or inadequate salary for the Pullman porter, we should not care to travel far or often in his car without crossing his palm with an adequate piece of silver. And, by the way, if the porters are to be put on an adequate salary basis, why not the same thing for the red caps who hustle our baggage and see that we get the right train and the right berth? Also it might be a good thing for the waiters. As for the waiters, however, we should, if we withheld a tip, be a little suspicious of the soup the next time we sat at the table even if we knew our waiter was receiving a respectable salary.

WHETHER GOD IS?[1]

Hilaire Belloc

Let us drop the word and the idea of cause, and call our argument, "The Argument from the Nothingness of Nothingness." I think in that form it will be admitted. Nothingness is not. Not only can it not move, it cannot be: for it is not.

If this be not true, then all thought ends and all effort at the

[1]From *The Question and the Answer,* Science and Culture Series. The Bruce Publishing Company, Copyright.

discovery of truth fails at its first step. Shall we grant that out of nothingness nothing can come, that nothingness cannot in any conceivable sense however impersonal, produce? I think we must. It follows (and we are not living in a queer age, that we should have to beg for an axiom so elementary!), it follows, I say, that where there is increment, that increment has come from somewhere.

The greater contains the less and not the less the greater. You can draw a quart of water out of a two-gallon pail full of water, but you cannot draw two gallons of water from a quart pot full of water. If we see issuing from one particular thing another thing greater in volume or in character, we may be absolutely certain that the lesser did not produce the greater, for nothing comes from nothingness. Nothingness is impotent to produce. If we do in point of fact draw two gallons of water from a measure *apparently* only containing a quart, we can be absolutely certain that the quart pot is in some way being replenished all the time, is in communication with a supply of water sufficient to give us our two gallons.

Now, all about us, Nature presents this singular phenomenon of the greater apparently proceeding from the less; of increment: increment of idea, of number, of character: the complex from the simple, the tree from the seed, and so on.

Growth, to put it in a word, is manifest everywhere. There is also the converse process of decay, of the complex becoming simple and life falling back into dead matter, and the rest. That does not prevent the fact that the process of addition is present; increment must be done before it can be undone, and the addition must have come from somewhere.

If we say that the tree is "potentially" present in the simple seed, we are only using a metaphor. It is not really present. It came somehow, and it is something greater, something more, than what it came from. That addition could not come into being were it not actually present somewhere already. And this argument that out of nothing, nothing comes, and that therefore the lesser cannot produce the greater is of supreme, absolute, and vital value when we consider the twin phenomena of consciousness and intelligence.

That which cannot think could not of itself produce that which does think, nor that which thinks less produce that which thinks more. Unconsciousness could not have produced consciousness, nor that which is less conscious have produced that which is more conscious.

Consciousness *is,* no one can deny it. Intelligence *is,* no one can deny that. Also unconsciousness *is,* or at any rate lesser and lesser degrees of consciousness; also the lack of intelligence *is,* that is, the inability to think — the inability of a thing to contemplate itself — or at any rate an ability so slight that we can find no trace of it. If you can say that a beefsteak thinks, you are talking nonsense. But if you say that a man (who is in part a beefsteak, being of flesh) thinks, you are saying what is known to be true. If you say that a lump of iron is conscious, you are, in common sense, talking nonsense. You may, if you like, imagine that there are some rudiments of consciousness present everywhere throughout the universe; that cannot be disproved, and some who have been very determined to deny God have gone so far as to affirm that consciousness is thus present everywhere even in the apparently least conscious things. That idea is at the back of the great Epicurean philosophy, which keeps on cropping up in the mouths of lesser men than the ancients. The great Lucretius talked like that, and so did the absurd Haeckel, of our own time.

Well, I say that this affirmation that Nature is conscious cannot be disproved. If you like to say that there is a sort of elementary consciousness just above zero even in the deadest matter, you can do so, though it will be pretty clear to all who hear you that you are taking refuge in a very desperate affirmation for which you have no sort of ground, and that you would not be saying such things unless you were determined not to admit their opposite. You are like a man presented with seventeen independent witnesses, no one in communication with another and all testifying in various ways to the identity of a murderer, but a man so determined not to admit the murderer to be guilty that he would rather believe all the seventeen to be liars, or all the seventeen to be suffering each and every one of them from illusion than give up his fixed conviction. And if he says that of seventeen, he can logically say it of seventeen million.

But let it be so. The affirmation, though extravagant, is not a contradiction in terms; it is just barely conceivable that an overwhelming convergence of evidence should be false; it is just barely conceivable that though no trace of consciousness is discoverable in what we call unconsciousness, yet some such trace is there. Grant that, and even so you have these degrees of unconsciousness.

No one can deny that there is a fuller and fuller consciousness; that the grown man is more conscious than the baby, the baby than the embryo; the sensitive plant in a way more conscious than the seed from which it sprang. There has been addition. Something has appeared over and above; that something cannot have come out of nothing.

In other words, consciousness cannot have been made save by something itself conscious.

The process need not be repeated in the case of intelligence, for the same applies to intelligence as to consciousness. It certainly does not look as though a lump of iron could contemplate itself and reason upon itself. It certainly cannot do so in any intelligible sense. But even if you like to affirm that in some infinitesimally small degree it does, or that its ultimate material components do, at least you must admit that there are degrees in intelligence and that the higher intelligence cannot have come out of a lower. You cannot get your two gallons out of a quart.

It is this argument—even if there were no others—which enables us to affirm with certitude that nature is not sufficient to herself, unless we include under the term "Nature" something of the highest consciousness and the highest intelligence which has lain behind the phenomenon of the most advanced consciousness and intelligence apparent in ourselves and in our fellow beings. In other words, unless when we say "Nature" we mean "Nature including something which is of a consciousness at least as conscious as the highest degree of consciousness known to us," we are talking nonsense.

But to say, "at least as conscious as this, at least as intelligent as this" is not enough. Since there are degrees in consciousness and intelligence there is an ascending series, and to such an ascending series it is impossible, in reason, to put a limit. I see, coming from somewhere, increment upon increment of consciousness and intelligence and therefore the power to produce increment. To any one degree of increase, the highest known to us, there may be and can be a fuller increase. I am fuller of consciousness in one mood than another. It is nonsense to affirm that I shall never feel another mood of still sharper, fuller consciousness. I thought out things more clearly and thoroughly yesterday than I do today when I am fatigued. It is nonsense to say that I may not be able in some later hour to think more clearly and thoroughly than today. I cannot as yet solve such and such a problem. It is nonsense to say that on this account it is insoluble.

Again: I found so and so the most intelligent man I ever met. It is nonsense to say that there can be no man more intelligent. I found so and so the most vital. It is nonsense to say, "There can be no man more full of vitality — that is, of consciousness." No limits can be set to the process. Were even all men fully known to you, it would be nonsense to say that some creature other than man might not be more conscious and intelligent than the most conscious and intelligent man.

There is, then, some consciousness and intelligence of a degree indefinitely greater, "greater than any assignable degree of magnitude" than others, and "greater than any assignable degree of magnitude" is but the modern cautious compromise for what a more robust generation called "infinite." When, in mathematics, we say that such and such a series increases to a number "greater than any assignable number," we are saying "increases to infinity." Whenever we say that two lines will not meet though they be produced to a distance "greater than any assignable distance" we are saying, "will not meet though infinitely produced."[2]

There is, then, somewhere in the universal All which we are contemplating, an infinitely great degree of consciousness and intelligence.

Now, consciousness and intelligence are functions of personality. That is what, *at the least,* we mean by a person — that there are present in it consciousness and intelligence. Hence, so far, a conscious and intelligent God.

But there is something more. Personality is recognized also by will. Personality, our own and that of our fellows, we know by experience to be. We are equally informed that it cannot be without a will. Our wills, like our consciousness and intelligence, are manifestly imperfect. It may even be argued (correspondingly)

[2]These are examples of things which are finite indeed, yet indefinitely capable of being increased, as is the case in mathematical quantities. But things indefinitely capable of being increased logically presupposes something that is strictly infinite, i.e., absolutely without any limits. *The Editor.*

that, as they are derivative, they have no independent existence and that our will is not free—and so not a true will. But, like consciousness and intelligence, it came from that which can so provoke such an increment, and argues the Infinite Person who has Infinite Consciousness and Intelligence and Infinite Will. There is at *least* one Will, as there is one Personality of this kind; if it were not so, then will, like consciousness and intelligence, would not even be present as an addition to the rest of being.

So far, then, God is an Infinite Person, of Consciousness, Intelligence, and Will, whence alone such continuity of these could have come.

KNOWLEDGE, LEARNING, AND PROFESSIONAL SKILL[1]

John Henry Newman

It were well if the English, like the Greek language, possessed some definite word to express, simply and generally, intellectual proficiency or perfection, such as "health," as used with reference to the animal frame, and "virtue," with reference to our moral nature. I am not able to find such a term; talent, ability, genius, belong distinctly to the raw material, which is the subject matter, not to that excellence which is the result of exercise and training. When we turn, indeed, to the particular kinds of intellectual perfection, words are forthcoming for our purpose, as, for instance, judgment, taste, and skill; yet even these belong, for the most part, to powers or habits bearing upon practice or upon art, and not to any perfect condition of the intellect, considered in itself. Wisdom, again, is certainly a more comprehensive word than any other, but it has a direct relation to conduct and to human life. Knowledge, indeed, and Science express purely intellectual ideas, but still not a state or quality of the intellect; for knowledge, in its ordinary

[1]From *The Idea of a University.*

sense, is but one of its circumstances, denoting a possession or a habit; and science has been appropriated to the subject matter of the intellect, instead of belonging in English, as it ought to do, to the intellect itself. The consequence is that, on an occasion like this, many words are necessary, in order, first, to bring out and convey what surely is no difficult idea in itself—that of the cultivation of the intellect as an end; next, in order to recommend what surely is no unreasonable object; and lastly, to describe and make the mind realize the particular perfection in which that object consists. Everyone knows particularly what are the constituents of health or of virtue; and everyone recognizes health and virtue as ends to be pursued; it is otherwise with intellectual excellence, and this must be my excuse, if I seem to anyone to be bestowing a good deal of labor on a preliminary matter.

In default of a recognized term, I have called the perfection or virtue of the intellect by the name of philosophy, philosophical knowledge, enlargement of mind, or illumination; terms which are not uncommonly given to it by writers of this day; but, whatever name we bestow on it, it is, I believe, as a matter of history, the business of a university to make this intellectual culture its direct scope, or to employ itself in the education of the intellect—just as the work of a hospital lies in healing the sick or wounded, of a riding or fencing school, or of a gymnasium, in exercising the limbs, of an almshouse, in aiding and solacing the old, of an orphanage, in protecting innocence, of a penitentiary, in restoring the guilty. I say, a university, taken in its bare idea, and before we view it as an instrument of the Church, has this object and this mission; it contemplates neither moral impression nor mechanical production; it professes to exercise the mind neither in art nor in duty; its function is intellectual culture; here it may leave its scholars, and it has done its work when it has done as much as this. It educates the intellect to reason well in all matters, to reach out toward truth, and grasp it.

* * *

This, I said in my foregoing Discourse, was the object of a university, viewed in itself, and apart from the Catholic Church, or from the State, or from any other power which may use it; and I illustrated this in various ways. I said that the intellect must have an excellence of its own, for there was nothing which had not its specific good; that the word *educate* would not be used of intellectual culture, as it is used, had not the intellect had an end of its own; that, had it not such an end, there would be no meaning in calling certain intellectual exercises "liberal," in contrast with "useful," as is commonly done; that the very notion of a philosophical temper implied it, for it threw us back upon research and system as ends in themselves, distinct from effects and works of any kind; that a philosophical scheme of knowledge, or system of sciences, could not, from the nature of the case, issue in any one definite art or pursuit, as its end; and that, on the other hand, the discovery and contemplation of truth, to which research and systematizing led, were surely sufficient ends, though nothing beyond them were added, and that they had ever been accounted sufficient by mankind.

Here, then, I take up the subject; and, having determined that the cultivation of the intellect is an end distinct and sufficient in itself, and that, so far as words go, it is an enlargement of illumination, I proceed to inquire what this mental breadth, or power, or light, or philosophy consists in. A hospital heals a broken limb or cures a fever: what does an institution effect, which professes the health, not of the body, not of the soul, but of the intellect? What is this good, which in former times, as well as our own, has been found worth the notice, the appropriation, of the Catholic Church?

I have then to investigate, in the Discourses which follow, those qualities and characteristics of the intellect in which its cultivation issues or rather consists; and, with a view of assisting myself in this undertaking, I shall recur to certain questions which have already been touched upon. These questions are three: viz., the relation of intellectual culture, first, to *mere* knowledge; secondly, to *professional* knowledge; and thirdly, to *religious* knowledge. In other words, are *acquirements* and *attainments* the scope of a university education? or *expertness in particular arts and pursuits?* or *moral and religious proficiency?* or something besides these three? These questions I shall examine in succession, with the purpose I have mentioned; and I hope to be excused, if, in this anxious undertaking, I am led to repeat what, either in these Discourses or elsewhere, I have already put upon paper. And first, of *Mere Knowl-*

edge, or Learning, and its connection with intellectual illumination or Philosophy.

* * *

I suppose the *prima facie* view which the public at large would take of a university, considering it as a place of education, is nothing more or less than a place for acquiring a great deal of knowledge on a great many subjects. Memory is one of the first developed of the mental faculties; a boy's business when he goes to school is to learn; that is, to store up things in his memory. For some years his intellect is little more than an instrument for taking in facts, or a receptacle for storing them; he welcomes them as fast as they come to him; he lives on what is without; he has his eyes ever about him; he has a lively susceptibility of impressions; he imbibes information of every kind; and little does he make his own in a true sense of the word, living rather upon his neighbors all around him. He has opinions, religious, political, and literary, and, for a boy, is very positive in them and sure about them; but he gets them from his schoolfellows, or his masters, or his parents, as the case may be. Such as he is in his other relations, such also is he in his school exercises; his mind is observant, sharp, ready, retentive; he is almost passive in the acquisition of knowledge. I say this in no disparagement of the idea of a clever boy. Geography, chronology, history, language, natural history, he heaps up the matter of these studies as treasures for a future day. It is the seven years of plenty with him; he gathers in by handfuls, like the Egyptians, without counting; and though, as time goes on, there is exercise for his argumentative powers in the elements of mathematics, and for his taste in the poets and orators, still, while at school, or at least till quite the last years of his time, he acquires, and little more; and when he is leaving for the university, he is mainly the creature of foreign influences and circumstances, and made up of accidents, homogeneous or not, as the case may be. Moreover, the moral habits which are a boy's praise, encourage and assist this result; that is, diligence, assiduity, regularity, despatch, persevering application; for these are the direct conditions of acquisition, and naturally lead to it. Acquirements, again, are emphatically producible, and at a moment; they are a something to show, both for master and scholar; an audience, even though ignorant themselves of the subjects of an examination, can comprehend when questions are answered and when they are not. Here again is a reason why mental culture is in the minds of men identified with the acquisition of knowledge.

The same notion possesses the public mind, when it passes on from the thought of a school to that of a university: and with the best of reasons so far as this, that there is not true culture without acquirements, and that philosophy presupposes knowledge. It requires a great deal of reading, or a wide range of information, to warrant us in putting forth our opinions on any serious subject; and without such learning the most original mind may be able indeed to dazzle, to amuse, to refute, to perplex, but not to come to any useful result or any trustworthy conclusion. There are indeed persons who profess a different view of the matter, and even act upon it. Every now and then you will find a person of vigorous or fertile mind, who relies upon his own resources, despises all former authors, and gives the world, with the utmost fearlessness, his views upon religion, or history, or any other popular subject. And his works may sell for a while; he may get a name in his day; but this will be all. His readers are sure to find in the long run that his doctrines are mere theories, and not the expression of facts, that they are chaff instead of bread, and then his popularity drops as suddenly as it rose.

Knowledge, then, is the indispensable condition of expansion of mind, and the instrument of attaining to it; this cannot be denied, it is ever to be insisted on; I begin with it as a first principle; however, the very truth of it carries men too far, and confirms to them the notion that it is the whole of the matter. A narrow mind is thought to be that which contains little knowledge; and an enlarged mind, that which holds a great deal; and what seems to put the matter beyond dispute is the fact of the great number of studies which are pursued in a university, by its very profession. Lectures are given on every kind of subject; examinations are held; prizes awarded. There are moral, metaphysical, physical professors; professors of languages, of history, of mathematics, of experimental science. Lists of questions are published, wonderful for their range and depth, variety and difficulty; treatises are written, which carry upon their very face the evidence of extensive reading or multifarious information; what, then, is wanting for mental culture to a person of large reading and scientific attainments? what is grasp of mind but acquirement? where shall philosophical repose be found, but in the consciousness and enjoyment of large intellectual possessions?

And yet this notion is, I conceive, a mistake, and my present business is to show that it is one, and that the end of a liberal education is not mere knowledge, or knowledge considered in its *matter,* and I shall best attain my object, by actually setting down some cases, which will be generally granted to be instances of the process of enlightenment or enlargement of mind, and others which are not, and thus, by the comparison, you will be able to judge for yourselves, Gentlemen, whether knowledge, that is, acquirement, is after all the real principle of the enlargement, or whether that principle is not rather something beyond it.

* * *

For instance, let a person whose experience has hitherto been confined to the more calm and unpretending scenery of these islands, whether here or in England, go for the first time into parts where physical nature puts on her wilder and more awful forms, whether at home or abroad, as into mountainous districts; or let one who has ever lived in a quiet village go for the first time to a great metropolis — then I suppose he will have a sensation which perhaps he never had before. He has a feeling not in addition or increase of former feelings, but of something different in its nature. He will perhaps be borne forward, and find for a time that he has lost his bearings. He has made a certain progress, and he has a consciousness of mental enlargement; he does not stand where he did, he has a new center, and a range of thoughts to which he was before a stranger.

Again, the view of the heavens which the telescope opens upon us, if allowed to fill and possess the mind, may almost whirl it round and make it dizzy. It brings in a flood of ideas, and is rightly called an intellectual enlargement, whatever is meant by the term.

And so again, the sight of beasts of prey and other foreign animals, their strangeness, the originality (if I may use the term) of their forms and gestures and habits and their variety and independence of each other, throw us out of ourselves into another creation, and as if under another Creator, if I may so express the temptation which may come on the mind. We seem to have new faculties, or a new exercise for our faculties, by this addition to our knowledge; like a prisoner, who, having been accustomed to wear manacles or fetters, suddenly finds his arms and legs free.

Hence physical science generally, in all its departments, as bringing before us the exuberant riches and resources, yet the orderly course, of the universe, elevates and excites the student, and at first, I may say, almost takes away his breath, while in time it exercises a tranquilizing influence upon him.

Again, the study of history is said to enlarge and enlighten the mind, and why? because, as I conceive, it gives it a power of judging of passing events, and of all events, and a conscious superiority over them, which before it did not possess.

And in like manner, what is called seeing the world, entering into active life, going into society, traveling, gaining acquaintance with the various classes of the community, coming into contact with the principles and modes of thought of various parties, interests, and races, their views, aims, habits, and manners, their religious creeds and forms of worship—gaining experience how various yet how alike men are, how low-minded, how bad, how opposed, yet how confident in their opinions; all this exerts a perceptible influence upon the mind, which it is impossible to mistake, be it good or be it bad, and is popularly called its enlargement.

And then again, the first time the mind comes across the arguments and speculations of unbelievers, and feels what a novel light they cast upon what he has hitherto accounted sacred; and still more, if it gives in to them and embraces them, and throws off as so much prejudice what it has hitherto held, and, as if waking from a dream, begins to realize to its imagination that there is now no such thing as law and the transgression of law, that sin is a phantom, and punishment a bugbear, that it is free to sin, free to enjoy the world and the flesh; and still further, when it does enjoy them, and reflects that it may think and hold just what it will, that "the world is all before it where to choose," and what system to build up as its own private persuasion; when this torrent of willful thoughts rushes over and inundates it, who will deny that the fruit of the tree of knowledge, or what the mind takes for knowledge, has made it one of the gods, with a sense of expansion and elevation—an intoxication in reality, still, so far as the subjective state of the mind goes, an illumination? Hence the fanaticism of individuals or nations who suddenly cast off their Maker. Their eyes are opened; and, like the judgment-stricken king in the tragedy, they see two suns, and a magic universe, out of which they look back upon their former state of faith and innocence with a sort of contempt and indignation, as if they were then but fools, and the dupes of imposture.

On the other hand, religion has its own enlargement, and an enlargement, not of tumult, but of peace. It is often remarked of uneducated persons, who have hitherto thought little of the unseen world, that, on their turning to God, looking into themselves, regulating their hearts, reforming their conduct, and meditating on death and judgment, heaven and hell, they seem to become, in point of intellect, different beings from what they were. Before, they took things as they came, and thought no more of one thing than another. But now every event has a meaning; they have their own estimate of whatever happens to them; they are mindful of times and seasons, and compare the present with the past; and the world, no longer dull, monotonous, unprofitable, and hopeless, is a various and complicated drama, with parts and an object, and an awful moral.

* * *

Now for these instances, to which many more might be added, it is plain, first, that the communication of knowledge certainly is either a condition or the means of that sense of enlargement or enlightenment, of which at this day we hear so much in certain quarters: this cannot be denied; but next, it is equally plain that such communication is not the whole of the process. The enlargement consists, not merely in the passive reception into the mind of a number of ideas hitherto unknown to it, but in the mind's energetic and simultaneous action upon and toward and among those new ideas which are rushing in upon it. It is the action of a formative power, reducing to order and meaning the matter of our requirements; it is a making the objects of our knowledge subjectively our own, or, to use a familiar word, it is a digestion of what we receive into the substance of our previous state of thought; and without this no enlargement is said to follow. There is no enlargement, unless there be a comparison of ideas one with another, as they come before the mind, and a systematizing of them. We feel our minds to be growing and expanding *then,* when we not only learn, but refer what we learn to what we know already. It is not the mere addition to our knowledge that is the illumination; but the locomotion, the movement onward, of that mental center, to which both what we know and what we are learning, the accumulating mass of our acquirements, gravitates. And therefore a truly great intellect, and recognized to be such by the common opinion of mankind, such as the intellect of Aristotle, or of St. Thomas, or of Newton, or of Goethe (I purposely take instances within and without the Catholic pale, when I would speak of the intellect as such), is one which takes a connected view of old and new, past and present, far and near, and which has an insight into the influence of all these one on another; without which there is no whole, and no center. It possesses the knowledge, not only of things, but also of their mutual and true relations; knowledge, not merely considered as acquirement, but as philosophy.

Accordingly, when this analytical, distributive, harmonizing process is away, the mind experiences no enlargement, and is not reckoned as enlightened or comprehensive, whatever it may add to its knowledge. For instance, a great memory, as I have already said, does not make a philosopher, any more than a dictionary can be called a grammar. There are men who embrace in their minds a vast multitude of ideas, but with little sensibility about their real relations toward each other. These may be antiquarians, annalists, naturalists; they may be learned in the law; they may be versed in statistics; they are most useful in their own place; I should shrink from speaking disrespectfully of them; still, there is nothing in such attainments to guarantee the absence of narrowness of mind. If they are nothing more than well-read men, or men of information they have not what specially deserves the name of culture of mind, or fulfills the type of liberal education.

In like manner, we sometimes fall in with persons who have seen much of the world, and of the men, who, in their day, have played a conspicuous part in it, but who generalize nothing, and have no observation, in the true sense of the word. They abound in information in detail, curious and entertaining, about men and things; and, having lived under the influence of no very clear or settled principles, religious or political, they speak of everyone and everything only as so many phenomena which are complete in themselves and lead to nothing, not discussing them, or teaching any truth, or instructing the hearer, but simply talking. No one would say that these persons, well informed as they are, had attained to any great culture of intellect or to philosophy.

The case is the same still more strikingly where the persons in question are beyond dispute men of inferior powers and deficient education. Perhaps they have been much in foreign countries, and they receive, in a passive, otiose, unfruitful way, the various facts which are forced upon them there. Seafaring men, for example, range from one end of the earth to the other; but the multiplicity of external objects which they have encountered forms no symmetrical and consistent picture upon their imagination; they see the tapestry of human life, as it were, on the wrong side, and it tells no story. They sleep, and they rise up, and they find themselves now in Europe, now in Asia; they see visions of great cities and wild regions; they are in the marts of commerce, or amid the islands of the South; they gaze on Pompey's Pillar, or on the Andes; and nothing which meets them carries them forward or backward, to any idea beyond itself. Nothing has a drift or relation; nothing has a history or a promise. Everything stands by itself, and comes and goes in its turn, like the shifting scenes of a show, which leave the spectator where he was. Perhaps you are near such a man on a particular occasion, and expect him to be shocked or perplexed at something which occurs; but one thing is much the same to him as another, or, if he is perplexed, it is as not knowing what to say, whether it is right to admire, or to ridicule, or to disapprove, while conscious that some expression of opinion is expected from him; for in fact he has no standard of judgment at all, and no landmarks to guide him to a conclusion. Such is mere acquisition, and, I repeat, no one would dream of calling it philosophy.

Instances such as these confirm, by the contrast, the conclusion I have already drawn from those which preceded them. That only is true enlargement of mind which is the power of viewing many things at once as one whole, of referring them severally to their true place in the universal system, of understanding their respective values, and determining their mutual dependence. Thus is that form of universal knowledge, of which I have on a former occasion spoken, set up in the individual intellect, and constitutes its perfection. Possessed of this real illumination, the mind never views any part of the extended subject matter of knowledge without recollecting that it is but a part, or without the associations which spring from this recollection. It makes everything in some sort lead to everything else; it would communicate the image of the whole to every separate portion, till that whole becomes in imagination like a spirit, everywhere pervading and penetrating its component parts, and giving them one definite meaning. Just as our bodily organs, when mentioned, recall their function in the body, as the word *creation* suggests the Creator, and *subjects* a sovereign, so, in the mind of the philosopher, as we are abstractedly conceiving of him, the elements of the physical and moral world, sciences, arts, pursuits, ranks, offices, events, opinions, individualities, are all viewed as one, with correlative functions, and as gradually by successive combinations converging, one and all, to the true center.

To have even a portion of this illuminative reason and true philosophy is the highest state to which nature can aspire, in the way of intellect; it puts the mind above the influences of chance and necessity, above anxiety, suspense, unsettlement, and superstition, which is the lot of the many. Men whose minds are possessed with some one object, take exaggerated views of its importance, are feverish in the pursuit of it, make it the measure of things which are utterly foreign to it, and are startled and despond if it happens to fail them. They are ever in alarm or in transport. Those, on the other hand, who have no object or principle whatever to hold by, lose their way, every step they take. They are thrown out, and do not know what to think or say, at every fresh juncture; they have no view of persons, or occurrences, or facts, which come suddenly upon them, and they hand upon the opinion of others, for want of internal resources. But the intellect which has been disciplined to the perfection of its powers, which knows, and thinks while it knows, which has learned to leaven the dense mass of facts and events with the elastic force of reason, such an intellect cannot be partial, cannot be exclusive, cannot be impetuous, cannot be at a loss, cannot but be patient, collected, and majestically calm, because it discerns the end in every beginning, the origin in every end, the law in every interruption, the limit in each delay; because it ever knows where it stands, and how its path lies from one point to another. It is the τετράγωνος of the Peripatetic,[2] and has the *nil admirari*[3] of the Stoic—

> *Felix qui potuit rerum cognoscere causas,*
> *Atque metus omnes, et inexorabile fatum,*
> *Subjecit pedibus, strepitumque Acherontis avari.*[4]

There are men who, when in difficulties, originate at the moment vast ideas or dazzling projects; who, under the influence of excitement, are able to cast a light, almost as if from inspiration, on a subject or course of action which comes before them; who have a sudden presence of mind equal to any emergency, rising with the occasion, and an undaunted magnanimous bearing, and an energy and keenness which is but made intense by opposition. This is genius, this is heroism; it is the exhibition of a natural gift which no culture can teach, at which no Institution can aim; here, on the contrary, we are concerned, not with mere nature, but with training and teaching. That perfection of the intellect which is the result of education, and its *beau ideal,* to be imparted to individuals in their respective measures, is the clear, calm, accurate vision and comprehension of all things, as far as the finite mind can embrace them, each in its place, and with its own characteristics upon it. It is almost prophetic from its knowledge of history; it is almost heart-searching from its knowledge of human nature; it has almost supernatural charity from its freedom from littleness and prejudice; it has almost the repose of faith, because nothing can startle it; it has almost the beauty and harmony of heavenly contemplation, so intimate is it with the eternal order of things and the music of the spheres.

* * *

And now, if I may take for granted that the true and adequate

---

[2]Aristotle had described the excellent man as "foursquare."

[3]"Be astonished by nothing."

[4]"Happy he who has learned the causes of all things, and tramples under his feet every fear, inexorable fate itself, and the roar of hungry Acheron." (Virgil, *Georgics,* Bk. 2.)

end of intellectual training and of a university is not learning or acquirement, but rather, is thought or reason exercised upon knowledge, or what may be called philosophy, I shall be in a position to explain the various mistakes which at the present day beset the subject of university education.

I say then, if we would improve the intellect, first of all, we must ascend; we cannot gain real knowledge on a level; we must generalize, we must reduce to method, we must have a grasp of principles, and group and shape our acquisitions by means of them. It matters not whether our field of operation be wide or limited; in every case, to command it is to mount above it. Who has not felt the irritation of mind and impatience created by a deep, rich country, visited for the first time, with winding lanes, and high hedges, and green steeps, and tangled woods, and everything smiling indeed, but in a maze? The same feeling comes upon us in a strange city, when we have no map of its streets. Hence you hear of practised travelers, when they first come into a place, mounting some high hill or church tower, by way of reconnoitering its neighborhood. In like manner, you must be above your knowledge, not under it, or it will oppress you; and the more you have of it, the greater will be the load. The learning of a Salmasius or a Burmann,[5] unless you are its master, will be your tyrant. *Imperat aut servit;*[6] if you can wield it with a strong arm, it is a great weapon; otherwise,

Vis consili expers
Mole ruit sua.[7]

And in thus speaking, I am not denying that a strong and ready memory is in itself a real treasure; I am not disparaging a well-stored mind, though it be nothing besides, provided it be sober, any more than I would despise a bookseller's shop: it is of great value to others, even when not so to the owner. Nor am I banishing, far from it, the possessors of deep and multifarious learning from my ideal university; they adorn it in the eyes of men; I do

[5]Philologists, Salmasius at the University of Leyden (died 1653), Burmann at Utrecht (died 1742).

[6]It either commands or serves.

[7]Force without discretion falls by its own weight. (Horace, *Odes*, III, 4.)

but say that they constitute no type of the results at which it aims; that it is no great gain to the intellect to have enlarged the memory at the expense of faculties which are indisputably higher.

* * *

Nor, indeed, am I supposing that there is any great danger, at least in this day, of overeducation; the danger is on the other side. I will tell you, Gentlemen, what has been the practical error of the last twenty years — not to load the memory of the student with a mass of undigested knowledge, but to force upon him so much that he has rejected all. It has been the error of distracting and enfeebling the mind by an unmeaning profusion of subjects; of implying that a smattering in a dozen branches of study is not shallowness, which it really is, but enlargement, which it is not; of considering an acquaintance with the learned names of things and persons, and the possession of clever duodecimos, and attendance on eloquent lecturers, and membership with scientific institutions, and the sight of the experiments of a platform and the specimens of a museum — that all this was not dissipation of mind, but progress. All things now are to be learned at once, not first one thing, then another, not one well, but many badly. Learning is to be without exertion, without attention, without toil; without grounding, without advance, without finishing. There is to be nothing individual in it; and this, forsooth, is the wonder of the age. What the steam engine does with matter, the printing press is to do with mind; it is to act mechanically, and the population is to be passively, almost unconsciously enlightened, by the mere multiplication and dissemination of volumes. Whether it be the schoolboy, or the schoolgirl, or the youth at college, or the mechanic in the town, or the politician in the senate, all have been the victims in one way or other of this most preposterous and pernicious of delusions. Wise men have lifted up their voices in vain; and at length, lest their own institutions should be outshone and should disappear in the folly of the hour, they have been obliged, as far as they could with a good conscience, to humor a spirit which they could not withstand, and make temporizing concessions at which they could not but inwardly smile.

It must not be supposed that, because I so speak, therefore I have some sort of fear of the education of the people: on the contrary, the more education they have, the better, so that it is really education. Nor am I an enemy to the cheap publication of scientific and literary works, which is now in vogue: on the contrary, I consider it a great advantage, convenience, and gain; that is, to those to whom education has given a capacity for using them. Further, I consider such innocent recreations as science and literature are able to furnish will be a very fit occupation of the thoughts and the leisure of young persons, and may be made the means of keeping them from bad employments and bad companions. Moreover, as to that superficial acquaintance with chemistry, and geology, and astronomy, and political economy, and modern history, and biography, and other branches of knowledge, which periodical literature and occasional lectures and scientific institutions diffuse through the community, I think it a graceful accomplishment, and a suitable, nay, in this day a necessary accomplishment, in the case of educated men. Nor, lastly, am I disparaging or discouraging the thorough acquisition of any one of these studies, or denying that, as far as it goes, such thorough acquisition is a real education of the mind. All I say is, call things by their right names, and do not confuse together ideas which are essentially different. A thorough knowledge of one science and a superficial acquaintance with many, are not the same thing; a smattering of a hundred things or a memory for detail, is not a philosophical or comprehensive view. Recreations are not education; accomplishments are not education. Do not say, the people must be educated, when, after all, you only mean, amused, refreshed, soothed, put into good spirits and good humor, or kept from vicious excesses. I do not say that such amusements, such occupations of mind, are not a great gain; but they are not education. You may as well call drawing and fencing education, as a general knowledge of botany or conchology. Stuffing birds or playing stringed instruments is an elegant pastime, and a resource to the idle, but it is not education; it does not form or cultivate the intellect. Education is a high word; it is the preparation for knowledge, and it is the imparting of knowledge in proportion to that preparation. We require intellectual eyes to know withal, as bodily eyes for sight. We need both objects and organs intellectual; we cannot gain them without setting about it; we cannot gain them in our sleep, or by haphazard. The best telescope does not dispense with eyes; the printing press or the lecture room will assist us greatly, but we must be true to ourselves, we must be parties in the work. A university is, according to the usual designation, an Alma Mater, knowing her children one by one, not a foundry, or a mint, or a treadmill.

* * *

This process of training, by which the intellect, instead of being formed or sacrificed to some particular or accidental purpose, some specific trade or profession, or study or science, is disciplined for its own sake, for the perception of its own proper object, and for its own highest culture, is called Liberal Education; and though there is no one in whom it is carried as far as is conceivable, or whose intellect would be a pattern of what intellects should be made, yet there is scarcely anyone but may gain an idea of what real training is, and at least look toward it, and make its true scope and result, not something else, his standard of excellence; and numbers there are who may submit themselves to it, and secure it to themselves in good measure. And to set forth the right standard, and to train according to it, and to help forward all students toward it according to their various capacities, this I conceive to be the business of a university.

Now this is what some great men are very slow to allow; they insist that education should be confined to some particular and narrow end, and should issue in some definite work, which can be weighed and measured. They argue as if everything, as well as every person, had its price; and that where there has been a great outlay, they have a right to expect a return in kind. This they call making education and instruction "useful," and Utility becomes their watchword. With a fundamental principle of this nature, they very naturally go on to ask, what there is to show for the expense of a university; what is the real worth in the market of the article called "a liberal education," on the supposition that it does not teach us definitely how to advance our manufactures, or to improve our lands, or to better our civil economy; or again, if it does not at once make this man a lawyer, that an engineer, and that a surgeon; or at least if it does not lead to discoveries in chemistry, astronomy, geology, magnetism, and science of every kind.

* * *

You will see what I mean by the parallel of bodily health. Health is a good in itself, though nothing came of it, and is especially worth seeking and cherishing; yet, after all, the blessings which attend its presence are so great, while they are so close to it and so redound back upon it and encircle it, that we never think of it except as useful as well as good, and praise and prize it for what it does, as well as for what it is, though at the same time we cannot point out any definite and distinct work or production which it can be said to effect. And so as regards intellectual culture, I am far from denying utility in this large sense as the end of education, when I lay it down, that the culture of the intellect is a good in itself and its own end; I do not exclude from the idea of intellectual culture what it cannot but be, from the very nature of things; I only deny that we must be able to point out, before we have any right to call it useful, some art, or business, or profession, or trade, or work, as resulting from it, and its real and complete end. The parallel is exact: as the body may be sacrificed to some manual or other toil, whether moderate or oppressive, so may the intellect be devoted to some specific profession; and I do not call *this* the culture of the intellect. Again, as some member or organ of the body may be so inordinately used and developed, so may memory, or imagination, or the reasoning faculty; and *this* again is not intellectual culture. On the other hand, as the body may be tended, cherished, and exercised, with a simple view to its general health, so may the intellect also be generally exercised in order to its perfect state; and this *is* its cultivation.

Again, as health ought to precede labor of the body, and as a man in health can do what an unhealthy man cannot do, and as of this health the properties are strength, energy, agility, graceful carriage and action, manual dexterity, and endurance of fatigue, so in like manner general culture of mind is the best aid to professional and scientific study, and educated men can do what illiterate cannot; and the man who has learned to think and to reason and to compare and to discriminate and to analyze, who has refined his taste, and formed his judgment, and sharpened his mental vision, will not indeed at once be a lawyer, or a pleader, or an orator, or a statesman, or a physician, or a good landlord, or a man of business, or a soldier, or an engineer, or chemist, or a geologist, or antiquarian, but he will be placed in that state of intellect in which he can take up any one of the sciences or callings I have referred to, or any other for which he has a taste or special talent, with an ease, a grace, a versatility, and a success, to which another is a stranger. In this sense then, and as yet I have said but a very few words on a large subject, mental culture is emphatically *useful.*

If, then, I am arguing, and shall argue, against professional or scientific knowledge as the sufficient end of a university education, let me not be supposed, Gentlemen, to be disrespectful toward particular studies, or arts, or vocations, and those who are engaged in them. In saying that law or medicine is not the end of a university course, I do not mean to imply that the university does not teach law or medicine. What indeed can it teach at all, if it does not teach something particular? It teaches *all* knowledge by teaching all *branches* of knowledge, and in no other way. I do but say that there will be this distinction as regards a professor of law, or of medicine, or of geology, or of political economy, in a university and out of it, that out of a university he is in danger of being absorbed and narrowed by his pursuit, and of giving lectures which are the lectures of nothing more than a lawyer, physician, geologist, or political economist; whereas in a university he will just know where he and his science stand—he has come to it, as it were, from a height, he has taken a survey of all knowledge, he is kept from extravagance by the very rivalry of other studies, he has gained from them a special illumination and largeness of mind and freedom and self-possession, and he treats his own, in consequence, with a philosophy and a resource which belongs not to the study itself but to his liberal education.

This, then, is how I should solve the fallacy, for so I must call it, by which Locke and his disciples would frighten us from cultivating the intellect, under the notion that no education is useful which does not teach us some temporal calling, or some mechanical art, or some physical secret. I say that a cultivated intellect, because it is a good in itself, brings with it a power and a grace to every work and occupation which it undertakes, and enables us to be more useful, and to a greater number. There is a duty we owe to human society as such, to the state to which we belong, to the sphere in which we move, to the individuals toward whom we are variously related, and whom we successively encounter in life; and that philosophical or liberal education, as I have called it, which is the proper function of a university, if it refuses the foremost place to professional interests, does but postpone them to the formation of the citizen, and, while it subserves the larger interests of philanthropy, prepares also for the successful prosecution of those merely personal objects which at first sight it seems to disparage.

* * *

Today I have confined myself to saying that that training of the intellect which is best for the individual himself, best enables him to discharge his duties to society. The philosopher, indeed, and the man of the world differ in their very notion, but the methods by which they are respectively formed are pretty much the same. The philosopher has the same command of matters of thought, which the true citizen and gentleman has of matters of business and conduct. If, then, a practical end must be assigned to a university course, I say it is that of training good members of society. Its art is the art of social life, and its end is fitness for the world. It neither confines its views to particular professions on the one hand, nor creates heroes or inspires genius on the other. Works, indeed, of genius fall under no art; heroic minds come under no rule; a university is not a birthplace of poets or of immortal authors, of founders of schools, leaders of colonies, or conquerors of nations. It does not promise a generation of Aristotles or Newtons, of Napoleons or Washingtons, of Raphaels or Shakespeares, though such miracles of nature it has before now contained within its precincts. Nor is it content, on the other hand, with forming the critic or the experimentalist, the economist or the engineer, though such too it includes within its scope. But a university training is the great ordinary means to a great but ordinary end; it aims at raising the intellectual tone of society, at cultivating the public mind, at purifying the national taste, at supplying true principles to popular enthusiasm and fixed aims to popular aspiration, at giving enlargement and sobriety to the ideas of the age, at facilitating the exercise of political power, and refining the intercourse of private life. It is the education which gives a man a clear conscious view of his own opinions and judgments, a truth in developing them, an eloquence in expressing them, and a force in urging them. It teaches him to see things as they are, to go right to the point, to disentangle a skein of thought, to detect what is sophistical, and to discard what is irrelevant. It prepares him to fill any post with credit, and to master any subject with facility. It shows him how to accommodate himself to others, how to throw himself into their state of mind, how to bring before them his own, how to influence them, how to come to an understanding with them, how to bear with them. He is at home in any society, he has common ground with every class; he knows when to speak and when to be silent; he is able to converse, he is able to listen; he can ask a question pertinently, and gain a lesson seasonably, when he has nothing to impart himself; he is ever ready, yet never in the way; he is a pleasant companion, and a comrade you can depend upon; he knows when to be serious and when to trifle, and he has a sure tact which enables him to trifle with gracefulness and to be serious with effect. He has the repose of a mind which lives in itself, while it lives in the world, and which has resources for its happiness at home when it cannot go abroad. He has a gift which serves him in public, and supports him in retirement, without which good fortune is but vulgar, and with which failure and disappointment have a charm. The art which tends to make a man all this, is, in the object which it pursues, as useful as the art of wealth or the art of health, though it is less susceptible of method, and less tangible, less certain, less complete in its result.

GAS-HOUSE POETRY[1]

Michael Earls, S.J.

There is a bleak-looking structure down in the valley, a huge cylindrical blur across the landscape, a vaunting monster amid gentle cottages in the village. It is the gas house. The chimney,

[1]From *Under College Towers,* by permission of the author.

like a Bolshevist pencil stuck boldly into the air, emits occasionally a smear of flame, the explosive puff from the exhaust. The flare-up attracts no notice in the clear, steady light of daytime, but in the darkness of night the sudden brilliance startles the itinerants of the neighborhod.

There you have the imagistic symbol of the free-versist; there is the technique of ninety per cent of what is clamorously termed "modern poetry"—the detached, the occasional flare-up like some scarlet word or crimson line rising out of a waste of words in the ode or lyric. It strikes attention for a moment, only this and nothing more; and quickly it dies away in the dissipation of multiplied nothingnesses and is buried deep in the circumambient waste of commonplace lines and the flat marshes of banalities. Free verse (I must repeat that I am looking at what is boisterously called "the modern school") resembles art only as a scarecrow stands for a man; it is a thing, not a king, of shreds and patches. It has unity only "by accident," like the oneness of a cord of wood; but it is not the tree, structurally organized, with a vital in-ness through root and trunk, flower and fruit.

Let it not be imagined here, as pedantic free-versists may shout back, that we postulate for poetry or even good verse the mechanics of rhyme and fixed rhythm, either the elaborate rhyme-system of Gaelic poetry (A.D. 800), or the rhythmical maneuvers of Greek choruses (450 B.C.). Every amateur reader in English literature knows that there are abundant specimens of good poetry, on either side of the Victorian period, without rhyme or "footed" rhythms: Coventry Patmore with "The Toys," for instance, and Joyce Kilmer with "A Blue Valentine." But these odes and lyrics and ballads do not lack the processes of organization, the norms of art, the vital energy of living emotions and ecstasy, the wholesome exultation in the lyrism and an eye in fine frenzy rolling. This is the test of the poet—that he should see life steadily and see it whole, as Arnold said of Sophocles.

Let us be honest and admit that the ecstasy of much of the free verse today seems to be a replica of the pitiable mouthings, the insistent ejaculations of inmates in an insane asylum, the lyrism of a psychiatric ward. The mechanics of "the average" free-verse product seems to have the movement of a St. Vitus dance, done in a sort of vertigo. This modern school needs the vitriolic censure of a

Juvenal, who even cried over the quantities of parchment wasted by the "moderns" of his day. Or should we take the attitude of the laughing philosopher at the patchy pomposity of our modernistic versifiers, at their supercilious scoffing of the three R's — rhyme, rhythm, and reason; and let us add another, restraint; for true art selects, elects, and perfects on the ground of restraint.

As a laughing philosopher, Mr. Chesterton punctures the mummer manners of these moderns. From his essay on Pope, written long ago, a reader might have felt that Mr. Chesterton was exaggerating the excess baggage of the free-versist; but the twenty years between his laugh and the present exhibitions show that he was looking clearly at the horizon. If in that green wood the prospect was so ridiculous, what is it now in the dry! Said Chesterton: "Supposing that a lyric poet of the new school really had to deal with such an idea as that expressed in Pope's line about Man:

> A being darkly wise and rudely great.

Is it really so certain that he would go deeper into the matter than that old antithetical jingle goes? . . . The contemporary poet, in his elaborately ornamental book of verses, would produce something like the following:

> A creature
> Of feature
> More dark, more dark, more dark than skies.
> Yea, darkly wise, yea, darkly wise;
> Darkly wise as a formless fate.
> And if he be great,
> If he be great, then rudely great,
> Rudely great as a plough that plies,
> And darkly wise, and darkly wise."

One might suppose, as I have said, that Mr. Chesterton was jesting with the manner; but we find his contention verified in repeated pages of free verse, almost every second page. Anthologies, with mock heroic seriousness, parade them. Here is a typical one (I do not give the author's name, for I know that he has done verse that has not "this freedom"):

We have a one-room home,
You have a two-room, three-room, four-room.
We have a one-room home
because a one-room home is all we have.
We have a one-room home
because a one-room home holds all we have.
We have a one-room home
because we do not want
a two-room, three-room, four-room.
If we had a two-room, three-room, four-room
we would need more than a one-room home.
We have a one-room home.
We like a one-room home.

Now if that is mid-Broadway manner (and it is selected from an anthology called *Today's Poetry*), give us back the mid-Victorian at its full, or Celtic twilight in all its dimness, or puffs of mythology from old Parnassus. If it is a cradle-song, for the author places it among "Berceuse Ariettes," it is better adapted for a tipster rocking a boat.

Again, in the unabashed apologetics of the free-versist, the claim is made that their matter and manner "reflect contemporary life." Bless the mark! What has most of the poetry of our Western world done in the past but faithfully reflect the life of its day, breathing the spirit of the age, copying from the body of the times the tone and gestures to the manner born? I say most of that poetry; for, of course, the allegorical and romantic forms, in lyric or epic, aim at idealizations. Must we know contemporary life only in its freckles, men only with abnormal idiosyncrasies, roads only with mud, over which the poet must not throw his Walter Raleigh cloak? Is contemporary life merely a body with skin-blotches, and no soul to it capable of rational exaltations and courageous aspirations?

More specifically, take two themes that are frequent types of the material affected by these parodists of so-called contemporary life: a broken-hearted girl, suicide in the Thames or the Seine; and again, a frail woman working in "sweat-shop" conditions. Surely this is their common matter; yet life, even before our contemporaries, has had numerous instances of these tragic and sorrowful conditions. Compare, or rather contrast, the treatment of these themes by the free-versist and the genuine poet. From the former, what hysterical shrieks, what scarlet flashes, what unavailing repetitions and vulgar affectation of sordidness, unavailing for the living or the dying or the dead. On the other page, witness the service of poetry when it has to deal with those motifs. The reader may find the very examples in two lyrical ballads by Thomas Hood, "The Bridge of Sighs" and "The Song of the Shirt." Since they are too lengthy for present insertion here, I must ask the reader to review these two specimens and see how poetry treats themes that are maltreated by free verse. Moreover, be it noted that Hood was no mid-, but pre-Victorian. There are repetitions of word or phrase; note, however, that the reiterations count into an artistic growth and progress. Here are withal rhyme, rhythm, reason, and restraint: and what healthy tones are here embodied for sociological culture; what pity, that covers the dead with graceful feeling and enheartens the living for better things. Did not "The Song of the Shirt" bring about a Parliamentary reform of conditions among tenement workers?

Oh, Men, with Sisters dear!
Oh, Men with Mothers and Wives!
It is not linen you're wearing out
But human creatures' lives!
Stitch — stitch — stitch,
In poverty, hunger, and dirt,
Sewing at once, with a double thread,
A Shroud as well as a Shirt.

One more sample in the contrast will suffice. Who does not know Lamb's "The Old Familiar Faces"? It is and is likely to be in every well-selected anthology. It has no rhyme, it moves in varying rhythm; yet it is not free verse, for it contains "the thing" that is of the essence of poetry:

I have had playmates, I have had companions,
In my days of childhood, in my joyful school-days;
All, all are gone, the old familiar faces.

Ghost-like I paced round the haunts of my childhood,
Earth seemed a desert I was bound to traverse,
Seeking to find the old familiar faces.

Let a modern try to improve on that and what is the result? We do not have to search Mr. Chesterton for the response, for we can find the "effort" done, and, I may presume, achieved with the pompous self-satisfaction of the modern school in the *Spoon River Anthology*. Lamb's poem sings its universal appeal under a few general statements; and the Spoon River verse gurgles waterishly in its unappealing details, as, for instance, this first dip into it:

Where are Elmer, Herman, Bert, Tom and Charley,
The weak of will, the strong of arm, the clown, the boozer, the fighter?
All, all are sleeping on the hill.
One passed in a fever.
One was burned in a mine.
One was killed in a brawl,
One died in a jail.
One fell from a bridge toiling for children and wife —
All, all are sleeping, sleeping, sleeping on the hill.
Where are Ella, Kate, Mag, Lizzie and Edith,
The tender heart, the simple soul, the loud, the proud, the happy one?
All, all are sleeping on the hill.

Since that is a page of the modern school, let us return to the ancients with their cesuras and iambics, and to the formal couplets of Pope and Dryden: Since that is freedom, let us have the slavery of old approved laws of the art of literature. Verselibrism, which is the ritual of much of the modern school, seems to be a disposition against laws in every department — artistic, grammatical, ethical, and religious. It protests the restraint of the artist's brush or chisel; it employs only a kodak to go slumming. Its images and diction belong to a world which has drifted from calm thinking, from endurance in labor, from sanity in appreciation. Free verse is in the class with music that is jazz, with dress that is bizarre, with conduct that is burlesque. Like the gas-house flare, it gives a spectral glow for a moment; but the darkness of night continues. These bounders of the modern school contribute nothing permanent to the delightful thoughts or the cultural adages of mankind. To quote the affable Bert Leston Taylor:

I read a great deal of verse libre,
And images scan by the score,

But never a line,
Be it ever so fine,
Is added to memory's store.

Yet this is a test of great poetry, namely, that it brings forth, in beauty of expression, thoughts worthy of the memory of mankind; as Newman says of a great author: "He expresses what all feel but all cannot say; and his sayings pass into proverbs among his people, and his phrases become household words and idioms of their daily speech, which is tesselated with the rich fragments of his language, as we see in foreign lands the marbles of Roman grandeur worked into the walls and pavements of modern palaces."

Fifty years hence the present hubbub of the so-called modern school will not be noticed in the anthologies, except for archeological wonderment. But many of the mid-Victorians will be there; and, in goodly numbers, the despised "artificialities" of the Age of Classicism, and the sneered-at lyrics of the Caroline and Elizabethan periods. The modern school is already old. The ephemeral glare of the gas house is dead. The stars still shine.

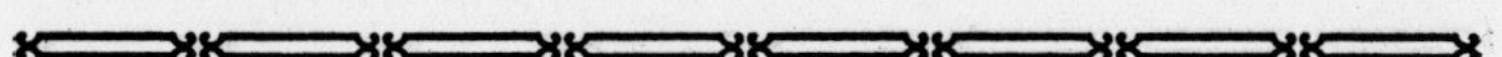

III. DESCRIPTION

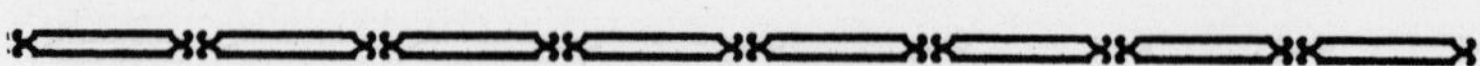

A. Brief Descriptions

1. Buildings and Places
2. Persons
3. Nature

B. Longer Descriptions

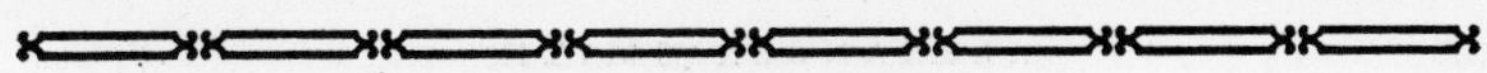

A. BRIEF DESCRIPTIONS

1. Buildings and Places

❦

DREAMTHORP[1]

Alexander Smith

It matters not to relate how or when I became a denizen of Dreamthorp; it will be sufficient to say that I am not a born native, but that I came to reside in it a good while ago now. The several towns and villages in which, in my time, I have pitched a tent did not please, for one obscure reason or another: this one was too large, t'other too small; but when on a summer evening about the hour of eight, I first beheld Dreamthorp, with its westward-looking windows painted by sunset, its children playing in the single straggling street, the mothers knitting at the open doors, the fathers standing about in long white blouses, chatting or smoking; the great tower of the ruined castle rising high into the rosy air, with a whole troop of swallows—by distance made as small as gnats—skimming about its rents and fissures—when I first beheld all this, I felt instinctively that my knapsack might be taken off my shoulders, that my tired feet might wander no more, that at last, on the planet, I had found a home. From that evening I have dwelt here, and the only journey I am like now to make, is the very inconsiderable one, so far at least as distance is concerned, from the house in which I live to the graveyard beside the ruined castle. There, with the former habitants of the palace, I trust to sleep quietly enough, and nature will draw over our heads her coverlet of green sod, and tenderly tuck us in, as a mother her sleeping ones,

[1]From *Dreamthorp and Other Essays.*

so that no sound from the world shall ever reach us, and no sorrow trouble us any more.

The village stands far inland; and the streams that trot through the soft green valleys all about have as little knowledge of the sea as the three-years' child of the storms and passions of manhood. The surrounding country is smooth and green, full of undulations; and pleasant country roads strike through it in every direction, bound for distant towns and villages, yet in no hurry to reach them. On these roads the lark in summer is continually heard; nests are plentiful in the hedges and dry ditches; and on the grassy banks, and at the feet of the bowed dikes, the blue-eyed speedwell smiles its benison on the passing wayfarer. On these roads you may walk for a year and encounter nothing more remarkable than the country cart, troops of tawny children from the woods, laden with primroses, and at long intervals — for people in this district live to a ripe age — a black funeral creeping in from some remote hamlet; and to this last the people reverently doff their hats and stand aside. Death does not walk about here often, but when he does, he receives as much respect as the squire himself. Everything round one is unhurried, quiet, mossgrown, and orderly. Season follows in the track of season, and one year can hardly be distinguished from another. Time should be measured here by the silent dial, rather than by the ticking clock, or by the chimes of the church. Dreamthorp can boast of a respectable antiquity, and in it the trade of the builder is unknown. Ever since I remember, not a single stone has been laid on the top of another. The castle, inhabited now by jackdaws and starlings, is old; the chapel which adjoins it is older still; and the lake behind both, and in which their shadows sleep, is, I suppose, as old as Adam. A fountain in the market place, all mouths and faces and curious arabesques — as dry, however, as the castle moat — has a tradition connected with it; and a great noble, riding through the street one day several hundred years ago, was shot from a window by a man whom he had injured. The death of this noble is the chief link which connects the place with authentic history. The houses are old, and remote dates may yet be deciphered on the stones above the doors; the apple trees are mossed and ancient; countless generations of sparrows have bred in the thatched roofs, and thereon have chirped out their lives. In every room of the place men have been born, men have died. On Dreamthorp centuries have fallen, and have left no more trace than have last winter's snowflakes. This commonplace sequence and flowing on of life is immeasurably affecting. That winter morning when Charles lost his head in front of the banqueting hall of his own palace, the icicles hung from the eaves of the houses here, and the clown kicked the snowballs from his clouted shoon, and thought but of his supper when, at three o'clock, the red sun set in the purple mist. On that Sunday in June while Waterloo was going on, the gossips, after morning service, stood on the country roads discussing agricultural prospects, without the slightest suspicion that the day passing over their heads would be a famous one in the calendar. Battles have been fought, kings have died, history has transacted itself; but, all unheeding and untouched, Dreamthorp has watched apple trees redden and wheat ripen, and smoked its pipe, and quaffed its mug of beer, and rejoiced over its newborn children and with proper solemnity carried its dead to the churchyard. As I gaze on the village of my adoption, I think of many things very far removed, and seem to get closer to them. The last setting sun that Shakespeare saw reddened the windows here, and struck warmly on the faces of the hinds coming home from the fields. The mighty storm that raged while Cromwell lay a-dying made all the oak woods groan about here, and tore the thatch from the very roofs I gaze upon. When I think of this, I can almost, so to speak, lay my hand on Shakespeare and on Cromwell. These poor walls were contemporaries of both, and I find something affecting in the thought. The mere soil is, of course, far older than either, but *it* does not touch one in the same way. A wall is the creation of a human hand, the soil is not.

This place suits my whim, and I like it better year after year. As with everything else, since I began to love it I find it gradually growing beautiful. Dreamthorp — a castle, a chapel, a lake, a straggling strip of gray houses, with a blue film of smoke over all — lies embosomed in emerald. Summer, with its daisies, runs up to every cottage door. From the little height where I am now sitting, I see it beneath me. Nothing could be more peaceful. The wind and the birds fly over it. A passing sunbeam makes brilliant a white gable-end, and brings out the colors of the blossomed apple tree beyond, and disappears. I see figures in the street, but hear them not. The hands on the church clock seem always pointing to one hour. Time has fallen asleep in the afternoon sunshine. I make a frame of my fingers, and look at my picture. On the walls of the next Academy's Exhibition will hang nothing half so beautiful!

My village is, I think, a special favorite of summer's. Every window sill in it she touches with color and fragrance; everywhere she wakens the drowsy murmurs of the hives; every place she scents with apple blossom. Traces of her hand are to be seen on the weir beside the ruined mill; and even the canal, along which the barges come and go, has a great white water lily asleep on its olive-colored face. Never was velvet on a monarch's robe so gorgeous as the green mosses that beruff the roofs of farm and cottage, when the sunbeam slants on them and goes. The old road out toward the common, and the hoary dikes that might have been built in the reign of Alfred, have not been forgotten by the generous adorning season; for every fissure has its mossy cushion, and the old blocks themselves are washed by the loveliest gray-green lichens in the world, and the large loose stones lying on the ground have gathered to themselves the peacefullest mossy coverings. Some of these have not been disturbed for a century. Summer has adorned my village as gaily, and taken as much pleasure in the task, as the people of old, when Elizabeth was queen, took in the adornment of the Maypole against a summer festival. And, just think, not only Dreamthorp, but every English village she has made beautiful after one fashion or another — making vivid green the hill slope on which straggling white Welsh hamlets hang right opposite the sea; drowning in apple blossom the red Sussex ones in the fat valley. And think, once more, every spear of grass in England she has touched with a livelier green; the crest of every bird she has burnished; every old wall between the four seas has received her mossy and licheny attentions; every nook in every forest she has sown with pale flowers, every marsh she has dashed with the fires of the marigold. And in the wonderful night the moon knows, she hangs — the planet on which so many millions of us fight, and sin, and agonize, and die — a sphere of glowworm light.

EMILY'S HOME[1]

Charles Dickens

"Yon's our house, Mas'r Davy!"

I looked in all directions, as far as I could stare over the wilderness, and away at the sea, and away at the river, but no house could *I* make out. There was a black barge, or some other kind of superannuated boat, not far off, high and dry on the ground, with an iron funnel sticking out of it for a chimney and smoking very cosily; but nothing else in the way of a habitation that was visible to *me.*

"That's not it?" said I. "That ship-looking thing?"

"That's it, Mas'r Davy," returned Ham.

If it had been Aladdin's palace, roc's egg and all, I suppose I could not have been more charmed with the romantic idea of living in it. There was a delightful door cut in the side, and it was roofed in, and there were little windows in it; but the wonderful charm of it was that it was a real boat which had, no doubt, been upon the water hundreds of times, and which had never been intended to be lived in, on dry land. That was the captivation of it to me. If it had ever been meant to be lived in, I might have thought it small, or inconvenient, or lonely; but never having been designed for any such use, it became a perfect abode.

It was beautifully clean inside, and as tidy as possible. There was a table, and a Dutch clock, and a chest of drawers, and on the chest of drawers there was a tea tray with a painting on it of a lady with a parasol, taking a walk with a military-looking child who was trundling a hoop. The tray was kept from tumbling down by a a Bible; and the tray, if it had tumbled down, would have smashed a quantity of cups and saucers and a teapot that were grouped around the book. On the walls there were some common colored pictures, framed and glazed, of Scripture subjects, such as I have never seen since in the hands of pedlars, without seeing the whole interior of Peggotty's brother's house again, at one view. Abraham in red going to sacrifice Isaac in blue, and Daniel in yellow cast into a den of green lions, were the most prominent of these. Over

[1]From *David Copperfield.*

the little mantel-shelf was a picture of the *Sarah Jane* lugger, built at Sunderland, with a real little wooden stern stuck on to it; a work of art, combining composition with carpentry, which I considered to be one of the most enviable possessions that the world could afford. There were some hooks in the beams of the ceiling, the use of which I did not divine then; and some lockers and boxes and conveniences of that sort, which served for seats and eked out the chairs.

All this, I saw in the first glance after I crossed the threshold—childlike, according to my theory—and then Peggotty opened a little door and showed me my bedroom. It was the completest and most desirable bedroom ever seen—in the stern of the vessel; with a little window, where the rudder used to go through; a little looking-glass, just the right height for me, nailed against the wall, and framed with oyster shells; a little bed, which there was just room enough to get into; and a nosegay of seaweed in a blue mug on the table. The walls were whitewashed as white as milk, and the patchwork counterpane made my eyes quite ache with its brightness. One thing I particularly noticed in this delightful house was the smell of fish; which was so searching, that when I took out my pocket handkerchief to wipe my nose, I found it smelt exactly as if it had wrapped up a lobster. On my imparting this discovery in confidence to Peggotty, she informed me that her brother dealt in lobsters, crabs, and crawfish; and I afterwards found that a heap of these creatures, in a state of wonderful conglomeration with one another, and never leaving off pinching whatever they laid hold of, were usually to be found in a little wooden outhouse where the pots and kettles were kept.

MEMORIES OF HOME[1]

Charles Dickens

And now I see the outside of our house, with the latticed bedroom windows, standing open to let in the sweet-smelling air, and the

[1]From *David Copperfield.*

ragged old rook's nests still dangling in the elm trees at the bottom of the front garden. Now I am in the garden at the back, beyond the yard where the empty pigeon-house and dog kennel are — a very preserve of butterflies, as I remember it, with a high fence and a gate and padlock; where the fruit clusters on the trees, riper and richer than fruit has ever been since, in any other garden, and where my mother has gathered some in a basket, while I stand by, bolting further gooseberries, and trying to look unmoved. A great wind rises, and the summer is gone in a minute. We are playing in the winter twilight, dancing about the parlor. When my mother is out of breath and rests herself in an elbow-chair, I watch her winding her bright curls about her fingers, and straightening her waist, and nobody knows better than I do that she likes to look well and is proud of being so pretty.

A PICTURESQUE HOUSE[1]

George Eliot

Imagine a rambling, patchy house, the best part built of gray stone, and red-tiled, a round tower jutting at one of the corners, the mellow darkness of its conical roof surmounted by a weather-cock making an agreeable object either amidst the gleams and greens of summer or the low-hanging clouds and snowy branches of winter; the ground shady with spreading trees; a great cedar flourishing on one side, backward some Scotch firs on a broken bank where the roots hung naked, and beyond, a rookery: on the other side a pool overhung with bushes where the water fowl fluttered and screamed: all around, a vast meadow which might be called a park, bordered by an old plantation and guarded by stone lodges which looked like little prisons.

[1]From *Daniel Deronda.*

THE TOWN OF ST. OGG'S[1]

George Eliot

A wide plain, where the broadening floss hurries on between its green banks to the sea, and the loving tide, rushing to meet it, checks its passage with an impetuous embrace. On this mighty tide the black ships — laden with the fresh-scented fir planks, with rounded sacks of oil-bearing seed, or with the dark glitter of coal — are borne along to the town of St. Ogg's, which shows its aged, fluted red roofs and the broad gables of its wharves between the low wooded hill and the river brink, tingeing the water with a soft February sun.

THE RED-ROOM[1]

Charlotte Brontë

The red-room was a spare chamber, very seldom slept in; I might say never, indeed, unless when a chance influx of visitors at Gateshead Hall rendered it necessary to turn to account all the accommodation it contained: yet it was one of the largest and stateliest chambers in the mansion. A bed, supported on massive pillars of mahogany, hung with curtains of deep-red damask, stood out like a tabernacle in the center; the two large windows, with their blinds always drawn down, were half shrouded in festoons and falls of similar drapery; the carpet was red; the table at the foot of the bed was covered with a crimson cloth; the walls were a soft fawn

---

[1]From *Mill on the Floss.*

[1]From *Jane Eyre.*

color, with a blush of pink in it; the wardrobe, the toilet table, the chairs, were of darkly polished old mahogany. Out of these deep surrounding shades rose high, and glared white, the piled-up mattresses and pillows of the bed, spread with a snowy Marseilles counterpane. Scarcely less prominent was an ample, cushioned easy-chair near the head of the bed, also white, with a footstool before it, and looking, as I thought, like a pale throne.

This room was chill, because it seldom had a fire; it was silent, because remote from the nursery and kitchens; solemn, because it was known to be so seldom entered. The housemaid alone came here on Saturdays, to wipe from the mirrors and the furniture a week's quiet dust; and Mrs. Reed herself, at far intervals, visited it to review the contents of a certain secret drawer in the wardrobe, where were stored divers parchments, her jewel casket, and a miniature of her deceased husband; and in those last words lies the secret of the red-room — the spell which kept it so lonely in spite of its grandeur.

Mr. Reed had been dead nine years; it was in this chamber he breathed his last; here he lay in state; hence his coffin was borne by the undertaker's men; and since that day a sense of dreary consecration had guarded it from frequent intrusion.

My seat, to which Bessie and the bitter Miss Abbot had left me riveted, was a low ottoman near the marble chimney-piece; the bed rose before me; to my right hand there was the high, dark wardrobe, with subdued, broken reflections varying the gloss of its panels; to my left the muffled windows; a great looking-glass between them repeated the vacant majesty of the bed and room. . . . All looked colder and darker in that visionary hollow than in reality; and the strange little figure there gazing at me, with a white face and arms specking the gloom, and glittering eyes of fear moving where all else was still, had the effect of a real spirit. I thought it like one of the tiny phantoms, half fairy, half imp, Bessie's evening stories represented as coming up out of lone, ferny dells in moors, and appearing before the eyes of belated travelers.

ATHENS, THE EYE OF GREECE[1]

John Henry Newman

A confined triangle, perhaps fifty miles its greatest length, and thirty its greatest breadth; two elevated rocky barriers, meeting at an angle; three prominent mountains, commanding the plain—Parnes, Pentelicus, and Hymettus; an unsatisfactory soil; some streams, not always full—such is about the report which the agent of a London company would have made of Attica. He would report that the climate was mild; the hills were limestone; there was plenty of good marble; more pasture land than at first survey might have been expected, sufficient certainly for sheep and goats; fisheries productive; silver mines once, but long since worked out; figs fair; oil first-rate; olives in profusion. But what he would not think of noting down, was, that that olive tree was so choice in nature and so noble in shape, that it excited a religious veneration; and that it took so kindly to the light soil, as to expand into woods upon the open plain, and to climb up and fringe the hills. He would not think of writing word to his employers, how that clear air, of which I have spoken, brought out, yet blended and subdued, the colors on the marble, till they had a softness and harmony, for all their richness, which in a picture looks exaggerated, yet is after all within the truth. He would not tell how that same delicate and brilliant atmosphere freshened up the pale olive, till the olive forgot its monotony, and its cheek glowed like the arbutus or beech of the Umbrian hills. He would say nothing of the thyme and thousand fragrant herbs which carpeted Hymettus; he would hear nothing of the hum of its bees; nor take much account of the rare flavor of its honey, since Gozo and Minorca were sufficient for the English demand. He would look over the Ægean from the height he had ascended; he would follow with his eye the chain of islands, which, starting from the Sunian headland, seemed to offer the fabled divinities of Attica, when they would visit their Ionian cousins, a sort of viaduct thereto across the sea; but that fancy would not

[1]From *Historical Sketches*.

occur to him, nor any admiration of the dark violet billows with their white edges down below; nor of those graceful, fanlike jets of silver upon the rocks, which slowly rise aloft like water spirits from the deep, then shiver, and break, and spread, and shroud themselves, and disappear, in a soft mist of foam; nor of the gentle, incessant heaving and panting of the whole liquid plain; nor of the long waves, keeping steady time, like a line of soldiery, as they resound upon the hollow shore — he would not deign to notice that restless living element at all, except to bless his stars that he was not upon it. Nor the distinct detail, nor the refined coloring, nor the graceful outline and roseate golden hue of the jutting crags, nor the bold shadows cast from Otus or Laurium by the declining sun; our agent of a mercantile firm would not value these matters even at a low figure.

ENGLISH COTTAGES[1]

John Ruskin

The principal thing worthy of observation in the lowland cottage of England is its finished neatness. The thatch is firmly pegged down, and mathematically leveled at the edges; and, though the martin is permitted to attach its humble domicile, in undisturbed security, to the eaves, he may be considered as enhancing the effect of the cottage, by increasing its usefulness and making it contribute to the comfort of more beings than one. The whitewash is stainless, and its rough surface catches a side light as brightly as a front one: the luxuriant rose is trained gracefully over the window; and the gleaming lattice, divided not into heavy squares, but into small pointed diamonds, is thrown half open, as is just discovered by its glance among the green leaves of the sweet brier, to admit the breeze, that, as it passes over the flowers, becomes full of their fragrance. The

[1]From *The Poetry of Architecture.*

light wooden porch breaks the flat of the cottage face by its projection; and a branch or two of wandering honeysuckle spread over the low hatch. A few square feet of garden and a latched wicket, persuading the weary and dusty pedestrian, with excessive eloquence, to lean upon it for an instant and request a drink of water or milk, complete a picture, which, if it be far enough from London to be unspoiled by town sophistications, is a very perfect thing in its way. The ideas it awakens are agreeable, and the architecture is all that we want in such a situation. It is pretty and appropriate; and if it boasted of any other perfection, it would be at the expense of its propriety.

AN ENGLISH CATHEDRAL[1]

John Ruskin

And now I wish that the reader, before I bring him into St. Mark's Place, would imagine himself for a little time in a quiet English cathedral town, and walk with me to the west front of its cathedral. Let us go together up the more retired street, at the end of which we can see the pinnacles of one of the towers, and then through the low gray gateway with its battlemented top and small latticed window in the center, into the inner private-looking road or close, where nothing goes in but the carts of the tradesmen who supply the bishop and the chapter, and where there are little shaven grass-plots, fenced in by neat rails, before old-fashioned groups of somewhat diminutive and excessively trim houses, with little oriel and bay windows jutting out here and there, and deep wooden cornices and eaves painted cream color and white, and small porches to their doors in the shape of cockleshells, or little, crooked, thick, indescribable wooden gables warped a little on one side; and so forward till we come to larger houses, also old-fashioned, but of red brick, and with gardens behind them, and fruit walls, which show here

[1]From *Stones of Venice*.

and there, among the nectarines, the vestiges of an old cloister arch or shaft; and looking in front on the cathedral square itself, laid out in rigid divisions of smooth grass and gravel walk, yet not uncheerful, especially on the sunny side, where the canon's children are walking with their nurserymaids. And so, taking care not to tread on the grass, we will go along the straight walk to the west front, and there stand for a time, looking up at its deep-pointed porches and the dark places between their pillars where there were statues once, and where the fragments, here and there, of a stately figure are still left, which has in it the likeness of a king, perhaps indeed a king on earth, perhaps a saintly king long ago in heaven; and so higher and higher up to the great moldering wall of rugged sculpture and confused arcades, shattered, and gray, and grisly with heads of dragons and mocking fiends, worn by the rains and swirling winds into yet unseemlier shape, and colored on their stony scales by the deep russet-orange lichen, melancholy gold; and so, higher still, to the bleak towers, so far above that the eye loses itself among the bosses of their traceries, though they are rude and strong, and only sees, like a drift of eddying black points, now closing, now scattering, and now settling suddenly into invisible places among the bosses and flowers, the crowd of restless birds that fill the whole square with that strange clangor of theirs, so harsh and yet so soothing, like the cries of birds on a solitary coast between the cliffs and sea.

THE EXTERIOR OF ST. MARK'S[1]

John Ruskin

We will push fast [through the lounging group of English and Austrians] into the shadow of the pillars at the end of the "Bocca di Piazza,"[2] and then we forget them all; for between those pillars

[1]From *The Stones of Venice.*
[2]"Mouth of the Square," leading into the wide opening before St. Mark's.

there opens a great light, and, in the midst of it, as we advance slowly, the vast tower of St. Mark seems to lift itself visibly forth from the level field of checkered stones; and, on each side, the countless arches prolong themselves into ranged symmetry, as if the rugged and irregular houses that pressed together above us in the dark alley had been struck back into sudden obedience and lovely order, and all their rude casements and broken walls had been transformed into arches charged with goodly sculpture, and fluted shafts of delicate stone.

And well may they fall back, for beyond those troops of ordered arches there rises a vision out of the earth, and all the great square seems to have opened from it in a kind of awe that we may see it far away; a multitude of pillars and white domes, clustered into a long low pyramid of colored light; a treasure heap it seems, partly of gold, and partly of opal and mother-of-pearl, hollowed beneath into five great vaulted porches, ceiled with fair mosaic, and beset with sculpture of alabaster, clear as amber and delicate as ivory — sculptures fantastic and involved, of palm leaves and lilies, and grapes and pomegranates, and birds clinging and fluttering among the branches, all twined together into an endless network of buds and plumes; and, in the midst of it, the solemn forms of angels, sceptered, and robed to the feet, and leaning to each other across the gates, their figures indistinct among the gleaming of the golden ground through the leaves beside them, interrupted and dim, like the morning light as it faded back among the branches of Eden, when first its gates were angel-guarded long ago. And round the walls of the porches there are set pillars of variegated stones, jasper and porphyry, marbles, that half refuse and half yield to the sunshine, Cleopatralike, "their bluest veins to kiss" — the shadow, as it steals back from them, revealing line after line of azure undulation, as a receding tide leaves the waved sand; their capitals rich with interwoven tracery, rooted knots of herbage, and drifting leaves of acanthus and vine, and mystical signs, all beginning and ending in the Cross; and above them, in the broad archivolts, a continuous chain of language and of life — angels, and the signs of heaven, and the labors of men, each in its appointed season upon the earth; and above these, another range of glittering pinnacles, mixed with white arches edged with scarlet flowers — a confusion of delight amid which the breasts of the Greek horses are seen blazing in their breadth of golden strength, and the St. Mark's lion, lifted on a blue field covered with stars, until at last, as if in ecstasy, the crests of the arches break into a marble foam, and toss themselves far into the blue sky in flashes and wreaths of sculptured spray, as if the breakers on the Lido shore had been frost-bound before they fell, and the sea-nymphs had inlaid them with coral and amethyst.

THE MOSLEM QUARTER[1]

A. W. Kinglake

The Moslem quarter of a city is lonely and desolate; you go up and down, and on, over shelving and hillocky paths through the narrow lanes walled in by blank, windowless dwellings; you come out upon an open space strewed with the black ruins that some late fire has left; you pass by a mountain of castaway things, the rubbish of centuries, and on it you see numbers of big, wolflike dogs lying torpid under the sun, with limbs outstretched to the full, as if they were dead; storks or cranes, sitting fearless upon the low roofs, look gravely down upon you; the still air that you breathe is loaded with the scent of citron and pomegranate rinds scorched by the sun, or (as you approach the bazaar) with the dry, dead perfume of strange spices. You long for some signs of life, and tread the ground more heavily, as though you would wake the sleepers with the heel of your boot; but the foot falls noiseless upon the crumbling soil of an eastern city, and silence follows you still. Again and again you meet turbans, and faces of men, but they have nothing for you — no welcome — no wonder — no wrath — no scorn; they look upon you as we do upon a December's fall of snow — as a "seasonable," unaccountable, uncomfortable work of God that may have been sent for some good purpose, to be revealed hereafter.

[1]From *Eothen.*

THE HOUSE OF USHER[1]

Edgar Allan Poe

During the whole of a dull, dark, and soundless day in the autumn of the year, when the clouds hung oppressively low in the heavens, I had been passing alone, on horseback, through a singularly dreary tract of country; and at length I found myself, as the shades of evening drew on, within view of the melancholy House of Usher. I know not how it was — but with the first glimpse of the building, a sense of insufferable gloom pervaded my spirit. I say insufferable; for the feeling was unrelieved by any of that half pleasurable, because poetic, sentiment, with which the mind usually receives even the sternest natural images of the desolate or terrible. I looked upon the scene before me — upon the mere house, and the simple landscape features of the domain — upon the bleak walls — upon the vacant and eyelike windows — upon a few rank sedges — and upon a few white trunks of decayed trees — with an utter depression of soul which I can compare to no earthly sensation more properly than to the after-dream of the reveler upon opium — the bitter lapse into everyday life — the hideous dropping off of the veil. There was an iciness, a sinking, a sickening of the heart — an unredeemed dreariness of thought which no goading of the imagination could torture into aught of the sublime. What was it — I paused to think — what was it that so unnerved me in the contemplation of the House of Usher? It was a mystery all insoluble; nor could I grapple with the shadowy fancies that crowded upon me as I pondered. I was forced to fall back upon the unsatisfactory conclusion, that while, beyond doubt, there *are* combinations of very simple natural objects which have the power of thus affecting us, still the analysis of this power lies among considerations beyond our depth. It was possible, I reflected, that a mere different arrangement of the particulars of the scene, of the details of the picture, would be sufficient to modify, or perhaps to annihilate, its capacity for sorrowful im-

[1]From *The Fall of the House of Usher.*

pression; and acting upon this idea, I reined my horse to the precipitous brink of a black and lurid tarn that lay in unruffled luster by the dwelling, and gazed down — but with a shudder even more thrilling than before — upon the remodeled and inverted images of the gray sedge, and the ghastly tree stems, and the vacant and eyelike windows.

OXFORD

Matthew Arnold

Oxford. Beautiful city! so venerable, so lovely, so unravaged by the fierce intellectual life of our century, so serene!

"There are our young barbarians, all at play!"

And yet, steeped in sentiment as she lies, spreading her gardens to the moonlight, and whispering from her towers the last enchantments of the Middle Age, who will deny that Oxford, by her ineffable charm, keeps ever calling us nearer to the true goal of all of us, to the ideal, to perfection — to beauty, in a word, which is only truth seen from another side? — nearer, perhaps, than all the science of Tübingen. Adorable dreamer, whose heart has been so romantic! who hast given thyself so prodigally, given thyself to sides and to heroes not mine, only never to the Philistines! home of lost causes, and forsaken beliefs, and unpopular names, and impossible loyalties? What example could ever so inspire us to keep down the Philistine in ourselves, what teacher could ever so save us from that bondage to which we are all prone, that bondage which Goethe, in his incomparable lines on the death of Schiller, makes it his friend's highest praise (and nobly did Schiller deserve the praise) to have left miles out of sight behind him — the bondage of "*was uns alle bändigt, das Gemeine!*" She will forgive me, even if I have unwittingly drawn upon her a shot or two aimed at her unworthy son; for she is generous, and the cause in which I fight is, after all, hers. Apparitions of a day, what is our puny warfare against the Philistines, compared with the warfare which this queen of romance has been waging against them for centuries, and will wage after we are gone?

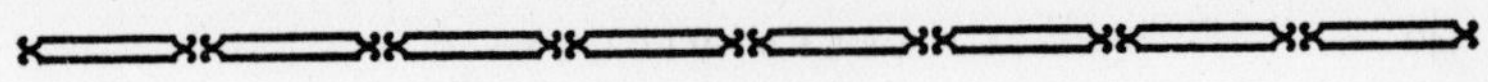

A. BRIEF DESCRIPTIONS

2. Persons

CAPTAIN AHAB[1]

Herman Melville

Captain Ahab stood upon his quarter-deck. There seemed no sign of common bodily illness about him, nor of the recovery from any. He looked like a man cut away from the stake, when the fire has overrunningly wasted all the limbs without consuming them, or taking away one particle from their compacted aged robustness. His whole high, broad form, seemed made of solid bronze, and shaped in an unalterable mold, like Cellini's cast Perseus. Threading its way out from among his gray hairs, and continuing right down one side of his tawny scorched face and neck, till it disappeared in his clothing, you saw a slender rodlike mark, lividly whitish. It resembled that perpendicular seam sometimes made in the straight, lofty trunk of a great tree, when the upper lightning tearingly darts down it, and without wrenching a single twig, peels and grooves out the bark from top to bottom, ere running off into the soil, leaving the tree still greenly alive, but branded. Whether that mark was born with him, or whether it was the scar left by some desperate wound, no one could certainly say.

So powerfully did the whole grim aspect of Ahab affect me, and the livid brand which streaked it, that for the first few moments I hardly noted that not a little of this overbearing grimness was owing to the barbaric white leg upon which he partly stood. It had previously come to me that this ivory leg had at sea been fashioned from the polished bone of the sperm whale's jaw. "Aye, he was dis-

[1]From *Moby Dick*.

masted off Japan," said the old Gay-Head Indian once; "but like his dismasted craft, he shipped another mast without coming home for it. He has a quiver of 'em."

I was struck with the singular posture he maintained. Upon each side of the *Pequod's* quarter-deck, and pretty close to the mizzen shrouds, there was an auger hole, bored about half an inch or so, into the plank. His bone leg steadied in that hole; one arm elevated, and holding by a shroud; Captain Ahab stood erect, looking straight out beyond the ship's ever-pitching prow. There was an infinity of firmest fortitude, a determinate, unsurrenderable willfulness, in the fixed and fearless, forward dedication of that glance. Not a word he spoke; nor did his officers say aught to him; though by all their minutest gestures and expressions, they plainly showed the uneasy, if not painful, consciousness of being under a troubled master-eye. And not only that, but moody stricken Ahab stood before them with an apparently eternal anguish in his face; in all the nameless regal overbearing dignity of some mighty woe.

THE ARTFUL DODGER[1]

Charles Dickens

The boy who addressed this inquiry to the young wayfarer, was about his own age: but one of the queerest-looking boys that Oliver had ever seen. He was a snub-nosed, flat-browed, common-faced boy enough; and as dirty a juvenile as one would wish to see; but he had about him all the airs and manners of a man. He was short of his age: with rather bow-legs, and little sharp, ugly eyes. His hat was stuck on the top of his head so lightly, that it threatened to fall off every moment—and would have done so, very often, if the wearer had not had a knack of every now and then giving his head a sudden twitch, which brought it back to its old place again. He wore a man's coat, which reached nearly to his heels. He had turned

[1]From *Oliver Twist.*

the cuffs back, halfway up his arm, to get his hands out of the sleeves: apparently with the ultimate view of thrusting them into the pockets of his corduroy trousers; for there he kept them. He was, altogether, as roystering and swaggering a young gentleman as ever stood four feet six, or something less, in his bluchers.

DANTE[1]

Thomas Carlyle

To me it is a most touching face; perhaps of all faces that I know, the most so. Lonely there, painted as on vacancy, with the simple laurel wound round it; the deathless sorrow and pain, the known victory which is also deathless — significant of the whole history of Dante! I think it is the mournfulest face that ever was painted from reality; an altogether tragic, heart-affecting face. There is in it, as a foundation of it, the softness, tenderness, gentle affection as of a child; but all this is as if congealed into sharp contradiction, into abnegation, isolation, proud hopeless pain. A soft ethereal soul looking out so stern, implacable, grimtrenchant, as from imprisonment of thick-ribbed ice! Withal it is a silent pain too, a silent scornful one: the lip is curled in a kind of godlike disdain of the thing that is eating-out his heart — as if it were withal a mean, insignificant thing, as if he whom it had power to torture and strangle were greater than it. The face of one wholly in protest, and lifelong unsurrendering battle, against the world. Affection all converted into indignation: an implacable indignation; slow, equable, silent, like that of a god! The eye too, it looks out as in a kind of *surprise,* a kind of inquiry, Why the world was of such a sort? This is Dante: so he looks, this "voice of ten silent centuries," and sings us "his mystic unfathomable song."

[1]From *Heroes and Hero Worship.*

BEATRIX DESCENDING THE STAIRS[1]

William Makepeace Thackeray

This laughing colloquy took place in the hall of Walcote House: in the midst of which is a staircase that leads from an open gallery, where are the doors of the sleeping chambers; and from one of these, a wax candle in her hand, and illuminating her, came Mistress Beatrix—the light falling indeed upon the scarlet riband which she wore, and upon the most brilliant white neck in the world.

Esmond had left a child and found a woman, grown beyond the common height; and arrived at such a dazzling completeness of beauty, that his eyes might well show surprise and delight at beholding her. In hers there was a brightness so lustrous and melting, that I have seen a whole assembly follow her as if by an attraction irresistible; and that night the great Duke was at the playhouse after Ramillies, every soul turned and looked (she chanced to enter at the opposite side of the theater at the same moment) at her, and not at him. She was a brown beauty; that is, her eyes, hair, and eyebrows and eyelashes were dark; her hair curling with rich undulations and waving over her shoulders; but her complexion was as dazzling white as snow in sunshine; except her cheeks, which were a bright red, and her lips which were of a still deeper crimson. Her mouth and chin, they said, were too large and full, and so they might be for a goddess in marble, but not for a woman whose eyes were fire, whose look was love, whose voice was the sweetest low song, whose shape was perfect symmetry, health, decision, activity, whose foot as it planted itself on the ground, was firm but flexible, and whose motion, whether rapid or slow, was always perfect grace—agile as a nymph, lofty as a queen—now melting, now imperious, now sarcastic—there was no single movement of hers but was beautiful. As he thinks of her, he who writes feels young again, and remembers a paragon.

---

[1]From *Henry Esmond.*

So she came holding her dress with one fair rounded arm, and her taper before her, tripping down the stair to greet Esmond.

ADAM BEDE[1]

George Eliot

On a heap of those soft shavings a rough gray shepherd dog had made himself a pleasant bed, and was lying with his nose between his forepaws, occasionally wrinkling his brow to cast a glance at the tallest of the five workmen, who was carving a shield in the center of a wooden mantel piece. It was to this workman that the strong baritone belonged which was heard above the sound of plane and hammer singing,

Awake, my soul, and with the sun
Thy daily stage of duty run;
Shake off dull sloth. . . .

Here some measurement was to be taken which required more concentrated attention, and the sonorous voice subsided into a low whistle, but it presently broke out again with renewed vigor —

Let all thy converse be sincere,
Thy conscience as the noonday clear.

Such a voice could only come from a broad chest, and the broad chest belonged to a large-boned, muscular man nearly six feet high, with a back so flat and a head so well poised that when he drew himself up to take a more distant survey of his work, he had the air of a soldier standing at ease. The sleeve rolled up above the

[1]From *Adam Bede.*

elbow showed an arm that was likely to win the prize for feats of strength; yet the long supple hand, with its broad finger tips, looked ready for works of skill. In his tall stalwartness Adam Bede was a Saxon, and justified his name; but the jet-black hair, made the more noticeable by its contrast with the light paper cap, and the keen glance of the dark eyes that shown from under strongly marked, prominent, and mobile eyebrows, indicated a mixture of Celtic blood. The face was large and rough-hewn, and when in repose had no other heartily than such as belongs to an expression of good-humored honest intelligence.

FACES IN LIGHT AND SHADE[1]

Thomas Hardy

The brilliant lights and sooty shades which struggled upon the skin and clothes of the persons standing round caused their lineaments and general contours to be drawn with Dureresque vigor and dash. Yet the permanent moral expression of each face it was impossible to discover, for as the nimble flames towered, nodded, and swooped through the surrounding air, the blots of shade and flakes of light upon the countenances of the group changed shape and position endlessly. All was unstable; quivering as leaves, evanescent as lightning. Shadowy eye sockets, deep as those of a death's head, suddenly turned into pits of luster; a lantern jaw was cavernous, then it was shining; wrinkles were emphasized to ravines, or obliterated entirely by a changed ray. Nostrils were dark wells; sinews in old necks were gilt moldings; things with no particular polish on them were glazed; bright objects, such as the tip of a furze-hook one of the men carried, were as glass; eyeballs glowed like little lanterns. Those nature had depicted as merely quaint

[1]From *The Return of the Native.*

became grotesque, the grotesque became preternatural; for all was in extremity.

MAJOR PENDENNIS[1]
William Makepeace Thackeray

At a quarter past ten the Major invariably made his appearance in the best blacked boots in all London, with a checked morning cravat that never was rumpled until dinner time, a buff waistcoat which bore the crown of his sovereign on the buttons, and linen so spotless that Mr. Brummel himself asked the name of his laundress, and would probably have employed her had not misfortunes compelled that great man to fly the country. Pendennis's coat, his white gloves, his whiskers, his very cane, were perfect of their kind as specimens of the costume of a military man *en retraite*. At a distance, or seeing his back merely, you would have taken him to be not more than thirty years old: it was only by a nearer inspection that you saw the factitious nature of rich brown hair, and that there were a few crow's feet round about the somewhat faded eyes of his handsome mottled face. His nose was of the Wellington pattern. His hands and wristbands were beautifully long and white. On the latter he wore handsome gold buttons given to him by his Royal Highness, the Duke of York, and on the others more than one elegant ring, the chief and largest of them being emblazoned with the famous arms of Pendennis.

[1]From *Pendennis.*

ARTHUR PENDENNIS[1]

William Makepeace Thackeray

Arthur was about sixteen years old, we have said, when he began to reign; in person, he had what his friends would call a dumpy figure, but his mamma styled it a neat little figure. His hair was of a healthy brown color, which looks like gold in the sunshine; his face was round, rosy, freckled, and good-humored, his whiskers were decidedly of a reddish hue; in fact, without being a beauty, he had such a frank, good-natured kind face, and laughed so merrily at you out of his honest blue eyes, that no wonder Mrs. Pendennis thought him the pride of the whole country. Between the ages of sixteen and eighteen he rose from five feet six to five feet eight inches in height, at which altitude he paused. But his mother marveled at it. He was three inches taller than his father. Was it possible that any man could grow to be three inches taller than Mr. Pendennis?

SHELLEY[1]

Edward John Trelawny

After a long stop at that city of painted palaces, anxious to see the poet, I drove to Pisa alone. I arrived late, and, after putting up my horse at the inn and dining, hastened to the Tre Palazzi, on the Lung, Arno, where the Shelleys and Williamses lived on different flats under the same roof, as is the custom on the continent. The

[1]From *Pendennis.*

[1]From *Recollections of the Last Days of Shelley and Byron.*

Williamses received me in their earnest, cordial manner; we had a great deal to communicate to each other, and were in loud and animated conversation, when I was rather put out by observing in the passage near the open door, opposite to where I sat, a pair of glittering eyes steadily fixed on mine; it was too dark to make out whom they belonged to. With the acuteness of a woman, Mrs. Williams's eyes followed the direction of mine, and, going to the doorway, she laughingly said:

"Come in, Shelley; it's only our friend Tre just arrived."

Swiftly gliding in, blushing like a girl, a tall, thin stripling held out both his hands; and, although I could hardly believe, as I looked at his flushed, feminine, and artless face, that it could be the poet, I returned his warm pressure. After the ordinary greetings and courtesies, he sat down and listened. I was silent from astonishment. Was it possible this mild-looking, beardless boy could be the veritable monster at war with all the world? — excommunicated by the fathers of the Church, deprived of his civil rights by the fiat of a grim Lord Chancellor, discarded by every member of his family, and denounced by the rival sages of our literature as the founder of a Satanic school? I could not believe it; it must be a hoax. He was habited like a boy, in a black jacket and trousers, which he seemed to have outgrown, or his tailor, as is the custom, had most shamefully stinted him in his "sizings." Mrs. Williams saw my embarrassment, and to relieve me asked Shelley what book he had in his hand. His face brightened, and he answered, briskly:

"Calderón's *Mágico Prodigioso*. I am translating some passages in it."

"Oh, read it to us!"

Shoved off from the shore of commonplace incidents that could not interest him, and fairly launched on a theme that did, he instantly became oblivious of everything but the book in his hand. The masterly manner in which he analyzed the genius of the author, his lucid interpretation of the story, and the ease with which he translated into our language the most subtle and imaginative passages of the Spanish poet, were marvelous, as was his command of the two languages. After this touch of his quality, I no longer doubted his identity. A dead silence ensued; looking up, I asked:

"Where is he?"

Mrs. Williams said, "Who? — Shelley? Oh, he comes and goes like a spirit, no one knows when or where."

THE MOURNERS[1]

Sir Walter Scott

In the inside of the cottage was a scene which our Wilkie alone could have painted with the exquisite feeling of nature that characterizes his enchanting productions.

The body was laid in its coffin within the wooden bedstead which the young fisher had occupied while alive. At a little distance stood the father, whose rugged, weather-beaten countenance, shaded by his grizzled hair, had faced many a stormy night and night-like day. He was apparently revolving his loss in his mind with that strong feeling of painful grief, peculiar to harsh and rough characters, which almost breaks forth into hatred against the world, and all that remain in it after the beloved object is withdrawn. The old man had made the most desperate efforts to save his son, and had only been withheld by main force from renewing them at a moment when, without the possibility of assisting the sufferer, he must himself have perished. All this apparently was boiling in his recollection. His glance was directed sidelong toward the coffin, as to an object on which he could not steadfastly look, and yet from which he could not withdraw his eyes. His answers to the necessary questions which were occasionally put to him were brief, harsh, and almost fierce. His family had not yet dared to address to him a word, either of sympathy or consolation. His masculine wife, virago as she was, and absolutely mistress of the family, as she justly boasted herself, on all ordinary occasions, was, by this great loss, terrified into silence and submission, and compelled to hide from

[1]From *The Antiquary.*

her husband's observation the bursts of her female sorrow. As he had rejected food ever since the disaster had happened, not daring herself to approach him, she had that morning, with affectionate artifice, employed the youngest and favorite child to present her husband with some nourishment. His first action was to push it from him with an angry violence that frightened the child; his next, to snatch up the boy and devour him with kisses. "Ye'll be a bra' fallow, and ye be spared, Patie—but ye'll never—never can be—what he was to me!—He has sailed the coble wi' me since he was ten years auld; and there wasna the like o' him drew a net betwixt this and Buchan-ness. They say folks maun submit—I will try."

And he had been silent from that moment until compelled to answer the necessary questions we have already noticed. Such was the disconsolate state of the father.

In another corner of the cottage, her face covered by her apron, which was flung over it, sat the mother, the nature of her grief sufficiently indicated by the wringing of her hands and the convulsive agitation of the bosom which the covering could not conceal. Two of her gossips, officiously whispering into her ear the commonplace topic of resignation under irremediate misfortune, seemed as if they were endeavoring to stun the grief which they could not console.

The sorrow of the children was mingled with wonder at the preparations they beheld around them and at the unusual display of wheaten bread and wine, which the poorest peasant, or fisher, offers to the guests on these mournful occasions; and thus their grief for their brother's death was almost already lost in admiration of the splendor of his funeral.

But the figure of the old grandmother was the most remarkable of the sorrowing group. Seated on her accustomed chair, with her usual air of apathy and want of interest in what surrounded her, she seemed every now and then mechanically to resume the motion of twirling her spindle—then to look toward her bosom for the distaff, although both had been laid aside. She would then cast her eyes about as if surprised at missing the usual implements of her industry, and appear struck by the black color of the gown in which they had dressed her, and embarrassed by the number of persons by whom she was surrounded—then, finally, she would raise her head with a ghastly look and fix her eyes upon the bed which contained the coffin of her grandson, as if she had at once, and for the first time, acquired sense to comprehend her inexpressible calamity. These alternate feelings of embarrassment, wonder, and grief, seemed to succeed each other more than once upon her torpid features. But she spoke not a word, neither had she shed a tear; nor did one of the family understand, either from look or expression, to what extent she comprehended the uncommon bustle around her. Thus she sat among the funeral assembly like a connecting link between the surviving mourners and the dead corpse which they bewailed—a being in whom the light of existence was already obscured by the encroaching shadows of death.

LUCY DESBOROUGH[1]

George Meredith

She was indeed sweetly fair, and would have been held fair among rival damsels. . . . The soft rose in her cheeks, the clearness of her eyes, bore witness to the body's virtue; and health and happy blood were in her bearing. Had she stood before Sir Austin among rival damsels, that Scientific Humanist, for the consummation of his System, would have thrown her the handkerchief for his son. The wide summer hat, nodding over her forehead to her brows seemed to flow with the flowing heavy curls, and those fire-threaded mellow curls, only half-curls, waves of hair call them, rippling at the ends, went like a sunny red-veined torrent down her back almost to her waist: a glorious vision to the youth, who embraced it as a flower of beauty and read not a feature. There were curious features of color in her face for him to have read. Her brows, thick and brownish against a soft skin showing the action of the blood, met in the bend of a bow, extending to the temples long and level: you saw that she was fashioned to peruse the sights of earth, and

[1]From *Ordeal of Richard Feverel.*

by the pliability of her brows that the wonderful creature used her faculty, and was not going to be a statue to the gazer. Under the dark thick brows an arch of lashes shot out, giving a wealth of darkness to the full frank blue eyes, a mystery of meaning—more than brain was ever meant to fathom: richer, henceforth, than all mortal wisdom to Prince Ferdinand. For when nature turns artist, and produces contrasts of color on a fair face, where is the Sage, or what the Oracle, shall match the depth of its lightest look?

THOMAS NEWCOME'S "ADSUM"

William Makepeace Thackeray

The days went on, and our hopes for the Colonel's recovery, raised sometimes, began to flicker and fail. One evening the Colonel left his chair for his bed in pretty good spirits, but passed a disturbed night, and the next morning was too weak to rise. Then he remained in his bed and his friends visited him there. . . .

One afternoon in early spring, Thomas Newcome began to wander more and more. He talked louder; he gave the word of command, spoke Hindustanee as if to his men. Ethel and Clive were with him, and presently his voice sank into faint murmurs.

At the usual evening hour the chapel bell began to toll, and Thomas Newcome's hands feebly beat time. And just as the last bell struck, a peculiar sweet smile shone over his face, and he lifted up his head a little, and quickly said "Adsum!" and fell back. It was the word we used at school, when names were called; and lo, he, whose heart was as that of a little child, had answered his name, and stood in the presence of The Master.

A. BRIEF DESCRIPTIONS

3. Nature

❦

THE BIRD

John Ruskin

We will take the bird first. It is little more than a drift of the air brought into form by plumes; the air is in its quills, it breathes through its whole frame and flesh, and glows with air in its flying, like blown flame: it rests upon the air, subdues it, surpasses it, outraces it;—*is* the air, conscious of itself, conquering itself, ruling itself.

Also, in the throat of the bird is given the voice of the air. All that in the wind itself is weak, wild, useless in sweetness, is knit together in its song. As we may imagine the wild form of the cloud closed into the perfect form of the bird's wings; so the wild voice of the cloud into its ordered and commanded voice; unwearied, rippling through the clear heaven in its gladness, interpreting all intense passion through the soft spring nights, bursting into acclaim and rapture of choir at daybreak, or lisping and twittering among the boughs and hedges through heat of day, like little winds that only make the cowslip bells shake, and ruffle the petals of the wild rose.

Also, upon the plumes of the bird are put the colors of the air: on these the gold of the cloud, that cannot be gathered by any covetousness; the rubies of the clouds, that are not the price of Athena, but *are* Athena; the vermillion of the cloud-bar, and the flame of the cloudcrest, and the snow of the cloud, and its shadow, and the melted blue of the deep wells of the sky—all these, seized by the creating spirit, and woven by Athena herself into films and threads of plume; with wave on wave following and fading along breast, and throat, and opened wings, infinite as the dividing of the foam and the sifting of the sea-sand; — even the white down of the cloud seeming to flutter up between the stronger plumes, seen, but too soft for touch.

MARSEILLES IN AUGUST[1]

Charles Dickens

There was no wind to make a ripple on the foul water within the harbor, or on the beautiful sea without. The line of demarcation between the two colors, black and white, showed the point which the pure sea would not pass; but it lay as quiet as the abominable pool, with which it never mixed. Boats without awnings were too hot to touch; ships blistered at their moorings; the stones of the quays had not cooled, night or day, for months. Hindoos, Russians, Chinese, Spaniards, Portuguese, Englishmen, Frenchmen, Genoese, Neapolitans, Venetians, Greeks, Turks, descendants from all the builders of Babel, come to trade at Marseilles, sought the shade alike — taking refuge in any hiding place from a sea too intensely blue to be looked at, and a sky of purple, set with one great flaming jewel of fire.

The universal stare made the eyes ache. Toward the distant line of Italian coast, indeed, it was a little relieved by light clouds of mist, slowly rising from the evaporation of the sea; but it softened nowhere else. Far away the staring roads, deep in dust, stared from the hillside, stared from the hollow, stared from the interminable plain. Far away the dusty vines overhanging wayside cottages, and the monotonous wayside avenues of parched trees without shade, drooped beneath the stare of earth and sky. So did the horses with drowsy bells, in long files of carts, creeping slowly toward the interior; so did their recumbent drivers when they were awake, which rarely happened; so did the exhausted laborers in the fields. Everything that lived or grew was oppressed by the glare, except the

[1]From *Little Dorrit.*

lizard passing swiftly over rough stone walls, and the cicala, chirping his dry, hot chirp, like a rattle. The very dust was scorched brown, and something quivered in the atmosphere as if the air itself were panting.

Blinds, shutters, curtains, awnings, were all closed and drawn to keep out the stare. Grant it but a chink or keyhole, and it shot in like a white-hot arrow. The churches were the freest from it. To come out of the twilight of pillars and arches—dreamily dotted with winking lamps, dreamily peopled with ugly old shadows piously dozing, spitting, and begging—was to plunge into a fiery river and swim for life to the nearest strip of shade. So, with people lounging and lying wherever shade was, with but little hum of tongues or barking of dogs, with occasional jangling of discordant church bells, and rattling of vicious drums, Marseilles, a fact to be strongly smelt and tasted, lay broiling in the sun.

JURA PASTURES[1]

John Ruskin

It is a spot which has all the solemnity, with none of the savageness of the Alps; where there is a sense of a great power beginning to be manifested in the earth, and of a deep and majestic concord in the rise of the long low lines of piny hills; the first utterance of those mighty mountain symphonies, soon to be more loudly lifted and wildly broken along the battlements of the Alps. But their strength is as yet restrained; and the far-reaching ridges of pastoral mountain succeed each other, like the long and sighing swell which moves over quiet waters from some far-off stormy sea. And there is a deep tenderness pervading that vast monotony. The destructive forces and the stern expression of the central ranges are alike withdrawn. No frost-ploughed, dust-encumbered paths of ancient glacier fret the soft Jura pastures; no splintered heaps of ruin break the fair ranks of the forests; no pale, defiled, or furious rivers rend

[1]From *The Seven Lamps of Architecture, The Lamp of Memory.*

their rude and changeful ways among her rocks. Patiently, eddy by eddy, the clear green streams wind along their well-known beds; and under the dark quietness of the undisturbed pines, there spring up, year by year, such company of joyful flowers as I know not the like of among all the blessings of the earth. It was springtime, too; and all were coming forth in clusters crowded for very love; there was room enough for all, but they crushed their leaves into all manner of strange shapes only to be nearer each other. There was the wood anemone, star after star, closing every now and then into nebulæ; and there was the oxalis, troop by troop, like virginal processions of the *Mais de Marie,* the dark vertical clefts in the limestone choked up with them as with heavy snow, and touched with ivy on the edges—ivy as light and lovely as the vine; and, ever and anon, a blue gush of violets, and cowslip bells in sunny places; and in the more open ground the vetsh and comfrey, and mezeron, and the small sapphire buds of the *Polygala Alpina,* and the wild strawberry, just a blossom or two all showered amidst the golden softness of deep, warm, amber-colored moss.

SNOW IN CRANFORD[1]

Mrs. Gaskell

The lights came on in Cranford Street. It was snowing, after many days of rain, and the flakes came down gently, driven by no wind. The snow beautified the street which was a short one of no particular pretensions, though decent enough for such men as a high-school professor, the cashier of a bank, a chief draftsman for Renslers'. But the houses, which in the rain seemed to try hard to keep up appearances, now had to make no effort. The snow made all trim and jolly, intensified the glow of the lamps in windows, made it somehow an event to walk up the steps into any of these houses.

[1]From *Cranford.*

AN AUGUST DAY[1]

George Eliot

The eighteenth of August was one of these days, when the sunshine looked brighter in all eyes for the gloom that went before. Grand masses of cloud were hurried across the blue, and the great round hills behind the Chase seemed alive with their flying shadows; the sun was hidden for a moment, and then shown out warm again, like a recovered joy; the leaves, still green, were tossed off the hedgerow trees by the wind; around the farmhouses there was a sound of clapping doors; the apples fell in the orchards; and the stray horses on the green sides of the lanes and on the common had their manes blown about their faces.

EGDON HEATH[1]

Thomas Hardy

Egdon Heath was a vast tract of uninclosed wild. The heaven being spread with a stretch of whitish cloud shutting out the sky and the earth with the darkest vegetation, their meeting line at the horizon was clearly marked. The spot was a near relation of night. The somber stretch of rounds and hollows seemed to rise and meet the evening gloom in pure sympathy, the health exhaling darkness as rapidly as the heavens precipitated it. Egdon was aroused to reciprocity; for the storm was its lover, and the wind its friend. It became the home of strange phantoms.

It was at present a place perfectly accordant with man's nature —neither ghastly, hateful, nor ugly; neither commonplace, un-

---

[1]From *Adam Bede.*

[1]From *The Return of the Native.*

meaning, nor tame; but, like man, slighted and enduring; and withal singularly colossal and mysterious in its swarthy monotony. Solitude seemed to look out of its countenance. It had a lonely face, suggesting tragical possibilities. Civilization was its enemy; and ever since the beginning of vegetation its soil had worn the same antique brown dress, the natural and invariable garment of the particular formation. In its venerable one coat lay a certain vein of satire on human vanity in clothes.

TREES IN THE STORM[1]

Thomas Hardy

A single vast gray cloud covered all the country, from which the small rain and mist had just begun to blow down in wavy sheets, alternately thick and thin. The trees of the fields and plantations writhed like miserable men as the air wound its way swiftly among them: the lowest portions of their trunks, that had hardly ever been known to move, were visibly rocked by the fiercer gusts, distressing the mind by its painful unwontedness, as when a strong man is seen to shed tears. Lowhanging boughs went up and down; high and erect boughs went to and fro; the blasts being so irregular and divided into so many cross-currents, that neighboring branches of the same tree swept the skies in independent motions, crossed each other, or became entangled. Across the open spaces flew flocks of green and yellowish leaves, which after traveling a long distance from their parent trees, reached the ground, and lay there with their undersides upward.

---

[1]From *Under the Greenwood Tree.*

LAKE LOUISE[1]

Rupert Brooke

You may watch the water and the peaks all day, and never see the same view twice. In the lake, everchanging, is Beauty herself, as nearly visible to mortal eyes as she may ever be. The water, beyond the flowers, is green, always a different green. Sometimes it is tranquil, glassy, shot with blue, of a peacock tint. Then a little wind awakes in the distance, and ruffles the surface, yard by yard, covering it with a myriad tiny wrinkles, till the lake is milky emerald, while the rest still sleeps. And, at length, the whole is astir, and the sun catches it, and Lake Louise is a web of laughter, the opal distillation of all the buds of all the spring. On either side go up the dark processional pines, mounting to the sacred peaks, devout, kneeling, motionless, in an ecstasy of homely adoration, like the donors and their families in a Flemish picture. Among these you may wander for hours by little rambling paths, over white and red and golden flowers, and, continually, you spy little lakes, hidden away, each a shy, soft jewel of a new strange tint of green or blue, mutable and lovely. . . . And beyond all is the glacier and the vast fields and peaks of eternal snow.

A STORM AT SEA[1]

Joseph Conrad

It was January, and the weather was beautiful—the beautiful sunny winter weather that has more charm than in the summer-

[1]From *Letters from America;* reprinted by permission of the publishers, Charles Scribner's Sons.

[1]From *Youth;* reprinted by permission of the publishers, Doubleday, Doran and Company, Inc.

time, because it is unexpected, and crisp, and you know it won't, it can't, last long. It's like a windfall, like a godsend, like an unexpected piece of luck.

It lasted all down the North Sea, all down Channel; and it lasted till we were three hundred miles or so to the westward of the Lizards: then the wind went round to the sou'west and began to pipe up. In two days it blew a gale. The *Judea,* hove to, wallowed on the Atlantic like an old candlebox. It blew day after day: it blew with spite, without interval, without mercy, without rest. The world was nothing but an immensity of great foaming waves rushing at us, under a sky low enough to touch with the hand and dirty like a smoked ceiling. In the stormy space surrounding us there was as much flying spray as air. Day after day and night after night there was nothing round the ship but the howl of the wind, the tumult of the sea, the noise of water pouring over her deck. There was no rest for her and no rest for us. She tossed, she pitched, she stood on her head, she sat on her tail, she rolled, she groaned, and we had to hold on while on deck and cling to our bunks when below, in a constant effort of body and worry of mind.

THE BURNING SHIP[1]

Joseph Conrad

Between the darkness of earth and heaven she was burning fiercely upon a disk of purple sea shot by the blood-red play of gleams; upon a disk of water glittering and sinister. A high, clear flame, an immense and lonely flame, ascended from the ocean, and from its summit the black smoke poured continuously at the sky. She burned furiously; mournful and imposing like a funeral pile kindled in the night, surrounded by the sea, watched over by the stars. A magnificent death had come like a grace, like a gift, like a reward to

[1]From *Youth;* reprinted by permission of the publishers, Doubleday, Doran and Company, Inc.

that old ship at the end of her laborious days. The surrender of her weary ghost to the keeping of stars and sea was stirring like the sight of a glorious triumph. The masts fell just before daybreak, and for a moment there was a burst and turmoil of sparks that seemed to fill with flying fire the night patient and watchful, the vast night lying silent upon the sea. At daylight she was only a charred shell, floating still under a cloud of smoke and bearing a glowing mass of coal within.

Then the oars were got out, and the boats forming in a line moved round her remains as if in procession—the longboat leading. As we pulled across her stern a slim dart of fire shot out viciously at us, and suddenly she went down, head first, in a great hiss of steam. The unconsumed stern was the last to sink; but the paint had gone, had cracked, had peeled off, and there were no letters, there was no word, no stubborn device that was like her soul, to flash at the rising sun her creed and her name.

THE PELT OF SAND[1]

John Masefield

He rose up again to take stock of his whereabouts and to see if he could see a train hand. He saw the trucks forging and jolting ahead. Beyond the trucks, both in front and behind, were the high, closed, yellow wooden Occidental freightcars, marked with capacity marks in dull red. The train lurched and jangled along the desert in a ceaseless pelt of sand. The sand was merciless and pitiless, a little and a little and a little. The chaparral bowed a little to it, the cactus seemed to put back its ears. Everything was dry with it, gritty, cracked, burnished. The persistence of its small annoyance told on all things. As the dropping of water wears the stone, so the

[1]From John Masefield's *Sard Harker;* by permission of The Macmillan Company, publishers.

pelting of the sand wore the spirit. Sard remembered what he had heard of these northers: how the children are kept from school lest they should mutiny, and how men, maddened by that insistent patting, will strike and kill. The thought crossed his mind that if he had to walk back along the track in that pelting, that annoyance of the tiny hands pat-pat-patting on face and hands would be soon unbearable. Even there, sheltered in the truck, it came pat-pat-patting, flying like a little dry-shot over the sides, filtering up through cracks in the bottom, and dancing there, like grains in a spring, till they were flung away. From time to time the dry, quiet pat-pat-patting deepened to a noise of water, with a roaring and a swish, into which the train joggled, lurched, jangled and clanked, and which it at last seemed to tread down and overroar.

B. LONGER DESCRIPTIONS

LANDSCAPES OF TURNER[1]

John Ruskin

Stand upon the peak of some isolated mountain at daybreak, when the night mists first rise off the plains, and watch their white and lakelike fields as they float in level bays and winding gulfs about the island summits of the lower hills, untouched yet by more than dawn, colder and more quiet than a windless sea under the moon of midnight; watch when the first sunbeam is sent upon the silver channels, how the foam of their undulating surface parts and passes away; and down under their depths, the glittering city and green pasture lie like Atlantis, between the white paths of winding rivers; the flakes of light falling every moment faster and broader among the starry spires, as the wreathed surges break and vanish above them, and the confused crests and ridges of the dark hills shorten their gray shadows upon the plain. Has Claude given this? Wait a little longer, and you shall see those scattered mists rallying in the ravines, and floating up toward you, along the winding valleys, till they couch in quiet masses, iridescent with the morning light, upon the broad breasts of the higher hills, whose leagues of massy undulation will melt back and back into that robe of material light, until they fade away, lost in its luster, to appear again above, in the serene heaven, like a wild, bright, impossible dream, foundationless and inaccessible, their very bases vanishing in the unsubstantial and mocking blue of the deep lake below. Has Claude given this? Wait yet a little longer, and you shall see those mists gather themselves into white towers, and stand like fortresses along the promontories, massy and motionless, only piled with every instant

[1]From *Modern Painters*.

higher and higher into the sky, and casting longer shadows athwart the rocks; and out of the pale blue of the horizon you will see forming and advancing a troop of narrow, dark, pointed vapors, which will cover the sky, inch by inch, with their gray network, and take the light off the landscape with an eclipse which will stop the singing of the birds and the motion of the leaves together; and then you will see horizontal bars of black shadow forming under them, and lurid wreaths create themselves, you know not how, along the shoulders of the hills; you never see them form, but when you look back at a place which was clear an instant ago, there is a cloud on it, hanging by the precipices, as a hawk pauses over his prey. Has Claude given this? And then you will hear the sudden rush of the awakened wind, and you will see those watch-towers of vapor swept away from their foundations, and waving curtains of opaque rain let down to the valleys, swinging from the burdened clouds in black, bending fringes, or pacing in pale columns along the lake level, grazing its surface into foam as they go. And then, as the sun sinks, you shall see the storm drift for an instant from off the hills, leaving their broad sides smoking, and loaded yet with snow-white, torn, steamlike rags of capricious vapor, now gone, now gathered again; while the smoldering sun, seeming not far away, but burning like a red-hot ball beside you, and as if you could reach it, plunges through the rushing wind and rolling cloud with headlong fall, as if it meant to rise no more, dyeing all the air about it with blood. Has Claude given this? And then you shall hear the fainting tempest die in the hollow of the night, and you shall see a green halo kindling on the summit of the eastern hills, brighter—brighter yet, till the large white circle of the slow moon is lifted up among the barred clouds, step by step, line by line; star after star, she quenches with her kindling light, setting in their stead an army of pale, penetrable, fleecy wreaths in the heaven, to give light upon the earth, which move together, hand in hand, company by company, troop by troop, so measured in their unity of motion, that the whole heaven seems to roll with them, and the earth to reel under them. Ask Claude, or his brethren, for that. And then wait yet for one hour, until the east again becomes purple, and the heaving mountains, rolling against it in darkness, like waves of a wild sea, are drowned one by one in the glory of its burning; watch the white glaciers blaze in their winding paths about the mountains, like mighty serpents with scales of fire; watch the columnar peaks of solitary snow, kindling downward, chasm by chasm, each in itself a new morning; their long avalanches cast down in keen streams brighter than the lightning, sending each his tribute of driven snow, like altar-smoke, up to the heaven; the rose-light of their silent domes flushing that heaven about them and above them, piercing with purer light through its purple lines of lifted cloud, casting a new glory on every wreath as it passes by, until the whole heaven — one scarlet canopy — is interwoven with a roof of waving flame, and tossing, vault beyond vault, as with the drifted wings of many companies of angels; and then, when you can look no more for gladness, and when you are bowed down with fear and love of the Maker and Doer of this, tell me who has best delivered this His message unto men!

THE FLIGHT OF THE KING[1]

Thomas Carlyle

On Monday night, the twentieth of June, 1791, about eleven o'clock, there is many a hackney-coach, and glass-coach (*carrosse de remise*), still rumbling, or at rest, on the streets of Paris. But of all glass-coaches, we recommend this to thee, O Reader, which stands drawn up in the Rue de l'Échelle, hard by the Carrousel and out-gate of the Tuileries; in the Rue de l'Échelle that then was; "opposite Ronsin the saddler's door," as if waiting for a fare there! Not long does it wait: a hooded dame, with two hooded children has issued from Villequier's door, where no sentry walks, into the Tuileries Court-of-Princes; into the Carrousel; into the Rue de l'Échelle; where the glass-coachman readily admits them; and again waits. Not long; another dame, likewise hooded or shrouded, leaning on a servant, issues in the same manner; bids the servants good

[1]From *The French Revolution.*

night; and is, in the same manner, by the glass-coachman, cheerfully admitted. Whither go so many dames? 'Tis his Majesty's *Couchée,* Majesty just gone to bed, and all the palace-world is retiring home. But the glass-coachman still waits; his fare seemingly incomplete.

By and by, we note a thick-set individual, in round hat and peruke, arm in arm with some servant, seemingly of the runner or courier sort; he also issues through Villequier's door; starts a shoebuckle as he passes one of the sentries, stoops down to clasp it again; is however, by the glass-coachman, still more cheerfully admitted. And *now,* is his fare complete? Not yet; the glass-coachman still waits.—Alas! and the false chambermaid has warned Gouvion that she thinks the royal family will fly this very night; and Gouvion distrusting his own glazed eyes, has sent express for Lafayette; and Lafayette's carriage, flaring with lights, rolls this moment through the inner arch of the Carrousel—where a lady shaded in broad gypsy hat, and leaning on the arm of a servant, also of the runner or courier sort, stands aside to let it pass, and has even the whim to touch a spoke of it with her *badine*—light little magic rod which she calls *badine,* such as the beautiful then wore. The flare of Lafayette's carriage rolls past: all is found quiet in the Court-of-Princes; sentries at their post; Majesties' apartments closed in smooth rest. Your false chambermaid must have been mistaken? Watch thou, Gouvion, with Argus' vigilance; for, of a truth, treachery is within these walls.

But where is the lady that stood aside in gypsy hat, and touched the wheel-spoke with her *badine?* O reader, that lady that touched the wheel-spoke was the queen of France! She has issued safe through that inner arch, into the Carrousel itself; but not into the Rue de l'Échelle. Flurried by the rattle and rencounter, she took the right hand not the left; neither she nor her courier knows Paris; he indeed is no courier, but a loyal stupid *ci-devant* bodyguard disguised as one. They are off, quite wrong, over the Pont Royal and River; roaming disconsolate in the Rue de Bac; far from the glass-coachman, who still waits. Waits, with flutter of heart; with thoughts—which he must button close up, under his jarvie surtout!

Midnight clangs from all the city steeples; one precious hour has been spent so; most mortals are asleep. The glass-coachman waits; and in what mood! A brother jarvie drives up, enters into conversation; is answered cheerfully in jarvie dialect: the brothers of the whip exchange a pinch of snuff; decline drinking together, and part with good night. Be the heavens blest! here at length is the queen-lady, in gypsy hat; safe after perils; who has had to inquire her way. She too is admitted; her courier jumps aloft, as the other, who is also a disguised bodyguard, has done; and now, O Glass-coachman of a thousand — Count Fersen, for the reader sees it is thou — drive!

Dust shall not stick to the hoofs of Fersen: crack! crack! the glass-coach rattles, and every soul breathes lighter. But is Fersen on the right road? Northeastward, to the Barrier of Saint-Martin and Metz Highway, thither were we bound: and lo, he drives right northward! The royal individual, in round hat and peruke, sits astonished; but right or wrong, there is no remedy. Crack, crack, we go incessant, through the slumbering city. Seldom, since Paris rose out of mud, or the long-haired kings went in bullock carts, was there such a drive. Mortals on each hand of you, close by, stretched out horizontal, dormant; and we alive and quaking! Crack, crack, through the Rue de Grammont; across the Boulevard; up the Rue de la Chaussée d'Antin — these windows, all silent, of Number 42, were Mirabeau's. Toward the Barrier not of Saint-Martin, but of Clichy on the utmost north! Patience, ye royal individuals; Fersen understands what he is about. Passing up the Rue de Clichy, he alights for one moment at Madame Sullivan's: "Did Count Fersen's coachman get the Baroness de Korff's Berline?" — "Gone with it an hour-and-half ago," grumbles responsive the drowsy Porter. — "*C'est bien.*" Yes, it is well; — though had not such hour-and-half been *lost,* it were still better. Forth therefore, O Fersen, fast, by the Barrier de Clichy; then eastward along the Outer Boulevard, what horses and whipcord can do!

Thus Fersen drives, through the ambrosial night. Sleeping Paris is now all on the right hand of him; silent except for some snoring hum: and now he is eastward as far as the Barrier de Saint-Martin; looking earnestly for Baroness de Korff's Berline. This heaven's Berline he at length does descry, drawn up with its six horses, his own German coachman waiting on the box. Right, thou good German: now haste, whither thou knowest! — And as for us of the glass-coach, haste too, O haste; much time is already lost! The august glass-coach fare, six insides, hastily packs itself into the new

Berline; two bodyguard couriers behind. The glass-coach itself is turned adrift, its head toward the city; to wander whither it lists — and be found next morning tumbled in a ditch. But Fersen is on the new box, with its brave new hammer-cloths; flourishing his whip; he bolts forward toward Bondy. There a third and final bodyguard courier of ours ought surely to be, with post-horses ready-ordered. There likewise ought that purchased Chaise, with the two waiting-maids and their band-boxes, to be; whom also her Majesty could not travel without. Swift, thou deft Fersen, and may the heavens turn it well!

Once more, by heaven's blessing, it is all well. Here is the sleeping Hamlet of Bondy; Chaise with waiting-women; horses all ready, and postilions with their churn-boots, impatient in the dewy dawn. Brief harnessing done, the postilions with their churn-boots vault into the saddles; brandish circularly their little noisy whips. Fersen, under his jarvie-surtout, bends in lowly silent reverence of adieu; royal hands wave speechless inexpressible response; Baroness de Korff's Berline, with the Royalty of France, bounds off: forever, as it proved. Deft Fersen dashes obliquely Northward, through the country, toward Bougret; gains Bougret, finds his German coachman and chariot waiting there; cracks off, and drives undiscovered into unknown space. A deft active man, we say; what he undertook to do is nimbly and successfully done.

THE MICAWBERS[1]

Charles Dickens

It was a little inn where Mr. Micawber put up, and he occupied a little room in it, partitioned off from the commercial room, and strongly flavored with tobacco smoke. I think it was over the kitchen, because a warm, greasy smell appeared to come up through the

[1]From *David Copperfield.*

chinks in the floor, and there was a flabby perspiration on the walls. I know it was near the bar, on account of the smell of spirits and jingling of glasses. Here, recumbent on a small sofa, underneath a picture of a racehorse, with her head close to the fire, and her feet pushing the mustard off the dumb-waiter at the other end of the room, was Mrs. Micawber, to whom Mr. Micawber entered first saying, "My dear, allow me to introduce to you a pupil of Doctor Strong's."

I noticed, by-the-by, that although Mr. Micawber was just as much confused as ever about my age and standing, he always remembered, as a genteel thing, that I was a pupil of Dr. Strong's.

Mrs. Micawber was amazed, but very glad to see me. I was very very glad to see her too, and, after an affectionate greeting on both sides, sat down on the small sofa near her.

"My dear," said Mr. Micawber, "if you will mention to Copperfield what our present position is, which I have no doubt he will like to know, I will go and look at the paper the while, and see whether anything turns up among the advertisements."

"I thought you were at Plymouth, ma'am," I said to Mrs. Micawber, as he went out.

"My dear Master Copperfield," she replied, "we went to Plymouth."

"To be on the spot," I hinted.

"Just so," said Mrs. Micawber — "to be on the spot. But the truth is, talent is not wanted in the Custom House. The local influence of my family was quite unavailing to obtain any employment in that department for a man of Mr. Micawber's abilities. They would rather *not* have a man of Mr. Micawber's abilities. He would only show the deficiency of the others. Apart from which," said Mrs. Micawber, "I will not disguise from you, my dear Master Copperfield, that when that branch of my family which settled in Plymouth became aware that Mr. Micawber was accompanied by myself, and by little Wilkens and his sister, and by the twins, they did not receive him with that ardor which he might have expected, being so newly released from captivity. In fact," said Mrs. Micawber, lowering her voice — "this is between ourselves — our reception was cool."

"Dear me!" I said.

"Yes," said Mrs. Micawber. "It is truly painful to contemplate mankind in such an aspect, Master Copperfield, but our reception was decidedly cool. There is no doubt about it. In fact, that branch of my family which is settled in Plymouth became quite personal to Mr. Micawber, before we had been there a week."

I said, and thought, that they ought to be ashamed of themselves.

"Still, so it was," continued Mrs. Micawber. "Under such circumstances, what could a man of Mr. Micawber's spirit do? But one obvious course was left — to borrow of that branch of my family the money to return to London, and to return at any sacrifice."

"Then you all came back again, ma'am?" I said.

"We all came back again," replied Mrs. Micawber. "Since then, I have consulted other branches of my family on the course which it is most expedient for Mr. Micawber to take — for I maintain that he must take some course, Master Copperfield," said Mrs. Micawber argumentatively. "It is clear that a family of six, not including a domestic, cannot live upon air."

"Certainly, ma'am," said I.

"The opinion of those other branches of my family," pursued Mrs. Micawber, "is, that Mr. Micawber should immediately turn his attention to coals."

"To what, ma'am?"

"To coals," said Mrs. Micawber — "to the coal trade. Mr. Micawber was induced to think, on inquiry, that there might be an opening for a man of his talent in the Medway coal trade. Then, as Mr. Micawber very properly said, the first step to be taken clearly was, to come and *see* the Medway. Which we came and saw. I say 'we,' Master Copperfield; for I never will," said Mrs. Micawber with emotion — "I never will desert Mr. Micawber."

I murmured my admiration and approbation.

"We came," repeated Mrs. Micawber, "and saw the Medway. My opinion of the coal trade on that river is, that it may require talent, but that it certainly requires capital. Talent, Mr. Micawber has; capital, Mr. Micawber has not. We saw, I think, the greater part of the Medway; and that is my individual conclusion. Being so near here, Mr. Micawber was of opinion that it would be rash not to come on and see the cathedral — firstly, on account of its being so well worth seeing, and our never having seen it; and secondly, on account of the great probability of something turning up in a cathedral town. We have been here," said Mrs. Micawber, "three days. Nothing has, as yet, turned up; and it may not surprise you, my dear Master Copperfield, so much as it would a stranger, to know that we are at present waiting for a remittance from London to discharge our pecuniary obligations at this hotel. Until the arrival of that remittance," said Mrs. Micawber with much feeling, "I am cut off from my home (I allude to lodgings in Pentonville), from my boy and girl, and from my twins."

I felt the utmost sympathy for Mr. and Mrs. Micawber in this anxious extremity, said as much to Mr. Micawber, who now returned — adding that I only wished I had money enough to lend them the amount they needed. Mr. Micawber's answer expressed the disturbance of his mind. He said, shaking hands with me, "Copperfield, you are a true friend; but when the worst comes to worst, no man is without a friend who is possessed of shaving materials." At this deadful hint Mrs. Micawber threw her arms round Mr. Micawber's neck, and entreated him to be calm. He wept; but so far recovered, almost immediately, as to ring the bell for the waiter, and bespeak a hot kidney pudding and a plate of shrimps for breakfast in the morning.

When I took my leave of them, they both pressed me so much to come and dine before they went away that I could not refuse. But as I knew I could not come next day, when I should have a good deal to prepare in the evening, Mr. Micawber arranged that he would call at Doctor Strong's in the course of the morning (having a presentiment that the remittance would arrive by that post), and propose the day after, if it would suit me better. Accordingly, I was called out of school next forenoon, and found Mr. Micawber in the parlor, who had called to say that the dinner would take place as proposed. When I asked him if the remittance had come, he pressed my hand and departed.

As I was looking out of the window that same evening, it surprised me, and made me uneasy, to see Mr. Micawber and Uriah Heep walk past arm in arm — Uriah humbly sensible of the honor that was done him, and Mr. Micawber taking a bland delight in extending his patronage to Uriah. But I was still more surprised when I went to the little hotel next day at the appointed dinner-hour, which was four o'clock, to find, from what Mr. Micawber said, that he had gone home with Uriah, and had drunk brandy-and-water at Mrs. Heep's.

"And I'll tell you what, my dear Copperfield," said Mr. Micawber, "your friend Heep is a young fellow who might be attorney-general. If I had known that young man at the period when my difficulties came to a crisis, all I can say is, that I believe my creditors would have been a great deal better managed than they were."

I hardly understood how this could have been, seeing that Mr. Micawber had paid them nothing at all as it was; but I did not like to ask. Neither did I like to say that I hoped he had not been too communicative to Uriah, or to inquire if they had talked much about me. I was afraid of hurting Mr. Micawber's feelings, or at all events, Mrs. Micawber's, she being very sensitive; but I was uncomfortable about it, too, and often thought about it afterwards.

We had a beautiful little dinner — quite an elegant dish of fish, the kidney-end of a loin of veal roasted, fried sausage-meat, a partridge, and a pudding. There was wine, and there was strong ale; and after dinner, Mrs. Micawber made us a bowl of hot punch with her own hands.

Mr. Micawber was uncommonly convivial. I never saw him such good company. He made his face shine with the punch, so that it looked as if it had been varnished all over. He got cheerfully sentimental about the town, and proposed success to it; observing that Mrs. Micawber and himself had been made extremely snug and comfortable there, and that he never should forget the agreeable hours they had passed in Canterbury. He proposed me afterwards; and he, and Mrs. Micawber, and I, took a review of our past acquaintance, in the course of which we sold the property all over again. Then I proposed Mrs. Micawber — or, at least, said modestly, "If you'll allow me, Mrs. Micawber, I shall now have the pleasure of drinking your health, ma'am." On which Mr. Micawber delivered an eulogium on Mrs. Micawber's character, and said she had ever been his guide, philosopher, and friend; and that he would recommend me, when I came to a marrying-time of life, to marry such another woman, if such another woman could be found.

As the punch disappeared, Mr. Micawber became still more friendly and convivial. Mrs. Micawber's spirits becoming elevated, too, we sang, "Auld Lang Syne." When we came to "Here's my trusty fiere," we all joined hands round the table; and when we declared we would "tak' a right gude willie-waught," and hadn't the least idea what it meant, we were really affected.

In a word, I never saw anybody so thoroughly jovial as Mr. Micawber was, down to the very last moment of the evening, when I took a hearty farewell of himself and his amiable wife. Consequently I was not prepared, at seven o'clock next morning, to receive the following communication, dated half-past nine in the evening, a quarter of an hour after I had left him:

"My Dear Young Friend:

"The die is cast—all is over. Hiding the ravages of care with a sickly mask of mirth, I have not informed you, this evening, that there is no hope of the remittance! Under these circumstances, alike humiliating to contemplate, and humiliating to relate, I have discharged the pecuniary liability contracted at this establishment by giving a note of hand, made payable fourteen days after date, at my residence, Pentonville, London. When it becomes due, it will not be taken up. The result is destruction. The bolt is impending, and the tree must fall.

"Let the wretched man who now addresses you, my dear Copperfield, be a beacon to you through life. He writes with that intention and in that hope. If he could think himself of so much use, one gleam of day might, by possibility, penetrate into the cheerless dungeon of his remaining existence—though his longevity is, at present (to say the least of it), extremely problematical.

"This is the last communication, my dear Copperfield, you will ever receive.

"From
"The
"Beggared Outcast,
"Wilkins Micawber."

I was so shocked by the contents of this heart-rending letter that I ran off directly toward the little hotel, with the intention of taking it on my way to Doctor Strong's, and trying to soothe Mr. Micawber with a word of comfort. But, halfway there, I met the London coach, with Mr. and Mrs. Micawber up behind; Mr. Micawber, the very picture of tranquil enjoyment, smiling at Mrs. Micawber's conversation, eating walnuts out of a paper bag, with a bottle sticking out of his breast pocket. As they did not see me, I thought it best, all things considered, not to see them. So, with a great weight taken off my mind, I turned into a by-street that was the nearest way to school, and felt, upon the whole, relieved that they were gone — though I still liked them very much, nevertheless.

THE GUILLOTINE[1]

Charles Dickens

Along the Paris streets, the death-carts rumble, hollow and harsh. Six tumbrils carry the day's wine to La Guillotine. All the devouring and insatiate Monsters imagined since imagination could record itself, are fused in the one realization, Guillotine. And yet there is not in France, with its rich variety of soil and climate, a blade, a leaf, a root, a spring, a peppercorn, which will grow to maturity under conditions more certain than those that have produced this horror. Crush humanity out of shape once more, under similar hammers, and it will twist itself into the same tortured forms. Sow the same seed of rapacious license and oppression over again, and it will surely yield the same fruit according to its kind.

Six tumbrils roll along the streets. Change these back again to what they were, thou powerful enchanter, Time, and they shall be seen to be the carriages of absolute monarchs, the equipages of feudal nobles, the toilettes of flaring Jezebels, the churches that are not my father's house but dens of thieves, the huts of millions of starving peasants! No; the great magician who majestically works out the appointed order of the Creator, never reverses his transformations. "If thou be changed into this shape by the will of God," say the seers to the enchanted, in the wise Arabian stories, "then remain so! But, if thou wear this form through mere passing conjuration, then resume thy former aspect!" Changeless and hopeless, the tumbrils roll along.

As the somber wheels of the six carts go round, they seem to plough up a long crooked furrow among the populace in the streets. Ridges of faces are thrown to this side and to that, and the

[1]From *A Tale of Two Cities.*

ploughs go steadily onward. So used are the regular inhabitants of the houses to the spectacle, that in many windows there are no people, and in some the occupation of the hands is not so much as suspended, while the eyes survey the faces in the tumbrils. Here and there, the inmate has visitors to see the sight; then he points his finger, with something of the complacency of a curator or authorized exponent, to this cart and to that, and seems to tell who sat here yesterday, and who there the day before.

Of the riders in the tumbrils, some observe these things, and all things on their last roadside, with an impassive stare; others, with a lingering interest in the ways of life and men. Some, seated with drooping heads, are sunk in silent despair; again, there are some so heedful of their looks that they cast upon the multitude such glances as they have seen in theaters, and in pictures. Several close their eyes, and think, or try to get their straying thoughts together. Only one, and he is a miserable creature, of a crazed aspect, is so shattered and made drunk by horror, that he sings, and tries to dance. Not one of the whole number appeals by look or gesture, to the pity of the people.

There is a guard of sundry horsemen riding abreast of the tumbrils, and faces are often turned up to some of them, and they are asked some question. It would seem to be always the same question, for, it is always followed by a press of people toward the third cart. The horsemen abreast of that cart, frequently point out one man in it with their swords. The leading curiosity is, to know which is he; he stands at the back of the tumbril with his head bent down, to converse with a mere girl who sits at the side of the cart, and holds his hand. He has no curiosity or care for the scene about him, and always speaks to the girl. Here and there in the long street of St. Honoré, cries are raised against him. If they move him at all, it is only to a quiet smile, as he shakes his hair a little more loosely about his face. He cannot easily touch his face, his arms being bound.

On the steps of a church, awaiting the coming up of the tumbrils, stands the Spy and the prison-sheep. He looks into the first of them: not there: He looks into the second: not there. He already asks himself, "Has he sacrificed me?" when his face clears, as he looks into the third.

"Which is Evrémonde?" says a man behind him.

"That. At the back there."

"With his hand in the girl's?"

"Yes."

The man cries, "Down, Evrémonde! To the Guillotine all aristocrats! Down, Evrémonde!"

"Hush, hush!" the Spy entreats him, timidly.

"And why not, citizen?"

"He is going to pay the forfeit: it will be paid in five minutes more. Let him be at peace."

But the man continuing to exclaim, "Down, Evrémonde!" the face of Evrémonde is for a moment turned toward him. Evrémonde then sees the Spy, and looks attentively at him, and goes his way.

The clocks are on the stroke of three, and the furrow ploughed among the populace is turning round, to come on into the place of execution, and end. The ridges thrown to this side and to that, now crumble in and close behind the last plough as it passes on, for all are following to the Guillotine. In front of it, seated in chairs, as in a garden of public diversion, are a number of women, busily knitting. On one of the foremost chairs, stands The Vengeance, looking about for her friend.

"Thérèse!" she cries, in her shrill tones. "Who has seen her? Thérèse Defarge!"

"She never missed before," says a knitting-woman of the sisterhood.

"No; nor will she miss now," cries The Vengeance, petulantly. "Thérèse!"

"Louder," the woman recommends.

Ay! Louder, Vengeance, much louder, and still she will scarcely hear thee. Louder yet, Vengeance, with a little oath or so added, and yet it will hardly bring her. Send other women up and down to seek her, lingering somewhere; and yet, although the messengers have done dread deeds, it is questionable whether of their own wills they will go far enough to find her!

"Bad Fortune!" cries The Vengeance, stamping her foot in the chair, "and here are the tumbrils! And Evrémonde will be despatched in a wink, and she not here! See her knitting in my hand, and her empty chair ready for her. I cry with vexation and disappointment!"

As The Vengeance descends from her elevation to do it, the tumbrils begin to discharge their loads. The ministers of Sainte Guillotine are robed and ready. Crash!—A head is held up, and the knitting-women who scarcely lifted their eyes to look at it a moment ago when it could think and speak, count One.

The second tumbril empties and moves on; the third comes up. Crash!—And the knitting-women, never faltering or pausing in their work, count Two.

The supposed Evrémonde descends, and the seamstress is lifted out next after him. He has not relinquished her patient hand in getting out, but still holds it as he promised. He gently places her with her back to the crashing engine that constantly whirrs up and falls, and she looks into his face and thanks him.

"But for you, dear stranger, I should not be so composed, for I am naturally a poor little thing, faint of heart; nor should I have been able to raise my thoughts to Him who was put to death, that we might have hope and comfort here today. I think you were sent to me by Heaven."

"Or you to me," says Sydney Carton. "Keep your eyes upon me, dear child, and mind no other object."

"I mind nothing while I hold your hand. I shall mind nothing when I let it go, if they are rapid."

"They will be rapid. Fear not!"

The two stand in the fast-thinning throng of victims, but they speak as if they were alone. Eye to eye, voice to voice, hand to hand, heart to heart, these two children of the Universal Mother, else so wide apart and differing, have come together on the dark highway, to repair home together, and to rest in her bosom.

"Brave and generous friend, will you let me ask you one last question? I am very ignorant, and it troubles me—just a little."

"Tell me what it is."

"I have a cousin, an only relative and an orphan, like myself, whom I love very dearly. She is five years younger than I, and she lives in a farmer's house in the south country. Poverty parted us, and she knows nothing of my fate—for I cannot write—and if I could, how should I tell her! It is better as it is."

"Yes, yes; better as it is."

"What I have been thinking as we came along, and what I am still thinking now, as I look into your kind strong face which gives me so much support, is this:—If the Republic really does good to the poor, and they come to be less hungry, and in all ways to suffer less, she may live a long time: she may even live to be old."

"What then, my gentle sister?"

"Do you think:" the uncomplaining eyes in which there is so much endurance, fill with tears, and the lips part a little more and tremble: "that it will seem long to me, while I wait for her in the better land where I trust both you and I will be mercifully sheltered?"

"It cannot be, my child; there is no Time there, and no trouble there."

"You comfort me so much! I am so ignorant. Am I to kiss you now? Is the moment come?"

"Yes."

She kisses his lips; he kisses hers; they solemnly bless each other. The spare hand does not tremble as he releases it; nothing worse than a sweet, bright constancy is in the patient face. She goes next before him — is gone; the knitting-women count Twenty-Two.

"I am the Resurrection and the Life, saith the Lord: he that believeth in Me, though he were dead, yet shall he live: and whosoever liveth and believeth in Me shall never die."

The murmuring of many voices, the upturning of many faces, the pressing on of many footsteps in the outskirts of the crowd, so that it swells forward in a mass, like one great heave of water, all flashes away. Twenty-Three.

❦

SIEGE OF THE BASTILLE[1]

Thomas Carlyle

. . . To describe this Siege of the Bastille (thought to be one of the most important in History) perhaps transcends the talent of mortals. Could one but, after infinite reading, get to understand so much as the plan of the building! But there is open Esplanade, at

[1]From *The French Revolution.*

the end of the Rue Saint-Antoine; there are such Forecourts, *Cour Avancée, Cour de l'Orme,* arched Gateway (where Louis Tournay now fights); then new draw-bridges, dormant-bridges, rampart-bastions, and the grim Eight Towers; a labyrinthic Mass, high-frowning there, of all ages from twenty years to four hundred and twenty—beleaguered, in this its last hour, as we said, by mere Chaos come again! Ordinance of all calibers; throats of all capacities; men of all plans, every man his own engineer: seldom since the war of Pygmies and Cranes was there seen so anomalous a thing. Half-pay Elie is home for a suit of regimentals; no one would heed him in colored clothes: half-pay Hulin is haranguing Gardes Françaises in the Place de Grève. Frantic Patriots pick up the grapeshots; bear them, still hot (or seemingly so), to the Hôtel-de-Ville—Paris, you perceive, is to be burnt! Flesselles is "pale to the very lips," for the roar of the multitude grows deep. Paris wholly has got to the acme of its frenzy; whirled, all ways, by panic madness. At every street-barricade, there whirls simmering a minor whirlpool—strengthening the barricade, since God knows what is coming; and all minor whirlpools play distractedly into the grand Fire-Mahlstrom which is lashing round the Bastille.

And so it lashes and it roars. Cholat the wine-merchant has become an impromptu cannoneer. See Georget, of the Marine Service, fresh from Brest, ply the King of Siam's cannon. Singular (if we were not used to the like): Georget lay, last night, taking his ease at his inn; the King of Siam's cannon also lay, knowing nothing of *him,* for a hundred years. Yet now, at the right instant, they have got together, and discourse eloquent music. For, hearing what was toward, Georget sprang from the Brest Diligence, and ran. Gardes Françaises also will be here, with real artillery: were not the walls so thick!—Upward from the Esplanade, horizontally from all neighboring roofs and windows, flashes one irregular deluge of musketry, without effect. The Invalides lie flat, firing comparatively at their ease from behind stone; hardly through portholes, show the tip of a nose. We fall, shot; and make no impression!

Let conflagration rage; of whatsoever is combustible! Guard-rooms are burnt, Invalides mess-rooms. A distracted "Peruke-maker with two fiery torches" is for burning "the salt-peters of the Arsenal"—had not a woman run screaming; had not a Patriot, with some tincture of Natural Philosophy, instantly struck the wind out of him (butt of musket on pit of stomach), overturned barrels, and stayed the devouring element. A young beautiful lady, seized escaping in these Outer Courts, and thought falsely to be De Launay's daughter, shall be burnt in De Launay's sight; she lies swooned on a paillasse: but again a Patriot, it is brave Aubin Bonnemère the old soldier, dashes in, and rescues her. Straw is burnt; three cartloads of it, hauled thither, go up in white smoke: almost to the choking of Patriotism itself; so that Elie had, with singed brows, to drag back one cart; and Réole the "gigantic haberdasher" another. Smoke as of Tophet; confusion as of Babel; noise as of the Crack of Doom!

LONDON IN 1685[1]

Thomas Babington Macaulay

He who then rambled to what is now the gayest and most crowded part of Regent Street found himself in a solitude, and was sometimes so fortunate as to have a shot at a woodcock. On the north the Oxford road ran between hedges. Three or four hundred yards to the south were the garden walls of a few great houses which were considered as quite out of town. On the west was a meadow renowned for a spring from which, long afterward, Conduit Street was named. On the east was a field not to be passed without a shudder by any Londoner of that age. There, as in a place far from the haunts of men, had been dug, twenty years before, when the great plague was raging, a pit into which the dead carts had nightly shot corpses by scores. It was popularly believed that the earth was deeply tainted with infection and could not be disturbed without imminent risk to human life. No foundations were laid there till two generations had passed without any return of the pestilence, and till the ghastly spot had long been surrounded by buildings.

[1]From *History of England.*

We should greatly err if we were to suppose that any of the streets and squares then bore the same aspect as at present. The great majority of the houses, indeed, have, since that time, been wholly, or in great part, rebuilt. If the most fashionable parts of the capital could be placed before us, such as they then were, we should be disgusted by their squalid appearance, and poisoned by their noisome atmosphere. In Covent Garden a filthy and noisy market was held close to the dwellings of the great. Fruit women screamed, carters fought, cabbage stalks and rotten apples accumulated in heaps at the thresholds of the Countess of Berkshire and of the Bishop of Durham.

The center of Lincoln's Inn Fields was an open space where the rabble congregated every evening, within a few yards of Cardigan House and Winchester House, to hear mountebanks harangue, to see bears dance, and to set dogs at oxen. Rubbish was shot in every part of the area. Horses were exercised there. The beggars were as noisy and importunate as in the worst governed cities of the Continent. A Lincoln's Inn mumper was a proverb. The whole fraternity knew the arms and liveries of every charitably disposed grandee in the neighborhood and, as soon as his lordship's coach and six appeared, came hopping and crawling in crowds to persecute him. These disorders lasted, in spite of many accidents, and of some legal proceedings, till, in the reign of George II, Sir Joseph Jekyll, Master of the Rolls, was knocked down and nearly killed in the middle of the square. Then at length palisades were set up, and a pleasant garden laid out.

St. James's Square was a receptacle for all the offal and cinders, for all the dead cats and dead dogs of Westminster. At one time a cudgel player kept the ring there. At another time an impudent squatter settled himself there, and built a shed for rubbish under the windows of the gilded saloons in which the first magnates of the realm, Norfolk, Ormond, Kent, and Pembroke, gave banquets and balls. It was not till these nuisances had lasted through a whole generation, and till much had been written about them, that the inhabitants applied to Parliament for permission to put up rails, and to plant trees.

When such was the state of the region inhabited by the most luxurious portion of society, we may easily believe that the great body of the population suffered what would now be considered as insupportable grievances. The pavement was detestable; all foreigners cried shame upon it. The drainage was so bad that in rainy weather the gutters soon became torrents. Several facetious poets have commemorated the fury with which these black rivulets roared down Snow Hill, and Ludgate Hill, bearing to Fleet Ditch a vast tribute of animal and vegetable filth from the stalls of butchers and green-grocers. This flood was profusely thrown to right and left by coaches and carts. To keep as far from the carriage road as possible was therefore the wish of every pedestrian. The mild and timid gave the wall. The bold and athletic took it. If two roisterers met, they cocked their hats in each other's faces, and pushed each other about till the weaker was shoved toward the kennel. If he was a mere bully he sneaked off, muttering that he should find a time. If he was pugnacious, the encounter probably ended in a duel behind Montague House.

The houses were not numbered. There would indeed have been little advantage in numbering them; for of the coachmen, chairmen, porters, and errand boys of London, a very small proportion could read. It was necessary to use marks which the most ignorant could understand. The shops were therefore distinguished by painted signs, which gave a gay and grotesque aspect to the streets. The walk from Charing Cross to Whitechapel lay through an endless succession of Saracens' Heads, Royal Oaks, Blue Bears, and Golden Lambs, which disappeared when they were no longer required for the direction of the common people.

When the evening closed in, the difficulty and danger of walking about London became serious indeed. The garret windows were opened, and pails were emptied, with little regard to those who were passing below. Falls, bruises, and broken bones were of constant occurrence. For, till the last year of the reign of Charles II, most of the streets were left in profound darkness. Thieves and robbers plied their trade with impunity; yet they were hardly so terrible to peaceable citizens as another class of ruffians. It was a favorite amusement of dissolute young gentlemen to swagger by night about the town, breaking windows, upsetting sedans, beating quiet men, and offering rude caresses to pretty women. Several dynasties of these tyrants had, since the Restoration, domineered over the streets. The Muns and Tityre Tus had given place to the Hectors, and the Hectors had been recently succeeded by the Scourers.

At a later period arose the Nicker, the Hawcubite, and the yet more dreaded name of Mohawk. . . .

The machinery for keeping the peace was utterly contemptible. There was an act of Common Council which provided that more than a thousand watchmen should be constantly on the alert in the city, from sunset to sunrise, and that every inhabitant should take his turn of duty. But this act was negligently executed. Few of those who were summoned left their homes; and those few generally found it more agreeable to tipple in alehouses than to pace the streets.

It ought to be noticed that, in the last year of the reign of Charles II, began a great change in the police of London, a change which has perhaps added as much to the happiness of the body of the people as revolutions of much greater fame. An ingenious projector, named Edward Heming, obtained letters patent conveying to him, for a term of years, the exclusive right of lighting up London. He undertook, for a moderate consideration, to place a light before every tenth door, on moonless nights, from Michaelmas to Lady day, and from six to twelve of the clock. Those who now see the capital all the year round, from dusk to dawn, blazing with a splendor beside which the illuminations for La Hogue and Blenheim would have looked pale, may perhaps smile to think of Heming's lanterns, which glimmered feebly before one house in ten during a small part of one night in three. But such was not the feeling of his contemporaries. His scheme was enthusiastically applauded, and furiously attacked. The friends of improvement extolled him as the greatest of all the benefactors of his city. What, they asked, were the boasted inventions of Archimedes when compared with the achievement of the man who had turned the nocturnal shades into noonday? In spite of these eloquent eulogies the cause of darkness was not left undefended. There were fools in that age who opposed the introduction of what was called the new light as strenuously as fools in our age have opposed the introduction of vaccination and railroads, as strenuously as the fools of an age anterior to the dawn of history doubtless opposed the introduction of the plough and of alphabetical writing. Many years after the date of Heming's patent there were extensive districts in which no lamp was seen.

We may easily imagine what, in such times, must have been the state of the quarters of London which were peopled by the outcasts of society. Among those quarters one had attained a scandalous pre-eminence. On the confines of the City and the Temple had been founded, in the thirteenth century, a House of Carmelite Friars, distinguished by their white hoods. The precinct of this house had, before the Reformation, been a sanctuary for criminals and still retained the privilege of protecting debtors from arrest. Insolvents consequently were to be found in every dwelling, from cellar to garret. Of these a large proportion were knaves and libertines, and were followed to their asylum by women more abandoned than themselves. The civil power was unable to keep order in a district swarming with such inhabitants; and thus Whitefriars became the favorite resort of all who wished to be emancipated from the restraints of the law. Though the immunities legally belonging to the place extended only to cases of debt, cheats, false witnesses, forgers, and highwaymen found refuge there. For amidst a rabble so desperate no peace officer's life was in safety. At the cry of "Rescue" bullies with swords and cudgels, and termagant hags with spits and broomsticks, poured forth by hundreds; and the intruder was fortunate if he escaped back into Fleet Street, hustled, stripped, and pumped upon. Even the warrant of the Chief Justice of England could not be executed without the help of a company of musketeers. Such relics of the barbarism of the darkest ages were to be found within a short walk of the chambers where Somers was studying history and law, of the chapel where Tillotson was preaching, of the coffee house where Dryden was passing judgment on poems and plays, and of the hall where the Royal Society was examining the astronomical system of Isaac Newton.

THE HORIZON[1]

Alice Meynell

To mount a hill is to lift with you something lighter and brighter than yourself or than any meaner burden. You lift the world, you raise the horizon; you give a signal for the distance to stand up. It

[1]By permission of Charles Scribner's Sons, Publishers.

is like the scene in the Vatican when a Cardinal, with his dramatic Italian hands, bids the kneeling groups to arise. He does more than bid them. He lifts them, he gathers them up, far and near, with the upward gesture of both arms; he takes them to their feet with the compulsion of his expressive force. Or it is as when a conductor takes his players to successive heights of music. You summon the sea, you bring the mountains, the distances unfold unlooked-for wings and take an even flight. You are but a man lifting his weight upon the upward road, but as you climb the circle of the world goes up to face you.

Not here or there, but with a definite continuity, the unseen unfolds. This distant hill outsoars that less distant, but all are on the wing, and the plain raises its verge. All things follow and wait upon your eyes. You lift these up, not by the raising of your eyelids, but by the pilgrimage of your body. "Lift thine eyes to the mountains." It is then that other mountains lift themselves to your human eyes.

It is the law whereby the eye and the horizon answer one another that makes the way up a hill so full of universal movement. All the landscape is on pilgrimage. The town gathers itself closer, and its inner harbors literally come to light; the headlands repeat themselves; little cups within the treeless hills open and show their farms. In the sea are many regions. A breeze is at play for a mile or two, and the surface is turned. There are roads and curves in the blue and in the white. Not a step of your journey up the height that has not its replies in the steady motion of land and sea. Things rise together like a flock of many-feathered birds.

But it is the horizon, more than all else, you have come in search of; that is your chief companion on your way. It is to uplift the horizon to the equality of your sight that you go high. You give it a distance worthy of the skies. There is no distance, except the distance in the sky, to be seen from the level earth; but from the height is to be seen the distance of this world. The line is sent back into the remoteness of light, the verge is removed beyond verge, into a distance that is enormous and minute.

So delicate and so slender is the distant horizon that nothing less near than Queen Mab and her chariot can equal its fineness. Here on the edges of the eyelids, or there on the edges of the world — we know no other place for things so exquisitely made, so thin, so small and tender. The touches of her passing, as close as dreams, or the utmost vanishing of the forest or the ocean in the white light between the earth and the air; nothing else is quite so intimate and fine. The extremities of a mountain view have just such tiny touches as the closeness of closing eyes shut in.

On the horizon is the sweetest light. Elsewhere color mars the simplicity of light; but there color is effaced, not as men efface it, by a blur or darkness, but by mere light. The bluest sky disappears on that shining edge; there is not substance enough for color. The rim of the hill, of the woodland, of the meadowland, of the sea—let it only be far enough—has the same absorption of color; and even the dark things drawn upon the bright edges of the sky are lucid, the light is among them, and they are mingled with it. The horizon has its own way of making bright the penciled figures of forests, which are black but luminous.

On the horizon, moveover, closes the long perspective of the sky. There you perceive that an ordinary sky of clouds—not a thunder sky—is not a wall but the underside of a floor. You see the clouds that repeat each other grow smaller by distance; and you find a new unity in the sky and earth that gather alike the great lines of their designs to the same distant close. There is no longer an alien sky, tossed up in unintelligible heights.

Of all the things that London has forgone, the most to be regretted is the horizon. Not the bark of the trees in its right color; not the spirit of the growing grass, which has in some way escaped from the parks; not the smell of the earth unmingled with the odor of soot; but rather the mere horizon. No doubt the sun makes a beautiful thing of the London smoke at times, and in some places of the sky; but not there, not where the soft sharp distance ought to shine. To be dull there is to put all relations and comparisons in the wrong, and to make the sky lawless.

A horizon dark with storm is another thing. The weather darkens the line and defines it, or mingles it with the raining cloud; or softly dims it, or blackens it against a gleam of narrow sunshine in the sky. The stormy horizon will take wing, and the sunny. Go high enough, and you can raise the light from beyond the shower, and the shadow from behind the ray. Only the shapeless and lifeless smoke disobeys and defeats the summons of the eyes.

Up at the top of the seaward hill your first thought is one of some compassion for sailors, inasmuch as they see but little of their sea.

A child on a mere Channel cliff looks upon spaces and sizes that they cannot see in the Pacific, on the ocean side of the world. Never in the solitude of the blue water, never between the Cape of Good Hope and Cape Horn, never between the Islands and the West, has the seaman seen anything but a little circle of sea. The Ancient Mariner, when he was alone, did but drift through a thousand narrow solitudes. The sailor has nothing but his mast, indeed. And but for his mast he would be isolated in as small a world as that of a traveler through the plains.

A close circlet of waves is the sailor's famous offing. His offing hardly deserves the name of horizon. To hear him you might think something of his offing, but you do not so when you sit down in the center of it.

As the upspringing of all things at your going up the heights, so steady, so swift is the subsidence at your descent. The further sea lies away, hill folds down beyond hill. The whole upstanding world, with its looks serene and alert, its distant replies, its signals of many miles, its signs and communications of light, gathers down and pauses. This flock of birds which is the mobile landscape wheels and goes to earth. The Cardinal weighs down the audience with his downward hands. Farewell to the most delicate horizon.

THE ROCKIES[1]

Rupert Brooke

At Calgary, if you can spare a minute from more important matters, slip beyond the hurrying white city, climb the golf links, and gaze west. A low bank of dark clouds disturbs you by the fixity of its outline. It is the Rockies, seventy miles away. On a good day, it is said, they are visible twice as far, so clear and serene is this air. Five hundred miles west is the coast of British Columbia, a region

[1]From *Letters from America.* Copyright, 1916, by Charles Scribner's Sons. Reprinted by permission of the publishers.

with a different climate, different country, and different problems. It is cut off from the prairies by vast tracts of wild country and uninhabitable ranges. For nearly two hundred miles the train pants through the homeless grandeur of the Rockies and the Selkirks. Four or five hotels, a few huts or tents, and a rare mining-camp — that is all the habitation in many thousands of square miles. Little even of that is visible from the train. That is one of the chief differences between the effect of the Rockies and that of the Alps. There, you are always in sight of a civilization which has nestled for ages at the feet of those high places. They stand, enrobed with worship, and grander by contrast with the lives of men. These unmemoried heights are inhuman — or rather, irrelevant to humanity. No recorded Hannibal has struggled across them; their shadow lies on no remembered literature. They acknowledge claims neither of the soul nor of the body of man. He is a stranger, neither nature's enemy nor her child. She is there alone, scarcely a unity in the heaped confusion of these crags, almost without grandeur among the chaos of earth.

Yet this horrid and solitary wildness is but one aspect. There is beauty here, at length, for the first time in Canada, the real beauty that is always too sudden for mortal eyes, and brings pain with its comfort. The Rockies have a remoter, yet a kindlier, beauty than the Alps. Their rock is of a browner color, and such rugged peaks and crowns as do not attain snow continually suggest gigantic castellations, or the ramparts of Titans. Eastward, the foothills are few and low, and the mountains stand superbly. The heart lifts to see them. They guard the sunset. Into this rocky wilderness you plunge, and toil through it hour by hour, viewing it from the rear of the observation car. The observation car is a great invention of the new world. At the end of the train is a compartment with large windows, and a little platform behind it, roofed over, but exposed otherwise to the air. On this platform are sixteen little perches, for which you fight with Americans. Victorious, you crouch on one, and watch the ever-receding panorama behind the train. It is an admirable way of viewing scenery. But a day of being perpetually drawn backward at a great pace through some of the grandest mountains in the world has a queer effect. Like life, it leaves you with a dizzy irritation. For, as in life, you never see the glories till they are past, and then they vanish with incredible rapidity. And if you crane to see the dwindling further peaks, you miss the new splendors.

The day I went through most of the Rockies was, by some standards, a bad one for the view. Rain scudded by in forlorn, gray showers, and the upper parts of the mountains were wrapped in cloud, which was but rarely blown aside to reveal the heights. Sublimity, therefore, was left to the imagination; but desolation was most vividly present. In no weather could the impression of loneliness be stronger. The pines drooped and sobbed. Cascades, born somewhere in the dun firmament above, dropped down the mountainsides in ever-growing, white treads. The rivers roared and plunged with aimless passion down the ravines. Stray little clouds, left behind when the wrack lifted a little, ran bleating up and down the forlorn hillsides. More often, the clouds trailed along the valleys, a long procession of shrouded, melancholy figures, seeming to pause, as with an indeterminate, tragic, vain gesture, before passing out of sight up some ravine.

Yet desolation is not the final impression that will remain of the Rockies and the Selkirks. I was advised by various people to "stop off" at Banff and at Lake Louise, in the Rockies. I did so. They are supposed to be equally the beauty spots of the mountains. How perplexing it is that advisers are always so kindly and willing to help, and always so undiscriminating. It is equally disastrous to be a skeptic and to be credulous. Banff is an ordinary little tourist resort in mountainous country, with hills and a stream and snow peaks beyond. Beautiful enough, and invigorating. But Lake Louise —Lake Louise is of another world. Imagine a little round lake 6,000 feet up, a mile across, closed in by great cliffs of brown rock, round the shoulders of which are thrown mantles of close, dark pine. At one end the lake is fed by a vast glacier, and its milky, tumbling stream; and the glacier climbs to snow fields of one of the highest and loveliest peaks in the Rockies, which keeps perpetual guard over the scene. To this place you go up three or four miles from the railway. There is the hotel at one end of the lake, facing the glacier; else no sign of humanity. From the windows you may watch the water and the peaks all day, and never see the same view twice. In the lake, ever-changing, is Beauty herself, as nearly visible to mortal eyes as she may ever be. The water, beyond the flowers, is green, always a different green. Sometimes it is tranquil, glassy, shot with blue, of a peacock tint. Then a little wind awakes in the distance, and ruffles the surface, yard by yard, covering it with a myriad tiny wrinkles, till half the lake is milky emerald, while the rest still sleeps. And, at length, the whole is astir, and the sun catches it, and Lake Louise is a web of laughter, the opal distillation of all the buds of all the spring. On either side go up the dark, processional pines, mounting to the sacred peaks, devout, kneeling, motionless, in an ecstasy of homely adoration, like the donors and their families in a Flemish picture. Among these you may wander for hours by little rambling paths, over white and red and golden flowers, and, continually, you spy little lakes, hidden away, each a shy, soft jewel of a new strange tint of green or blue, mutable and lovely. . . . And beyond all is the glacier and the vast fields and peaks of eternal snow.

If you watch the great white cliff, from the foot of which the glacier flows — seven miles away, but it seems two — you will sometimes see a little puff of silvery smoke go up, thin, and vanish. A few seconds later comes the roar of terrific, distant thunder. The mountains tower and smile unregarding in the sun. It was an avalanche. And if you climb any of the ridges or peaks around, there are discovered other valleys and heights and ranges, wild and desert, stretching endlessly away. As day draws to an end the shadows on the snow turn bluer, the crying of innumerable waters hushes, and the immense, bare ramparts of westward-facing rock that guard the great valley win a rich, golden-brown radiance. Long after the sun has set they seem to give forth the splendor of the day, and the tranquillity of their centuries, in undiminished fullness. They have that other-worldly serenity which a perfect old age possesses. And as with a perfect old age, so here, the color and the light ebb so gradually out of things that you could swear nothing of the radiance and glory gone up to the very moment before the dark.

It was on such a height, and at such hour as this, that I sat and considered the nature of the country in this continent. There was perceptible, even here, though less urgent than elsewhere, the strangeness I had noticed in woods by the St. Lawrence, and on the banks of the Delaware (where are red-haired girls who sing at dawn), and in British Columbia, and afterwards among the brown hills and colossal trees of California, but especially by that lonely, golden beach in Manitoba, where the high-stepping little brown deer run down to drink, and the wild geese through the evening go flying and crying. It is an empty land. To love the country here —mountains are worshipped, not loved—is like embracing a wraith. A European can find nothing to satisfy the hunger of his heart. The air is too thin to breathe. He requires haunted woods, and the friendly presence of ghosts. The immaterial soil of England is heavy and fertile with the decaying stuff of past seasons and generations. Here is the floor of a new wood, yet uncumbered by one year's autumn fall. We Europeans find the Orient stale and yet too luxuriantly fetid by reason of the multitude of bygone lives and thoughts, oppressive with the crowded presence of the dead, both men and gods. So, I imagine, a Canadian would feel our woods and fields heavy with the past and the invisible, and suffer claustrophobia[2] in an English countryside beneath the dreadful pressure of immortals. For his own forests and wild places are wind-swept and empty. That is their charm, and their terror. You may lie awake all night and never feel the passing of evil presences, nor hear printless feet; neither do you lapse into slumber with the comfortable consciousness of those friendly watchers who sit invisibly by a lonely sleeper under an English sky. Even an Irishman would not see a row of little men with green caps lepping along beneath the fireweed and the golden daisies; nor have the subtler fairies of England found these wilds. It has never paid a steamship or railway company to arrange for their emigration.

In the bush of certain islands of the South Seas you may hear a crashing on windless noons, and, looking up, see a corpse swinging along head downward at a great speed from tree to tree, holding by its toes, grimacing, dripping with decay. Americans, so active in this life, rest quiet afterwards. And though every stone of Wall Street have its separate Lar,[3] their kind have not gone out beyond city lots. The maple and the birch conceal no dryads, and Pan has never been heard among these reed beds. Look as long as you like upon a cataract of the New World, you shall not see a white arm in the foam. A godless place. And the dead do not return. That is why there is nothing lurking in the heart of the shadows, and no human mystery in the colors, and neither the same joy nor the kind of peace in dawn and sunset that older lands know. It is, in-

[2]*Claustrophobia,* morbid dread of confined places.
[3]*Lar,* a tutelary divinity, spirit of a dead ancestor.

deed, a new world. How far away seem those grassy, moonlit places in England that have been Roman camps or roads, where there is always serenity, and the spirit of a purpose at rest, and the sunlight flashes upon more than flint! Here one is perpetually a first-comer. The land is virginal, the wind cleaner than elsewhere, and every lake newborn, and each day is the first day. The flowers are less conscious than English flowers, the breezes have nothing to remember, and everything to promise. There walk, as yet, no ghosts of lovers in Canadian lanes. This is the essence of the gray freshness and brisk melancholy of this land. And for all the charm of those qualities, it is also the secret of a European's discontent. For it is possible, at a pinch, to do without gods. But one misses the dead.

AN IRISH GARDEN[1]

Katharine Tynan

Somewhere about 1868 my father acquired the lands and house of Whitehall, Clondalkin, where my later childhood and youth were to be spent. The house had once belonged to Curran, the great Irish lawyer and patriot, whose daughter, Sarah, should have married Robert Emmet. It was a small cottage building with little windows under immense overhanging eaves of thatch and a hall door within a porch of green trellis. There was a very quaint little lawn in front in which grew an immense tree-peony, a fuschia as big, and a great many Portugal laurels and laurestinus. The cottage was flanked by a building of two stories. The lower story was the kitchen of the cottage. Its green door opened on a long strip of courtyard. There was a stone bench by the door, useful for many things.

Our first summer there was 1869, when we three children were there in charge of a nurse. The house had not yet been altered to accommodate a family. Of the two-story edifice only one fourth be-

[1]By permission of Devin-Adair Company, the authorized publishers.

longed to us. My father's steward and his wife lived in half the lower story and the upper floor. What had been a door of communication was boarded up and filled in with a row of shelves.

Our kitchen was a true toy-kitchen. It was whitewashed and floored with red tiles. One little window with a deep sill looked down the strip of courtyard: another, exactly alike, looked into an orchard which, I think now, must have been a fairyland. There was a settle under one window on which a child could stand and read by the hour, her book laid open on the deep sill which propped her elbows when she would lean with her hands in her curls.

My mother had pantries full of china, beautiful old china for the most part, and that sent down for our use was a delicate embossed china with a pattern in grayish brown of all manner of seashells. The pieces stood on the little rows of shelves and they seem to me a part of the enchantment of the place. From the kitchen a door opened into the dining room. Beyond that was a hall, from which three little bedrooms opened: beyond that a drawing-room, with a glass door leading into an old walled garden full of flowers and fruit. Close by the end gable of the house, a green paling atop of a low white wall overlooked the orchard, and there was a wicket gate to the orchard round the corner just out of sight.

It must have been one of the few great summers that come to Ireland. The cottage was wrapped up in monthly roses and woodbine — honeysuckle is the clover blossom in Ireland — fuschias, jessamine, and the hardy yellow Scotch rose. These put out tendrils and climbed the thatch. In one room a tendril had come through the window and boldly climbed a wall and spread, and no one had detached it.

In the orchard and the garden the low fruit trees stood thick. They were mainly apple trees. Three sorts I keep in my memory. One was the Irish peach, of which there were several. A little low, gnarled one which had planted itself among the flower beds at some prehistoric period is in my mind as though it had life. Its fruit ripened first and it bore well. The apples, though they were small, were of a delicious flavor. Long after the peach-apples were done there was a tree hanging over our summerhouse, the fruit of which yellowed with the autumn leaves and were so many honey morsels. There was a third tree with apples of a pale green, the sides broadly ribbed and mottled with spots. I have no name for these delights, and a tragedy befell—for in the autumn following that summer the trees were thinned, and the most beautiful were cut down. No one thought of consulting the children, who had the best knowledge of good and bad fruit after all.

Fortunately the little tree in the flower beds survived and, so far as I know, still survives. Spanish iris clustered about its feet, with forget-me-nots and wall flowers and narcissi, with masses of pansies. The beds with their box borders made a most intricate pattern, all the tiny walks leading toward the summerhouse. There was a deal of greenery, as there always is in an Irish garden: and when the lilies sprang up every July they looked like rows of young angels.

Was it in '68 or was it in '69? Whatever year it was it was the great summer. Think of a pack of children who had lived in the town and only had the country by snatches turned loose a whole summer in this place packed with old-fashioned delights.

The little rooms were very flowery. Because we were on the ground floor perhaps, with only a nurse in charge, we had our windows shuttered of nights. A long slit of light used to come between the shutters in the golden mornings, suffusing the room with a green and golden light.

For a time we had a perilous delight, for a bull grazed in the orchard and would sometimes lift his head to roar quite at the windowpane. You can imagine the delighted terror of the child who lay abed, the formidable beast only separated from her by a thin sheet of glass: and what a joy it was to peep through the slit in the shutters at the immense head with its splendid curls, knowing oneself unseen, but not unapprehended, for the bull would occasionally paw the earth as though scenting an enemy, and utter a roar like thunder.

That summer we learned all the country delights, having only known them before by snatches. There was a big farmyard and a hayyard or rickyard. The rickyard is always associated in my mind with Hans Andersen's *Ugly Duckling,* which I must have read at the time. I always imagined the Ugly Duckling's mother sitting hatching her eggs under the great docks in the rickyard. Side by side with it ran the very pond where the Ugly Duckling met with one of his most terrifying adventures. The pond was much overgrown and deep enough to make it an adventure to reach the islet in the midst, on which a water-hen lived and reared her brood. On a summer day when all was still you would see the little ones taking to the water, just emerged from the egg, their brothers and sisters yet perhaps in the eggs only chipping beneath the mother's breast.

There too was a well, clear and cool, which had the reputation of never drying up even in the hottest summer. It was cool and dark under its hood of stone over which wet lichens and waterweeds had grown. It smelt of streams and freshness, a mirage for London in the hot days. We used to dip in a jug or pail and bring up little silvery minnows—"pinkeens" we call them—swimming round and round in the cool pure water. The well was fed from the mountains and the water chattered over beds of jewels in all the ditches. It was always summer there in my thoughts of it. The snail in his shell hanging on the thorn had a most wonderful house of opal iridescence. There were little blue moths, which I have never seen in England, flying about among the flowers, and black or brown butterflies with blotches of crimson on their wings. There must have been autumn though, for I remember the crab apples in the hedgerows, a fairy fruit for beauty, and the quickes-berries hanging like drops of blood. I remember the loneliness of autumnal fields after the reaping was over, the gathering of blackberries and mushrooms, the pleasant terror of the Moat, which was a fairy rath, in the heart of it a dry quarry where the biggest and juiciest blackberries grew. Gathering them one never liked to be far from one's companions, lest harm befell. In the evening when it was dark it was pleasant to steal out and see the darkness of the Moat at a distance: and when the misted harvest moon rose above it we thought it was a fairy fire and it afforded us a marvel for many days to come. Then there were the ripe apples, so to be sure it must have been autumn sometime.

Every Sunday morning our excellent nurse trailed the whole family off to Mass. We used to take a short cut, being always rather pressed for time, across a field in which grazed the bull—his name was Young Leviathan, and he deserved it—that bellowed at our ears. There must have been seven or eight children for the intrepid woman to convey unhurt. We were happy when the bull grazed in a remote corner from the pathway. What a scurry it used to be! There was a gate leading from the field on the road, which was padlocked: and the gap by which we emerged had a steep descent. The bull usually discovered us before we were clear. I have a vivid memory of his charge as I tumbled down the steep ditch. That was the occasion, I think, on which another child lost her shoe, leaving it to the tender mercies of the bull. We used to return by a safe detour, which was slower and less exciting. I have often wondered since at the hardihood of that nurse.

The village "innocent" used sometimes to put in his foolish head terrifying us at our games. He looked like Smike in the Hablot K. Browne illustrations to *Nicholas Nickleby* and he had a mordant wit. He made remarks about your personal appearance unless you were very civil. He and his kind have for the greater part disappeared or been gathered into asylums. Not all. Back again in Ireland I meet a God's fool from time to time as I walk the country lanes, a ruddy-faced, weather-beaten man who talks incessantly with a running laugh between the speech. Sometimes his talk is unintelligible — but again it is of the immortality of the soul. "The kingdom of heaven's within you. The soul's its own place and can make heaven or hell. The soul or the mind: it's all the same. But where does the soul go when it's out of the body — tell me that."

He sums up Irish intolerance of disagreement in a pregnant phrase. "Over there," he says, waving his hand across the Irish Sea, "you can say what you like. But here they'd knock the gob off you."

That autumn after the golden summer I had my first intimate experience of death. We had gone back to town and then hurriedly returned to the country because of the illness of the elder sister just home from the convent school and only awaiting impatiently the time when she might return to its novitiate. It was October then and the country was in ruins — only a few late apples on the trees and the wind and the rain bringing down the last leaves. That eldest sister was my first love. I thought her the most wonderful creature. Something of the innocency and fragrance of the convent hung about her, making her elusive, saint-like. She had brought home her sheaves, among them a glass-topped table painted with flowers behind which silver foil gave depths of light to the colors. I hung over that table entranced. She had her drawings — and I was not critical. Various triumphs of needlework in the shape of cushions, anti-massars, tea-cosies, and the like, dazzled me. She sang "The Bridge," words by Longfellow, and my heart wept tears as I listened. I am not sure that it does not weep now. I had to hide behind window curtains to conceal my agitation when she sang.

She was just a brief, lovely vision. I have no memory of her at all before that vacation. She knew I adored her and she petted me. She let me see just a glimpse of her supernatural secret. It made me determined to be a nun, and the determination lasted for a good dozen years afterward. There was something heavenly in the vision, something of long convent corridors, dazzlingly clean, flooded with light and air, sweet with the smell of lilies and a thought of incense, of little convent cells naked and pure, of convent gardens, places where

> The Brides of Christ
> Lie hid, emparadised.

I was allowed to wait on her the first day of her illness, and she must have been a little delirious, for she talked of strange things and then apologized gently. How I loved to be her servant, her slave!

Then we were back in the country again and it was sad. I lived with my nose in a book. Sometimes my father came with a disturbed face. There was a talk of a crisis. "Next Tuesday about will be the crisis. Till after that we cannot hope for good tidings."

I read and read incessantly. The nurse, who was a somewhat harassing person, let me be. I suppose that she was glad that one of us should be off her hands. I was reading *Picciola, the Prison Flower,* in my favorite place for reading now that the wet autumn had come, kneeling on a table in front of one of the deep-set little windows of the cottage, on the sill of which rested my open book and my elbows. Below the window was the stone bench upon which the beggars used to take a seat, or the tinker when he mended our pots and pans. There I had sat and shelled peas for a summer's day dinner, and had eaten the peas as I shelled them, giving up only a basket of empty pods to my justly enraged nurse.

There came father, with a more disturbed face than ever, working as we looked at him, his voice tangled in his throat. "Mary is dead," he said, and rushed away into the rain. Desolation swept my soul for a space. I do not know how long. Presently, with a sensation of guilt, I returned to the reading of *Picciola, the Prison Flower*. Even for death a book did not fail of comfortable distraction in those days when heaven was a vision of storybooks to be read incessantly without any troublesome elder intervening.

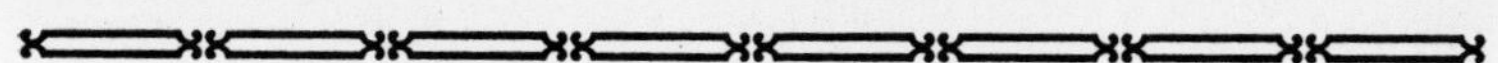

IV. NARRATIVE

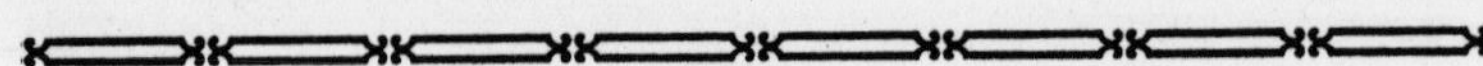

A. Informal Narrative

B. Formal Narrative

A. INFORMAL NARRATIVE

EARLY READING[1]

Leigh Hunt

My books were a never-ceasing consolation to me, and such they have ever continued. My favorites, out of school hours, were Spenser, Collins, Gray, and the *Arabian Nights*. Pope I admired more than loved; Milton was above me; and the only play of Shakespeare's with which I was conversant was *Hamlet,* of which I had a delighted awe. Neither then, however, nor at any time, have I been as fond of dramatic reading as of any other, though I have written many dramas myself, and have even a special propensity for so doing; a contradiction for which I have never been able to account. Chaucer, who has since been one of my best friends, I was not acquainted with at school, nor till long afterwards. *Hudibras* I remember reading through at one desperate plunge, while I lay incapable of moving, with two scalded legs. I did it as a sort of achievement, driving on through the verses without understanding a twentieth part of them, but now and then laughing immoderately at the rhymes and similes, and catching a bit of knowledge unawares. I had a schoolfellow of the name of Brooke, afterwards an officer in the East India Service — a grave, quiet boy, with a fund of manliness and good-humor. He would pick out the ludicrous couplets, like plums; such as those on the astrologer —

> Who deals in destiny's dark counsels,
> And sage opinions of the moon sells;

And on the apothecary's shop —

> With stores of deleterious med'cines,
> Which whosoever took is dead since.

[1]From *The Autobiography of Leigh Hunt.*

He had the little thick duodecimo edition, with Hogarth's plates —dirty, and well read, looking like Hudibras himself. I read through, at the same time, and with little less sense of it as a task, Milton's *Paradise Lost*. The divinity of it was so much "Heathen Greek" to us. Unluckily, I could not taste the beautiful "Heathen Greek" of the style. Milton's heaven made no impression; nor could I enter even into the earthly catastrophe of his man and woman. The only two things I thought of were their happiness in Paradise, where (to me) they eternally remained; and the strange malignity of the devil, who, instead of getting them out of it, as the poet represents, only served to bind them closer. He seemed an odd shade to the picture. The figure he cut in the engravings was more in my thoughts than anything said of him in the poem. He was a sort of human wild beast, lurking about the garden in which they lived; though, in consequence of the dress given him in some of the plates, this man with a tail occasionally confused himself in my imagination with a Roman general. I could make little of it. I believe, the plates impressed me altogether much more than the poem. Perhaps they were the reason why I thought of Adam and Eve as I did; the pictures of them in their paradisaical state being more numerous than those in which they appear exiled. Besides, in their exile they were together; and this constituting the best thing in their paradise, I suppose I could not so easily get miserable with them when out of it. I had the same impression from Dr. Johnson's *Rasselas*. I never thought of anything in it but the Happy Valley. I might have called to mind, with an effort, a shadowy something about disappointment, and a long remainder of talk which I would not read again, perhaps never thoroughly did read. The Happy Valley was new to me, and delightful, and everlasting; and there the princely inmates were everlastingly to be found.

THE DEATH OF SOCRATES[1]

Plato

Now the hour of sunset was near, for a good deal of time had passed while he was within. When he came out, he sat down with us again after his bath, but not much was said. Soon the jailer, who was the servant of the Eleven, entered and stood by him, saying: To you, Socrates, whom I know to be the noblest and gentlest and best of all who ever came to this place, I will not impute the angry feelings of other men, who rage and swear at me, when, in obedience to the authorities, I bid them drink the poison — indeed, I am sure that you will not be angry with me; for others, as you are aware, and not I, are to blame. And so fare you well, and try to bear lightly what must needs be — you know my errand. Then bursting into tears he turned away and went out.

Socrates looked at him and said: I return your good wishes, and will do as you bid. Then turning to us, he said, How charming the man is: since I have been in prison he has always been coming to see me, and at times he would talk to me, and was as good to me as could be, and now see how generously he sorrows on my account. We must do as he says, Crito; and therefore let the cup be brought, if the poison is prepared: if not, let the attendant prepare some.

Yet, said Crito, the sun is still upon the hill tops, and I know that many a one has taken the draught late, and after the announcement has been made to him, he has eaten and drunk, and enjoyed the society of his beloved; do not hurry — there is time enough.

Socrates said: Yes, Crito, and they of whom you speak are right in so acting, for they think that they will be gainers by the delay; but I am right in not following their example, for I do not think that I should gain anything by drinking the poison a little later; I should only be ridiculous in my own eyes for sparing and saving a life which is already forfeit. Please then to do as I say, and not to refuse me.

Crito made a sign to the servant, who was standing by; and he went out, and having been absent for some time, returned with the

[1]From the translation of the *Phædo* by Benjamin Jowett.

jailer carrying the cup of poison. Socrates said: You, my good friend, who are experienced in these matters, shall give me directions how I am to proceed. The man answered: You have only to walk about until your legs are heavy, and then to lie down, and the poison will act. At the same time he handed the cup to Socrates, who in the easiest and gentlest manner, without the least fear or change of color or feature, looking at the man with all his eyes, Echecrates, as his manner was, took the cup and said: What do you say about making a libation out of this cup to any god? May I, or not? The man answered: We only prepare, Socrates, just so much as we deem enough. I understand, he said: but I may and must ask the gods to prosper my journey from this to the other world—even so—and so be it according to my prayer. Then raising the cup to his lips, quite readily and cheerfully he drank off the poison. And hitherto most of us had been able to control our sorrow; but now when we saw him drinking, and saw too that he had finished the draught, we could no longer forbear, and in spite of myself my own tears were flowing fast; so that I covered my face and wept, not for him, but at the thought of my own calamity in having to part from such a friend. Nor was I the first; for Crito, when he found himself unable to restrain his tears, had got up, and I followed; and at that moment, Apollodorus, who had been weeping all the time, broke out in a loud and passionate cry which made cowards of us all. Socrates alone retained his calmness: What is this strange outcry? he said. I sent away the women mainly in order that they might not misbehave in this way, for I have been told that a man should die in peace. Be quiet then, and have patience. When we heard his words we were ashamed, and refrained our tears; and he walked about until, as he said, his legs began to fail, and then he lay on his back, according to the directions, and the man who gave him the poison now and then looked at his feet and legs; and after a while he pressed his foot hard, and asked him if he could feel; and he said, No; and then his leg, and so upwards and upwards, and showed us that he was cold and stiff. And then he felt them himself, and said: When the poison reaches the heart, that will be the end. He was beginning to grow cold about the groin, when he uncovered his face, for he had covered himself up, and said—they were his last words—he said: Crito, I owe a cock to Asclepius; will you remember to pay the debt? The debt shall be paid, said Crito; is there anything else? There was no answer to this question; but in a minute or two a movement was heard, and the attendants uncovered him; his eyes were set, and Crito closed his eyes and mouth.

Such was the end, Echecrates, of our friend; concerning whom I may truly say, that of all the men of his time whom I have known, he was the wisest and justest and best.

THE LONDON FIRE

Samuel Pepys

September 2, 1666. (Lord's day.) Some of our maids sitting up late last night to get things ready against our feast today, Jane called us up about three in the morning to tell us of a great fire they saw in the city. So I rose and slipped on my nightgown and went to her window, and thought it to be on the backside of Marke Lane at the farthest; but, being unused to such fires as followed, I thought it far enough off; and so went to bed again and to sleep. About seven rose again to dress myself, and there looked out at the window and saw the fire not so much as it was and further off. So to my closet to set things to rights after yesterday's cleaning. By and by Jane comes and tells me that she hears that above 300 houses have been burned down tonight by the fire we saw, and that it is now burning down all Fish Street, by London Bridge. So I made myself ready presently and walked to the Tower, and there got up upon one of the high places, Sir J. Robinson's little son going up with me; and there I did see the houses at that end of the Bridge all on fire, and an infinite great fire on this and the other side the end of the Bridge; which, among other people, did trouble me for poor little Michell and our Sarah on the bridge. So down with my heart full of trouble to the Lieutenant of the Tower, who tells me that it begun this morning in the King's baker's house in Pudding Lane, and that it hath burned down St. Magnus's Church and most part of Fish Street already. So I down to the waterside, and there got a boat and through Bridge, and there saw a lamentable fire. Poor Michell's house, as far as the Old Swan, already burned that way, and the fire running further, that, in a very little time, it got as far as the Steele-yard, while I was there. Everybody endeavoring to remove their goods, and flinging into the river, or bringing them into lighters that lay off; poor people staying in their houses as long as till the very fire touched them, and then running into boats, or clambering from one pair of stairs, by the waterside, to another. And, among other things, the poor pigeons, I perceive, were loath to leave their houses, but hovered about the windows and balconies till they burned their wings and fell down. Having stayed and in an hour's time seen the fire rage every way, and nobody, to my sight, endeavoring to quench it but to remove their goods and leave all to the fire; and having seen it get as far as the Steele-yard, and the wind mighty high, and driving it into the city; and everything, after so long a drought, proving combustible even the very stones of churches; and, among other things, the poor steeple by which pretty Mrs.—— lives, and whereof my old schoolfellow Elborough is parson, taken fire in the very top and there burned till it fell down, I to Whitehall, with a gentleman with me, who desired to go off from the Tower, to see the fire, in my boat; and there up to the King's closet in the Chapel, where people come about me, and I did give them an account dismayed them all, and word was carried in to the King. So I was called for, and did tell the King and Duke of York what I saw, and that unless His Majesty did command houses to be pulled down, nothing could stop the fire. They seemed much troubled, and the King commanded me to go to my Lord Mayor from him and command him to spare no houses but to pull down before the fire every way. . . .

About four o'clock in the morning, my Lady Batten sent me a cart to carry away all my money and plate and best things to Sir W. Rider's at Bednall Green, which I did, riding myself in my nightgown, in the cart; and, Lord! to see how the streets and the highways are crowded with people running and riding, and getting of carts at any rate to fetch away things. I find Sir W. Rider tired with being called up all night, and receiving things from several friends. His house full of goods, and much of Sir W. Batten's and Sir W. Pen's. I am eased at my heart to have my treasure so well secured. Then home, and with much ado to find a way, nor any sleep all this night to me nor my poor wife. But then all this day she and I and all my people laboring to get away the rest of our things, and did get Mr. Tooker to get me a lighter to take them in, and we did carry them, myself some, over Tower Hill, which was by this time full of people's goods, bringing their goods thither; and down to the lighter, which lay at the next quay above the Tower Dock. And here was my neighbor's wife, Mrs. ——, with her pretty child and some few of her things, which I did willingly give away to be saved with mine; but there was no passing with anything through the postern, the crowd was so great. The Duke of York come this day by the office and spoke to us, and did ride with his guard up and down the city to keep all quiet, he being now General and having the care of all. . . .

Up by break of day to get away the remainder of my things, which I did by a lighter at the Iron Gate; and by hands so full that it was the afternoon before we could get them all away. Sir W. Pen and I to the Tower Street, and there met the fire burning three or four doors beyond Mr. Howell's, whose goods, poor man, his trays, and dishes, shovels, etc., were flung all along Tower Street in the kennels, and people working therewith from one end to the other; the fire coming on in that narrow street on both sides with infinite fury. Sir W. Batten, not knowing how to remove his wine, did dig a pit in the garden and laid it in there; and I took the opportunity of laying all the papers of my office that I could not otherwise dispose of. And in the evening Sir W. Pen and I did dig another and put our wine in it; and I my parmazan[1] cheese, as well as my wine and some other things. This night, Mrs. Turner, who, poor woman, was removing her goods all this day, good goods, into the garden, and knows not how to dispose of them, and her husband supped with my wife and me at night, in the office, upon a shoulder of mutton from the cook's without any napkin or anything, in a sad manner, but were merry. Only now and then, walking into the garden, saw how horribly the sky looks, all on a fire in the night, was enough to put us out of our wits; and, indeed, it was extremely dreadful, for it looks just as if it was at us, and the whole heaven on fire. I after supper walked in the dark down to Tower Street and there saw it all on fire, at the Trinity House on

[1]Made in Parma, Italy.

that side and the Dolphin Tavern on this side, which was very near us; and the fire with extraordinary vehemence. Now begins the practice of blowing up houses in Tower Street, those next the Tower, which at first did frighten people more than anything; but it stopped the fire where it was done, it bringing down the houses to the ground in the same places they stood, and then it was easy to quench what little fire was in it, though it kindled nothing almost. W. Hewer this day went to see how his mother did and comes late home, telling us how he hath been forced to remove her to Islington, her house in Pye Corner being burned; so that the fire is not so far that way, and to the Old Bailey,[2] and was running down to Fleet Street; and Paul's is burned, and all Cheapside. I wrote to my father this night, but the post-house being burned, the letter could not go.

I lay down in the office again upon W. Hewer's quilt, being mighty weary and sore in my feet with going till I was hardly able to stand. About two in the morning my wife calls me up and tells me of new cries of fire, it being come to Barking Church, which is the bottom of our lane. I up; and finding it so, resolved presently to take her away, and did, and took my gold, which was about £2,350, W. Hewer, and Jane down by Proundy's boat to Woolwich; but, Lord! what a sad sight it was by moonlight to see the whole city almost on fire, that you might see it as plain at Woolwich as if you were by it. There, when I come, I find the gates shut but no guard kept at all; which troubled me because of discourses now begun that there is a plot in it and that the French had done it. I got the gates open and to Mr. Sheldon's, where I locked up my gold and charged my wife and W. Hewer never to leave the room without one of them in it, night or day. So back again, by the way seeing my goods well in the lighters at Deptford and watched well by people. Home, and whereas I expected to have seen our house on fire, it being now about seven o'clock, it was not. But to the fire, and there find greater hopes than I expected; for my confidence of finding our office on fire was such that I durst not ask anybody how it was with us till I come and saw it was not burned.

[2]*Vetus Ballium,* area of Central Criminal Court.

ON SOCIAL WORK AND KANGAROOS[1]

Worth Tuttle

During the winter you hear vague hints about it; in early spring the murmurs become insistent; by midsummer there is no escape. The Joan of Arc Club, the Pollyannas, and the little Liberties must go to Bronx Park Zoo! They make intricate plans whereby each individual may see the animal dearest to its imagination, and the day is set — a selection involving, in our polyglot neighborhood, the Mosaic Law, the Papal Bull, and the Lutheran doctrine. We are going to Bronx Park Zoo!

You mention it casually at dinner. You note the incredulous expressions and the ominous silence of the older, more seasoned workers, but you pay little heed. All winter you have been inwardly scornful of their lack of enthusiasm for instructive recreational work.

And yet — when the chosen day dawns clear and warm you are aware of a shameful hope dying. But at 3:25, when you look from the office window on to an empty playground, a new one springs up in your heart. At 3:30 you glance out again. The playground swarms. It resounds with cries of "Teacher, we're ready! We're ready, Teacher!" They are shiny as to face, a bit ragged as to some clothes and a bit dressy as to others — net and lace confirmation dresses rubbing against dirty ginghams, unadorned heads bobbing about next to hats of Sicilian lace, trimmed with tenement-made flowers. They carry bottles of water, lemons, and pink paper bags from Rose Sternhill's mother's store. "It's so sick we get on the subway train, Teacher!" "We got some for you, Teacher!" You hear a titter behind you and turn to glare at your fellow workers in a group at the door, but you start off with a wildly beating heart.

"My mother says it six o'clock I mus' be home, Teacher!" "Gertrude Krumpea's gotta take her little brother, Teacher! Oh, Teacher, Gertrude's gotta take —" You look at Gertrude, smiling sturdily up at you, and decide that her Teutonic efficiency can handle that fat little four-year-old clinging to her skirt.

[1]Reprinted from *The Atlantic Monthly,* 1925, with permission.

You begin to count them. Everybody begins. You think there are twenty-three. Only twenty-three! Gertrude says there are twenty-four, without even glancing up from her little brother's nose she is then attending. Gertrude is right. You shoo them toward the car line.

You accept tolerantly the sally of the young and facetious conductor of the trolley and assure him that they *are* all yours. You begin to seat them. Then, as you drop wearily into the space Margaret Maggochi and Mary Fiorito have been fighting to preserve for you, the conductor yells maliciously, "This way out! *This* way! Here, you! Let em' off! *Let 'em off!*" You raise your voice above his to tell Ida Mongolies and Gussie Turgel that they cannot go out by the window, and with the aid of the facetious young conductor you get 'em off.

Hurrying before the wheels of two impatient trucks, you assure Rose Koleck that indeed he was a nice man, grab Gussie from the jaws of death of the on-going trolley, give Margaret her two pennies to squander on gum at the subway entrance, and drive them down the steps, refusing one stick of gum.

They scream at the darkness below and rush back. Gertrude asks whether this is like hell. You assure her that it is, and count out twenty-three nickels from the store in your pocket. They put hands over ears as a train approaches, and again rush at you. You scream silently that the train will not hurt them if they let it alone, and pull Teresa Astarita — and Gussie — back from the edge. You count them again. There are thirty-one. You beg them to stand still one minute, just one minute!

When they are seated in two long neat rows in the car, awed into wide-eyed quietness, you are glad. Glad that for once the collective blankness of the subway faces has been broken, wrinkled into separate expressions of surprise, sympathy, consternation. The old gentleman on your right asks with keen interest about the lemons and the water bottles. Anna Romano has begun on her lemon, greedily. You begin to believe, oh, to believe absolutely, in the dark tales she has told of the time she went on the subway before — "So sick I was my mother thought I would die on her!" Her skin is a greenish white. You glance hastily away. Rose Sternhill is beginning on hers, and the same threatening pallor is spreading beneath her dark eyes.

Ida Mongolies punches Gussie Turgel in the side, or so Gussie says. There is violent discord and endless ethical discussion. You try to arbitrate, and understand in a flash why nothing can be accomplished at Geneva. The owners of the disturbed expressions begin to get off, station after station, and you become less self-conscious about the hue of complexions. What happens now will be a family affair. The subway becomes an "El" just there and you smile benignly at the unified shout of delight, as though it were a surprise you had had especially prepared.

You drag Gussie from her conversation with the guard, who looked like the candyman on her corner, and marshal them through the gate of Bronx Park.

You beg them not to waste all their excitement on the bison. You lead the way to Bearland. You try, agilely, to be at every cage in response to every query. You look frantically at the placards and, feeling infinitely wise, introduce each slouching beast by name, age, and habitat; and, on further inquiry, you explain where he sleeps, when he sleeps, what he eats and when. What he *likes* to eat? Oh, what he gets! While that novel idea is being absorbed you take them to the indoor mammals.

With shrieks of joy they discover revolving doors. They play merry-go-round. They want to play tag with the tigers. They mimic the monkeys until the monkeys drop despondently from their swings and eye *them* with an increasing interest. You continue to be zoölogically intelligent, question-proof, until Anna Romano, in her even, monotonous voice, pointing to the girth of the hippopotamus, asks, "Teather, what's in his belly?" Colombo Polombo saves you by announcing firmly that she must see a kangaroo. She studied about one in her geography and, though she doesn't believe there is such a thing, there was a *picture* of it. You assure her that there are kangaroos and that in due time she shall see one and then you suggest fresh air.

Outside on a bench you refuse hunks of Italian bread and lollipops and little almond cakes—they've been in Rose Sternhill's mother's store for weeks awaiting this day. Colombo again mentions kangaroos. You reassure her and let Gussie and America Fuligini go for water. Water! Everybody goes for water! "Ain't a bit o' fun in Central Park," pipes Tessie D'Est, the traveled; "can't get a drink there a-tall."

Colombo Polombo must see a kangaroo. There is nothing more important than that. You search a guard. He waves vaguely toward the west. You grasp Colombo by one hand and order the other twenty-two to follow. Gertrude leads them, smiling, her fat little brother asleep in her arms.

But between Colombo and her heart's desire are gray foxes, and peacocks, and swans, and the parrot house, and reptiles! You look at your watch. Five forty-five! You pull them away from the crocodiles and make them skip, in spite of Teresa's blistered heel and Angelina's hurt toe. You see a giraffe and a zebra. You call Colombo's attention to them particularly. But Colombo's hopeful expression is drowned in tears. You say, "Colombo, I'm terribly sorry"—and you look steadily away. Your hand is dropped.

The returning train is empty, and a song of thanksgiving rises in your heart. You refuse to scoop any of the chocolate out of Gussie's palm and relax in the joy of achievement. "Look at Anna, Teacher, oh, look at Anna. She's sick on you!" You look. Her head flops, and she is green. You hasten with her to the vestibule. You hold her head, but you speak heartlessly: "Anna, stand up now and behave yourself!" There is a tug at your skirt. Rose Sternhill is there, and Carmela Gillio, empty bottles and lemon skins in their lax hands. You resort to threats: "If you children get sick, I shall never take you out again!" They raise weak eyes to your granitelike face. . . .

In the wee small hours around eight o'clock you drag yourself up many winding tenement stairs, returning each child by hand to each bowing and smiling mother, and wonder not at their gratitude. Wearily you take yourself to the House, where cool, well-groomed, and smiling fellow workers inquire pleasantly into your afternoon.

In the dark hour of three you awake. Somebody has spoken in a hauntingly unsatisfied voice about seeing a kangaroo, and when you doze again a frieze of kangaroos goes loping round about your tired head.

THE VIPER[1]

George Borrow

It happened that my brother and myself were playing one evening in a sandy lane, in the neighborhood of this Pett camp; our mother was at a slight distance. All of a sudden a bright yellow, and, to my infantine eye, beautiful and glorious object made its appearance at the top of the bank from between the thick quickset, and, gliding down, began to move across the lane to the other side, like a line of golden light. Uttering a cry of pleasure, I sprang forward, and seized it nearly by the middle. A strange sensation of numbing coldness seemed to pervade my whole arm, which surprised me the more as the object to the eye appeared so warm and sunlike. I did not drop it, however, but, holding it up, looked at it intently, as its head dangled about a foot from my hand. It made no resistance; I felt not even the slightest struggle; but now my brother began to scream and shriek like one possessed. "Oh, mother, mother!" said he, "the viper!—my brother has a viper in his hand!" He then, like one frantic, made an effort to snatch the creature away from me. The viper now hissed amain, and raised its head, in which were eyes like hot coals, menacing, not myself, but my brother. I dropped my captive, for I saw my mother running toward me; and the reptile, after standing for a moment nearly erect, and still hissing furiously, made off, and disappeared. The whole scene is now before me as vividly as if it occurred yesterday—the gorgeous viper, my poor, dear, frantic brother, my agitated parent, and a frightened hen clucking under the bushes; and yet I was not three years old.

[1]From *Lavengro.*

THE REJOICING DESERT[1]

Helen Parry Eden

Blessed Albertus Magnus, more recently known to the Calendar as St. Albert the Great, was one of those unfortunate saints who get covered up with odd stories like an old castle with ivy. The castle is as solid as the rock on which it is built; but what with the thickness of the ivy and the chattering of the jackdaws that live in it, you hardly get a chance of seeing it or speaking about it quietly and it runs considerable risk of becoming forgotten altogether. There was an amazing quantity of such overgrowth and bickering about Blessed Albertus, even in his own lifetime. People said he was a wizard, and they were word-perfect as to the details of his wizardry. They painted a white horse on the side of a tower in the market-place of his native town and said that as a little boy Albert, and Albert alone, could lead that horse about. They pretended that he had a magic cup in which he had but to pour wine or water and the sick man who sipped it was cured. They made out that beside his own cell in the Convent of Cologne, he had a little room hidden away, full of strange animals and fantastic instruments and uncanny vessels of glass. They said that there was a scarlet curtain in one corner of it, behind which stood a talking figure which could say "Salve! Salve! Salve!" This, they would assure you, had taken Blessed Albertus thirty years to make. They boasted that the Four Crowned Martyrs, the patron saints of masons, had traced him out the plans of Cologne Cathedral; though all the world knows that it was Gerard of Riel, who travelled in France first and worked in a timberyard afterwards, to whom the plans of Cologne Cathedral are owing. Finally they told the story of the Magic Garden. And this is perhaps true in the same fashion as the story of Jotham the son of Jerubbaal which begins: "The trees went forth to anoint themselves a king." This story — which you will find in the ninth chapter of the Book of Judges — is what Origen calls an enigma. It is true underneath; but it is not very likely to have been true on

[1]From *Whistles of Silver,* Science and Culture Series, The Bruce Publishing Company (Copyrighted).

top, though it is told as if it had been. And it is to present you with the key to this enigma of mine that I have called it "The Rejoicing Desert" instead of, quite simply, "The Garden of Blessed Albertus."

In the year twelve hundred and forty-nine, just after Christmas, young William the Emperor arrived at Cologne with a great train, to venerate the relics of the Three Kings and lay on their shrine an offering toward the new cathedral. For the old Roman church which held the bodies of the Magi had been partly burnt the year before, and all Christendom was concerned that the new one should be finer than the old. Everyone loved the Three Kings of Cologne: kings because they were kings, and sages because they were sages, and ordinary folk because they were the first people outside Jewry to find the King of kings in His stable. It was only befitting, then, that their bodies should be surrounded by gold and myrrh and frankincense in a fine cathedral till the Last Day, seeing that they had brought gold and myrrh and frankincense to the unknown Baby of Bethlehem.

Well, the Emperor heard his Mass in the half-burnt cathedral; and when they asked him what he would like to do afterwards, he said he had thought of calling on Blessed Albertus in his cell in the Stolkstrasse. Hither he accordingly turned (it was only a step from the shrine) with his knights and his nobles and his pages in attendance, and they all jangled up the stairs and knocked at friar's door. Blessed Albertus opened it at once and the Emperor saluted him courteously; and with some trepidation—for it is a fearful thing to tamper with the powers of darkness—suggested that they had come to see a sample of his magic. Blessed Albertus put aside the insinuation in the most deferential and tactful manner, and proposed a gentle saunter in the Convent grounds as the best way of passing the half-hour between then and dinner-time.

The day, you remember, was the sixth of January; the place, a town in North Germany! The Emperor looked over the friar's shoulder at the little oblong of freezing sky outside the cell-window and hesitated. The nobles in the passage (who were out of sight but could hear all that was going on inside) shrugged their shoulders and tapped their foreheads suggestively. A few of the less polite had the impudence to stamp on the flag-stones to show that they were none too warm where they were. Judge of their disgust when the Emperor's voice said cheerily, "With all my heart, Reverend Sir." And they had to flatten themselves against the walls of the corridor to let the friar pass with the Emperor after him. Then they closed in behind and followed, as best they might, down the staircase.

Once on the ground floor they traversed a freezing cloister which evidently ran round the four sides of a courtyard; though, for that matter, they could not see out at all for the exterior arches of the cloister were glazed and the glass was covered with frost. The hindermost nobles pulled their furred hoods over their heads, and those who had hitherto carried them over their arms put them on. The grandees, however, who were nearest the Emperor, had to suffer for their gentility and stay bareheaded—as was only right. All of a sudden the company stopped. Blessed Albertus was unbolting the huge iron-clamped door that led from the cloister to the quadrangle. It opened outwards—and a great blaze of scent and sunlight and the songs of birds streamed into that sepulchral place. The friar stood back with a grave inclination against the door; and the Emperor and his suite stepped out into the most wonderful garden that was ever seen.

Now it takes Lord Bacon to blazon a garden. I am no hand at it at all. So you can each make up the garden to your liking. But you must not forget a single flower you fancy, for you may be sure that it was there. There was every sort of fruit and that "dead mellow," as my old nurse used to say; and the very butterflies were so drowsy with honey that they would have been taken for petals themselves if they had not opened and shut their wings. Seven fountains were drizzling musically into their marble basins, and rare swans and little crested ducks were steering about under the spray. But what took that company's fancy most was a fine banquet spread in front of a grove of lemon trees; and when Blessed Albertus had said grace (to the great reassurance of not a few of his guests) they all sat down, while pages in scarlet-and-camel-colored hose (*tibialibus scarlatis camelinisque* says the chronicler) came out from behind the bushes with course after course of dainties.

What a banquet it was! There was a roasted peacock, tail and all, opposite the Emperor, and the mightiest salmon ever cooked in front of Blessed Albertus. The sound of viols and citholes and other sweet-stringed instruments mingled with the trills of the birds and the tinkling of the fountains, and the revelry of the nobles rose higher and higher as the feast proceeded. But at last the grace-cup went round and the Emperor got up to leave the table. The nobles rose simultaneously. And then, lo and behold, the whole thing went out like a candle! Flowers, butterflies, birds, fountains, pages, and banquets—all vanished. They stood in a gaunt quadrangle like two rows of children ready for "Nuts and May," with nothing whatsoever between them, or around them, but the drifting snow.

Such is the story of the Garden of Blessed Albertus or (as I prefer to call it) "The Rejoicing Desert." For I think myself it is no lie, but an enigma of the Grace of God according to the saying of the Prophet Isaias: "The land that was desolate and impassable shall be glad and the desert shall rejoice and blossom like a lily." And if you tell me that it should not be "lily" but "rose," I can only answer that you are using the Authorized Version of King James and I the Vulgate of St. Jerome; and there is no sense in falling out about the flowers as long as we agree upon the Desert. For the desert, as St. Augustine says, is the solitude of a man's soul and only the magic of sanctity can make it blossom. And the magic of sanctity is nothing but the goodwill of a mortal added to the Grace of God.

THE CITY THAT NEVER WAS[1]

Michael Williams

I had reached my home; I let myself in and got noiselessly to bed. I suppose it was nearly four o'clock when at last my excited brain ceased its working, and sleep came.

And almost at once I came awake again—vaguely wondering what was the matter?

The big bed in which I lay was trying its best to imitate a buck-

[1]By permission of the author.

ing broncho and to throw me out of the window, toward which it was lurching. The air itself seemed to be pulling at me, with invisible fingers clutching from all directions at once, but unevenly; the plaster was falling in big chunks; and there was a vast crescendic roaring noise, incomprehensible: a vast sea of sound.

There was the commingling of the crash of falling walls, the tumbling of millions of bricks, the rending and cracking and splintering of wood, the shattering of windowglass by the hundreds of thousands of sheets and panes, and myriads of other sounds. All these were based, as it were, on another, unwordable sound, which was the roaring of the earthquake — the groaning of the very earth itself.

What a racket!

It was like — well, it was like — let me see, now it was like — oh, heavens above, *I don't know what it was like!* Nobody knows. Fancy a billion big drays, loaded with iron rails, passing along over rough cobblestones, with the rails clangorously falling, and the windows of all the houses being shattered by the concussions, and then fancy — but, no, you can't! Neither can I. That noise is not to be conjured up by fancy — it can only be remembered.

Yet that terrible noise was nothing at all — a mere trifle, a trivial incident, a bagatelle, compared to the impression of the earthquake *as earthquake,* if I may so express myself.

But how can I tell you? I really cannot tell you!

For there was something about that shock that struck, deeper than any sound could penetrate, into the substance of your soul. — You know how it is when we try to suggest some tremendous emotion or altogether unusual sense of calamity — we say, "It was as if the earth moved under our feet," or, "It was as if the earth trembled."

So what can we say — what is there left to say — when the earth in fact *does* move under our feet, when actually the earth *does* tremble?

For we are so accustomed to the earth being — well, reliable, trustworthy: safe, sane, and conservative, so to speak. We are so used to being its boss, to using it as we please, plowing and digging it, sowing and reaping it, building our cities with its own stuff, brick and stone and wood — without a murmur from it, without any tricks being played with us, such as the untamable sea and the mysterious air and that dangerous character, fire, take pleasure in perpetrating. We're up against trouble all the time in our dealings with water, and fire, and air — but we consider the earth a straight, clear-cut proposition.

So when *it* cuts loose. . . . Oh, I give it up! There aren't any words for what you feel in an earthquake shock.

Here's a bit of a hint. Suppose you were on a ship at sea, on a long, long voyage, so that the motion, the fluidity, the freedom of movement, were part of your very being — you are saturated with motion — and suddenly the water becomes a solid substance, and the air becomes rigid, and the ship stops and is held without a quiver, like a toy ship frozen inside a block of ice. Well, the solid earth, that morning in San Francisco, was behaving like the unstable sea —

Oh, but what's the use! The feeling simply can't be described. It dates back to chaos — to a time before there was any law and order or solid substance. This upheaval of the primal powers that bind atom to atom, cell to cell, organism to organism, star to star, and universe to universe, throughout all creation in cohesion, and balance, and system, leaves in the mind that has experienced it a memory which is unique, and a sensation which lies altogether outside the limits of category. Only those who have gone through a 'quake can understand me. I'll just add this, however — that we who have gone through a big 'quake understand what other people can only think they understand, namely, that the foundation, the underlying principle, of all material things from the ultimate atom to the biggest star in the heavens is nothing that can be seen or touched or handled or known by any sense, but is forever imponderable, and unnamable, and eternally inscrutable. We hint at it in such terms as the cosmic ether, polarity, gravitation, and so forth, and so on. Some of us, however, are still old-fashioned enough to say, the Hand of God.

At any rate it was shaking the city of San Francisco that bright, still dawn, and beneath the falling timbers and stones men and women and children were being crushed to death by hundreds. At a score of points fire was springing up. And there was no water with which the fires could be quenched in this first stage. The water-supplying system had been put out of business by the shock. I have been told that the water mains were not properly constructed, any more than the ruined City Hall was properly constructed—that in both jobs there had been rich, fat graft. You see? It was as if the corruption of the city's life had corroded its very bones, eaten into its very physical structure, so that in the hour of its calamity it lacked the power to save itself. As we now know, if the fires could have been controlled in those first few hours, huge as was the damage of the earthquake, it would have been a trifle in comparison with that which was inflicted by the fire—that fire which was the worst this fire-ravaged world has witnessed, so far as history can show.

* * *

My little daughter was in the crib by the bed. Her mother gathered her up quickly in her arms, and I arched myself above them both, to ward off the plaster, or the universe, I didn't know which. Our baby boy was in the adjoining room, in a crib by the bedside of a friend who lived with us; a lady who appeared a second or two after the start of the trouble, in her nightdress, in the doorway. She was a maiden lady from New England; so you see how unconventional this occasion must have been. She it was who gave a name to it.

"Earthquake!" she said.

I had vaguely thought of an explosion; of a sudden and awful storm approaching, or a flood, a tidal wave; but, sure enough, now I understood that it was an earthquake. When you come back from sleep after only an hour, you are not as bright-minded as you'd like to be able to say you were.

"The baby!" cried the lady in the doorway.

Then, as neither the plaster nor the universe had crushed us so far, I ceased my imitation of a cat with its back arched, and ran into the outer room.

The force of the shock had been much greater there. All the furniture was crowding into the middle of the room and trying to play a clumsy game of leap-frog. It was bright daylight of a perfect April day outside, but the blinds were drawn in the room and the light was dim, mild, and milky. And through this placid, opalescent light I saw the wide, untroubled eyes of the baby boy, who was perfectly calm, looking at me. He was like a philosopher from some other planet nonchalantly observing a queer human being in pajamas scrambling over a mountain of furniture, in a room which was apparently trying to turn itself inside out. I have often wondered what can go on in the mind of a child in such a moment.

* * *

The earthquake came a little after five. It lasted eighteen seconds. According to the scientific gentlemen, it appears that the Coast Range Mountains along a line of some three hundred miles shrugged their shoulders, or made a slight gesture, as it were, and cities and towns and villages along that line behaved very much as a child's building blocks behave when he pulls the tablecloth on which they are stacked. Mount Tamalpais, a mass of how many billions of tons only science can tell you, shifted its position. Redwood trees three or four thousand years old were split wide open. Torrents and springs of water or sand leaped from the broken and tortured earth. Landslides streamed down the hills. Trees were overthrown. All this, outside the city. As for the city—Well, let me return to my own adventures; it is hopeless to attempt the description of the city's fate, just yet.

The house I lived in was an old wooden structure, solidly and honestly made. Like all such, it swayed and shook; plaster fell, shelves were emptied; but there was no serious damage. Honestly made steel buildings also stood the racket.

Before the shock had finished its course by more than a few seconds, we were in the street; part of the fantastic multitude disgorging out of doorways up and down all the streets of the city. Some, but these were the few, were dressed; housewives or servants or workers early astir; but the most of us were in all the stages of extraordinary dishabille. There was a vacant lot not far from the house, and to this we ran, and soon the place was crowded with fat men in nighties, women with children in their arms, blankets about some of them, others merely in their nightgowns; and all sorts and conditions of men, women, and children.

There was a brief pause, as it were; a scant breathing spell, and then, very suddenly, my heart tried to jump out of my mouth, and then seemed to fall back, fluttering like a wounded creature.

Another earthquake had begun . . . again the earth, and the air, and all that was upon earth, and in the air, was throbbing, was swaying, was quivering, was palpitating enormously. It was frightful! But thank God, it didn't last so long, nor was it nearly so severe as the first one. Nevertheless, it shook down walls that had been weakened by the other shock, and bricks from chimneys came raining down, and people who had ventured back into their houses came rushing out in fresh dismay. Some of them didn't come out again; falling walls or beams pinning them down, killed or badly injured, caught, in some places, like animals in pits or dead-fall traps.

There came a fresh wave of people rushing through the streets, but we remained in the open space.

And up the middle of the street, a little bit later, there walked two well-dressed men — Orientals, or mulattoes — looking as if they had been up all night waiting for this moment. They were proclaiming the end of the world. It was Judgment Day, they cried; the Book was open, the Book of Life and Death; and they bade us fall upon our knees and pray. And, really, you know — we weren't sure they were not right. Truly, it was like the end of things mortal. Somebody, looking at the wall of fire marching toward us, later on; that strangely silent, quietly busy advance of a wall of flame, said: "Yes, it surely must be Judgment Day." Somebody else replied: "And this must be the gates of hell."

It ought to have been a perfectly tremendous moment. I suppose . . . but it wasn't.

The trouble was, that we couldn't believe our prophet. Daylight, I expect, is not congenial to belief in prophets, even when the daylight is one of a day of disaster. There seems to be something in us, something that belongs to our very life — perhaps it is the force of life itself — that utterly refuses to believe in death until death itself says: "Here I am." Even if April 18, 1906, really had been Doomsday, you couldn't have got us to believe it, out there in San Francisco, not if a regiment of black prophets had been on the job.

I saw a few troubled faces here and there amid the crowd, but the trouble was more what you might feel when somebody acts indecorously than anything deeper.

"That mutt must be crazy," I heard a fat man wheezing near me. "Somebody ought to make him shut up — or knock his block off," answered the man the fat chap spoke to. "Say, even if he is right what business has he to try to scare folks?"

Personally, I felt quite indifferent. Maybe the prophet was right. Quite likely he was. But if this was the end of the world — oh, very well, it was the end of the world — but we might just as well carry on, without any fuss.

And that, you might say, was the common, the general feeling, not only there in Geary Street, but throughout the city, and not only then, as we recovered from the first stunning confusion of the shock, but later on, throughout all the terrible days that followed. It was not that we were indifferent to fears and horrors and disasters; not at all; nor was it that we were endowed with heroic courage to overcome all things. No, that was not the case. We were full of fears, all the time. I think there was hardly one of us who didn't keep in mind the dark horror of a tidal wave. Others, I know from what they told me, felt that at any moment the earth might open and swallow them. The menace of shaky walls loomed always over us. In the first few days, there came more than forty minor shocks, and each shock sent many nervously disordered person temporarily insane. The sand hills toward the sea were full of wandering, harmless, mad folk; talking and muttering to themselves, or sitting on the ground staring at the smoke and crimson reflections of the fire in the sky. And we knew the fear of plague, and of pestilence, and starvation, and sudden death. And always there were circulating the most dreadful rumors. We believed them, too, more or less. Why not? Anything might happen, after what had already happened. Anything at all. Nothing was impossible. We heard that Los Angeles had been wiped out completely. Mount Rainier was in eruption; torrents of lava were covering the north country with burning lakes. Chicago had been swallowed by Lake Michigan. The catastrophe was country-wide; maybe it was universal; for London had been smitten, so we heard. There were no telegraph wires working for days, of course, but only a few of us were aware of this. Anyhow, rumors, as we all know, whether false or true, do not need telegraph wires in order to travel about; they seem to use the all-pervading ether, like the waves of the wireless. Or else they spread through telepathy.

But, all the same, we did not get badly excited. We were bewildered; some of us were bedazed; we were all nerve shaken, and we all had our own particular fears to face — but, taking us altogether, by and large, taking us as a crowd of human beings — as a mob, if you like — as a multitude — we stood everything mighty well. There was a calmness; there was a grave, yet kindly, almost smiling kind of acceptance of the situation on the part of the people as a whole, the memory of which remains with me like the memory of noble and harmonic music. For, after all, you see, there was something in San Francisco which the 'quake could not overthrow, nor even agitate very seriously — and this thing was the intangible something which is the spirit of human nature — the spirit of human life — which shows itself in human nature's unbreakable habit of keeping busy at the business of living on in this world just as long as there is any shred of world left on which to live. What is that inner something? That inmost assurance? Mere instinct? Self-preservation? The will-to-live? Or is it Faith?

Anyhow — we do, we will carry on. Some day we'll know why.

* * *

By-and-by, I ventured back into the house, wondering what moment it would fall in upon me, and secured my clothes. My wife — being one of those extraordinary women whom nothing frightens — except mice — also went back and cooked breakfast.

Then I started to walk toward the office, but on my way I learned that the fire chief had been killed, that the water mains of the city were out of business, and that great fires had started in many directions, and were joining, spreading, and marching along. So I knew, right then and there, that the real name of this calamity was not earthquake, but fire; and I knew that it would march along without any other force being able to stop it. Not remembering the width of Van Ness Avenue (one can't think of everything in such moments, not even a newspaperman!), I thought that the whole city was doomed. So my first duty was toward those waiting me in Geary Street. On my journey to them I spent what little money I had in buying condensed cream, chocolate, bread, canned stuff, health food (of a particular brand, indispensable to a one-year-old baby with a weak digestive machine) and trifles of that sort, which I stuffed into the recesses of a canvas shooting coat which I had thrown on that morning, with some vague notion, no doubt, of dressing appropriately. And as I watched the great crowds pouring onward before the drive of flame for the most part so silently, so calmly; dragging trunks, bedsteads, carts, baby carriages, easy-chairs, bundles, baskets, bags, caged parrots, stuffed owls, books, tools, bedclothes, loaves of bread, live chickens, statues of the saints, jugs, guns, and all manner of things — as I watched this strange multitude, moving through a stranger silence, the silence of a city in which no trolley cars were thundering, I remembered, with gratitude to the giver of all good thoughts, that there were soldiers, Uncle Sam's regular soldiers, out at the Presidio, and that a very good place for a married man and his family to seek for lodging would be a tent near those soldiers. For, like many others, I dreaded looting on the grand scale, and starving mobs, and scarlet anarchy.

Again we ventured into the house, up to the top floor. From the windows at the back we saw the dome of the City Hall against a sky beginning to blacken with smoke, and lurid with flame; a dome like a sinister skeleton, stripped to its ribs of steel; looking like a gigantic bird cage; and I saw the flames south of Market Street, and out in the Mission, and toward the foot of Geary Street.

Then began that awful tramp to the Presidio, pushing one child in the baby carriage, with the other carried in our arms, or in the foot of the carriage, and dragging all that we could manage to drag, wrapped up in a quilt; up hill, and down hill; that terrible tramp to the Presidio. For a man who had come West in order to patch up a hole in his lungs, it was tough work; but I didn't think so then. For when you imagine that at any moment the earth may open and swallow you up, at one bite (as we heard it had been doing in many places), or when the sea is expected to send in a tidal wave, as it was libellously accused of having done elsewhere, why, you cease to take much interest in your minor or major ailments. Many a bedridden invalid leaped clear out of bed that morning and didn't go back again; cured by the shock.

What I chiefly worried about was my lack of money. Strange, I know, that a wandering writer should feel such a worry; all the traditions of Bohemia go against the fact; but yet, so it was, and the first man I knew by sight was called upon at once to make me a loan. It was Tom Dillon, the Hatter (I present him with this advertisement with immense satisfaction). He didn't know me; but, just like a true San Franciscan, he did not enquire too closely into this panhandling demand, he simply, out of the goodness of a San Franciscan's heart, put a twenty-dollar gold piece in my hand. (It was a long, long time before he got it back; but if I ever make any money I think I will walk up and down Third Street some night, and give away twenty dollars to the toughest-looking hoboes I can discover, and then ask them all to spend at least part of it in drinking the health of Tom Dillon.)

Then I bought more food. I point with pride to this fact. I proclaim it; I write it down in a book that once in his life, at least, a writing man who from the dim beginnings down all the colored years had sought the far trails of high Romance through all the western world, was practical! As a result, we did not have to join the bread-line! But there were millionaires, and capitalists, and even canny politicians, who did.

We obtained a tent, though thousands of late comers were disappointed. All through that night I kept a revolver near my hand, as the thousands of feet went pounding, pounding, pounding—pounding without cessation, pounding all night long, pounding like dull yet mighty drumming, pounding like the sustained and awful susurrance of a mighty ocean—as the crowds poured in from the flaming city. Fifty miles inland and far out at sea that tremendous blaze illuminated the night, reflected back from the huge canopy of smoke that overspread the sky, although elsewhere it was a starry night, bland and still. Detonations of dynamite now and then thudded through the pounding.

With the morning I left my family, and struck out for my office. The three morning newspapers joined forces that day, and produced a joint issue. I got across the bay to Oakland and reported to the superior editors, who were foregathered there, and was immediately ordered back to San Francisco in command of a company of reporters and camera men, to set up local headquarters, and begin the task of news gathering. The paper was to be printed in Oakland.

We obtained a small tow-boat, which the twenty-odd men on board crowded badly. Among our number was Mr. Samuel Shortridge, the lawyer, who had begged his way across in our company as nobody save soldiers, physicians, priests, nurses, newspapermen, and other regular assistants at disasters, was permitted to get back into the city once he had left it.

It was a gay trip. Our skipper turned out to be blind drunk, and our boat went staggering, and turning eccentric half-circles, and now and then trying to turn a somersault, through a heavy sea. At last two of us had to stand on either side of the wheel, holding up our skipper and making him steer some sort of reasonable course for the other side.

We ricocheted our way close to Alcatraz Island. Telegraph Hill, Nob Hill, Russian Hill, were blazing like cosmic torches, gigantic tongues of red fire going up straight into the still air beneath the black canopy of smoke.

Mr. Shortridge has a very deep voice and a singularly impressive deliberation and distinctness of utterance. He is a celebrated orator. He felt moved to make a speech on this occasion. He said, staring at the three burning hills: "Lord God Almighty!"

I have heard many speeches; thousands of them I suppose. Perhaps ten of them were good speeches. But this one remains unique at once in its appropriateness and its effect upon those who heard it. All vain words were banished; all useless thoughts were swept away. Today I may string words together, so long after that mighty moment; but then only the high names of God could fit the occasion.

We landed near Fort Mason. I at once set about the business of hiring headquarters. After several vain efforts I finally succeeded in striking a great bargain; I hired Harbor View Park, the whole establishment. This comprised a bathing beach, a bowling alley, a barroom, a well-stocked larder, enclosed by a high fence. It is vanished now.

I also hired a motor car and sent a reporter — better known today as Frederick Ferdinand Moore, war correspondent and novelist — to the Presidio for my family. I had heard that the absence of sanitary arrangements among the herded thousands in Golden Gate Park and the Presidio threatened to cause an outbreak of disease. In Harbor View Park we would be safe.

In less than an hour Moore was back again, with my wife and children.

Less than half an hour later, a mounted army officer rode to the gate and demanded speech with whoever was in authority.

"You must immediately vacate these premises," said he, when I appeared. "The United States Army wants them, as a detention camp for contagious diseases. The smallpox patients will be here within the hour."

We heard and perforce obeyed. Very luckily, right at the moment, a tugboat from Santa Cruz put in at the little wharf, and I at once hired it for a despatch boat, to carry copy and orders back and forward between Oakland and San Francisco. So I sent my family across the bay, together with a large number of other refugees. I did not see wife or children again during the next three weeks.

Then came the new search for headquarters. It was ended quickly. Mr. Shortridge, hearing of our predicament, solved it out of hand. He placed his own large and beautiful home completely at my disposal. He threw in his Chinese cook, to make the job complete. So in this luxurious office, sleeping three in a bed with Ah Fung to cook for us, we lived as newspapermen have rarely lived before. Each day a special detail went out, not for news but for grub. The day's work was over at six or seven o'clock, because the copy had to go over to Oakland very early. Then we foregathered from our various jobs, and ate a wonderful dinner, and fleeted the evening hours away with card games, and stories, a punch bowl, and Mr. Shortridge's gorgeous grand piano, the one he had bought especially for Paderewski, his client. Every now and then a shock of earthquake would make the house rock and quiver. Sometimes these blows were so heavy that we went running into the street. Then we would go back again and Freddy Moore, or somebody, would play ragtime, in between the shocks, and we would sing:

Through a small Irish town,
Marched a troop of renown,
In the year seventeen hundred and forty;
With a hip, hip, hurray, and a hip, hip, hurray,
Tirri-row, did-a-dow, did-a-row-dow!

Ours was the only house in all the district permitted to burn lights after eight or nine o'clock; and under our glowing windows, on the steps, and along the curb, the neighbors would gather, listening to our songs, and taking comfort, I think, in our jollity. One night we gave a dinner to our host; ah, such a dinner! We brewed an earthquake punch. The whole city was scoured for materials. Somebody went up the hill to Mayor Schmitz's house and returned with beer, and a bottle of Scotch. Into the big bowl went beer, and Scotch, and benedictine, and rye, and a bottle of champagne, and brandy, and creme de menthe — anything, and everything.

* * *

But if we newspapermen had special opportunities to be gay, San Francisco in general was also high-hearted despite the darkness, and the dread of doom.

The fire had on the third day been stopped at Van Ness Avenue.

How many had been lost in the tumbling of walls, and the destruction of cheap tenement houses, and, still more, in the abominable lodging houses south of Market Street and on Barbary Coast, will never be known till the real Doomsday happens along; but many hundreds are known to have perished. As Mary Austin says: "Large figures of adventure moved through the murk of these days — Denman going out with his gun and holding up express wagons with expensively saved goods, which were dumped out on sidewalks that food might be carried to unfed hundreds; Father Ramm cutting away the timbers on St. Mary's tower, while the red glow crept across the cross out of reach of the hose; and the humble sacrifices — the woman who shared her full breasts with the child of another whose fountain had failed from weariness and fright — would that I had her name to hold in remembrance!"

Those were indeed brave, colored, splendid days! San Francisco's soul will be richer and stronger and warmer and more human till the end of time because of them. They were days when the dream of Utopia, the fabled epoch of the Golden Age, of human brotherhood, were perhaps as nearly realized as ever upon this troubled world.

Save for those whom death had struck with loss and pain, through taking away loved ones, the vast majority of San Franciscans were not merely stoical — they were gallantly brave, romantically chivalrous, superbly generous. In my goings about through the worst of the stricken districts, I saw many instances of loss and disaster, but my memory of those days is not stained with a single incident of cowardice or of meanness.

The obvious thing to say, is that social conventions and distinctions were laid aside; well, so they were, but that only expresses a small part of the truth. After all, the only place where men are truly, quite literally equal, is in their souls. God made us all, and when the red ruin was raging from the water front on toward Van Ness Avenue, a line of fire ten miles wide, at times, and later, when amid the shards and dust and smoke of the vanished city, men and women no longer felt that Doomsday was upon them, they acted toward each other as fellow creatures, as human beings, not merely as employer and employee, rich man, poor man, beggar man, thief.

* * *

Will Irwin wrote an excellent description of Old San Francisco, which he called "The City-That-Was." Well, the glimpses of Paradise, or of Utopia, which came to me while San Francisco, riven and shattered, was being bound, as it were, upon the monstrous pyre of its burning, was a vision of the City-That-Never-Was — the city of the world-wide dream — the city which John of Patmos saw descending out of heaven to earth — out of aspiration into accomplishment — out of the ideal into reality — the city of peace and of brotherly love — of the kingdom of God come upon earth. The City that never was — that never, never was — yet which surely is to be — which surely is to be!

* * *

Perhaps I saw everything magnified by my own mood — colored by my own desire — nevertheless, it is true that for several marvelous days in San Francisco we lived as people might live if they but willed it so — we lived a life of good-will. Nearly all the artificial barriers and distinctions with which we isolate class from class and person from person were thrown down more effectually than the 'quake threw down the walls of houses — the walls of evil houses and the walls of churches together. For days, there was no use for money — there was nothing to buy or sell. Rich and poor were no longer either rich or poor. The bread line was no respecter of persons. The women of the Tenderloin were cared for by virtuous women. Food was in common. He who had not asked and he who had gave. Your neighbor was as yourself. You did not see the mote in his eye for there was no distorting beam in yours. Generosity—kindness—pity—mercy—tenderness—all the brave and beautiful angels of the heart of man walked in the streets of the shattered city. Oh, yes, there were exceptions, no doubt. I've heard of them—but I did not myself see them—but it is God's own truth I'm telling you when I say that the great disaster which for several days shut off San Francisco from the world that still went on in the ordinary way, brought out what is best, and what is strongest, and what will finally prevail in mankind—that which is good. Those three or four days, despite all the dreadful things that happened, were days of the Golden Age returned again—and to me their memories remain as prophecies of the time to come, when we shall all together so live without change or shadow of turning.

Indeed, it almost seemed as if Goethe's dream was realized, and that San Francisco had been shocked out of its egoism and had found in the midst of this apocryphal overthrowal the poet's spring of goodness, and had become quite literally the City of Brotherly Love, the City of Peace—the City-That-Never-Has-Been. . . .

Ah me!

It was wonderful to hear city officials who were more than merely suspected of the most brazen graft declare that for them, "The history of San Francisco begins on April 18, 1906!" It was thrilling to see worn foes and bitterly opposed factions uniting in the new bonds of mutual service.

It was sublime!

* * *

And it was also evanescent as a dream.

Violent reformations of cities or of individuals are dramatic, but impermanent. . . .

I well remember how frantically we had to work, one night not long after the worst of the disaster was over, to hurry the news to Oakland, where our paper was being printed, that the Board of City Supervisors had just jammed through a very nefarious piece of special-privilege legislation. . . .

— And we know how soon afterwards the malodorous graft cases made the name of San Francisco scandalous throughout civilization.

No. Apparently it requires something more profound, more energetic, than an earthquake, to reform a city, or a soul. An earthquake may destroy; yes; and so will many other things. . . .

But what will save us?

B. FORMAL NARRATIVE

ETHAN BRAND[1]

Nathaniel Hawthorne

Bartram the lime-burner, a rough, heavy-looking man, begrimed with charcoal, sat watching his kiln, at nightfall, while his little son played at building houses with the scattered fragments of marble, when, on the hillside below them, they heard a roar of laughter, not mirthful, but slow, and even solemn, like a wind shaking the boughs of the forest.

"Father, what is that?" asked the little boy, leaving his play, and pressing betwixt his father's knees.

"Oh, some drunken man, I suppose," answered the lime-burner; "some merry fellow from the barroom in the village, who dared not laugh loud enough within doors lest he should blow the roof of the house off. So here he is, shaking his jolly sides at the foot of Graylock."

"But, father," said the child, more sensitive than the obtuse, middle-aged clown, "he does not laugh like a man that is glad. So the noise frightens me!"

"Don't be a fool, child!" cried his father gruffly. "You will never make a man, I do believe; there is too much of your mother in you. I have known the rustling of a leaf startle you. Hark! Here comes the merry fellow now. You shall see that there is no harm in him."

Bartram and his little son, while they were talking thus, sat watching the same limekiln that had been the scene of Ethan Brand's solitary and meditative life, before he began his search for the Unpardonable Sin. Many years, as we have seen, had now elapsed, since that portentous night when the IDEA was first devel-

[1]From *The Snow Image and Other Tales.*

oped. The kiln, however, on the mountainside stood unimpaired, and was in nothing changed since he had thrown his dark thoughts into the intense glow of its furnace, and melted them, as it were, into the one thought that took possession of his life. It was a rude, round, towerlike structure, about twenty feet high, heavily built of rough stones, and with a hillock of earth heaped about the larger part of its circumference; so that the blocks and fragments of marble might be drawn by cartloads, and thrown in at the top. There was an opening at the bottom of the tower, like an ovenmouth, but large enough to admit a man in a stooping posture, and provided with a massive iron door. With the smoke and jets of flame issuing from the chinks and crevices of this door, which seemed to give admittance into the hillside, it resembled nothing so much as the private entrance to the infernal regions, which the shepherds of the Delectable Mountains were accustomed to show to pilgrims.

There are many such limekilns in that tract of country, for the purpose of burning the white marble which composes a large part of the substance of the hills. Some of them, built years ago, and long deserted, with weeds growing in the vacant round of the interior, which is open to the sky, and grass and wild flowers rooting themselves into the chinks of the stones, look already like relics of antiquity, and may yet be overspread with the lichens of centuries to come. Others, where the lime-burner still feeds his daily and night-long fire, afford points of interest to the wanderer among the hills, who seats himself on a log of wood or a fragment of marble, to hold a chat with the solitary man. It is a lonesome, and, when the character is inclined to thought, may be an intensely thoughtful, occupation; as it proved in the case of Ethan Brand, who had mused to such strange purposes, in days gone by, while the fire in this very kiln was burning.

The man who now watched the fire was of a different order, and troubled himself with no thoughts save the very few that were requisite to his business. At frequent intervals he flung back the clashing weight of the iron door, and, turning his face from the insufferable glare, thrust in huge logs of oak, or stirred the immense brands with a long pole. Within the furnace were seen the curling and riotous flames, and the burning marble, almost molten with the intensity of heat; while without, the reflection of the fire quivered on the dark intricacy of the surrounding forest, and showed in the foreground a bright and ruddy little picture of the hut, the spring beside its door, the athletic and coal-begrimed figure of the lime-burner, and the half-frightened child, shrinking into the protection of his father's shadow. And when again the iron door was closed, then reappeared the tender light of the half-moon, which vainly strove to trace out the indistinct shapes of the neighboring mountains; and, in the upper sky, there was a flitting congregation of clouds, still faintly tinged with the rosy sunset, though thus far down into the valley the sunshine had vanished long and long ago.

The little boy now crept still closer to his father, as footsteps were heard ascending the hillside, and a human form thrust aside the bushes that clustered beneath the trees.

"Halloo! what is it?" cried the lime-burner, vexed at his son's timidity, yet half infected by it. "Come forward, and show yourself, like a man, or I'll fling this chunk of marble at your head!"

"You offer me a rough welcome," said a gloomy voice, as the unknown man drew nigh. "Yet I neither claim nor desire a kinder one, even at my own fireside."

To obtain a distincter view, Bartram threw open the iron door of the kiln, whence immediately issued a gush of fierce light, that smote full upon the stranger's face and figure. To a careless eye there appeared nothing very remarkable in his aspect, which was that of a man in a coarse, brown, country-made suit of clothes, tall and thin, with the staff and heavy shoes of a wayfarer. As he advanced, he fixed his eyes—which were very bright—intently upon the brightness of the furnace, as if he beheld, or expected to behold, some object worthy of note within it.

"Good evening, stranger," said the lime-burner; "whence come you, so late in the day?"

"I come from my search," answered the wayfarer; "for, at last, it is finished."

"Drunk!—or crazy!" muttered Bartram to himself. "I shall have trouble with the fellow. The sooner I drive him away, the better."

The little boy, all in a tremble, whispered to his father, and begged him to shut the door of the kiln, so that there might not be so much light; for that there was something in the man's face which he was afraid to look at, yet could not look away from. And, indeed, even the lime-burner's dull and torpid sense began to be impressed by an indescribable something in that thin, rugged, thoughtful visage, with the grizzled hair hanging wildly about it, and those deeply sunken eyes, which gleamed like fires within the entrance of a mysterious cavern. But, as he closed the door, the stranger turned toward him, and spoke in a quiet, familiar way that made Bartram feel as if he were a sane and sensible man, after all.

"Your task draws to an end, I see," said he. "This marble has already been burning three days. A few hours more will convert the stone to lime."

"Why, who are you?" exclaimed the lime-burner. "You seem as well acquainted with my business as I am myself."

"And well I may be," said the stranger; "for I followed the same craft many a long year, and here, too, on this very spot. But you are a newcomer in these parts. Did you never hear of Ethan Brand?"

"The man that went in search of the Unpardonable Sin?" asked Bartram, with a laugh.

"The same," answered the stranger. "He has found what he sought, and therefore he comes back again."

"What! then you are Ethan Brand himself?" cried the lime-burner, in amazement. "I am a newcomer here, as you say, and they call it eighteen years since you left the foot of Graylock. But, I can tell you, the good folks still talk about Ethan Brand, in the village yonder, and what a strange errand took him away from his limekiln. Well, and so you have found the Unpardonable Sin?"

"Even so!" said the stranger calmly.

"If the question is a fair one," proceeded Bartram, "where might it be?"

Ethan Brand laid his finger on his own heart.

"Here!" replied he.

And then, without mirth in his countenance, but as if moved by an involuntary recognition of the infinite absurdity of seeking throughout the world for what was the closest of all things to himself, and looking into every heart, save his own, for what was hidden in no other breast, he broke into a laugh of scorn. It was the same slow, heavy laugh that had almost appalled the lime-burner when it heralded the wayfarer's approach.

The solitary mountainside was made dismal by it. Laughter, when out of place, mistimed, or bursting forth from a disordered state of feeling, may be the most terrible modulation of the human voice. The laughter of one asleep, even if it be a little child—the madman's laugh — the wild, screaming laugh of a born idiot — are sounds that we sometimes tremble to hear, and would always willingly forget. Poets have imagined no utterance of fiends or hobgoblins so fearfully appropriate as a laugh. And even the obtuse lime-burner felt his nerves shaken, as this strange man looked inward at his own heart, and burst into laughter that rolled away into the night, and was indistinctly reverberated among the hills.

"Joe," said he to his little son, "scamper down to the tavern in the village, and tell the jolly fellows there that Ethan Brand has come back, and that he has found the Unpardonable Sin!"

The boy darted away on his errand, to which Ethan Brand made no objection, nor seemed hardly to notice it. He sat on a log of wood, looking steadfastly at the iron door of the kiln. When the child was out of sight, and his swift and light footsteps ceased to be heard treading first on the fallen leaves and then on the rocky mountain path, the lime-burner began to regret his departure. He felt that the little fellow's presence had been a barrier between his guest and himself, and that he must now deal, heart to heart, with a man who, on his own confession, had committed the one only crime for which Heaven could afford no mercy. That crime, in its indistinct blackness, seemed to overshadow him. The lime-burner's own sins rose up within him, and made his memory riotous with a throng of evil shapes that asserted their kindred with the Master Sin, whatever it might be, which it was within the scope of man's corrupted nature to conceive and cherish. They were all of one family; they went to and fro between his breast and Ethan Brand's, and carried dark greetings from one to the other.

Then Bartram remembered the stories which had grown traditionary in reference to this strange man, who had come upon him like a shadow of the night, and was making himself at home in his old place, after so long absence that the dead people, dead and buried for years, would have had more right to be at home, in any familiar spot, than he. Ethan Brand, it was said, had conversed with Satan himself in the lurid blaze of this very kiln. The legend had been matter of mirth heretofore, but looked grisly now. According to this tale, before Ethan Brand departed on his search, he had been accustomed to evoke a fiend from the hot furnace of the limekiln, night after night, in order to confer with him about the Unpardonable Sin; the man and the fiend each laboring to frame the image of some mode of guilt which could neither be atoned for nor forgiven. And, with the first gleam of light upon the mountain-top, the fiend crept in at the iron door, there to abide the intensest element of fire, until again summoned forth to share in the dreadful task of extending man's possible guilt beyond the scope of Heaven's else infinite mercy.

While the lime-burner was struggling with the horror of these thoughts, Ethan Brand rose from the log, and flung open the door of the kiln. The action was in such accordance with the idea in Bartram's mind, that he almost expected to see the Evil One issue forth, red-hot from the raging furnace.

"Hold! hold!" cried he, with a tremulous attempt to laugh; for he was ashamed of his fears, although they overmastered him. "Don't, for mercy's sake, bring out your Devil now!"

"Man!" sternly replied Ethan Brand, "what need have I of the Devil? I have left him behind me, on my track. It is with such halfway sinners as you that he busies himself. Fear not, because I open the door. I do but act by old custom, and am going to trim your fire, like a lime-burner, as I was once."

He stirred the vast coals, thrust in more wood, and bent forward to gaze into the hollow prison-house of the fire, regardless of the fierce glow that reddened upon his face. The lime-burner sat watching him, and half suspected his strange guest of a purpose, if not to evoke a fiend, at least to plunge bodily into the flames, and thus vanish from the sight of man. Ethan Brand, however, drew quietly back, and closed the door of the kiln.

"I have looked," said he, "into many a human heart that was seven times hotter with sinful passions than yonder furnace is with fire. But I found not there what I sought. No, not the Unpardonable Sin!"

"What is the Unpardonable Sin?" asked the lime-burner; and then he shrank farther from his companion, trembling lest his question should be answered.

"It is a sin that grew within my own breast," replied Ethan Brand, standing erect, with a pride that distinguishes all enthusiasts of his stamp. "A sin that grew nowhere else! The sin of an intellect that triumphed over the sense of brotherhood with man and reverence for God, and sacrificed everything to its own mighty claims! the only sin that reserves a recompense of immortal agony! Freely, were it to do again, would I incur the guilt. Unshrinkingly I accept the retribution!"

"The man's head is turned," muttered the lime-burner to himself. "He may be a sinner, like the rest of us — nothing more likely — but, I'll be sworn, he is a madman too."

Nevertheless, he felt uncomfortable at this situation, alone with Ethan Brand on the wild mountainside, and was right glad to hear the rough murmur of tongues, and the footsteps of what seemed a pretty numerous party, stumbling over the stones and rustling through the underbrush. Soon appeared the whole lazy regiment that was wont to infest the village tavern, comprehending three or four individuals who had drunk flip beside the barroom fire through all the winters, and smoked their pipes beneath the stoop through all the summers, since Ethan Brand's departure. Laughing boisterously, and mingling all their voices together in unceremonious talk, they now burst into the moonshine and narrow streaks of firelight that illuminated the open space before the limekiln. Bartram set the door ajar again, flooding the spot with light, that the whole company might get a fair view of Ethan Brand, and he of them.

There, among other old acquaintances, was a once ubiquitous man, now almost extinct, but whom we were formerly sure to encounter at the hotel of every thriving village throughout the country. It was the stage agent. The present specimen of the genus was a wilted and smoke-dried man, wrinkled and red-nosed, in a smartly cut, brown, bobtailed coat, with brass buttons, who for a length of time unknown, had kept his desk and corner in the barroom, and was still puffing what seemed to be the same cigar that he had lighted twenty years before. He had great fame as a dry joker, though, perhaps, less on account of any intrinsic humor than from a certain flavor of brandy toddy and tobacco smoke, which impregnated all his ideas and expressions, as well as his person. Another well-remembered though strangely altered face was that of Lawyer Giles, as people still called him in courtesy; an elderly ragamuffin, in his soiled shirt sleeves and tow-cloth trousers. This poor fellow had been an attorney, in what he called his better days, a sharp practitioner, and a great vogue among the village litigants; but flip, and sling, and toddy, and cocktails, imbibed at all hours, morning, noon, and night, had caused him to slide from intellectual to various kinds and degrees of bodily labor, till, at last, to adopt his own phrase, he slid into a soap vat. In other words, Giles was now a soap boiler, in a small way. He had come to be but the fragment of a human being, a part of one foot having been chopped off by an ax, and an entire hand torn away by the devilish grip of a steam engine. Yet, though the corporeal hand was gone, a spiritual member remained; for, stretching forth the stump, Giles steadfastly averred that he felt an invisible thumb and fingers with as vivid a sensation as before the real ones were amputated. A maimed and miserable wretch he was; but one, nevertheless, whom the world could not trample on, and had no right to scorn, either in this or any previous stage of his misfortunes, since he had still kept up the courage and spirit of a man, asked nothing in charity, and with his one hand—and that the left one—fought a stern battle against want and hostile circumstances.

Among the throng, too, came another personage, who, with certain points of similarity to Lawyer Giles, had many more of difference. It was the village doctor; a man of some fifty years, whom, at an earlier period of his life, we introduced as paying a professional visit to Ethan Brand during the latter's supposed insanity. He was now a purple-visaged, rude, and brutal, yet half-gentlemanly figure, with something wild, and desperate in his talk, and in all the details of his gesture and manners. Brandy possessed this man like an evil spirit, and made him as surly and savage as a wild beast, and as miserable as a lost soul; but there was supposed to be in him such wonderful skill, such native gifts of healing, beyond any which medical science could impart, that society caught hold of him, and would not let him sink out of its reach. So, swaying to and fro upon his horse, and grumbling thick accents at the bedside, he visited all the sick-chambers for miles about among the mountain towns, and sometimes raised a dying man, as it were, by miracle, or quite as often, no doubt, sent his patient to a grave that was dug many a year too soon. The doctor had an everlasting pipe in his mouth, and, as somebody said, in allusion to his habit of swearing, it was always alight with hell-fire.

These three worthies pressed forward, and greeted Ethen Brand each after his own fashion, earnestly inviting him to partake of the contents of a certain black bottle, in which, as they averred, he would find something far better worth seeking for than the Unpardonable Sin. No mind, which has wrought itself by intense and solitary meditation into a high state of enthusiasm, can endure the kind of contact with low and vulgar modes of thought and feeling to which Ethan Brand was now subjected. It made him doubt—and, strange to say, it was a painful doubt—whether he had indeed found the Unpardonable Sin and found it within himself. The whole question on which he had exhausted life, and more than life, looked like a delusion.

"Leave me," he said bitterly, "ye brute beasts, that have made yourselves so, shrivelling up your souls with fiery liquors! I have done with you. Years and years ago, I groped into your hearts, and found nothing there for my purpose. Get ye gone!"

"Why, you uncivil scoundrel," cried the fierce doctor, "is that the way you respond to the kindness of your best friends? Then let me tell you the truth. You have no more found the Unpardonable Sin than yonder boy Joe has. You are but a crazy fellow—I told you so twenty years ago—neither better nor worse than a crazy fellow, and a fit companion of old Humphrey, here!"

He pointed to an old man, shabbily dressed, with long white hair, thin visage, and unsteady eyes. For some years past this aged person had been wandering about among the hills, inquiring of all travelers whom he met for his daughter. The girl, it seemed, had gone off with a company of circus performers; and occasionally tidings of her came to the village, and fine stories were told of her glittering appearance as she rode on horseback in the ring, or performed marvellous feats on the tight-rope.

The white-haired father now approached Ethan Brand, and gazed unsteadily into his face.

"They tell me you have been all over the earth," said he, wringing his hands with earnestness. "You must have seen my daughter, for she makes a grand figure in the world, and everybody goes to see her. Did she send any word to her old father, or say when she was coming back?"

Ethan Brand's eye quailed beneath the old man's. That daughter, from whom he so earnestly desired a word of greeting, was the Esther of our tale, the very girl whom, with such cold and remorseless purpose, Ethan Brand had made the subject of a psychological experiment, and wasted, absorbed, and perhaps annihilated her soul, in the process.

"Yes," murmured he, turning away from the hoary wanderer; "it is no delusion. There is an Unpardonable Sin!"

While these things were passing, a merry scene was going forward in the area of cheerful light, beside the spring and before the door of the hut. A number of the youth of the village, young men and girls, had hurried up the hillside, impelled by curiosity to see Ethan Brand, the hero of so many a legend familiar to their childhood. Finding nothing, however, very remarkable in his aspect—nothing but a sunburnt wayfarer, in plain garb and dusty shoes, who sat looking into the fire, as if he fancied pictures among the coals—these young people speedily grew tired of observing him. As it happened, there was other amusement at hand. An old German Jew, traveling with a diorama on his back, was passing down the mountain road towards the village just as the party turned aside from it, and, in hopes of eking out the profits of the day, the showman had kept them company to the lime-kiln.

"Come, old Dutchman," cried one of the young men, "let us see your pictures, if you can swear they are worth looking at!"

"Oh yes, Captain," answered the Jew—whether as a matter of courtesy or craft, he styled everybody Captain—"I shall show you, indeed, some very superb pictures!"

So, placing his box in a proper position, he invited the young men and girls to look through the glass orifices of the machine, and proceeded to exhibit a series of the most outrageous scratchings and daubings, as specimens of the fine arts, that ever an itinerant showman had the face to impose upon his circle of spectators. The pictures were worn out, moreover, tattered, full of cracks and wrinkles, dingy with tobacco smoke, and otherwise in a most pitiable condition. Some purported to be cities, public edifices, and ruined castles in Europe; others represented Napoleon's battles and Nelson's sea fights; and in the midst of these would be seen a gigantic, brown, hairy hand—which might have been mistaken for the Hand of Destiny, though, in truth, it was only the showman's—pointing its forefinger to various scenes of the conflict, while its owner gave historical illustrations. When, with much merriment at its abominable deficiency of merit, the exhibition was concluded, the German bade little Joe put his head into the box. Viewed through the magnifying glasses, the boy's round, rosy visage assumed the strangest imaginable aspect of an immense Titanic child, the mouth grinning broadly, and the eyes and every other feature overflowing with fun at the joke. Suddenly, however, that merry face turned pale, and its expression changed to horror, for this easily impressed and excitable child had become sensible that the eye of Ethan Brand was fixed upon him through the glass.

"You make the little man to be afraid, Captain," said the German Jew, turning up the dark and strong outline of his visage, from his stooping posture. "But look again, and, by chance, I shall cause you to see somewhat that is very fine, upon my word!"

Ethan Brand gazed into the box for an instant, and then starting back, looked fixedly at the German. What had he seen? Nothing, apparently; for a curious youth, who had peeped in almost at the same moment, beheld only a vacant space of canvas.

"I remember you now," muttered Ethan Brand to the showman.

"Ah, Captain," whispered the Jew of Nuremberg, with a dark smile, "I find it to be a heavy matter in my showbox—this Unpardonable Sin! By my faith, Captain, it has wearied my shoulders, this long day, to carry it over the mountain."

"Peace," answered Ethan Brand sternly, "or get thee into the furnace yonder!"

The Jew's exhibition had scarcely concluded, when a great elderly dog—who seemed to be his own master, as no person in the company laid claim to him—saw fit to render himself the object of public notice. Hitherto, he had shown himself a very quiet, well-disposed old dog, going round from one to another, and, by way of being sociable, offering his rough head to be patted by any kindly hand that would take so much trouble. But now, all of a sudden, this grave and venerable quadruped, of his own mere notion, and without the slightest suggestion from anybody else, began to run round after his tail, which, to heighten the absurdity of the proceeding, was a great deal shorter than it should have been. Never was seen such a headlong eagerness in pursuit of an object that could not possibly be attained; never was heard such a tremendous outbreak of growling, snarling, barking, and snapping—as if one end of the ridiculous brute's body were at deadly and most unforgivable enmity with the other. Faster and faster, round about went the cur; and faster and still faster fled the unapproachable brevity of his tail; and louder and fiercer grew his yells of rage and animosity; until, utterly exhausted, and as far from the goal as ever, the foolish old dog ceased his performance as suddenly as he had begun it. The next moment he was as mild, quiet, sensible, and respectable in his deportment, as when he first scraped acquaintance with the company.

As may be supposed, the exhibition was greeted with universal laughter, clapping of hands, and shouts of encore, to which the canine performer responded by wagging all that there was to wag of his tail, but appeared totally unable to repeat his very successful effort to amuse the spectators.

Meanwhile, Ethan Brand had resumed his seat upon the log, and moved, it might be, by a perception of some remote analogy between his own case and that of this self-pursuing cur, he broke into the awful laugh, which, more than any other token, expressed the condition of his inward being. From that moment, the merriment of the party was at an end; they stood aghast, dreading lest the inauspicious sound should be reverberated around the horizon, and that mountain would thunder it to mountain, and so the horror be prolonged upon their ears. Then, whispering one to another that it was late — that the moon was almost down — that the August night was growing chill — they hurried homewards, leaving the lime-burner and little Joe to deal as they might with their unwelcome guest. Save for these three human beings, the open space on the hillside was a solitude, set in a vast gloom of forest. Beyond that darksome verge, the firelight shimmered on the stately trunks and almost black foliage of pines, intermixed with the lighter verdure of sapling oaks, maples, and poplars, while here and there lay the gigantic corpses of dead trees, decaying on the leaf-strewn soil. And it seemed to little Joe — a timorous and imaginative child — that the silent forest was holding its breath, until some fearful thing should happen.

Ethan Brand thrust more wood into the fire, and closed the door of the kiln; then looking over his shoulder at the lime-burner and his son, he bade, rather than advised, them to retire to rest.

"For myself, I cannot sleep," said he. "I have matters that it concerns me to meditate upon. I will watch the fire, as I used to do in the old time."

"And call the Devil out of the furnace to keep you company, I suppose," muttered Bartram, who had been making intimate acquaintance with the black bottle above mentioned. "But watch, if you like, and call as many devils as you like! For my part, I shall be all the better for a snooze. Come, Joe!"

As the boy followed his father into the hut, he looked back at the wayfarer, and the tears came into his eyes, for his tender spirit had an intuition of the bleak and terrible loneliness in which this man had enveloped himself.

When they had gone, Ethan Brand sat listening to the crackling of the kindled wood, and looking at the little spirits of fire that issued through the chinks of the door. These trifles, however, once so familiar, had but the slightest hold of his attention, while deep within his mind he was reviewing the gradual but marvellous change that had been wrought upon him by the search to which he had devoted himself. He remembered how the night dew had fallen upon him—how the dark forest had whispered to him—how the stars had gleamed upon him—a simple and loving man, watching his fire in the years gone by, and ever musing as it burned. He remembered with what tenderness, with what love and sympathy for mankind, and what pity for human guilt and woe, he had first begun to contemplate those ideas which afterwards became the inspiration of his life; with what reverence he had then looked into the heart of man, viewing it as a temple originally divine, and, however desecrated, still to be held sacred by a brother; with what awful fear he had deprecated the success of his pursuits, and prayed that the Unpardonable Sin might never be revealed to him. Then ensued that vast intellectual development, which, in its progress, disturbed the counterpoise between his mind and heart. The Idea that possessed his life had operated as a means of education; it had gone on cultivating his powers to the highest point of which they were susceptible; it had raised him from the level of an unlettered laborer to stand on a starlit eminence, whither the philosophers of the earth, laden with the lore of universities, might vainly strive to clamber after him. So much for the intellect! But where was the heart? That, indeed, had withered—had contracted—had hardened—had perished! It had ceased to partake of the universal throb. He had lost his hold of the magnetic chain of humanity. He was no longer a brotherman, opening the chambers of the dungeons of our common nature by the key of holy sympathy, which gave him a right to share in all its secrets; he was now a cold observer, looking on mankind as the subject of his experiment, and, at length, converting man and woman to be his puppets, and pulling the wires that moved them to such degrees of crime as were demanded for his study.

Thus Ethan Brand became a fiend. He began to be so from the moment that his moral nature had ceased to keep the pace of improvement with his intellect. And now, as his highest effort and inevitable development—as the bright and gorgeous flower, and rich, delicious fruit of his life's labor—he had produced the Unpardonable Sin!

"What more have I to seek? what more to achieve?" said Ethan Brand to himself. "My task is done, and well done!"

Starting from the log with a certain alacrity in his gait and ascending the hillock of earth that was raised against the stone circumference of the lime-kiln, he thus reached the top of the structure. It was a space of perhaps ten feet across, from edge to edge, presenting a view of the upper surface of the immense mass of broken marble with which the kiln was heaped. All these innumerable blocks and fragments of marble were red-hot and vividly on fire, sending up great spouts of blue flame, which quivered aloft and danced madly, as within a magic circle, and sank and rose again, with continual and multitudinous activity. As the lonely man bent forward over this terrible body of fire, the blasting heat smote up against his person with a breath that, it might be supposed, would have scorched and shriveled him up in a moment.

Ethan Brand stood erect, and raised his arms on high. The blue flames played upon his face, and imparted the wild and ghastly light which alone could have suited its expression; it was that of a fiend on the verge of plunging into his gulf of intensest torment.

"O Mother Earth," cried he, "who art no more my mother, and into whose bosom this frame shall never be resolved! O mankind, whose brotherhood I have cast off, and trampled thy great heart beneath my feet! O stars of heaven, that shone on me of old, as if to light me onward and upward!—farewell all, and forever. Come, deadly element of Fire—henceforth my familiar frame! Embrace me, as I do thee!"

That night the sound of a fearful peal of laughter rolled heavily through the sleep of the lime-burner and his little son; dim shapes of horror and anguish haunted their dreams, and seemed still present in the rude hovel when they opened their eyes to the daylight.

"Up, boy, up!" cried the lime-burner, staring about him. "Thank Heaven, the night is gone, at last; and rather than pass such another, I would watch my limekiln, wide-awake, for a twelvemonth. This Ethan Brand, with his humbug of an Unpardonable Sin, has done me no such mighty favor, in taking my place!"

He issued from the hut, followed by little Joe, who kept fast hold of his father's hand. The early sunshine was already pouring its gold upon the mountaintops; and though the valleys were still in shadow, they smiled cheerfully in the promise of the bright day that was hastening onward. The village, completely shut in by hills, which swelled away gently about it, looked as if it had rested peacefully in the hollow of the great hand of Providence. Every dwelling was distinctly visible; the little spires of the two churches pointed upward, and caught a fore-glimmering of brightness from the sun-gilt skies upon their gilded weathercocks. The tavern was astir, and the figure of the old, smoke-dried stage agent, cigar in mouth, was seen beneath the stoop. Old Graylock was glorified with a golden cloud upon his head. Scattered likewise over the breasts of the surrounding mountains, there were heaps of hoary mist, in fantastic shapes, some of them far down into the valley, others high up toward the summits, and still others, of the same family of mist or cloud, hovering in the gold radiance of the upper atmosphere. Stepping from one to another of the clouds that rested on the hills, and thence to the loftier brotherhood that sailed in air, it seemed almost as if a mortal man might thus ascend into the heavenly regions. Earth was so mingled with sky that it was a daydream to look at it.

To supply that charm of the familiar and homely, which Nature so readily adopts into a scene like this, the stagecoach was rattling down the mountain road, and the driver sounded his horn, while echo caught up the notes, and intertwined them into a rich and varied and elaborate harmony, of which the original performer could lay claim to little share. The great hills played a concert among themselves, each contributing a strain of airy sweetness.

Little Joe's face brightened at once.

"Dear father," cried he, skipping cherrily to and fro, "that strange man is gone, and the sky and the mountains all seem glad of it!"

"Yes," growled the lime-burner, with an oath, "but he has let the fire go down, and no thanks to him if five hundred bushels of lime are not spoiled. If I catch the fellow hereabouts again, I shall feel like tossing him into the furnace!"

With his long pole in his hand, he ascended to the top of the kiln. After a moment's pause, he called to his son:

"Come up here, Joe!"

So little Joe ran up the hillock, and stood by his father's side. The marble was all burnt into perfect, snow-white lime. But on its surface, in the midst of the circle—snow-white, too, and thoroughly converted into lime—lay a human skeleton, in the attitude of a person who, after long toil, lies down to long repose. Within the ribs—strange to say—was the shape of a human heart.

"Was this fellow's heart made of marble?" cried Bartram, in some perplexity at this phenomenon. "At any rate, it is burnt into what looks like special good lime; and, taking all the bones together, my kiln is half a bushel the richer for him."

So saying, the rude lime-burner lifted his pole, and, letting it fall upon the skeleton, the relics of Ethan Brand were crumbled into fragments.

A MUNICIPAL REPORT[1]

O. Henry

Fancy a novel about Chicago or Buffalo, let us say, or Nashville, Tennessee! There are just three big cities in the United States that are "story cities"—New York, of course, New Orleans, and, best of the lot, San Francisco.—*Frank Norris.*

East is East, and West is San Francisco, according to Californians. Californians are a race of people; they are not merely inhabitants of a state. They are the Southerners of the West. Now, Chicagoans are no less loyal to their city; but when you ask them why, they stammer and speak of lake fish and the new Odd Fellows' Building. But Californians go into detail.

---

[1]From *Strictly Business*. Copyright, 1904, by Doubleday, Doran & Company, Inc. Used by permission of the publishers.

Of course they have, in the climate, an argument that is good for half an hour while you are thinking of your coal bills and heavy underwear. But as soon as they come to mistake your silence for conviction, madness comes upon them, and they picture the city of the Golden Gate as the Bagdad of the New World. So far, as a matter of opinion, no refutation is necessary. But, dear cousins all (from Adam and Eve descended), it is a rash one who will lay his finger on the map and say: "In this town there can be no romance — what could happen here?" Yes, it is a bold and a rash deed to challenge in one sentence history, romance, and Rand and McNally.

NASHVILLE. — A city, port of delivery, and the capital of the State of Tennessee, is on the Cumberland River and on the N. C. & St. L. and the L. & N. railroads. This city is regarded as the most important educational center in the South.

I stepped off the train at 8 p.m. Having searched the thesaurus in vain for adjectives, I must, as a substitution, hie me to comparison in the form of a recipe.

Take of London fog, 30 parts; malaria, 10 parts; gas leaks, 20 parts; dewdrops gathered in a brickyard at sunrise, 25 parts; odor of honeysuckle, 15 parts. Mix.

The mixture will give you an approximate conception of a Nashville drizzle. It is not so fragrant as a mothball nor as thick as pea soup; but 'tis enough — 'twill serve.

I went to a hotel in a tumbril. It required strong self-suppression for me to keep from climbing to the top of it and giving an imitation of Sidney Carton. The vehicle was drawn by beasts of a bygone era and driven by something dark and emancipated.

I was sleepy and tired, so when I got to the hotel I hurriedly paid it the fifty cents it demanded (with approximate lagniappe, I assure you). I knew its habits; and I did not want to hear it prate about its old "marster" or anything that happened "befo' de wah."

The hotel was one of the kind described as "renovated." That means twenty thousand dollars' worth of new marble pillars, tiling, electric lights and brass cuspidors in the lobby, and a new L. & N. timetable and a lithograph of Lookout Mountain in each one of the great rooms above. The management was without reproach, the attention full of exquisite Southern courtesy, the service as slow as the progress of a snail and as good-humored as Rip Van Winkle. The food was worth traveling a thousand miles for. There is no other hotel in the world where you can get such chicken livers *en brochette*.

At dinner I asked a Negro waiter if there was anything doing in town. He pondered gravely for a minute, and then replied: "Well, boss, I don't really reckon there's anything at all doin' after sundown."

Sundown had been accomplished; it had been drowned in the drizzle long before. So that spectacle was denied me. But I went forth upon the streets in the drizzle to see what might be there.

It is built on undulating grounds; and the streets are lighted by electricity at a cost of $32,470 per annum.

As I left the hotel there was a race riot. Down upon me charged a company of freedmen, or Arabs, or Zulus, armed with — no, I saw with relief that they were not rifles, but whips. And I saw dimly a caravan of black, clumsy vehicles; and at the reassuring shouts, "Kyar you anywhere in the town, boss, fuh fifty cents," I reasoned that I was merely a "fare" instead of a victim.

I walked through long streets, all leading uphill. I wondered how those streets ever came down again. Perhaps they didn't until they were "graded." On a few of the "main streets" I saw lights in stores here and there; saw street cars go by conveying worthy burghers hither and yon; saw people pass engaged in the art of conversation; and heard a burst of semi-lively laughter issuing from a soda-water and ice-cream parlor. The streets other than "main" seemed to have enticed upon their borders houses consecrated to peace and domesticity. In many of them lights shone behind discreetly drawn window shades; in a few, pianos tinkled orderly and irreproachable music. There was, indeed, little "doing." I wished I had come before sundown. So I returned to my hotel.

In November, 1864, the Confederate General Hood advanced against Nashville, where he shut up a National force under General Thomas. The latter then sallied forth and defeated the Confederates in a terrible conflict.

All my life I have heard of, admired, and witnessed the fine marksmanship of the South in its peaceful conflicts in the tobacco-chewing regions. But in my hotel a surprise awaited me. There were twelve bright, new, imposing, capacious brass cuspidors in the great lobby, tall enough to be called urns and so wide-mouthed that the crack pitcher of a lady baseball team should have been able to throw a ball into each of them at five paces distant. But, although a terrible battle had raged and was still raging, the enemy had not suffered. Bright, new, imposing, capacious, untouched, they stood. But, shades of Jefferson Brick! the tile floor — the beautiful tile floor! I could not avoid thinking of the battle of Nashville, and trying to draw, as in my foolish habit, some deductions about hereditary marksmanship.

Here I first saw Major (by misplaced courtesy) Wentworth Caswell. I knew him for a type the moment my eyes suffered from the sight of him. A rat has no geographical habitat. My old friend, A. Tennyson, said, as he so well said almost everything:

> Prophet, curse me the blabbing lip,
> And curse me the British vermin, the rat.

Let us regard the word "British" as interchangeable *ad lib.* A rat is a rat.

This man was hunting about the hotel lobby like a starved dog that had forgotten where he had buried a bone. He had a face of great acreage, red, pulpy, and with a kind of sleepy massiveness like that of Buddha. He possessed one single virtue — he was smoothly shaven. The mark of the beast is not indelible upon a man until he goes about with a stubble. I think that if he had not used his razor that day I would have repulsed his advances, and the criminal calendar of the world would have been spared the addition of one murder.

I happened to be standing within five feet of a cuspidor when Major Caswell opened fire upon it. I had been observant enough to perceive that the attacking force was using Gatlings instead of squirrel rifles; so I side-stepped so promptly that the Major seized the opportunity to apologize to a noncombatant. He had the blabbing lip. In four minutes he had become my friend and had dragged me to the bar.

I desire to interpolate here that I am a Southerner. But I am not one by profession or trade. I eschew the string tie, the slouch hat, the Prince Albert, the number of bales of cotton destroyed by Sherman, and plug chewing. When the orchestra plays "Dixie" I do not cheer. I slide a little lower on the leather-cornered seat and—well—order another Würzburger and wish that Longstreet had—but what's the use?

Major Caswell banged the bar with his fist, and the first gun at Fort Sumter reëchoed. When he fired the last one at Appomattox I began to hope. But then he began on family trees, and demonstrated that Adam was only a third cousin of a collateral branch of the Caswell family. Genealogy disposed of, he took up, to my distaste, his private family matters. He spoke of his wife, traced her descent back to Eve, and profanely denied any possible rumor that she may have had relations in the land of Nod.

By this time I began to suspect that he was trying to obscure by the noise the fact that he had ordered the drinks, on the chance that I would be bewildered into paying for them. But when they were down he crashed a silver dollar loudly upon the bar. Then, of course, another serving was obligatory. And when I had paid for that I took leave of him brusquely; for I wanted no more of him. But before I had obtained my release he had prated loudly of an income that his wife received, and showed a handful of silver money.

When I got my key at the desk the clerk said to me courteously: "If that man Caswell has annoyed you, and if you would like to make a complaint, we will have him ejected. He is a nuisance, a loafer, and without any known means of support, although he seems to have money most of the time. But we don't seem to be able to hit upon any means of throwing him out legally."

"Why, no," said I, after some reflection; "I don't see my way clear to make a complaint. But I would like to place myself on record as asserting that I do not care for his company. Your town," I continued, "seems to be a quiet one. What manner of entertainment, adventure, or excitement have you to offer to the stranger within your gates?"

"Well, sir," said the clerk, "there will be a show here next Thursday. It is—I'll look it up and have the announcement sent up to your room with the ice water. Good-night."

After I went up to my room I looked out of the window. It was only about ten o'clock, but I looked upon a silent town. The drizzle continued, spangled with dim lights, as far apart as currants in a cake sold at the Ladies' Exchange.

"A quiet place," I said to myself, as my first shoe struck the ceiling of the occupant of the room beneath mine. "Nothing of the life here that gives color and variety to the cities in the East and West. Just a good, ordinary, humdrum, business town."

Nashville occupies a foremost place among the manufacturing centers of the country. It is the fifth boot and shoe market in the United States, the largest candy and cracker manufacturing city in the South, and does an enormous wholesale dry goods, grocery, and drug business.

I must tell you how I came to be in Nashville, and I assure you the digression brings as much tedium to me as it does to you. I was traveling elsewhere on my own business, but I had a commission from a Northern literary magazine to stop over there and establish a connection between the publication and one of its personal contributors, Azalea Adair.

Adair (there was no clue to the personality except the hand writing) had sent in some essays (lost art!) and poems that had made the editors swear approvingly over their one-o'clock luncheon. So they had commissioned me to round up said Adair and corner by contract his or her output at two cents a word before some other publisher offered her ten or twenty.

At nine o'clock the next morning, after my chicken livers *en brochette* (try them if you find that hotel), I strayed out into the drizzle, which was still on for an unlimited run. At the first corner, I came upon Uncle Caesar. He was a stalwart Negro older than the pyramids, with gray wool and a face that reminded me of Brutus, and a second afterwards of the late King Cetewayo. He wore the most remarkable coat that I ever had seen or expected to see. It reached to his ankles and had once been a Confederate gray in color. But rain and sun and age had so variegated it that Joseph's coat, beside it, would have faded to a pale monochrome. I must linger with that coat, for it has to do with the story—the story that is so long in coming, because you can hardly expect anything to happen in Nashville.

Once it must have been the military coat of an officer. The cape of it had vanished, but all adown its front it had been frogged and tasseled magnificently. But now the frogs and tassels were gone. In their stead had been patiently stitched (I surmise by some surviving "black mammy") new frogs made of cunningly twisted common hempen twine. This twine was frayed and disheveled. It must have been added to the coat as a substitute for vanished splendors, with tasteless but painstaking devotion, for it followed faithfully the curves of the long-missing frogs. And, to complete the comedy and pathos of the garment, all its buttons were gone save one. The second button from the top alone remained. The coat was fastened by other twine strings tied through the buttonholes and other holes rudely pierced on the opposite side. There was never such a weird garment so fantastically bedecked and of so many mottled hues. The lone button was the size of a half dollar, made of yellow horn and sewed on with coarse twine.

This Negro stood by a carriage so old that Ham himself might have started a hack-line after he left the ark with the two animals hitched to it. As I approached he threw open the door, drew out a feather duster, waved it without using it, and said in deep, rumbling tones:

"Step right in, suh; ain't a speck of dust in it—jus' got back from a funeral, suh."

I inferred that on such gala occasions carriages were given an extra cleaning. I looked up and down the street and perceived that there was little choice among the vehicles for hire that lined the curb. I looked in my memorandum book for the address of Azalea Adair.

"I want to go to 861 Jessamine Street," I said, and was about to step into the hack.

But for an instant the thick, gorilla-like arm of the old Negro barred me. On his massive and saturnine face a look of sudden suspicion and enmity flashed for a moment. Then, with quickly returning conviction, he asked blandishingly: "What are you gwine there for, boss?"

"What is that to you?" I asked a little sharply.

"Nothin', suh, jus' nothin'. Only it's a lonesome kind of part of town and few folks ever has business there. Step right in. The seat is clean—jes' got back from a funeral, suh."

A mile and a half it must have been to our journey's end. I could hear nothing but the fearful rattle of the ancient hack over the uneven brick paving; I could smell nothing but the drizzle, now further flavored with coal smoke and something like a mixture of tar and oleander blossoms. All I could see through the streaming windows were two rows of dim houses.

The city has an area of 10 square miles; 181 miles of streets of which 137 miles are paved; a system of waterworks that cost $2,000,000, with 77 miles of mains.

Eight-sixty-one Jessamine Street was a decayed mansion. Thirty yards back from the street it stood, outmerged in a splendid grove of trees and untrimmed shrubbery. A row of box bushes overflowed and almost hid the paling fence from sight; the gate was kept closed by a rope noose that encircled the gatepost and the first paling of the gate. But when you got inside you saw that eight-sixty-one was a shell, a shadow, a ghost of former grandeur and excellence. But in the story, I have not yet got inside.

When the hack had ceased from rattling and the weary quadrupeds came to a rest, I handed my Jehu his fifty cents with an additional quarter, feeling a glow of conscious generosity as I did so. He refused it.

"It's two dollars, suh," he said.

"How's that?" I asked. "I plainly heard you call out at the hotel: 'Fifty cents to any part of the town.'"

"It's two dollars, suh," he repeated obstinately. "It's a long ways from the hotel."

"It is within the city limits and well within them," I argued. "Don't think that you have picked up a greenhorn Yankee. Do you see those hills over there?" I went on, pointing toward the east (I could not see them, myself, for the drizzle); "well, I was born and raised on their other side. You old fool nigger, can't you tell people from other people when you see 'em?"

The grim face of King Cetewayo softened. "Is you from the South, suh? I reckon it was them shoes of yourn fooled me. They is somethin' sharp in the toes for a Southern gen'l'man to wear."

"Then the charge is fifty cents, I suppose?" said I inexorably.

His former expression, a mingling of cupidity and hostility, returned, remained ten seconds, and vanished.

"Boss," he said, "fifty cents is right; but I *needs* two dollars, suh; I'm *obleeged* to have two dollars. I ain't *demandin'* it now, suh, after I knows whar you's from; I'm jus' sayin' that I *has* to have two dollars tonight, and business is mighty po'."

Peace and confidence settled upon his heavy features. He had been luckier than he had hoped. Instead of having picked up a greenhorn, ignorant of rates, he had come upon an inheritance.

"You confounded old rascal," I said, reaching down to my pocket, "you ought to be turned over to the police."

For the first time I saw him smile. He knew; he *knew;* HE KNEW.

I gave him two one-dollar bills. As I handed them over I noticed that one of them had seen parlous times. Its upper right-hand corner was missing, and it had been torn through the middle, but joined again. A strip of blue tissue paper, pasted over the split, preserved its negotiability.

Enough of the African bandit for the present: I left him happy, lifted the rope, and opened the creaky gate.

The house, as I said, was a shell. A paintbrush had not touched it in twenty years. I could not see why a strong wind should not have bowled it over like a house of cards until I looked again at the trees that hugged it close — the trees that saw the battle of Nashville and still drew their protecting branches around it against storm and enemy and cold.

Azalea Adair, fifty years old, white-haired, a descendant of the cavaliers, as thin and frail as the house she lived in, robed in the cheapest and cleanest dress I ever saw, with an air as simple as a queen's, received me.

The reception room seemed a mile square, because there was nothing in it except some rows of books, on unpainted white-pine bookshelves, a cracked marble-top table, a rag rug, a hairless horsehair sofa, and two or three chairs. Yes, there was a picture on the wall, a colored crayon drawing of a cluster of pansies. I looked around for the portrait of Andrew Jackson and the pinecone hanging basket, but they were not there.

Azalea Adair and I had conversation, a little of which will be repeated to you. She was a product of the old South, gently nurtured in the sheltered life. Her learning was not broad, but was deep and of splendid originality in its somewhat narrow scope. She had been educated at home, and her knowledge of the world was derived from inference and by inspiration. Of such is the precious, small group of essayists made. While she talked to me I kept brushing my fingers, trying, unconsciously, to rid them guiltily of the absent dust from the half-calf backs of Lamb, Chaucer, Hazlitt, Marcus Aurelius, Montaigne, and Hood. She was exquisite, she was a valuable discovery, nearly everybody nowadays knows too much — oh, so much too much — of real life.

I could perceive clearly that Azalea Adair was very poor. A house and a dress she had, not much else, I fancied. So, divided between my duty to the magazine and my loyalty to the poets and essayists who fought Thomas in the valley of the Cumberland, I listened to her voice, which was like a harpsichord's, and found that I could not speak of contracts. In the presence of the nine Muses and the three Graces one hesitated to lower the topic to two cents. There would have to be another colloquy after I had regained my commercialism. But I spoke of my mission, and three o'clock of the next afternoon was set for the discussion of the business proposition.

"Your town," I said, as I began to make ready to depart (which is the time for smooth generalities), "seems to be a quiet, sedate place. A home town, I should say, where few things out of the ordinary ever happen."

It carries an extensive trade in stoves and hollow ware with the West and South, and its flouring mills have a daily capacity of more than two thousand barrels.

Azalea Adair seemed to reflect.

"I have never thought of it that way," she said, with a kind of sincere intensity that seemed to belong to her. "Isn't it in the still, quiet places that things do happen? I fancy that when God began to create the earth on the first Monday morning one could have leaned out one's window and heard the drops of mud splashing from His trowel as He built up the everlasting hills. What did the noisiest project in the world—I mean the building of the tower of Babel—result in finally? A page and a half of Esperanto in the *North American Review.*"

"Of course," I said platitudinously, "human nature is the same everywhere; but there is more color—er—more drama and movement and—er—romance in some cities than in others."

"On the surface," said Azalea Adair. "I have traveled many times round the world in a golden airship wafted on two wings—print and dreams. I have seen (on one of my imaginary tours) the Sultan of Turkey bowstring with his own hands one of his wives who had uncovered her face in public. I have seen a man in Nashville tear up his theater tickets because his wife was going out with her face covered—with rice powder. In San Francisco's Chinatown I saw the slave girl Sing Yee dipped slowly, inch by inch, in boiling almond oil to make her swear she would never see her American lover again. She gave in when the boiling oil had reached three inches above her knee. At a euchre party in East Nashville the other night, I saw Kitty Morgan cut dead by seven of her schoolmates and lifelong friends because she had married a house painter. The boiling oil was sizzling as high as her heart; but I wish you could have seen the fine little smile that she carried from table to table. Oh, yes, it is a humdrum town. Just a few miles of red-brick houses and mud stores and lumber yards."

Someone knocked hollowly at the back of the house. Azalea Adair breathed a soft apology and went to investigate the sound. She came back in three minutes with brightened eyes, a faint flush on her cheeks, and ten years lifted from her shoulders.

"You must have a cup of tea before you go," she said, "and a sugar cake."

She reached and shook a little iron bell. In shuffled a small Negro girl about twelve, barefoot, not very tidy, glowering at me with thumb in mouth and bulging eyes.

Azalea Adair opened a tiny, worn purse and drew out a dollar bill, with the upper right-hand corner missing, torn in two pieces and pasted together again with a strip of blue tissue paper. It was one of the bills I had given the piratical Negro—there was no doubt of it.

"Go up to Mr. Baker's store on the corner, Impy," she said, handing the girl the dollar bill, "and get me a quarter of a pound of tea—the kind he always sends me—and ten cents' worth of sugar cakes. Now, hurry. The supply of tea in the house happens to be exhausted," she explained to me.

Impy left by the back way. Before the scrape of her hard, bare feet had died away on the back porch, a wild shriek—I was sure it was hers—filled the hollow house. Then the deep, gruff tones of an angry man's voice mingled with the girl's further squeals and unintelligible words.

Azalea Adair rose without surprise or emotion and disappeared. For two minutes I heard the hoarse rumble of the man's voice; then something like an oath and a slight scuffle, and she returned calmly to her chair.

"This is a roomy house," she said, "and I have a tenant for part of it. I am sorry to have to rescind my invitation to tea. It was impossible to get the kind I always use at the store. Perhaps tomorrow Mr. Baker will be able to supply me."

I was sure that Impy had not had time to leave the house. I inquired concerning street-car lines and took my leave. After I was well on my way I remembered that I had not learned Azalea Adair's name. But tomorrow would do.

That same day I started in on the course of iniquity that this uneventful city forced upon me. I was in the town only two days, but in that time I managed to lie shamelessly by telegraph, and to be an accomplice — after the fact, if that is the correct legal term — to a murder.

As I rounded the corner nearest my hotel the Afrite coachman of the polychromatic, nonpareil coat seized me, swung open the dungeony door of his peripatetic sarcophagus, flirted his feather duster, and began his ritual: "Step right in, boss. Carriage is clean — jus' got back from a funeral. Fifty cents to any —"

And then he knew me and grinned broadly. " 'Scuse me, boss; you is de gen'l'man what rid out with me dis mawnin'. Thank you kindly, suh."

"I am going out to eight-sixty-one again tomorrow afternoon at three," said I, "and if you will be here, I'll let you drive me. So you know Miss Adair?" I concluded, thinking of my dollar bill.

"I belonged to her father, Judge Adair, suh," he replied.

"I judge that she is pretty poor," I said. "She hasn't much money to speak of, has she?"

For an instant I looked again at the fierce countenance of King Cetewayo, and then he changed back to an extortionate old Negro hack-driver.

"She ain't gwine to starve, suh," he said slowly. "She has reso'ces, suh; she has reso'ces."

"I shall pay you fifty cents for the trip," said I.

"Dat is puffeckly correct, suh," he answered humbly. "I jus' *had* to have dat two dollars dis mawnin', boss."

I went to the hotel and lied by electricity. I wired the magazine: "A. Adair holds out for eight cents a word."

The answer that came back was: "Give it to her quick, you duffer."

Just before dinner "Major" Wentworth Caswell bore down upon me with the greetings of a long-lost friend. I have seen few men whom I have so instantaneously hated, and of whom it was so difficult to be rid. I was standing at the bar when he invaded me; therefore I could not wave the white ribbon in his face. I would have paid gladly for the drinks, hoping, thereby to escape another; but he was one of those despicable, roaring, advertising bibbers who must have brass bands and fireworks attend upon every cent that they waste in their follies.

With an air of producing millions he drew two one-dollar bills from a pocket and dashed one of them upon the bar. I looked once more at the dollar bill with the upper right-hand corner missing, torn through the middle, and patched with a strip of blue tissue paper. It was my dollar bill again. It could have been no other.

I went up to my room. The drizzle and the monotony of a dreary, eventless Southern town had made me tired and listless. I remember that just before I went to bed I mentally disposed of the mysterious dollar bill (which might have formed the clue to a tremendously fine detective story of San Francisco) by saying to myself sleepily: "Seems as if a lot of people here own stock in the Hack-Driver's Trust. Pays dividends promptly, too. Wonder if —" Then I fell asleep.

King Cetewayo was at his post the next day, and rattled my bones over the stones out to eight-sixty-one. He was to wait and rattle me back again when I was ready.

Azalea Adair looked paler and cleaner and frailer than she had looked on the day before. After she had signed the contract at eight cents per word, she grew still paler and began to slip out of her chair. Without much trouble I managed to get her up on the antediluvian horsehair sofa and then I ran out to the sidewalk and yelled to the coffee-colored pirate to bring a doctor. With a wisdom that I had not suspected in him, he abandoned his team and struck off up the street afoot, realizing the value of speed. In ten minutes he returned with a grave, gray-haired, and capable man of medicine. In a few words (worth much less than eight cents each) I explained to him my presence in the hollow house of mystery. He bowed with stately understanding and turned to the old Negro.

"Uncle Caesar," he said calmly, "run up to my house and ask Miss Lucy to give you a cream pitcher full of fresh milk and half a tumbler of port wine. And hurry back. Don't drive — run. I want you to get back sometime this week."

It occurred to me that Dr. Merriman also felt a distrust as to the speeding powers of the land-pirate's steeds. After Uncle Caesar was gone, lumberingly, but swiftly, up the street, the doctor looked me over with great politeness and as much careful calculation until he had decided that I might do.

"It is only a case of insufficient nutrition," he said. "In other words, the result of poverty, pride, and starvation. Mrs. Caswell has many devoted friends who would be glad to aid her, but she will accept nothing except from that old Negro, Uncle Caesar, who was once owned by her family."

"Mrs. Caswell!" said I, in surprise. And then I looked at the contract and saw that she had signed it "Azalea Adair Caswell."

"I thought she was Miss Adair," said I.

"Married to a drunken, worthless loafer, sir," said the doctor. "It is said that he robs her even of the small sums that her old servant contributes toward her support."

When the milk and wine had been brought, the doctor soon revived Azalea Adair. She sat up and talked of the beauty of the autumn leaves that were then in season, and their height of color. She referred lightly to her fainting seizure as the outcome of an old palpitation of the heart. Impy fanned her as she lay on the sofa. The doctor was due elsewhere, and I followed him to the door. I told him that it was within my power and intentions to make a reasonable advance of money to Azalea Adair on future contributions to the magazine, and he seemed pleased.

"By the way," he said, "perhaps you would like to know that you have had royalty for a coachman. Old Caesar's grandfather was a king in Congo. Caesar himself has royal ways, as you may have observed."

As the doctor was moving off I heard Uncle Caesar's voice inside: "Did he git bofe of them two dollars from you, Mis' Zalea?"

"Yes, Caesar," I heard Azalea Adair answer weakly.

And then I went in and concluded business negotiations with our contributor. I assumed the responsibility of advancing fifty dollars, putting it as a necessary formality in binding our bargain. And then Uncle Caesar drove me back to the hotel.

Here ends all of the story as far as I can testify as a witness. The rest must be only bare statements of facts.

At about six o'clock I went out for a stroll. Uncle Caesar was at his corner. He threw the door of his carriage, flourished his duster, and began his depressing formula: "Step right in, suh. Fifty cents to anywhere in the city—hack's puffickly clean, suh—jus' back from a funeral—"

And then he recognized me. I think his eyesight was getting bad. His coat had taken on a few more faded shades of color, the twine strings were more frayed and ragged, the last remaining button—the button of yellow horn—was gone. A motley descendant of kings was Uncle Caesar!

About two hours later I saw an excited crowd besieging the front door of the drug store. In a desert where nothing happens this was manna; so I edged my way inside. On an extemporized couch of empty boxes and chairs was stretched the mortal corporeality of Major Wentworth Caswell. A doctor was testing him for the immortal ingredient. His decision was that it was conspicuous by its absence.

The erstwhile Major had been found dead on a dark street and brought by curious and ennuied citizens to the drug store. The late human being had been engaged in terrific battle—the details showed that. Loafer and reprobate though he had been, he had been also a warrior. But he had lost. His hands were yet clinched so tightly that his fingers would not be opened. The gentle citizens who had known him stood about and searched their vocabularies to find some good words, if it were possible, to speak of him. One kind-looking man said, after much thought: "When 'Cas' was about fo'teen he was one of the best spellers in school."

While I stood there the fingers of the right hand of "the man that was," which hung down the side of a white-pine box, relaxed, and dropped something at my feet. I covered it with one foot quickly, and a little later on I picked it up and pocketed it. I reasoned that in his last struggle his hand must have seized that object unwittingly and held it in a death grip.

At the hotel that night the main topic of conversation, with the possible exceptions of politics and prohibition, was the demise of Major Caswell. I heard one man say to a group of listeners:

"In my opinion, gentlemen, Caswell was murdered by some of those no-account niggers for his money. He had fifty dollars this afternoon which he showed to several gentlemen in the hotel. When he was found the money was not on his person."

I left the city the next morning at nine, and as the train was crossing the bridge over the Cumberland River, I took out of my pocket a yellow-horn overcoat button the size of a fifty-cent piece, with frayed ends of coarse twine hanging from it, and cast it out of the window into the slow, muddy waters below.

I wonder what's doing in Buffalo!

THE PAWNSHOP[1]

John S. Sexton

She came to the Jew's place on a night in late November. It had been raining all that day and toward evening a raw robustrious wind came in from the sea. Outside the Jew's tiny refuge, his pawnshop, the icy flood from gray heavens was flung with the velocity of silver spears along Crew Street; the ancient thoroughfare drummed with mighty beat of it. Water boiled along the gutters and foamed at the ancient filth congested there; rejected food scraps, stale newspapers, bits of rusty clothing, and much which was plain untidy dirt. In that weather and at that hour no lights showed along Crew Street, but all its people knew the Jew's place and every one knew that he was accessible at all hours.

The Jew sat drowsing over a newspaper written in the language of his people. He was nearsighted and his rheumed eyes blinked at the sheet through thick spectacles perched on the bridge of his high-arched nose. A pot-bellied stove filled with sea coal warmed him. Its ridiculous swollen sides were red with heat, and heat radiated blisteringly through the stuffy room, but the Jew was old and the slow cold blood in his veins found comfort in the unbearable place.

The wind was out of the northwest that night, and the door of

[1]*The Catholic World*, Copyright, 1926, by The Missionary Society of St. Paul the Apostle in the State of New York. By Permission.

his rusty shop opened outward; so when the girl came in the door slammed shut behind her with a vicious cheated force. The ramshackle place shook with the impact and waked him from his musing. She stood at the threshold, a slender half-drowned wisp of a girl, coughing and holding a nondescript cloak about her narrow chest.

The Jew lifted himself from his stool and shuffled unsteadily behind his counter. He stood there waiting for her, fingering thoughtfully the fringe of his long white-shot beard. She was not of Crew Street. He knew Crew Street, and she was different. He looked at her through his nickel-rimmed spectacles with his habitual expression of dim kindliness. "Yes?" he said with a rising inflection.

Then, her eyes avoiding his face, the girl drew her hand from under her cloak and showed what it had concealed. She held up before him a string of pearls, let him look at them for a moment, then let them fall into the ruck on his counter. The pawnbroker, for all his humble calling, had the fine instinct of the born lapidary. Even before his palsied fingers had picked up the string from the plush-bottomed watch box, where it had fallen, he knew the pearls were not genuine. But he held the beads, caressing them with his moving fingers, and saying nothing. She coughed, a dry unnatural little sound, sheer nervousness, but either could not or would not be the first to speak.

"To borrow or to sell?" he asked gently.

"To borrow, please," she answered.

"These are synthetic," said the Jew, who, watching her closely, saw her face blanch. In this shop it had happened this way so many, many times, but the girl was so young—her white-faced distress bothered the gentle old man. He spread his hands in a wide Semitic gesture. "If they were genuine," he explained with gentle courtesy, "they would be worth much, perhaps thousands and thousands of dollars. These are worth," he hesitated, "possibly forty dollars."

She threw her right hand over her heart, and looked him through and through, her dark eyes enormous in her small rain-drenched face. Each was unreal to the other, the Christian, a bit of flotsam tossed by the storm into a Jew's pawnshop, the Jew with the face of Anton Lang. By every tradition in his class and race, as she had been taught them, he must be deceiving. Yet intuitively she knew he was speaking the truth. There was no guile in that venerable old face which looked so like the illustrations she had seen in a dog-eared, forgotten book in her mother's house.

The odd mingling of supplication and contempt in her attitude changed and became apparent in her face. She flung the cloak over her shoulder; its damp heaviness oppressed her.

"What shall I do?" she asked in her low, suppressed voice.

The old man looked at her sorrowfully. She was so young. If she had volunteered the story of the reason for her need he would have suspected her. But in his experience her very silence was proof of her suffering sincerity. His fumbling fingers handling the beads found a striking peculiarity in their arrangement, and he raised them closer to his nearsighted gaze. They were arranged, he noted, not in a straight uninterrupted coil, but in sequences; there were ten, then one, ten, then one. This occurred five times; then the string met and joined, and from their intersection depended four pearls and a cross. Interested, the Jew lifted the cross and studied the figure, the figure of a Man naked except for a loin cloth. His hands fixed at the arms of the cross. The old man thought he understood this, he had heard of this. But he was not sure.

"Tell me," he asked her gently, "why are the pearls arranged in this form? What is this?"

A slow dull red showed against the ivory whiteness of her skin and he knew he had displeased her.

"If you do not wish to tell me . . ." said the Jew quickly.

"It's a rosary," the girl whispered.

The old man looked at her, musingly. "And you come to me with this?"

The iron restraint the girl had imposed on herself broke. She took one step toward him and gripped the counter; the knuckles of her two hands showed white under the pressure. "Give me back my beads," she flashed at him, sobbing. "Oh, if I'd ever known it would be like this! Give me my beads and let me go."

The old man pushed the skull cap to the back of his head, exposing the bald spot at the crown. His thin fingers thoughtfully explored the wilderness of his great untidy beard and the look he fixed on her was full of pity.

"How much must you have?" he asked softly.

She spoke rapidly and nervously. "I thought it would be easy. My mother thought these were worth hundreds, you know such things happen. Even if I sold them they would not bring what I need and I shall never, never sell them." The unhappy young voice softened. "You've been kind to me but you cannot help me. Please give them to me and let me go."

"Would fifty dollars be enough," the old man persisted gently.

"Oh, yes," the girl said breathlessly.

The dim eyes looked at her for a long moment through the comic spectacles. Then the Jew nodded as if satisfied at what he had found. He stooped beneath his counter, picked at some recess invisible to her from where she stood, and emerged with a small drawer heaped with a miscellany composed of wrinkled bills, copper pledge medals, and coins from many lands. His shaking fingers separated some bills from the untidy heap and pushed them across to her. But, even yet, she could not believe it.

"I cannot sell," she reminded him piteously.

"I know," he nodded gravely.

"You have not even asked me why I need this."

He smiled with his eyes. "Your need is great, that is enough."

She picked up the money and thrust it deep in an inner pocket of the cloak. "You are so good," she said humbly.

The old man lowered his head. He heard the door close and knew she must be gone. Then he set his elbows on the counter, and resting his venerable beard in his cupped hands stared at the rosary. The murky gleam from the worn filaments of the light above him showed on the pretty thing on which he had just loaned money in excess of its market worth. The crucifix fascinated him; he had seen one before; he had never handled one or seen it so close. His brow set in wrinkles of deepest abstraction and for a long time, in the silence of his little shop, he looked at the Man on the cross. Then he sighed.

"God," he said to himself, deeply troubled, "one God, God of Abraham, and Isaac, and Jacob, tell me, have I done wrong?"

A CHRISTMAS PRESENT FOR A LADY[1]

Myra Kelly

It was the week before Christmas, and the First-Reader Class, in a lower East-Side school, had, almost to a man, decided on the gifts to be lavished on "Teacher." She was quite unprepared for any such observance on the part of her small adherents, for her first study of the roll book had shown her that its numerous Jacobs, Isidores, and Rachels belonged to a class to which Christmas Day was much as other days. And so she went serenely on her way, all unconscious of the swift and strict relation between her manner and her chances. She was, for instance, the only person in the room who did not know that her criticism of Isidore Belchatosky's hands and face cost her a tall "three for ten cents" candlestick and a plump box of candy.

But Morris Mogilewsky, whose love for Teacher was far greater than the combined loves of all the other children, had as yet no present to bestow. That his "kind feeling" should be without proof when the lesser loves of Isadore Wishnewsky, Sadie Gonorowsky, and Bertha Binderwitz were taking the tangible but surprising forms which were daily exhibited to his confidential gaze was more than he could bear. The knowledge saddened all his hours, and was the more maddening because it could in no wise be shared by Teacher, who noticed his altered bearing and tried with all sorts of artful beguilements to make him happy and at ease. But her efforts served only to increase his unhappiness and his love. And he loved her! Oh, how he loved her! Since first his dreading eyes had clung for a breath's space to her "like man's shoes" and had then crept timidly upward past a black skirt, a "from silk" apron, a red "jumper," and "from gold" chain to her "light face," she had been mistress of his heart of hearts. That was more than three months ago. How well he remembered the day!

His mother had washed him horribly, and had taken him into the big red schoolhouse, so familiar from the outside, but so full of unknown terrors within. After his dusty little shoes had stumbled

[1]From *Little Citizens* by Myra Kelly, copyright 1902, 1904, 1924, by permission of Doubleday, Doran and Company, Inc.

over the threshold he had passed from ordeal to ordeal until, at last, he was torn in mute and white-faced despair from his mother's skirts.

He was then dragged through long halls and up tall stairs by a large boy, who spoke to him disdainfully as "greenie," and cautioned him as to the laying down softly and taking up gently of those poor, dusty shoes, so that his spirit was quite broken and his nerves were all unstrung when he was pushed into a room full of bright sunshine and of children who laughed at his frightened little face. The sunshine smote his timid eyes, the laughter smote his timid heart, and he turned to flee. But the door was shut, the large boy gone, and despair took him for its own.

Down upon the floor he dropped, and wailed, and wept, and kicked. It was then that he heard, for the first time, the voice which now he loved. A hand was forced between his aching body and the floor, and the voice said.

"Why, my dear little chap, you mustn't cry like that. What's the matter?"

The hand was gentle and the question kind, and these, combined with a faint perfume suggestive of drug stores and barber shops—but nicer than either—made him uncover his hot little face. Kneeling beside him was a lady, and he forced his eyes to that perilous ascent; from shoes to skirt, from skirt to jumper, from jumper to face, they trailed in dread uncertainty, but at the face they stopped—they had found rest.

Morris allowed himself to be gathered into the lady's arms and held upon her knee, and when his sobs no longer rent the very foundations of his pink and wide-spread tie, he answered her question in a voice as soft as his eyes, and as gently sad.

"I ain't so big, and I don't know where is my mama."

So, having cast his troubles on the shoulders of the lady, he had added his throbbing head to the burden, and from that safe retreat had enjoyed his first day at school immensely.

Thereafter he had been the first to arrive every morning, and the last to leave every afternoon; and under the care of Teacher, his liege lady, he had grown in wisdom and love and happiness, but the greatest of these was love. And now, when the other boys and girls were planning surprises and gifts of price for Teacher, his hands were as empty as his heart was full. Appeal to his mother met with denial prompt and energetic.

"For what you go und make, over Christmas, presents? You ain't no Krisht; you should better have no kind feelings over Krishts, neither; your papa could to have a mad."

"Teacher ain't no Krisht," said Morris stoutly; "all the other fellows buys her presents, and I'm loving mit her, too; it's polite I gives her presents the while I'm got such a kind feeling over her."

"Well, we ain't got no money for buy nothings," said Mrs. Mogilewsky sadly. "No money, und your papa, he has all times a scare he shouldn't to get no more, the while the boss"—and here followed incomprehensible, but depressing, financial details, until the end of the interview found Morris and his mother sobbing and rocking in each other's arms. So Morris was helpless, his mother poor, and Teacher all unknowing.

And now the great day, the Friday before Christmas, has come, and the school is, for the first half hour, quite mad. Doors open suddenly and softly to admit small persons, clad in wondrous ways and bearing wondrous parcels. Room 18, generally so placid and so peaceful, is a howling wilderness full of brightly colored, quickly changing groups of children, all whispering, all gurgling, and all hiding queer bundles. A newcomer invariably causes a diversion; the assembled multitude, athirst for novelty, falls upon him and clamors for a glimpse of his bundle and a statement of its price.

Teacher watches in dumb amaze. What can be the matter with the children? They can't have guessed that the shrouded something in the corner is a Christmas tree? What makes them behave so queerly, and why do they look so strange? They seem to have grown stout in a single night, and Teacher, as she notes this, marvels greatly. The explanation is simple, though it comes in alarming form. The sounds of revelry are pierced by a long, shrill yell, and a pair of agitated legs spring suddenly into view between two desks. Teacher, rushing to the rescue, notes that the legs form the unsteady stem of an upturned mushroom of brown flannel and green braid, which she recognizes as the outward seeming of her cherished Bertha Binderwitz; and yet, when the desks are forced to disgorge their prey, the legs restored to their normal position are found to support a fat child—and Bertha was best described as "skinny"—in a dress of the Stuart tartan tastefully trimmed with purple. Investigation proves that Bertha's accumulative taste in dress is an established custom. In nearly all cases the glory of holiday attire is hung upon the solid foundation of everyday clothes as bunting is hung upon a building. The habit is economical of time, and produces a charming embonpoint.

Teacher, too, is more beautiful than ever. Her dress is blue, and "very long down, like a lady," with bands of silk and scraps of lace distributed with the eye of art. In her hair she wears a bow of what Sadie Gonorowsky, whose father "works by fancy goods," describes as "black from plush ribbon — cost ten cents."

Isidore Belchatosky, relenting, is the first to lay tribute before Teacher. He comes forward with a sweet smile and a tall candlestick — the candy has gone to its long home — and Teacher for a moment cannot be made to understand that all that length of bluish-white china is really hers "for keeps."

"It's tomorrow holiday," Isidore assures her; "and we give you presents, the while we have a kind feeling. Candlesticks could to cost twenty-five cents."

"It's a lie. Three for ten," says a voice in the background, but Teacher hastens to respond to Isidore's test of her credulity:

"Indeed, they could. This candlestick could have cost fifty cents, and it's just what I want. It is very good of you to bring me a present."

"You're welcome," says Isidore, retiring; and then, the ice being broken, the First Reader Class in a body rises to cast its gifts on Teacher's desk, and its arms around Teacher's neck.

Nathan Horowitz presents a small cup and saucer; Isidore Applebaum bestows a large calendar for the year before last; Sadie Gonorowsky brings a basket containing a bottle of perfume, a thimble, and a bright silk handkerchief; Sara Schrodsky offers a pen wiper and a yellow celluloid collar button, and Eva Kidansky gives an elaborate nasal douche, under the pleasing delusion that it is an atomizer.

Once more sounds of grief reach Teacher's ears. Rushing again to the rescue, she throws open the door and comes upon woe personified. Eva Gonorowsky, her hair in wildest disarray, her stocking fouled, ungartered, and down-gyved to her ankle, appears before her teacher. She bears all the marks of Hamlet's excitement, and many more, including a tear-stained little face and a gilt saucer clasped to a panting breast.

"Eva, my dearest Eva, what's happened to you *now?*" asks Teacher, for the list of ill chances which have befallen this one of her charges is very long. And Eva wails forth that a boy, a very big boy, had stolen her golden cup "what I had for you by present," and has left her only the saucer and her undying love to bestow.

Before Eva's sobs have quite yielded to Teacher's arts, Jacob Spitsky presses forward with a tortoise-shell comb of terrifying aspect and hungry teeth, and an air showing forth a determination to adjust it in its destined place. Teacher meekly bows her head; Jacob forces his offering into her long-suffering hair, and then retires with the information, "Cost fifteen cents, Teacher," and the courteous phrase — by etiquette prescribed — "Wish you health to wear it." He is plainly a hero, and is heard remarking to less favored admirers that "Teacher's hair is awful softy, and smells off of perfumery."

Here a big boy, a very big boy, enters hastily. He does not belong to Room 18, but he has long known Teacher. He has brought her a present; he wishes her a merry Christmas. The present, when produced, proves to be a pretty gold cup, and Eva Gonorowsky, with renewed emotion, recognizes the boy as her assailant and the cup as her property. Teacher is dreadfully embarrassed; the boy not at all so. His policy is simple and entire denial, and in this he perseveres, even after Eva's saucer has unmistakably proclaimed its relationship to the cup.

Meanwhile the rush of presentation goes steadily on. Other cups and saucers come in wild profusion. The desk is covered with them, and their wrappings of purple tissue paper require a monitor's whole attention. The soap, too, becomes urgently perceptible. It is of all sizes, shapes, and colors, but of uniform and dreadful power of perfume. Teacher's eyes fill with tears — of gratitude — as each new piece, or box, is pressed against her nose, and Teacher's mind is full of wonder as to what she can ever do with all of it. Bottles of perfume vie with one another and with the all-pervading soap until the air is heavy and breathing grows laborious, while pride swells the hearts of the assembled multitude. No other teacher has so many helps to the toilet. None other is so beloved.

Teacher's aspect is quite changed, and the "blue long down like a lady dress" is almost hidden by the offerings she has received. Jacob's comb has two massive and bejeweled rivals in the "softy hair." The front of the dress, where aching or despondent heads are wont to rest, is glittering with campaign buttons of American celebrities, beginning with James G. Blaine and extending into modern history as far as Patrick Divver, Admiral Dewey, and Captain Dreyfus. Outside the blue belt is a white one, nearly clean, and bearing in "sure 'nough golden words" the curt, but stirring, invitation, "Remember the Maine." Around the neck are three chaplets of beads, wrought by chubby fingers and embodying much love, while the waistline is further adorned by tiny and beribboned aprons. Truly, it is a day of triumph.

When the wastepaper basket has been twice filled with wrappings and twice emptied; when order is emerging out of chaos; when the Christmas tree has been disclosed and its treasures distributed, a timid hand is laid on Teacher's knee and a plaintive voice whispers, "Say, Teacher, I got something for you"; and Teacher turns quickly to see Morris, her dearest boy charge, with his poor little body showing quite plainly between his shirtwaist buttons and through the gashes he calls pockets. This is his ordinary costume, and the funds of the house of Mogilewsky are evidently unequal to an outer layer of finery.

"Now, Morris, dear," says Teacher, "you shouldn't have troubled to get me a present; you know you and I are such good friends that —"

"Teacher, yis, ma'am," Morris interrupts, in a bewitching rising inflection of his soft and plaintive voice; "I know you got a kind feeling by me, and I couldn't to tell even how I'm got a kind feeling by you. Only it's about that kind feeling I should give you a present. I didn't" — with a glance at the crowded desk — "I didn't to have no soap nor no perfumery, and my mama, she couldn't to buy none by the store; but Teacher, I'm got something awful nice for you by present."

"And what is it, deary?" asks the already rich and gifted young person. "What is my new present?"

"Teacher, it's like this: I don't know; I ain't so big like I could to know" — and, truly, God pity him! he is passing small — "it ain't for boys — it's for ladies. Over yesterday on the night comes my papa on my house, and he gives my mama the present. Sooner she looks on it, sooner she has a awful glad; in her eye stands tears, und she says, like that — out of Jewish — 'Thanks,' un' she kisses my papa a kiss. Und my papa, *how* he is polite! he says — out of Jewish, too — 'You're welcome, all right,' un' he kisses my mama a kiss. So my mama, she sets and looks on the present, und all the time she looks she has a glad over it. Und I didn't to have no soap, so you could to have the present."

"But did your mother say I might?"

"Teacher, no ma'am; she didn't say like that un' she didn't to say *not* like that. She didn't to know. But it's for ladies, un' I didn't to have no soap. You could to look on it. It ain't for boys."

And here Morris opens a hot little hand and discloses a tightly-folded pinkish paper. As Teacher reads it he watches her with eager, furtive eyes, dry and bright, until hers grow suddenly moist, when his promptly follow suit. As she looks down at him, he makes his moan once more:

"It's for ladies, und I didn't to have no soap."

"But, Morris, dear," cries Teacher unsteadily, laughing a little, and yet not far from tears, "This is ever so much nicer than soap — a thousand times better than perfume; and you're quite right, it is for ladies, and I never had one in all my life before. I am so very thankful."

"You're welcome, all right. That's how my papa says; it's polite," says Morris proudly. And proudly he takes his place among the very little boys, and loudly he joins in the ensuing song. For the rest of that exciting day he is a shining point of virtue in a slightly confused class. And at three o'clock he is at Teacher's desk again, carrying on the conversation as if there had been no interruption.

"Und my mama," he says insinuatingly — "she kisses my papa a kiss."

"Well?" says Teacher.

"Well," says Morris, "you ain't never kissed me a kiss, und I seen how you kissed Eva Gonorowsky. I'm loving mit you too. Why don't you never kiss me a kiss?"

"Perhaps," suggests Teacher mischievously, "perhaps it ain't for boys."

But a glance at her "light face," with its crown of surprising combs, reassures him.

"Teacher, yis, ma'am; it's for boys," he cries as he feels her arms about him, and sees that in her eyes, too, "stands tears."

"It's polite you kisses me a kiss over that for ladies' present."

Late that night Teacher sat in her pretty room — for she was, unofficially a greatly pampered young person — and reviewed her treasures. She saw that they were very numerous, very touching, very whimsical, and very precious. But above all the rest she cherished a frayed pinkish paper, rather crumpled and a little soiled. For it held the love of a man and woman and a little child, and the magic of a home, for Morris Mogilewsky's Christmas present for ladies was the receipt for a month's rent for a room on the top floor of a Monroe Street tenement.

THE FATHER[1]

Björnstjerne Björnson

The man whose story is here to be told was the wealthiest and most influential person in his parish; his name was Thord Overaas. He appeared in the priest's study one day, tall and earnest.

"I have gotten a son," said he, "and I wish to present him for baptism."

"What shall his name be?"

"Finn — after my father."

"And the sponsors?"

They were mentioned, and proved to be the best men and women of Thord's relations in the parish.

"Is there anything else?" inquired the priest, and looked up.

The peasant hesitated a little.

"I should like very much to have him baptized by himself," said he finally.

"That is to say on a week day?"

[1]Used by permission of the translator, Professor R. B. Anderson, Madison, Wisconsin.

"Next Saturday, at twelve o'clock noon."

"Is there anything else?" inquired the priest.

"There is nothing else"; and the peasant twirled his cap, as though he were about to go.

Then the priest arose. "There is yet this, however," said he and walking toward Thord, he took him by the hand and looked gravely into his eyes: "God grant that the child may become a blessing to you!"

One day sixteen years later, Thord stood once more in the priest's study.

"Really, you carry your age astonishingly well, Thord," said the priest; for he saw no change whatever in the man.

"That is because I have no troubles," replied Thord.

To this the priest said nothing, but after a while he asked: "What is the pleasure this evening?"

"I have come this evening about that son of mine who is to be confirmed tomorrow."

"He is a bright boy."

"I did not wish to pay the priest until I heard what number the boy would have when he takes his place in church tomorrow."

"He will stand number one."

"So I have heard; and here are ten dollars for the priest."

"Is there anything else I can do for you?" inquired the priest, fixing his eyes on Thord.

"There is nothing else."

Thord went out.

Eight years more rolled by, and then one day a noise was heard outside of the priest's study, for many men were approaching, and at their head was Thord, who entered first.

The priest looked up and recognized him.

"You come well attended this evening, Thord," said he.

"I am here to request that the banns may be published for my son; he is about to marry Karen Storliden, daughter of Gudmund, who stands here beside me."

"Why, that is the richest girl in the parish."

"So they say," replied the peasant, stroking back his hair with one hand.

The priest sat a while as if in deep thought, then entered the names in his book, without making any comments, and the men wrote their signatures underneath. Thord laid three dollars on the table.

"One is all I am to have," said the priest.

"I know that very well; but he is my only child; I want to do it handsomely."

The priest took the money.

"This is now the third time, Thord, that you have come here on your son's account."

"But now I am through with him," said Thord, and folding up his pocketbook he said farewell and walked away.

The men slowly followed him.

A fortnight later, the father and son were rowing across the lake, one calm day, to Storliden to make arrangements for the wedding.

"This thwart is not secure," said the son, and stood up to straighten the seat on which he was sitting.

At the same moment the board he was standing on slipped from under him; he threw out his arms, uttered a shriek, and fell overboard.

"Take hold of the oar!" shouted the father, springing to his feet and holding out the oar.

But when the son had made a couple of efforts he grew stiff.

"Wait a moment!" cried the father, and began to row toward his son.

Then the son rolled over on his back, gave his father one long look, and sank.

Thord could scarcely believe it; he held the boat still, and stared at the spot where his son had gone down, as though he must surely come to the surface. There rose some bubbles, then some more, and finally one large one that burst; and the lake lay there as smooth and bright as a mirror again.

For three days and three nights people saw the father rowing round and round the spot, without taking either food or sleep; he was dragging the lake for the body of his son. And toward morning of the third day he found it, and carried it in his arms up over the hills to his gard.

It might have been about a year from that day, when the priest, late one autumn evening, heard someone in the passage outside the door, carefully trying to find the latch. The priest opened the door, and in walked a tall, thin man, with bowed form and white hair. The priest looked long at him before he recognized him. It was Thord.

"Are you out walking so late?" said the priest, and stood still in front of him.

"Ah, yes! it is late," said Thord, and took a seat.

The priest sat down also, as though waiting. A long, long silence followed. At last Thord said:

"I have something with me that I would like to give to the poor; I want it to be invested as a legacy in my son's name."

He rose, laid some money on the table, and sat down again. The priest counted it.

"It is a great deal of money," said he.

"It is half the price of my gard. I sold it today."

The priest sat long in silence. At last he asked, but gently:

"What do you propose to do now, Thord?"

"Something better."

They sat there for a while, Thord with downcast eyes, the priest with his eyes fixed on Thord. Presently the priest said, slowly and softly:

"I think your son has at last brought you a true blessing."

"Yes, I think so myself," said Thord, looking up while two big tears coursed slowly down his cheeks.

THE SIRE DE MALÉTROIT'S DOOR[1]

Robert Louis Stevenson

Denis de Beaulieu was not yet two-and-twenty, but he counted himself a grown man, and a very accomplished cavalier into the bargain. Lads were early formed in that rough, warfaring epoch; and when one has been in a pitched battle and a dozen raids, has killed one's man in an honorable fashion, and knows a thing or

[1]By permission of Charles Scribner's Sons.

two of strategy and mankind, a certain swagger in the gait is surely to be pardoned. He had put up his horse with due care, and supped with due deliberation; and then, in a very agreeable frame of mind, went out to pay a visit in the gray of the evening. It was not a very wise proceeding on the young man's part. He would have done better to remain beside the fire or go decently to bed. For the town was full of the troops of Burgundy and England under a mixed command; and though Denis was there on safe-conduct, his safe-conduct was like to serve him little on a chance encounter.

It was September, 1429; the weather had fallen sharp; a flighty piping wind, laden with showers, beat about the township; and the dead leaves ran riot along the streets. Here and there a window was already lighted up; and the noise of men-at-arms making merry over supper within, came forth in fits and was swallowed up and carried away by the wind. The night fell swiftly; the flag of England, fluttering on the spire-top, grew ever fainter and fainter against the flying clouds — a black speck like a swallow in the tumultuous, leaden chaos of the sky. As the night fell the wind rose, and began to hoot under archways and roar amid the treetops in the valley below the town.

Denis de Beaulieu walked fast and was soon knocking at his friend's door; but though he promised himself to stay only a little while and make an early return, his welcome was so pleasant, and he found so much to delay him, that it was already long past midnight before he said good-by upon the threshold. The wind had fallen again in the meanwhile; the night was as black as the grave; not a star, nor a glimmer of moonshine, slipped through the canopy of cloud. Denis was ill-acquainted with the intricate lanes of Chateau Landon; even by daylight he had found some trouble in picking his way; and in this absolute darkness he soon lost it altogether. He was certain of one thing only — to keep mounting the hill; for his friend's house lay at the lower end, or tail, of Chateau Landon, while the inn was up at the head, under the great church spire. With this clew to go upon he stumbled and groped forward, now breathing more freely in open spaces where there was a good slice of sky overhead, now feeling along the wall in stifling closes. It is an eerie and mysterious position to be thus submerged in opaque blackness in an almost unknown town. The silence is terrifying in its possibilities. The touch of cold window bars to the exploring hand startles the man like the touch of a toad; the inequalities of the pavement shake his heart into his mouth; a piece of denser darkness threatens an ambuscade or a chasm in the pathway; and where the air is brighter, the houses put on strange and bewildering appearances, as if to lead him farther from his way. For Denis, who had to regain his inn without attracting notice, there was real danger as well as mere discomfort in the walk; and he went warily and boldly at once, and at every corner paused to make an observation.

He had been for some time threading a lane so narrow that he could touch a wall with either hand when it began to open out and go sharply downward. Plainly this lay no longer in the direction of his inn; but the hope of a little more light tempted him forward to reconnoiter. The lane ended in a terrace with a bartizan wall, which gave an outlook between high houses, as out of an embrasure, into the valley lying dark and formless several hundred feet below. Denis looked down, and could discern a few treetops waving and a single speck of brightness where the river ran across a weir. The weather was clearing up, and the sky had lightened, so as to show the outline of the heavier clouds and the dark margin of the hills. By the uncertain glimmer, the house on his left hand should be a place of some pretensions; it was surmounted by several pinnacles and turret-tops; the round stern of a chapel, with a fringe of flying buttresses, projected boldly from the main block; and the door was sheltered under a deep porch carved with figures and overhung by two long gargoyles. The windows of the chapel gleamed through their intricate tracery with a light as of many tapers, and threw out the buttresses and the peaked roof in a more intense blackness against the sky. It was plainly the hotel of some great family of the neighborhood; and as it reminded Denis of a town house of his own at Bourges, he stood for some time gazing up at it and mentally gauging the skill of the architects and the consideration of the two families.

There seemed to be no issue to the terrace but the lane by which he had reached it; he could only retrace his steps, but he had gained some notion of his whereabouts, and hoped by this means to hit the main thoroughfare and speedily regain the inn. He was reckoning without the chapter of accidents which was to make this night memorable above all others in his career; for he had not gone back above a hundred yards before he saw a light coming to meet him, and heard loud voices speaking together in the echoing narrows of the lane. It was a party of men-at-arms going the night round with torches. Denis assured himself that they had all been making free with the wine bowl, and were in no mood to be particular about safe-conducts or the niceties of chivalrous war. It was as like as not that they would kill him like a dog and leave him where he fell. The situation was inspiriting but nervous. Their own torches would conceal him from sight, he reflected; and he hoped that they would drown the noise of his footsteps with their own empty voices. If he were but fleet and silent, he might evade their notice altogether.

Unfortunately, as he turned to beat a retreat, his foot rolled upon a pebble; he fell against the wall with an ejaculation, and his sword rang loudly on the stones. Two or three voices demanded who went there—some in French, some in English; but Denis made no reply, and ran the faster down the lane. Once upon the terrace, he paused to look back. They still kept calling after him, and just then began to double the pace in pursuit, with a considerable clank of armor, and great tossing of the torchlight to and fro in the narrow jaws of the passage.

Denis cast a look around and darted into the porch. There he might escape observation, or—if that were too much to expect—was in a capital posture whether for parley or defense. So thinking, he drew his sword and tried to set his back against the door. To his surprise, it yielded behind his weight; and though he turned in a moment, continued to swing back on oiled and noiseless hinges, until it stood wide open on a black interior. When things fall out opportunely for the person concerned, he is not apt to be critical about the how or why, his own immediate personal convenience seeming a sufficient reason for the strangest oddities and revolutions in our sublunary things; and so Denis, without a moment's hesitation, stepped within and partly closed the door behind him to conceal his place of refuge. Nothing was further from his thoughts than to close it altogether; but for some inexplicable reason—perhaps by a spring or a weight—the ponderous mass of oak whipped itself out of his fingers and clanked to, with a formidable rumble and a noise like the falling of an automatic bar.

The round, at that very moment, debouched upon the terrace and proceeded to summon him with shouts and curses. He heard them ferreting in the dark corners; the stock of a lance even rattled along the outer surface of the door behind which he stood; but these gentlemen were in too high a humor to be long delayed, and soon made off down a corkscrew pathway which had escaped Denis's observation, and passed out of sight and hearing along the battlements of the town.

Denis breathed again. He gave them a few minutes' grace for fear of accidents, and then groped about for some means of opening the door and slipping forth again. The inner surface was quite smooth, not a handle, not a molding, not a projection of any sort. He got his finger nails round the edges and pulled, but the mass was immovable. He shook it, it was as firm as a rock. Denis de Beaulieu frowned and gave vent to a little noiseless whistle. What ailed the door? he wondered. Why was it open? How came it to shut so easily and so effectually after him. There was something obscure and underhand about all this, that was little to the young man's fancy. It looked like a snare; and yet who could suppose a snare in such a quiet by-street and in a house of so prosperous and even noble an exterior. And yet—snare or no snare, intentionally or unintentionally—here he was, prettily trapped; and for the life of him he could see no way out of it again. The darkness began to weigh upon him. He gave ear; all was silent without, but within and close by he seemed to catch a faint sighing, a faint sobbing rustle, a little stealthy creak—as though many persons were at his side, holding themselves quite still, and governing even their respiration with the extreme of slyness. The idea went to his vitals with a shock, and he faced about suddenly as if to defend his life. Then, for the first time, he became aware of a light about the level of his eyes and at some distance in the interior of the house—a vertical thread of light, widening toward the bottom, such as might escape between two wings of arras over a doorway. To see anything was a relief to Denis; it was like a piece of solid ground to a man laboring in a morass; his mind seized upon it with avidity; and he stood staring at it and trying to piece together some logical conception of his surroundings. Plainly there was a flight of steps ascending from his own level to that of this illuminated doorway; and indeed he thought he could make out another thread of light, as fine as a needle and as faint as phosphorescence, which might very well be reflected along the polished wood of a handrail. Since he had begun to suspect that he was not alone, his heart had continued to beat with smothering violence, and an intolerable desire for action of any sort had possessed itself of his spirit. He was in deadly peril, he believed. What could be more natural than to mount the staircase, lift the curtain, and confront his difficulty at once? At least he would be dealing with something tangible; at least he would be no longer in the dark. He stepped slowly forward with outstretched hands, until his foot struck the bottom step; then he rapidly scaled the stairs, stood for a moment to compose his expression, lifted the arras, and went in.

He found himself in a large apartment of polished stone. There were three doors; one on each of three sides; all similarly curtained with tapestry. The fourth side was occupied by two large windows and a great stone chimneypiece, carved with the arms of the Malétroits. Denis recognized the bearing, and was gratified to find himself in such good hands. The room was strongly illuminated; but it contained little furniture except a heavy table and a chair or two, the hearth was innocent of fire, and the pavement was but sparsely strewn with rushes clearly many days old.

On a high chair beside the chimney, and directly facing Denis as he entered, sat a little old gentleman in a fur tippet. He sat with legs crossed and his hands folded, and a cup of spiced wine stood by his elbow on a bracket on the wall. His countenance had a strongly masculine cast; not properly human, but such as we see in the bull, the goat, or the domestic boar; something equivocal and wheedling, something greedy, brutal, and dangerous. The upper lip was inordinately full, as though swollen by a blow or a toothache; and the smile, the peaked eyebrows, and the small, strong eyes were quaintly and almost comically evil in expression. Beautiful white hair hung straight all round his head, like a saint's, and fell in a single curl upon the tippet. His beard and moustache were the pink of venerable sweetness. Age, probably in consequence of inordinate precautions, had left no mark upon his hands; and the Malétroit hand was famous. It would be difficult to imagine anything at once so fleshy and so delicate in design; the taper, sensual fingers were like those of one of Leonardo's women; the fork of the thumb made a dimpled protuberance when closed; the nails were perfectly shaped, and of a dead, surprising whiteness. It rendered his aspect tenfold more redoubtable, that a man with hands like these should keep them devoutly folded like a virgin martyr —that a man with so intent and startling an expression of face should sit patiently on his seat and contemplate people with an unwinking stare, like a god, or a god's statue. His quiescence seemed ironical and treacherous, it fitted so poorly with his looks.

Such was Alain, Sire de Malétroit.

Denis and he looked silently at each other for a second or two.

"Pray step in," said the Sire de Malétroit. "I have been expecting you all the evening."

He had not risen, but he accompanied his words with a smile and a slight but courteous inclination of the head. Partly from the smile, partly from the strange musical murmur with which the Sire prefaced his observation, Denis felt a strong shudder of disgust go through his marrow. And what with disgust and honest confusion of mind, he could scarcely get words together in reply.

"I fear," he said, "that this is a double accident. I am not the person you suppose me. It seems you were looking for a visit; but for my part, nothing was further from my thoughts—nothing could be more contrary to my wishes—than this intrusion."

"Well, well," replied the old gentleman indulgently, "here you are, which is the main point. Seat yourself, my friend, and put yourself entirely at your ease. We shall arrange our little affairs presently."

Denis perceived that the matter was still complicated with some misconception, and he hastened to continue his explanation.

"Your door . . ." he began.

"About my door?" asked the other, raising his peaked eyebrows. "A little piece of ingenuity." And he shrugged his shoulder. "A hospitable fancy! By your own account, you were not desirous of making my acquaintance. We old people look for such reluctance now and then; when it touches our honor, we cast about until we find some way of overcoming it. You arrive uninvited, but, believe me, very welcome."

"You persist in error, sir," said Denis. "There can be no question between you and me. I am a stranger in this countryside. My name is Denis, damoiseau de Beaulieu. If you see me in your house, it is only—"

"My young friend," interrupted the other, "you will permit me to have my own ideas on that subject. They probably differ from yours at the present moment," he added with a leer, "but time will show which of us is in the right."

Denis was convinced he had to do with a lunatic. He seated himself with a shrug, content to wait the upshot; and a pause ensued, during which he thought he could distinguish a hurried gabbing as of prayer from behind the arras immediately opposite him. Sometimes there seemed to be but one person engaged, sometimes two; and the vehemence of the voice, low as it was, seemed to indicate either great haste or an agony of spirit. It occurred to him that this piece of tapestry covered the entrance to the chapel he had noticed from without.

The old gentleman meanwhile surveyed Denis from head to foot with a smile, and from time to time emitted little noises like a bird or a mouse, which seemed to indicate a high degree of satisfaction. This state of matters became rapidly insupportable; and Denis, to put an end to it, remarked politely that the wind had gone down.

The old gentleman fell into a fit of silent laughter, so prolonged and violent that he became quite red in the face. Denis got upon his feet at once, and put on his hat with a flourish.

"Sir," he said, "if you are in your wits, you have affronted me grossly. If you are out of them, I flatter myself I can find better employment for my brains than to talk with lunatics. My conscience is clear; you have made a fool of me from the first moment; you have refused to hear my explanations; and now there is no power under God will make me stay here any longer; and if I cannot make my way out in a more decent fashion, I will hack your door in pieces with my sword."

The Sire de Malétroit raised his right hand and wagged it at Denis with the fore and little fingers extended.

"My dear nephew," he said, "sit down."

"Nephew!" retorted Denis, "you lie in your throat"; and he snapped his fingers in his face.

"Sit down, you rogue!" cried the old gentleman, in a sudden harsh voice, like the barking of a dog. "Do you fancy," he went on, "that when I had made my little contrivance for the door I had stopped short with that? If you prefer to be bound hand and foot till your bones ache, rise and try to go away. If you choose to remain a free young buck, agreeably conversing with an old gentleman — why, sit where you are in peace, and God be with you."

"Do you mean I am a prisoner?" demanded Denis.

"I state the facts," replied the other. "I would rather leave the conclusion to yourself."

Denis sat down again. Externally he managed to keep pretty calm; but within, he was now boiling with anger, now chilled with apprehension. He no longer felt convinced that he was dealing with a madman. And if the old gentleman was sane, what, in God's name, had he to look for? What absurd or tragical adventure had befallen him? What countenance was he to assume?

While he was thus unpleasantly reflecting, the arras that overhung the chapel door was raised, and a tall priest in his robes came forth and, giving a long, keen stare at Denis, said something in an undertone to Sire de Malétroit.

"She is in a better frame of spirit?" asked the latter.

"She is more resigned, messire," replied the priest.

"Now the Lord help her, she is hard to please!" sneered the old gentleman. "A likely stripling — not ill-born — and of her own choosing, too? Why, what more would the jade have?"

"The situation is not usual for a young damsel," said the other, "and somewhat trying to her blushes."

"She should have thought of that before she began the dance! It was none of my choosing, God knows that: but since she is in it, by our lady, she shall carry it to the end." And then addressing Denis, "Monsieur de Beaulieu," he asked, "may I present you to my niece? She has been waiting your arrival, I may say, with even greater impatience than myself."

Denis had resigned himself with a good grace — all he desired was to know the worst of it as speedily as possible; so he rose at once, and bowed in acquiescence. The Sire de Malétroit followed his example and limped, with the assistance of the chaplain's arm, toward the chapel door. The priest pulled aside the arras, and all three entered. The building had considerable architectural pretensions. A light groining sprang from six stout columns, and hung down in two rich pendants from the center of the vault. The place terminated behind the altar in a round end, embossed and honeycombed with a superfluity of ornament in relief, and pierced by many little windows shaped like stars, trefoils, or wheels. These windows were imperfectly glazed, so that the night air circulated freely in the chapel. The tapers, of which there must have been half a hundred burning on the altar, were unmercifully blown about; and the light went through many different phases of brilliancy and semi-eclipse. On the steps in front of the altar knelt a young girl richly attired as a bride. A chill settled over Denis as he observed her costume; he fought with desperate energy against the conclusion that was being thrust upon his mind; it could not — it should not — be as he feared.

"Blanche," said the Sire, in his most flutelike tones, "I have brought a friend to see you, my little girl; turn round and give him your pretty hand. It is good to be devout; but it is necessary to be polite, my niece."

The girl rose to her feet and turned toward the newcomers. She moved all of a piece; and shame and exhaustion were expressed in every line of her fresh young body; and she held her head down and kept her eyes upon the pavement, as she came slowly forward. In the course of her advance, her eyes fell upon Denis de Beaulieu's feet — feet of which he was justly vain, be it remarked, and wore in the most elegant accouterment even while traveling. She paused — started, as if his yellow boots had conveyed some shocking meaning — and glanced suddenly up into the wearer's countenance. Their eyes met, shame gave place to horror and terror in her looks; the blood left her lips; with a piercing scream she covered her face with her hands and sank upon the chapel floor.

"That is not the man!" she cried. "My uncle, that is not the man!"

The Sire de Malétroit chirped agreeably. "Of course not," he said, "I expected as much. It was so unfortunate you could not remember his name."

"Indeed," she cried, "indeed, I have never seen this person till this moment — I have never so much as set eyes upon him — I never wish to see him again. Sir," she said, turning to Denis, "if you are a gentleman, you will bear me out. Have I ever seen you — have you ever seen me — before this accursed hour?"

"To speak for myself, I have never had that pleasure," answered the young man. "This is the first time, messire, that I have met with your engaging niece."

The old gentleman shrugged his shoulders.

"I am distressed to hear it," he said. "But it is never too late to begin. I had little more acquaintance with my own late lady ere

I married her; which proves," he added, with a grimace, "that these impromptu marriages may often produce an excellent understanding in the long run. As the bridegroom is to have a voice in the matter, I will give him two hours to make up for lost time before we proceed with the ceremony." And he turned toward the door, followed by the clergyman.

The girl was on her feet in a moment. "My uncle, you cannot be in earnest," she said. "I declare before God I will stab myself rather than be forced on that young man. The heart rises at it; God forbids such marriages; you dishonor your white hair. Oh, my uncle, pity me! There is not a woman in all the world but would prefer death to such a nuptial. Is it possible," she added, faltering—"is it possible that you do not believe me—that you still think this"—and she pointed at Denis with a tremor of anger and contempt—"that you still think *this* to be the man?"

"Frankly," said the old gentleman, pausing on the threshold, "I do. But let me explain to you once for all, Blanche de Malétroit, my way of thinking about this affair. When you took it into your head to dishonor my family and the name that I have borne, in peace and war, for more than threescore years, you forfeited, not only the right to question my designs, but that of looking me in the face. If your father had been alive, he would have spat on you and turned you out of doors. His was the hand of iron. You may bless your God you have only to deal with the hand of velvet, mademoiselle. It was my duty to get you married without delay. Out of pure goodwill, I have tried to find your own gallant for you. And I believe I have succeeded. But before God and all the holy angels, Blanche de Malétroit, if I have not, I care not one jackstraw. So let me recommend you to be polite to our young friend; for upon my word, your next groom may be less appetizing."

And with that he went out, with the chaplain at his heels; and the arras fell behind the pair.

The girl turned upon Denis with flashing eyes.

"And what, sir," she demanded, "may be the meaning of all this?"

"God knows," returned Denis, gloomily. "I am a prisoner in this house, which seems full of mad people. More I know not; and nothing do I understand."

"And pray how came you here?" she asked.

He told her as briefly as he could. "For the rest," he added, "perhaps you will follow my example, and tell me the answer to all these riddles, and what, in God's name, is like to be the end of it."

She stood silent for a little, and he could see her lips tremble and her tearless eyes burn with a feverish luster. Then she pressed her forehead in both hands.

"Alas, how my head aches!" she said wearily—"to say nothing of my poor heart! But it is due to you to know my story, unmaidenly as it must seem. I am called Blanche de Malétroit; I have been without father or mother for—oh! for as long as I can recollect, and indeed I have been most unhappy all my life. Three months ago a young captain began to stand near me every day in church. I could see that I pleased him; I am much to blame, but I was so glad that anyone should love me; and when he passed me a letter, I took it home with me and read it with great pleasure. Since that time he has written many. He was so anxious to speak with me, poor fellow! and kept asking me to leave the door open some evening that we might have two words upon the stair. For he knew how much my uncle trusted me." She gave something like a sob at that, and it was a moment before she could go on. "My uncle is a hard man, but he is very shrewd," she said at last. "He has performed many feats in war, and was a great person at court, and much trusted by Queen Isabeau in old days. How he came to suspect me I cannot tell; but it is hard to keep anything from his knowledge; and this morning, as we came from Mass, he took my hand into his, forced it open, and read my little billet, walking by my side all the while. When he finished, he gave it back to me with great politeness. It contained another request to have the door left open; and this has been the ruin of us all. My uncle kept me strictly in my room until evening, and then ordered me to dress myself as you see me—a hard mockery for a young girl, do you not think so? I suppose, when he could not prevail with me to tell him the young captain's name, he must have laid a trap for him: into which, alas! you have fallen in the anger of God. I looked for much confusion; for how could I tell whether he was willing to take me for his wife on these sharp terms? He might have been trifling with me from the first; or I might have made myself too cheap in his eyes. But truly I had not looked for such a shameful punishment as this! I could not think that God would let a girl be so disgraced before a young man. And now I tell you all; and I can scarcely hope that you will not despise me."

Denis made her a respectful inclination.

"Madam," he said, "you have honored me by your confidence. It remains for me to prove that I am not unworthy of the honor. Is Messire de Malétroit at hand?"

"I believe he is writing in the salle without," she answered.

"May I lead you thither, madam?" asked Denis, offering his hand with his most courtly bearing.

She accepted it; and the pair passed out of the chapel, Blanche in a very drooping and shamefast condition, but Denis strutting and ruffling in the consciousness of a mission, and the boyish certainty of accomplishing it with honor.

The Sire de Malétroit rose to meet them with an ironical obeisance.

"Sir," said Denis, with the grandest possible air, "I believe I am to have some say in the matter of this marriage; and let me tell you at once, I will be no party to forcing the inclination of this young lady. Had it been freely offered to me, I should have been proud to accept her hand, for I perceive she is as good as she is beautiful; but as things are, I have now the honor, messire, of refusing."

Blanche looked at him with gratitude in her eyes; but the old gentleman only smiled and smiled, until his smile grew positively sickening to Denis.

"I am afraid," he said, "Monsieur de Beaulieu, that you do not perfectly understand the choice I have offered you. Follow me, I beseech you, to this window." And he led the way to one of the large windows which stood open on the night. "You observe," he went on, "there is an iron ring in the upper masonry, and reeved through that, a very efficacious rope. Now, mark my words: if you should find your disinclination to my niece's person insurmountable, I shall have you hanged out of this window before sunrise. I shall only proceed to such an extremity with the greatest regret, you may believe me. For it is not at all your death that I desire, but my niece's establishment in life. At the same time, it must come to that if you prove obstinate. Your family, Monsieur de Beaulieu, is very well in its way; but if you sprang from Charlemagne, you should not refuse the hand of a Malétroit with impunity — not if she had been as common as the Paris road — not if she were as hideous as the gargoyle over my door. Neither my niece nor you, nor my own private feelings, move me at all in this matter. The honor of my house has been compromised; I believe you to be the guilty person, at least you are now in the secret; and you can hardly wonder if I request you to wipe out the stain. If you will not, your blood be on your own head! It will be no great satisfaction to me to have your interesting relics kicking their heels in the breeze below my windows, but half a loaf is better than no bread, and if I cannot cure the dishonor, I shall at least stop the scandal."

There was a pause.

"I believe there are other ways of settling such imbroglios among gentlemen," said Denis. "You wear a sword, and I hear you have used it with distinction."

The Sire de Malétroit made a signal to the chaplain, who crossed the room with long silent strides and raised the arras over the third of the three doors. It was only a moment before he let it fall again; but Denis had time to see a dusky passage full of armed men.

"When I was a little younger, I should have been delighted to honor you, Monsieur de Beaulieu," said Sire Alain; "but I am now too old. Faithful retainers are the sinews of age, and I must employ the strength I have. This is one of the hardest things to swallow as a man grows up in years; but with a little patience, even this becomes habitual. You and the lady seem to prefer the salle for what remains of your two hours; and as I have no desire to cross your preference, I shall resign it to your use with all the pleasure in the world. No haste!" he added, holding up his hand, as he saw a dangerous look come into Denis de Beaulieu's face. "If your mind revolt against hanging, it will be time enough two hours hence to throw yourself out of the window or upon the pikes of my retainers. Two hours of life are always two hours. A great many things may turn up in even as little a while as that. And, besides, if I understand her appearance, my niece has something to say to you. You will not disfigure your last hours by a want of politeness to a lady?"

Denis looked at Blanche, and she made him an imploring gesture.

It is likely that the old gentleman was hugely pleased at this symptom of an understanding; for he smiled on both, and added sweetly: "If you will give me your word of honor, Monsieur de Beaulieu, to await my return at the end of the two hours before attempting anything desperate, I shall withdraw my retainers, and let you speak in greater privacy with mademoiselle."

Denis again glanced at the girl, who seemed to beseech him to agree.

"I give you my word of honor," he said.

Messire de Malétroit bowed, and proceeded to limp about the apartment, clearing his throat the while with that odd musical chirp which had already grown so irritating in the ears of Denis de Beaulieu. He first possessed himself of some papers which lay upon the table; then he went to the mouth of the passage and appeared to give an order to the men behind the arras; and lastly he hobbled out through the door by which Denis had come in, turning upon the threshold to address a last smiling bow to the young couple, and followed by the chaplain with a hand lamp.

No sooner were they alone than Blanche advanced toward Denis with her hands extended. Her face was flushed and excited, and her eyes shone with tears.

"You shall not die!" she cried, "you shall marry me after all."

"You seem to think, madam," replied Denis, "that I stand much in fear of death."

"Oh, no, no," she said, "I see you are no poltroon. It is for my own sake—I could not bear to have you slain for such a scruple."

"I am afraid," returned Denis, "that you underrate the difficulty, madam. What you may be too generous to refuse, I may be too proud to accept. In a moment of noble feeling toward me, you forgot what you perhaps owe to others."

He had the decency to keep his eyes on the floor as he said this, and after he had finished, so as not to spy upon her confusion. She stood silent for a moment, then walked suddenly away, and falling on her uncle's chair, fairly burst out sobbing. Denis was in the acme of embarrassment. He looked round, as if to seek for inspiration, and seeing a stool, plumped down upon it for something to do. There he sat, playing with the guard of his rapier, and wishing himself dead a thousand times over, and buried in the nastiest kitchen-heap in France. His eyes wandered around the apartment, but found nothing to arrest them. There were such wide spaces between furniture, the light fell so badly and cheerlessly over all, the dark outside air looked in so coldly through the windows, that he thought he had never seen a church so vast, nor a tomb so melancholy. The regular sobs of Blanche de Malétroit measured out the time like the ticking of a clock. He read the device upon the shield over and over again, until his eyes became obscured; he stared into shadowy corners until he imagined they were swarming with horrible animals; and every now and again he awoke with a start, to remember that his last two hours were running, and death was on the march.

Oftener and oftener, as the time went on, did his glance settle on the girl herself. Her face was bowed forward and covered with her hands, and she was shaken at intervals by the convulsive hiccough of grief. Even thus she was not an unpleasant object to dwell upon, so plump and yet so fine, with a warm brown skin, and the most beautiful hair, Denis thought, in the whole world of womankind. Her hands were like her uncle's; but they were more in place at the end of her young arms, and looked infinitely soft and caressing. He remembered how her blue eyes had shone upon him, full of anger, pity, and innocence. And the more he dwelt on her perfections, the uglier death looked, and the more deeply was he smitten with penitence at her continued tears. Now he felt that no man could have the courage to leave a world which contained so beautiful a creature; and now he would have given forty minutes of his last hour to have unsaid his cruel speech.

Suddenly a hoarse and ragged peal of cockcrow rose to their ears from the dark valley below the windows. And this shattering noise in the silence of all around was like a light in a dark place, and shook them both out of their reflections.

"Alas, can I do nothing to help you?" she said, looking up.

"Madam," replied Denis, with a fine irrelevancy, "if I have said anything to wound you, believe me, it was for your own sake and not for mine."

She thanked him with a tearful look.

"I feel your position cruelly," he went on. "The world has been bitter hard on you. Your uncle is a disgrace to mankind. Believe me, madam, there is no young gentleman in all France but would be glad of my opportunity, to die in doing you a momentary service."

"I know already that you can be very brave and generous," she answered. "What I *want* to know is whether I can serve you—now or afterwards," she added, with a quaver.

"Most certainly," he answered with a smile. "Let me sit beside you as if I were a friend, instead of a foolish intruder; try to forget how awkwardly we are placed to one another; make my last moments go pleasantly; and you will do me the chief service possible."

"You are very gallant," she added, with a yet deeper sadness, "very gallant, and it somehow pains me. But draw nearer, if you please; and if you find anything to say to me, you will at least make certain of a very friendly listener. Ah! Monsieur de Beaulieu," she broke forth—"ah! Monsieur de Beaulieu, how can I look you in the face?" And she fell to weeping again with a renewed effusion.

"Madam," said Denis, taking her hand in both of his, "reflect on the little time I have before me, and the great bitterness into which I am cast by the sight of your distress. Spare me, in my last moments, the spectacle of what I cannot cure even with the sacrifice of my life."

"I am very selfish," answered Blanche. "I will be braver, Monsieur de Beaulieu, for your sake. But think if I can do you no kindness in the future—if you have no friends to whom I could carry your adieux. Charge me as heavily as you can; every burden will lighten, by so little, the invaluable gratitude I owe you. Put it in my power to do something more for you than weep."

"My mother is married again, and has a young family to care for. My brother Guichard will inherit my fiefs; and if I am not in error, that will content him amply for my death. Life is a little vapor that passeth away, as we are told by those in holy orders. When a man is in a fair way and sees all life open in front of him, he seems to himself to make a very important figure in the world. His horse whinnies to him; the trumpets blow and the girls look out of window as he rides into town before his company; he receives many assurances of trust and regard—sometimes by express in a letter—sometimes face to face, with persons of great consequence falling on his neck. It is not wonderful if his head is turned for a time. But once he is dead, were he as brave as Hercules or as wise as Solomon, he is soon forgotten. It is not ten years since my father fell, with many other knights around him, in a very fierce encounter, and I do not think that any one of them, nor so much as the name of the fight, is now remembered. No, no, madam, the nearer you come to it, you see that death is a dark and dusty corner, where a man gets into his tomb and has the door shut after him till the judgment day. I have few friends just now, and once I am dead I shall have none."

"Ah, Monsieur de Beaulieu!" she exclaimed, "you forget Blanche de Malétroit."

"You have a sweet nature, madam, and you are pleased to estimate a little service far beyond its worth."

"It is not that," she answered. "You mistake me if you think I am easily touched by my own concerns. I say so, because you are the noblest man I have ever met; because I recognize in you a spirit that would have made even a common person famous in the land."

"And yet here I die in a mousetrap — with no more noise about it than my own squeaking," answered he.

A look of pain crossed her face, and she was silent for a little while. Then a light came into her eyes, and with a smile she spoke again.

"I cannot have my champion think meanly of himself. Anyone who gives his life for another will be met in Paradise by all the heralds and angels of the Lord God. And you have no such cause to hang your head. For — pray, do you think me beautiful?" she asked, with a deep flush.

"Indeed, madam, I do," he said.

"I am glad of that," she answered heartily. "Do you think there are many men in France who have been asked in marriage by a beautiful maiden — with her own lips — and who have refused her to her face? I know you men would half despise such a triumph! but believe me, we women know more of what is precious in love. There is nothing that should set a person higher in his own esteem; and we women would prize nothing more dearly."

"You are very good," he said; "but you cannot make me forget that I was asked in pity and not for love."

"I am not so sure of that," she replied, holding down her head. "Hear me to an end, Monsieur de Beaulieu. I know how you must despise me; I feel you are right to do so; I am too poor a creature to occupy one thought of your mind, although, alas! you must die for me this morning. But when I asked you to marry me, indeed, and indeed, it was because I respected and admired you, and loved you with my whole soul, from the very moment that you took my part against my uncle. If you had seen yourself, and how noble you looked, you would pity rather than despise me. And now," she went on, hurriedly checking him with her hand, "although I have laid aside all reserve and told you so much, remember that I know your sentiments toward me already. I would not, believe me, being nobly born, weary you with importunities into consent. I too have a pride of my own: and I declare before the holy mother of God, if you should now go back from your word already given, I would no more marry you than I would marry my uncle's groom."

Denis smiled a little bitterly.

"It is a small love," he said, "that shies at a little pride."

She made no answer, although she probably had her own thoughts.

"Come hither to the window," he said with a sigh. "Here is the dawn."

And indeed the dawn was already beginning. The hollow of the sky was full of essential daylight, colorless and clean; and the valley underneath was flooded with a gray reflection. A few thin vapors clung in the coves of the forest or lay along the winding course of the river. The scene disengaged a surprising effect of stillness, which was hardly interrupted when the cocks began once more to crow among the steadings. Perhaps the same fellow who had made so horrid a clangor in the darkness not half an hour before, now sent up the merriest cheer to greet the coming day. A little wind went bustling and eddying among the treetops underneath the windows. And still the daylight kept flooding insensibly out of the east, which was soon to grow incandescent and cast up that red-hot cannon ball, the rising sun.

Denis looked out over all this with a bit of a shiver. He had taken her hand, and retained it in his almost unconsciously.

"Has the day begun already?" she said; and then, illogically enough: "the night has been so long! Alas! what shall we say to my uncle when he returns?"

"What you will," said Denis, and he pressed her fingers in his.

She was silent.

"Blanche," he said, with a swift, uncertain, passionate utterance, "you have seen whether I fear death. You must know well enough that I would as gladly leap out of that window into the empty air as to lay a finger on you without your free and full consent. But if you care for me at all do not let me lose my life in a misapprehension; for I love you better than the whole world; and though

I will die for you blithely, it would be like all the joys of Paradise to live on and spend my life in your service."

As he stopped speaking, a bell began to ring loudly in the interior of the house; and a clatter of armor in the corridor showed that the retainers were returning to their post, and the two hours were at an end.

"After all that you have heard?" she whispered, leaning toward him with her lips and eyes.

"I have heard nothing," he replied.

"The captain's name was Florimond de Champdivers," she said in his ear.

"I did not hear it," he answered, taking her supple body in his arms, and covered her wet face with kisses.

A melodious chirping was audible behind, followed by a beautiful chuckle, and the voice of Messire de Malétroit wished his new nephew a good-morning.

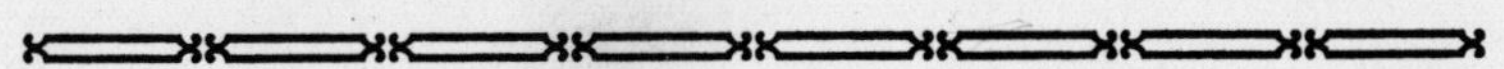

V. LETTERS

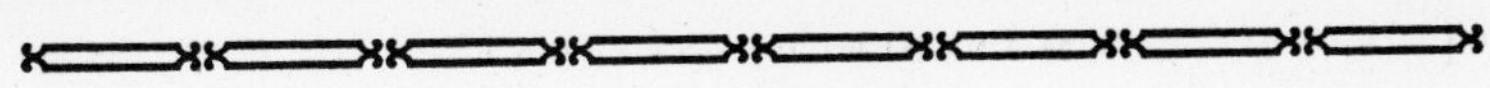

V. LETTERS

MARCUS TULLIUS CICERO TO ATTICUS

There is nothing I need so much just now as someone with whom I may discuss all my anxieties, someone with whom I may speak quite frankly and without pretenses. My brother, who is all candor and kindness, is away. Metellus is empty as the air, barren as the desert. And you, who have so often relieved my cares and sorrows by your conversation and counsel, and have always been my support in politics and my confidant in all private affairs, the partner of all my thoughts and plans — where are you?

I am so utterly deserted that I have no other comfort but in my wife and daughter and dear little Cicero. For those ambitious friendships with great people are all show and tinsel, and contain nothing that satisfies inwardly. Every morning my house swarms with visitors; I go down to the Forum attended by troops of friends; but in the whole crowd there is no one with whom I can freely jest, or whom I can trust with an intimate word. It is for you that I wait; I need your presence; I even implore you to come.

I have a load of anxieties and troubles, of which, if you could listen to them in one of our walks together, you would go far to relieve me. I have to keep to myself the stings and vexations of my domestic troubles; I dare not trust them to this letter and to an unknown courier. I don't want you to think them greater than they are, but they haunt and worry me, and there is no friendly counsel to alleviate them. As for the republic, though my courage and will toward it are not diminished, yet it has again and again itself evaded remedy. If I were to tell you all that has happened since you went away, you would certainly say that the Roman state must be nearing its fall. The Clodian scandal was, I think, the first episode after your departure. On that occasion, thinking that I had an opportunity of cutting down and restraining the licentiousness of the young men, I exerted myself with all my might, and brought into play every power of my mind, not in hostility to an individual, but in the hope of correcting and healing the state. But a venal and profligate verdict in the matter has brought upon the republic the gravest injury. And see what has taken place since.

A consul has been imposed upon us whom no one, unless a philosopher like ourselves, can look at without a sigh. What an injury that is! Again, although a decree of the senate with regard to bribery and corruption has been passed, no law has been carried through; and the senate has been harassed beyond endurance and the Roman knights have been alienated. So, in one year, two pillars of the republic, which had been established by me alone, have been overturned; the authority of the senate has been destroyed and the concord of the two orders has been violated.

MADAME DE SÉVIGNÉ TO HER DAUGHTER[1]

My Dear Child:

I have been here but three hours, and already take my pen to talk to you. I left Paris with the Abbé, Hélène, Hébert, and Marphise, so that I might get away from the noise and bustle of the town until Thursday evening. I want to have perfect quietness, in which to reflect. I intend to fast for many good reasons, and to walk much to make up for the long time I have spent in my room; and above all, I want to discipline myself for the love of God.

But, my dear daughter, what I shall do more than all this, will be to think of you. I have not ceased to do so since I arrived here; and being quite unable to restrain my feelings, I have betaken my-

[1]The letters of Madame de Sévigné (1626–1696) number over a thousand and were mainly written to the daughter referred to here, Madame de Grignan. The extant correspondence extends over a quarter of a century and is famous in literature.

self to the little shady walk you so loved, to write to you, and am sitting on the mossy bank where you so often used to lie. But, my dear, where in this place have I not seen you? Do not thoughts of you haunt my heart everywhere I turn?—in the house, in the church, in the field, in the garden—every spot speaks to me of you. You are in my thoughts all the time, and my heart cries out for you again and again. I search in vain for the dear, dear child I love so passionately; but she is 600 miles away, and I cannot call her to my side. My tears fall, and I cannot stop them. I know it is weak, but this tenderness for you is right and natural and I cannot be strong.

I wonder what your mood will be when you receive this letter; perhaps at that moment you will not be touched with the emotions I now feel so poignantly, and then you may not read it in the spirit in which it was written. But against that I cannot guard, and the act of writing relieves my feelings at the moment—that is at least what I ask of it. You would not believe the condition into which this place has thrown me.

Do not refer to my weakness, I beg of you; but you must love me, and have respect for my tears, since they flow from a heart which is full of you.

THE REV. P. J. DE SMET, S.J., TO CANON DE LA CROIX[1]

April 16, 1855.

Reverend Sir:

You will undoubtedly be gratified to have some news of the mission of St. Francis Hieronymo among the Osages, to whom you were the first to announce the consolations of the everlasting Gospel. The seed of salvation which you planted, and which was after-

[1]From *Western Missions and Missionaries*. Owing to the great length of this letter extracts only could be taken and linked together.

wards neglected, has not been sterile. You are acquainted with the difficulties of the Osage mission. Being in the neighborhood of the boundary line of the United States, these Indians learn to adopt, very easily, all the vices of the whites, without joining to them any of their virtues. They forget the frugality and simplicity which formerly characterized them, and give themselves up to intemperance and the perfidiousness of civilized life. However, every year a considerable number of adults enter the bosom of the Church; a great number of children receive baptism, and as they often die very young, they are so many innocent souls who intercede in heaven for the conversion of their unhappy parents, buried in the grossest superstition and idolatry of paganism.

In the spring of 1852 an epidemic malady, which made great ravages, became for a large number (although weakening the power of their nation) a blessed occasion of salvation.

Heaven accorded its benedictions to the efforts of Father Bax[2] and his companions in this painful ministry. Of nearly 1,500 savages, who were swept away by the epidemic, all, with a very few exceptions, had the happiness of being fortified by the last sacraments of the Church before dying. Seized, at last, himself with symptoms of the illness, Father Bax continued his ordinary labors, and dragged himself around to visit the sick and dying. His zeal would not suffer him to attend to himself. Strength soon failed him. He was dying while still laboring! He was obliged, at last, to consent to allow himself to be transported about forty miles from the mission, to Fort Scott, a military post, where one of the most skillful physicians of the United States Army then resided. It was too late, all the cares of the doctor proved useless. The good religious, the indefatigable missionary, was a fruit ripe for heaven. At the end of six weeks he died as he had lived. His last aspirations showed still his unfading zeal for the conversion of his dear savages.

There are but two Fathers to visit the different Osage villages, situated at the distance of fifty and seventy miles from each other. The toils and fatigues of the holy ministry there are excessive. The catechumens must be instructed, the neophytes sustained, the sick and dying visited, and continual efforts made to convert obstinate

[2]Father Bax received the highest commendation in the annual message of the President of the United States in 1854. The Indians knew him by the beautiful Osage name: "The Father-Who-Is-All-Heart."

adults. Amid so many obstacles, so many privations and difficulties, the missionaries find also sweet consolations in the fruits which the Lord deigns to grant to their labors. Every year they baptize among the Osages about two hundred and fifty persons.

We cannot without sighing cast a look over the immense Indian territory, which stretches far away to the Rocky Mountains. There a great number of nations still continue their errant life. There remains but a feeble ray of hope that they will obtain spiritual aid. It is not because the field is barren; it has been already explored by the Fathers Hoeken and Point, both of the Society of Jesus, and by the Rev. Messrs. Bellecourt and Ravoux. I have gone over its whole extent at different periods. All the missionaries declare unanimously, that everywhere, in all their visits, they have been received with the most touching deference by the savages; that the various tribes have testified the deepest interest in our holy religion. Several thousand children and a great number of adults, particularly among the Blackfeet, the Crows, the Sioux, Poncahs, Ricaries, Minataries, Cheyennes, and the Rapahoes, have already been regenerated into the holy waters of baptism. The personal and material means have hitherto been wanting for beginning therein durable establishments. The Indians year after year renew their invitations. We shall continue to supplicate the Master of the Vineyard, to deign to send us auxiliaries, so as to diffuse our missions in this extensive region. "The harvest is great, but the laborers are few."

ABRAHAM LINCOLN TO MRS. BIXBY

November 21, 1864.

Dear Madame:

I have been shown in the files of the War Department a statement of the Adjutant-General of Massachusetts that you are the mother of five sons who have died gloriously on the field of battle. I feel how weak and fruitless must be any words of mine which should attempt to beguile you from the grief of a loss so overwhelming. But I cannot refrain from tendering to you the consolation that may be found in the thanks of the Republic they died to save. I pray that our heavenly Father may assuage the anguish of your bereavement, and leave you only the cherished memory of the loved and lost, and the solemn pride that must be yours to have laid so costly a sacrifice upon the altar of freedom.

Yours very sincerely and respectfully,

Abraham Lincoln.

SAMUEL JOHNSON TO THE EARL OF CHESTERFIELD

February 7, 1755.

TO THE RIGHT HONORABLE THE EARL OF CHESTERFIELD

My Lord, I have been lately informed, by the proprietor of the *World*, that two papers, in which my Dictionary is recommended to the public, were written by your lordship. To be so distinguished is an honor, which, being very little accustomed to favors from the great, I know not well how to receive, or in what terms to acknowledge.

When, upon some slight encouragement, I first visited your lordship, I was overpowered, like the rest of mankind, by the enchantment of your address, and could not forbear to wish that I might boast myself *Le vainqueur du vainqueur de la terre*—that I might obtain that regard for which I saw the world contending; but I found my attendance so little encouraged, that neither pride nor modesty would suffer me to continue it. When I had once addressed your lordship in public, I had exhausted all the art of pleasing which a retired and uncourtly scholar can possess. I had done all that I could; and no man is well pleased to have his all neglected, be it ever so little.

Seven years, my lord, have now passed, since I waited in your outward rooms, or was repulsed from your door; during which time I have been pushing on my work through difficulties, of which it is useless to complain, and have brought it, at last, to the verge of publication, without one act of assistance, one word of encouragement, or one smile of favor. Such treatment I did not expect, for I never had a patron before.

The shepherd in "Virgil" grew at last acquainted with Love, and found him a native of the rocks.

Is not a patron, my lord, one who looks with unconcern on a man struggling for life in the water, and, when he has reached ground, encumbers him with help? The notice which you have been pleased to take of my labors had it been early, had been kind; but it has been delayed till I am indifferent and cannot enjoy it; till I am solitary, and cannot impart it; till I am known, and do not want it. I hope it is no very cynical asperity, not to confess obligations where no benefit has been received, or to be unwilling that the public should consider me as owing that to a patron, which Providence has enabled me to do myself.

Having carried on my work thus far with so little obligation to any favorer of learning, I shall not be disappointed though I shall conclude it, if less be possible, with less; for I have been long wakened from that dream of hope, in which I once boasted myself with so much exultation,

My Lord, your lordship's most humble,
Most obedient servant,

Sam. Johnson

MRS. DELANY TO MRS. DEWES[1]

Delville, Feb. 22, 1752.

I am more astonished at Mrs. Chapone's not liking Dr. Young's Night Thoughts, than at any thing I have met with for a great while. I should have thought such sublimity, such exalted piety,

[1]From *Autobiography and Correspondence of Mrs. Delany.*

such a true spirit of poetry, would have charmed her and made amends for some obscurities and some few sinkings which I must confess there are in some parts of them. I read them carefully over this summer to the Dean, and we were both charmed with them, and could not help wondering at their being so little attended to and liked; the way I have always accounted for it is, the horror that most people have of dying, so that instead of preparing themselves for an event that must come, they drive the thought away as far as they can, not considering how much more dreadful that must make the fatal hour when it arrives. Amongst the numberless mercies of God, surely none is greater than the gradual weaning us from the world, which everybody that lives rationally must be sensible of. A strong desire of living and enjoying the world is implanted in us; without it we could not support the thousand shocks we meet with in our progress; but as years increase upon us, that desire lessens; we see how transient and unsatisfactory most of our pursuits and enjoyments are; we feel that our perfect happiness cannot be made out in this life, and that perfect joys are reserved for another! Why should we then be terrified at a dissolution (if we endeavor to perform our duty, and not neglect the true means of salvation), that is to make us forever happy, and open the doors of everlasting life?

You did not tell me Mrs. Roach was a widow. I don't know by your account whether I am to condole or congratulate her upon it. If you find no real bad in her, some fantastic ways may be diverting; the chief service you want of her is to teach the children French. I am glad you are going to work covers to your chairs; I think you must alter your pattern, for as they will have more wearing and washing than the bed or curtains, I fear your cloth work will not be firm enough. The border will be too broad for the chairs, something of the same kind of border to the bed with the mosaic pattern in the middle, and instead of cloth, fill up part of it with stitches in thread; but don't you want your coverlid first?

WILLIAM COWPER TO MRS. NEWTON

Olney, November 23, 1782.

Accept my thanks for the trouble you take in vending my poems, and still more for the interest you take in their success. To be approved by the great, as Horace observed many years ago, is fame indeed.

The winter sets in with great severity. The rigor of the season, the advanced price of grain, are very threatening to the poor. It is well with those than can feed upon a promise, and wrap themselves up warm in the robe of salvation. A good fireside and a well-spread table are but very indifferent substitutes for those better accommodations; so very indifferent, that I would gladly exchange them both for the rags and the unsatisfied hunger of the poorest creature that looks forward with hope to a better world, and weeps tears of joy in the midst of penury and distress.

What a world is this! How mysteriously governed, and in appearance left to itself! One man, having squandered thousands at a gaming-table, finds it convenient to travel; gives his estate to somebody to manage for him; amuses himself a few years in France and Italy; returns, perhaps, wiser than he went, having acquired knowledge which, but for his follies, he would never have acquired; again makes a splendid figure at home, shines in the senate, governs his country as its minister, is admired for his abilities, and, if successful, adored at least by a party. When he dies, he is praised as a demigod, and his monument records everything but his vices.

The exact contrary of such a picture is to be found in many cottages at Olney. I have no need to describe them; you know the characters I mean. They love God, they trust Him, they pray to Him in secret, and, though He means to reward them openly, the day of recompense is delayed. In the meantime, they suffer everything that infirmity and poverty can inflict upon them. Who would suspect, that has not a spiritual eye to discern it, that the fine gentleman was one whom his Maker had in abhorrence, and the wretch last mentioned dear to Him as the apple of His eye?

It is no wonder that the world, who are not in the secret, find themselves obliged, some of them, to doubt a Providence, and others absolutely to deny it, when almost all the real virtue there is in it is to be found living and dying in a state of neglected obscurity, and all the vices of others cannot exclude them from worship and honor. But behind the curtain the matter is explained, very little, however, to the satisfaction of the great.

THOMAS GRAY TO HIS MOTHER

Amiens, April, 1739.

We left Dover at noon, and with a pretty brisk gale reached Calais by five. This is an exceeding old, but very pretty town, and we hardly saw anything there that was not so new and so different from England that it surprised us agreeably. We went the next morning to the great church, and were at high Mass, it being Easter Monday. In the afternoon we took a post-chaise for Boulogne, which was only eighteen miles farther.

This chaise is a strange sort of conveyance, resembling an ill-shaped chariot, only with the door opening before, instead of the side; three horses draw it, one between the shafts, and the other two on each side, on one of which the postillion rides and drives, too. This vehicle will, upon occasion, go fourscore miles a day; but Mr. Walpole, being in no hurry, chooses to make easy journeys of it, and we go about six miles an hour. They are no very graceful steeds, but they go well, and through roads which they say are bad for France, but to me they seem gravel walks and bowling greens. In short, it would be the finest traveling in the world were it not for the inns, which are most terrible places indeed.

The country we have passed through hitherto has been flat, open, but agreeably diversified with villages, fields well cultivated, and little rivers. On every hillock is a windmill, a crucifix, or a Virgin Mary dressed in flowers and a sarcenet robe; one sees not many people or carriages on the road; now and then, indeed, you meet a strolling friar, a countryman, or a woman riding astride on a little ass, with short petticoats and a great headdress of blue wool.

THOMAS GRAY TO THE SAME

Lyons, October 13, 1739.

We have been to see a famous monastery, called the Grand Chartreuse, and had no reason to think our time lost. After having traveled seven days, very slow (for we did not change horses, it being impossibe for a chaise to go post in these roads), we arrived at a little village among the mountains of Savoy, called Echelles; from thence we proceeded on horses, who are used to the way, to the mountain of the Chartreuse. It is six miles to the top; the road runs winding up it, commonly not six feet broad; on one hand is the rock, with woods of pine-trees hanging overhead; on the other, a monstrous precipice, almost perpendicular, at the bottom of which rolls a torrent, that sometimes is tumbling among the fragments of stone that have fallen from on high, and sometimes precipitating itself down vast descents with a noise like thunder, which is made still greater by the echo from the mountains on each side, concurs to form one of the most solemn, the most romantic, and the most astonishing scenes I ever beheld. Add to this the strange views made by the crags and cliffs on the other hand, the cascades that in many places throw themselves from the very summit down into the vale and the river below.

This place St. Bruno chose to retire to, and upon its very top founded the convent, which is the superior of the whole order. When we came there, the two fathers who are commissioned to entertain strangers (for the rest must neither speak to one another nor to anyone else) received us very kindly, and set before us a repast of dried fish, eggs, butter, and fruits, all excellent in their kind, and extremely neat. They pressed us to spend the night there, and to stay some days with them; but this we could not do, so they led us about their house, which is like a little city, for there are 100 fathers, besides 300 servants, that make their clothes, grind their corn, press their wine, and do everything among themselves. The whole is quite orderly and simple; nothing of finery, but the wonderful decency and the strange situation more than supply the place of it.

CHARLES LAMB TO WILLIAM WORDSWORTH

January 30, 1801.

I ought before this to have replied to your very kind invitation to Cumberland. With you and your sister I could gang anywhere; but I am afraid whether I shall ever be able to afford so desperate a journey. Separate from the pleasure of your company, I don't much care if I never see a mountain in my life. I have passed all my days in London, until I have formed as many and intense local attachments as any of you mountaineers can have done with dead Nature. The lighted shops of the Strand and Fleet Street; the innumerable trades, tradesmen, and customers, coaches, wagons, playhouses; all the bustle and wickedness round about Covent Garden; the very women of the Town; the watchmen, drunken scenes, rattles; life awake, if you awake, at all hours of the night; the impossibility of being dull in Fleet Street; the crowds, the very dirt and mud, the sun shining upon houses and pavements, the printshops, the old bookstalls, parsons cheapening books, coffee houses, steams of soups from kitchens, the pantomimes—London itself a pantomime and a masquerade—all these things work themselves into my mind, and feed me, without a power of satiating me. The wonder of these sights impels me into night-walks about her crowded streets, and I often shed tears in the motley Strand from fullness of joy at so much life. All these emotions must be strange to you; so are your rural emotions to me. But consider, what must I have been doing all my life, not to have lent great portions of my heart with usury to such scenes?

My attachments are all local, purely local. I have no passion (or have had none since I was in love, and then it was the spurious engendering of poetry and books) for groves and valleys. The rooms where I was born, the furniture which has been before my eyes all my life, a bookcase which has followed me about like a faithful dog (only exceeding him in knowledge), wherever I have moved, old chairs, old tables, streets, squares, where I have sunned myself, my old school — these are my mistresses. Have I not enough, without your mountains? I do not envy you. I should pity you, did I not know that the mind will make friends of anything. Your sun, and moon, and skies, and hills, and lakes, affect me no more, or scarcely come to me in more venerable characters, than as a gilded room with tapestry and tapers, where I might live with handsome visible objects. I consider the clouds above me but as a roof beautifully painted, but unable to satisfy my mind: and at last, like the pictures of the apartment of a connoisseur, unable to afford him any longer a pleasure. So fading upon me, from disuse, have been the beauties of nature, as they have been confinedly called; so ever fresh, and green, and warm are all the inventions of men, and assemblies of men in this great city. I should certainly have laughed with dear Joanna.

Give my kindest love and my sister's to D. and yourself; and a kiss from me to little Barbara Lewthwaite. Thank you for liking my play.

C.L.

JANE CARLYLE TO HER AUNT[1]

Chelsea, September 5, 1836.

My dear Aunt:

I got into that mail the other night with as much repugnance and trepidation as if it had been a Phalaris' brazen bull, instead of a Christian vehicle, invented for purposes of mercy — not of cruelty.

[1]Jane Welsh Carlyle was the wife of Thomas Carlyle.

There were three besides myself when we started, but two dropped off at the end of the first stage, and the rest of the way I had, as usual, half of the coach to myself. My fellow-passenger had the highest of all terrestrial qualities, which for me a fellow passenger can possess — he was silent. I think his name was Roscoe, and he read sundry long papers to himself, with the pondering air of a lawyer.

We breakfasted at Lichfield, at five in the morning, on muddy coffee and scorched toast, which made me once more lyrically recognize in my heart (not without a sigh of regret) the very different coffee and toast with which you helped me out of my headache. At two there was another stop of ten minutes, that might be employed in lunching or otherwise. Feeling myself more fevered than hungry, I determined on spending the time in combing my hair and washing my face and hands with vinegar. In the midst of this solacing operation I heard what seemed to be the Mail running its rapid course, and quick as lightning it flashed on me, "There it goes! and my luggage is on the top of it, and my purse is in the pocket of it, and here am I stranded on an unknown beach, without so much as sixpence in my pocket to pay for the vinegar I have already consumed!" Without my bonnet, my hair hanging down my back, my face half dried, and the towel, with which I was drying it, firmly grasped in my hand, I dashed out — along, down, opening wrong doors, stumbling over steps, cursing the day I was born, still more the day on which I took a notion to travel, and arrived finally at the bar of the Inn, in a state of excitement bordering on lunacy. The barmaids looked at me "with wonder and amazement." "Is the coach gone?" I gasped out. "The coach? Yes!" "Oh! and you have let it away without me! Oh! stop it, cannot you stop it?" and out I rushed into the street, with streaming hair and streaming towel, and almost brained myself against — the Mail! which was standing there in all stillness, without so much as horses in it! What I had heard was a heavy coach. And now, having descended like a maniac, I ascended again like a fool, and dried the other half of my face, and put on my bonnet, and came back "a sadder and wiser" woman.

I did not find my husband at the "Swan with Two Necks"; for we were in a quarter of an hour before the appointed time. So I had my luggage put on the backs of two porters, and walked on to Cheapside, where I presently found a Chelsea omnibus. By-and-by, however, the omnibus stopped, and amid cries of "No room, sir," "Can't get in," Carlyle's face, beautifully set off by a broad-brimmed white hat, gazed in at the door, like the Peri, who, "at the Gate of Heaven, stood disconsolate." In hurrying along the Strand, pretty sure of being too late, amidst all the imaginable and unimaginable phenomena which the immense thoroughfare of a street presents, his eye (Heaven bless the mark!) had lighted on my trunk perched on the top of the omnibus, and had recognized it. This seems to me one of the most indubitable proofs of genius which he ever manifested. Happily, a passenger went out a little further on, and then he got in.

My brother-in-law had gone two days before, so my arrival was most well timed. I found all at home right and tight; my maid seems to have conducted herself quite handsomely in my absence; my best room looked really inviting. A bust of Shelley (a present from Leigh Hunt), and a fine print of Albert Dürer, handsomely framed (also a present), had still further ornamented it during my absence. I also found (for I wish to tell you all my satisfaction) every grate in the house furnished with a supply of colored clippings, and the holes in the stair carpet all darned, so that it looks like new. They gave me tea and fried bacon, and staved off my headache as well as might be. They were very kind to me, but, on my life, everybody is kind to me, and to a degree that fills me with admiration. I feel so strong a wish to make you all convinced how very deeply I feel your kindness, and just the more I would say, the less able I am to say anything.

God bless you all. Love to all, from the head of the house down to Jonny.

Your affectionate

Jane W. Carlyle.

JANE DE QUINCEY TO THOMAS DE QUINCEY[1]

Wednesday, May 17, 1809.

Mary has been reproaching me the whole week for not writing to you, which is a great shame, because your last letter was to her; and, besides, you owe me some three or four already. After all, I don't know what it is she is so desirous I should impart to you, except that there is no reason why you should not come to us in ten days, as you say, or in one day if you please; but I conclude there is no reason for repeating so old a truth, that we are always supremely happy in the honor and pleasure, &c., &c., &c.

I observe you always say ten days, a distance which as regularly recedes so that it is constantly at the same standing. We have heard of you today; that is, from your favored friend, Miss Wordsworth, through Mrs. Kelsall. When shall we hear anything more of this beautiful cottage? I can't approve of the sitting room being upstairs. Why did it not open on a sloping lawn, buried in the shade of venerable beeches, through which one should here and there discover the lake with the western sun sinking into it? Here indeed would be a retreat worthy a philosopher! I should like to know how you will pass your time — whether you mean to bury yourself in total seclusion, or only in an elegant retirement, embellished with every unsophisticated pleasure. I can tell you that you will never endure it alone for two months. I should much like to know Miss Wordsworth, and see what sort of a woman you admire. I look with no small pleasure to the seeing all the divine things in Grasmere which you mention. I think that pleasure which I *feel* from beautiful country, or from anything in country not strictly beautiful which I have associated, however remotely, with my ideas of fine scenery, would have power to arouse and delight me even at moments (if such there were) when every other thing would be disgusting to me.

---

[1]Jane de Quincey was the sister of the English essayist De Quincey. The letter is taken from the *De Quincey Memorials,* edited by A. H. Japp, New York, 1891.

I think you will be pleased with our views from Westhay, though they are certainly of a very mild sort of beauty, and may appear tame after the northern sublimity. If you have any dislike to the worldly bustle of removing, I again conjure you to come immediately, since our time is finally fixed for leaving Clifton entirely at or rather before Midsummer, and cannot now be altered, because this house is *let* from that period, and therefore we must leave whether we are so disposed or not. You can go with us to Westhay if you please, for we shall have rooms enough finished, though the house will be half full of workmen. How often have I told you that "hope deferred maketh the heart sick"? I am sure no mortal ever had so many prayers, adjurations, and imprecations showered upon them in vain as you have had. Above all things remember the Bible, as you value your peace on earth. I hope you will bring some books with you, for we are in a dry and barren soil, where to this hour I believe it is the fashion to talk of nothing but "Marmion" and "Caelebs." I suppose we shall have some more of Walter Scott's stolen goods *soon*. Do you know anything of him? or can he prosecute me for a libelist if I say he borrows his ideas often, his words even, sometimes? You have not told us whether you understand Spanish. Mary has got the most stupid master in the world, and so unlike a noble Spaniard, he might rather pass for a low and vulgar Francese. Have you any Italian books with you? I can get none, and I much wish to increase my slight acquaintance with the language. People sometimes argue with me that there is no use in learning Italian and Spanish, because there are so few books worth reading. You have given me a different idea; at all events they are so easy to learn, and I have not the dislike that people in general have to languages.

Do you remember that you are to teach me German? We hear by letters from India that my Uncle is just made a Major, so we expect he will come home. Richard is still in the Baltic with Admiral Keats. I fear you have never written to Miss Brotherton. Oh, if you break your promises to the fair unknown as you do to us, you will certainly be disgraced. I long to question you on some interesting topics which in a letter you would elude, but the truth cannot escape my penetrating eye. Can you tell me why Foster has never brought out the book which you said was preparing? I suppose it will never come now. I do not think even of inquiring for the "Friend." Adieu.—Your ever affectionate sister,

Jane De Quincey.

THOMAS MACAULAY TO HIS SISTER

London, May 30, 1831.

Well, my dear, I have been to Holland House. I took a glass coach, and arrived, through a fine avenue of elms, at the great entrance toward seven o'clock. The house is delightful—the very perfection of the old Elizabethan style—a considerable number of very large and very comfortable rooms, rich with antique carving and gilding, but carpeted and furnished with all the skill of the best modern upholsterers. The library is a very long room—as long, I should think, as the gallery at Rothley Temple—with little cabinets for study branching out of it, warmly and snugly fitted up, and looking out on very beautiful grounds. The collection of books is not, like Lord Spencer's, curious; but it contains almost everything that one ever wished to read. I found nobody there when I arrived but Lord Russell, the son of the Marquess of Tavistock. We are old House of Commons friends; so we had some very pleasant talk, and in a little while in came Allen, who is warden of Dulwich College, and who lives almost entirely at Holland House. He is certainly a man of vast information and great conversational powers. Some other gentlemen dropped in, and we chatted till Lady Holland made her appearance. Lord Holland dined by himself on account of his gout. We sat down to dinner in a fine long room, the wainscot of which is rich with gilded coronets, roses, and portcullises. There were Lord Albermarle, Lord Alvanley, Lord Russell, Lord Mahon—a violent Tory, but a very agreeable companion and a very good scholar. There was Cradock, a fine fellow, who was the Duke of Wellington's aide-de-camp in 1815, and some other people whose names I did not catch. What, however, is more to the purpose, there was a most excellent dinner. I have always heard that Holland House is famous for its good cheer, and certainly the reputation is not unmerited. After dinner Lord Holland was wheeled in and placed very near me. He was extremely amusing and good-natured.

In the drawing-room I had a long talk with Lady Holland about the antiquities of the house, and about the purity of the English language wherein she thinks herself a critic. I happened, in speaking about the Reform Bill, to say that I wished that it had been possible to form a few commercial constituencies, if the word *constituency* were admissible. "I am glad you put that in," said her ladyship. "I was just going to give it you. It is an odious word. Then there is *talented,* and *influential,* and *gentlemanly.* I never could break Sheridan of *gentlemanly,* though he allowed it to be wrong." We talked about the word *talents* and its history. I said that it had first appeared in theological writing, that it was a metaphor taken from the parable in the New Testament, and that it had gradually passed from the vocabulary of divinity into common use. I challenged her to find it in any classical writer on general subjects before the Restoration, or even before the year 1700. I believe I might safely have gone down later. She seemed surprised by this theory, never having, so far as I could judge, heard of the parable of the talents. I did not tell her, though I might have done so, that a person who professes to be a critic in the delicacies of the English language ought to have the Bible at his fingers' ends.

She is certainly a woman of considerable talents and great literary acquirements. To me she was excessively gracious; yet there is a haughtiness in her courtesy which, even after all that I had heard of her, surprised me. The centurion did not keep his soldiers in better order than she keeps her guests. It is to one "Go," and he goeth; and to another "Do this," and it is done. "Ring the bell, Mr. Macaulay." "Lay down that screen, Lord Russell; you will spoil it." "Mr. Allen, take a candle and show Mr. Cradock the picture of Bonaparte." Lord Holland is, on the other hand, all kindness, simplicity, and vivacity. He asked me in a very friendly manner about my father's health, and begged to be remembered to him.

When my coach came, Lady Holland made me promise that I would on the first fine morning walk out to breakfast with them and see the grounds; and, after drinking a glass of very good iced lemonade, I took my leave, much amused and pleased. The house certainly deserves its reputation for pleasantness, and her ladyship used me, I believe, as well as it is her way to use anybody. Ever yours,

T.B.M.

EUGÉNIE DE GUÉRIN TO MAURICE DE GUÉRIN[1]

I am furious with the gray cat. The mischievous beast has made away with a little half-frozen pigeon, which I was trying to thaw by the side of the fire. The poor little thing was just beginning to come round; I meant to tame him; he would have grown fond of me; and there is my whole scheme eaten up by a cat! This event, and all the rest of today's history, has passed in the kitchen. Here I take up my abode all the morning and a part of the evening, ever since I am without Mimi.[2] I have to superintend the cook; sometimes papa comes down, and I read to him by the oven, or by the fireside, some bits out of the *Antiquities of the Anglo-Saxon Church*. This book struck Pierril[3] with astonishment. *"Que de mouts aqui dédins!* What a lot of words there are inside it!" This boy is a real original. One evening he asked me if the soul was immortal; then afterwards, what a philosopher was. We had got upon great questions, as you see. When I told him that a philosopher was a person who was wise and learned: "Then, mademoiselle, you are a philosopher." This was said with an air of simplicity and sincerity which might have made even Socrates take it as a compliment; but it

[1]These extracts are taken from the Journal of Eugénie de Guérin, written for her brother Maurice alone, and thus partaking of the nature of a letter. No eye but his ever saw them during the course of her lifetime. *C'est pour un* ("It is for one") she wrote, or as she again expresses it, her thoughts were poured out "before God and one human being," and this with the utmost charm and freedom, for "God has made our souls of one piece." The sections quoted here date from November, 1834, and somewhat later periods.

[2]The familiar name of her sister Marie.

[3]A servant boy at Le Cayla.

made me laugh so much that my gravity as catechist was gone for that evening. A day or two ago Pierril left us, to his great sorrow: his time with us was up on Saint Brice's day. Now he goes about with his little dog, truffle-hunting. If he comes this way I shall go and ask him if he still thinks I look like a philosopher.

* * *

Today [December 9, 1834] I have been warming myself at every fireside in the village. It is a round which Mimi and I often make, and in which I take pleasure. Today we have been seeing sick people, and holding forth on doses and sickroom drinks. "Take this, do that"; and they attend to us just as if we were the doctor. We prescribed shoes for a little thing who was amiss from having gone barefoot; to the brother, who, with a bad headache, was lying quite flat, we prescribed a pillow; the pillow did him good, but I am afraid it will hardly cure him. He is at the beginning of a bad feverish cold: and these poor people live in the filth of their hovels like animals in their stable; the bad air poisons them. When I come home to Le Cayla I seem to be in a palace.

* * *

Cloaks, clogs, umbrellas, all the apparatus of winter, went with us this morning to Andillac, where we have passed the whole day; some of it at the curé's house, the rest in church. How I like this life of a country Sunday, with its activity, its journeys to church, its liveliness! You find all your neighbors on the road; you have a curtsey from every woman you meet, and then, as you go along, such a talk about the poultry, the sheep and cows, the good man and the children! My great delight is to give a kiss to these children, and see them run away and hide their blushing faces in their mother's gown. They are alarmed at *las dounaïsèlos,*[4] as at a being of another world. One of these little things said the other day to its grandmother, who was talking of coming to see us: *"Minino,* you mustn't go to that castle; there is a black hole there." What is the reason that in all ages the noble's château has been an object of

[4]The young lady.

terror? Is it because of the horrors that were committed there in old times? I suppose so.

* * *

This morning I was up before daylight, dressed quickly, said my prayers, and started with Marie for Cahuzac.[5] When we got there, the chapel was occupied, which I was not sorry for. I like not to be hurried, and to have time, before I go in, to lay bare my soul before God. This often takes me a long time, because my thoughts are apt to be flying about like these autumn leaves. At ten o'clock I was on my knees, listening to words the most salutary that were ever spoken; and I went away, feeling myself a better being. Every burden thrown off leaves us with a sense of brightness; and when the soul has lain down the load of its sins at God's feet, it feels as if it had wings. What an admirable thing is confession! What comfort, what light, what strength is given me every time after I have said, *I have sinned*.

FATHER FABER TO LADY MINNA F. HOWARD

Feast of St. Nicholas, 1850.

My dearest Minna:

So you are seven years old, and you have made up your mind to be a nun. Well now, what must you do? Must you put on a strange dress, and cut all your hair off, and go into a convent, and live a hard life? No! not just yet. By-and-by, with our dearest Lady's blessing, it may be so. "But then," as you always, always say, "but then I cannot wait so many, many years." Well, Sister Minna of the Infant Jesus! you need not wait. I will tell you how to be a nun, at once, directly, in the Hotel Bellevue, and with the consent of papa and mamma. Now, I am sure this will both please and surprise you, and it will make V. open her eyes, and noisy M. be quiet.

[5]She refers here to a visit to the little church in this town to make her weekly confession.

"How am I to be made a nun of directly?" Sister Minna! Sister Minna! What is it to be a nun? Listen. To be a nun is to love no one else but Jesus, and to love Him always, and very much, and to love everybody else, papa, mamma, sisters, boy, Father Wilfrid, and all the world, because Jesus loves them so much. This is being a nun. When Sister Minna likes her own will and loves her own way, then she is not a nun. When Sister Minna does not do what she is told, or does it complainingly, then she is not a nun. When Sister Minna says an angry word, then she is not a nun. But when Sister Minna loves Jesus, oh, so much, so very, very much; and when she is always asking her dear Mother in heaven to make her love Jesus more and more, then she is a nun, a real, real nun! So you see you can be a nun whenever you like. O dear! how many questions this letter will make you ask!

And now, good-by, dearest Minna! I pray the dear little Jesus in Mary's arms to take care of you, the dear little Jesus who is the great, great God, for all He is so little. O Minna! if the huge God could love you and me so much that He could become a little Baby, helpless as Ethel says, for you and me, why do not we both love Him ten hundred thousand million times more than we do? Get an answer ready for that question, Minna!

Yours most affectionately,

F. W. Faber.

JOYCE KILMER TO THE REV. JAMES J. DALY, S.J.[1]

October 7, 1912.

My dear Father Daly:

I hope that I interpret your letter of September 20th correctly in thinking that it means that you will permit me to write to you occasionally, and that you will write to me in return. Of course I

[1]This letter was written before the poet's entrance into the Catholic Church. It is printed by courtesy of the Reverend Father Daly.

know that your work occupies much of your time, and that you have pleasanter uses for your leisure than writing letters to some one you have not seen. So do not feel obliged by courtesy to answer me at length.

I am glad that you like some of my work. I am afraid that my review of Francis Thompson's Essays will disappoint you. It appeared in yesterday's *Times,* with its concluding paragraphs (which were of some length) deleted. This made the article more unsatisfactory than it was in its original form. The fault was my own, however, for I knew the amount of space allowed me.

Since I wrote to you last, I have left the employ of Funk and Wagnall's, so I no longer have the pleasant company of our friend Grey. We lunch together now and then, but I am sorry to see him so infrequently. My present occupation is that of assistant editor of *The Churchman,* an Anglican weekly paper. It is a church newspaper, with some literary features. I am glad to say that we hope to print some of Miss Guiney's poems this winter. I will clip them and send them to you. Did Grey tell you that I was not of your Communion? I hope that this knowledge will not shut me out of your regard.

Your remarks, in your last letter, on the fact that many of our most famous writers today are anti-Christian, are certainly justified. Still, do you not think that a reaction is coming? Already we have Chesterton, and Belloc, and Bazin, and Miss Guiney, and Father Vincent McNabb, and a number of other brilliant writers who not as theologians but purely as literary artists express a fine and wholesome faith. People are beginning to tire of cheap eroticism and "realism" and similar absurdities.

But the flood of putrid literature still pours from the presses. Here on my desk as I write lies *The* —— by ——. This man was for a time a Methodist preacher, then a Congregationalist, and now he is writing against Christianity. He is a vulgarian and a liar; his book is written in wretched English, it is full of grotesque and obvious falsities — and it is in its *third edition!* I have read the book through (400 pages) and I am so sick of the fellow's cheap blasphemies that I cannot quiet myself enough to review it in printable words. I understand now thoroughly the custom of having books burned by the common hangman. It was not necessarily because the books were dangerous, or likely to lead people astray — it was just because they were essentially evil, things to be put out of the way. Well, we can't have *The* —— burned, but you must pray for me to get words fiery enough to consume the book utterly when I review it!

JOYCE KILMER TO THE SAME[1]

January 9, 1914.

Dear Father Daly:

At last I have leisure to thank you for your Christmas gifts. I did not know that such beautiful cards were made. How is it that in Prairie du Chien — a place of which the name suggests Indians and tomahawks and Dead Wood Stage-coaches — you can procure better cards than I can get in New York? The medals are highly valued — the workmanship on them is admirable — they will be worn properly as soon as I can afford to buy some silver chains — and that will be next Tuesday.

The Church refuses to live up to its reputation. In the first place, no one ever tried to proselyte me. I hung on the edge, but my Catholic friends would not push. I had to jump. And now that I'm in, the Church still refuses to live up to its reputation. The priest who received me warned me that I'd be shocked by the begging of the parish clergy. I wish I could find a real begging priest. My pastor, begs not half enough.

Seriously, I think the Church is slandered more by educated Catholic laymen than by Protestants. Even when I was a Protestant, I was pained by some things that Catholics of my acquaintance said about the Church. Surely there should be reticence about family scandals.

Of course you understand my conversation. I am beginning to understand it. I believed in the Catholic position, the Catholic view of ethics and aesthetics, for a long time. But I wanted something

[1]This letter was written after the poet's entrance into the Catholic Church. It is printed by courtesy of the Reverend Father Daly.

not intellectual, some conviction not mental — in fact I wanted Faith.

Just off Broadway, on the way from the Hudson Tube Station, to the Times Building there is a Church, called the Church of the Holy Innocents. Since it is in the heart of the Tenderloin, this name is strangely appropriate — for there surely is need of youth and innocence. Well, every morning for months I stopped on my way to the office and prayed in this church for faith. When faith did come, it came, I think, by way of my little paralyzed daughter. Her lifeless hands led me; I think her tiny still feet know beautiful paths. You understand this and it gives me a selfish pleasure to write it down.

I was very glad of your criticism of "The Young Poet Who Killed Himself." I need some stricter discipline, I think, and it's hard to get it. I enjoy my confessor's direction very much, he is a fine old Irishman with no nonsense about him. But I need to be called a fool, I need to have some of the conceit and sophistication knocked out of me. I suppose you think this is "enthusiasm" — that much-heralded danger of converts. Perhaps it is, but I don't think so. I know I'm glad I live two miles from the church, because its excellent for a lazy person like myself to be made to exert himself for religion. And I wish I had a stern medieval confessor — the sort of person one reads about in anti-Catholic books — who would inflict real penances. The saying of Hail Marys and Our Fathers is no penance, it's a delight.

Forgive this egotistical letter! I am praying that the New Year may bring you much happiness.

JOHN AYSCOUGH TO HIS MOTHER[1]

September 18, 1914.

I am writing you this short note, not because I have anything much to say, as I wrote you and Christie a long letter each, yester-

[1]From *John Ayscough's Letters to His Mother.* With permission of P. J. Kenedy & Sons, New York, 1919.

day, but simply because I have the opportunity, and may not have another for ever so long.

We are still at the farm that was a Preceptory of Knights Templars: but may get the order to move at any moment.

A lot of wounded came in this morning, but we were able to send them on within an hour or two. Meanwhile I chatted to most of them and gave Extreme Unction to a dying German prisoner. He was only twenty-one, a sad-faced, simple country lad from Prussian Poland, with no more idea why he should be killed or should kill anyone else, than a sheep or a cow. He was horribly wounded by shell fire on Sunday, and had lain out in the rain ever since, till our people found him in the woods last night (this is Thursday). Isn't it horrible to picture? Starving, drenched, bleeding, so torn and shot in the buttock as to be unable to drag himself out of the woods. So his wounds had gangrened, and he must die. He could only lie on his face: he was fully conscious and joined in where he could in the responses of the office of Extreme Unction; but I know nothing more awful than the broken-hearted patience of such lads: the whole sad face, the dumb eyes, the agonized posture — without cry, or moan; if ever anything was an appeal to heaven from a brother's blood, crying from the earth, this was one. . . .

JOHN AYSCOUGH TO THE SAME[1]

Wednesday Night, September 8, 1915.

This morning I posted to you by the French civil post at Chartres a letter I wrote you there last night: but I do not know whether you will receive it before this one or after. I need only repeat that letter so far as to explain that I have long been anxious to visit Chartres, whose cathedral is one of the most ancient, beautiful, and interesting in France — or indeed in any country: and so today is

[1]From same source as its preceding letter.

Our Lady's birthday, and the great feast day there. I went yesterday so as to be able to say Mass in the shrine there today.

I have so many different cards of it that I shall send them in at least two batches — perhaps in three: but none are duplicates, and I would like you to keep them all.

I said Mass in the shrine at six-thirty this morning. The chapel is in the crypt, which was crowded with hundreds of pilgrims who all went to Holy Communion. It was wonderfully impressive and devotional, almost like saying Mass in one of the Roman catacombs. After Mass I went to the hotel for breakfast, then went to High Mass sung in the cathedral itself. The Archbishop "assisted" at the throne, and I was in the stalls, and saw the function beautifully. It was fine in itself and the setting glorious. The vast church was crammed with pilgrims, the music was solemn and good — pure Gregorian, and the ceremonies were carried out with perfection: quite one of the scenes that one can never forget.

After luncheon I went to visit two other churches, St. Pierre and St. Aignau: both very fine and very ancient. The stained glass at the cathedral, and at St. Pierre, is splendid, and hard to rival, being of the eleventh and thirteenth centuries, very rich, though somewhat somber in effect, of very dark coloring, and making the church darker than is usual.

After another farewell visit to the cathedral I caught an express train back here, and found my Garden House very homely and comfortable.

I do not think any cards can quite convey the singular loveliness and charm of Chartres Cathedral. Every moment one looked at it, from whatever point of view, its beauty seemed to become more entrancing, and it stands well, not shut in by mean houses as many Continental cathedrals are. Rouen is not comparable to it: Chartres being much earlier, and much purer in style, less florid and less heavy. The city of Rouen does not attract me a bit; it is big, noisy, crowded, and very dirty, whereas Chartres is brilliantly clean and cheerful, stands high, and though the streets are often very ancient and winding, they are gay, and at the same time quiet. Though it has forty thousand inhabitants it is a regular country town, with no manufactures or tall chimneys and no slush or grime. Round the cathedral there seems to reign a smiling calm, that the caw of countless jackdaws upon the towers only makes more peaceful and more gay. The weather was perfect, very brilliant sunshine, and not too hot, though a great deal warmer than it has been for weeks. . . .

But I must go to bed now, and so wishing you none but happy dreams and praying hard, hard, that we may soon be together again. . . .

ROBERT L. STEVENSON TO SIDNEY COLVIN[1]

My Dear Sidney Colvin:

The journey which this little book is to describe was very agreeable and fortunate for me. After an uncouth beginning, I had the best of luck to the end. But we are all travelers in what John Bunyan calls the wilderness of this world — all, too, travelers with a donkey; and the best that we find in our travels is an honest friend. He is a fortunate voyager who finds many. We travel, indeed, to find them. They are the end and the reward of life. They keep us worthy of ourselves; and when we are alone, we are only nearer to the absent.

Every book is, in an intimate sense, a circular letter to the friends of him who writes it. They alone take his meaning; they find private messages, assurances of love, and expressions of gratitude, dropped for them in every corner. The public is but a generous patron who defrays the postage. Yet though the letter is directed to all, we have an old and kindly custom of addressing it on the outside to one. Of what shall a man be proud, if he is not proud of his friends? And so, my dear Sidney Colvin, it is with pride that I sign myself affectionately yours,

R. L. S.

[1]The dedication for his book *Travels with a Donkey in the Cévennes.* By permission of Charles Scribner's Sons.

MRS. HELEN PARRY EDEN TO FATHER O'DOWD[1]

To the Very Reverend William Bernard O'Dowd,
once Warden of St. Charles's House, Oxford,
this book, in accordance with an old promise,
is joyfully dedicated.

My dear Father O'Dowd:

It is now over twelve years since you died, yet I should no more think of dedicating this book to your memory than I should think of offering my prayers to the memory of God. As surely as He lives, you live; and I have no doubt whatsoever about either verity. No one has been less obscured for me by death than you have; and our friendship has remained such as St. Augustine extolled to Martianus: "A bond between lovers and well-wishers in all things human and divine . . . a bond truly immortal, seeing that it binds not only friend to friend but both to God."

Of course our conversation nowadays is a trifle one-sided; but this, thanks to your ecclesiastical deliberation and my feminine intrepidity, it always was. And here, it seems, I may fitly remind you of the unique occasion when you took an unabashed initiative and proposed for yourself the poor compliment I am paying you now. A much-loved mutual friend was modestly disclaiming the dedication of this book's predecessor, when you scattered his scruples and my blushes with "I only wish someone would dedicate a book to me!" I promised you the next book then and there. And here, after twelve years, it is.

Well, two of us are far enough away from the scene of that promise. But here within earshot, almost, of the Angelus we used to hear together, I fulfill the compact of that Oxfordshire afternoon. "Devotion," says St. Thomas, "may be given to all God's friends whether alive or dead"; but in the case of ecclesiastics it is more

[1]Letter of Dedication written for her book *Whistles of Silver,* Science and Culture Series, The Bruce Publishing Company. Copyrighted.

tactful to profess devotion to the dead than the living, and it is easier for me now than it would have been twelve years ago, to sign myself, dear Father O'Dowd, your devoted

Helen Parry Eden.

Woodstock, 1932.

ST. THÉRÈSE TO HER SISTER CELINE

August 15, 1892.

My dear little Sister:

To write to you today I am obliged to steal a little time from our Lord. He will forgive, because it is of Him that we are going to speak together. The vast solitudes and enchanting views which unfold themselves before you ought to uplift your soul. I do not see those things, and I content myself by saying with St. John of the Cross in His Spiritual Canticle:

In Christ I have the mountains,
The quiet, wooded valleys.

Lately I have been thinking what I could undertake for the salvation of souls, and these simple words of the Gospel have given me light. Pointing to the fields of ripe corn, Jesus once said to His disciples: "Lift up your eyes and see the fields, for they are already white with the harvest";[1] and again: "The harvest indeed is great, but the labourers are few; pray ye therefore the Lord of the harvest that He send forth labourers."[2]

Here is a mystery indeed! Is not Jesus all-powerful? Do not creatures belong to Him who made them? Why does He deign to say: "Pray ye the Lord of the harvest that He send forth labour-

[1]John iv. 35.
[2]Matt. ix. 37, 38.

ers"? It is because His love for us is so unsearchable, so tender, that He wishes us to share in all He does. The Creator of the Universe awaits the prayer of a poor little soul to save a multitude of other souls, ransomed, like her, at the price of His Blood.

Our vocation is not to go forth and reap in Our Father's fields.[3] Jesus does not say to us: "Look down and reap the harvest." Our mission is even more sublime. "Lift up your eyes and see," saith our Divine Master, "see how in heaven there are empty thrones. It is for you to fill them. . . . You are as Moses praying on the mountain, so ask Me for labourers and they shall be sent. I only await a prayer, a sigh!" Is not the apostolate of my prayer, so to speak, higher than that of the spoken word? It is for us by prayer to train workers who will spread the glad tidings of the Gospel and who will save countless souls—the souls to whom we shall be the spiritual Mothers. What, then, have we to envy in the priests of the Lord?

[3]St. Thérèse belonged to a strictly cloistered Order.

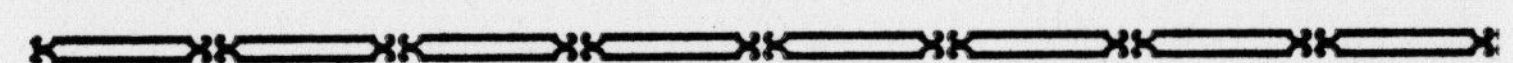

INDEX

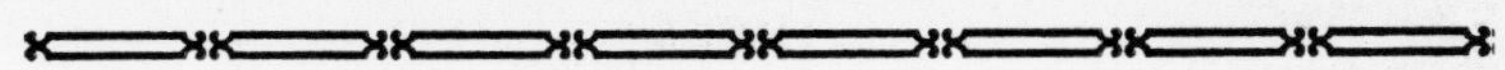

INDEX